THE I TATTI
RENAISSANCE LIBRARY

James Hankins, General Editor

FLAVIO

ITALY ILLUMINATED

VOLUME II

ITRL 75

BIONDO FLAVIO
✦ ✦ ✦
ITALY ILLUMINATED
VOLUME II ✦ BOOKS V–VIII

EDITED AND TRANSLATED BY

JEFFREY A. WHITE

THE I TATTI RENAISSANCE LIBRARY
HARVARD UNIVERSITY PRESS
CAMBRIDGE, MASSACHUSETTS
LONDON, ENGLAND
2016

Series design by Dean Bornstein

Library of Congress Cataloging-in-Publication Data
Biondo Flavio, 1392–1463.
[Italia illustrata. English & Latin]
Italy illuminated / Biondo Flavio ; edited and translated by Jeffrey A. White.
v. <1> — (ITRL ; 20)
Latin text with English translation.
Includes bibliographical references and index.
Contents: v. 1, bks. 1–4.
ISBN 0-674-01743-9 (cloth : alk. paper)
1. Italy — Description and travel — Early works to 1800.
2. Italy — History — To 1500 — Early works to 1800.
3. Humanism — Italy — Early works to 1800.
4. Italy — Biography — Early works to 1800.
5. Italy — Genealogy — Early works to 1800.
I. White, Jeffrey A.   II. Title.   III. I Tatti Renaissance library ; 20.
DG422.B56 2005
945 — dc22   2005046070

Contents

৯৯৪৯

Book V

Book VI

Book VII

Book VIII

BLONDI FLAVII FORLIVIENSIS ITALIAE ILLVSTRATAE LIBRI VIII

BIONDO FLAVIO OF FORLÌ ITALY ILLUMINATED IN EIGHT BOOKS

[Volume II: Books V–VIII]

LIBER V

Regio septima. Lombardia[1]

1   Perducta est superiore libro Romandiola hinc ad sinistram Scultennae amnis ripam, inde ad Melariam agri Ferrariensis vicum,
certos ultra citraque Padum limites suos. Lombardiae nunc opera
est impendenda. Id nomen a Longobardis tractum esse constat.
Quando enim Carolus Magnus et Adrianus primus pontifex Romanus nomen (ut diximus) Romandiolae indiderunt, hanc quoque
partem Italiae aliquando (dictam prius Galliam Cisalpinam) voluerunt censeri nomine Lombardiae, quod a Longobardis ad decem et octo supra ducentos annos fuerat occupata. Sicque eam
Romana ecclesia ab ipso tempore citra suis in monumentis per
annos sexcentos quinquaginta fecit appellari. Et quamquam Verona, Vicentia, Padua, et Tarvisium civitates, ac omnis regio
Aquileiensis ecclesiae ab eisdem quoque Longobardis semper fuerint possessae, certa tamen nobis ratione, quam ipsas descripturi
regiones afferemus, quatuor illae civitates cum aliquot aliis, Marchia Tarvisina et reliqua pars Italiae illi adiacens (cum Aquileiensis
tum Forojulii regio) ab eo tempore fuerunt[2] nominatae.

2   Sunt Lombardiae fines Scultenna et Padus amnes, Apenninus
et Alpes citra Padum, et ultra eum quicquid intra Alpes Benacum-
que lacum et amnem Mincium ipso clauditur Pado. Igitur ad
Scultennae dexteram qua influit Formigo torrens fossae immixtus
a Mutina defluenti Bomportus est vicus. Infra est Finale oppidum,
ad quod ea[3] quam diximus aquarum moles, Rheno, Scultenna,

BOOK V

Region 7. Lombardy

In the last book, I took Romagna as far as the left bank of the 1
Scoltenna on one side and to the village of Melara in Ferrarese territory on the other, its two furthest fixed points on the near and
far side of the Po.[1] Now we must turn to Lombardy. The name of
the region is generally agreed to derive from the *Longobardi* or
"Lombards": when Charlemagne and Pope Adrian I gave Romagna its name (as we said above),[2] they also decided at some
stage to have this part of Italy, which had earlier been called *Gallia
Cisalpina*, designated "Lombardy," because it had been occupied by
the Lombards for 218 years. From that time onward, for 650 years,
the Church of Rome has called the region by this name in its
documents. And though the cities of Verona, Vicenza, Padua, and
Treviso, and all the lands of the Church of Aquileia, had always
been held by the Lombards, those four cities nevertheless, along
with several others — for a particular reason which I shall mention
when I come to describe those areas — were designated as part of
the March of Treviso, and the rest of Italy lying next to it as the
regions of Aquileia and Friuli.

The borders of Lombardy are the rivers Scoltenna and Po, the 2
Apennines and the Alps on the near side of the Po, and all the
land bounded by the Po itself up to the Alps, Lake Garda, and the
river Mincio. And so on the right bank of the river Scoltenna,
where the stream Formigine flows into it after merging with the
canal that runs down from Modena, stands the village of Bomporto. Below Bomporto is the town of Finale Emilia, where the
mass of waters we spoke of — a great many streams which now
join the rivers Reno, Scoltenna and Formigine — go to form the

Formigine et plerisque torrentibus coeuntibus, Fossam efficit Fistorenam, ultima Padusae ostia facientem, apud Bondenum oppidum, ubi opinor fuisse Bondomacum, quem Plinius lingua Gallica ideo sic appellatum affirmat quod immensum ibi Padus profundum habeat. Scultenna fluvius vetustum id nomen supra viam Aemiliam nunc retinet, infra Panarius appellatur. Estque is fluvius apud quem ad annum salutis sexcentesimum et septuagesimum, proelio inter Ravennates et Longobardos commisso, cecidisse in Ravennatium partibus octo milia ostendimus in *Historiis.* Cui interius ad sinistram adiacent Spilimbertum, Vignola, Maranum, et in Apennino Fananum, per quod oppidum arduus est in Etruriam ad Pistoriam trames.

3   Formigo dehinc torrens apud Spezanum oriundus Mutinam attingit vetusti et in historiis frequentati nominis civitatem, quam Livius libro XXXIX dicit fuisse cum Pisauro et Parma deductam a Romanis coloniam. Et libro CXVIII idem Livius scribit M. Antonium obsedisse Mutinae D.[4] Brutum, et cum missi ad eum de pace legati parum valuissent, populum Romanum saga sumpsisse. Infra autem libro CXIX idem Livius: causa malorum fuit, cum C.[5] Octavius D.[6] Brutum ab obsidione Antonii liberasset, senatus ipsi Bruto triumphum decrevit, levi mentione habita militum Octaviani. Quare iratus et Antonio ac Lepido reconciliatus Romam cum exercitu venit, et annos agens decem et novem consul est creatus. Tradit autem Plinius exire Mutinensi agro statis diebus Vulcanum. Eam Mutinam, quae nunc exstat, novam esse, et vetustae fundamenta pauxillum distare constat. Quis autem vel hanc aedificaverit novam vel fuerit veterem demolitus, non invenimus. Certum tamen habemus ipsam, quae nunc est, trecentesimo quinquagesimo abhinc anno non fuisse, et utriusque solum annis ante reaedificationem quadringentis munitionibus in urbem coactis ca-

Fistorena canal, creating the farthest mouth of the Po at the town of Bondeno. This, I think, was the location of *Bondomacus*, so called in the Gallic tongue, according to Pliny, because the Po's depths are unfathomable there.[3] The river Scoltenna still keeps its ancient name south of the Aemilian Way, but to the north it is called the Panaro. In my *Histories*, I showed that this was the river where in 670 CE the men of Ravenna and the Lombards joined battle, with the loss of eight thousand men on the Ravennate side.[4] Further inland, along the left bank of the Panaro, lie Spilamberto, Vignola, Marano sul Panaro, and in the Apennines the town of Fanano, through which passes a steep path that leads to Pistoia in Tuscany.

Then comes the Formigine stream, which rises at Spezzano di 3 Fiorano and goes to Modena, an ancient city often mentioned in historical works. Livy says in Book XXXIX that Modena was a colony founded by the Romans, along with Pesaro and Parma.[5] And in Book CXVIII he writes that Mark Antony laid siege to Decimus Brutus in Modena and that, when the peace envoys that had been sent to him made little headway, the Roman People readied themselves for war.[6] Also, further on, in Book CXIX, Livy again writes: the cause of the trouble was that although Gaius Octavius had relieved Antony's siege of Decimus Brutus, the Senate actually awarded the triumph to Brutus, with scant mention of Octavian's soldiers. Taking offense at this, Octavian reconciled himself with Antony and Lepidus and went with his army to Rome, where he was elected consul at the age of nineteen.[7] Pliny tells us that fire issues from the ground in the territory of Modena on fixed days.[8] People generally agree that present-day Modena is new and that the remains of ancient Modena are some little way off, though I cannot discover who built the new city or demolished the old one. But I am sure that the present town did not exist 350 years ago, and that for 400 years before it was rebuilt, neither location had defenses sufficient to constitute a city. Its

ruisse. In historiis enim Gothorum Longobardorumque nusquam eius nomen invenitur, cum Bononiae, Tanneti, Brixilli, et Parmae nomina ibidem sint frequentia. Qua ratione in ea divisione terrarum Italiae quam Carolus Magnus et Ludovicus ac alii filii et nepotes Romana cum ecclesia fecerunt, in neutrius partium sortem haec ipsa civitas venit. Unde nec pontifici Romano censum pendet nec ab imperatore aliquam dependentiam habet.

4   Fecit hactenus Padusa palus ut sinistram Padi ripam a Primariis Ostiis ad Bondenum describere nequiverimus. Post Bondenum quinto miliario in Padi ripa est Stellata, vicus arcem habens, unde catena in alteram trahitur e regione Pado appositam arcem, quibus praesidiis marchiones Estenses Padi integri et utriusque eius ripae claustra communiunt et defensant. Sermedum in hac Padi ripa sequitur vetusti nominis oppidum, per quod Antonini Pii *Itinerarius liber* ostendit iter fuisse a Patavio Adeustoque Concordiam oppidum et inde Bononiam accessuris. Quae ratio facit ut non dubitem ramum, qui sub Ficarolo ceteris maior a Pado scinditur, nedum per Antonini tempora sed neque diu postea, sicut in *Romandiola* diximus, fuisse. Post Sermedum in Padi ripa est Reverum, novum oppidum e regione Ostiliae situm, quod Ludovicus Gonzaga marchio Mantuanus, validissimis communitum moenibus, pulcherrima domo ornare perseverat. Intus est Mirandula, et interius Corrigia oppidum, nobilis Corrigiorum familiae patria. Post est Carpum[7] opulentissimum oppidum, nobilis Piorum familiae domicilium.

5   Primus deinceps fluvius, integer et solus, Padum illabitur Sicla, cui ad sinistram imminet[8] Nuvolaria vicus, Turris, Aqualonga, Saxolum, et, ubi torrente Dollo augetur, Salcinum,[9] et ad Dollum sub Apennino Fraxanorium, et in Apennino Peregrinum, qua ar-

name is not to be found in the histories of the Goths and Lombards, even though the names of Bologna, Taneto, Brescello, and Parma often come up there. It was on that account that in the division of the lands of Italy which Charlemagne (and Louis and his other sons and grandsons) made with the Church of Rome, the city was assigned to neither party. In consequence she pays no tribute to the Roman pontiff and is at the same time entirely independent of the emperor.

The swamp of the Po has so far kept me from surveying the left 4 bank of the river, from the Po di Primaro to Bondeno. Five miles beyond Bondeno, on the banks of the Po, is the town of Stellata with its fortress. From there a chain is strung to another fortress on the river directly opposite, and from these strongholds the Marquises d'Este fortify and protect the defenses of the whole river and both its banks. Sermide, an ancient town, follows Stellata on this side of the Po. The *Itinerarium* of Antoninus Pius shows that the route from Padua and Este for those heading for the town of Concordia and then Bologna lay through here.[9] This accounts for my conviction that the largest branch of the Po, which splits off below Ficarolo, did not exist in the time of Antoninus Pius nor for long afterward, as I said in my discussion of Romagna.[10] Along the banks of the Po after Sermide is Revere, a modern town situated opposite Ostiglia. The Marquis of Mantua, Lodovico Gonzaga, has given the town mighty fortifications, and he continues to grace it with his beautiful residence.[11] Mirandola is inland, and further inland lies the town of Correggio, homeland of the illustrious Correggio family. Then one comes to the wealthy town of Carpi, seat of the illustrious family of the Pio.[12]

Next there is the Secchia, the first river that flows into the Po 5 entire and by itself. Near its left bank is the village of Novellara, then Torre, Acqualonga, Sassuolo, and, where the river is swollen by the stream Dolo, Saltino, and, on the Dolo at the foot of the Apennines, Frassinoro, and, in the Apennines, S. Pellegrino in

duus item est in Etruriam et Lunensem agrum saltus. Apud Salcinum[10] etiam altero Sicla dextrorsum augetur torrente, cui adiacent oppida Carponetum, Volognum,[11] et in Apennino Piolum. Ad Siclae dexteram est Sancti Benedicti celebre monasterium a gloriosa Matildi comitissa aedificatum. Intus Sancti Martini oppidum, et, ubi Fossam Taram Crustulus illabitur torrens, Regiolum. Interius ad dexteram Roberia, ad sinistram Lora, Baesium, et sub Apennino Castrum Novum.

6   Ad Crustuli sinistram in via Aemilia est Regium Lepidum civitas, quam cum Mutina obtinet Estensis marchio Ferrariae. Etsi vero haec civitas satis est vetusta, quam Lepidum per scelestissimi triumviratus tempora aedificasse constat, tamen (sicut de Mutina diximus) nomen eius in nullis Gothorum aut Longobardorum historiis reperitur, cum Parmae, Tanneti, Bononiae, et Brixilli nomina eisdem in historiis frequentia inveniantur: ut non absurde videamur suspicari ne aliquot saeculis destructa manserit aut immunita. Frontinus enim in *Strategematibus* scribit: 'in legionem, quae Regium Lepidum oppidum iniussu ducis diruerat, animadversum est ita ut quatuor milia custodiae tradita necarentur. Praeterea senatus consulto cautum est ne quem ex eis sepeliri vel lugere fas esset.'[12] Superius sunt Palus et Sarcha, et ad dexteram Gipsum, et Canossa, in quo oppido gloriosam Matildim comitissam in *Historiis* ostendimus VII Gregorium pontificem Romanum ab insidiis et violentia Henrici III imperatoris tutatam fuisse, et Henricum postea decalciatis pedibus et nudo capite per mediam hiemem de nivibus et glacie veniam a pontifice impetrasse. Sequitur in ripa Padi Guardastallum olim, nunc Guastalla, quo in oppido miratus sum pontifices Romanos Urbanum et Pascalem (utrumque nominis ordine secundum) ante annos trecentos duo concilia celebrasse. Unde crediderim, illo quod tunc fuerit oppido destructo, novum

Alpe, where there is a high wooded pass into Tuscany and the Lunigiana. At Saltino, the Secchia is also augmented by another stream flowing into it from the right,[13] on which lie Carpineti, Vologno, and, in the Apennines, Piolo. To the right of the Secchia is the famous monastery of S. Benedetto, built by the glorious countess Matilda.[14] Inland is the town of S. Martino, and, where the Crostolo stream flows into the Tara canal, Reggiolo. Further inland, on the right, is Rubiera, and on the left Lora, Baiso, and under the Apennines Castelnovo ne' Monti.

The city of Reggio nell'Emilia is on the left bank of the Cros- 6 tolo on the Aemilian Way, a possession, like Modena, of the Marquis d'Este of Ferrara. Though the city really is very old—Lepidus is generally held to have built it in the time of the wicked Triumvirate—yet its name, as we said in the case of Modena, is not to be found in any of the histories of the Goths or Lombards, though the names of Parma, Taneto, Bologna, and Brescello often occur in those documents:[15] we may well suspect that it was destroyed or remained unfortified for several centuries. In any case, Frontinus writes in his *Stratagems*: "Punishment of the legion that destroyed the town of Regium Lepidum against the orders of their commander was so extreme that four thousand men were taken into custody and executed. The Senate passed a further measure forbidding any of them to be given burial or mourning rites."[16] Higher up are Palude and Sarca, and, to the right, Gesso, and the town of Canossa, where, as I showed in my *Histories*, the glorious Countess Matilda protected Pope Gregory VII from the intrigues and violence of the Emperor Henry III. Later, standing on the snow and ice unshod and bareheaded in the depths of winter, Henry begged and won the pope's forgiveness.[17] There follows on the banks of the Po the present-day Guastalla, formerly *Guardastallum*: I was surprised to find that three hundred years ago popes Urban II and Paschal II held two councils in the town.[18] That inclines me to think that the town of those days was de-

hoc postea aedificatum fuisse. Deinceps est Brixillum, vetusti et in historiis celebrati nominis oppidum, nunc incivile, cuius arcem Corrigienses nobilis Lombardiae familia magnifici apparatus ornatam aedificiis inhabitant. Primus vero omnium Rotharis Longobardorum rex Brixillum (quod Ravennatibus suberat) cum vi cepisset, demolitus est. Eodemque bello a Longobardis materia plancisque communitum, Ravennates, iniecto igni, penitus desertarunt.

7   Tannetum fuit oppidum Aemiliam inter viam et Brixillum Regio urbi propinquum, de quo Livius libro XXI infra scripta habet, quae potuerunt Mutinae esse communia: 'Triumviri ad deducendas colonias missi, Placentiae moenibus diffisi, Mutinam confugerunt. Legati ad Boios missi violati sunt. Mutina obsessa. Et simulatum de pace agi, missique ad eam tractandam a Gallis comprensi. L. Manlius imperator effusum agmen ad Mutinam ducit. Et in silvis (quae tunc circa Mutinam erant) caesi sunt Romanorum octingenti. Ceteri Tannetum petierunt.' Et (sicut in regione *Romandiola* Sassinam describentes Boiorum eam caput diximus) ostendit Livius libro XXI Tannetum fuisse Boiorum oppidum his verbis: 'Ita divisae copiae, Boisque in agrum suum Tannetum profectis.' Apudque id oppidum Longobardorum equitum decem milia, quae Narses patricius copiarum Iustiniani imperatoris dux mercede conducta primum in Italiam duxit, Totilam Gothorum regem (sicut in *Historiis* diximus) superatum interfecerunt. Eo denique paulo post in loco idem Narses Bucellinum ducem Gallicum magnas regis Metensium copias adversum imperatorias legiones ducentem, magna illius exercitus facta occidione, superavit. Scribitque Livius in censu Italiae, qui Vespasiani imperatoris edicto habitus est, virum unum Brixilli repertum fuisse qui centum XX annos natus esset.

stroyed and the present one was built later on. Next comes Brescello, an ancient town much celebrated in history, but now de-
cayed. The noble family of the Correggio of Lombardy live in the
fortress there, fitted out with magnificent buildings. Brescello, being subject to Ravenna, was destroyed when Rothari, the first king
of all the Lombards, took it by storm.[19] The Lombards gave the
town timber defenses in the course of the same war, but the
Ravennati set it alight and laid waste to it.

Taneto was a town between the Aemilian Way and Brescello,   7
near the city of Reggio. Livy in Book XXI writes about it as follows (a passage that applies to Modena too):[20] "The triumvirs sent
out to found the colonies mistrusted the defenses of Piacenza and
took refuge in Modena. Legates sent to the Boii were treated with
violence, and Modena put under siege. The Gauls made a show of
seeking peace, but those who were dispatched to arrange it were
seized by them. The commander Lucius Manlius led a disorderly
troop of soldiers to Modena and eight hundred of the Romans
were killed in the forests which then surrounded the town. The
rest made for Taneto."[21] And in Book XXI (as in our description
of Sarsina in *Romagna*, where we called it the capital of the Boii),[22]
Livy shows that Taneto was a town of the Boii in this passage:
"And so the armies separated, the Boii departing for their own territory of Taneto."[23] It was near this town that the ten thousand
Lombard cavalry which the patrician Narses, commander of the
troops of the Emperor Justinian, had first hired and brought
into Italy, defeated and killed Totila, the king of the Goths, as
mentioned in our *Histories*.[24] Finally, at Taneto shortly afterward,
Narses also defeated the Frankish captain Buccellinus, who was
leading the vast forces of the king of Metz against the imperial legions, with great slaughter of their army.[25] Livy writes of the census of Italy carried out by order of the emperor Vespasian that a
man was discovered at Brescello who was 120 years old.[26]

8   Post Brixillum Lentia fluvius Padum illabitur, ad cuius sinistram intus est Guardasionum. Superius, Rossana. Defluit postea
in Padum Parma fluvius, ad cuius dexteram est Colornium tollera-
tae bis aetate[13] nostra durissimae obsidionis fama notum. Intus via
Aemilia est Parma civitas vetusta, Romanorum colonia, quam Livius libro XL simul cum Pisauro et Mutina deductam fuisse
ostendit; eam fluvius Parma dividit. Quae praeclara admodum
urbs plerosque viros praestantes habuit,[14] sed maxime duobus,
Cassio poeta et altero centurione Cassio, ornata fuit. Macro-
biumque, cuius exstant doctrina pleni de *Saturnalibus* libri, Parmensem fuisse legimus, in cuius sepulchro Parmae celebri nostra
aetate conditus est Blasius Parmensis philosophus non incelebris.
Quatuor ipsa urbs ornata est magnatum familiis, amplissimi[15] eius
agri oppida ferme omnia dicione tenentibus magnumque[16] alenti-
bus equitatum: Rossis, Corrigiensibus, Palavicinis, ac Vitalensi-
bus. Qui, cum uni dominio parent, et Lombardiae aditum et ipsam custodiunt civitatem. Cum vero quicquam in provincia aut
inter se ipsos acciderit tumultus,[17] divisos secum quadrifariam
cives et omnem provinciam motibus involvunt. Auctor vero est
Plinius, cum imperator Vespasianus Italiae populos describi face-
ret, inventos fuisse duos Parmae, quorum uterque viginti quinque
supra centum annos vixisset. Et Martialis poeta ostendit agrum
Parmensem semper antea (sicut nunc est) bene pascuum fuisse:
'Tondet et innumeros Gallica Parma greges.'

9   Interius ad Parmae amnis sinistram, Sapellum, Chaesta, et Brotium oppida sunt, et sub Apennino est Belforte. Ad dexteram,
Bagantiano torrenti Parmam augenti Calestanum adiacet. Tarus
exinde fluvius Padum illabitur. Cui intus ad sinistram, ubi Conio
torrente augetur, Fornovum, superius vero Complanum, Sancta
Maria, et (ad ortum fluvii) Citium castella sunt. Ad dexteram autem Solegnanum, et Bargum, quem[18] Alpem Bardonis olim fuisse

Beyond Brescello, the river Enza flows into the Po, on whose   8
left bank, inland, is Guardasone. Further up is Rossena. Then the
river Parma flows down into the Po: on its right bank is Colorno,
notable for having endured two very hard sieges in our time.[27] Inland along the Aemilian Way is the ancient city of Parma, through
the middle of which flows the Parma river. Livy shows in Book
XL that it was founded as a Roman colony at the same time as
Pesaro and Modena.[28] This famous city has had many noteworthy men, but has been graced by two in particular, Cassius the
poet and another Cassius, the centurion.[29] We read that Macrobius, whose learned books on the *Saturnalia* are still extant, was a
man of Parma. In Macrobius's famous tomb at Parma was laid in
our own time Biagio Pelacani, a philosopher himself not without
fame.[30] The city is distinguished by four great families, which hold
in their sway nearly all the towns of its extensive territory and support a great number of cavalry, the Rossi, da Correggio, Pallavicini,
and San Vitali. When these families serve one overlord, they hold
the key to Lombardy and to the city itself. But when some inci-
dent takes place in the region and they fall out among themselves,
their ructions involve the whole area and cause the citizens to split
into four factions. Pliny tells us that when the emperor Vespasian
had the peoples of Italy surveyed, two men were found at Parma
who had both lived for 125 years.[31] And the poet Martial shows us
that the lands of Parma have always been good for grazing, as they
still are: "And Gallic Parma shears innumerable flocks."[32]

Further inland along the left bank of the river Parma are the   9
towns of Sapello, Chesta, and Brozzo, and, beneath the Apennines, Belforte.[33] On the right, Calestano lies on the stream
Baganza, a tributary of the river Parma. Then the river Taro flows
into the Po. Inland to the left of the Taro are the fortresses of
Fornovo di Taro (where the Taro is swollen by the stream of the
Ceno), and further up Compiano, S. Maria del Taro, and at the
source, Cisa. On the right of the Taro are Solignano and Bardone:

dictum invenio, in quo Liutprandus Longobardorum rex monasterium, quod Barcetum dicitur, aedificavit. Ad Conii sinistram et ubi Ocha torrens illum influit, est Stoparinum, post Ramugola[19] et Cornus, et ad Conii ortum est Ruinum, sub quo est Carisium. Medio quod Tarum amnem et proximum torrentem Ardam interiacet spatio, in via Aemilia Burgus est Doninius, nobile oppidum. Infra est Buschetum[20] novum oppidum. Ad Ardae[21] vero sinistram Soargia est, intusque Columbanium, et in via Aemilia est Fidentiola, oppidum nobile vetustique nominis. De quo Livius libro LXXXVIII: 'Sulla Carbonem, exercitu ad Clusium, ad Faventiam Fidentiolamque caeso, Italia expulit.' Ad dexteram est nobile oppidum Arquata, vinum habens omnium regionis suavissimum. Sequitur Nura fluvius, ad cuius dexteram est intus Carminium, Ripa, et Rovengonum,[22] ad sinistram Roncoverum, et sub Apennino Nucetum.

10   Post amnem Nuram primus Padum illabitur fluvius Trebia, ad cuius ostium est Placentia. Quam Q. Asconius Pedianus tradit ordine quinquagesimam et tertiam coloniam Romanorum deductam fuisse a P. Masone Asina, a Cn. Pompeio Strabone, et a P. Cornelio Scipione, triumviris. Suntque eo missa sex milia hominum, novi coloni, in quibus equites. Deducendi fuit causa ut opponerentur Gallis, qui eam partem Galliae tenebant. Livius autem libro XXI: 'Agro Gallorum capto, coloniae deductae sunt Placentia et Cremona.' Et libro XXVII: 'Hasdrubal, quod celeritate itineris profectum erat, id mora ad Placentiam, dum obsidet magis quam oppugnat, corrupit. Crediderat campestris oppidi facilem oppugnationem esse, et nobilitas coloniae induxerat eum.' Et libro XXVIII: 'Placentini et Cremonenses questi ad Senatum de agri populationibus quas fecerant Galli accolae. Iussit Senatus Manlio praetori ut curaret. Et decrevit Senatus ut, qui cives Placentini et

here I find the Alps were once called the Alps of Bardone, where Liutprand, the king of the Lombards, built a monastery called Berceto.[34] On the left bank of the Ceno, where the stream of the Oca flows into it, is Stoparino, and beyond that Ramugola and Cornio. At the source of the Ceno is Rovina, and below Rovina, Carisio. On the Aemilian Way, midway between the Taro and the next stream, the Arda, is the well-known town of Borgo S. Donnino.[35] Below Borgo is a modern town, Busseto. Soarza is on the left bank of the Arda, and further inland S. Colombano, and on the Aemilian Way Fiorenzuola, a fine ancient town.[36] Livy says of it in Book LXXXVIII: "Sulla destroyed Carbo's army at Chiusi, Faenza, and Fiorenzuola, and drove him out of Italy."[37] On the right of the Arda is the fine town of Castell'Arquato, with the sweetest wines of the region. The river Nure follows the Arda: inland on its right bank are Carmiano, Riva and Rivergaro; on the left, Roncovero and at the foot of the Apennines, Noceto.

The Trebbia is the next river to flow into the Po after the Nure, with Piacenza at its mouth. Quintus Asconius Pedianus tells us that Placentia was founded by the triumvirs Publius Maso Asina, Gnaeus Pompeius Strabo, and Publius Cornelius Scipio as the fifty-third Roman colony. Six thousand men were sent there, new colonists, among them men of the equestrian order. The reason for the foundation of the colony was to oppose the Gauls who controlled that part of Gallia Cisalpina.[38] Livy again in Book XXI: "Once the territory of the Gauls had been taken, the colonies of Placentia and Cremona were founded."[39] And in Book XXVII: "Hasdrubal wasted the advantage he had gained from the speed of his march by getting mired down at Placentia, laying it under siege rather than attacking it. He had thought that it would be easy to storm a town on the plains, and the celebrity of the colony had led him on."[40] And in Book XXVIII: "Citizens of Placentia and Cremona had complained to the Senate that the neighboring Gauls had laid waste to their lands. The Senate ordered the praetor

10

15

Cremonenses erant, in colonias mitterentur.' Trebellius Pollio in *Aureliani gestis rebus:* 'Cum autem Aurelianus vellet omnibus simul Marcomanis, facta exercitus sui constipatione, occurrere, tanta apud Placentiam clades accepta est ut Romanum paene solveretur imperium.' Scribit etiam Livius XXI fuisse apud Placentiam emporium ope magna munitum et valido firmatum praesidio, quod Hannibal expugnare nequivit. Id emporium fuerat a Romanis Bello Gallico munitum. Inde locum frequentaverant accolae mixti[23] undique ex finitimis populis, quos proelio superatos Hannibal crudelissime diripuit. Ornata fuit Placentia T. Tinca oratore Placentino (sicut Cicero in *Bruto* dicit) dicacissimo. Idemque Cicero *Pro Murena* dicit patrem L. Pisonis eius qui fuit C. Julii Caesaris socer fuisse Placentinum et Bello Marsico faciendis armis praefuisse. Et diu post habuit Gregorium X pontificem Romanum, qui Lugdunense concilium celebravit. Isque pontifex celeberrimus post multa gloriose in ecclesia Dei gesta Aretii obiit et sepultus est, ubi saepe miraculis coruscavit. Scribitque Plinius, cum Vespasiani imperatoris edicto census Italiae haberetur, virum unum Placentiae repertum fuisse qui XXX centumque vixisset annos. Eaque civitas ad annum salutis XLIX supra ducentesimum et millesimum a Palavicinis nobilibus subiecta fuit, cum numquam prius cuique alteri subdita fuisset qui non Italiae omnis aut saltem Lombardiae totius dominium obtineret. Casus vero quos postea per aetatem nostram pertulit horrendos referre infinitum fuerit, sed satis superque[24] sit nunc clariores breviter explicare.

11   Post mortem Johannis Galeatii Vicecomitis, qui fuit primus Mediolani dux, intra duos annos Placentia octies praedae exposita fuit, ad eamque tunc devenit calamitatem ut nos ipsam perlustraverimus totam omni mortalium praeterquam unius publici hospitatoris habitatione destitutam. Et ad annum postea plus minus

Manlius to see to the matter. And the Senate decreed that all who were Placentine and Cremonese citizens should return to their colonies."[41] Trebellius Pollio says in his *History of Aurelian*: "But since Aurelian wanted by massing his forces together to meet the Marcomanni all at once, he suffered such a defeat at Placentia that the Roman empire was all but destroyed."[42] Livy writes, in Book XXI again, that the Romans built an elaborately fortified and strongly garrisoned supply station near Placentia, which Hannibal was unable to take by storm. The Romans had built the station during the Gallic War. It had since attracted numerous settlers from the various peoples dwelling in the vicinity, whom Hannibal defeated in battle and cruelly massacred.[43] Among its ornaments was the witty orator Titus Tincus, a Placentine, as Cicero calls him in the *Brutus*.[44] Cicero also says in *Pro Murena* that Lucius Piso, the father of Caesar's father-in-law, was from Placentia and had been put in charge of the manufacture of arms in the Social War.[45] Long afterward Piacenza produced the Roman pontiff Gregory X, who presided over the Council of Lyon.[46] This famous pope, after many glorious accomplishments in the Church of God, died and was buried at Arezzo, where he has inspired many miracles. Pliny writes that when the census was being taken by decree of the emperor Vespasian, a man was found at Piacenza who was 130 years old.[47] In 1249 CE the city came under the control of the noble Pallavicini family,[48] though it had never before been subject to anyone who did not hold sway over all of Italy, or at least over all of Lombardy. It would take an eternity to relate the terrible events that it afterward endured in our own times: it will be enough to give here an account of the more notable ones.

After the death of Gian Galeazzo Visconti, the first duke of 11 Milan,[49] Piacenza was sacked eight times in two years. At that point it was so devastated that I wandered around the entire city without finding a single human habitation, except for an inn. Some forty years later, when the people of Milan were unsuccess-

XL, Philippo Mediolanensium duce tertio vita functo, cum populus Mediolanensis se liberum esse parum fortunato consilio quaesivisset, Placentiaque Venetis se dedisset, in eam Mediolanenses arma verterunt. Franciscusque Sfortia, Mediolanensis populi ductor exercitus, illam durissima pressit obsidione. Defensabatur autem urbs a Thadeo Estense, quem Veneti cum duobus equitum totidemque peditum milibus praesidio illi[25] immiserant. Cum tamen populus in ea esset magnus, milia virorum octo, in Mediolanensium vero exercitu (praeter Sfortianos) militum decem milia erant: sub Francisco Piccinino, Guidacio Manfredo, Ludovico Vermi, Carolo Gonzaga, et aliis minoribus copiarum ductoribus, quos omnes cum Sfortia constat supra quindecim milia equitum peditumque habuisse.[26] Oppugnata vero est Placentia aliquot diebus copiis bipartitis, quod unis castris Sfortiani, aliis ceteri omnes, tenderent,[27] et muri utrobique bombardis aperti sunt. Forte autem fortuna accidit Padum continuis aliquot dierum imbribus auctum adeo intumescere ut naves ad moenia appellerentur: quam ob occasionem tertio navali proelio urbs oppugnari coepta; et Guidacio Gonzagaeque id muneris est iniunctum; captaque est magno impetu urbs praeclara. Tanta autem in diripiendo fuit rabies, tam effrenis libido ut nihil humani aut divini iuris aliter sit servatum quam si in barbariem quandam publico Dei principumque orbis Christiani edicto fuisset saeviendum. Et ne singulas percurram scelerum formas: ea quae alias in urbium direptione miserrima sunt visa, matronas violari, virgines parentum sinu evelli, inter minima Placentiae tunc sunt visa.

12   Secus Trebiam paulo supra Placentiam locus est insigni clade Romana, Sempronio cos., ab Hannibale inflicta notissimus. Et Trebia intus ad sinistram habet Runchuverum,[28] et superius Bobium, monasterio clarum beati abbatis Galli, quod ipse anno ad-

fully trying to gain their freedom following the death of the third duke, Filippo Maria,[50] they attacked Piacenza after it had surrendered to the Venetians.[51] Francesco Sforza, the captain of the Milanese army, subjected the city to a pitiless siege. The defense of the city was given to Taddeo d'Este, whom the Venetians had sent there with two thousand horse and the same number of infantry as a garrison. There were a large number of people in the city, eight thousand souls, but the Milanese army, apart from Sforza's men, amounted to ten thousand soldiers, and with Sforza's forces, and those of Francesco Piccinino, Guidaccio Manfredi, Ludovico dal Verme, Carlo Gonzaga, and the lesser commanders, they were reckoned to have had fifteen thousand horse and foot in all. Piacenza was put under attack by two sets of forces for several days, Sforza's men operating out of one camp, the rest from another. The city's walls were breached by artillery bombardments on both sides. By chance, however, the Po was swollen by several days of continuous rain, and rose so high that it reached the walls. This circumstance allowed the city to be attacked on a third front by naval forces, a task assigned to Manfredi and Gonzaga. With a mighty onslaught, the famous city was taken. Such was the fury and unbridled lust that took place in the sack of the city that human and divine law was no more respected than if the savagery were being visited on some barbarian place by open edict of God and the princes of Christendom. I do not mean to run through each and every crime that happened: every pitiable deed that has been seen in the sack of cities elsewhere — the rape of mothers, virgins torn from their parents' embrace — these were the least of the things seen then in Piacenza.

On the Trebbia a little further inland from Piacenza is the well- 12 known site of the notable defeat that Hannibal inflicted on the Romans under the consul Sempronius.[52] Further inland on the left the Trebbia has Roncovero and above it, Bobbio, famous for the monastery of the abbot St. Gall, which he himself con-

ventus Longobardorum in Italiam LXXXVII Adaloaldi[29] Theo-
dolindae reginae filii et ipsius reginae impensa aedificavit. Ubi vero
torrente Avanto Trebia augetur, est Organascum,[30] superius ad
dexteram Octunum, Rovenum,[31] et ad Trebiae fontem Monbru-
num, qua in Ligures supra Genuam est trames. Ad Avanti vero
torrentis sinistram, ubi torrente Algretia augetur Sancti Johannis
oppidum, et in Apennino Talliolum est castellum. Dehinc in Padi
ripa sunt Tuni torrentis ostia, qui torrens in via Aemilia Sancti
Johannis agri Placentini oppidum attingit. Infra est ad dexteram
Bosenascum, ulterius ad Padum Stella, et ad torrentis Copae[32]
ostia Bricolanum. Ad huiusque torrentis sinistram intus est Clastidium, illud[33] Poenorum secundo bello Punico horreum, nunc me-
diocre oppidum. De quo Livius, XXI: 'Hannibal, inopia quae per
hostium agros euntes nusquam praeparatis commeatibus maior in
dies excipiebat, ad Clastidium vicum, quo magnum frumenti numerum congesserant Romani, mittit. Ibi, cum vim pararent, spes
facta proditionis nec sane magno pretio—nummis[34] aureis quadringentis datis P. Brundisino[35] praefecto praesidii corrupto—traditur Hannibali Clastidium. Id horreum fuit Poenis sedentibus ad
Trebiam.' Illud autem oppidum et adiacentes civitates per id secundi belli Punici tempus fuisse Ligurum dicionis ostendit Livius,
XXII: 'Q. Minucius in laevam Italiae ad Inferum Mare flexit iter,
geminoque exercitu educto a Liguribus orsus[36] est bellum. Oppida
Clastidium et Litubium, utraque Ligurum, et duae gentis eiusdem

structed, eighty-seven years after the coming of the Lombards into Italy, at the expense of Adoald, son of queen Theodolinda, and of the queen herself.[53] Ponte Orgonasco is located where the torrent Aveto flows into the Trebbia; further up on the right bank of the river are Ottone and Rovegno, and at its source Montebruno, where there is a track into Liguria, to the north of Genoa. To the left of the Aveto, where it is joined by the stream Allegrezze, is the town of San Giovanni, and in the Apennines the castle of Tagliolo.[54] Along the banks of the Po is the mouth of the stream Tidone, which passes by the town of Castel San Giovanni, on the Aemilian Way in the territory of Piacenza. Below it on the right is Bosnasco. Further inland, near the Po, is Stella, and at the mouth of the stream Coppa, Bricolano. Inland on the left bank of the Coppa is Casteggio, that granary of the Carthaginians in the second Punic War, now a modest village. In Book XXI Livy writes of it: "Shortage of food grew ever more serious as they made their way through the lands of the enemy, since they had not laid by provisions anywhere in advance. Hannibal accordingly sent men on ahead to the village of Clastidium, where the Romans had stored a great quantity of grain. As the Carthaginians prepared to assault the town, hope arose that it would be betrayed, and, sure enough, at no great expense — the commander of the garrison, Publius of Brundisium, was corrupted with a bribe of four hundred gold pieces — Clastidium was handed over to Hannibal. The town served as the Carthaginians' granary as they camped on the Trebbia."[55] Livy shows in Book XXII that that town and the adjacent cities were under the sway of the Ligurians throughout the second Punic War: "Quintus Minucius altered his course to head for the left side of Italy, toward the Tyrrhenian, and when a double army was led out of Liguria, began hostilities. The towns of Clastidium and Litubium, both Ligurian towns, and the Celeiates and Cerdiciates, two groups of the same people, surrendered. And the

civitates, Celelates Cordiciatesque,[37] sese dediderunt. Et tum omnia cis Padum, praeter Gallos Boios, Ligurum sub dicione erant.'

13   Superius sunt Trochoneum et Turris. Influit inde Padum Staf-
fola torrens, ad cuius ostia est Albianum. Supra ad sinistram Naz-
zanum, et Vorcum ad dexteram, intus Vogheria, oppidum nunc
opulentissimum. Torrens inde habetur Coronus, ad cuius sinistram intus est Cassium, ad dexteram superius Muleta et Castellarium.[38] Fluvius sequitur Schirmia, supra cuius ostia ad sinistram
est Castrum Novum oppidum, et ipsum opulentissimum, quo insignem Borsium Estensem Philippus Anglus Mediolanensium dux
donavit. Supra est Terdona[39] civitas vetus, quam ad annum nunc
LX supra ducentesimum Federicus Barbarossus imperator vastavit. Superius ad Schirmiae sinistram Seravallis, quod oppidum
Philippi Mediolanensium tertii ducis dono possidet Blasius Age-
reus Genuensis, quem res maritimis expeditionibus bene gestae
clarum fecerunt. Et supra eam sunt Insula, Bissuda, et in Apennino Torrillia. Sequitur amnis Tanarus duodecim auctus torrentibus, quorum quatuor ad sinistram, ad dexteram octo accipit.

14   Ad Tanarum amnem ora incipit celebris nunc Monsferratus
appellata, cuius fines sunt hinc Padus, inde Apenninus, et Tanarus
ipse a fonte suo ad ostia quibus fertur in Padum, et superiori in
parte montes Moncalerio proximi, ubi Pedemontium incipit. Fer-
ratensisque ora paene omnis marchionibus est subdita in Italia
nobilissimis, qui ex Palaeologis Constantinopolitanis imperatoribus oriundi quinquaginta iam et centum annis eam possederunt
oram.[40] Supersuntque fratres quatuor: Johannes, Guilielmus, Bonifacius, et Theodorus sedis Apostolicae notarius. Etsi vero omnes
litteris sunt ornati, tresque natu maiores arma cum laude tractarunt, Guilielmus tamen pluribus per Italiam bellis interfuit.

15   Locorum eius orae ordinem sequi et simul digniora copiosius
describere operosum fuerit atque impeditum nimis opus. Quare

whole region on this side of the Po, except for the Gallic Boii, was then under the control of the Ligurians."⁵⁶

Further up are Tronchonero and Torre. Then the stream Staf- 13 fora flows into the Po, with Albano at its mouth. Above Albano on the left bank of the Staffora is Nazzano, and on the right Varzi, and inland Voghera, now a very prosperous town. Next one comes upon the stream Curone, on whose left bank inland is Ca- sei Gerola, and on the right, higher up, Muleta and Castellaro. The river Scrivia follows, above whose mouth, on the left, is the town of Castelnuovo Scrivia, also very prosperous, which was given by Filippo, count of Angera and duke of Milan, to the illus- trious Borso d' Este.⁵⁷ Above Castelnuovo is the ancient city of Tortona, which was destroyed by the emperor Barbarossa 260 years ago. Higher up on the left bank of the Scrivia is Serravalle, a town that Biagio Assereto of Genoa, whose naval victories have made him famous, holds by gift of Filippo III, duke of Milan. And above Serravalle are Isola del Cantone, Busalla, and in the Apennines, Torriglia. Next comes the river Tanaro, which is fed by twelve streams, four on the left and eight on the right.

At the river Tanaro begins the celebrated region now known as 14 Monferrato: it is bounded on the one side by the Po, on the other by the Apennines, by the Tanaro itself from its source to the mouths that take it into the Po, and in its upper stretch by the mountains beside Moncalieri, where Piedmont begins.⁵⁸ Almost all of the region of Monferrato is subject to the noblest marquises of Italy, descendants of the Paleologi emperors of Constantinople, who have held the region for the last 150 years.⁵⁹ Four brothers are living still, Giovanni, Guglielmo, Bonifacio, and Teodoro, notary of the Apostolic See.⁶⁰ All have attained distinction in letters, and the three elder brothers have won glory in arms, yet Guglielmo has been the most involved in wars throughout Italy.

To trace the sites of this region in order and at the same 15 time give a full description of the more important ones would be a

summatim quaecumque videbuntur digniora explicabimus. Ad
Padi ripam sunt Bassignana (ubi ponte iunctus est Padus), et Va-
lentia vel — uti Plinius appellat — Valentium, quod primo Forum
Fulvii dicebatur, deinde Pomarum, Frassinetum, Casale Sancti
Evasii, quod per aetatem nostram ornatum fuit Facino Cane, pot-
entissimo rei bellicae ductore. Deinceps habentur Pons Sturiae,
Caminum, Gabianum, Verrucula, Sanctus Raphael, Gassinum, et
Moncalerium[41] oppida, ac Salutia illustrium Marchionum eius
cognominis patria, in qua principem nunc habemus litteris et omnimoda virtute conspicuum Ludovicum. Et secundum amnis Tanari ripam post Bassignanam sunt Mons Castellus et Panonum[42]
oppida, deinceps Bergolium, et altera potior eiusdem civitatis pars,
Alexandria, quam Mediolanenses, Placentini, et Cremonenses, ut
Papiensibus inimicis commodius obesse possent, ad annum salutis
LXV supra centesimum et millesimum aedificarunt et, ut novae
urbi ac facto suo maior accederet auctoritas, eam a tertio Alexandro tunc Romano pontifice Alexandriam vocaverunt. Supra eam[43]
sunt oppida Felicianum et Morum,[44] deinceps Asta, civitas malo
usurae quaestu opulenta, quam nunc obtinet dux Aurelianensis
Francorum stirpe regia oriundus. Et inde habentur oppida Guarene, Monticellum, Sancta Victoria, et Pollentium, ubi Cn. Plancius[45] cos. a M. Antonio superatus interfectusque fuit. Superius
sunt Ceva oppidum nobile et sui marchionatus oppida et castella,
inter quae Tanarus fluvius ortum habet. Deinceps per Tanari sinistram descendendo obvia est Alba, Civitas Pompeiana a Plinio
appellata, inde Rocha Tanari oppidum. Et supra, ubi Burmida
fluvius Tanarum amnem illabitur, sunt ad sinistram oppida Castel-
latium, Cassine, deinceps Aquae civitas. Supraque eam sunt Basta-
nium, Curtismilium, et Carium, oppida nobilium Scramporum:
quibus locis oppida continent[46] et castella marchionum Charrec-

laborious task and altogether too difficult to accomplish. I shall therefore set out in summary fashion all those that seem noteworthy. On the banks of the Po are Bassignana, where a bridge crosses the river, and Valenza or *Valentium,* as Pliny calls it, earlier known as *Forum Fulvii*.[61] There follow Pomaro Monferrato, Frassinetto, and Casale Monferrato,[62] notable in our time for Facino Cane, mightiest of military commanders.[63] Then come the towns of Pontestura, Camino, Gabiano, Verrua, San Raffaele, Gassino Torinese, and Moncalieri; then Saluzzo, homeland of the marquises of that name, where now we have Ludovico, a prince remarkable for his learning and virtue of every kind.[64] On the banks of the river Tanaro beyond Bassignana are the towns of Montecastello and Panone, then Bergolo, and another more important part of the same district, Alessandria. The city was built in 1165 CE by the Milanese, Piacentines, and Cremonese to help keep their enemies the Pavians in check. To give the new city and their founding of it a greater measure of prestige, they named it Alessandria after the reigning pope Alexander III.[65] Beyond Alessandria are the towns of Felizzano and Mori, then the city of Asti, grown rich on the ill-gotten gains of usury; it is now a possession of the duke of Orléans, scion of the royal house of France.[66] And then one comes upon the towns of Guarene, Monticello, S. Vittoria d'Alba, and Pollenzo, where the consul Gnaeus Plancius was defeated by Mark Antony and slain.[67] Higher up still are the fine town of Ceva and the towns and castles of the marquisate of Ceva, among which the river Tanaro has its source. Then as one descends along the left-hand bank of the Tanaro, one comes to Alba, called *Civitas Pompeiana* by Pliny,[68] then the town of Rocchetta Tanaro. Above Rocchetta, where the river Bormida flows into the Tanaro, there are on the left the towns of Castellazzo Bormida, Cassine, then the city of Acqui Terme. Above Acqui there are Bistagno, Cortemilia, and Cairo Montenotte, towns of the noble Scarampo; in this region are also found the towns and castles of the marquises del Carretto,

tensium in Apennino sita et ad Genuensium occidentalem Riperiam continentia.

16 Infra vero torrens Borbus ad dexteram Damianum[47] et ad fontem habet Canachium, cui proximum est oppidum Carmagnola. Quod aetate nostra ornatum fuit Francisco cognomine Carmagnola, quo excellentissimo rei bellicae ductore Philippus Mediolanensium dux tertius, si diutius bene uti scivisset, rem Venetam Florentinamque in maximum discrimen perduxisset. Post haec Padus sequitur, qui in sinistro duorum cornuum, quae sub ortu suo efficit, habet Uncinum, et in dextero Cricium. Inter quae duo oppida est ipse Padi ortus, quem Plinius fontem Visundum appellat, dicitque eum mediis diebus aestivis, velut interquiescentem, semper arescere. Et arduus, a quo fons ipse scatet,[48] mons Vesulus a priscis est appellatus, ex quo primum nasci et ab Alpibus discedere incipit Apenninus. Padum amnem, a Vergilio libro VI Eridanum appellatum, Servius grammaticus scribit ideo a poetis dici apud inferos nasci, quia nascatur in Apennino in Mare Inferum verso. Sed contrarium esse videmus, cum ea pars Apennini, ex qua ortum habet, sit in Mare Superum versa. Quod autem postea Servius subiungit verum est: Eridanum fuisse dictum a Solis filio in curru fulminato, quem male regebat; postea sorores flentes versas in populos.

17 Sed iam transeundum est ad aliam Lombardiae partem, quae olim dicta est Italia Transpadana, de qua Plinius: 'Transpadana Italia addita faba, sine qua nihil conficiunt.' Et ubi de rapis libro XVII tractat, dicit: 'tertius hic Transpadanis fructus.' Primusque illi[49] est in Padi ripa Mincius noti vetustique et a Vergilio celebratissimi nominis, fluvius lacu Benaco effusus. Mincio ad sinistram prope Padum est Governum oppidum,[50] apud quem locum pri-

set in the Apennines and bordering on the Genoese Riviera di
Ponente.[69]

Inland the stream Borbore has S. Damiano d'Asti to the right,   16
and at its source, Canale, next to which is the town of Carmagnola, notable in our time for that excellent general Francesco
Bussone da Carmagnola. If Filippo Maria, the third duke of Milan, had been able to make good use of him for longer, he would
have posed a great danger to Venice and Florence.[70] After these
towns, the Po continues with two arms forming below its source,
Oncino on the left one, and Crissolo on the right. Between the
two towns is the source of the Po itself. Pliny calls this spring *Visundum*, and he says that at midday in summer it always dries up,
as if it were having a rest.[71] The sheer mountain from which this
spring wells up was called *Mons Vesulus* by the ancients. It is here
that the Apennines first rise up and split off from the Alps. The
grammarian Servius writes that the river Po (which Vergil in Book
VI calls the Eridanus) is said by poets to arise in the Underworld
because it rises where the Apennine range turns toward the Under
Sea. But we see that the opposite is the case, since the part of the
Apennines where the Po has its source is turned toward the Upper
Sea.[72] However, Servius's subsequent observation is true: the Po
was called the Eridanus from the son of the Sun, who was blasted
by lightning in his chariot when he lost control of it. His sisters
were later changed into poplars as they wept for him.[73]

Now we must cross over to the other side of Lombardy, the   17
part which was once called Transpadane Italy, on which Pliny
writes: "Transpadane Italy, the bean added — nothing is prepared
in the kitchen without it."[74] And when Pliny discusses the turnip
in Book XVII, he says: "This is the third-ranking product of the
land north of the Po."[75] The first river of Transpadane Italy along
the banks of the Po is the ancient and well-known Mincio, much
celebrated by Vergil, which flows out of Lake Garda. On the left
bank of the Mincio near the Po lies the town of Governolo, where

mus Leo papa Attilam Hunnorum regem, qui 'flagellum Dei' dictus est, ne ulterius Italiam ingrederetur suae sanctitatis gravitate deterruit. Et ubi Mincius palude emittitur Mantuam urbem circumdante, Formigosa est castellum. Mantuam urbem vetustissimam ab Etruscis conditam et unam fuisse XII coloniarum, quas superius ex Livio Patavino docuimus trans Apenninum ab ea gente missas, magis constat quam ut alia indigeat probatione, praesertim cum poeta insignis Vergilius civis eius id orbi faciat notissimum, diffusiusque eius urbis narret originem: 'Mantua dives avis, sed non genus omnibus unum,' et cetera. Unde satis fuerit cum Martiali coquo dixisse: 'Marone felix Mantua est.' Livius libro XXII: 'Ita divisae copiae, Boisque in agrum suum Tannetum profectis, Insubres Cenomannique super amnis Mincii ripam consederunt. Infra mille passuum[51] et Cornelius cos. eidem flumini castra applicuit.' Et libro XXIIII prodigia enumerans, quae anno V secundi belli Punici fuerunt, dicit: 'Mantuae stagnum effusum Mincio amni cruentum visum.'

18 Passa est pridem Mantua calamitates maximas praeter illas quae Vergiliano versu sunt notissimae: 'Mantua, vae! miserae nimium vicina Cremonae.' Nam ab Attila, Gothis, Longobardis, et Chachanno Bavarorum rege eam quandoque dirutam, quandoque spoliatam, quandoque moenibus apertis immunitam fuisse relictam in *Historiis* ostendimus. Mantuae per Caroli Magni tempora sanguis Christi miraculosus apparuit, ad quem visendum II Leo papa se contulit, et inde in Germaniam ad Carolum accessit. Carolusque Calvus Magni filius Mantuae veneno interiit, quod Hebraeus medicus pecunia corruptus dedit. Eadem quoque in urbe II Nicolaus pontifex Romanus concilium celebravit, in quo confirmata est constitutio de pontificis Romani electione a cardinalibus facienda. Interfuitque concilio Matildis gloriosa, in cuius po-

Pope Leo I stopped Attila the Hun, the so-called Scourge of God, from further incursions into Italy by the force of his holiness.[76] The castle of Formigosa is situated at the point where the Mincio emerges from the marshes surrounding Mantua. I showed above on the evidence of Livy of Padua that the ancient city of Mantua was founded by Etruscans as one of the twelve colonies settled by them across the Apennines,[77] and the fact is too firmly established to need further confirmation, especially since her citizen, the famous poet Vergil, makes this plain to all and sundry in telling at length the story of the city's origin: "Mantua rich in forebears, yet not of a single stock," etc.[78] So it is enough to say with the cook Martial: "Mantua is blessed with Vergil."[79] Livy writes in Book XXII: "And so the armies separated: while the Boii departed for their own territory of Taneto, the Insubrians and Cenomani encamped on the banks of the river Mincio. The consul Cornelius pitched his own camp on the same river less than a mile away."[80] And in Book XXIII, where he lists the prodigies of the fifth year of the Second Punic War, Livy says: "At Mantua the swamp that the river Mincio drains into appeared to be made of blood."[81]

Mantua has suffered great calamities in the past, quite apart from those familiar to us from the poetry of Vergil: "Alas for Mantua, too close to poor Cremona!"[82] I have shown in my *Histories* that at the hands of Attila, the Goths, the Lombards, and king Chachannus of the Bavarians, it has been at various times destroyed, pillaged, and had its walls breached and left defenseless.[83] In the time of Charlemagne, Christ's miraculous blood was displayed at Mantua: Pope Leo II went there to see it, before going on to Charlemagne in Germany.[84] It was at Mantua that Charlemagne's son, Charles the Bald, died from poison given him by a Jewish physician who had been bribed. Also in Mantua, Pope Nicholas II convened a council, at which the article that required popes to be elected by the College of Cardinals was confirmed.[85] The council was attended by the glorious Countess Matilda, in

18

testate ea urbs tunc erat. Obiit in ea nuper praestantissimus princeps Johannes Franciscus Gonzaga bello et pace clarissimus, virtute cuius et proximarum Lombardiae civitatum infortuniis per aetatem nostram opibus Mantua populoque quam multis ante fuerit saeculis plenior est facta. Estque illi superstes Paula uxor, feminarum aetatis nostrae cum propter humanitatem eius ac prudentiam singularem tum propter religionem praecipuam celeberrima.[52] Et huiusmodi parentum laudibus respondentes Ludovicus marchio Carolusque frater, etsi arma cum laude tractant, litteris tamen exornantur. Quibus eos et fratres ac sorores imbuit vir doctissimus ac omnimoda virtute conspicuus Feltrensis Victorinus. Episcopum item et civem nunc habet Mantua praestantissimum Galeacium Caprianum, litteris, honestate, et prudentia ornatissimum.

19   Mincium amnem ponte iungit Valegium oppidum. Supra ad lacus emissorium est Piscaria magni portorii oppidum, arce et ponte magnifici operis a Scaligeris olim Veronensibus communitum. Isque pro Benaco Gardae lacus nunc appellatus est. Vergilius: 'Quos patre Benaco velatus harundine glauca Mincius infesta ducebat in aequora puppi.' Benacus vero oppida et vicos habet ad dexteram, Lagisium Gardamque, a quo nomen accipit, et Turrim, Malsesinum,[53] et Turbolum, sub quo illum intrat Sarcha fluvius in Tridentinis montibus oriundus. Estque is Turboli vicus turri munitus debilissima, ad quem primaria *Historiarum* nostrae aetatis pars pro miraculo narrat triremes Venetorum Philippensi bello altissimis traductas montibus in Benacum fuisse dimissas. Sarchae item ad dexteram sunt castella et vici: Archus, Drenna, Madrusium, et ad parvi lacus quem in montibus facit dexteram Vocianum, superiusque in valle Pontionum, et ad fluvii Sarchae fontem

whose power the city then was. The excellent prince Gianfrancesco Gonzaga, famous in war as in peace, died there not long ago.
Thanks to his virtues and to the misfortunes of the nearby Lombard cities, Mantua has become more populous and powerful in
our time than it has been for many centuries. His wife Paola survives him, most celebrated of the women of our age both for her
humanity and singular wisdom and for her extraordinary piety.
Their sons, the marquis Ludovico and his brother Carlo, mirror
the virtues of their parents and, though soldiers of distinction,
nevertheless have great literary accomplishments, something inspired in them, along with their brothers and sisters, by Vittorino
da Feltre, that man of outstanding learning and virtue of every
sort.[86] Mantua now has the excellent citizen Galeazzo Cavriani as
its bishop, remarkable for his culture, good character and good
sense.[87]

A bridge crosses the river Mincio at the town of Valeggio. 19
Above it, at the outlet of the lake, is Peschiera del Garda, a town
that derives much income from its customs tolls. It is defended by
an imposing castle and a bridge built by the Scaligeri, formerly of
Verona.[88] The lake, once known as Benacus, is now called Garda.
Vergil writes of the men "whom the Mincius with its veil of gray
reeds carried down to the sea in their fighting ships from father
Benacus."[89] Lake Garda has the following towns and villages on
the right: Lazise, and Garda (from which the lake takes its name),
Torri del Benaco, Malcesine, and Torbole. Beneath Torbole the
river Sarca, which rises in the mountains of the Trentino, flows
into Lake Garda. The village of Torbole has no more than a very
weak tower to defend it. The first section of my *History* of the
present age tells the miraculous tale of how in the war against
Filippo Maria Visconti Venetian triremes were hauled over the
tops of the mountains and launched from here on to Lake Garda.[90]
To the right of the Sarca, there are more castles and villages: Arco,
Drena, Castel Madruzzo, and, to the right of the little lake that

Sancta Maria. Ad Mincii autem sinistram sunt Rivalta,[54] Goidum, intusque Volta, et Capriana. Ad lacus vero sinistram: Rivoltella, Desentianum, Minervium, et, in sinus quem facit lacus angulo, Salodium. Post ea in circuitu, Madernum, Gargnanum,[55] Lucionium,[56] et Riva nobilissimum regionis oppidum, quod in *Historiis Longobardorum* legimus sic appellatum fuisse a rivo sanguinis, qui factus est cum rex Longobardorum Grimoaldus Francos Italiam per Tridentum ingressos magna occidione in proelio superasset. Superius ad Sarchae sinistram, Tiennium[57] et Cadarcionum, et[58] in lacus insula Sermionum.

20   Ultra Mincium per Padi ripam est Burgus Fortis, ubi Mantuanus marchio illum munitissimis hincinde custoditum arcibus catena claudit. Paulo supra sunt amnis Ollii ostia. Is fluvius lacu Sebuino (quem nunc Isei vocant) effusus brevi supra Padum tractu, ad dexteram Clesio augetur flumine, prope cuius ostia est oppidum Marcharia, et ad ipsa ostia, Calvatum castellum. Ad Clesii vero dexteram est Asola oppidum, et Morum, Monsclarusque, cui amplissima adiacet planities, ac Lunatum. Ad eiusque sinistram, Gavardum, Buarnum, Angosenium, superiusque Clesium tres augent torrentes: Toverus, Degnus, Biocolus. Ederum inde habetur castellum apud sui nominis lacum, quem sub Ludronio castello altissimis in montibus influit Chaffar torrens. Ad Clesii vero fontem Bargatium est oppidulum. At ad Ollii fluminis sinistram sunt Pons Vicus, Urcei Novi, Urcei Veteres oppida. Et supra ad Sebuinum est Isei oppidum, a quo lacus novum accepit nomen. Supra, ubi Ollius ipse[59] lacum influit, est Pisognum castellum, et, ubi torrente augetur Grinia, Buenum, superius Civitale et Bro-

the Sarca forms in the hills, Vezzano. Higher up in the valley is Pinzolo, and at the source of the Sarca, Madonna di Campiglio.[91] To the left of the Mincio, there are Rivalta sul Mincio, Goito, and further inland Volta and Cavriana. On the left side of Lake Garda are Rivoltella, Desenzano, Manerba, and in the corner of a bay in the lake, Salò. Past these, going round the lake, we come to Maderno, Gargnano, Limone, and Riva del Garda, the major town of the area. We read in the *History of the Lombards* that Riva was so named from the river of blood that formed when the Franks who had come down into Italy by way of Trent were routed in battle by Grimuald, king of the Lombards, and cut to pieces.[92] Higher up, to the left of the Sarca, are Tenno and Cavadeno. On an island in Lake Garda is Sirmione.

Beyond the Mincio on the banks of the Po is Borgoforte. The 20 Marquis of Mantua can block the river there with a chain strung between very strong fortresses set on either side.[93] A little above Borgoforte is the mouth of the Oglio. This river flows out of *Lacus Sebuinus*, now known as Lago d'Iseo. A short way above the Po it is joined by the river Chiese, near whose mouth is the town of Marcaria, and at the mouth itself, the castle of Calvatone. On the right bank of the Chiese are the towns of Asola, Casalmoro, Montichiari (with a large plain next to it), and Lonato. To the left of the Chiese there are Gavardo, Bione, Agnosine. Higher up three streams join the Chiese, the Toverno, Degnone, and Abbiocolo. Then comes Idro, the castle on the lake of the same name, into which, below the castle of Lodrone in the high mountains, the stream of the Caffaro flows. Then at the source of the Chiese lies the little town of Barghe. To the left of the Oglio, on the other hand, are the towns of Pontevico, Orzinuovi, Orzivecchi. Above them, on the Lago d'Iseo, is the town of Iseo, from which the lake takes its modern name. Further up, where the Oglio itself enters the lake, is the castle of Pisogne, and at the point where the stream Grigna joins the Oglio, Biennio, and above it Cividate Camuno

cium.[60] Ubi fontem habeat Ollius difficile est definire.[61] Nam cum
a Frigidolfo lacu (qui est in Alpibus) torrentes decidant duo: qui
ad sinistram est Frigidolfum nomen retinens, Ollium influit; qui
vero est ad dexteram, in alium cadit torrentem, a quo Ollium habere initium incolae affirmant. Cum item alter torrens apud Poggium castellum oriundus duorum, quos habet ramorum, altero ad
sinistram per Dialengum, Sanctum Bartholomaeum, Armicumque
et Cusiam, Vallis Solis loca, Abduam amnem,[62] altero ad dexteram
Ollium[63] illabitur, communem cum Abdua ortum Ollius habere
videtur. Sed ad inferiora amnis Ollius paulo supra Clesii ostia ad
sinistram habet Platinam, post Rebechum, inde Soncinum oppida, superius Palatiolum et Calebium. Ad lacusque sinistram,
Sarnagum, Pranorium,[64] Loarium, Monticulum, Gemium et Edo-
lium.

21   Medio quod Clesium et Ollium amnes interiacet spatio Brixia
est praepotens civitas, quam Iustinus ex Trogo dicit conditam
fuisse simul cum Mediolano et pluribus aliis civitatibus a Gallis
qui urbem Romam ceperunt. Sed Livius velle videtur eam fuisse
Cenomannorum olim, a quibus condita sit, caput. Est autem vetusto nomine et rebus apud eam gestis clara. Eam enim Livius
libro XXI fuisse Romanis auxilio his verbis scribit: 'L. Aemilius
imperator effusum agmen ad Mutinam ducit. Et in silvis (quae
tunc circa Mutinam erant) caesi sunt Romanorum LXXX. Ceteri
Tannetum petierunt. Sex signa militaria adempta. Fuere tunc auxilio Romanis Brixiani Galli adversus alios Gallos et Boios.' Et libro
XXII: 'Ita divisae copiae, Boisque in agrum suum Tannetum profectis, Insubres cum Cenomannis super amnis Mincii ripam
consederunt. Infra mille passuum[65] et Cornelius cos. eidem flu-

and Berzo.[94] It is difficult to determine where the Oglio has its source. For two streams descend from Lake Frigidolfo [Lago Nero] in the Alps: the one on the left, keeping the name Oglio Frigidolfo, flows down into the Oglio, while the stream on the right drops down into another torrent, and from this torrent the inhabitants are sure the Oglio originates. There is similarly a second stream, which rises at the castle of Poggio and also has two branches, that on the left passing through Ponte di Legno, S. Bartolomeo, Armico and Cusiano (places in the Val di Sole) into the river Adda, while its right-hand branch empties into the Oglio; so the rivers Oglio and Adda would seem to have a common source. In its lower reaches, the river Oglio has on the left, shortly after the point where the Chiese joins it, the towns of Piadena and later Robecco, then Soncino, and further up, Palazzolo and Castelli Calepio. On the left bank of the Lago d'Iseo are found Sarnico, Pianoro, Lovere, Monticolo, Cemmo, and Edolo.

In the tract of land that lies between the rivers Chiese and Oglio is the mighty city of Brescia, which Justin, following Trogus, says was founded by the Gauls who captured Rome, at the same time as Milan and many other cities.[95] But Livy seems to want Brescia to have been the former capital of the Cenomanni, and for them to have founded it.[96] It is in any case an ancient foundation and one with a distinguished history. In Book XXI Livy writes that it came to the assistance of the Romans, in these words: The commander Lucius Aemilius led a disorderly troop of soldiers to Modena, and eighty of the Romans were killed in the forests which then surrounded the town. The rest made for Taneto. Six battle standards were captured. The Gauls of Brescia then gave the Romans assistance against the other Gauls and the Boii.[97] And, in Book XXII: "And so the armies separated, the Boii departing for their own territory of Taneto, while the Insubrians and Cenomanni encamped on the banks of the river Mincio. The consul Cornelius pitched his own camp on the same river less than a mile

21

mini castra applicuit. Inde mittendo in vicos Cenomannorum Brixiamque, quae caput gentis erat, ut satis comperit, et cetera.' Nec tamen minus clara est reddita nuper obsidione quam[66] omnium aetatis nostrae durissimam Philippensi bello sub Francisci Barbari patricii Veneti, insignis viri, praefectura defensioneque pertulit.[67]

22   Brixiam praeterlabitur fluvius Mella, de scatentibus ubique per regionem fontibus aut rivis potius quam quatuor a torrentibus[68] illum influentibus non multis auctus aquis, quas ad nullum proximorum amnium integer perducit. Habet Mella ad dexteram Monpianum, Concisum, et Seretium castella, ad sinistram vero, ubi crescere incipit, Chorium, subinde Villam et Uncinum, et, ubi influit Broccus torrens, Broccium. Ad Brocci autem ortum Lodrinum[69] est. Ad fontemque Mormae torrentis Pesacium, secusque Mellae ipsius alveum Boratum et Coium. Ad Padi deinde alveum sequitur Dosiolum, et post[70] Vitelliana oppidum opibus populoque refertissimum, quod Vitellius imperator, direpta Cremona, dum Othonis Romae imperantis mortem cum proditoribus constitutam exspectat, pro castris primo habuit, postea ut pro oppido habitaretur, reliquit communitum. Superius est Sabloneta oppidum, a quo familia in Cremonensibus nobilis comitum Persiceti, quae nunc habet Brocardum litteris ornatissimum, duxit originem. Inde quinto milliario in Padi ripa est[71] Casale, quod cognomine dicunt Maius, oppidum populo frequentissimum.

23   Triginta inde milibus passuum abest Cremona, vetus Romanorum colonia simul cum Placentia (sicut Livius XXI scribit) deducta, quae—sicut Vergilius non de praeterito magis vere dixit quam de futuro vaticinatus fuit—multas saepenumero calamitates accepit,[72] quod post tempora Vergilii a Vitelliano[73] exercitu primum (ut diximus) direpta, et post annos circiter quadringentos a Gothis, inde ab Agilulfo[74] Longobardorum rege, et Sclavis illi mi-

away. Sending messengers into the villages of the Cenomani and to Brescia, which was the capital city of the tribe, he satisfied himself that," etc.[98] Nor was the fame of Brescia lessened by the siege — the hardest siege of any in our time — which it endured in the war with Filippo Maria Visconti, when it was defended by the noble Francesco Barbaro, the Venetian captain.[99]

The river Mella runs down past Brescia, its flow increased more   22 by the springs and rivulets that well up everywhere in the region than by the four streams that flow into it — with no great volume of water, which the Mella as a whole carries into none of the closest rivers. The Mella has on its right the castles of Mompiano, Concesio, and Sarezzo; on the left, where it begins to widen, Corio, and then Villa and Oncino, and where the stream Brozzo joins it, the village of Brozzo, and, at the source of the stream, Lodrino. At the source of the stream of Marma is Pezzaze, and on the course of the Mella itself, there are Burato and Collio. Along the course of the Po there follows Dosolo, and then Viadana, a thriving and populous town. After he had sacked Cremona and was waiting for the death of Otho, the reigning Roman emperor, which he had arranged with Otho's betrayers, the emperor Vitellius first used the place as his headquarters, and then had it fortified as a habitable town.[100] Further to the north is the town of Sabbioneta, where the Cremonese noble family of the Counts of Persico originated, notable now for the literary distinction of Broccardo Persico.[101] Five miles away from Sabbioneta along the Po is the populous town of Casale, nowadays called Casalmaggiore.

Thirty miles from Casale is the old Roman colony of Cremona,   23 which was founded at the same time as Placentia, as Livy says in Book XXI.[102] Cremona has often suffered great calamities — Vergil was as prophetic of the future of Cremona as he was clear on its past[103] — first being sacked by Vitellius's army after Vergil's time, as we mentioned, and then by the Goths some four hundred years later, then in turn by Agilulf king of the Lombards and by

litantibus per diem XII Septembris ad annum salutis circiter sexcentesimum et tricesimum eversa, et annis postea plus minus sex-
centis inde elapsis a Federico Barbarosso imperatore spoliata ac
immunita fuit derelicta. Nunc autem Blanchae Mariae dotalis
Francisco Sfortiae viro eius subiecta est.[75] Habuit ex vetustissimis
M. Furium poetam cognomine Bibaculum, et postea Quintilium
poetam Vergilio et Horatio familiarissimum, Eusebium quoque[76]
ecclesiasticorum dogmatum peritissimum. Habuit etiam[77] Gerar-
dum Sablonetium excellentem physicum et astronomum, qui,
Chaldaeas Graecasque aeque ac Latinas edoctus litteras, Avicen-
nae et Rasis (sive *Almansoris*) libros, qui nunc Latine leguntur,
transtulit ex Arabico. Et nuper habuit Johannem Balistarium prae-
ceptorem meum grammaticae, rhetoricae, et poeseos, quibus
adulescens ab eo imbutus fui, peritissimum. Habet[78] quoque cum
multos juri et medicinae deditos tum maxime Nicolaum, Placentinum episcopum, et Vincentium fratrem, Amidanos, cives eloquentia exornatos.

24   Supra Cremonam ad dexteram est Machastorma castellum
caede Cavalcaboum, quos Cabrinus Fundulus[79] crudelissime ibi
occidit, notissimum. Deinde proximo in[80] loco sunt ostia fluminis
Abduae. Intusque ad dexteram paucis supra Padum miliaribus
Abduam influit Serius amnis, ad cuius ostia imminet Abduae Picilionum[81] oppidum populo frequentatum, arcem habens inter primas munitioresque Lombardiae numerandam. Et ad Serii dexteram sunt Sanctus Sebastianus, Castilionum, Ruminengum,
Martinengum, et in montibus Ghisalbagum Seriacumque. Et inde
Vallis Seriana vicis plurimis frequentata. Ad Serii vero fluminis
sinistram primum est Crema oppidum nobile a Federico Barbarosso post afflictam Cremonam in eius civitatis damnum oppro-
briumque aedificatum, quo Veneti per foedera sunt potiti quae
cum Francisco Sfortia adversus Mediolanenses inierunt. Supra

Slavs fighting for him, the last on a September 12 around 630 CE. Six hundred years after that, Cremona was plundered and left stripped of its defenses by the emperor Frederick Barbarossa. Now, however, Cremona has passed into the hands of Francesco Sforza with the dowry of his wife Bianca Maria.[104] In antiquity it numbered among its citizens the poet Marcus Furius Bibaculus and later the poet Quintilius, the friend of Vergil and Horace, and also Eusebius, the authority on ecclesiastical doctrine.[105] Cremona also claims Gerardo of Sabbioneta, the renowned physician and astronomer, who knew Syriac and Greek as well as he knew Latin, and translated the books of Avicenna and Rasis (that is, the *Al-mansor*)[106] from Arabic into the Latin in which we read them.[107] Cremona bore Giovanni Balestreri, too, an experienced teacher of grammar, rhetoric, and poetry, subjects in which he steeped me in my youth. There are many other Cremonese citizens besides who have devoted themselves to the law and medicine, in particular Niccolò Amidano, the bishop of Piacenza, and his brother Vincenzo, both men of great eloquence.[108]

Further up beyond Cremona on the right lies the castle of Mac-castorna, notorious for the slaughter of the Cavalcabò, whom Gabrino Fondulo had cruelly put to death there.[109] Neighboring it is the mouth of the river Adda. Inland to the right, a few miles above the Po, the river Serio flows into the Adda; overlooking the confluence is Pizzighettone, a populous town with a citadel reckoned to be one of the best and strongest in Lombardy. To the right of the Serio are San Sebastiano, Castelleone, Romanengo, Martinengo, and, in the hills, Ghisalba and Seriate. And then comes the Valle Seriana, crowded with many villages. To the left of the river Serio is first the well-known town of Crema, built by Frederick Barbarossa to weaken and degrade the city of Cremona after he had crushed that town; the Venetians have taken possession of Crema by the terms of the treaty that they entered into with Francesco Sforza against the Milanese. Above Crema are Nembro and

24

sunt Nemberium et Vertorium oppida, et ad fluvii fontem Bardionum.[82] Imminetque ostiis Abduae ad sinistram Castrum Novum cognomine Bucca[83] Abduae.

25   Interiusque quinquagesimo secundum amnis decursum milliario est Lauda civitas, quam Federicus Barbarossus Mediolano destructo aedificavit. Ornaturque ea civitas Ambrosio Vignatensi, iureconsulto in Lombardis praestantissimo bonarumque artium studiis deditissimo, et pariter Maphaeo Veggio doctissimo atque optimo viro, aliquotque editis operibus (partim metro partim oratione soluta) claro. Distat vero a praesenti Lauda civitate tertio milliario altera Lauda 'vetus' dicta, quam vulgo ferunt Cn. Pompeium aedificasse, datis ibi colonis primariis piratarum, quos duxerat in triumphum — quod quidem nullo invenimus in[84] loco. Quin potius Servius in Vergilii expositione est auctor piratas, partim in Graecia partim in Calabria, a Pompeio agros habuisse, nisi forte aliter voluisse videatur innuere Lucanus, in Primo, ubi facit Caesarem Arimini contionantem sic dicere: 'Quae sedes erit emeritis? Quae rura dabuntur quae noster veteranus aret? Quae moenia fessis? An melius fient piratae, Magne,[85] coloni?' Plinius vero[86] velle videtur eam urbem fuisse conditam a populis nomine Laeviis[87] et Maricis, qui fuerint[88] Transalpini, et tamen eam appellat Laudam Pompeianam. Raram autem apud veteres[89] eius urbis aut loci videmus fieri mentionem. Primus namque post[90] Plinium locus in quo Laudae civitatis nomen legatur est ubi nos Odoacris Herulorum regis adventum in Italiam describentes diximus — quod et aliunde accepimus — Orestem patricium, Augustuli imperatoris genitorem, apud Laudam Odoacri congressum ab eoque superatum Papiam confugisse.

26   Supra Laudam Abduae imminet Cassianum oppidum. Dehinc[91] regio est Mons Brigantius appellata, multis habitata viculis, et vini optimi castanearumque feracissima. Ubi vero Abduae mons

Vertova and at the source of the Serio, Bondione. Castelnuovo, called "Castelnuovo Bocca d'Adda," overlooks the mouth of the Adda on the left.

Further inland, fifty miles up the course of the river Adda, is 25 the city of Lodi, which Frederick Barbarossa built following his destruction of Milan. These days Lodi can boast of Ambrogio Vignati, the leading jurisconsult of Lombardy and one who devotes himself to the study of the liberal arts,[110] and also Maffeo Vegio, a man at once upright and learned, famous for a number of works he has published, some in meter and some in prose.[111] Three miles from the present city of Lodi is a second Lodi, called "Lodi Vecchio," which is generally said to have been built by Pompey, when the pirate chieftains that he led in his triumph were assigned as its colonists, but I can find no source for this information. Servius, in fact, in his commentary on Vergil says that the pirates had lands from Pompey in Greece and in Calabria: unless Lucan is hinting at another interpretation in Book I, where he has Caesar addressing his troops at Rimini thus: "What homes will there be for their retirement? What lands will be given for our veterans to plow? What walls to shelter the weary? Or would pirates, Pompey, make better colonists?"[112] In any event Pliny would have it that the city of Lodi Vecchio was founded by transalpine peoples called the Laevii and Marici, and yet he calls her 'Lauda Pompeiana.'[113] But we find that the city and the place are seldom mentioned by the ancients. Apart from Pliny, the first mention of the city of Lodi that one reads is in the episode where we described the descent of Odoacer, king of the Heruli, into Italy, writing that the patrician Orestes, the father of the emperor Augustulus, fought Odoacer at Lodi, was beaten by him, and fled to Pavia, as we have found in other sources too.[114]

Above Lodi, the town of Cassano d'Adda overlooks the river 26 Adda. Beyond Cassano there is a territory called the Brianza, occupied by many small towns and productive of fine wine and

ipse imminet, Brippium est oppidum quod Veneti obtinent. Et supra varios inter colles Abduam dextrorsum illabitur Brembus amnis, cuius in convalle[92] inter montes castella sunt[93] et vici: Sanctus Petrus, Menium, Angum,[94] Sanctus Peregrinus, Sanctus Johannes, et Platia. Contra Brembi vero amnis ostia est Vavarium castellum et intus Gorgontiola. Attrahit deinde ex lacu Lario, nunc Comi dicto, Abdua sinum, quem Leuci lacum dicunt. Estque ad lacus ipsius emissorium,[95] qua fluvius Abdua in mediterranea exit, Leucum oppidum, ubi pons eum iungit amnem. Et secundum lacus dexteram superius sunt Abbatia et[96] Mandellum, deinceps Lernium, Varena, Bollanum, Corcenum, Prona, et ubi Abdua ipse ex Alpibus cadens Larium influit, est Colungum.[97] Supraque sunt Morbengum, Stationa, Tiranum, Machum, et (ubi communem Abduae cum Ollio fontem esse diximus) sub Frigidolfo Burinum. Sunt etiam ad Abduae lacum influentis sinistram Postalesium, Xundrum, et supra lacunam, quae Abduae fons a multis esse creditur, Posclavinum.

27 Medio autem quod Abduam influentes Serium et Brembum fluvios interest spatio editissimis in montibus est Bergomus[98] civitas vetusta a Gallis simul cum Mediolano et Brixia et Verona eodemque tempore (sicut Pompeius Trogus dicit) aedificata. Plinius tamen eam urbem Oromoniorum stirpis esse affirmat, sicut infra in Como dicemus.[99] Quae Gasparino Bergomensi rhetore et grammatico exornata est. Eo item spatio quod Brembum, Serium, Abduamque amnes et Bergomenses intercedit montes, regio est Glarea Abduae appellata. In qua sunt castella:[100] Trivilium, Mozanica, et (quae supra sunt dicta) Ruminengum, Martinengum, et Caravagium proelio insigne omnium aetatis nostrae memorabilissimo, in quo Mediolanensis tunc rei publicae exercitus copias Venetorum (equitum XII, peditum IIII milia)[101] fregit fuditque, vel pot-

chestnuts. Where the Brianza itself abuts on the Adda is the town of Brivio, which is in Venetian hands. Beyond that, making its way through the hills, the river Brembo empties from the right into the Adda. In its valley among the hills are the castles and villages of Ponte San Pietro, Almenno, Zogno, San Pellegrino Terme, San Giovanni Bianco, and Piazzolo. Over against the mouth of the river Brembo is the castle of Vaprio and, further inland, Gorgonzola. The river Adda forms a bay of *Lacus Larius* (now known as Lake Como) which is called the Lago di Lecco. At the outlet of the lake, where the Adda flows out into the interior, is the town of Lecco, with a bridge crossing the river. Further up along the right bank of the lake are Abbadia Lariana and Mandello del Lario, then Lierna, Varenna, Bellano, Corenno, Piona. The town of Colico lies at the point where the Adda descends from the Alps and flows into Lake Como. Above it are Morbegno, Stazzona, Tirano, Mazzo di Vitellina; and under Frigidolfo (which we mentioned as the site of the common source of the rivers Adda and Oglio)[115] is Bormio. To the left of the Adda as it flows into Lake Como there are also Postalesio and Sondrio, and, above the lake that many believe is the source of the Adda, Poschiavino.[116]

In the high mountains between the rivers Serio and Brembo, tributaries of the Adda, lies the ancient city of Bergamo, built (as Trogus says) by the Gauls, like Milan, Brescia, and Verona, and at the same time.[117] Yet Pliny states that this city was a foundation of the *Oromonii*, as I mention below in the case of Como.[118] Bergamo can boast Gasparino Barzizza, the rhetorician and teacher.[119] Between the rivers Brembo, Serio, and Adda and the hills of Bergamo is the district called Gera d'Adda, with the castles of Treviglio and Mozzanica, and, as we mentioned above,[120] Rominengo, Martinengo, and Caravaggio, the last famous for the most notable battle of our time, in which the army of the Republic of Milan (as it then was) smashed and routed the Venetian forces of twelve thousand horses and four thousand infantry, or rather, took most

27

ius maiori ex parte cepit. Sequitur[102] ad Padi dexteram Belzoio-
sum villa opulentissima, quam Philippi Angeli Mediolanensium
III ducis dono obtinet Ludovicus Cunii comes, Albricum eius
nominis[103] tertium et Malatestam, comitum Cunii (sicut ostendimus) clarissimorum reliquias, in ea fovens.

28   Post ea sunt ostia Umbronis fluminis, quod Eupilum lacus Larii (sive Comensis) partem exonerat. Et Umbro quidem primum
habet ad dexteram castellum Villalantem, dehinc Sanctum Angelum, et intus longe supra Canturium oppidum. Superius vero
Comum est civitas vetusta, lacui Lario, cui dat cognomen,[104] contigua. Ea a Gallis cum Mediolano, Brixia, et Verona (sicut Trogus
scribit) condita fuit. Civemque[105] habuit paterna origine Plinium,
quem mutatus incolatus vocari fecit Veronensem. Is scribit Comum et Bergomum Oromoniorum[106] stirpis fuisse Catonem tradere ac fateri eius[107] se gentis originem ignorasse. Quam postea
docuit Cornelius Alexander, affirmans ortam fuisse in Graecia,
interpretatione nominis indicante quod vitam in montibus[108] de-
gant. Catullusque poeta innuere videtur Caecilium poetam fuisse
Comensem hoc epigrammate: 'Poetae tenero, meo sodali velim
Caecilio, papyre, dicas: Veronam veniat, Novi relinquens Comi
moenia Lariumque litus. Nam quasdam volo cogitationes amici
accipiat sui meique. Quare si sapiet, viam vorabit.' Plinius autem[109]
Comi consuetus[110] fontem esse dicit in Comensi qui singulis horis
semper intumescit ac residet. Et idem affirmat Abduam amnem
lacum Larium supernatare. Quodque nunc quoque usu cognosci-
tur: lapidem esse dicit in Comensi qui cavatur tornaturque co-
quendis cibis. *Longobardorum* quoque habent *historiae* in lacu Lario
insulam esse, quae Comacina appellaretur, in qua legimus Franci-
lionem primo ducem Romanum, postea aliquos Gothorum et

of them prisoner.[121] On the right bank of the Po there follows the opulent estate of Belgioioso, which Ludovico, Count of Cunio, now holds as fief from Filippo Maria Visconti, third Duke of Milan, and there he raises Alberico III and Malatesta, scions of the famous counts of Cunio, as I related.[122]

Then comes the mouth of the river Lambro, which drains the   28 waters of Lago di Pusiano, a part of *Lacus Larius* (Lake Como). The Lambro has on its right bank first the castle of Villanterio, then S. Angelo Lodigiano, and much further inland, the town of Cantù. Further up again is the ancient city of Como on the edge of Lake Como, to which it gives its name. Como was founded by the Gauls, along with Milan, Brescia, and Verona, as Trogus writes.[123] Pliny the Elder was a citizen of Como through his father's family, though a change of residence led to his being called a Veronese. Pliny writes that according to Cato, Como and Bergamo derived from Oromonian stock — though Cato admitted that he did not know where they came from.[124] Later, Cornelius Alexander revealed their origin by stating that they came from Greece, the name implying that they passed their lives in the mountains.[125] Catullus the poet seems to be suggesting that his fellow poet Caecilius was a man of Como in this epigram: "Dear letter, tell my friend Caecilius, poet of love, to leave the walls of Novum Comum and the shores of Larius and come to Verona. For I want him to share some thoughts of his friend and mine. If he has any sense, he'll eat up the road."[126] Pliny, who knew the town well, says that in the district of Como there is a spring that wells up once an hour and then subsides.[127] Pliny also affirms that the river Adda flows across the surface of Lake Como.[128] And — something that is still known to be in use today — he says that there is a stone in the Como area that is hollowed out and turned on the lathe for cooking food.[129] The *History of the Lombards* speaks of an island called Comacina on Lake Como, where, as we learn, the Roman captain Francio in the first place and then some of the

Longobardorum reges, multas conservasse divitias — et forte maiores omnibus quae ab illo tempore alicubi in Italia fuerint congregatae. Eaque insula, nunc nobis ignota, non longe a domo aberat vel oppido vel vico. Scribit etiam Plinius Transpadanam Italiam iuxta Alpes Larium lacum habere amoenum arbusto agro, ad quem ciconiae non transvolant. Sunt ad eam lacus partem, qui[111] a maioribus appellatur Eupilus, dextera in parte Fenium, Palantium, Ripa, Nesium, Lesenium, et qua se lacus in Abduam flectit, Belasium.

29   Ab Umbronis fluvii ostiis parvo supra Padum tractu est Sanctus Columbanus oppidum, dehinc via Laudensi a Mediolano est Melegnanum. Inde Vicus Mercatus populo frequentissimus, et superius Modoetia nobilissimum totius Lombardiae oppidum, in quo servat absurda consuetudo, ab trecentis annis introducta, Caesares Germanos corona ferrea in Romanos reges imperatoresque insigniri. Id oppidum prius ex parvo amplissimum reddidit Theodericus rex Ostrogothorum primus, palatio in eo magnificentissimi operis aedificato, dehinc Theodolinda Longobardorum regina insignis (ad quam beatus Gregorius *Dialogorum* libros scripsit), basilica[112] beati Johannis Baptistae sumptuosissimi operis superbissimaque in eodem exstructa.[113]

30   Supra Modoetiam vero Umbroni fluvio adiacet Charratum. Secus Comum autem ad Umbronis ex lacu Eupilo ortum Brissia influit torrens, ad cuius ortum castella sunt Murgum, Canossium, et Vatallum. At secundum lacus[114] Larii (vel Comi) sinistram castella sunt: Sennobium, Arcinium, Campus, et ubi torrens Aqua Seria influit, Monasium, dehinc Rasonegum, Gundum, Gravidona, Domassium, Iera, et Soregium, ac, ubi fluvius lacum influit, est Senolegum.[115] Supra torrentem quoque sunt oppida Larium, Victoria, et dehinc castellum Clavenna,[116] apud quam Plinius dicit Curiam Raetiarum fuisse. Ea vero montana regio cur olim Raetia fuerit appellata Iustinus in Trogo sic docet: Tusci a Gallis pulsi

Gothic and Lombard kings kept a mass of treasure—greater treasures, perhaps, than have been gathered anywhere in Italy since that time.[130] This island, now unknown to us, was not far from their residence, a town or a village.[131] Pliny also writes of Lake Como in Transpadane Italy next to the Alps as being a pleasant place with wooded fields, which storks will not fly across.[132] On that part of the lake called Eupilus by our ancestors are, on the right, Fenio, Palanzo, Riva Faggetto, Nesso, Lezzeno, and where the lake bends toward the Adda, Bellagio.

A short way above the Po from the mouth of the river Lambro   29
is the town of San Colombano al Lambro, and beyond that, Melagnano on the road to Lodi from Milan. Then comes the lively town of Vimercate, and, higher up, Monza, the most famous town of all Lombardy. There they keep the strange custom, as they have for three hundred years, of crowning the German Caesars as Roman kings and emperors with the iron crown.[133] Theodoric, the first king of the Ostrogoths, made this insignificant place into an important town with the construction there of a magnificent palace,[134] as later did the famous Queen of the Lombards Theodolinda (to whom St. Gregory dedicated his *Dialogues*) by building the lavish and imposing cathedral of St. John the Baptist at Monza.[135]

Carate Brianza lies on the Lambro north of Monza. Where the   30
river rises out of the Lago di Pusiano, the stream Breggia flows beside Como;[136] at its source are the castles of Muggio, Caneggio, and Vacallo. Along the left side of *Lacus Larius* (Lake Como) are the castles of Cernobbio, Argegno, Campo, and, where the stream Acquaseria empties into Lake Como, Menaggio, then S. Maria Rezzonico, Dongo, Gravedona, Domaso, Gera Lario, Sorico. Samolaco is situated where the river flows into the lake. Above the Acquaseria are Lario, Vittoria, and then the castle of Chiavenna, where Pliny tells us the city of Curia of the Raeti was.[137] Justin in his *Epitome* of Trogus explains why this mountain region was for-

sedibus Alpes occupavere et Raetorum[117] gentem sic ab eorum
duce appellatam condidere. Fueruntque hi populi bifariam in primam et secundam Raetiam divisi. Ad alterum vero Curiae latus[118]
Casatium est, et in extremo lacus angulo Megiulla castellum.

31   Ad dexteram autem Padi ripam post Umbronem prima habentur Ticini ostia. Is fluvius Verbanum lacum, quem nunc Maiorem
dicunt, exonerat. Adiacetque ei[119] ad dexteram quarto supra ostium milliario civitas, nunc Papia, Ticinum nomine vetustiore,
quam Plinius velle videtur fuisse conditam a populis Laeviis et
Maricis, qui fuerunt Transalpini. Sed quantum licet ex Livii scriptis coniicere: Ticinum urbs, quo tempore Hannibal in Italiam venit, nondum erat. Nam libro XXI sic habet: Iam tamen Scipio
Padum traiecerat, ad Ticinum amnem motis castris. Et infra: 'Cum
utrimque ad certamen accensi militum animi essent, Romani
ponte Ticinum iungunt, tutandique pontis causa castellum super-
imponunt.' Et inferius: 'Auxitque pavorem consulis vulnus, pericu-
lumque intercursu tum pubescentis filii pulsatum.[120] Hic erat iuve-
nis Africanus.' Dicimus itaque non potuisse fieri[121] quin, si Papia
tunc fuisset (aut Ticinum) urbs, eius nomen aliquo loco[122] Livius
posuisset, nec pontem Romani fecissent factoque castellum impo-
suissent.

32   Eam civitatem Attila rex Hunnorum direptam vastavit. Et cum
paulo post instaurata esset, Odoacer Herulorum rex Orestem patricium, Augustuli imperatoris genitorem, in eo[123] obsessum vique
captum interfecit. Ticinumque urbs crudeliter direpta atque vastata est, fuitque in ea tum caedes maxima[124] civium Romanorum
quanta numquam[125] alibi post Romani imperii inclinationem com-

merly called Raetia, because when the Etruscans were driven from their lands by the Gauls, they found a home in the Alps, originating a nation named the Raeti after their chief.[138] These people split into two, forming Raetia prima and Raetia secunda. On the other side of Curia is Casaccia, and in the furthest stretch of the lake the castle Mezzola.

On the right bank of the Po beyond the river Lambro, the first 31 river mouths are those of the Ticino. The river drains *Lacus Verbanus*, nowadays called Lago Maggiore. Four miles above the mouth the city of Pavia lies on its right bank. Pavia was formerly called Ticinum, and Pliny apparently thought it was founded by the Laevii and Marici, peoples from the other side of the Alps.[139] But as far as I can tell from the writings of Livy, the city of Ticinum was not yet in existence when Hannibal entered Italy. For in Book XXI he says: "Scipio, however, had by now crossed the Po, having moved his camp up to the river Ticinus."[140] And below: "When the spirits of the soldiers on both sides had been whetted for the struggle, the Romans threw a bridge over the Ticinus and erected a fort besides for its protection."[141] And further on again: "And to add to their fear, the consul was wounded and was only saved from danger by the intervention of his son, who was just reaching manhood; this youth was Scipio Africanus."[142] I therefore say that it is impossible that Livy would not somewhere have named Pavia (or Ticinum) if it had existed at that time, and that the Romans would not have built a bridge, or set a fort over it once they had done so.

Attila, king of the Huns, sacked and laid waste to the city of 32 Ticinum. A little later, when the city had recovered, the king of the Heruli Odoacer laid siege there to the nobleman Orestes, father of Augustulus, took him by force, and had him killed.[143] Ticinum was cruelly sacked and laid waste, with vast slaughter of Roman citizens—greater than any that had happened since the fall of the Roman Empire. About 120 years after that, Alboin, the

missa fuerat. Cuius rei similem[126] ad annum inde circiter[127] cente-simum et vicesimum voverat se facturum Alboinus rex primus Longobardorum, nimia Papiensium resistentia fastiditus. Sed cum ipso in ingressu equus sub eo collapsus surgere nequiret, admoni-tus a comite suo, viro bono,[128] mutavit sententiam,[129] equusque il-lico surgens illum in urbem detulit incolumem. Rudolfo[130] autem Burgundo Italiae regnum occupante, per VII Stephani Romani pontificis tempora Hungari, Salodo duce, Italiam ingressi, Papiam obsessam[131] captamque ferro ignique vastarunt.

33   Alunda fuit adulescentula nobilis et pulcherrima, Papiae (in-certo nobis iure) dominio potita, quam Ugo Arelatensis Italiae rex Lothario filio dedit uxorem. Eoque mortuo, III Berengarius, Ugoni in Italiae regno successor, Papia potitus, mulierem carcere tenuit. Interea Agapitus pontifex Romanus Italiaeque proceres et populi, Berengarii et Alberti filii tyrannidem exosi, Ottonem pri-mum ex Germania in Italiam vocaverunt. Isque cum armatorum milibus quinquaginta veniens, Berengario et Alberto deiectis, Alundam carcere eductam matrimonio sibi copulavit. Tumque[132] Italia a malis, quae diu fuerat perpessa,[133] respirare coepit. Pertha-rit Longobardorum rex monasterium Sanctae Agathae et Theodo-linda regina ecclesiam Sanctae Mariae ad Perticas in ea civitate construxerunt. Et Luthprandus[134] Longobardorum rex ossa beati Augustini ex Sardinia Papiam, ubi venerantissime servantur, de-ferri curavit. Idemque rex monasterium Beati[135] Petri, 'Cellula Aurea' appellatum, et apud Holonam (ubi curiam reges saepe te-nuerunt) monasterium Sancti Anastasii Martyris aedificavit. Gon-diberta regina ecclesiam Sancti Johannis Baptistae et Petrus epis-copus, Luthprandi[136] regis consangineus, ecclesiam Sancti Savini Papiae construxerunt. Eam urbem situ et aëris salubritate amoe-nissimam reges Ostrogothorum et postea Longobardorum libenter incoluerunt. Qua ratione apud eam multa praeclare sunt gesta a

first king of the Lombards, vowed to do the same, infuriated by the citizens' stubborn resistance to him.[144] But as he was actually entering the city, his horse collapsed under him and was unable to get up. On the advice of a one of his attendants, a good man, he changed his mind, and there and then his horse got to its feet and carried him safely into the city. When Rudolf of Burgundy occupied the kingdom of Italy in the time of the Roman pontiff Stephen VII,[145] the Huns under their chieftain Salodus burst into Italy, besieged and captured Pavia, and destroyed it with fire and sword.

Alonda was a beautiful young woman of high birth who took 33 possession of Pavia, though what claim she had on it is not clear to me. Hugh of Arles, the king of Italy, gave her to his son Lothair in marriage, and when Lothair died, Berengar III, Hugh's successor as king of Italy, took over Pavia and put Alonda in prison. Meanwhile the Roman pontiff Agapetus II and the rulers and peoples of Italy came to detest the tyranny of Berengar and his son Albert, and invited Otto I to come to Italy from Germany. Arriving with fifty thousand soldiers, Otto overthrew Berengar and Albert, freed Alonda from prison and married her.[146] At that point Italy began to recover from the troubles she had suffered so long. Perctarit the king of the Lombards built the monastery of St. Agatha, and Queen Theodolinda the church of Santa Maria in Pertica in that city. Liutprand, the king of the Lombards, had the bones of St. Augustine brought from Sardinia to Pavia, where they are kept with great reverence. Perctarit also built the monastery of St. Peter called the *Cellula Aurea*,[147] and at Olona, where the kings often held court,[148] the monastery of Sant'Anastasio the Martyr. At Pavia Queen Gondiberta built the church of St. John the Baptist, and Bishop Peter, a relative of king Liutprand, the church of S. Savino.[149] The Ostrogothic kings, and later the Lombard kings, favored Pavia as their residence for its attractive situation and wholesome air. For that reason it was the scene of many

nobis in *Historiis*, praeter haec,[137] accuratissime scripta. Ornavit eam vero[138] maximisque prosecutus est spiritualibus adiumentis Epiphanius episcopus Aquileia oriundus, qui sex milia captivorum Mediolanensium a Francorum rege liberari impetravit. Et Johannes Romanus pontifex nominis ordine duodevigesimus, qui a Bonifacio, Ferrutii filio, pontifice adulterino captus in arcemque Sancti Angeli coniectus diem vi adhibita obiit, civis fuit Papiensis. Habet quoque nunc Papia in gymnasiis multos iuris[139] civilis et pontificii ac philosophiae et medicinae scientia claros, sed ex civibus Catonem Saccium et Sillanum Nigrum civili deditos iuri et bonarum artium studiis exornatos.

34   Adiacet Ticino[140] amni intus ad dexteram[141] et fossae manufactae ab eodem fluvio ductae haeret Abbiagrassum. Superiusque est Vigivenum Petri Candidi, litteras Graecas ac Latinas edocti ac editis operibus clari, patria, inde Cuccionum, et paulo post Sextium lacui Verbano propinquum. Qua in parte illum[142] duo minores augent lacus, ex quibus[143] qui est ad dexteram Lugani lacus, qui ad sinistram Sancti Iulii appellatur. Ad Verbani (sive Maioris) lacus dexteram Angleria primum est oppidum, a quo Vicecomitum familia originem traxit. Recedit vero intus ad dexteram eius lacus partem Varesium oppidum populo frequentissimum. Supra curvatus est bifariam Verbanus (sive Maior) lacus, Lugani ea in parte appellatus, eique[144] adiacent Brosinum, Portus, Caput Laci, Campionum, Ostenum, et Porleccia. Et ubi Lavenus influit amnis, sunt ad lacus undas: Sessa, Morchum, et Luganum, a quo lacus nomen accepit. Ticinum[145] autem ad sinistram parvo supra Padum tractu torrens influit Gravalonus, ad cuius sinistram est Gropetum. Intusque sunt Mortaria oppidum nobile et Laumellum nunc exile sed opulentissimum olim oppidum, multis[146] celebratum (praesertim Longobardorum) historiis. Nam Theodolinda, Autaris Longobardorum regis relicta, Agilulfum Taurinensem ducem

remarkable events, of which, apart from those mentioned here, I have given a detailed account in my *History*.[150] The bishop Epiphanius from Aquileia gave luster to the city and added greatly to its spiritual appeal. He won the release of six thousand Milanese prisoners from the king of the Franks.[151] The Roman pope John XVIII was a citizen of Pavia; he was seized and imprisoned in the Castel Sant'Angelo by the false pope Boniface, son of Ferruccio, and met a violent end there.[152] Pavia also now has in its schools many distinguished practitioners of canon and civil law, philosophy and medicine. Among these, Catone Sacco and Sillano Negri, exponents of civil law and devotees of the liberal arts, are citizens of Pavia.[153]

Further inland, to the right of the river Ticino, lies Abbiate-   34
grasso, situated on a man-made canal that runs off from the Ti-cino.[154] Higher up is Vigevano, the home town of Pier Candido Decembrio, famous for his mastery of Greek and Latin letters and for his writings.[155] Then comes Cuggiono, and soon after Sesto Calende near Lago Maggiore. In this region, two smaller lakes feed into Lago Maggiore: the one to the right of the lake is called the Lago di Lugano, to the left, the Lago di San Giulio. The first town on the right of *Lacus Verbanus* (or Lago Maggiore), is An-gera, where the Visconti family originated. Inland, set back from the lake to the right, is the populous town of Varese. Above Varese, the part of *Lake Verbanus* (Maggiore) called the Lago di Lugano stretches round in two directions, and along this lie Brusino, Porto Ceresio, Capolago, Campione d'Italia, Osteno, and Porlezza. Where the river Laveno flows into the lake, there are at the lakeside Sessa, Morcote, and Lugano, from which the lake takes its name. To the left, not far above the Po, the torrent Gra-vellone flows into the Ticino, and to its left is Gropello Cairoli. Inland is the well-known town of Mortara and then Lomello, not much of a town now, but once very wealthy and celebrated in many histories, in particular the *History of the Lombards*:[156] It was at

apud Laumellum sibi in maritum et—Longobardis ut permiserunt—in regem ascivit. A Laumelloque nomen habet omnis ea paeninsula, regio[147] *quae Padum Ticinumque et Verbanum intercedit lacum*,[148] aliquot oppidulis vicisque frequentata: in qua linum gigni et multum et optimum Plinius est auctor.

35   Interius est Novaria, civitas vetusta a Vertamacoris Vocontium (sicut vult Plinius) aedificata,[149] quae Albucio Silo claro oratore (sicut tradit Eusebius) Octaviani imperatoris temporibus[150] ornata fuit. Et ad annum salutis octavum supra millesimum trecentesimum[151] habuit Dulcinum haeresiarcham, in quem cum Clemens V pontifex Romanus animadvertendum censuisset, ipse in montes, qui Novariae altissimi imminent, cum sectatoribus quingentis se contulit. Eosque saltuosus natura et paene inaccessibilis locus fuisset tutatus, ni superveniens solito maior nix plurimam eorum partem fame ac frigore mortem fecisset oppetere. Dulcinusque et Margarita uxor cum reliquis, eo confecti incommodo, in potestatem venerunt. Nec tamen errori ut abrenuntiarent adduci[152] potuerunt quin Margarita in conspectu mariti mutilata et ipse item pari laceratus supplicio, in proposito pertinaces, tot paene mortes quot habebant[153] membra perpessi sunt. Mons namque Bosus nomine, Cottiarum Alpium promontorium, ceteros superans Italiae montes, ad ipsum verticem, quem semper continuatis etiam aestate nivibus tectum habet, omnino inaccessibilis est. Eique haeret contiguus paulo celsitudine demissior mons, nunc ab hoc Dulcini[154] facto Gazarorum appellatus, in summo cuius vertice et ad eum locum in quo se continuerant haeretici, sacellum nunc est Sancti Bernardi vocabulo appellatum.[155] Adiacentque eius montis radicibus ad aversam partem Triverium, Cozola, et Crepacorum, agri Vercellensis oppida et castella.

36   Ad Ticini item undas est Castellettum, et paulo supra lacus Verbanus (seu Maior) ad emissorium, a quo Gravalonus amnis ortum habet, sinum efficit, quem Mergotii lacum dicunt.[156] Illabuntur torrentes duo Grais Alpibus defluentes, eorumque alter[157]

Lomello that Theodolinda, widow of the Lombard king Authari, took Agilulf the duke of Turin as her husband and—as the Lombards allowed—as king.[157] The whole peninsula, the region *lying between the Po, the Ticino and Lago Maggiore* with a scattering of a few small towns and villages, takes its name from Lomello.[158] Pliny says it produces large quantities of excellent flax.[159]

Further inland is the ancient city of Novara, built, according to 35 Pliny, by the Vertamacori of the Vocontes.[160] In the time of the emperor Augustus, Eusebius tells us, it was graced by the famous orator Albutius Silus.[161] In the year 1308, Novara harbored the heretical ringleader Dolcino.[162] When the Roman pontiff Clement V decided to have him punished, Dolcino retreated into the high mountains that overlook Novara along with five hundred of his followers. The wooded and inaccessible nature of the place would have kept them safe but for unusually heavy snows, which caused the great majority of them to die from starvation and cold. In their weakened state, Dolcino, his wife Margherita and other survivors were taken prisoner. They could not, however, be brought to renounce their heretical beliefs, and unswerving in their resolve, Margherita was mutilated before her husband and he too was likewise dismembered, each limb suffering a little death. Monte Boso is an outlier of the Cottian Alps and the highest mountain in Italy.[163] Its summit is wholly inaccessible, being covered by constant snow even in summer. A somewhat smaller mountain adjoins it nearby, called Gazzada now after Dolcino's activities.[164] At the very top of the summit (on the spot where the heretics stayed) is a little chapel named after St. Bernard. At the foot of this mountain and facing it are towns and castles of the territory of Vercelli: Trivero, Coggiola, and Crevacuore.

Likewise on the banks of the Ticino is Castelletto;[165] a little 36 above, at an outlet of *Lacus Verbanus* (Lago Maggiore) where the river Gravellone rises, Maggiore forms a gulf which is called the Lago di Mergozzo.[166] Two rivers flow down from the Graian Alps

Tonsa dicitur, alter, quod per Sancti Iulii lacum transeat, eius lacus retinet nomen. Nam eo in lacu insula est a Sancti Iulii ecclesia (sicut et lacus) appellata. Visunturque ibi confessoris Iulii reliquiae miraculis coruscantes. Suntque ad lacus Mergotii sinistram: Omagnum, Acabrium, Aimum, Boguinum; et ad dexteram: Upaium atque Appellium. Tonsae autem ad sinistram, Vergonta est, et supra in Alpibus Domussula, quam nunc Domodussulam appellant. Estque unus ex quatuor tramitibus quibus[158] a Mediolano in Gallias sive Germaniam itur.[159] Ad Tonsae vero dexteram Mergotium est, a quo sinus nomen accipit,[160] et ad eandem sinus dexteram Palantia. Sequunturque secundum Verbanum lacum oppida et castella: Canobium, Brisagum, Ascona, Carnium, Gardola. Et ubi Ticinus ex Alpibus Grais cadens lacum Sebuinum influit, castellum est nomine Magainum.

37 Descripsimus supra duos amnes Padum illabentes, hinc Umbronem inde Ticinum, et simul docuimus quibus in locis uterque amnis — ex Sebuino[161] hic, ex Eupilo ille — ortum ducat. Dumque loca explicuimus ipsis vel fluminibus vel lacubus adiacentia, mediam liquimus intactam planitiem omnium Italiae populis frequentissimam. In qua Mediolanum est civitas potentissima, quam, nostro iudicio, insulse opinati sunt quidam inde dictam, quod in medio Padi, Ticini, Abduae, et Umbronis amnium sit sita, cum alia sit in Gallia eiusdem nominis civitas, cuius fines nullis amnibus coercentur.[162] Originem vero habuit Mediolanum Lombardiae, ut[163] Livius Patavinus et Trogus Pompeius narrant, a Gallis qui, duce Brenno, in Italiam descenderunt. Populique loca incolentes, in quibus est aedificata, Insubres appellabantur, de quibus L. Florus ex Livio dicit: Galli Insubres, ferini et immensi corporis Alpium accolae, saepe alias, sed Viridomaro duce, iuraverant[164] se non soluturos baltea, nisi in Capitolio. Aemilius victor eos domuit.

into the Lago di Mergozzo: one of them is called the Toce, the other takes the name of the lake through which it flows, the Lago di S. Giulio. There is an island in the lake named, like the lake itself, after the church of S. Giulio. The remains of the Confessor Julius are to be seen there, vibrant with miracles.[167] To the left of Lago di Mergozzo, there are Omegna, Gabbio, Ameno, Buccione, and to the right Opaglio and Pella. To the left of the Toce is Pieve Vergonte, and further up in the Alps, Domussula, nowadays called Domodossola. Domodossola is one of four routes that lead from Milan into France or Germany. To the right of the Toce is Mergozzo (after which the bay is named), and Pallanza, likewise on the right. Beside Lago Maggiore, there are the following towns and castles, Cannobio, Brissago, Ascona, Locarno, Gordola. Where the river Ticino descends from the Graian Alps and enters the lake, there is a castle called Magadino.[168]

I surveyed above the two rivers that flow into the Po, the Lambro on one side and the Ticino on the other, and in doing so mentioned the sources on which they draw, Lago Maggiore for the Ticino and Lago di Pusiano for the Lambro. I described the places adjacent to these rivers and lakes, but left out the plain that lies between them, the most populous of all in Italy. Here is the mighty city of Milan, which some think — absurdly, in my judgment — was so named because it lies in the middle of the rivers Po, Ticino, Adda and Lambro. But there is another city of the same name in France, which unlike Milan is not bordered by any rivers.[169] The Milan in Lombardy, as Livy and Pompeius Trogus tell us, originated with the Gauls who descended into Italy under the leadership of Brennus.[170] The people who dwelt in the territory in which Milan was founded were called Insubres. Florus, following Livy, speaks of the Insubrian Gauls who dwell in the Alps, savage in appearance and massive in size; on various occasions, but specially under the leadership of Viridomarus, they swore that they would not put down their swords till they were on the Capitoline.

37

57

Nec videmus alia fuisse Italiae loca, in quibus facilius coaluerit mortalium multitudo tanta, quantam Insubres primum, dehinc[165] Mediolanenses, omnibus temporibus[166] habuerunt. Roma enim quem Mediolanensi multo maiorem habuit populum non modo non genuit, verum aëris semper ab ipsius origine insalubris dispositione id agente, neque confluentem ex tota Italia collatamque et vi ductam ex toto orbe mortalium exuberantiam bene conservavit.[167]

38   Quae apud Insubres Mediolanensesque post[168] eam conditam urbem historici gesta scribunt, hic referre operosissimum esset. Sed nostro insistentes instituto, indices earum rerum ponemus. Scribit Eusebius in *Temporum supputationibus* Statium Caecilium comoediarum scriptorem clarum fuisse Insubrem Gallum et Ennii contubernalem, et existimasse quosdam ipsum[169] fuisse Mediolanensem. Scribit Livius *Ab urbe condita*[170] libro XX exercitum Romanum[171] tunc primum ultra Padum fuisse ductum, et Gallos Insubres aliquot proeliis superatos in deditionem tunc primum venisse, quod quidem ad annos Romae Urbis conditae CCCCLX fuisse videtur. Trigesimus inde Livii liber habet Magonem, Hannibalis fratrem, in agro Insubrium vulneratum,[172] dum in Africam per legatos revocatus[173] navigaret, apud Corsicam obiisse. Et Liber XXXI habet L. Furium praetorem Romanum Gallos Insubres rebellantes et Hamilcarem Poenum in ea parte molientem acie vicisse, Hamilcareque occiso, milia hominum triginta sex caesa fuisse. Et Liber XXXI[174] habet Cornelium Cethegum cos. Gallos Insubres proelio fudisse, pauloque post L. Furium Purpureonem et Claudium Marcellum Boios et Insubres Gallos subegisse, Marcellumque triumphasse. Post eum vero triumphum urbs Mediolanensis annis ferme quingentis[175] pacatissima atque adeo florens fuit ut illam principes Romani (quoad per occupationes licuit) inhabitaverint: Nerva, Trajanus, Hadrianus, Maximianus, Philippus, Constantinus III, Constans et Constantinus IV (qui dictus est

Aemilius defeated and pacified them.[171] I do not find that there was any other region of Italy where such a vast populace (at first the Insubrians, latterly the Milanese) were so easily united: Rome's population was much larger than Milan's, but not only did she not produce it herself but, owing to the unwholesome climate that persisted from her very foundation, she quite failed to preserve the masses that streamed into her from all Italy or were forcibly introduced from all over the world.

It would a very large task to recount here all that the historians write about the deeds of the Insubrians and Milanese following the city's foundation. But I shall keep to my usual practice and touch on the main points of their history. Eusebius in his *Chronicles* writes that the famous comic poet Caecilius Statius was an Insubrian Gaul and the comrade of Ennius, and that some have supposed that he was Milanese.[172] Livy writes in Book XX of his *History of Rome* that the Roman army first crossed the Po, and the Insubrian Gauls first surrendered after defeat in a number of battles, in what seems to have been 460 AUC.[173] We then find in Livy Book XXX that having been wounded in Insubrian territory, Hannibal's brother Mago was recalled by legates and died in Corsica while he was sailing back to Africa.[174] In Book XXXI, Livy has the Roman praetor Lucius Furius conquering the rebellious Insubrian Gauls in battle as well as Hamilcar the Carthaginian, who was operating in the area. Hamilcar was killed and thirty-six thousand men slain.[175] In Book XXXI again, we find the consul Cornelius Cethegus routing the Insubrians in battle, and soon afterward Lucius Furius Purpureo and Claudius Marcellus subjugating the Boii and the Insubrian Gauls, Marcellus celebrating a triumph.[176] After that triumph, the city of Milan remained entirely at peace for nearly five hundred years, and was sufficiently prosperous that a number of Roman emperors resided there, as far as their business allowed: Nerva, Trajan, Hadrian, Maximian, Philip, Constantine III, Constans and Constantine IV (known as Gal-

38

Gallus), Jovianus, Theodosius, Valens et Valentinianus. Iulianumque, Galli fratrem, Mediolani Caesarem appellatum fuisse tradit Eusebius.

39   Post eam vero tam diuturnam felicitatem primas passum est molestias Mediolanum, beato Ambrosio adhuc superstite. Arianis (sicut ipse in *Homeliis* scribit) infestantibus, quorum persecutiones ut declinaret, in Illyricum exsul se contulit. Post seram vero (sicut Eusebius tradit) Auxentii[176] mortem, Ambrosio Mediolani episcopo in suam sedem restituto, omnis Italia ad rectam Christi fidem est conversa. Paulo tamen post Attila Italiam ingressus, cum omnem afflixisset Venetiam, Mediolanum quoque diruit. Instaurataque tunc parum quievit bellis agitata, quae Ostrogothi cum Iustiniani imperatoris ducibus gesserunt. Quibus in bellis, ut Gothis resisteret et in partibus Iustiniani imperatoris duraret, Mediolanum eas pertulit difficultates et angustias quae hominibus vix tolerabiles[177] esse videntur. Et tamen superante[178] famis acerbitate deditionem, tunc etiam sicut et nunc, invitam fecit. A Longobardis autem eadem urbs non quidem destructa umquam, sed maximis molestiis agitata est. Illisque a Carolo Magno domitis regnoque privatis, Mediolanum annis trecentis et sexaginta[179] sub Italiae et Romae regibus imperatoribusque quasi liberum floruit, nullas interim magnas passum agitationes quousque Federicus Barbarossus imperator ad annum salutis quintum et sexagesimum supra millesimum et centesimum[180] eam diruit et solo aequavit. Populum autem in sex tribus portarum nomine divisum sex loca decem ad minus distantia passuum milibus[181] habitare coegit. Sexto autem abinde anno, cum Federicus bello a Franciae regibus pro tertii Alexandri pontificis Romani salute agitaretur, Mediolanenses a Parmensibus Placentinisque adiuti repetitam patriam tanto reaedificarunt animorum ardore ut intra triennium ditior, populo frequentior potentiorque solito facta videretur.

lus),[177] Jovian, Theodosius, Valens and Valentinian I. Eusebius tells us that Gallus's brother Julian was acclaimed emperor in Milan.[178]

After this long period of prosperity, Milan's troubles began during the lifetime of St. Ambrose. Under attack from the Arians, as he writes in his *Homilies*, Ambrose went into exile in Illyria to avoid being persecuted by them. When Auxentius at length died (as Eusebius tells us),[179] and Ambrose was restored to his episcopal see in Milan, the whole of Italy returned to orthodox Christian belief. A little later, however, Attila descended into Italy, wreaking destruction throughout the Veneto and then destroying Milan. Though it was rebuilt at the time, Milan had little peace, being wracked by the wars that the Ostrogoths waged on the emperor Justinian's generals. In those wars, Milan suffered hardships and privations almost beyond human endurance as she tried to hold off the Goths and to stay loyal to the emperor Justinian. Still, in the end the rigors of famine overcame her and she surrendered, unwillingly then as she has more recently. The city was never actually destroyed by the Lombards, but did endure terrible suffering. After Charlemagne conquered the Lombards and stripped them of their kingdom, Milan effectively flourished as a free city under kings of Italy and Roman emperors for 360 years. She faced no great setbacks in that period until the emperor Frederick Barbarossa destroyed the city, razing it to the ground in the year 1165. He divided the people into six tribes named after the city gates and compelled them to live in six different places at least ten miles from Milan. But six years later, while Frederick was preoccupied with the war waged by the kings of France on behalf of the Roman pontiff Alexander III,[180] the Milanese reclaimed their city with the help of the people of Parma and Piacenza, and rebuilt it with such vigor that within the space of three years, it appeared richer, more populous, and more powerful than before.

39

40   Habuit vero centum et quinquaginta annis[182] mirabile incrementum — adeo ut nisi Turrianorum Vicecomitumque civilia
obstitissent dissidia, omni Lombardia facile fuerit potitura. Anno
autem salutis septuagesimo sexto supra millesimum et ducentesimum[183] Vicecomites, pulsis Turrianis, Mediolani tyrannide sunt
potiti. Et anno abinde LXXIV sextus Clemens Romanus pontifex
cum a Ludovico Bavaro imperatore adulterino multis agitaretur
molestiis, in illius damnum dedecusque Luchinum Vicecomitem
Romanae ecclesiae in Mediolano vicarium et eius germanum Johannem Mediolani archiepiscopum creavit. Annoque abinde plus
minus quinquagesimo Johannes Galeacius Vicecomes primus ab
imperatore dux Mediolani in ea familia est constitutus, princeps
certe regno et imperio potius quam eo ducatu solo dignus, cum
propter insignes alias virtutes tum maxime quod doctrina et virtutibus excultos viros apud se habere atque extollere curavit. Omnium autem externorum quos dilexerit, primus fuit Petrus Candianus[184] patria Cretensis, qui primum[185] Novariensis episcopus,
tum[186] Mediolanensis archiepiscopus, deinde Romanae ecclesiae
cardinalis, et demum, summus pontifex factus, Alexander V nomine[187] est appellatus. Isque vir omnium sui saeculi doctissimus,
quo tempore Johannes ipse Galeacius[188] ducatu Mediolani a Venceslao[189] Lucimburgensi Romanorum rege ornatus est, orationem
habuit doctrina et variarum rerum copia redundantem, quae, inter
multa ornamentum urbis Mediolani continentia, haec habet: Mediolanum physico naturali situ suo ab incendiis caumatum et fri-
gorum rigoribus aequaliter abesse, ac propterea locum totius orbis
temperatissimum, aëremque serenissimum, et aquarum in puteis
et fontibus salubritatem obtinere, cum tamen lacus pulcherrimi
decem et septem, et sexaginta quatuor flumina terrae superficiem
irrigantia in illius agro reperiantur. Dicitque idem pontifex Bar-
nabam, Pauli condiscipulum et comitem, primum fuisse Mediolanensis ecclesiae episcopum, cui paulo post successerit beatus

For 150 years Milan enjoyed miraculous growth—so much so   40
that, had not the civil disorders provoked by the Torriani and the
Visconti stood in the way, she would easily have gained control of
all of Lombardy.[181] In the year 1276, the Visconti drove the Torriani out and won absolute mastery over Milan. Seventy-four years
later, the Roman pontiff Clement VI was suffering continuous
provocations at the hands of the false emperor Louis of Bavaria,
and so to damage and discredit him, Clement made Luchino Visconti the vicar of the Roman church in Milan and Luchino's
brother Giovanni archbishop of Milan. And about fifty years after
that, Gian Galeazzo Visconti was installed by the emperor as
Duke of Milan, the first of that family.[182] He was a prince surely
more deserving of a kingdom or an empire than of that mere
duchy, owing to his many signal qualities, in particular because he
took care to keep and promote at his court men notable for their
learning and virtue. Foremost of all the foreigners that he loved
was Pietro Candiano of Crete, who was first bishop of Novara,
then archbishop of Milan, then cardinal of the Roman Church,
and finally named supreme pontiff as Alexander V.[183] When Gian
Galeazzo was invested with the Duchy of Milan by Wenceslaus of
Luxembourg, King of the Romans, Candiano, the most erudite
man of his time, delivered an address full of learning and variety
of matter. Among its many points in praise of the city are these:
Milan is protected from fiery heat and biting cold alike by its natural physical situation. On that account it occupies the most equa-
ble spot in all the world, with cloudless skies and wholesome waters in her wells and springs; notwithstanding, seventeen beautiful
lakes and sixty-four rivers watering the face of the land are found
in its territory. The prelate goes on to say that Barnabas, the fellow
disciple and companion of Paul, was the first bishop of Milan,
who was succeeded not long afterward by the famous Doctor of
the Church St. Ambrose—and Ambrose converted St. Augustine

Ambrosius doctor ecclesiae celeberrimus, a quo sanctus Aurelius Augustinus, doctor et ipse excellentissimus, in ipso Mediolano ad fidem Christi conversus fuit.

41   Johanne Galeacio et post eum duobus filiis, Johanne Maria primum et postea Philippo Maria (qui tertius dux fuit) vita functis, populus Mediolanensis in libertatem se erigens, post asperam insignemque famem bello perpessam urbem dedidit Francisco Sfortiae Attendulo, ex[190] Cutignola Romandiolae Sfortia primo patre oriundo, cuius decorat roboratque[191] principatum Maria Blanca uxor, Philippo tertio duce nata, regio titulo fastuque dignissima. Genuit Mediolanensis urbs Alexandrum secundum tertiumque Urbanum ex nobili gente Cribella ac Caelestinum IV, pontifices Romanos, Datiumque[192] episcopum suum, qui vir, si beato Gregorio credimus, sanctus et doctus, patriae (cuius fuit amantissimus) plurimum profuit. Imperite vero scripsit Alexander V pontifex Romanus Valerianum et Galienum imperatores Mediolani genitos fuisse. Sed Aelius Spartianus scribit avum paternum Didii Iuliani imperatoris fuisse Mediolanensem. Et Iulius Capitolinus dicit Valerianum iuniorem non natum sed sepultum fuisse Mediolani. Et Flavius Eutropius in *Alterius Valeriani gestis rebus* tradit acceptam fuisse cladem sub Aureliano a Marcomanis per errorem. Nam dum is a fronte non curat occurrerunt subito erumpentibus, dumque illos a dorso persequi parat, omnia circa Mediolanum vastata sunt. *Postea quoque et ipsi Marcomani superati sunt.*[193]

42   Fuerunt etiam patrum nostrorum memoria Mediolanenses iureconsulti excellentes: Obertus de Orto, qui eam composuit iuris civilis partem quae *Usus feudorum* appellatur, et Christoforus Castillioneus, iureconsultorum suae aetatis facile princeps, ac Johannes itidem Castillioneus episcopus Vicentinus. Et paulo post ad nostram pervenerunt aetatem viri duo eleganter docti, ordinis Sancti Augustini unus, Sancti Francisci alter: e quibus[194] ille Andreas

(another great Doctor of the Church) to the Christian faith in Milan itself.[184]

Following the death of Gian Galeazzo and of his two sons, first 41 Giovanni Maria and then the third duke Filippo Maria, the people of Milan regained their independence.[185] But after suffering extraordinarily harsh starvation in the war, they surrendered the city to Francesco Attendolo Sforza, who was born at Cotignola in Romagna to his father Attendolo Sforza the elder. Francesco's wife Maria Bianca, daughter of Duke Filippo Maria, and worthy in her own right of royal estate and title, adds grace and strength to his rule. The city of Milan gave birth to the popes Alexander II, Urban III (a member of the noble Crivelli family), and Celestine IV, and also her bishop Datius, a pious and learned man who performed great services for his homeland, according to St. Gregory.[186] Pope Alexander V was in fact wrong to say that the emperors Valerian and Gallienus were born at Milan, but Aelius Spartianus writes that the paternal grandfather of the emperor Didius Julianus was Milanese.[187] Julius Capitolinus further says that the younger Valerian was buried, though not born, at Milan.[188] And Flavius Eutropius tells us in *The History of the Younger Valerian* that the Romans suffered a disaster at the hands of the Marcomanni in the reign of Aurelian owing to a miscalculation: for while he neglected to meet them face to face during a sudden invasion, instead preparing to pursue them from the rear, they wrought great devastation in all the region around Milan. *Later on, however, the Marcomanni themselves were conquered as well.*[189]

There have also been in our fathers' time prominent Milanese 42 jurisconsults: Oberto dall'Orto, who put together the part of civil law called *Feudal Usage*,[190] and Cristoforo da Castiglione,[191] far and away the leading jurisconsult of his day, and also Giovanni da Castiglione, bishop of Vicenza, of the same family. A little later, two men of great learning lived in our own time, one Augustinian, the other Franciscan: the Augustinian Andrea Biglia and the Fran-

Bilius, hic Antonius Raudensis appellati aliquot ediderunt opera quid ipsi dicendo et scribendo valeant[195] absque meo testimonio ostendentia. Ornat quoque patriam Joseph Biprius sacris saecularibusque litteris apprime eruditus.

43   Sed ad propositum iter nostrum: post Ticini ostia[196] Padus longo tractu nullo flumine ad dexteram augetur. Est vero inter proximum Scicidam et Sancti Iulii lacum torrens Gogna apud Cochium oriundus et ad Sanctam Martham Neblosamque cursum perdens. Ad Padi autem ripam, ubi Scicida fluvius ostia habet, Bremide oppidum, et ad eius fluvii dexteram Palestrum, superiusque Romagnum oppida inveniuntur. Ad Scicidae autem sinistram, priusquam Sarvus influat torrens, sunt Vercellae civitas vetus, Apollineae a Martiali coquo poeta appellatae et quas Plinius a Saluiis Libiciis ortas tradit. Tenuerunt autem Saluii populi montes Niceae supereminentes. De hac urbe Plinius: 'Exstat lex censoria Vintimiliarum aurifodinae, quae in Vercellensi agro cavabatur, ne plus quinque M[197] hominum in opere aurum faciendi publicani haberent.' Et Eusebius Caesariensis, in *Temporum supputationibus*, tradit Eusebium Vercellensem episcopum sacrorum dogmatum peritia claruisse. Nosque *Historiarum* secundo ostendimus Valentinianum tertium, Constantii comitis ex Galla Placidia filium, misisse Ardaburum orientis praefectum adversus Castinum comitem, Johannis adulterini imperatoris ducem, et, proelio apud Vercellas commisso, Castinum superatum captumque fuisse.

44   Superius ad eandem sinistram Scicidae adhaeret Burgus, Sarvoque ad dexteram Andurnum. Ad sinistram est Bedulium. Dehinc ad Padum est Tridinum oppidum, Brolia patrum nostrorum aetate celeberrimo militum ductore ornatum et monasterio Lucedi amplissimo.[198] Duria Baltea[199] proxime habetur amnis, apud Hastubiam in Alpibus oriundus. Cui amni inferius adiacet[200] Crescentinum nobile oppidum, superius Salugiae, et paulo supra est

ciscan Antonio da Rho published numbers of works which show their powers of literary expression without any commendation of mine.[192] Giuseppe Brivio, an expert in sacred and secular learning, is another ornament of his Milanese homeland.[193]

But to return to my itinerary: for a long stretch beyond the mouth of the Ticino, no river joins the Po on the right. Between the Sesia, the next river, and the Lago di S. Giulio, there is the stream called Agogna, which rises at Cocquio; its course becomes unclear at Santa Marta and Nibbiola. The town of Breme is found on the banks of the Po where the Sesia joins it. On the right bank of the Sesia are the towns of Palestro and, further up, Romagnano Sesia. On the left bank of the Sesia, before the Cervo flows into it, is the ancient city of Vercelli, which Martial calls *Vercellae Apollineae*,[194] and which Pliny tells us took its beginnings from the Saluii Libicii.[195] The Saluii people dwelt in the mountains that overlook Nice. Of that city Pliny writes: "There is extant a ruling of the censors relating to a goldmine being excavated in the territory of Vercelli at Ventimiglia: tax farmers were not to have more than five thousand men engaged in the task of producing gold."[196] Eusebius of Caesarea in his *Chronicles* tells us that Eusebius the bishop of Vercelli was noted for the depth of his sacred learning.[197] In Book II of my *Histories*, I mentioned that Valentinian III, the son of Count Constantius[198] by Galla Placidia, sent the Prefect of the East, Ardaburus, against Count Castinus, general of the bogus emperor Joannes, and that when battle was joined at Vercelli, Castinus was vanquished and captured.[199]

Above Vercelli, likewise on left bank of the river Sesia, is Borgosesia, and on the right of the Cervo, Andorno: on its left is Biella. Then comes the town of Trino on the Po, ornamented in our fathers' day by the famous general Broglia[200] and by the magnificent Abbazia di Lucedio.[201] The Dora Baltea is the next river, rising in the Alps at Entrèves. The fine town of Crescentino lies on the Dora in its lower reaches, and Saluggia further up; a little

43

44

67

Eporedia[201] a bonis equorum domitoribus lingua Gallica (sicut Plinio placet) appellata.[202] Quam idem affirmat Populum Romanum Sibyllinis libris admonitum ac iussum condidisse. Dehinc ascendendo per vallem Augustae[203] Praetoriae itinere unius diei est Mons Jovettus.

45   Et supra est Augusta Praetoria iuxta geminas Alpium fores sita, Graias atque Peninas, quibus Herculem et Poenos transisse Plinius asserit Graios opinari. Apudque eam incisus fuit marmore titulus ille pergrandis populos enumerans, quos Caesar Augustus in Alpibus subegit. Dicitque Plinius Cottianas civitates XII non fuisse additas titulis Augusti quia nihil hostile commiserant. Geminas autem fores, Graias atque Peninas, nunc appellant alteras Montem Jovis (ubi monasterium est nobilissimum Sancto Bernardo dicatum), alteras[204] Columnam Jovis, qua via iter est ad vallem Tarantasiae Allobrogum, quam quidem vallem Isara[205] amnis excipit. Ad sinistramque Duriae Balteae amnis[206] oppidum est Mazadium. Orcus dehinc fluvius Padum illabitur, cui ad ostium est Clavassium[207] nobile oppidum. Ad dexteramque superius Sancti Martini, ad sinistram vero Sancti Benedicti de Fructeria, habentur oppida.[208]

46   Duriae autem Ripariae amnis Padum deinceps illabentis proxima haeret ostio Taurinum[209] civitas vetustissima, per quam primum Hannibalem Italiam ingressum venisse Livius XXI ostendit: 'Taurini Galli proxima gens erat in Italiam digresso.' Et infra: 'Peropportune . . . Taurinis,[210] proximae genti, adversus Insubres motum bellum erat . . . inde ex stativis moverat Hannibal, Taurinorumque unam urbem, caput eius gentis, quia[211] volentis in amicitiam non venerat, vi expugnavit.' Duriae[212] Ripariae fluvio ad dexteram oppida Lancium et Bellegerium, ad sinistram Ciriacum[213] et Druentum sunt proxima. Eoque in terrarum spatio quod Padum binasque Durias et Alpes interiacet est regio Canapicium appellata, in qua tres nobilium familiae oppida possident et cas-

further up again is Ivrea, which takes its name from the Gallic term for good breakers of horses, according to Pliny. Pliny also tells us that the Roman people founded Ivrea at the bidding of the Sibylline Books.[202] A day's journey from there up the Val d'Aosta lies Montjovet.

Above Montjovet is Aosta, situated at the twin portals of the   45 Alps, the Graian and the Pennine, through which, as Pliny tells us, the Greeks believe that Hercules and the Carthaginians passed over into Italy.[203] At Aosta was cut in marble that great inscription which lists the Alpine peoples subdued by Caesar Augustus. Pliny says that twelve towns of the Cottiani were omitted from Augustus's inscription as having taken no part in the hostilities.[204] These twin gateways into the Alps, the Graian and the Pennine, are now called Monte di Giove (the site of the famous monastery of St. Bernard) and Colonna di Giove respectively. The latter leads into the valley of the Tarantaise in the territory of the Allobroges, which is occupied by the river Isère. On the left bank of the Dora Baltea is the town of Mazzé. Then comes the river Orco, with the notable town of Chivasso where it joins the Po. Above Chivasso are found the towns of San Martino on the right and San Benigno di Fruttuaria on the left.[205]

Then comes the ancient city of Turin, which lies at the mouth   46 of the Dora Riparia as it flows into the nearby Po. Livy relates in Book XXI that Hannibal came through here when he first entered Italy: "The Taurine Gauls were the first tribe that Hannibal met as he entered Italy," and later: "Very opportunely, the Taurini, the neighboring tribe, had started a war against the Insubres . . . Then Hannibal broke camp and stormed the chief city of the Taurini, because they were unwilling to enter into alliance with him."[206] Hard by the Dora Riparia are the towns of Lanzo and Balangero on the right, and on the left Cirié and Druento.[207] In the land bounded by the Po, the two Dora rivers, and the Alps is a region called Canavese. Three families of nobles control the

tella, Valpergani, Sancti Martini, et Sancti Georgii comites. Nec longe absunt a Taurino Sangoni amnis in Padum labentis ostia, cui ad dexteram haerent oppida Ripolum et Aviliana (inter quae est celebre monasterium Sancti Antonii de Renverso), et Sanctus Ambrosius oppidulum.

47   Et paulo supra[214] civitas est Secusa. Superiusque ad Sangoni amnis ortum est Sessanna. Clusiola[215] posthac amnis Padum illabitur, eique[216] proximum ad sex milia passuum[217] est Pinnarolum nobile oppidum, nobili item monasterio exornatum. Superiusque Petrosa oppidum, et ad fontem sinistrorsum est oppidum Pragelatum. Cui amni Bricarasium primo, post Mons Bobius dextrorsum, haeret.[218] Post Clusiolam Pelix fluvius Clusono auctus Padum illabitur Panchalerium inter et Villam Francam, oppida populis frequentata. Fuitque Panchalerium olim Augusta Taurinorum[219] ex antiqua Ligurum stirpe,[220] apud quam Plinius dicit Padum primo navigabilem esse. Et Villa Franca primum ponte Padum sublicio est complexa. Pado autem fonti suo iam propinquanti oppida[221] sunt proxima Revellum et Paisana, et ad supremi ultimique torrentis illum illabentis fontem (ut diximus) oppidum est Cricium.[222] Deinceps sunt Alpium iuga, et ea quidem quae Hannibal Italiam ingressurus aceto rupit.[223]

towns and castles of the region, the counts of Valperga, San Martino, and San Giorgio. Not far from Turin is the mouth of the Sangone, a river that flows into the Po; on its right bank lie the towns of Rivoli and Avigliana (between which is the famous monastery of S. Antonio di Ranverso),[208] and the little town of Sant'Ambrogio di Torino.

A little further on is the city of Susa, and higher still is Sessanna, at the source of the river Sangone. Thereafter the river Chiusella flows into the Po, from where it is six miles to the well-known town of Pinerolo, itself graced by a well-known monastery.[209] Above Pinerolo is the town of Perosa Argentina, and to the left at the source the town of Pragelato. On the river to the right are sited first Bricherasio, then Bobbio Pellice. After the Chiusella, the river Pellice (into which the Chisone empties) flows into the Po between the populous towns of Pancalieri and Villafranca Piemonte. Pancalieri was Augusta of the Taurini, a people of ancient Ligurian stock, where Pliny says the Po is first navigable.[210] At Villafranca was the pile bridge that first spanned the Po. Near the source of the Po are the towns of Revello and Paesana, and at the source of the last and highest torrent that flows down into the Po there is, as I said [§16], the town of Crissolo. After that there are the Alpine ridges, the very ones that Hannibal split open with vinegar as he descended into Italy.[211]

47

LIBER VI

Regio octava. Venetiae[1]

1 Lombardia ad finem perducta, si hactenus servatum morem sequi volumus, ad proximorum Pado amnium ostia revertendum esset. Sed cum ab ultimis Padi ostiis 'Ad Fornaces' appellatis ad stagnantes ad mare Adriaticum Aquas Gradatas (in quas Athesis Meduacusque et Timavus amnes defluunt) fines Ducatus Venetiarum urbis aquae salsae obtineant, ipsas Venetias eisdem salsis aquis circumdatas priusquam Marchiam Tarvisinam et Aquileiensem (sive Foroiuliensem)[2] regiones describi necesse est. Postea namque in sicco melius persequemur ostia cursusque fluviorum,[3] secundum ripas quorum, ex nostro instituto, eas[4] regiones ipsarumque loca[5] certius inveniemus.

2 Venetias, civitatem in intimo Adriatici maris sinu sitam, ad annum salutis quinquagesimum sextum supra quadringentesimum fuisse conditam (quo anno Athila rex Hunnorum Aquileiam diruit) docuimus in *Historiis*. Habet autem eius ducatus regio longitudinem[6] milium octoginta, ab Aquis olim Gradatis [7] ad Lauretum, oppidum a Vitali Faledro aedificatum, nunc autem Pado proximum, ubi Ad Fornaces diximus Padi ostia appellari. Latitudo autem varia nullos habet alios terminos quam quousque cedentes recedentesque maris aquae ad siccum stagnando perveniunt.

3 Eius regionis diverso modo non nulli meminerunt vetusti scriptores. Antoninus enim Pius in *Romani imperii provinciarum regionumque itinerario*, cum a Ravenna Aquileiam per Altinum iter describeret, haec nunc Venetiarum stagna appellat septem maria quod a Ravenna Altinum usque septem vada essent navi transmittenda. Et Vergilius, quod diffuse in Patavii descriptione infra ostendemus, ubi Patavii aedificationem ab Antenore factam narrat,

BOOK VI

Region 8. Venice

Having finished Lombardy, to maintain my previous practice   1
would involve returning to the mouths of the rivers closest to the
Po. But seawater forms the boundary of the duchy of Venice from
the furthest mouth of the Po (called "Ai Fornaci")[1] to the lagoons
of San Canzian d'Isonzo on the Adriatic, a sea fed by the rivers
Adige, Brenta and Timavo; so I shall have to describe the city of
Venice itself—equally surrounded by seawater—before dealing with
the regions of the March of Treviso and Aquileia (or Friuli). It will
be better to have separate treatment of the mouths and courses of
the rivers on the *terrafirma*, so as to give a more accurate account of
those regions and the places along their banks, as is my custom.[2]

Venice is a city situated on an inner bay of the Adriatic. As I   2
wrote in my *History*, it was founded in 456 CE, the year that Attila
king of the Huns destroyed Aquileia.[3] The duchy is eighty miles
long, from San Canzian to Loreo, a town built long ago by Vitale
Falier[4] now very close to the Po, by the mouth of the river we
called above "Ai Fornaci." The breadth of the region is variable, its
only boundaries being the marshes formed by the waves of the sea
as they advance and recede toward and away from dry land.[5]

A number of ancient writers mention this region in various   3
connections. Antoninus Pius in his *Itinerary of the Provinces and Regions of the Roman Empire* describes the route from Ravenna to Aquileia via Altino, and calls what are now the lagoons of Venice "the
seven seas," because seven shallows had to be crossed by ship in
traveling from Ravenna to Altino.[6] And as I shall show in detail in
my description of Padua below, when Vergil tells the story of the
building of Padua by Antenor, he says: "and he sailed past the

sic habet: 'Et fontem superare Timavi, unde per ora novem vasto cum murmure montis, it mare praeruptum et pelago premit arva sonanti.' Mare enim quod per ora novem it praeruptum et premit arva pelago sonanti, est hoc totum quod a Pado ad Aquas Gradatas litus rumpens, colles eius poetice a Vergilio 'montes' appellatos inter ipsa vada linquit, quae nunc litora appellamus. Insulae eo conclusae spatio; quae habitantur, varios habuerunt conditores, qui in unicam hanc Venetiarum civitatem opes et consilia contulerunt.

4   Unde hanc Venetiarum civitatem pro una regione non immerito a nobis positam esse intelleget, qui considerabit non modo opes eius cuiuscumque alterius regionis Italicae opibus aequiparandas esse sed etiam[8] multas fuisse urbes, multa oppida, quorum excidio haec unica sit condita: Aquileiam, Altinum, Concordiam, Patavium, Montem Silicis, Opitergium, Eracliam, Equilium, Gradum, Caprulas, et Lauretum; quamquam et ex Vincentia, Verona, Mantua, Brixia, Mediolano, et Papia ab Athila afflictis et ab aliis Italiae civitatibus, praesertim urbe Roma diversis in persecutionibus nobiles et potentiores quosque Venetias a principio confugisse, in *Historiis* abunde docuimus. Igitur Aquileienses primi Gradum, Concordienses condidere Caprulas. Altinates, sicut urbem suam in sex portas divisam habebant, sex quoque in stagnorum insulis oppida condiderunt: Torcellum, Maiorbum, Burianum, Amoriacum, Constantiacum, et Aimanum. Patavinorum pars Rivum Altum et postea Dorsum Durum. Montesilicenses Atestinique[9] Methamauchum, Albiolam, Pelestrinam (sive, ut Plinius appellat, Philistinam), et Fossam Clodiam, quae nunc est civitas Clugia.

5   Crevit autem ilico ab ipso conditionis initio Veneta civitas quia non a pastoribus, sicut Roma, sed a potentioribus ditioribusque

source of the Timavus; from here through nine mouths, echoing loudly from the mountain, the sea bursts forth headlong and sweeps the field with booming flood."[7] Now the sea "which bursts forth headlong through nine mouths and sweeps the field with booming flood" is the whole stretch that beats on the shore from the Po to San Canzian, its hills — poetically termed "mountains" by Vergil — petering out among the shallows which we now call "lidos." Islands are set within these spaces. The inhabited ones had various founders, who joined their resources and wisdom together in the single city of Venice.

Anyone who considers not just that the wealth of Venice matches that of any other region of Italy, but also that many towns and cities were destroyed to found this one city — Aquileia, Altino, Concordia, Padua, Monselice, Oderzo, Eraclea, Iesolo, Grado, Caorle, Loreo — will appreciate the justness of my treating it as if it were a region of Italy in itself; it is also true, as I have abundantly shown in my *Histories*, that various nobles and potentates have from the very beginning sought refuge in Venice, men from Vicenza, Verona, Mantua, Brescia, from Milan and Pavia, all cities that suffered at the hands of Attila, and from other cities of Italy too, notably Rome during periods of persecution.[8] So it was that the citizens of Aquileia first founded Grado,[9] and those of Concordia Caorle. The people of Altino used to have their city divided into six districts after their gates; so likewise they founded six towns on the islands of the lagoons: Torcello, Mazzorbo, Burano, Amoriaco, Costanziaco and Ammiana.[10] A group from Padua founded Rialto, and later on Dorsoduro.[11] Men from Monselice and Este founded Malamocco, Albiella, and Pellestrina (or Philistina, as Pliny calls it),[12] and the Fossa Clodia, today the city of Chioggia.[13]

The city of Venice began to expand as soon as it was founded, being inhabited from the outset not by shepherds, as Rome was, but by the powerful and wealthy citizens of the former region of

4

5

regionis olim Venetiae fuit a principio, sicut diximus, habitata. Primus externorum Venetiis ornandis attulit adiumentum Narses eunuchus patricius, primi Iustiniani imperatoris copiarum in Italiam adversus Gothos missarum dux, qui, quod Veneti eum traducendis a Tarvisio Ravennam copiis navigio iuvissent postquam subegerat Gothos, ecclesias Sancti Theodori et Geminiani de capite Brolii in Venetiis aedificavit.

6   Quin etiam anno ipsius conditae centesimo et tricesimo secundo Arnulfus, rex Longobardorum, Patavium civitatem, post Totilense excidium a praedicto[10] Narsete eunucho Ravennatibusque instauratam, igni ferroque absumpsit. Et quotquot primae cladi superfuerant ac in patria coaluerant Patavini, secunda transmigratione in stagna Venetiarum confugientes, Rivum Altum impleverunt et Olivolense Castrum (ubi nunc Castellanum[11] est episcopium) condidere; atque eo tempore Sancti Martini et Sancti Iohannis in Bragula ecclesias construxerunt. Mirum vero est et summo extollendum laudis praeconio potuisse a tot tamque diversis urbium et oppidorum populis conditam civitatem annis[12] propemodum mille hanc quam retinent rem publicam conservare.

7   Nec tamen rerum humanarum condicionis adeo fuit expers haec civitas quin per singulas quasque aetates 'suos,' ut inquit poeta, 'manes fuerit perpessa.' Quam ob rem eius incrementa summatim (sicut in ceteris facimus Italiae civitatibus) explicando, labores quoque et difficultates pariter ostendemus; et ne in aliarum urbium, quas in hac condenda destrui contigit, negotio ulterius laborandum sit, omnia simul contexemus ut facta inter condendum destruendumque variatio certior[13] habeatur. Nec incongruum videtur a scissa patriarchali dignitate inchoare quod eam scimus in rebus Italiae semper momenti plurimum habuisse.

Venetia, as I said above. The first foreigner to add to the splendor of Venice was the noble eunuch Narses, who commanded the troops that the emperor Justinian I sent into Italy against the Goths. After he had subjugated the Goths, he built the churches of S. Teodoro and S. Gemignano at the head of the Broglio in Venice because the Venetians had helped him ferry his troops from Treviso to Ravenna.[14]

One hundred and thirty-two years after the foundation of Venice, the Lombard king Arnulf razed the city of Padua with fire and sword, after it had been rebuilt by the eunuch Narses mentioned above and by the people of Ravenna, following its earlier destruction by Totila. All the Paduans who had survived the first disaster and reunited in their homeland took flight again to the lagoons of Venice, congregating around Rialto and founding the castle of Olivolo, where the cathedral of Castello now stands. It was at that time that they built the churches of S. Martino and S. Giovanni in Bragora.[15] It is a wonderful thing and deserving of the highest praise that a state founded by peoples of such diverse cities and towns was able to preserve its republic for close on a thousand years, as it still does. 6

Not that the city was exempt from the common lot of mankind: through each of her several ages, she has in fact had to "endure her own ghosts," as the poet says.[16] And so as I touch on the main points of her development, as I do for the other cities of Italy, I shall portray the troubles and difficulties that she suffered along with the rest of them. So as not to get sidetracked by dealing with the other cities that chanced to be destroyed as Venice was being founded, I shall weave everything into one narrative in order to give a clearer picture of the ebb and flow of creation and destruction. It seems reasonable to begin with the division of the patriarchate, since by common consent this has always been something of the utmost importance in the affairs of Italy. 7

8   Ad annum salutis sexcentesimum decimum Gisulfus, dux Fo-
roiulianus, consensu Agilulfi, Lombardorum regis, elegit Iohannem abbatem in patriarcham Veteris Aquileiae, Candiano superstite patriarcha Novae Aquileiae (quae apud Gradum fuerat a
Romanis pontificibus constituta). Et anno inde quinto partium
consensu constitutum est ut qui esset Aquileiae patriarcha omnem
continentis regionem moderaretur, qui esset apud Gradum, omni
huic quae nunc est Venetiarum ducatus regioni praeesset. Quartodecimo abinde anno, cum Rotharis,[14] Longobardorum rex, Opitergium civitatem diruisset, eius civitatis episcopus nomine
Magnus ad stagna confugiens, consensu et auctoritate Severini,
pontificis Romani, ac Eraclii imperatoris, civitatem condidit quae
ab ipso imperatore Eraclea est appellata. Eodem[15] anno Paulus,
Altini episcopi, cum populo suo qui cladibus superfuerat, Torcellum se conferens, sedem, ibi quae nunc exstat, Severini, pontificis
Romani, auctoritate firmavit. Cuius pontificis consensu pariter
Patavinus episcopus, Arrianam haeresim (quae tunc in multis Italiae locis fervebat) declinans, sedem episcopalem in Methamauchum transtulit. Quo anno, foedere inter Longobardos regem et
duces ac Venetiarum civitatem[16] icto, declaratum est ut tota terrestris Venetia ab Abdua ad aquas salsas Lombardia et quicquid in
ipsis esset salsis aquis Venetiae appellarentur.

9   Ad annum vero salutis sexcentesimum et quinquagesimum
Constantius imperator, Eraclii filius, Torcellum veniens ut Romam
accederet, vicum qui est in Torcello primarius Constantiacum de
suo nomine voluit appellari. Eraclea civitate interim aucta, eius
populi pars in vicinam commigrans insulam Equilium condidit
civitatem. Cum autem annis duobus et triginta supra ducentos
Venetiae variam sub tribunis habuissent gubernationis formam,
primus earum dux in Eraclea et civis Eracleanus, Paulinus, anno
salutis sexcentesimo nonagesimo septimo a patriarcha, episcopis,
clero, tribunis, proceribus et plebeis creatus est, qui dux, foedere
cum Longobardis icto, Eracleae fines a Plave Maiore ad Minorem

In 610 CE, with the approval of the Lombard king Agilulf, Gi-   8
sulf, the duke of Friuli, appointed the abbot John patriarch of Old
Aquileia, while Candianus, the patriarch of New Aquileia (which
had been founded by the popes at Grado), was still alive. Five
years later the parties came to an agreement that the patriarch of
Aquileia would rule all the mainland of the region and that the
patriarch of Grado would hold sway over the area which is now
the duchy of Venice.[17] Fourteen years after that, when the Lombard king Rothari had sacked the city of Oderzo, Magnus, the
bishop of the town, fled to the lagoon and with the approval and
authority of Pope Severinus and the emperor Heraclius founded a
city there, named Eraclea after the emperor.[18] In the same year,
Paul the bishop of Altino took such of his people as had survived
the disaster and went to Torcello, founding there an episcopal seat,
which still exists today, with the approval of the pope.[19] Likewise
with the consent of Severinus, the bishop of Padua rejected the
Arianism that was then raging in much of in Italy, and transferred
his episcopal seat to Malamocco.[20] That same year, according to
the terms of a treaty struck between the king and dukes of the
Lombards and the city of Venice, it was declared that all of mainland Veneto from the river Adda to the salt waters would be
called Lombardy, and all that was embraced by these salt waters
Venetia.[21]

In 650 CE, the emperor Constantius, son of Heraclius, came to   9
Torcello on his way to Rome and named the chief settlement on
Torcello Constantiacum after himself.[22] The city of Eraclea having
grown in the meantime, some of her people migrated to a nearby
island and founded the city of Iesolo.[23] After the passage of 232
years, when Venetia had various forms of government under tribunes, the first doge Paulinus, an Eraclean citizen, was elected at
Eraclea by the patriarch, bishops, clergy, tribunes, nobles and com-
moners in 697 CE.[24] As doge he struck a treaty with the Lombards
and extended the territory of Eraclea from the Piave to the Piave-

produxit. Et anno inde undevigesimo Ursus item Eracleanus dux mortuo Paulino suffectus est, qui anno septimo ducatus civili in tumultu occisus est: sicque laborum suorum Veneti initia habere coeperunt.[17]

10   Nam, eo ducatus nomine antiquato, Dominicus Leo Magister militum attributa ducatus potestate creatus est, cui post annum primum defuncto suffectus Felix Cornicula Magister militum similiter[18] est dictus. (Et tertius item Iulianus Ceparius ac quartus Iohannes Fabriciacus Magistri militum sunt dicti.) Sed hic civili item tumultu magistratu depositus oculisque privatus est. Ad annumque salutis postea septingentesimum quadragesimumque secundum Deusdedit, Ursi quondam ducis interfecti filius, mutata ab Eraclea in Methamauchum sede et magisterii militum nomine exploso, Dux est dictus, qui anno ducatus tertiodecimo, cum ad Brintae amnis ostia castellum aedificare coepisset, in tyrannidis suspicionem venit et tumultu exorto depositus fuit excaecatus; eique in ducatu suffectus Galla anno quartodecimo tumultu captus oculosque est effossus, novaque subinde regiminis forma est facta: nam creato duce[19] Dominico Monegario Methamauchensi, duo annales 'Tribuni ad Clavum'[20] pari potestate consessuri fuere creati. Et tamen hic etiam Dux post annum in tumultu oculos simul cum ducatu amisit.

11   Ad Eracleanosque item res Veneta rediit et Mauritius Dux est factus, qui post annum malo exemplo filium ducatus consortem assumpsit. Quo annno primus Adrianus papa Obeliabatum Olivolensi ecclesiae primum dedit episcopum, a quo Sancti Moysi ecclesia aedificata est. Iniecit vero Mauritius dux in Iohannem patriarcham Gradensem manus adeo violentas ut brevi ille[21] obierit; suffectusque patriarcha Fortunatus, conspiratione contra ducem in praedecessoris sui ultionem inita, exorto tumultu pulsus in Fran-

sella.²⁵ On the death of Paulinus nineteen years later, another Eraclean, Orso, succeeded as doge, but he was killed in an insurrection in the seventh year of his reign.²⁶ So began the troubles of the
Venetians.

The title of doge having been set aside, Dominicus Leo was   10
elected "Magister Militum" with all the powers of a doge. He died
after his first year in office, however, and was succeeded by Felix
Cornicula, who was given the same title.²⁷ Julianus Ceparius was
named as the third Magister Militum, and Johannes Fabriciacus
the fourth. But following another riot, Fabriciacus was deposed
from the magistracy and blinded.²⁸ Later, in 742 CE, Teodato, the
son of the murdered former Doge Orso, was again named Doge,
after the title Magister Militum was abandoned and the ducal seat
moved from Eraclea to Malamocco.²⁹ In his thirteenth year in office, as he began to build a castle at the mouth of the river Brenta,
he fell under suspicion of aiming at tyranny: civil unrest again followed, and Teodato was deposed and blinded.³⁰ His successor
Galla was also seized in a rebellion and had his eyes put out in the
fourteenth year of his rule.³¹ After that a new form of government
was brought in, with Domenico Monegario of Malamocco being chosen Doge and two annual "Tribuni ad Clavum" elected to
preside alongside him with equal power.³² Notwithstanding, this
Doge too lost his office along with his eyes in a riot the following
year.³³

The government of Venetia again reverted to the Eracleans,   11
Maurizio being made doge, but he set a bad precedent by taking
on his son as coruler after a year.³⁴ In that year Pope Adrian I gave
the church of Olivolo its first bishop, the Obeliabato who built the
church of S. Moisè.³⁵ However, Giovanni the patriarch of Grado
suffered such violent treatment at the hands of the doge Maurizio
that he died soon afterward,³⁶ being succeeded as patriarch by
Fortunatus. Fortunatus fomented a conspiracy against the doge to
avenge his predecessor but was forced to flee to France after rioting

ciam se contulit. Deiecti tamen ducatu sunt Mauritius Dux et filius, et illis unicus Obelerius tunc tribunus Methamauchensis in
Venetiarum ducatu est suffectus. Eodem anno[22] qui erat salutis
octingentesimus quartus Obelerius dux civili tumultu patria pulsus Tarvisium se contulit ubi, ab exsulibus Venetis iterum dux
creatus,[23] Beatum fratrem ducatus consortem accepit.

12   Interea Pipinus, Caroli Magni filius, rex Italiae a primo Adriano
pontifice Romano constitutus anno salutis octingentesimo nono,
in Italiam veniens, hinc patriarcha Fortunato inde Obelerio et
Beato instigantibus, bello Venetos agitare coepit. Qui proelio apud
Tarvisium commisso superati cum Carolo Magno et Pipino filio,
rege Italiae, per foedera convenerunt. In quo actum est:[24] ut Obelerius Beatusque duces apud Methamauchum exsularent. Nec
tamen invenio aliquem a Carolo et Pipino magistratum adminis-
trandis Venetiarum rebus fuisse impositum. Eodem autem anno
Eracleam Veneti destruxerunt, unde maxima nobilium pars, qui
postea Venetias usque in haec tempora gubernarunt, in urbem
confluens illam auxere. Pariterque eodem anno Aquileienses in
Venetiarum urbem populariter commigrarunt ut tunc secunda
Venetiarum urbis conditio fuisse videatur.

13   Eoque anno Agnellus Particiacus Eracleanus primus dux fuit
qui in Rivo Alto insula electus palatium ducale nunc exstans aedificavit; pariterque eodem anno apud Olivolense Castrum exsistens
cathedralis ecclesia ab eo castello appellata est Castellana, et pro
Veneta Rivus Altus civitas dici coepta. Agnellus exinde[25] Dux tertio qui secutus est anno Eracleam reaedificans ambitu strictiorem
appellavit Civitatem Novam, quod et nunc (ratione episcopatus
magis quam habitationum) retinet nomen. Idemque Agnellus, filiis suis duobus assumptis in ducatus consortes, monasterium
Sancti Zachariae aedificavit, ubi eius[26] sancti corpus reliquiasque
locavit. Ursus autem episcopus ecclesiam suam Castellanam Sancti
Petri vocabulo decoravit, quo tempore eius consanguinei Sancti

broke out. Maurizio and his son were in any case stripped of their ducal office, and Obelerio, then Tribune of Malamocco, succeeded them as sole doge of Venice.[37] In that same year, 804 CE, he was driven from his homeland by civil strife and went to Treviso, where he was again elected doge by Venetian exiles and took his brother Beato as coruler.[38]

Meanwhile Charlemagne's son Pippin, created king of Italy by Pope Adrian I in 809 CE, entered Italy and started to wage war on the Venetians, encouraged by the patriarch Fortunatus on the one hand and by the doges Obelerio and Beato on the other. When the Venetians were beaten in battle at Treviso, they came to an agreement with Charlemagne and Pippin that the doges Obelerio and Beato would live in exile at Malamocco. Yet I cannot discover anyone that was imposed as magistrate by Charlemagne and Pippin to administer the Venetian government.[39] That same year the Venetians razed Eraclea to the ground,[40] and the great majority of the nobles who have governed Venice from that day to this streamed from there into the city, swelling its population. The citizens of Aquileia likewise migrated to the city *en masse* in that year, so that Venice really seems to have experienced a second foundation on that occasion.

In that year Agnello Participazio of Eraclea, elected doge on the island of Rialto, was the first to build the ducal palace that still stands today, and in the same year again the present cathedral at the fortress of Olivolo was called the "Castellana" after the castle, and the city began to be called Rialto instead of Venice.[41] Three years later doge Agnello rebuilt Eraclea on a more modest scale and called it Cittanova, the name it still bears today (for its being the seat of a bishopric rather than its buildings).[42] This Agnello took on his sons as corulers of the duchy,[43] and built the monastery of S. Zaccaria, in which he installed the saint's body and relics.[44] The bishop Orso graced his church in Castello with the name of S. Pietro; it was at this time that his kinsmen built the

12

13

Severi et Sancti Laurentii ecclesias in Geminis Insulis construxere. Conspirarunt vero adversum tres hos duces, patrem et filios, Iohannes Tornaricus et Bonus Bragadinus,[27] qui capti convictique et appensi patibulo interierunt; et tamen eorum de quibus sumptum erat supplicium agnati per id temporis Sancti Danielis ecclesiam construxerunt. Ad octingentesimum autem et[28] vigesimum septimum salutis annum defuncto Agnello Iustinianus Particiacus in ducatu solus est suffectus. Anno cuius secundo Beati Marci corpus Venetias[29] ex Asia est delatum, eoque qui secutus est anno cum Iustinianus obiisset, Iohannes frater dux est suffectus, quo anno Beati Marci ecclesia est aedificata.

14   Et per id temporis, ducto in Methamauchum exercitu, Obelerius ibi exsul occisus et civitas est destructa; cuius demolitionis caedisque Obelerii causa factum est ut vocatus in Franciam Iohannes dux accesserit, eoque absente Castellanus episcopus duoque cives Rivi Alti civitatis curam administrationis ducali attributa potestate gesserunt. Iohannes autem dux Francia reversus, civilique tumultu ducatu deiectus, et indecenter attonsus[30] maestitia diem obiit. Proximo deinde anno qui fuit salutis octingentesimus tricesimus sextus,[31] Petrus Trundonicus a[32] Pola oriundus Dux est creatus, qui Iohannem filium ducatus consortem habuit, ecclesiamque Sancti Pauli aedificavit. Quartoque abinde anno Sclavi Caprulas, Venetorum urbem, vi captam destruxerunt, Sergio (qui dictus est 'Os Porci') tunc pontifice Romano, in quo anno episcopus Maurus ecclesiam Sanctae Margaritae exstruxit. Petro Trundonico vita functo, Iohannes filius ducatum solus obtinuit, quem a Sancti Zachariae ecclesia redeuntem populus tumultu concitato occidit et in eadem ecclesia sepelivit, anno salutis octingentesimo quadragesimo[33] quarto.

15   Eratque Ursus Particiacus solemni tunc more electus, cum defuncti ducis famuli palatium populo non prius reddidere quam Pupuliam[34] sibi insulam certa cum immunitate habitandam impetravere. Ursusque dux anno ducatus sui tertiodecimo Iohannem

churches of S. Severo and S. Lorenzo on twin islands.[45] Giovanni Tornarico and Bono Bragadin formed a conspiracy against the doges, father and sons, but they were caught and condemned and died hung from the gallows. Notwithstanding, relations of the executed men built the church of S. Daniele at this time.[46] Following the death of Agnello in 827, Giustiniano Participazio succeeded him as sole doge.[47] In Giustiniano's second year as doge, the body of St. Mark was brought to Venice from Asia;[48] and the year after that, Giustiniano died and his brother Giovanni succeeded him as doge. In that year was built the church of S. Marco.[49]

About this time an army was led against Malamocco, and   14 Obelerio in exile there was slain and the city destroyed.[50] Owing to the destruction of the city and the murder of Obelerio, the doge Giovanni was summoned to France. When he went there, in his absence the bishop of Castello and two citizens administered the government of the city of Rialto with powers of the doge.[51] But when doge Giovanni returned from France, he was deposed in civil unrest and died of grief after being shamefully shorn of his hair.[52] In the year that followed, 836 CE, Pietro Tradonico of Pola was elected doge: he took his son Giovanni as coruler, and built the church of S. Polo.[53] Four years later, the Slavs captured and destroyed Caorle, a Venetian town, in the pontificate of Sergius (known as "Bocca di Porco"),[54] in the same year that the bishop Mauro built the church of S. Margarita.[55] When Pietro Tradonico died, his son Giovanni became sole doge; as Giovanni returned from the church of S. Zaccaria, the people killed him in a riot and buried him in that same church in the year 844 CE.[56]

Orso Participazio was duly elected in the time-honored man-   15 ner, though the attendants of the late doge Giovanni refused to surrender the palace to the people until they got the island of Poveglia to live on and a guarantee of immunity.[57] In the thirteenth year of his rule, Orso took his son Giovanni as coruler; it

filium ducatus consortem accepit, qui[35] campanas duodecim anno salutis octingentesimo septuagesimo[36] imperatori Graecorum misit: fueruntque eae[37] campanae quas primum Graecia[38] vidit. Gessit vero Ursus iste dux maximas res non minus Italiae quam Venetis gloriosas. Nam Saraceni, spoliata inflammataque Ancona, omnem Italiae oram quae inde ad Hydruntum intercedit pariter afflixerunt, in quos Tarentini sinus oram vastare parantes, cum Ursus duxisset, superarunt Christiani; fugataque inde classis Saracena Gradum urbem invasit: tuncque Ursus, qui illorum terga fuerat insecutus, repulsos a Grado[39] non prius persequi destitit quam omnis Italiae ora in Superum Mare versa reddita est pacatissima. Urso duce mortuo, Iohannes filius Dux solus Comaclum civitatem de Ravennatibus cepit, et anno inde tertio Petrum fratrem suum ducatus consortem habere obtinuit, qui novus dux ecclesias Sanctorum Cornelii et Cypriani in Methamauchensi litore aedificavit. Sed ambo duces intra tertium qui secutus est annum ducatu se abdicarunt.

16   Creatus est autem ad annum salutis octingentesimum octuagesimum septimum Petrus Candianus, vir praestantissimus, quem Sclavi uno superati altero redintegrato proelio interfecerunt, Iohannesque Particiacus, quem ducatu se abdicasse ostendimus, ut seditioni occurreret in[40] urbe fatiscenti[41] ducatum resumpsit; cumque eum sexto deposuisset mense, suffectus est Dux ad annum octingentesimum octuagesimum octavum Petrus cognomine Tribunus quo anno reges duos Italia, posthabitis Francis, ex Italicis habere coepit: Berengarium Foroiuliensem et Guidonem Spoletanum ducem. Anno autem inde tertio,[42] Petrus dux[43] urbis[44] Venetiarum partem muro cinxit a Rivo Castelli usque ad ecclesiam Sanctae Mariae in Iubanico ibique Canalem Maiorem ferrea clausit catena, cuius capita hinc ad Sanctae Mariae inde ad Sancti Gregorii ecclesias obserabantur.[45] Hic annus Italiae infelicissimus fuit quod Hungari a Tarvisio Mediolanum usque omnia caedibus incendiisque foedarunt et stagna Venetorum pelliciatis navibus

was Orso who sent twelve bells to the Greek emperor in 870, the
first bells seen in Greece.[58] Doge Orso really did great things, accomplishments no less glorious for Italy than for Venice. For the
Saracens had pillaged Ancona and burned it down, and they were
likewise harrying all the Italian coast from there to Otranto: as
they made ready to lay waste to the coast of the gulf of Taranto,
the Christians under Orso's leadership won the upper hand.
Beaten back from Taranto, the Saracen fleet attacked the city of
Grado. Orso then pursued them and beat them back from Grado,
not letting up his onslaught until the whole Adriatic coast of Italy
was returned to peace.[59] When he died, his son Giovanni reigned
alone: he seized the city of Comacchio from Ravenna,[60] and three
years later contrived to attach his brother Pietro to himself as coruler. The new doge Pietro built the churches of S. Cornelio and
S. Cipriano on the shore of Malamocco. But two years later both
doges abdicated.[61]

Now the dauntless Pietro Candiano was elected doge in 887.   16
The Slavs had been beaten by him in a first battle, but killed him
in a second when renewed fighting broke out;[62] and Giovanni Participazio, whose abdication we noted above, took up the dogeship
once again to counter civil discord in the exhausted city.[63] When
he laid down the office six months later, Pietro Tribuno succeeded
him as doge in 888: this was the year in which Italy started to have
two Italian kings, replacing Frankish ones, Berengar of Friuli and
Guido duke of Spoleto.[64] Three years later, the doge Pietro Tribuno enclosed part of the city in walls, from Rio di Castello to the
church of S. Maria Zobenigo. At that point he closed off the
Grand Canal with an iron chain, securing the ends to the afore-
mentioned church of S. Maria on the near side and to S. Gregorio
on the other.[65] This year was a disastrous one for Italy since the
Hungarians laid waste with fire and sword to everything from
Treviso to Milan. They forced their way into the Venetian lagoons
in ships hastily constructed out of hides and laid waste to Cit-

tumultuarie fabricatis ingressi Civitatem Novam Clugiamque et Caput Aggeris populati sunt. Eos tamen Berengarius rex cum quindecim armatorum milibus aliquantulum repressit et tandem, omni paene amisso exercitu, ingenti data pecunia ut in Hungariam redirent delinivit.

17   Petro Tribuno ducatus sui anno vicesimo tertio vita functo successit Ursus Particiacus secundus. Cuius temporibus[46] Conradus Alemannus[47] ex ea gente primus, licet papali confirmatione caruerit, imperium tamen invasit; et, rebus Italiae[48] fluctuantibus, Saraceni maiorem eius partem occupaverunt. Successitque huic post vicesimum annum in ducatu alter Petrus Candianus, qui ob Italiae imperiique debilitatem nactus occasionem[49] primus Venetorum potentiam in Liburnis Dalmatisque auxit et, Genua tunc a Saracenis spoliata, Veneti mari Italorum potentissimi[50] esse ceperunt: quam quidem potentiam usque in haec tempora ob Imperii Romani (tam Graeci quam Latini) inclinationem auxerunt. Nam Germani imperatores, etsi terra quandoque aliquam, nullam tamen umquam mari potentiam habuerunt. Itaque deinceps in hac Venetiarum regione brevitati consulentes nihil aliud quam motus intestinos aut nova aedificia,[51] quod nostri est propositi, attingemus.

18   Ottonis secundi imperatoris temporibus ad annum salutis nongentesimum septuagesimum quartum Veneti Petrum Candianum ducem deicere cupientes, cum ille se in palatio tueretur, iniecto igni[52] pice et sulpure mixto, et palatium et Sancti Marci, Sancti Theodori, Sanctae Mariae in Iubanico ecclesias, et[53] plus quam trecentas civium domos penitus[54] combusserunt; duxque cum filio et complicibus[55] est interfectus. Haec autem omnia aedificia suffectus illi Dux Petrus Urseolus, vir optimus, instauravit, qui Gradum quoque civitatem instauratam muro cinxit. Quo item tempore monasterium Sancti Georgii a Iohanne Mauroceno monacho est amplificatum. Ad annum vero salutis millesimum et nonum magnae olim Adriae urbis reliquias, apud Lauretum superatos Adrienses, Veneti tanta confecerunt occidione ut dies

tanova, Chioggia, and Cavarzere. King Berengar held them back
for a while with fifteen thousand armed men, however, and at
length, when he had lost nearly his entire army, paid them a huge
sum of money to induce them to return to Hungary.[66]

Orso Participazio II succeeded the doge Pietro Tribuno, dead   17
after a reign of twenty-two years. In Pietro's time, the German
Conrad I seized control of the Empire, though without the pope's
endorsement. Owing to the unsettled state of affairs in Italy, the
Saracens took over the greater part of it.[67] Pietro Candiano II succeeded Orso, who had ruled for twenty years.[68] Italy and the Empire being enfeebled, Pietro took the opportunity to extend Venetian hegemony over Croatia and Dalmatia. The Saracens had at
that time reduced Genoa to ruins, so Venice started to become the
dominant Italian naval power, and that power has continued to
increase to the present day, as the power of the Empire, East and
West, has continued to decline. The German emperors may have
had some power on land, but they never enjoyed any at sea. And
so henceforth in the interest of brevity and in line with my plan, I
shall treat only Venice's internal developments and new buildings.

During the reign of emperor Otto II, in 974 CE, the Vene-   18
tians formed a desire to depose the doge Pietro Candiano. When
he barricaded himself in the ducal palace for protection, they
launched incendiary devices made of pitch and sulfur and completely burned down the palace, as well as churches of S. Marco,
S. Teodoro, and S. Maria Zobenigo and the homes of more than
three hundred citizens. The doge, along with his son and associates, was killed.[69] But the excellent Pietro Orseolo, who succeeded
him as doge, rebuilt all those structures,[70] and rebuilt and walled
the city of Grado.[71] At this period too the monk Giovanni Morosini enlarged and enriched the monastery of S. Giorgio Maggiore.[72] At Loreo in 1009, the Venetians conquered and slaughtered the citizens of Adria, the remnants of a once great city, so
much so that that was the last day of a city for which the Adriatic

ille ultimus fuerit civitati a qua mare Adriaticum est appellatum. Quo item anno Pepus, patriarcha Aquileiensis, Gradum civitatem dolo captam destruxit, sed eam Veneti iterum ilico instaurarunt.[56] Anno autem inde vicesimo Dominicus Urseolus, pulso armis Petro Barbolano, Dux factus tertio die Ravennam metu confugit, Dominicusque Flabonicus tunc exsul in patriamque revocatus Dux[57] illi suffectus est. Et ad annum quadragesimum tertium supra millesimum Pepus patriarcha Aquileiensis, noni Benedicti pontifici auctoritate atque consensu, Gradum sibi subicit, ecclesias diruit, urbemque spoliat, et[58] Veneti vero eiusdem pontificis auctoritate illam instaurant. Annoque inde quadragesimo Dominicus Contarenus Dux monasterium Sancti Nicolai in litore et propinquo loco monasterium Sancti Angeli aedificavit. Ad centesimum vero atque millesimum salutis annum incendia bina Venetiis fuerunt, quibus parochiales ecclesiae ad viginti simul cum parochianorum domibus arserunt, quo tempore Methamaucensis civitas inundatione maris atque incendio vastata et paene submersa est, terrae motusque superveniens Venetias ubique afflixit.

19   Tertiodecimo autem abinde anno quintus Henricus imperator, Verona Venetias veniens situmque[59] et regionem civitatis[60] admiratus, Venetias *regnum* appellari decrevit, eoque qui secutus est anno Marcus Iulianus monasterium Virginis de Caritate exstruxit. Duodecimoque ab illo ⟨anno⟩ Veneti[61] Motonio Peloponensi sunt potiti, Petrusque Gatilosus ecclesiam Sancti Clementis et hospitale in Canalis Orphani ripa aedificavit. Undevicesimoque inde anno[62] turris campanaria Sancti Marci excitata est.

20   Sed nec adeo continuari[63] potuit quies inchoata quin ad annum salutis primum et septuagesimum supra millesimum et centesimum[64] Vitalis Michael Dux fuerit interfectus. Augebantur tamen in dies Venetorum opes mirabili incremento. Ad annum namque[65] sextum et nonagesimum supra millesimum et centesimum[66] Veneti, Francis bello sociati, urbis Constantinopolitanae dominio sunt potiti; et anno inde quadragesimo ecclesia Sancti Francisci

sea was named.[73] In the same year, the patriarch of Aquileia, Pepus, captured the city of Grado by stratagem and destroyed it,[74] but the Venetians immediately rebuilt it once more.[75] Twenty years later, Domenico Orseolo expelled Pietro Barbolano by force of arms and became doge, but after three days he took fright and fled to Ravenna;[76] the exile Domenico Flabanico was called home and succeeded him as doge.[77] In 1043 the patriarch of Aquileia Pepus, on the authority and with the consent of pope Benedict IX, took control of Grado, razing the churches to the ground and sacking the city; yet the Venetians, again on Benedict's authority, restored it.[78] Forty years later the doge Domenico Contarini built the monastery of S. Niccolò al Lido and the monastery of S. Angelo nearby.[79] In the year 1100 Venice suffered two fires in which about twenty parish churches burned down, together with the homes of their parishioners. In that period the city of Malamocco was devastated by sea flooding and fire and was nearly submerged, and an earthquake damaged the whole of Venetia on top of that.[80]

19 Thirteen years later the emperor Henry V came to Venice from Verona. He was struck with wonder at the site and surroundings of the city, and gave Venice the title of "kingdom."[81] A year later, Marco Giuliano built the monastery of Santa Maria della Carità.[82] Twelve years after that, the Venetians gained control of Modone in the Peloponnese.[83] Pietro Gatiloso built the church of S. Clemente and the Hospital on the banks of the Canal dell'Orfano;[84] and nineteen years later the campanile of S. Marco was erected.[85]

20 But the peace that had set in was not to continue, for in 1171 CE, the doge Vitale Michiel was murdered.[86] Yet the wealth of Venice was daily increasing at an astonishing pace. In 1196 the Venetians entered into military alliance with the French and won control of the city of Constantinople.[87] Forty years later, the church of S. Francesco was built in Venice[88] and the monastery of S. Cipriano

Venetiis et monasterium Sancti Cypriani in Torcello aedificatum;
undetricesimoque inde anno pons Rivi Alti subliceus est construc-
tus. Quo tempore, cum duplicatum esset Venetiis moliturae vectigal, populus in tumultum concitus arma cepit. Sed, his[67] qui se
duces incentoresque ingerebant captis eculeoque appensis, quies
ilico civitati reddita est. Maiorem vero plurimique faciendum anno
inde undequinquagesimo[68] tumultum urbs Veneta sensit, cum
Baiamons Teupolus, rerum novarum cupidus, una cum Quirinis,
Barociis, Doris, Badoariis, et Basiliis regnum affectavit, in quos
pro demeritis publico consilio animadversum est, quiesque civilis
et concordia in haec usque tempora, annis duodequadraginta supra centum, Venetiis fuit. Sed iam satis multa de Venetiarum origine ac, inter ipsam constituendam rem publicam, vel aedificatis
vel dirutis civitatibus et oppidis sunt dicta. Ad viros itaque eiusdem, ex nostro more institutoque, veniamus.

21   Habuit semper hactenus urbs Veneta viros maritimorum bellorum et mercaturae gloria claros, sed ante patrum aetatem nullo
decorata est viro litteris ornato, praeterquam Andrea Dandulo
duce, quem Francisci Petrarchae testimonio doctum fuisse scimus.
Patrum vero memoria Carolus Zenus Venetorum[69] non solum aetatis suae sed priorum quoque saeculorum litteris ornatissimus et
rebus bello gestis adeo clarus fuit ut alter Camillus merito a Venetis appellaretur,[70] quandoquidem Clugiensi bello quod cum Venetis Genuenses difficillimum ac periculosissimum gessere, unico
navali proelio felicissime gesto,[71] Genuenses a Venetis etiam eo
bello vinci posse primus docuit et omni eo bello hostium ferociam
sua fortitudine constantiaque compescuit; demumque Bucicar-
dum, regis Francorum navalis exercitus supremum ducem, dum
opem Patavinis afferre cuperet, proelio ingenti gloriosissimoque
superavit. Quae omnia Leonardus Iustinianus funebri luculentis-
sima oratione et Petrus Paulus Vergerius elegantissimis duabus
epistulis copiosissime prosecuti sunt.

on Torcello;[89] twenty-nine years later the bridge at the Rialto was constructed on wooden piles.[90] At this time the people rioted and took up arms when the tax on milling grain was doubled, but the ringleaders and agitators were captured and put to the rack, on which peace returned to the city at once.[91] Venice in truth experienced a greater and much more serious upheaval forty-nine years later when the revolutionary Bajamonte Tiepolo sought to launch a coup in concert with the Querini, Barozzi, Dori, Badoer, and Basegio. Their misdeeds were fittingly punished by public resolution, and civil peace and quiet has prevailed in Venice from that day to this, 138 years later. But we have said more than enough about the origin of Venice and of the towns and cities built or destroyed while the Venetian state was in process of formation. And so in line with my normal practice, let us turn to considering the men she produced.

Venice has always had, and still has, men famous for naval warfare and trade, but before our fathers' time, no one of distinction in the arts added luster to her, with the exception of the doge Andrea Dandolo, whom we know to have been a scholar on the testimony of Francesco Petrarca.[92] But in our fathers' day the outstanding literary figure, of his own and earlier times, was Carlo Zeno, who was justly called the second Camillus by the Venetians for his glorious military exploits. For example, during the difficult and dangerous war of Chioggia which the Genoese fought against the Venetians, with a single triumphant naval engagement Zeno was the first to show that the Venetians could actually beat the Genoese in that war, throughout which he held the enemy's savagery in check with his bravery and steadiness. Finally, in a vast and glorious battle, Zeno overcame Boucicault, the grand admiral of the fleet of the king of France,[93] who was trying to relieve Padua. All these exploits are dealt with at great length by Leonardo Giustinian in his splendid funeral speech,[94] and by Pier Paolo Vergerio in two elegant epistles.[95]

22   Fuit et paulo post Zacharias Tarvisanus,[72] vir doctrina consilioque celeberrimus, oratio cuius exstans coram Gregorio duodecimo[73] pontifice Romano habita, *Pro ecclesiae unione* suadenda, illum eloquentissimum fuisse ostendit. Hoc autem saeculo multos ipsi ac praestantissimos novimus:[74] e quibus Petrus Aemilianus episcopus Vincentinus litteris multum fuit sed prudentia plurimum decoratus;[75] Leonardus vero Iustinianus, magno vir nobilique ingenio inter alia humanitatis Latina et Graeca studia primum musicae adulescens iuvenisque deditus, dulcissimis materna lingua carminibus peritissimeque compositis[76] omnem replevit Italiam, dehinc natu grandior, scripto et pronuntiatione tam Latina quam vulgari et materna[77] eloquentissimus et senator gravissimus et[78] in administratione rei publicae potentissimus fuit; Marcus quoque Lippomanus iure consultus Graecas, Chaldaeas, Hebraeasque litteras aeque ac Latinas egregie doctus erat; Paulusque Venetus religiosus dialecticos nostri saeculi superavit, paucisque[79] in philosophia cedens theologus quoque[80] insignis est habitus; Franciscus etiam Barbadicus gravis, optimus, ac propemodum sanctus et Daniel Victurius,[81] cives splendidissimi, fuerunt humanitatis litteris haud quaquam[82] mediocriter eruditi.

23   Petrum Lauredanum rebus bello gestis clarissimum, quem Veneti alterum Claudium Marcellum in sua patria appellare possunt, hoc in loco a nobis poni mirabuntur qui meminerint eum Latinae linguae prima etiam rudimenta[83] penitus ignorasse. Sed eius ingenium non duximus merita laude fraudandum, quod omnia quae per aetatem suam mari gesta sunt (quorumque ipse magna pars fuit) et maris, portuositatis,[84] navigandique rationem vulgari scripto copiosissime prosecutus est. Sed dum eos ex mortuis qui in patria claruerunt doctos perquirimus, dignitatem maximam Venetorum narrando postposuimus.

A little later there was Zaccaria Trevisan, a man celebrated for 22 his learning and judgment. There exists an oration delivered before Pope Gregory XII urging the reunification of the Church which reveals his considerable eloquence.[96] In our own time I myself have come to know many extraordinary individuals. Of these, the bishop of Vicenza Pietro Emiliani was notable for his learning but even more so for his judgment.[97] Leonardo Giustinian, a man of great and noble character, his cultural pursuits in Latin and Greek apart, was first of all in youth and young manhood devoted to music: he filled all Italy with the prettiest songs cleverly composed in his mother tongue; in more mature years, he was as eloquent in Latin as in *volgare*, in writing and in speech; and as senator he was influential and eminently capable in the administration of the Republic.[98] The legal scholar Marco Lippomano was also impressively learned, in Greek, Syriac, and Hebrew literature as much as in Latin.[99] The cleric Paul of Venice was superior to the dialecticians of our time, and scarcely fell short of any in philosophy; he was accounted a distinguished theologian as well.[100] The influential, noble and almost saintly Francesco Barbarigo and Daniele Vettori, those splendid citizens, were by no means uninstructed in the literature of the humanities.[101]

Pietro Loredan is famous for his military achievements, and 23 well might the Venetians call him a second Marcellus in their own land. But the reader who recalls that he was wholly unacquainted with even the first rudiments of Latin will be surprised to find me putting him in such company. But I was determined that his genius should not be cheated of the praise that is his due, because everything that was achieved at sea in his time (much of it his own doing) and the theoretical basis of seamanship, harbor construction and navigation was dealt with at length in his *volgare* writings.[102] In seeking out those learned men of the past who have won fame in their native land, I have left till last an account of the greatest honor to come the way of the Venetians.

24   Fuerunt ex gente Corraria duodecimus Gregorius pontifex Romanus et Antonius nepos eius,[85] Romanae ecclesiae cardinalis, ea uterque morum et vitae sanctimonia quae privatos quoque[86] celebres reddere potuisset. Fuerunt ex Maurocena et Landa gente cardinales duo virtutibus litterisque ornatissimi. Alterum vero pontificem ex Condulmaria gente paulo post habuere Veneti,[87] Eugenium quartum, cuius gesta ex nostris Historiis[88] orbi notissima eum praeteritis Romanis pontificibus etiam praestantissimis parem aliorumque reliqua turba multo digniorem fuisse ostendunt.[89]

25   Quantum autem ad doctrinam litterasque attinet (quibus hoc in catalogo primas partes tribuimus), etsi Eugenius pontifex[90] nec iuri nec alicui doctrinae praecipue[91] perdiscendae animum adiecerit,[92] doctorum tamen ecclesiae, oratorumque et historicorum[93] Latinorum libros omnes et legit assidue et, quo erat mirabili ingenio, acutissime[94] intellexit. *Isque unicum ex Condulmaria gente sua ad cardinalatus dignitatem sublimavit Franciscum, qui Portuensis simul et Veronensis episcopus et Romanae ecclesiae vicecancellarius, humanitate in primis praeditus atque prudentia, primum multis iam annis in cardinalium collegio obtinet locum.[95] Et pariter humo extulit Ludovicum Blasio patre medico Venetum, a patriarchatu cui praeest Aquileiensem appellatum, per quem sedis apostolicae camerarium singularis prudentiae virum rem ecclesiasticam saecularem in primis administrari voluit.[96]* Ornavit autem cardinalatus dignitate Petrum Barbum, ex sorore nepotem, qui adulescens optimus tanta duodecim hactenus annis humanitate atque etiam integritate et simul liberalitate est usus ut et alter Titus Vespesianus et, quod illi tribuebatur, 'deliciae humani generis' sit appellatus: vir autem factus, titulo Sancti Marci est ornatus et patrio[97] cognomine cardinalis Venetiarum dictus.

26   Superestque Venetiis Franciscus Foscarus, dux omni virtutum praeterquam litterarum gloria ornatissimus. Supersunt et cives

Pope Gregory XII was a member of the Correr family, as was   24
the pope's nephew Antonio, a cardinal of the Roman church: both
men were possessed of such probity of character and style of life as
would have lent them distinction in private life as well.[103] Two
cardinals eminent in virtue and letters came from the families of
the Morosini and the Lando.[104] Soon afterward the Venetians had
a second pontiff, Eugenius IV, from the family of the Condulmer:
his achievements, made known to the world in my *Histories*, show
him the peer of even the greatest popes who preceded him, and
worthier by far than the common run of the rest.

This listing of mine has given pride of place to learning and   25
literature. In this sphere, though pope Eugenius did not devote
himself to a thorough study of the law or of any particular branch
of knowledge, he nevertheless read assiduously all the books of the
Latin church fathers, orators and historians, and thanks to his
marvelous intelligence, he had an excellent grasp of them. *He raised
to the estate of cardinal just one of the Condulmer family,*[105] *Francesco,
who was at the same time bishop of Porto and of Verona and vicechancellor of the Holy Roman Church; with his extraordinary humanity
and sagacity, he has for many years now held the leading position in the
College of cardinals. Eugenius likewise raised from humble beginnings
Ludovico of Venice, son of the physician Biagio and called Da Aquileia
from his patriarchate. Eugenius chose this man of singular sagacity to man-
age the affairs of the Church as Camerlengo of the Apostolic See.*[106] Eugenius also honored his nephew Pietro Barbo with the office of cardinalate. Barbo was his sister's son, and a youth of as yet twelve
years who behaved with such a mixture of affability, purity of
heart and generosity that he was hailed as a second Titus and, just
as Titus was, "the delight of mankind."[107] Arrived at manhood, he
was dignified with the *titulus* of San Marco, and known from his
city as the cardinal of Venice.

Venice today still has Francesco Foscari as its doge,[108] a man   26
distinguished in every field but letters. Of other contemporary

complures, e quibus Franciscus Barbarus adeo praestanti atque excellenti ingenio[98] est ut eius Graecae ac Latinae linguae doctrinam (ne an eloquentiam) editis operibus celebrem, vel in administranda re publica pietatem et sapientiam, an gestarum (praesertim apud Brixiam) rerum gloriam anteponam haud facile possim discernere.[99] Andreasque Maurocenus, bonarum artium studiis ornatus, sapientia et gubernandae rei publicae peritia gloriosus est.[100] Et Hermolaus Donatus, etsi administranda[101] re publica fuerit occupatissimus, litteris tamen[102] adeo est imbutus ut cum historiam teneat tum heroicos versus saepe composuerit elegantes. Pariterque[103] Zacharias Tarvisanus,[104] superioris Zachariae filius ac virtutis est heres. Barbonus[105] quoque[106] Maurocenus, Ludovicus Foscarenus, Vitalis Landus, Candianus Bollanus, iure consultissimi, Nicolausque Canalis, etsi iuri civili et simul rei publicae sint[107] dediti, tamen oratores poemataque et historias egregie callent.

27 Laurus etiam[108] Quirinus magnae[109] Graecarum Latinarumque litterarum peritiae iuris cognitionem addidit. Iohannem vero Cornelium (sive ut nunc corrupte eam appellant vetustam gentem 'Cornarium') doctum elegantemque moribus Venetiae habent. Paulus quoque Barbus cum ex equestri ordine tum ex Petri Barbi fratris Romanae ecclesiae cardinalis, viri integerrimi atque humanissimi, dignitate tum vero ex materna origine ab Eugenio pontifice ducta ingentem gloriam consecutus, illam bonarum artium studiis (quibus excellit) propriaque virtute accumulat.[110] Andreas Iulianus, bono vir ingenio, Bernardus Iustinianus Leonardo genitus, Hieronymus Barbadicus summo viro Francisco patre dignus,[111] Nicolausque Barbus litterarii ornamenti gloriam et laudem habent.

28 Quid quod in narrationis ordine in alterum[112] errorem incidamus,[113] qui Venetos ecclesiae praelatos saecularibus postposuimus? Sunt enim ex Venetis: episcopi Laurentius Castellanae eccle-

Venetian citizens we may single out Francesco Barbaro, a man of such surpassing genius that it is difficult to say whether one would give first place to his learning — perhaps rather, his eloquence — in Greek and Latin letters, as manifested in his famous writings, or to his dutifulness and sagacity in carrying out the republic's business, or to his exploits, particularly at Brescia;[109] Andrea Morosini, eminent in the liberal arts and a man conspicuous for his sagacity and skill in governing the republic;[110] Ermolao Donato, who though much involved with the public administration, is yet so instinct with letters that he is both a masterly student of history and a regular composer of elegant hexameters;[111] and Zaccaria Trevisan likewise, son of the elder Zaccaria and inheritor of his ability.[112] The jurists also, Barbone Morosini, Ludovico Foscarini, Vitale Lando, Candiano Bollani, and Niccolò Canal: though they are dedicated to civil law and to government, they are orators nonetheless and uncommonly knowledgeable in poetry and history.[113]

Lauro Quirini too combines knowledge of the law with mastery 27 of Greek and Latin literature.[114] Venice has as well Giovanni Cornelio (or Corner, as that ancient family is now corruptly known), a scholar of refined character.[115] Paolo Barbo too is already feted both for his membership of the Senate and for the dignities of his brother Pietro Barbo, the upright and cultured cardinal of the Roman church, as well as from his relationship with Pope Eugenius through his mother, to which he now adds the glory reaped from his talents in the liberal arts and from his own merits.[116] Andrea Zulian, that acute man,[117] Bernardo Giustiniani, the son of Leonardo,[118] Girolamo Barbarigo, worthy son of the excellent Francesco,[119] and Niccolò Barbo all enjoy the honor and praise of literary accomplishment.[120]

I suppose that in having my narrative deal first with Venetian 28 laymen rather than prelates of the church, I have fallen into another error. Of these Venice has Lorenzo and Fantin, bishops of

siae, Fantinusque Paduanae, viri doctrina et vitae[114] gravitate ac sapientia venerandi; est et Gregorius Corrarius, patrui pontificis nomen referens, sedis apostolicae protonotarius. Sunt etiam alii diversarum ecclesiarum episcopi: Hermolaus Barbarus Francisci nepos Tarvisanae, Petrus Monteus Brixianae, Iacobus Zenus Feltrensis ac Belunensis, Dominicusque Torcellanae, non solum iuris[115] civilis et pontificii ac theologiae doctrina (sicut eorum decet professionem) egregie eruditi verum ea quoque eloquentia praediti ut eius studiis aetate nostra praecipue deditos ceterisque peritiores scribendo dicendoque aequent.[116] Petrus etiam Thomasius et Venetorum et ceterorum quoque aetatis nostrae medicorum eloquentissimus habetur.[117] Sed iam nos invidiae nimis exposuit brevitatis habita ratio, quae[118] multos praeteriri fecit quos tanta civitas habet litterarum studiis vel imbutos vel operam impendentes.

Regio nona. Marchia Tarvisina[1]

1   Tribus earum quae supra a nobis descriptae sunt octo regionum, continentem esse ostendimus Marchiam Tarvisinam:[2] Romandiolae scilicet ad Melariae[3] Brigantinique paludes, Venetae urbi ad aquas salsas, et Lombardiae ad Mincium ac Benacum. Fecit tamen Benaci certius et copiosius describendi necessitas ut ad eius litoris dexteram[4] sita oppida et castella Lombardiae regioni, cuius esse non debent, adiunxerimus. Praedictis itaque trium regionum et Alpium ac Padi atque Lemini amnis contra Caprulas insulam in mare Adriaticum defluentis finibus conclusa erit Marchia Tarvisina.[5]

Castello and of Padua, men revered for their learning and upright living and wisdom.[121] There is Gregorio Correr, apostolic protonotary, who bears the name of his uncle the pope.[122] Then there are bishops of the various churches: Ermolao Barbaro, the nephew of Francesco and bishop of Treviso;[123] Pietro da Monte, bishop of Brescia;[124] Jacopo Zeno, bishop of Feltre and Belluno;[125] and Domenico, bishop of Torcello.[126] These men are not just deeply learned in civil and pontifical law and in theology, as befits their calling, but they also have an eloquence that makes them the match of our contemporaries whose specialty it is and who are more experienced in writing and speaking than the rest. Pietro Tommasi is regarded as the most eloquent of the physicians of our time — not just the physicians of Venice but all the rest as well.[127] But now the brevity that I have embraced on principle, which has obliged me to pass over many men of this great city who are expert in or students of the humanities, will have left me all too exposed to their indignation.

Region 9. March of Treviso

Three of the eight regions that I surveyed above border on the 1 March of Treviso, as I showed, namely Romagna at the marshes of Melara and Bergantino, the city of Venice at the sea, and Lombardy along the river Mincio and Lake Garda. The need to describe Garda in more depth and detail led me to attach the towns and castles on the lake's right-hand shore to the region of Lombardy, though they do not properly belong there. The March of Treviso, then, will be defined by the borders of the three regions just mentioned and by the Alps, the Po and the river Lemene that enters the Adriatic beside the island of Caorle.

2   Eam regionem (quandoque alias Galliae Cisalpinae, quandoque
Transpadanae Italiae partem, quandoque Venetiam appellatam)
Romanae ecclesiae monumenta esse volunt partem Dalmatiae
supra mare — ut nihil absurdius potuerit excogitari, cum nulla sui[6]
ex parte Dalmatia umquam[7] ad huius regionis fines pervenerit,[8]
quamquam par esse videtur absurditas maximas atque amplissimas
urbes Veronam et Patavium barbaro Marchiae vocabulo Tarvisiique titulo subiici.[9] Quam civitatem illae opulentia, potentatu, et
dignitate semper antea (sicut et nunc) longissime anteierunt.

3   Posterior tamen fuit indita ab ecclesia appellatio. Nam Longobardi, omnium qui Italiam invaserint[10] externorum superbissimi,
Romani imperii et Italiae dignitatem evertere ac omnino delere
conati, leges novas (quae alicubi in Italia exstant) condidere, mores,
ritus, gentium et rerum vocabula immutavere, ut affirmare au-
deamus locutionis Latinae Romanorum,[11] qua non solum[12] Italia[13]
sed Romano quoque imperio subiecti plerique populi utebantur,
mutationem factam in eam[14] vulgarem, cuius Italicis communis est
usus, Longobardorum temporibus[15] inchoasse. Idque incognitum
nobis quando opus De locutione Romana ad Leonardum Aretinum
edidimus. Postea didicimus, visis Longobardorum legibus, in quibus de mutatione facta multarum rerum vocabuli[16] tituli tracta-
tusque sunt positi. Quin etiam publicae administrationis et priva-
tim vivendi instituta accuratissime ab eisdem sunt mutata, et eo
usque illius[17] gentis processit insania ut, Romanarum[18] litterarum
charactere[19] penitus omisso,[20] novas ipsi et gentis barbariem sua
ineptia[21] indicantes cyphras pro litteris adinvenerint.[22]

4   Econtra vero Ostrogothi, aeque ac cives Romani Latinis litteris
delectati, nullam in illis barbariem effuderunt. Nam Theodoricus
rex primus Latine et Graece doctus fuit,[23] Amalasuntha[24] eius filia
doctior, Theodatus[25] rex tertius (et primi nepos) doctissimus,[26]

The region has been variously known as Cisalpine Gaul, 2
Transpadane Italy, or Venetia. Records of the Catholic church
would have it as part of Dalmatia "above-the-sea,"[1] though nothing
more absurd could be dreamed up, since no part of Dalmatia has
ever touched on the borders of the March of Treviso. But it seems
just as silly to have the mighty and splendid cities of Verona and
Padua nominally subject to Treviso and its barbarously named
"March." In wealth, power, and status, Verona and Padua have always far surpassed Treviso, in the past as they do today.

Be that as it may, that was the later name given to the region by 3
the church. In an attempt to overthrow and utterly destroy the
majesty of the Roman Empire and of Italy, the Lombards — most
arrogant of all the foreign invaders — laid down new laws (still in
force in some parts of Italy), customs, and rituals, and changed the
words for peoples and institutions, so that I dare say the change
undergone by the Latin language of the Romans, which was in use
not only in Italy but among most of the peoples subject to the Roman Empire, into the vernacular common to the Italian populace
began in the time of the Lombards. That was something I had not
realized when I published my book *On the Speech of the Romans*,
addressed to Leonardo Bruni.[2] I only learned it later when I had
looked at the laws of the Lombards, where there are entries and
discussions on the many things whose name was changed. The
Lombards in fact quite deliberately transformed the usages of public administration, and of private life too, reaching such a height of
madness that they abandoned the very letters of the Roman alpha-
bet and came up with novel ciphers to stand in for them, their
absurdity indicating the barbarousness of the race.[3]

The Ostrogoths, on the other hand, took as much pleasure in 4
Latin letters as Roman citizens, and did not adulterate them with
barbarisms. Theodoric, the first king, was learned in Latin and
Greek, his daughter Amalasuntha more so, and Theodahad, the
nephew of Theodoric and third Ostrogothic king, most of all,

quod Longobardorum vel regum vel principum virorum nemini contingit. Nullam vero aliam ab Ostrogothis factam fuisse mutationem hinc maxime credimus constare, quod Theodoricus et eum imitati reges ceteri Ostrogothorum cusi sua imagine nummi ambitione abstinentes aurum, aes, argentum prisco cudi Romanorum signo voluerunt.

5   Sed ad rem. Longobardi in ea Italiae parte maxima quam obtinebant regiones habuerunt quattuor a ducibus administratas, in quibus nullum successionis ius filiis[27] et nepotibus competebat: Beneventanam, Spoletinam, Taurinensem, et Foroiuliensem. Duasque opulentia et amplitudine superioribus pares, Anconitanam atque Tarvisinam, esse voluerunt ea affectas legis condicione ut, qui ex regibus aut gente Longobardorum qui eas concilii permissione decretove impetrasset,[28] filiis et agnatis successione possidendas relinquendi ius facultatemque haberet.[29] Nomenque hunc significans perpetuum magistratum in Longobarda barbarie marchionatus est appellatum.[30]

6   Quo autem tempore Carolus Magnus, sicut supra diximus, nomine indito Romandiolae Lombardiam voluit appellari regionem in qua regni sedem gens illa diutius habuerat, Romana Ecclesia hanc, de qua nunc agimus regionem, de Longobardis sumptam appellavit (ut diximus) Dalmatiam supra mare. Sed credo factum esse a minori nominis absurditate ut haec ipsa manserit appellatio Marchiae Tarvisinae.

7   Mincio eiusque, ut inquit Vergilius, 'Patre Benaco' ad sinistram relictis, nostrae descriptionis ad Padum[31] initium faciemus. Cui primum ad Mincii ostia imminet Sachetta vicus, Caprianensium familiae nobilis villa,[32] quam successione annis ducentis in cognatione continuata possederunt. Inferiusque est Seravallis arx principum Mantuanorum munitissima. A qua[33] passus mille abest Ostilia oppidum in regione primarium et[34] superbi operis arce, moenibus, ac ductis in circuitum[35] fossis conclusisque paludibus

something that never obtained among the kings or leaders of the Lombards. The Ostrogoths wrought no other changes, as I believe is most clearly shown by the fact that Theodoric, and the rest of the Ostrogothic kings in imitation of him, did not indulge an ambition to have coins made with their own image, but insisted on having the gold, bronze, and silver coinage struck with the ancient Roman designs.

But to return to our subject: in the large part of Italy that the Lombards controlled, they set up four regions governed by dukes, in which sons and grandsons had no right of succession, Benevento, Spoleto, Turin, and Friuli. There were two other regions comparable to these in wealth and extent, Ancona and Treviso, where they made it a legal condition that anyone who had taken possession of them by leave or decree of the kings or council of the Lombard nation would be able by right to pass them on to his sons or relations to hold in succession. In the barbarous terminology of the Lombards the name given to this hereditary magistracy is "marquisate."

As I mentioned above, when Charlemagne wanted to have the name Lombardy given to region where the Lombards had long been settled as rulers — the region then known as Romandiola — the Roman Church named the present region, which she had received from the Lombards, Dalmatia-above-the-Sea, as I said. But I suppose because it sounded less absurd, the name "March of Treviso" has stuck.

Leaving the river Mincio and its "father, Lake Garda," as Vergil has it,[4] behind us on the left, we begin our description at the Po. The first town on the Po at the mouth of the Mincio is Sacchetta, the famous villa of the Cavriani which they have held in their family for two hundred years. Below it is Serravalle a Po, a mighty fortress of the lords of Mantua. A mile further on is Ostiglia, the chief town of the region and one strongly protected by an imposing castle and walls, and by a circle of ditches and enclosed

munitissimum, quod a Veronensi populo (cuius agri iurium[36] fuit) ad annum salutis quinquagesimum undeciesque centenum[37] aedificatum marchiones Mantuani postea diutissime possederunt.

8   Amplaque et recta est ad vigesimum inde miliarium[38] Veronam usque via aliquot apud Ostiliam locis succisa, impositis pontibus arcibusque et castellis munitioni Ostiliensibus praesidioque futuris, perveniuntque[39] ad hos pontes paludis initia, quam in Romandiolae finibus descriptam Melariae Brigantinique agro diximus continere. Augentque (sicut ostendimus) eam paludem Tartarus et Menacus amnes, ex quibus[40] Tartarus in Veronensi agro ad Graecianum oriundus habet ad sinistram[41] Nugarolum, quae[42] Nugarolae nobili familiae Veronensi villa et primae originis patria fuit. Insula quoque[43] Porcaritia, et Gagium vicus eidem fluvio dextrorsum adiacent. At Menacus amnis, ortum ad Magnanum habens, Ceretam[44] vicum Praetellasque praeterfluit.

9   Inferius vero eadem palus (sicut in Adriae urbis vetustissimae descriptione ostendimus) augetur ab Athesis fluvii scissura ad Castagnarium appellata, eamque nos scissuram de[45] nostro hactenus omni in Italia servato more pro ostio Athesis sinistrorsum cogimur accipere. Is autem Athesis famae celebris fluvius (de quo Vergilius in *Bucolicis:*[46] 'Athesim vel propter amoenum') primum habet ad sinistram vicum Villam Bartolomaeum appellatum. Pauloque superius Athesi sinistrorsum haeret Liniacum oppidum populo opibusque plenum. Inde Athesi Zevedum adiacet oppidum brasicae et multae et dulcissimae feracissimum: adeo ut illi[47] Plinium credamus, si suam nunc incoleret Veronam, nec Sabellam in admiratione (ut scribit) crispam nec pullulantem cauliculis Aricinam,[48] nisi a suis Veronensibus vellet dissentire, praepositurum.

10   Eos vero vicies[49] mille passus, quos Veronam Ostiliamque diximus intercedere, campi quaquaversum excipiunt amplissimi aequissimique, in quibus rectae imminet viae vicus Insula Scali-

marshes: it was built in the year 1150 by the Veronese (in whose territory Ostiglia formerly was), but the marquises of Mantua have had possession of it for a very long time.[5]

A broad and straight road runs for twenty miles as far as Verona, though it is interrupted at various places around Ostiglia where bridges, towers and castles have been built to protect and defend the citizens of the place. The edge of the marshes (which I described in *Romagna* as bordering the territory of Melara and Bergantino) comes right up to these bridges.[6] The rivers Tartaro and Menago feed into these marshes, as I indicated:[7] of these rivers, the Tartaro, which rises in Veronese territory at Grezzana, has Nogarola on its left, which was the country estate and original home of the noble Nogarola family of Verona.[8] Isola Rizzo and the town of Gazzo lie on the river Tartaro, too, on the right.[9] The river Menago, with its source at Magnano, on the other hand, flows down by Cerea and the village of Pradelle. 8

Further down, as I showed in my treatment of the ancient city of Adria, these marshes are fed by a branch of the Adige called "a Castagnaro," and in line with the plan I have followed throughout all of Italy, I must take this as being the left-hand mouth of the Adige.[10] The famous river Adige (as Vergil in his *Georgics* has it: "or by the lovely Adige")[11] has first on its left a village called Villa Bartolomea. The wealthy and populous town of Legnago lies on the left of the Adige a little higher up. Next on the Adige is Zevio, a town that abounds in great quantities of succulent cabbage. If Pliny were alive now in his native Verona, I do not think he would favor (as he says he does) the crisp Sabine cabbages nor the cabbage of Aricia with its sprouting stalks over those of Zevio, unless he was prepared to part company with his fellow Veronese.[12] 9

The twenty miles that I mentioned as lying between Verona and Ostiglia are occupied on all sides by broad and level fields. On the straight road that runs through them is a village called Isola della Scala, so built up with the fortifications, churches and villas 10

gerum appellatus, communito praesidio ecclesiisque et Veronensium villis adeo ornatus ut, accedente populi quem habet multitudine, urbis potius quam oppidi speciem prae se ferat. Camposque hos (ut diximus, patentissimos) manufacta ab agricolatore raro impedit fossa adeo ut eos[50] natura committendis maximos inter exercitus proeliis de industria fecisse ac complanasse sit visa. Estque hic locus de quo Livius LXVIIII[51] ea habet, quae L. Flori breviatoris sui verbis libuit apponere: C. Marius Cimbros per hiemem Alpibus devolutos in campis Venetis usu iam vini et coctarum carnium mitigatos aggressus est. Et illis petentibus proximum diem pugnae statuit: inde LX milia ceciderunt, hinc tertio minus. Rex eorum Volerius pugnans interiit non inultus. Uxores eorum acerrimo bello captae, libertatem non impetrantes, suffocatis elisisque infantibus, mutuis vulneribus et capistris capelleis se necarunt. Quae victoria eodem die Romae per laureatos Castorem et Pollucem scita et celebrata fuit. Tigurini, qui Noricos Alpium tumulos insederant, fuga dispersi in latrocinia evanuerunt.

11   Theodoricus quoque Ostrogothorum rex primus Odoacrem Erulorum regem, qui Romam et Italiam annis iam octo occupaverat,[52] apud Soncium amnem (ubi primum ei[53] occurrit) recedere compulit. Deinde in campis Veronensibus ingenti proelio, quod tres continuatum est dies, superavit, factaque est maxima in utroque exercitu sed in Odoacris partibus maior caedes. Arnulfus[54] etiam Bavarorum[55] dux, ductis adversus Ugonem Burgundum Italiae regem copiis, a Veronensibus in urbem receptus atque rex appellatus est. Cumque Ugo ad Veronae recuperationem maximas duxisset copias, proelium his in Veronae campis est commissum in quo superavit Ugo, et Arnulfus[56] fugiens Veronam[57] portis a civibus est exclusus. Veronenses vero, rebellionis culpa in Racherium episcopum suum reiecta, veniam deprecati impetraverunt et episcopus Papiam relegatus est.

of the Veronese that, along with its considerable populace, it appears more like a city than a town. The ditches made by farmers scarcely impede passage over these open fields, so that nature might almost seem to have formed and leveled them for the express purpose of allowing great armies to join battle there. This is the place of which Livy in Book LXIX has the following to say, in the words of his abbreviator Lucius Florus: "The Cimbrians had come down from the Alps for the winter, growing soft from indulging in wine and cooked meat on the plains of Venice, when Gaius Marius attacked them. At their request he fixed the battle for the following day. Sixty thousand Cimbrians fell, a third fewer on our side. King Volerius of the Cimbrians died fighting but not unavenged. The wives of the Cimbrians, who were captured in the fierce fighting and denied release, smothered or crushed their babies to death and killed themselves by hacking at one another or strangling themselves with ropes made from their own hair. That same day the victory became known and celebrated in Rome by the statues of Castor and Pollux being decked with laurel. The Tigurini, who had settled into the Norican ranges of the Alps, fled and scattered, melting away and turning to brigandage."[13]

Theodoric the first king of the Ostrogoths here forced Odoacer, 11 king of the Heruli, who had occupied Rome and Italy for eight years, to beat a retreat at their first encounter at the river Isonzo. Then in a huge battle lasting for three days on the plains of Verona, Theodoric defeated him with great losses on both sides, but greater for Odoacer's army.[14] Arnulf too, king of the Bavarians, led his forces against Hugh of Burgundy, king of Italy, and was admitted into their city by the Veronese and named king. Hugh brought up a great force to recover the city, and battle was joined on these fields. Hugh proved victorious, and Arnulf was put to flight, thrust out of the gates of Verona by the citizenry. The Veronese put the blame for their treason onto their bishop Rather, who was exiled to Pavia after they had successfully sued for mercy.[15]

12   Sed ut iam ad Athesim redeamus: is fluvius, qua campi ad primos colles desinire incipiunt, Veronam dividit paene mediam. Quam urbem auctor est ex Trogo Pompeio Iustinus Gallos (qui urbem Romam ceperunt et pariter Mediolanum, Brixiam et Bergomum) aedificasse. Nec tamen minus cingit quam dividit Veronam Athesis, ut custodiae simul ornamentoque et subvehendis devehendisque mercibus et frugibus magno sit usui Veronensibus, quandoquidem supra infraque et circum ager sit praecipuae bonitatis, multa gignens in urbem convehenda: olei vim maximam, frumenta incolis in mercaturam superabundantia, vinorum varietatem atque praestantiam, pomorum omnis generis copiam, et lanam ceteras Italiae tenuitate[58] superantem, ut nulla sit Italiae regio, quae partem inde non accipiat indumentorum. Oleum quoque[59] cum ceterae agri partes tum maxime Benaci lacus dextera praestat ora, olearum consitis in silvae speciem amplissimae contecta, frumenta etiam[60] seminarius ager amplissimus undique patens mittit. Vinorum vero[61] praestantia, cum multis possit aliis ostendi rationibus, tum maxime uno extollitur argumento. Theodatus namque[62] Ostrogothorum rex tertius, cum sciret in Veronensi agro esse vinum (sicut Cassiodorus appellat) Accinaticum odoris saporisque suavissimi, illud Romam navibus Athesi in Superum mare delapsis comportari curavit. Libetque Cassiodori verba apponere: 'vinum etenim illud colore purpureo regium, sapore praecipuum, dulcedo cuius ineffabili suavitate sentitur, cum tamen tactus eius densitate pinguescat ut carneus liquor aut potio edibilis videatur.'

13   Pomorum autem[63] copiam, etsi nonnullae habent aliae civitates Italiae Veronensi parem, nullo tamen in loco tam grata odore[64] tamque varia specie inveniuntur. Sunt enim ex eis non nullae[65] quae perpetuitatem habent plurimi faciendam, cum senescentia tam serventur solida et illaesa ut florentibus et novellis commixta[66] manducentur. Vellerum vero[67] praestantiam greges ab herbarum et

But it is time to return to the river Adige, which runs more or   12
less through the middle of Verona at the point where the plains
merge into the foothills. According to Justin (based on Trogus),
the Gauls who captured Rome built this city, as they did at Milan,
Brescia, and Bergamo.[16] But the Adige not only divides Verona, it
also encircles it, serving at the same time as a defense and an ame-
nity. It is also very useful to the Veronese for transport up and
down the river of goods and crops, the land all around being of
exceptional quality and productive of much agricultural produce
for the supply of the city: great quantities of oil, copious grain for
the inhabitants to trade, a variety of good quality wines, fruit of all
sorts in abundance, and wool of a delicacy superior to the rest of
Italy's, so that there is no region of Italy that does not get a portion of its clothing from Verona. The territory of Verona provides
oil as well, in particular the part bordering on the right shore of
Lake Garda, which is covered by plantations of olive trees like a
great forest, and vast fields of seedlings stretching as far as the eye
can see bring forth grain. Many considerations attest to the excellence of Veronese wines, but this is the strongest argument, that
Theodatus, third king of the Ostrogoths, had a wine of the sweetest bouquet and savor that he knew in Veronese territory, the "Accinaticum" of Cassiodorus, shipped to Rome by way of the Adige
down into the Adriatic. I may quote Cassiodorus's actual words
here: "The wine is of a royal purple color with an outstanding
bouquet and an incomparable sweetness of taste, though on the
palate it has such a rich body that you might think it liquid meat
or an edible drink."[17]

Several other Italian cities can match Verona for abundance of   13
fruit, but nowhere else has such sweet-smelling fruit and of so
many different kinds. Some of them have a marvelous longevity,
since as they age they stay so firm and unbruised that they can be
eaten together with fresh fruit at its peak. Flocks of sheep derive the excellence of their wool from the special quality of the

pascuae praecipua nobilitate[68] accipiunt, quam[69] prata eius[70] campique aspectu[71] quoque amoenissimi naturae munere[72] praestant, cum tamen mons altissimus urbi supereminens Baldus nomine et eandem in[73] herbis suis et multo maiorem vim habeat. Cuius rei gratia herbilegi[74] undique confluentes multa herbarum radicumque genera animantium saluti opitulantia inde legant. Multae etiam ac variae[75] per agrum Veronensem perque oppida scaturiunt aquae, non minus ornamento a natura quam usui attributae, seu irrigationes, seu innumerabilia artificiorum genera, seu haustum ipsum[76] consideres, e quibus celebrem unius vim non reticendam esse censuimus. In valle, quam a telluris virtute et frugum praestantia Polizellam appellant, ubi Negarinae loco est nomen, mammae sunt ad aequam muliebribus formam de[77] saxo productae,[78] sub quarum papillis perpetuae stillant guttae.[79] Quibus[80] si lactans mulier papillas infuderit,[81] exsiccatus aliquo (ut fit) vel morbo vel casu alio illi humor lacteus revocatur.

14 Sed iam solidiora Veronae ornamenta, viros eius praestantes (sicut in caeteris urbibus), attingamus. Atque, ut religionem Christianam decet, Zenonem primum ponamus. Eum celebris sanctimoniae virum, qui in utriusque testamenti declarationem multa scripsit exstantia et eam quam imitatus est Ambrosianam eloquentiam redolentia, Verona praesulem habuit. Habuit et civem Aemilium Macrum poetam, quem in Asia obiisse Eusebius asserit. Habuit paulo post Catullum poetam, ac subinde Plinium utrumque saepe a nobis hac in *Italia* celebratos.[82] Et longe posteriori aetate genuit Verona[83] Rainaldum insignem (sicut Francisco Petrarchae placet) grammaticum, deinde Iohannem Madium iure consultum non incelebrem. Isque Madium genuit, nobis adulescentibus familiaritate coniunctum, iuri edisserendo defendendoque addictum, qui legum peritiae eloquentiam adiunxerat[84] adeo ut scriberet ornate, pronuntiaret suaviter, et in cunctis sese (quantum nostra[85] aetatis nostrae patitur exigitque consuetudo) bonum ostenderet oratorem. Medicos quoque genuit Verona suo saeculo[86]

grass and fodder, which the meadows and the equally delightful fields provide by nature's bounty, though the lofty mountain called Monte Baldo that towers above the city has grass of equal quality and even more energy. On that account herbalists flood in here from far and wide to pick the many kinds of grasses and roots that promote good health in animals. The countryside and towns of the Veronese teem with waters of many different kinds, a gift of nature both practical and attractive, bearing in mind its usefulness for irrigation, for trades of all sorts, or simply for drinking water. One of these in particular I cannot pass over in silence: in the Valpolicella (so called for the quality of its soil and the excellence of its produce), in a spot called Negarine, breasts like those of women have formed from the rock, and from the nipples drops of water continually drip: if a lactating woman's milk has dried up owing to some illness or other misfortune, as happens, it will be restored when she sprinkles the drops over her breasts.

But now let us turn, as we have with other cities, to Verona's 14 more substantial glories, her famous men. In first place, as Christian religion requires, let us place Zeno, a man of celebrated piety who was bishop of Verona. Much of his extant writing elucidates the Old and New Testament in a style redolent of the eloquence of his model Ambrose.[18] Verona also bore her citizen Aemilius Macer, the poet who died in Asia Minor, as we learn from Eusebius.[19] A little later, she had the poet Catullus, and then the two Plinies often mentioned in this *Italy Illuminated* of mine.[20] In a much later era, Verona bore Rainaldus the grammarian, a distinguished one in Petrarch's view,[21] then Giovanni Maggio, a jurist of a certain renown. He was the father of the Maggio who was my friend in youth. In his dedication to explaining and defending the law, Maggio joined such eloquence to his mastery of jurisprudence that he was a fine writer and a fluent speaker, and showed himself in every particular a good orator, so far as the habits of our age allow and demand.[22] Verona also bore the foremost physicians of

praestantissimos Avantium et Iacobum Lavagnolum, cuius nomen
refert et cognomen Iacobus equestris ordinis Lavagnolus humanitatis studiis et eloquentia exornatus. Bernardus quoque honesto
genitus Campaniae loco non parum[87] Veronae attulit ornamentum, qui medicus et philosophus[88] insignis tanta viguit memoria
ut Themistoclis instar nihil illi exciderit quod aut discere eum aut
attentius legere contigisset. Iohannes etiam Salernus ad equestris
dignitatis insignia doctrinam et facundiam socias addidit.

15   At res militaris praeclaros nobis ostentat viros, qui Veronae
laudes accumulant, quorum memoriae altior repetitio efficiet[89] ut
varios eius urbis casus referre cogamur. Floruerunt in ea praeclarae
familiae Monticuliensium et Sancti Bonifacii comitum.[90] Hique,
illos cum eiecissent, Azzonem Marchionem Estensem urbis dominio praefecerunt. Isque ad annum salutis millesimum ducentesimum[91] et duodecimum ab Ecelino de Romano vi eiectus Mantuanorum armis[92] restitutus est. Qua in restitutione durissimum
in Braida Veronae campo[93] proelium est commissum. Azzone
mortuo, Ecelinus ad annum millesimum ducentesimum[94] et vigesimum quintum Veronam obtinuit, qui immanissimus[95] omnium
tyrannus ducentos Veronenses, simul cum eo[96] carcere in quo tene-
bantur, uno combussit incendio. Cumque ei Veronae agenti (quod
in Patavio referemus) esset allatum Patavium sibi[97] rebellasse, duodecim milia Patavinorum,[98] quos militiae praetextu obsides secum
duxerat, diversis affectos cruciatibus in Verona occidit.

16   Eo autem apud Soncinum[99] Cremonensis agri oppidum inter-
fecto, Veronenses reductis Sancti Bonifacii comitibus in libertatem
erecti quietem nacti sunt, quae paucos continuata est annos,[100]
quod Scaligeri cives et ipsi Veronenses, sed per novi[101] Capitaneatus populi occasionem tyranni sunt effecti. Primusque omnium
Canisgrandis Scaliger, Dantis Franciscique Petrarchae amicitia

their generation, Avanzi and Jacopo Lavagnola, both of whose names have been taken over by ser Jacopo Lavagnola, a man of distinction in study of the humanities and eloquence.[23] Bernardus, too, born of a well-to-do family in Campania, brought no small glory to Verona: a remarkable physician and philosopher, his powers of memory were so strong that, like Themistocles, nothing escaped him that he had chanced to learn or noticed in his reading.[24] Giovanni Salerno likewise allied learning and eloquence to the insignia of his knightly rank.[25]

Then again, military events can show us famous men who 15 greatly added to Verona's glory, and going back further into history obliges us to deal with the city's varied vicissitudes. The distinguished families of the Montecchi and the counts of Sambonifacio were preeminent in Verona. When the Montecchi had driven out the counts of Sambonifacio, they installed Azzo marquis of Este as *podestà* of the city.[26] Ezzelino da Romano forcibly removed Azzo in 1212 CE, but the Mantuans restored him by dint of arms,[27] in the course of which a very hard battle was fought at Braida in the territory of Verona. On Azzo's death in 1225, Ezzelino, the cruelest of all tyrants, took control of the city and in a single conflagration burned to death two hundred Veronese, along with the jail in which they were being held. While Ezzelino was thus engaged in Verona, news was brought to him that Padua had revolted, as I shall mention under Padua. He had brought with him twelve thousand Paduans as hostages, supposedly for military purposes, and these he now put to death in Verona after torturing them in manifold ways.

When Ezzelino was killed at Soncino, a town in Cremonese 16 territory, however, the Veronese brought back the counts Sambonifacio and regained their independence, for a few years finding peace. But then the della Scala, themselves citizens of Verona, exploited the new position of Captain of the People to become tyrants. The first of them was Cangrande della Scala, better reputed

magis quam sua potentia notus, cum annis uno et quinquaginta[102] Veronae dominium tenuit,[103] civitatesque[104] interea Cremonam, Parmam, Regium, Vincentiam, Patavium, Feltrum, Civitatum, Tarvisium in potestatem redegit, Gonzagamque familiam dicioni Mantuae, eiectis Passarinis, imposuit. Sed et Scaligeri, cum annis LXX Veronae summo cum splendore dominati fuissent, ob varias in familia divisiones ter quaterque subortas, quandoque a Vicecomitibus Mediolanensibus quandoque a Charrariensibus Patavinis, patria pulsi sunt, quibus contentionum occasionibus[105] Veneti ea urbe, quam ab annis[106] iam XLV obtinent, sunt potiti. Luchinus Vermes Veronensis vir bello insignis Cretam insulam Venetis rebellem sua virtute vendicavit,[107] deinde, in Turchos Christi Dei nostri hostes profectus,[108] pugnans cecidit. Eiusque filius Iacobus Vermes patri haudquaquam dissimilis rem primi ducis Mediolani Iohannis Galeacii ab imminentibus periculis fortitudine et consilio saepe tutatus est. Armeniacique[109] comitem et Iohannem Hauchut Anglicum adversus Mediolanum maximo cum exercitu ruentes proelio apud Alexandriam commisso profligavit et, maxima caede commissa, Armeniacum cepit. Ea quoque expeditione, in qua Luchinus Vermes Cretam Veneto vendicavit[110] imperio, Georgius Caballus Veronensis eques praestantissimus militares ducens ordines navatae fortiter operae id retulit decus ut Senator a Venetis fuerit constitutus. Sed iam claudat Veronensium gloria digniorum aciem Guarinus, quem supra in eorum catalogo quos eloquentiam in nostrum saeculum longo postliminio reduxisse ostendimus merito laudum praeconio decoravimus: pictoriae artis peritum Verona superiori saeculo habuit Alticherium, sed unus superest,[111] qui fama ceteros nostri saeculi facile[112] antecellit, Pisanus nomine, de quo Guarini carmen exstat, qui Guarini Pisanus inscribitur.

for his friendship with Dante and Petrarch than for his exercise of power, despite the fact that he reigned over Verona for fifty-one years, during which he subdued the cities of Cremona, Parma, Reggio, Vicenza, Padua, Feltre, Cividale, and Treviso, expelled the Passarini from Mantua and subjected it to the Gonzaga family.[28] But though they reigned over Verona for seventy years with great brilliance, owing to various family quarrels that arose three or four times, the della Scala too were driven from their country, by the Visconti of Milan and at other times by the Carraresi of Padua. Taking advantage of these upheavals, the Venetians took control of the city, which they have now held for forty-five years. The valor of the famous Veronese soldier Lucchino dal Verme regained the island of Crete, which had revolted against the Venetians,[29] then attacked the Turks, the enemies of our Lord Christ, and fell fighting. Lucchino's son—who fell in no way short of his father—Jacopo dal Verme, by his bravery and good counsel often safe-guarded the state of Gian Galeazzo Visconti, the first duke of Milan, from the perils that threatened it.[30] When the Count of Armagnac and the Englishman John Hawkwood brought up a mighty army for an onslaught on Milan, Jacopo put them to flight in a bloody battle at Alessandria and took Armagnac prisoner.[31] And on the expedition where Lucchino dal Verme reclaimed Crete for the Venetian empire, the excellent Veronese knight Giorgio Cavalli won such glory for a task bravely discharged as he led his troops into battle that he was made a Senator by the Venetians.[32] But now let Guarino da Verona close the roll call of Veronese worthies, the man whom I singled out for deserved praise in my earlier catalog of those that restored eloquence to our generation after a long exile.[33] In the previous century, Verona had a master of the painter's art in Altichiero,[34] yet there is one still alive, Pisanello by name, whose fame far surpasses the other painters of our age. There is a poem by Guarino about him entitled "Guarino's Pisano."[35]

17   Gesta vero sunt vario eventu Veronae multa a nobis in *Historiis*
celebrata. Alboinum namque primum Longobardorum regem,
libro quarto, ostendimus uxoris Rosmondae insidiis ab Helmechilde in Verona occisum fuisse et utrosque adulteros Ravennae
quo confugerant, veneno mutue dato, interiisse. Et, in octavo,
diximus Theudelindam Grimoaldi Bavarorum regis filiam, ad
quam cum in praeclaram reginam devotissimamque Christianam
evasisset beatus Gregorius *Dialogorum* libros inscripsit, Veronae in
Sardicensi campo desponsatam fuisse. Estque, in XI, Veronenses,[113] Aldegisio Desiderii Longobardorum ultimi regis filio civitate (quam firmo tenebat praesidio) vi eiecto, Carolo Magno deditionem fecisse, eorumque exemplo omnem regionem[114] Carolo et
suis illico manum dedisse.[115] Aedificiis Verona mediocribus publice privatimque ornata theatrum habet ⟨prae⟩ ceteris quae ubique
exstent praeter Romanum amphitheatrum nunc Colosseum operis
magnificentia conspiciendum. Habet et pontes quatuor superbi
operis, Athesi impositos, et cathedralem ecclesiam non minus vetere decoram aedificio quam novo insignem *quod Franciscus Condul-
marius cardinalis vicecancellarius, Veronensis sicut et Portuensis ecclesiae
episcopus, nuperrime*[116] addidit.[117]

18   Supra Veronam Athesis sinistrorsum Pontonem[118] oppidum habet appositum, superiusque[119] Castrum Barchum nobile item oppidum, inde Cadenium, et, qua torrens Vallem Solis intersecans in
Athesim labitur, Mecium est oppidum, supraque illud Ignatum,
superiusque[120] Formigarium. Ad fontem vero Athesis in Alpibus
parvo sub lacu (quem fons ipse efficit) est oppidum Lamium.
Diximus supra, sinistram Athesis ripam describentes, eius ostium
ad Castagnarii scissuram (qua in Adriensium[121] paludes labitur)
necessario accipi designarique oportere. Nec aliter dicere aut scribere debuimus, quia quicquid ab ea scissura ad mare pertenditur[122]
in Romandiolae partibus est comprensum. Dexteram vero eius-

In my *Histories*, I recorded the many and varied events that took 17
place at Verona. In Book IV, for example, I described the murder
there of Alboin, first king of the Lombards, by Helmechilde,
thanks to the treachery of Alboin's wife Rosamund, and the death
by mutual poisoning of the adulterous couple at Ravenna, where
they had fled.[36] In Book VIII I noted that Theodolinda, daughter
of Grimoald, king of the Bavarians — to whom St. Gregory dedicated his *Dialogues* after she had become a famous queen and a
pious Christian — was married in the Campo di Sardi of Verona.[37]
In Book XI I noted that, after Aldegesius, son of Desiderius the
last king of the Lombards, had been driven out of the city, which
was being held for him by a strong garrison, the Veronese surrendered to Charlemagne, and that the whole region followed their
example and submitted to Charlemagne and his descendants on
the spot.[38] Verona is furnished with public and private buildings
of tolerable quality, but does have an absolutely magnificent theater which surpasses any other anywhere save for the amphitheater
at Rome now called the Colosseum. It also has four imposing
bridges over the Adige and a cathedral whose old structure is no
less remarkable than the additions *which the cardinal Vicechancellor
Francesco Condulmer (bishop of Verona as of Porto) recently made to it.*[39]

Above Verona on the left bank of the Adige lies the town 18
of Ponton, and above that Castelbarco, another fine town, then
Caino, and where a stream cuts across the Val di Sole and flows
into the Adige, there is the town of Mezzolombardo, and above
that, Egna, and higher still Castel Formiano. In the Alps at the
source of the Adige, beneath a small lake formed by the Adige itself, is the town of Lamium. I mentioned above in describing the
left bank of the Adige that one had to understand that the mouth
of the river is really at the turn it takes at Castagnaro, where it
flows into marshes of Adria, and that it should be so designated.[40]
And that was the correct way to put the matter, since everything
that extends from this bend to the sea is part of Romagna. In fact

dem[123] amnis ripam ab ipso mari Adriatico ad fontem usque totam
Marchiae Tarvisinae (cuius est) possumus applicare. Igitur qua
Athesis in mare labitur, ostium efficit portuosum quas 'Fossiones'
appellant.[124] Idque primum est eorum quae priscos 'septem maria'
diximus vocitasse. Adiacent intus huic amni, paludibus stagnisque
immixto, hinc Turris Nova praesidio et vectigalium custodiae apposita, inde Caput Aggeris, quod item praesidio[125] ducatus Venetiarum finibus institutae eius rei publicae initio ea in parte fuit
constructum.[126] Interius[127] Athesis bifurcatus peninsulam Rodigii
efficit, quae sinistrorsum in Romandiola superius est descripta.
Athesique dextrorsum, qua fluvius illabitur novus, adiacet Castrum
Baldum. Supra est Portus oppidum, quod Athesi a Liniaco divisum ponte illi coniungitur ut unum idemque oppidum censeantur.

19 Influit paulo supra Athesim amnis nomine Albus, cui dextrorsum Cereda haeret vicus in regione primarius. Sinistrorsum vero
sunt Arcellae supraque Sanctus Bonifacius oppidum, a quo nobili
Veronensium familiae fluxit cognomen, et superius est[128] Villanova. Deinde[129] supra fluminis Albi ostium adhaeret Athesi Porci-
lae oppidum, a quo parum distat amnis quem Montis Aurei nomine appellant ostium. Isque amnis fonte oritur uberrimo, cui in
Montis Aurei vico omnium regionis amoenissimo villa est ea ratione superaedificata, ut fons ipse media in aula scatens eam[130]
evomat vim aquarum, quae subito (intra lapidis iactum) molis
sufficit convolvendis. Suntque atterendo in farinam frumento et
bombicinis ⟨in⟩ conficiendas chartas comminuendis[131] tam frequentia amni superimposita aedificia[132] ut vix stadio colligendis
aquis invicem separentur. Sextoque inde miliario[133] abest Verona,
supra quam dextrorsum item haeret Athesi Pelusium oppidum, a
quo vallem vulgus dici existimat Pelosellam—licet eam a telluris

we may apply the term the March of Treviso to the whole right bank of the Adige (as indeed it is), all the way from the Adriatic to its source. Where the Adige flows into the sea, then, it makes a harbor mouth called Fossona: this is the first of those shallows that the ancients liked to call the "seven seas," as I said above.[41] Further inland, where it is mixed up with marshland and lagoons, the Adige has on the one side a new tower set up to safeguard and store customs tolls, and on the other Cavarzere, which was established when the Republic was founded to guard the borders of the Duchy of Venice in those parts. Further inland again, the forking of the Adige forms the peninsula of Rovigo, whose left side I surveyed above in *Romagna*.[42] Castelbaldo lies on the right bank of the Adige, where the new river flows into it. Above Castelbaldo is the town of Porto, which is separated from Legnago by the Adige but linked to it by a bridge, so that Porto and Legnago are reckoned as one and the same town.

A little higher up, a stream called Alpone flows into the Adige, on whose right bank lies the chief village of the area, Cerea. On the left are Arcole, and above Arcole the fine town of San Bonifacio, whence the noble Veronese family derives its name,[43] and above it is Villanova. Then comes the town of Porcile lying on the Adige above the mouth of the Alpone, not far from which is the mouth of the river called Montorio. That river rises from a copious spring in the village of Montorio, the most charming of the region. Over the spring a house has been built so that the river actually gushes up in the middle of the hall and generates such pressure of water that it serves at once to turn millwheels just a stone's throw away. To collect water for grinding grain into flour and for mashing rags for paper-making, these buildings have been built so close together over the river that for hundreds of yards there is scarcely any space between them. Verona is six miles from Montorio, and above Verona on the right bank of the Adige lies Pelusium, a town which is commonly thought to give Valpolicella

19

virtute et frugum praestantia Polizellam Guarinus existimet appellari. Licena deinde[134] est oppidum, et superius Rovoredum, apud
quod oppidum via scalpris monte excisa artum[135] viatoribus praebet iter validumque Veronensi agro ea in parte a Germanorum
insultibus est munimen.

20   Besenum deinde habetur oppidum, et superius (qua fluvius a
Pergine oppido defluens in Athesim cadit) est Tridentum, quam
urbem Iustinus scribit a Gallis qui urbem Romam ceperunt, sicut
et Veronam Vincentiamque, fuisse aedificatam. Apudque eam urbem auget Athesim amnis iuxta Pineam oppidum in Alpibus
oriundus, cui dextrorsum haeret Segozanum,[136] supraque[137] Par-
dasium[138] Menumque et ad sinistram Cavalesium et Visum ac
Chanacium.[139] Athesim item supra influit amnis apud Persono-
rium oppidum nobile oriundus. Cui amni Valesium, Foespergum,
et Cevedonum oppida sunt dextrorsum;[140] sinistrorsum vero est[141]
Clusa corrupte sed Latino verbo Clausura, ubi arctissimo aditu
trames Alpium est conclusus. Bolgianumque oppidum nobile parum ab Athesi recedens torrenti est appositum, qui a Sirentino[142]
oppido brevem cursum habet. Domus inde Nova oppidum, et superius est Maranum populo frequens oppidum, quod etsi in Italia
situm est, gentis locutione et moribus totum est Teutonicum potius quam Italicum. Deinceps sunt Alpium iuga, quorum aditibus
(et quidem arduis) in Germaniam est accessus.

21   Athesis cursu ab ostio in fontem[143] undique descripto, amnem,
quo eum[144] superius auctum esse diximus et cui 'Novo' flumini[145]
est appellatio, describi necesse est priusquam Meduacum[146] (sive
ut nunc appellant Bachilionem) assumamus ordine ostendendum.
Is fluvius nomine Novus, quem apud Castrum Baldum Athesim
illabi diximus, sinistrorsum attingit intus Coloniam oppidum populo opibusque plenissimum. Superiusque eidem haeret fluvio

its name, though Guarino thinks that it is called Polizella from the fertility of its soil and the high quality of its crops.[44] Then comes the town of Lizzana, and further up the town of Rovereto, where a road that has been carved out of the mountain gives wayfarers narrow passage and stout protection of the territory of Verona against attacks by Germans in the vicinity.

Next is the town of Beseno, and higher up, where a river flows   20
down from the town of Pergine into the Adige, is the city of Trent. Justin writes that it was built by the Gauls who captured the city of Rome, as well as Verona and Vicenza.[45] At Trent, a river that rises in the Alps near the town of Pinè flows into the Adige, and along this river on the right lie Segonzano, and above that, Predazzo and Moena, and to the left Cavalese, Vigo di Fassa and Canazei. Above these towns another river flows into the Adige, rising in the noble city of Bressanone: on this river lie to the right the towns of Valese, Fespergo, and Cevedone; to the left is Chiusa (a corruption of the Latin Clausura), where passage into the Alps is hemmed in by very narrow approaches. The fine town of Bolzano, not far from the Adige, lies on a stream whose brief course begins at the town of Sarentino. Then there is the town of Casa Nova, and above Nova is the populous town of Merano, which—though located in Italy—in the speech and customs of the inhabitants is wholly German rather than Italian. Then we have the Alpine peaks, through whose passes one enters with difficulty into Germany.

Having given a full description of the Adige from mouth to   21
source, I have now to describe the river that I said above flowed into it, called the Fiume Nuovo,[46] before taking up in turn the river Medoaco, or Bacchiglione as they now call it. This so-called New River, which as I said flows into the Adige at Castelbaldo,[47] skirts inland the rich and populous town of Cologna Veneta to the left. Above Cologna, Montebello Vicentino, another fine town, lies on the Fiume Nuovo, the wealthy and populous town of Brendola

Mons Bellus nobile item oppidum, et ad fontem sunt[147] Brendulae oppidum populo opibusque refertum. Brendulisque paulo infra ad amnis dexteram propinquum est Leonicum, populi opumque exuberantia civitatulae aequiparandum. Quod Omnebono cive ornatur litteris Graecis Latinisque apprime erudito et prae se mores ferente, quos a Victorino Feltrensi praeceptore[148] nutritus imbibit.

22   Ab Coloniaque in subiectas paludes Adeusto oppido vicinas instar fluvii currens fossa est[149] manufacta, apud quam Rovoredum et Montagnana[150] (oppidum regionis primarium) sunt sita. Ad eiusque fossae ostia, quibus in palades labitur, et paulo infra Locium Castellum, Meduacus (sive Bachilio) amnis proxime a nobis describendus alterum habet ostium. Attingitque illum sinistrorsum[151] Custodia oppidum populo frequentatum, medio in cuius suburbio fodinas esse inspeximus, per quas longo tractu in subterranea penetratur. Estque lapidis eius montis minera Tibertino lapidi adsimillima[152] ut — quod nullo in loco scriptum invenimus — nequaquam dubitemus saxa construendae conservandaeque urbi Patavinae vetustissimis olim temporibus inde excavata sumptaque fuisse. Et cum ea in caverna noxii olim servari consuevissent,[153] Custodia inde vicus est appellatus. Estque locus apud quem Guilielmum Ravennatem archiepiscopum, apostolicae sedis legatum, deseruerunt Bononienses milites, quorum opera usus Ecelinum de Romano Patavio eiecerat: qua ex re factum est[154] ut paulo post Ecelinus,[155] reassumptis viribus, vires Ecclesiae retuderit legatumque apud Gambaram Brixiani agri oppidum proelio superatum in carcerem coniecerit.

23   Supra Custodiam[156] Meduacus sive Bachilio Vincentiam dividit paene mediam, quae urbs a Gallis Romae incensoribus (sicut saepe supra diximus), cum Mediolano, Brixia, Bergomo, et Verona, fuit principio aedificata. Alius item fluvius Vincentiam illabitur, Tesina appellatus, qui apud Landrigum oppidum oriundus et apud Luxanum oppidum scissus alterum ramum, cui Barcanum

being at its source. Near Brendola, a little lower down on the right
bank of the river, is Lonigo, like a small city in the abundance of
its people and wealth. Lonigo is noted for her citizen Ognibene
Bonisoli da Lonigo, splendidly learned in Latin and Greek and a
paradigm of good character, which he took from his master Vittorino da Feltre.[48]

A canal has been constructed which runs like a river from Co-   22
logna to the swamps that border the town of Este; Roveredo di
Guà and Montagnana, the principal town of the region, are situated on it. At the mouth of the canal where it flows into the
swamps and a little below the castle of Lozzo, the river Medoaco,
also known as the Bacchiglione, which I shall describe next, has a
second mouth. The populous town of Costozza lies on the left
bank of the Medoaco: amid its suburbs I have seen pits that reach
far into the earth. The stone mined from the mountain there is
very much like travertine, and though I have seen it nowhere put
in writing, I am quite sure that the stone used for building and
repairing the city of Padua in ancient times was quarried here.
The town was called Costozza from the former custom of keeping
criminals in custody in this quarry. This is the place where the Bolognese soldiers deserted the Apostolic Legate Guglielmo, Archbishop of Ravenna, after they had helped him to expel Ezzelino da
Romano from Padua; and so it came about that Ezzelino, restored
to power not long afterward, smashed the forces of the Church,
defeated the Legate in battle at Gambara (a town in Brescian territory), and had him thrown into prison.

Above Costozza, the river Medoaco or Bacchiglione passes   23
practically through the middle of Vicenza. This is a city first
founded by the Gauls that burned down Rome, as we have often
said above, like their other foundations of Milan, Brescia, Bergamo, and Verona. Another river called the Tesina also flows by
Vicenza. It rises at the town of Landro and divides at the town of
Lusiano to form a second branch, on which a place called Barcano

haeret oppidum, facit. Eoque[157] Meduacum, priusquam Brentellas attingat, ingreditur. Genuit ex vetustis Vincentia Palaemonem (sicut Eusebio placet) insignem grammaticum, qui interrogatus quid inter 'guttam' et 'stillam'[158] interesset: 'Gutta,' inquit, 'stat, stilla cadit.' Nostra autem aetate illustrata est Vincentia Antonio Lusco, qui vir doctissimus eloquentissimusque et primus et solus, *In Orationibus Marci Tullii Ciceronis duodecim*, ars rhetoricae practicae[159] qua ratione a Tullio fuerit applicata tam clare tamque diffuse commentus est ut nihil magis nostros homines perdiscenda eloquentia iuvisse videatur. Exstant etiam viri eiusdem heroica quaedam carmina Vergilianam maiestatem carminum redolentia. Matthaeusque Bissarius iureconsultus, eloquentia et bonis artibus apprime eruditus, patriam exornat. Multa suppeterent in Vincentinorum laudem dicenda a ducentis annis gesta dum Patavinorum Veronensiumque pariter prope[160] vicinorum violentiae iniuriisque resistunt, sed unicum eos facinus abunde reddit ornatos:[161] quandoquidem primi fuere qui, Venetorum imperio sese sponte sua subiicientes, praeclaras urbes Patavium, Veronam, Brixiam Bergomumque et quicquid aliud illi nunc obtinent de Italia in potestatem eorum[162] venire plurimum adiuverunt.

24   Supra Vincentiam Meduaco adhaeret Caldognum oppidum, et superius fonti eius imminet oppidum Porcelletum. Meduacusque priusquam Custodiam attingat oppidum supra descriptum, altero scissus ramo fossas attingit quibus Brentellis est appellatio in munimentum Patavii[163] circumductas. Inde apud Vigentionum delapsus fertur in[164] oppidum Bubolentam. Defluens postea ad Pontem Longum continuato cursu stagnis se immiscet, a quibus alterno fluxu refluxuque (vel tractus[165] vel repulsus) in Fossam Clodiam se exonerat. Quae urbis Clugiae ab ea fossa appellatae portum efficit

is situated. From there the Tesina enters the Medoaco above Brentelle. Among the ancients, Vicenza gave birth, according to Eusebius, to the distinguished grammarian Palaemon, who when he was asked the difference between a drop and a drip, said that "a 'drop' is motionless, but a 'drip' falls."⁴⁹ In our own time Antonio Loschi too has added luster to Vicenza. Learned and eloquent, in his *On Twelve Orations of Marcus Tullius Cicero* he was the first and only writer to give such a brilliant and comprehensive disquisition on how Cicero applied theory to practical rhetoric that nothing has better helped the men of our era to master eloquence. Some of his hexameter poetry is also extant, redolent of the stateliness of Vergil's poems.⁵⁰ The jurisconsult Matteo Bissaro, surpassingly learned in eloquence and the good arts, is another ornament of his fatherland.⁵¹ Mere recitation of the many achievements of the Vicentines over the last two hundred years as they struggled against the onslaughts and injuries of their near neighbors the Paduans and Veronese in equal measure, would be sufficient praise for them, but a single feat renders them glorious: by being the first to place themselves voluntarily under the sway of the Venetians, they greatly assisted the passage of the famous cities of Padua, Verona, Brescia, Bergamo, and the rest of Venice's Italian dominions into the Venetian orbit.

Above Vicenza, the town of Caldogno sits on the river Medo 24
aco, and, higher up, the town of Porcellato overlooks the source of the river. Before reaching the town of Costozza described above, the Medoaco forks, its second branch connecting with the canal known as the Brentella, which was dug to defend Padua. Then the Medoaco feeds into the Vigenzone and carries on to the town of Bovolenta. After that it flows straight on down to Pontelongo and there merges with the marshes, from which as it is pushed or pulled with the ebb and flow of the tides, it is discharged into the canal of Chioggia. The canal forms the harbor of the city of Chioggia, which was named after it, the deepest harbor in the region.

omnium regionis profundissimum. Plinius namque Meduacum amnem in Fossam Clodiam labi docet.

25   Fuisse etiam Bachilionem amnem Meduacum Livii Patavini verbis ex decimo libet ostendere. 'Eodem anno classis Graecorum, Cleonymo duce Lacedaemonio, ad Italiae litora appulsa Thurio-rum[166] urbem in Sallentinis cepit. Adversus hunc hostem consul Aemilius missus proelio uno fugatum compulit in naves. Thu-riae[167] redditae veteri cultori, Sallentinoque agro pax parta. C.[168] Iunium Bubulcum dictatorem missum in Sallentinos in quibusdam annalibus invenio et Cleonymum, priusquam confligendum esset cum Romanis, Italia excessisse.[169] Circumvectus[170] inde Brundisii promontorium, medioque[171] sinu Adriatico ventis latus. Cum laeva importuosa Italiae litora, dextra Illyrici Liburnique et Histri gentes ferae et magna ex parte latrociniis maritimis infames terre-rent,[172] penitus ad litora Venetorum pervenit. Ibi, expositis paucis qui loca explorarent, cum audiisset tenue praetereundum[173] litus esse (quod praetergressis stagna ab tergo sint irrigua aestibus[174] maritimis), agros haud procul ⟨proximos⟩ campestres cerni, ulte-riora colles videri, esse ostium fluminis praealti quo circumagi naves in stationem tutam vidissent[175] (Meduacus amnis erat), eo invectam classem subire flumine adverso iussit. Gravissimas[176] na-vium non pertulit alveus fluminis. In minora navigia transgressa multitudo armatorum ad frequentes agros, tribus maritimis Pata-vinorum vicis colentibus eam oram, pervenit. Ibi egressi, praesidio levi navibus relicto, vicos expugnant, inflammant tecta, hominum pecudumque praedas agunt, et dulcedine praedandi longius usque

As you know, Pliny informs us that the river Medoaco flows into the canal of Chioggia.[52]

I should here point out that the river Meduacus was indeed the 25 Bacchiglione. To quote the Paduan Livy in Book X: "During the same year a Greek fleet commanded by Cleonymus the Lacedaemonian put in to the shores of Italy and seized the city of Thuriae in the country of the Salentini. The consul Aemilius was dispatched against this enemy, whom he routed in a single engagement and drove to his ships. Thuriae was restored to its old inhabitants, and peace was established in the Salentine territory. I find in some annals that Junius Bubulcus the dictator was sent among the Salentini, and that Cleonymus withdrew from Italy before it became necessary to fight the Romans. Rounding then the promontory of Brundisium, he was swept on by the winds in the mid gulf of the Adriatic, and dreading the harborless coasts of Italy on his left and on his right the Illyrians, Liburnians, and Istrians, — savage tribes and notorious most of them for their piracies — kept straight on until he reached the coasts of the Veneti. Having sent a small party ashore to explore the country, and learning that it was a narrow beach that extended in front of them, on crossing which one found behind it lagoons which were flooded by the tides; that not far off level fields could be made out, and that hills were seen rising beyond them, and that a river of great depth — the Meduacus — debouched there, into which they could bring round their ships to a safe anchorage — having learned all this, I say, he ordered the fleet to sail in and make its way up stream. But the channel would not admit the heaviest ships, and the multitude of armed men, passing over into the lighter vessels, kept on till they came to thickly inhabited fields; for three maritime villages of the Patavini were situated there along the riverbank. Disembarking there they left a small body of men to defend the boats, burned the houses, made spoil of men and cattle, and, lured on by the pleasant prospects of pillage, advanced to a greater and greater

a navibus procedunt. Haec ubi Patavium sunt nuntiata (semper autem eos in armis accolae Galli habebant), in duas partes iuventutem dividunt: altera[177] in regionem qua effusa populatio nuntiabatur,[178] altera, ne cui praedonum obvia fieret, altero itinere ad stationem navium (milia autem quatuordecim ab oppido aberant) ducta. In naves parvas, ignaris[179] custodibus interemptis, repentinus[180] impetus factus, territique nautae coguntur naves in alteram ripam amnis traiicere. Et in terra[181] prosperum aeque in palatos praedatores proelium fuerat: refugientibusque[182] ad stationem Graecis Veneti obsistunt.'

26   Dicimus ergo[183] praeteritum a Cleonymo[184] tenue litus ita protentum (quod praetergressis stagna a tergo essent aestibus maritima irrigua) ostiumque amnis praealti, quo invecta sit flumine adverso classis prope Patavium ad quatuordecim miliaria, satis ostendere[185] Meduacum fuisse amnem descriptum, cui Bachilioni fuit postea (estque nunc indita) appellatio. Neque enim alium habet regio fluvium ex agro Patavino in stagna marisve ostia delabentem, nisi forte eum quis proximum illi amnem nunc Brintam esse opinabitur, qui suam et ipse paucissimis cognitam fecit nominis mutationem.

27   Est enim Timavus priscorum scriptis, praesertim Vergilii, celebratus, quem saepe miratus sum viros nostri saeculi doctrinae fama celebres in Histris et Liburnis quaesivisse, errore abductos[186] atque ignoratione sensus Vergilii, quem volunt novem Timavo fontes suo in carmine attribuisse, cum potius Antenorem ille faciat a Troia Italiam petentem regna Liburnorum et Timavum superasse

distance from their ships. When word of these events was brought
to the Patavini, whom the vicinity of the Gauls kept always under
arms, they divided their young men into two divisions. One of
these marched into the region where the scattered marauding was
reported; the other, taking a different road, to avoid falling in with
any of the marauders, proceeded to the place where the ships were
moored, fourteen miles from the town. The latter party, slaying
the guards, who were unaware of their approach, made a rush for
the ships, and the terrified sailors were forced to get them over to
the other side of the stream. On land, too, the battle waged
against the straggling plunderers was equally successful, and when
the Greeks would have fled back to their station, the Veneti stood
in their way."[53]

I claim, then, that the long narrow beach over which Cle-   26
onymus passed (on crossing which one found behind it lagoons
flooded by the tides), and the mouth of a deep river where the
fleet put in facing the current some fourteen miles from Padua,
show clearly enough that the river described was the Meduacus,
which later acquired the name "Bacchiglione," as it is still called.
The region in fact has no other river flowing down from Paduan
territory into the lagoons or mouths of the sea, unless perhaps one
is to suppose that it was the next river along, now known as the
Brenta, and so a river that itself changed its name, though the
change was known to very few people.

The Timavus is celebrated in the writings of the ancients, par-   27
ticularly Vergil's. I have often been surprised that men of our time
famous for their learning have been led astray and looked for it in
Istria and Liburnia through misunderstanding Vergil's meaning.
They would have it that in his poem Vergil attributed nine sources
to the Timavus, whereas he actually writes that on his way to Italy
from Troy Antenor sailed by the kingdom of the Liburni and the
river Timavus, designated in poetic style by the phrase "the source
of the Timavus." For as Servius explains the term, "*fontem Timavi:*

amnem in ipso fontis nomine poetico more indicatum. Servius
enim id verbum exponens sic habet: 'fontem Timavi: amant poetae
rem unius sermonis circumlocutionibus ducere, ut pro "Troiam"
dicant "urbem Troianam." Sic modo pro "Timavo," "fontem Timavi," et paulo post "urbem Patavi" pro "Patavio."' Et 'ora novem
multi septem esse dicunt.' 'Superasse' autem ea parte unde (pro
qua) 'per ora novem mare it praeruptum et premit stagnorum arva'
(pro campis et planitie posita) 'sonanti pelago,' sicut semper sonare
videmus, cum litoris aut portus cuiuspiam fauces paulo violentior
commotiorque ingreditur, *vel dicamus cum Servio: 'pelago, id est aqua-*
rum multitudine.'[187] Eaque novem ora etiam nunc notissima sunt,
litoris Veneti aperturae,[188] quarum partem maximam a Ravennati
agro in Altinum prisci, et in primis Antoninus Pius imperator in
Itinerario, septem maria appellavere. Versus Vergilii, licet notissimi
sint, subiiciemus, cum prius Lucani de Timavo testimonium attu-
lerimus: 'Euganeo si vera fides memorantibus augur colle sedens,
Aponus terris ubi fumifer exit, atque Antenorei dispergitur unda
Timavi.' Si ergo unda Timavi Antenorei dispergitur prope Apo-
num nunc etiam notissimum et Patavio[189] propinquum, non oportuit in Histris illum aut Foroiuliensibus a nostris hominibus re-
quiri. Vergilius: 'Antenor potuit mediis elapsus Achivis Illyricos
penetrare sinus atque intima tutus regna Liburnorum et fontem
superare Timavi, unde per ora novem vasto cum murmure montis
it mare praeruptum et pelago premit arva sonanti.' Exstant quoque
carmina Musatti Patavini poetae tragici sepulchro inscripta, Timavum affirmantia Patavio propinquum esse: 'Condita a[190] Troiugenis
post diruta Pergama, tellus in mare fert Patavas (unde Timavus)
aquas: hunc genuit vatem.' Et Martialis coquus poeta:[191] 'Laneus[192]
Euganei lupus excipit ora Timavi.' Si ergo Timavus fuit Euganeus
necessario erit Brinta nunc Patavii fluvius. Nam idem Martialis

poets love to expand the sense of a single expression with circum-
locution, as, for example, when they say 'the Trojan city' for 'Troy.'
So now he says 'source of the Timavus' for 'Timavus,' and 'city
of Troy' for 'Troy,' and a little further on, 'city of Patavium' for
'Patavium.'"[54] Further, "Many say that Vergil's 'nine mouths' are
seven."[55] Vergil says "he sailed past the source of the Timavus," also
in that passage, "from here (using *unde* for *qua*) through nine
mouths, echoing loudly from the mountain, the sea bursts forth
headlong and pounds the fields (using *arva* for *campos* and *planitiem
positam*) with thundering flood," just as we see often happens when
a rough and turbulent sea enters into the mouth of a shore or
harbor of any sort — or let us say with Servius: "with the flood,
that is, with a mass of water."[56] These nine mouths are still familiar today, the openings on the Venetian shoreline, most of which,
from the countryside of Ravenna to Altino, the ancients (in particular the emperor Marcus Antoninus in his *Itinerary*) called the
"Seven Seas."[57] Though they are well known, I shall cite the verses
of Vergil, but first let me adduce the testimony of Lucan on the
Timavus: "If those who tell the tale may be believed, an augur sat
that day in the Euganean hills, where the smoking spring of Aponus issues from the ground and the Timavus, river of Antenor,
splits into channels."[58] Well, if "the Timavus, river of Antenor,
splits into channels" near Abano, which is still a well-known place
close to Padua, there is no need for the men of our day to look for
it in Istria or Friuli. Vergil says: "Antenor was able to slip through
the midst of the Argives, reach unscathed the bays of Illyria and
the inner realm of the Liburnians, and sail past the source of the
Timavus; from here through nine mouths, echoing loudly from
the mountain, the sea bursts forth headlong and pounds the fields
with thundering flood."[59] Verses of the tragic poet Albertino Mussato of Padua survive, too, inscribed on his tomb, and they con-
firm that the Timavus is close to Padua: "Settled by Trojans after
the destruction of Troy, the land carries its Paduan waters —

appellatione telluris Aponae Patavium significat hoc versu: 'cense-
tur Apona Livio suo tellus.' Et L. Florus haec[193] habet verba ex
quibus licet coniicere Timavum ab Arsia et finibus Italiae, in quibus nuper requirebatur, plurimum distare: Illyrici ab Alpium radicibus inter Arsiam et Timavum per Adriaticum litus effusi, regnante Teutana muliere.

28   Timavusque, ubi salsas attingit aquas, bifurcatus parte dextera
Pupiliam Methamaucumque petit, ubi portum efficit cum amplitudine tum etiam profunditate optimum. Rectiore autem ad sinistram cursu Venetam urbem mediam scindere solitus portum efficit
Venetum, cui munitissimae arces duae hinc et inde praesidio sunt
appositae. Sed haec pars, occlusis pridem ad Luciafusinam meati-
bus, in stagna paludesque diffunditur. Non fuisse autem Meduacum quem Timavum esse dicimus aut econtra praeter rationes
superiores[194] hinc maxime videtur constare: quod Plinius scribit
contra Timavum amnem insulam fuisse parvam in mari cum fontibus calidis, qui pariter cum aestu maris crescerent minueren-
turque. Et recto Brintae amnis cursui, quem naturaliter per mediam urbem Venetam habebat, oppositam fuisse constat insulam,
cui castellum Olivolense appellatum fuit impositum. Unde cathedralis ecclesia dicitur Castellana. Si vero calidi non apparent nunc
fontes, minime mirandum: quod non solum[195] in[196] litoreis et maritimis locis in quae maris saepe desaevit violentia sed in mediterraneis montanisque firmioribus multos aruisse fontes invenimus.

29   Timavusque supra Luciafusinam integer primum habet ad dexteram vicum Auriagum tabernis hospitatoriis frequentatum, ibique

whence the Timavus—into the sea: Padua gave birth to this poet."[60] And the poet Martial the cook: "The sea bass breasts the mouths of Euganean Timavus."[61] If the Timavus was Euganean, then, it must necessarily be the Brenta, the river of modern Padua.[62] Martial again designates Padua as "the land of Aponus," in the line, "the land of Aponus rests its reputation on its Livy."[63] Lucius Florus has the following to say, from which we may surmise that the Timavus is very distant from the river Arsa and the borders of Italy, where it has recently been sought: "the Illyrians under their queen Teutana spread all over the Adriatic coast, from the foothills of the Alps between the Arsa and the Timavus."[64]

When the Timavus reaches the salt lagoons, it splits into two. 28 The right-hand branch makes for Poveglia and Malamocco, where it forms a fine harbor, both wide and deep. Its more direct course to the left used to cut through the middle of Venice, where it creates the city's port, with two strong fortresses set on either side to defend it. But with its channels long since blocked off at Lizza Fusina, this stretch of the Timavus dissipates in lagoons and marshes. In addition to the reasons mentioned above, the strongest ground for our assertion that this river was the Timavus and not the Meduacus, or vice versa, is Pliny's statement that there was in the sea off the Timavus a small island with thermal springs that rose and fell with the tide.[65] It is common knowledge that there was an island opposite the direct course of the Brenta (the river's natural route through the middle of Venice), where there was a castle named Olivolo, from which the cathedral was known as "the church of Castello." If the hot springs are now no more to be seen, that is no surprise: we find that many springs have dried up, not just in coastland and beaches, which have often borne the brunt of the sea's violence, but in places in the middle of the countryside and in stable mountain areas too.

Above Lizza Fusina, the first village on the still undivided Ti- 29 mavus is Oriago on the right bank, which is crowded with inns for

Timavum illabitur Tegola[197] torrens, cui adiacet rus Peragum.[198] Deinceps Timavo sinistrorsum adiacet Strata oppidulum, a quo sexto milliario fossa manu facta Paduam compendio navigatur.

30   Eam urbem Italiae vetustissimam clarissimamque magis certum est Antenorem Troia profugum condidisse quam ut indigeat testimoniis. Versibus enim quos supra posuimus sic addit Vergilius: 'Hic tamen ille urbem Patavii[199] sedesque locavit.' Et Livius, Patavinorum decus, in primo idem seriose narrat. Cicero autem in *Philippicis* Patavinos dicit Romanis amicissimos fuisse, qui rei publicae difficillimis temporibus pecunia et armis iuverunt. Et Macrobius in *Saturnalibus*, ubi de fide servorum tractat, innuit Patavinos fuisse perhumanos, qui cum servis clementissime atque indulgentissime[200] se habuerunt, quandoquidem asserit, Asinio Pollione Patavinos cogente ut tributa conferrent, et propterea dominis latitantibus, neminem servorum fuisse inventum qui, libertate proposita, dominum proderet. Fuit autem postmodum Padua per felicissima stantis rei publicae tempora Romanorum colonia non eo modo deducta quo ceterae deducebantur, introductis novis populis in coloniam, sed datum est Paduanis ius Latii ut in designandis Romae magistratibus ferendi suffragii ius haberent, quod a Q. Asconio Pediano in expositionibus orationum Ciceronis habetur.

31   Ea vero describenda urbe, si prolixiores erimus, sua nos dignitas excusabit. Nullam enim aedificiorum pulchritudine, praesertim publicorum, in Italia similem ei[201] esse tenemus. Sunt tamen nova, quaecumque in ea nunc exstant (vel publica vel privata), quandoquidem ad quadringentesimum et trigesimum[202] salutis annum Athila rex Hunnorum ferro ignique vastatam reliquit immunitam, et a Narsete eunucho Ravennatibusque instauratam anno a prima dirutione vixdum centesimo Longobardi incensam penitus desertarunt.

travelers, and there the stream Tegola (on which the farm called Perage is situated) flows into the Timavus. Then the little town of Stra lies on the left bank of the Timavus; six miles from Stra there is a canal which provides quick passage to Padua.

The foundation of this city, the oldest and most famous in It- 30 aly, by the refugee from Troy Antenor is too well established to need supporting testimony. After the verses I quoted above, Vergil adds, "Yet here the famous Antenor founded the seat and city of Padua."[66] Livy in turn, the glory of Padua, tells the same story in Book I.[67] Cicero too in the *Philippics* says that the Paduans were very well disposed toward the Romans, and that they helped the Republic with money and arms in times of crisis.[68] Dealing with the faithfulness of slaves, Macrobius tells us in the *Saturnalia* that the Paduans were very civilized people who dealt with their slaves in a merciful and kindly way; he says, for example, that when Asinius Pollio was pressing the Paduans hard for tribute and their owners had for that reason gone into hiding, not one of their slaves could be found to betray his master, even when offered his freedom. Later, in the heyday of the Republic, Padua became a colony established not in the usual way, by the introduction of a new populace into the colony, but by the grant of the *ius Latii*, whereby the Paduans enjoyed the right to vote in the elections of magistrates at Rome: this matter is touched on in Asconius's commentaries on Cicero's orations.[69]

The importance of Padua will compensate for any prolixity on 31 my part as I describe the city. In my view no city in Italy can match it for the beauty of its buildings, especially public ones. Yet all the buildings public or private now in Padua are recent, because in 430 CE Attila the king of the Huns laid waste to it with fire and sword, leaving the city without defenses. Though it was restored by the eunuch Narses and the men of Ravenna, the Lombards again utterly devastated Padua with fire barely a hundred years after the first destruction.

32   Aucta vero est mirabili incremento Caroli Magni et filiorum
nepotumque imperii temporibus,[203] nec aliquod postea incommo-
dum sub Germanis imperatoribus accepit quousque Federici primi
Barbarossi temporibus Ecelinus de Romano, tyrannorum omnium
qui umquam fuerunt crudelissimus, ad annum salutis millesimum
ducentesimum trigesimum septimum[204] eam sibi subegit. Qui
praeter[205] commissas caedes alias proscriptionesque prope innume-
ras civium, ea usus est (de qua in Verona diximus) crudelitate raro
alias audita: caedis per varia cruciatuum genera perpetratae duodecim milium Patavinorum, quos Mantuanorum ingressurus[206] fines
sub militiae praetextu obsides secum duxerat. Paulo tamen postquam is tyrannus apud Soncinum interiit,[207] Charrarienses sub
capitaneatus titulo rerum in Patavio potiti sunt, qui eam urbem
annis paulo plus minus centum per varias successiones possessam
opulentiorem ornatioremque reddiderunt. Nam gentis Charrariae
opera maiori ex parte excitata ornataque fuerunt moenia, quibus
triplici circuitu Patavium communitur. Et licet eam per urbem
Timavus semper fuerit delapsus (quod Livius in X libro ostendit),
multis tamen variisque fossis magno et ingenti opere manu factis
aquae circum urbem et per diversa agri loca ornamento urbi com-
modoque futurae ab eisdem Charrariensibus sunt perductae.

33   Cum arx in urbe munitissima,[208] et coniunctum illi perductis
bracchiis palatium facile in Italis primarium, superbique operis
nonnulli in urbe pontes gentis eiusdem fuerint opera, Henricus
autem quartus imperator Germanicus cathedralem Patavii ecclesiam, quae exstat, aedificavit. Praetoriumque quo nullum in orbe
pulchrius esse tenemus,[209] cum esset casu crematum, speciosius
Veneti construxerunt, ossaque T. Livii conspicuo in eius fastigio
collocarunt. Insignis vero et cui rarissime sunt in Italia similes
beati Antonii basilica a Patavinis sub Romano imperio semiliberis

Padua underwent remarkable expansion in the time of the em-   32
pire of Charlemagne and his sons and grandsons, and suffered no
subsequent setbacks under the German emperors, until in the
days of Frederick I Barbarossa, Ezzelino da Romano, the cruelest
tyrant who ever lived, subjugated the city to himself in the year
1237 CE. Quite apart from the other murders he perpetrated and
the innumerable proscriptions of citizens, Ezzelino practiced a
cruelty seldom heard of elsewhere (as we mentioned under Verona)[70] in slaughtering by a variety of torments twelve thousand
Paduans that he had brought with him as hostages, under the
pretense that they were to fight for him as he prepared to invade Mantuan territory. Not long after the tyrant died at Soncino,
however, the Carraresi gained control of the government of Padua
as captains of the city, holding it over a number of generations for
about a hundred years and leaving it more prosperous and handsome.[71] It was largely thanks to the Carrara family that the triple
circuit of walls that protects Padua was raised and fortified. The
Timavus will have always flowed through the city, as Livy shows
in Book X,[72] but the Carrara themselves had water channeled
through the city and parts of the countryside in many different
canals which were constructed with enormous effort for the future
benefit and ornament of the city.

The same family was also responsible for the very strong for-   33
tress, the town hall (easily the finest in Italy), whose wings abutted
on to the fortress, and a number of urban bridges of superb workmanship, yet it was the German emperor Henry IV who built the
present cathedral of Padua.[73] The Venetians rebuilt the town hall,
which we reckon to be without peer in the world, even more hand-
somely after it had been accidentally burned down,[74] installing
Livy's bones in its pediment so as to be more easily seen. The famous basilica of St. Anthony, which scarcely has a rival in Italy,
was built by the Paduans when they were semi-autonomous in the
time of the Roman empire. It is well known that at various times

aedificata est. Parrochiales ecclesias quadraginta et mendicantium quatuor loca magnifici certe operis cives Patavinos diversis aedificasse temporibus constat. Est ea in urbe Iustinae Virginis templum, amplissimae cuius aedes mille in circuitu passus amplexae aquis circumluuntur; quod in vetustae aedis vestigio aedificatum fuisse hinc constat, quod effodientes ubique pulcherrima inveniunt lithostrota.[210] Eodemque in loco T. Livii sepulchrum aetate nostra repertum fuisse conspeximus ut credere liceat vetustum Iovis templum ibi fuisse in quo ipse Livius, in X, narrat spolia de Cleonymi Lacedaemonii[211] piratae victoria Patavium fuisse affixa reportata fuisse. Servat vero nunc idem templum Iustinae ipsius virginis Lucae Evangelistae, Maximi et Felicitatis, Mathiae Apostoli (super quem fors cecidit), Prosdocimique tutelaris Patavinorum sancti corpora et reliquias. Areas Patavium publicas quinque habet, nobilium scilicet et herbaticam, frumentariam, lignariam, et paleariam.[212] In eius quoque[213] gymnasio, omnium Italiae celeberrimo, aedes sunt amplissimae studentium quibus opes sint tenuiores auxilio deputatae.

34   Viros Patavium doctrina clarissimos genuit: T. Livium, cuius sepulchri—priusquam Romam accederet—sibi et filiis duobus uxorique positi saxum nuper vidimus litteras haudquaquam elegantes inscriptum: 'T. Livius Gaii filius sibi et suis Tito Livio, Titi filio, Prisco f.[214] T. Livio, T. f. Longo f., Cassiae Sextiae primae uxori.' Aliudque elegantiores maiusculas marmore incisas sepulchrum etiam Patavii in Iustinae Virginis vestibulo exstat titulis ornatum et[215] militiae cui ad decus utilitatemque fuit ascriptus,[216] et virtutis suae qui dissidentes Patavinos cives, in patriam reversus, ad concordiam revocavit: 'Vivens fecit T. Livius Liviae T. F. Quartae Legionis,[217] Halys[218] Concordialis Patavii sibi et suis omnibus.' Ratio autem, quae nos adduxit ut futuram in minore viro vanam

the citizens of Padua built forty parish churches and four magnificent houses of the mendicant orders. There is in the city a church
of the virgin Santa Giustina, whose extensive precinct, a mile in
circumference, is encircled by water. We know that it was built
among the remains of an ancient building from the fact that those
who dig there everywhere find mosaics of great beauty. I notice
that Livy's tomb was found at that very spot in our own day, so
one may well believe that a temple of Jupiter had been there:[75]
Livy himself says in Book X that the spoils from the victory over
the Spartan pirate Cleonymus were brought back to Padua and
hung up there.[76] This same church of S. Giustina preserves the
bodies and relics of the Evangelist Luke, Maximus and Felicity, the
Apostle St. Matthias (on whom "the lot fell"),[77] and Prosdocimus,
the patron saint of Padua. Padua has five public squares, namely,
the Piazze dei Signori, delle Erbe, della Frutta, della Legna, and
della Paglia. At the University of Padua, the most celebrated in
Italy, there are ample halls of residence set aside for the assistance
of scholars of limited means.

Padua has borne men of great fame for their learning — men   34
such as Livy, whose gravestone (made before he went to Rome) for
himself and his wife and two sons I recently saw, inscribed in
crude characters with these words: "Titus Livius, son of Gaius, set
this up for himself and for his sons, Titus Livius Priscus, son of
Titus, Titus Livius Longus, son of Titus, and for his first wife,
Cassia Sexta."[78] There is another marble sepulchral inscription at
Padua, also in the vestibule of S. Giustina, and carved in rather
better capital letters: these record his military service (which he
undertook with great distinction and success) as well as his courage in bringing harmony to the disputes among the citizens of
Padua when he returned to his native land. "T. Livius Halys, of
Livia the daughter of Titus, a soldier of the Fourth Legion, priest
of Concordia, had this inscription made at Padua for himself and
all his family in his lifetime."[79] But the reason that induced me to

huiusmodi diversitatis sepulchrorum curiositatem adhibuerimus, illa fuit, quod in primo[219] sepulchro omnes quos habuit Patavii degens, uxorem et filios, in successionem adnotavit. In altero autem omnibus dixit, qui filia[220] Romae esset auctus, quae Lucio Magio nupsit oratori Romano, de quo Seneca, *Declamationum* VIII, sic habet: Non puto quomodo Lucius Magius, gener Titi Livii, declamaverit, quamvis aliquo tempore suum populum habuit, cum illum homines non in ipsius honorem laudarent sed in soceri efferent. Fuitque is magnus[221] vir Livius, ad quem nobiles ex ultimis Hispaniarum[222] partibus venisse et, quos Romani nominis fama non moverat, eius hominis famam perduxisse beatus Hieronymus ex Plinio sumptum scribit.

35   Paulusque iurisconsultus apud vetustissimos celebratus fuit Patavinus. Et Martialis poeta duos dilexit Patavinos poetas Stellam et Flaccum his versibus: 'Verona licet audiente dicam, 'vicit, Maxime, passerem Catulli tanto Stella meus tuo Catullo quanto passere maior est columba.' Et infra: 'O mihi curarum pretium non vile[223] mearum, Flacce, Antenorei spes et alumne laris.' Catullus vero Volusium poetam Patavinum, qui secutus[224] Ennii exemplar rerum gestarum Populi Romani *Annales* carmine scripsit, damnare et vituperare conatus est his epigrammatibus: 'At Volusi[225] *Annales* Paduam morientur ad ipsam, et laxas scombris saepe dabunt tunicas.' Item alio loco: '*Annales* Volusi, cacata charta, votum solvite pro mea puella: nam sanctae Veneri Cupidinique[226] vovit, si sibi restitutus essem desissemque[227] truces vibrare iambos, electissima pessimi poetae scripta tardipedi deo daturam infelicibus ustulanda lignis. Et haec pessima se puella vidit iocose[228] lepide vovere[229] divis. Nunc o caeruleo creata ponto, quae sanctum Idalium Urios-

bring up the curious matter of the difference between these tomb inscriptions, which would be insignificant in the case of a lesser man, is this: in the case of the first, he listed in order all those (wife and sons) who were with him while he was living in Padua. But in the second he said "all his family," having had in addition a daughter while he was at Rome. That daughter married the Roman orator Lucius Magius, on whom Seneca remarks in *Declamations* VIII, "I do not think the style of declamation of Lucius Magius, Livy's son-in-law, [is relevant]: he did at one time have his followers, but men praised him not for himself but out of deference to his father-in-law."[80] This great man was Livy: basing himself on Pliny, St. Jerome writes that nobles came to visit him from furthest Spain and, though the fame of Rome left them unmoved, this man's fame drew them there.[81]

The jurisconsult Paulus, famous among the ancients, was a native of Padua.[82] The poet Martial expressed his love for the two Paduan poets Stella and Flaccus in these verses: "I shall speak, though Verona hear me: 'Stella's *Dove* has beaten Catullus's *Sparrow*, Maximus. My Stella is greater than your Catullus as much as the dove is greater than the sparrow.'"[83] And below: "Flaccus, in whom I find no mean reward for my pains, hope and child of Antenor's home."[84] In these epigrams Catullus sought to condemn and ridicule the Paduan poet Volusius, who followed the example of Ennius in writing the annals of Roman history in verse: "Volusius's *Annals* will die without even getting out of Padua and will provide plentiful loose tunics for mackerel."[85] And more of the same elsewhere: "*Annals* of Volusius, fecal folios, make good my girlfriend's vow. For she swore to holy Venus and to Cupid that if I were restored to her and stopped hurling my fierce iambs, she would offer up to the lame-footed god the choicest writings of the worst of poets to be burned alongside accursed logs. And in jest the girl saw that she was cleverly vowing to the gods the very worst of poems. Now, goddess born of the blue sea, who cherish holy

35

que[230] apertos, quaeque Anconam Cnidumque arundinosam colis,
quaeque Amathunta,[231] quaeque Golgos,[232] quaeque[233] Dyrrachium, Adriae tabernam, acceptum face redditumque votum, si
non illepidum neque invenustum est. At vos interea venite in
ignem, pleni turis et inficetiarum *Annales* Volusi, cacata charta.'

36   Petrum etiam de Apono[234] 'Conciliatorem' appellatum philosophiae et astronomiae usque ad magiae[235] suspicionem peritissimum Musattumque et Lovattum iure consultos poesi ornatos Patavium cives habuit. Franciscus Zabarella iure consultissimus et
Pileus de Prata, Romanae ecclesiae cardinales, dignitatem litteris
et prudentia ornaverunt. Marsilius quoque et paulo post Iohannes
Galeatiusque et Guilielmus Sophilici, Iohannes quoque[236] Horolo-
gius, et paulo post Antonius Cermisonus, excellentes medici, Patavium patriam exornarunt.

37   Agrum etiam habet Patavium non minus quam urbis aedificia
conspiciendum, quandoquidem montes in illo sunt excelsi nec
Alpes nec[237] Apenninum — quod nullo in Italiae loco alibi cerni-
tur — contingentes, et usque summa in cacumina vinetis olive-
tisque et consitis arboribus[238] tecti,[239] in quibus vina gignuntur
quae Plinius in intimo[240] Adriatico sinu optima describit. Gemu-
lam unum in cuius summitate mulieres Deo dicatae monasterium
habent a Beatrice Estensi virgine nobili aedificatum, et Vendam
alterum appellant monasterio ornatum, quod Montis Oliveti fratres inhabitant. Eisque[241] adiacent montibus colles Euganei fama
apud Latinos vates notissimi. Eam enim vatibus sedem fuisse innuit Martialis poeta his versibus: 'Si prius[242] Euganeas, Clemens,
Heliconis[243] in auras[244] pictaque pampineis videris arva iugis.' Et
Lucanus in primo: 'Euganeo, si vera fides memorantibus, augur
colle sedens.' Et cum vici villaeque multae hos contegant colles
tum maxime Arquatam populo frequentem vicum decorat Francisci Petrarchae praediolum, apud quod diutissime vixit multaque

Idalium and exposed Urii, who dwell in Ancona and reedy Cnidus, and in Amathus and in Golgi, and in Dyrrachium, rendezvous of the Adriatic, take the vow as duly paid and discharged, if it is not without charm or grace. But meanwhile, into the fire with you, *Annals* of Volusius, full of smoke and dullness, fecal folios."[86]

Other citizens of Padua were Pietro d'Abano, known as the   36 "Reconciler," a man so expert in philosophy and astronomy that he came under suspicion of sorcery, and Mussato and Lovati, both jurists with a gift for poetry.[87] The cardinals of the Roman Church, Francesco Zabarella, a leading jurisconsult, and Pileo da Prata have added the luster of letters and philosophy to their high station.[88] Marsilio di Santa Sofia, and slightly later Giovanni Galeazzo and Guglielmo,[89] and Giovanni Dondi dall'Orologio, and a little later again, Antonio Cermisone, all fine physicians, were a credit to their Paduan homeland.[90]

Padua also has a rural hinterland no less worthy of our atten-   37 tion than the buildings of the city, for the high mountains there are not connected to either the Alps or the Apennines, something that is not found elsewhere in Italy, and they are covered right up to the top with vineyards, olive groves, and orchards. In these mountains wines are produced which Pliny describes as the finest in the upper reaches of the Adriatic.[91] One of the mountains is called Monte Gemmola, on the summit of which nuns live in a convent built by the noble virgin Beatrice d'Este;[92] another, known as Monte Venda, is distinguished by a monastery inhabited by Olivetan monks. Beside those mountains lie the Euganean Hills much lauded by the Latin poets. The poet Martial intimates that the region was the home of bards in these verses: "If, Clemens, you see the Euganean tracts of Helicaon and the fields decked with vine trellises before I do . . ."[93] And Lucan in Book I: "If those who tell the tale may be believed, an augur sat that day in the Euganean hills . . . ."[94] Though there are many villages and estates spread over these hills, Petrarch's little holding gives special glory

scripsit. Estque eius sepulchrum marmoreo in sarcophago columnis quatuor sustentatum. Balneaque apud rus Euganeum etiam
nunc appellatum plurima visuntur, quae Theodericum regem Ostrogothorum muris conclusisse ac ornasse Cassiodorus est auctor,
in eisque herbas gigni scribit Plinius. De his etiam[245] poeta Martialis: 'Nullae sic tibi blandientur undae ac fontes Aponi rudes[246]
puellis.' Quibus vero ea opitulentur morbis Michael Savonarola
physicus celebris[247] opere in id edito disseruit.

38   Sed iam ad Timavum est redeundum. Is fluvius supra Liminam
vicum, ubi incipit esse integer, primum habet ad dexteram oppidum Citadellam, quod Patavini ad annum salutis millesimum
centesimum nonagesimum septimum[248] aedificarunt. Ulterius[249]
est Marostica, superius Bassianum, quae duo oppida populis sunt
frequentia. Supraque Bassianum Timavus, ubi Cisinum est oppidum, Cesino flumine augetur, in quod[250] Arcivagus[251] Vavorius-
que,[252] torrentes exigui, ex Alpibus delabuntur, Cisinusque apud
Premechum[253] oppidulum habet ortum. Timavo supra Cisinum ad
dexteram Grignum adiacet oppidum a torrente ibi augente dictum.
Ulterius oppidum habetur Ivanum,[254] supraque illud oritur Grig-
nus. Et superius emissorium lacus incubat Tusopum. Caldona-
cium deinceps oppidum et uni imminet lacui et aliis subiectum est
binis lacubus, a quibus tribus originem Timavus habet.

39   Primus post Timavum Musio fluvius stagna Venetorum apud
Mestre oppidum illabitur, cui ad sinistram Villa Nova primum est
proxima. Supraque paulo remotius Campus Sancti Petri oppidum
adiacet opulentum, eiusque fonti in montibus oppidulum imminet
Collis Musionis ab ipso fluvio appellatus. Ad dexteram vero Mu-

to the bustling village of Arquà, where he lived for the greatest length of time and wrote much.[95] His tomb is there, in the form of a marble sarcophagus resting on four columns. Baths are patronized in great numbers throughout the Euganean countryside, as it is still called today. We learn from Cassiodorus that Theodoric, king of the Ostrogoths, had them enclosed within walls and refurbished,[96] and Pliny writes that grasses grow in them.[97] Martial too writes about the baths: "No waters will charm you so much, not the springs of Aponus untried by maidens."[98] The celebrated physician Michele Savonarola has discussed the diseases that these baths can help in a work devoted to the subject.[99]

But it is time to get back to the Timavus. Above the village of 38 Limena, where it starts to be a single stream again, the river has Cittadella as the first town on its right, built by the Paduans in 1197. Beyond Cittadella is Marostica and further up Bassano, two populous towns. Above Bassano the river Cismon flows into the Timavus at the town of Cismon del Grappa, and two small streams, Senaiga and Vanoi, flow down from the Alps into the Cismon—the river Cismon actually rises at the little town of Primiero. Above the Cismon on the right, the town of Grigno (named after the stream that flows into the Timavus there) lies on the Timavus. Beyond Grigno comes the town of Castel Ivano, and the river Grigno rising above it. Higher up is the town of Tusopo nestling above the outlet of a lake. Then the town of Caldonazzo overlooks one lake and lies beneath two others: the three lakes together give rise to the Timavus.

The first river after the Timavus is the Musone, which enters 39 the Venetian lagoon at the town of Mestre. Next to Mestre, the first town you come to on the left of the river is Villa Nova. Above Villa Nova and a little further inland lies the prosperous town of Camposampiero, and sitting above the source of the Musone in the mountains is the hamlet of Colle Musone, named after the river. Inland on the right on the Musone lies the fine town of

147

sioni intus continent Castrum Francum nobile oppidum, superiusque Asola longe nobilius. Deinceps amnis est Silus, quem Plinius
asserit oriri in montibus Tarvisinis, apud Torcellum in stagna
cadens. Torcellumque civitatem, nunc episcopo ornatam doctissimo Dominico de Dominicis, supra Venetam[255] describentes regionem diximus aedificatam fuisse ex ruinis excidioque Altini.
Cuius vetustae urbis parva admodum vestigia ad eam continentis
partem, quae sinistrorsum Sili amnis ostio est apposita, nunc cernuntur. Altinique nomen primus veterum[256] ponit Plinius. Et post
eum[257] Martialis poeta tanti fecisse videtur Altini oppidi situm ut
dicat: 'Aemula Baianis Altini litora villis.' Antoninus vero Pius in
Itinerario, vias describens a Ravenna Aquileiam, dicit aut septem
maria recto a Ravenna secundum Adriatici litus ad Altinum trans-
mitti aut eos, qui per Bononiam, Sermedum, Ateustum Pataviam-
que terrestri petant itinere, Altinum primo dehinc[258] Aquileiam
accedere.

40   In eo autem quod[259] Musionem et Silum amnes interiacet spatio Novale est oppidum nobile, Silusque supra in mediterraneis
Tarvisium urbem dividit, cuius nomen prior inter vetustos habet
Plinius. Ostrogothorum vero temporibus[260] videtur initium fuisse
dignitatis[261] eius quam nunc habet. Nam cum Tothilae pater Veronam aeque ac Tarvisium dominio possideret, Tarvisii tamen conti-
nuo est moratus. Unde Tothila, qui postea quintus fuit Ostrogothorum rex et quidem praestantissimus, Tarvisii natus educatusque
est. Postea Longobardorum initio regni, cum Alboinus rex eius
gentis primus Italiam esset ingressus Aquileiamque (qualisqualis
tunc erat) et ceteras regionis urbes per deditionem cepisset, Tarvisium quia eius incolae deditionem tardiuscule obtulissent, spoliare
ac diruere constituerat nisi Felix illius[262] episcopus, vir timoratus
Ravennaque[263] oriundus, regis barbariem sua prudentia et precum
instantia delinisset. Ornataque nunc est ea civitas altero praestante

Castelfranco Veneto and, higher up and even grander, Asolo. Next is the river Sile, which Pliny tells us rises in the mountains of Treviso,[100] flowing down into the lagoon at Torcello. As I said when dealing with the Veneto region, the town of Torcello, ornamented now by the learned bishop Domenico Dominici, was built on the ruins of Altinum after its destruction.[101] Some scant traces of the old city of Altinum, which was located to the left of the mouth of the Sile, are still visible in that part of the mainland. Pliny was the first of the ancients to record the name of Altinum,[102] and after him the poet Martial evidently thought so well of the site of Altinum that he wrote: "The beaches of Altinum that rival the villas of Baiae."[103] In describing the routes from Ravenna to Aquileia in his *Itinerary*, Antoninus Pius says that one must either cross "the seven seas" in a straight line along the Adriatic coast, or for those making the journey on foot, first arrive at Altinum by way of Bologna, Sermide, Este, and Padua, and from there on to Aquileia.[104]

In the area that lies between the Musone and Sile rivers is the fine town of Noale. Above that, further inland, the Sile runs through the city of Treviso, first named by Pliny among the ancients.[105] The high standing that Treviso now enjoys seems to have begun in the time of the Ostrogoths, for though Totila's father controlled Verona just as he did Treviso, yet it was at Treviso that he lived on a permanent basis. So it came about that Totila, who later became the fifth — and indeed the most notable — king of the Ostrogoths, was born and brought up in Treviso.[106] Later, at the beginning of Lombard rule, when Alboin, the first king of that people, had invaded Italy and had received the surrender of Aquileia (such as it then was) and the other cities of the region, he decided to sack and destroy Treviso because her inhabitants had been rather slow to surrender; and he would have done so had not the city's devout bishop Felix, a native of Ravenna, softened the king's savagery with his prudence and unceasing prayers.[107] The

40

episcopo Hermolao Barbaro, qui (sicut decet episcopum) populo magis prodesse adnititur quam praeesse.

41   Regionem vero quam nunc describimus sub nomine absurdo Marchiae Tarvisinae et pariter proximam Forum Iulium, olim Galliae Cisalpinae partem, Plinius in regione Italiae decima posuit, quam Carnorum fuisse affirmat. Nam cum multa dixisset de fluvio Silo,[264] oppido Altino, flumine Liquentia, colonia Concordia, Taliavento, Anaxo,[265] Alsa, Natisone deque Aquileia colonia, subiungit: 'Carnorum haec regio fuit.' Quod vocabulum regiones ipsae alicubi etiam nostra aetate retinent.

42   Ad Sili fontem oppidulum est Casacorba. Deinceps Anaxum est flumen, cui nunc Plavi vulgatissima est appellatio. Ad eiusque ostia Equilium est insula stagnis paludibusque a continenti divisa. Fuitque ea in insula civitas eiusdem nominis ab Heracliensibus vicinis aedificata. Namque Heracleam in *Historiis* et in Veneta huius *Italiae* regione ostendimus fuisse post Aquileiae, Concordiae, et Altini demolitionem a dictarum urbium populis aedificatam, qui ab Heracleo illius tempestatis imperatore id nomen indiderint civitati. Sed Heraclienses inde Venetias commigrarunt ut nunc urbis vestigia requirantur. Equileique pariter, ubi mutato nomine Civitas dicitur Nova episcopio et quidem tenui nota, parvae et tenues reliquiae vix sciuntur. Anaxo (seu Plavi) fluvio ad sinistram adiacent oppida Venetium, Limina, et Aquorium. Et superius arduo in monte est Feltrum civitas episcopo nunc Iacobo ornata Zeno non minus doctrina quam gentis nobilitate conspicuo. Ad dexteram Plavis primum haeret oppidulum Madirium.[266] Inde in mediterraneis: Vetorium. Superiusque,[267] ubi eum[268] Varianus olim (nunc Calorius) auget fluvius, est oppidum Tesega,[269] eidemque amni Variano (sive Calorio) apposita est Belunum civitas

city is now ornamented by another outstanding bishop in the person of Ermolao Barbaro, who (as a bishop should) seeks rather to help his people than lord it over them.[108]

The region I am here describing under the absurd name of "the 41 March of Treviso" was placed by Pliny in the tenth region of Italy, along with the adjoining Friuli, which was once part of Cisalpine Gaul.[109] This tenth region, he tells us, was the territory of the Carni:[110] after speaking at length of the river Sile, the town of Altinum, the river Livenza,[111] the colony Concordia Sagittaria, the rivers Tagliamento, Piave, Ausa, and Natisone, and the colony of Aquileia, he adds, "This was the region of the Carni." Parts of these regions keep this name to this day.[112]

At the source of the Sile is the little town of Casacorba. Then 42 there is the river Anaxum, most commonly called the Piave nowadays.[113] At its mouth is Iesolo, an island separated from the mainland by lagoons and marshes. There used to be a town of the same name on the island, built by citizens of nearby Eraclea: I mentioned in my *Histories* and also in my account of the Veneto region in the present work that the people of Aquileia, Concordia, and Altinum built Eraclea after the destruction of their cities, and named the city after Heraclius, the emperor of the time.[114] But the inhabitants of Eraclea then migrated to Venice, so that traces of Eraclea now are difficult to find. The similarly scant and insignificant remains of Iesolo are also hard to make out: it underwent a change of name to Cittanova, with its own insignificant bishopric. The towns of Venezio, Limina, and Quero lie on the left bank of the river Anaxum or Piave. Above them on a steep mountain is the city of Feltre, notable for her current bishop Jacopo Zeno, a man no less distinguished for his learning than for his high birth.[115] Mandre is the first little town lying on the right bank of the Piave, and then further inland, Vidor. Higher up, where the present river Caorame (formerly the Varianus) flows into the Piave, is the town of Tesimo. And on this river Varianus or Cao-

vetustissima, quam Plinius ceterique scriptores Velunum appellant. Eidemque nunc cum Feltro[270] in eundem coniunctae episcopatum idem Zenus praeest episcopus.

43   Varianum vero (sive Calorium) amnem in Alpibus oriundum, quas Germanicae incolunt gentes, quinque augent torrentes, quorum convallibus[271] marginibusque castella vicique plures insunt barbaris nominibus appellati. Sed et, ubi Plavum diximus Variano (sive Calorio) incipere augeri, alter eam[272] influit amnis Cordovalus[273] et ipse ex summis defluens Alpibus, cui Falchachium Tabuliumque oppida et quam plures vici Germanica potius quam Italica nomina habentes adiacent.

44   Liquentia ad mare sequitur amnis vetusti nominis, quem ex montibus Opiterginis nasci Plinius est auctor. Eum nunc Liventiam appellant, habetque ostii bifariam divisi partem[274] ad easdem paludes quibus Equilium insulam a continenti diximus separari. Alteraque parte ad proxima Caprularum[275] insulae stagna paludesque delabitur. Ubi vero in dictas scinditur partes, ad dexteram Turricium est castellum. Interiusque, ubi Liquentiam sinistrorsum torrens auget Muttegus, Opitergium est nunc oppidulum. Quam vetusti nominis civitatem, simul cum Aquileia, Altino, et Concordia, ab Athila destructam et postea cum esset reaedificata a Longobardis eodem anno quo et Forum Pompilii, deletam[276] fuisse in *Historiis* ostendimus. Ad Muttegique[277] amnis fontem Conilianum est nobile ditissimumque oppidum. Liquentiam item dextrorsum Meduna auget fluvius, supremis in Alpibus Iuliis oriundus. Cui dextrorsum Corva, et supra ad Imculi torrentis fontem Portoneum, superiusque Prata, et in mediterraneis Porcilium, oppida sunt apposita. Prataque et Porcilium duabus (ut in regione) praestantibus nobilium familiis patrii cognominis exornantur. Ubi vero Liquen-

rame is set the ancient city of Belluno, which Pliny and the other writers all call "Velunum."[116] Zeno is now also in charge of Belluno, which has been amalgamated with Feltre into a single diocese.

Five smaller rivers flow into the river Varianus or Caorame, 43 which rises in the Alps settled by German peoples: on the valleys and banks of these rivers there are many castles and villages with barbarous names. But at the point where the Varianus or Caorame starts to flow into the Piave, as I mentioned, there is also a second river joining it, the Cordovale, likewise flowing down from the summits of the Alps itself. The towns of Falcade and Taibon lie on its banks, as well as a great number of villages that have German rather than Italian names.

On the coast the river anciently named Liquentia, nowadays 44 called the Livenza, which according to Pliny rises in the hills of Oderzo, comes next after the Piave.[117] It has a mouth that divides into two, one part being at the marshes that separate the island of Iesolo from the mainland that I mentioned above;[118] the other mouth flows into the lagoons and marshes near the island of Caorle. At the spot where the mouth splits into these two parts, the castle of Turrici is found on the right. Further inland, where the stream Monticano flows into the Livenza from the left, lies the little town of Oderzo. Attila destroyed the ancient city of Oderzo, along with Aquileia, Altinum, and Concordia, as I mentioned in my *Histories*,[119] and afterward, when it had been rebuilt, the Lombards destroyed it in the same year they destroyed Forlimpopoli.[120] At the source of the river Monticano is Coneglio, a fine and prosperous town. The Meduna flows into the Livenza from the right, a river that rises very high up in the Julian Alps. On the Meduna lie the towns of Corva on the right, and above it, at the source of the Noncello, Pordenone, and further up still Prata, and inland Porcia. Prata and Porcia each have a noble family—distinguished for provincial stock—that takes their name. Where the Meduna

tiam ipse auget Meduna amnis, Sacillum nobile ditissimumque est
oppidum. Ad Liquentiae sinistram supra Muttegi torrentis influxum est oppidum Buffolettum et supra, ubi Mesulus eam[278]
auget torrens, Cuvolonum[279] est oppidum. Superiusque[280] Seravalle. Sequitur Alsa vetusto nomine fluvius, nunc Liminus appellatus. Quod nomen eum inde crediderim nactum esse, quia (sicut
huius regionis principio diximus) et eius et Foroiulii limes a barbaris fuit dictus. Habetque ad ostium, quo in paludes stagnaque
exoneratur, Caprulas[281] insulam, in quam Opiterginos Athilae sae-
vitiam declinantes saepe alias ostendimus confugisse. Habetque
Alsa sive Liminus ad sinistram oppidum nomine Sextum.[282]

Regio decima. Foroiulium[1]

1 Sequitur regio Foroiuliensium, quos Plinius dicit dictos esse cognomine Transpadanos. Id Foroiulii nomen notissimum et quod
ante C. Iulii Caesaris tempora in ipsa regione inque[2] supereminentibus eidem Alpibus Iuliis inchoasse constat, unde post factam
Iapydum[3] aut Cisalpinae Galliae mutationem habuerit originem
ignoramus. Undecumque autem sit natum nostrae inhaerentes
divisioni regionis ipsius, quam tamen nonnulli Aquileiensem appellari volunt, initium ad Alsae seu Liminis[4] fluvii dexteram in-
choabimus. Cui primum[5] Portus Gruarius oppidum, dehinc[6] Cor-
devallem, et superius Porclanum[7] oppida sunt apposita.

2   Deinde[8] est Taliaventum prisci praesentisque nominis flumen,
quod Plinius dicit maius minusque fuisse, cum nunc unico in
Adriaticum ostio feratur. Sunt ei ad sinistram primum a ripa remotius oppidum Sanctus Vitus, inde[9] Valva castellum, et superius

joins the Livenza is the noble and prosperous town of Sacile. To the left of the Livenza, above where the river Monticano joins it, is the town of Portobuffole, and above that, where the river Meschio flows into it, the town of Cavolano. Above Cavolano is Seravalle. The Ausa comes next, to give it its ancient name, now called the Lemene: I imagine that it got this latter name from the fact that the barbarians declared it (as I said at the beginning of this region) the border [*limes*] between the March of Treviso and Friuli. At its mouth, where it discharges into the marshes and lagoons, the Lemene has the island of Caorle, where the inhabitants of Oderzo frequently took refuge from the savagery of Attila, as I have shown elsewhere. The Ausa or Lemene has to its left a town called Sesto.

Region 10. Friuli

Next comes the region of Friuli, whose inhabitants, Pliny says, [1] were given the additional name of "Transpadines."[1] The name Friuli is very widely known: it is commonly accepted that it came into use before Julius Caesar's time, in the region itself and in the Julian Alps which tower above it, but where its origins lay, after the name was changed from Iapydia and Gallia Cisalpina, I do not know. Wherever it came from, we shall keep to our division of the region (though some would have it called the territory of Aquileia), and make a beginning on it with the right bank of the river Ausa or Lemene. The first town on that bank is Portogruaro, followed by Cordovado and, further inland, Porchiano.

Then there is the river Tagliamento — the ancient and the modern [2] name. Pliny says there used to be a Greater and a Lesser Tagliamento, though it now reaches the Adriatic in a single channel.[2] On the left bank of the Tagliamento there are firstly San Vito al Tagliamento (though it is some way from the riverside), then the

in montibus Spilimbergum natura loci munitionibusque validissi-
mum et populo frequentatum. Dextrorsum vero haeret Taliavento
Tisana nobile munitissimumque item oppidum, et supra ab amnis
margine semotum Cuchagna, superiusque[10] in monte arduo Sanctus Daniel praestans in regione oppidum, et ad fontem in Alpibus
Dugonia est castellum. In ea litoris ubique inaequalis et maiori ex
parte stagnosi ora, torrens est in mare cadens, cui Palazolum in
mediterraneis castellum haeret, et stagno magnum in sinum reces-
sumque curvato piscosissimoque imminet Maranum oppidum populo frequentissimum. Torrenti autem stagnum illabenti[11] continet
Castelletum. Interius in mediterraneis oppidum nobile est Belgra-
dum superiusque Coldroitum.

3   At in maritimis est stagnis circumfusa Gradus insula, alter Venetiarum regionis et urbis limes, in quam et in *Historiis* et in ipsa[12]
Venetiarum descriptione saepenumero diximus Aquileienses, patria profugos, sese cum opibus et sacra supellectile recepisse et urbem aedificasse Gradensem, quam pluries dirutam reaedifica-
tamque tandem pauci nunc inhabitant.

4   Aquileia etiam, urbium quondam Italiae Transpadanae primaria
potentissimaque atque etiam pulcherrima, quintodecimo ⟨millia-
rio⟩, ut inquit Plinius, a mari semota[13] nunc paene derelicta est.
Nam praeter sacerdotes canonicos numero haud[14] multos ornatissima speciosissimaque in basilica divinae faciendae rei addictos,
praeter pastores piscatoresque rarissimos, nulli eam[15] nunc incolunt populi, ut vix castellulum tanta olim urbs nunc possit appellari. Suntque et ecclesia superius dicta et patriarchale atrium et
muri oppidulo circumducti et monasterium virginibus deputatum,
Peponis patriarchae operum reliquiae.

castle of Valvasone, and higher up in the hills, Spilimbergo whose natural situation and fortifications have made it immensely strong as well as populous. To the right of the Tagliamento are Latisana, likewise a fine town and well fortified, and above it and further from the river, Cucagna; higher up on a steep mountain is San Daniele, the chief town of the area. At the source of the Tagliamento in the Alps is the castle of Dognia. In the stretch of coast between the Lemene and Tagliamento, sinuous throughout and for the most part marshy, a stream flows into the sea, on which further inland lies a castle called Palazzolo della Stella. The populous town of Marano overlooks the lagoon, which is curved into a great concave bay and full of fish. On the stream as it enters the lagoon lies Castelletto. Upstream, further inland, is the fine town of Belgrado, and beyond that, Codroipo.

On the coast is the island of Grado, ringed by lagoons and 3 marking another border of the city of Venice and the Veneto region.[3] Both in my *Histories* and in the account of the Veneto in this work, I have often mentioned that the people of Aquileia betook themselves here when they fled from their homes, taking their property and sacred objects with them. Here they built the city of Grado, which was destroyed and rebuilt a number of times, but now has few inhabitants.[4]

Aquileia, too, situated fifteen miles from the sea according to 4 Pliny,[5] was once the most important and powerful of Transpadane Italian cities — and the most beautiful — but is now nearly derelict. Apart from a small number of canons required to carry out divine service in the elaborate and beautiful basilica there,[6] and a very few shepherds and fishermen, no people now live in Aquileia: and so the city that was once so great can scarcely be called a hamlet nowadays. As well as the basilica mentioned above, there are the Gallery of the Patriarchs, the walls surrounding the little town, and a convent assigned to nuns — this is what remains of the works of the Patriarch Pepo.[7]

5   Eam urbem qui prius condiderint non est memoriae proditum.
Livius autem in *Bello Macedonico* sic habet: 'Romae litterae Fabii[16]
magnam trepidationem fecerunt, eo maiorem quod paucos post
dies Marcellus tradito exercitu Fabio Romam cum venisset,[17] exercitum in Ligures traduci posse negavit,[18] quia bellum cum Histris
esset prohibentibus coloniam Aquileiam deduci.' Et paulo infra:
'Aquileia colonia Latina eodem anno in agro Gallorum est deducta.' Florere autem coepit quo tempore primum Romani sub-
igendis barbaris ad Danubium incolentibus manum apponere coeperunt. Unde Octavius Caesar Augustus, etsi maiorem bellorum
partem per legatos administravit, ut illis propinquior esset in his
Italiae partibus frequenter obversatus est. Nam Suetonius sic scribit: 'Reliqua bella per legatos administravit. Ut tamen quibusdam
Pannonicis atque Germanicis aut interveniret aut non longe abes-
set, Ravennam vel Mediolanum vel Aquileiam usque ab urbe progressus est.' Et Iulia eum comitata Aquileiae, abortu facto, puerum
amisit. Gloriosissime vero de Aquileia scribit Iulius Capitolinus in
Vita duorum Maximinorum his verbis: 'Praetereundum ne illud quidem est, quod tanta fide Aquileienses contra Maximinos pro se-
natu fuerunt ut funes de capillis mulierum facerent, cum defice-
rent nervi ad sagittas emittendas.' Et inferius asserit Capitolinus
nuntium,[19] qui ex Aquileia ad significandam Maximini mortem
Romam fuerat missus, tanto impetu, mutatis apud Ravennam
animalibus, cucurrisse ut quarta die Romam venerit.

6   Eius vero urbis amplitudo maxima unde processit, non iniucun-
dum aut inutile fuerit explicare. Primum legiones Romanas ibi
obversatas ut claustra Italiae tuerentur eam non peperisse opum
affluentiam quae fuit Aquileiae hinc constare videtur: quod nec
Ravenna neque Mediolanum neque in Gallis Massilia[20] aut in
Hispanis Tarraco, apud quas urbes Romanae legiones diutissime

Who first founded Aquileia has been lost to history. But in the 5
Macedonian War Livy has this to say: "At Rome, Fabius's letter created great trepidation, all the more so because a few days later,
when Marcellus reached Rome after handing over his army to Fabius, he said that they could not lead the army against the Ligurians because there was a war on with the Istrians, who were pre-
venting the foundation of a colony at Aquileia."[8] And a little later:
"A Latin colony, Aquileia, was established that same year in the
territory of the Gauls."[9] When the Romans first began to set their
hand to subduing the barbarians who lived along the Danube,
Aquileia began to come into her own. That is why Augustus,
though for the most part conducting his wars through deputies,
frequently traveled to these parts of Italy in order to be closer
to them. As Suetonius says: "He managed the rest of his wars
through deputies. But so that he might take part in some of the
Pannonian or German wars, or at least not be far distant from
them, he was for ever traveling from Rome to Ravenna or Milan
or Aquileia."[10] Julia, who accompanied him, had a miscarriage at
Aquileia and lost a son.[11] Julius Capitolinus in *The Two Maximini*
writes about Aquileia in splendid terms: "I must not fail to mention the exceptional loyalty of the citizens of Aquileia in support
of the Senate against the Maximini: they made cords out of their
women's hair when they ran out of bowstrings."[12] Capitolinus later
asserts that a messenger who had been sent to Rome from Aquileia to report the death of Maximinus raced with such speed
that he got to Rome in three days, with a change of horses at
Ravenna.[13]

It will be both pleasant and instructive to see how the city rose 6
to greatness. In the first place it is fairly clear that the riches which
Aquileia enjoyed were not produced by the legions stationed there
to defend the borders of Italy, since neither Ravenna nor Milan
nor Marseilles in France nor Tarragona in Spain, all places where
Roman legions were long stationed, reached such levels of opu-

fuerunt moratae, ad id opulentiae aut divitiarum potuerunt pervenire. Auxit igitur mirabili incremento et immense ditavit Aquileiam
orientalium occidentaliumque mercimoniorum mutua collatio[21] in
ea[22] instituta, quod nullus stante Aquileia locus alter circa Adriaticum mare fuit in cuius portu et diversorio occidentales orienta-
lesque pro commutandis mercandisque[23] et vendendis invicem rebus convenirent. Eadem[24] ratio Spinam olim urbem (ut inquit
Plinius, iuxta Padum et Ravennam a Diomede conditam), et ea
omnino destructa Adriam, quae mari Adriatico nomen dedit, et
postremo diruta Aquileia Venetias crescere, augeri, et mirum in
modum ditari fecit.

7   Longum nimis atque superfluum fuerit res apud Aquileiam
gestas ex nostro instituto recensere, quia id a nobis multis in locis
diligenter est factum. Sed virorum eius urbis ornamenta non duximus omittenda. Evangelista Marcus dum a beato Petro[25] apostolorum Christi principe in Alexandriam mitteretur navigaturusque
naves illic ex more (ut diximus) opperiretur, Aquileienses ad
Christi fidem convertit, sanctumque evangelium suum, cuius co-
dex manu eius exaratus[26] Venetiis nunc venerantissime servatur,
scripsit. Hermacorasque et ipse sanctus, ad Marci praedicationem
conversus a beato[27] Petro Aquileiae et omnis Venetiae protopraesul
institutus, omnem eam regionem Deo[28] nostro lucratus est: quem
Nero imperator (et simul Fortunatum subdiaconem) securi per-
cussit. Syrus exinde vir Aquileiensis doctissimus, Papiam ab Her-
macora missus, mira⟨e⟩[29] sanctitatis opera ibi edidit. Fuit et
Aquileiensis Chromatius, ad quem gloriosus Hieronymus multa
inscripsit[30] opera multasque exstantes dedit epistulas. Nihilque
fecisse videtur gloriosius Chromatius quam quod beati Hieronymi
notarios atque librarios sustentavit. Praestantem ultimo loco
Aquileiensem virum ponimus Rufinum, presbyterum Latinis
Graecisque litteris adeo eruditum ut eius, quae exstant, cum opera

lence and riches. In these circumstances it was rather the recip-
rocal exchange of merchandise from East and West that caused
Aquileia's incredible growth and immense wealth, since as long as
the city survived, there was nowhere else on the Adriatic in whose
port and lodgings westerners and easterners could meet to exchange and sell goods. The same process accounts for the growth,
expansion and extraordinary enrichment of the former city of
Spina (which, as Pliny says, was founded by Diomedes near
Ravenna and the Po),[14] and after Spina's wholesale destruction, of
Adria (the city which gave its name to the Adriatic), and finally,
following the demolition of Aquileia, of Venice.[15]

It would be tedious and superfluous to rehearse here, in our 7
usual manner, all that has taken place at Aquileia, things we have
already touched on in detail in many places. But I thought that the
glories her men have brought to the city should not be left out of
account. The Evangelist Mark was sent to Alexandria by St. Peter,
Prince of the Apostles of Christ. While he was waiting at Aquileia
(as usually happens) for a ship to sail on, as I said, he converted
the people of the town to the faith of Christ, and composed his
holy gospel, a manuscript of which, written in his own hand, is
now preserved with the utmost veneration at Venice. Another
saint, Hermagoras, had been converted by the preaching of St.
Mark, and was appointed bishop of Aquileia and all Venetia by St.
Peter, winning over the entire region for Our Lord. The emperor
Nero had him beheaded along with his deacon Fortunatus. The
learned Aquileian Syrus had been sent to Pavia by Hermagoras,
and he later performed works of wonderful saintliness there. Chromatius, to whom the glorious Jerome dedicated many works and
sent many extant letters, was also a man of Aquileia. And it seems
that nothing that Chromatius did was more glorious than maintaining Jerome's secretaries and copyists. The outstanding man of
Aquileia I leave till last: the priest Rufinus was so erudite in Latin
and Greek letters that his surviving works and translations I regard

tum translationes nullis cuiuspiam Ecclesiae doctoris operibus secunda,[31] eloquentia ornatuque, ducamus.

8   Visitur Aquileiae marmoreus lapis grandes elegantesque litteras
huiusmodi incisus: 'Imperator Caesar Augustus, Aquileiensium
restitutor et conditor, viam quoque geminam a porta usque ad
pontem, per tirones iuventutis novae Italiae sui[32] dilectus[33] posteri-
oris, longi temporis labe corruptam, munivit ac restituit.'

9   Adiacet sinistrorsum Aquileia Natisoni fluvio, cui nunc Lison-
tio est appellatio. Et eo, quod[34] ad Talliaventum amnem proximum
intercedit, campestri in spatio, supereminet Aquileiae ad triginta
milia passuum Utinum praestans ditissimumque regionis oppidum novi nominis, quod nec in Gothorum nec[35] Longobardorum
neque[36] propinquioribus[37] aetati nostrae rebus gestis[38] invenitur.
Hinc (quod vulgo fertur) Austrinos id[39] ad trecentesimum abhinc
annum condidisse credo. Eam enim regionem duces Austriae tunc
temporis obtinebant. Habet vero nunc Utinum Iacob[40] civem et
Aquileiae canonicum eloquentia ornatissimum. Suntque superius
ad primos colles Fafagna,[41] superiorique[42] loco in montibus Gle-
mona, vetusti quod Gothorum Longobardorumque historiae
habent nominis, oppidum. Et ad Natisonem est in montibus Ven-
tionum. Natisoni sinistrorsum est propinquum[43] Mons Falco oppidum regionis egregium arduo in monte situm, quod Theodericus rex Ostrogothorum primus aedificavit.

10   Superius celsos inter montes[44] est Civitas Austriae[45] nunc Cividale appellata, quam urbem, et aspectu veterrimam et (ut mon-
tuosa in regione) speciosam civilique[46] cultu habitatam, fuisse crediderim oppidum illud a Gallis prope Aquileiam aedificatum, de
quo Livius, Libro XXVIII, sic habet: 'Eodem anno Galli Transalpini transgressi in Venetiam sine populatione et bello haud procul
inde ubi nunc Aquileia est locum oppido condendo ceperunt. Le-
gatis Romanis trans Alpes missis responsum est: neque profectos

as second to none of the works of any Church Doctor in style and
elegance.[16]

A marble tablet is to be seen at Aquileia, inscribed in large and   8
graceful letters to this effect: "The Emperor Caesar Augustus, re-
storer and founder of Aquileia, has reinforced and restored as well
the double carriageway from city gate to bridge, which had been
ruined by long dereliction, using his own levy of recruits of the
youth of Italy."[17]

Aquileia lies to the left of the river Natisone, now known as the   9
Isonzo. In the fields that lie between the Isonzo and the next river,
the Tagliamento, lies Udine, the chief town of the region and the
richest, which rises above Aquileia some thirty miles away. The
name of the town is new, not being found in the histories of the
Goths or Lombards, nor in histories closer to our own time. For
this reason I believe that it was founded by the Austrians (as they
are commonly known) about three hundred years ago, the region
being under the control of the dukes of Austria at the time.[18]
Udine nowadays has among its citizens Jacopo, a canon of Aquileia highly distinguished for his eloquence.[19] Further inland in the
foothills there is Fagagna, and higher up in the mountains Ge-
mona del Friuli, an ancient town which you *will* find in the histories of the Goths and Lombards. Then in the hills there is Ven-
zone on the Natisone. Nearby on the left of the Natisone is the
fine provincial town of Monfalcone situated on a steep hill, which
was founded by Theodoric, the first king of the Ostrogoths.[20]

Further up in the high mountains is "Civitas Austriae," now   10
called Cividale. This city has a very ancient appearance, and for a
mountain town is handsome and civilized: I imagine it was the
town that the Gauls built near Aquileia, of which Livy in Book
XXVIII has this to say: "In the same year Transalpine Gauls,
crossing into Venetia without any devastation or war, took possession of a site for founding a town not far from where Aquileia now
stands. Roman envoys sent across the Alps received the reply that

ex auctoritate gentis eos nec quid in Italia facerent se scire.' Dirimitque urbs ipsa Germanos ab Italis certiore atque etiam celebratiore modo ceteris omnibus limitaneis vel urbibus vel oppidis, quae aut Gallis aut Germanis aut Sclavonibus ubique in Alpibus sunt conterminae, quod mores in illa et omnis vitae apparatus a Germanis omnino est dissonus. Supra Civitatem Austriae Natisoni continet Sofimbergum.[47] Tarro autem amni sub Civitate Austriae Natisonem illabenti et quem Plinius cum Natisone Aquileiam profluere dicit, ad fontem in Alpibus adiacet Vapochum. Et infra ad medium sui cursum celso in monte appositum est Dogrium. Et supra Montem Falconem, celsiore item sub Alpibus loco, Cormona[48] est oppidum in nostris *Longobardorum Historiis* celebratum.

11   Sed ad ea quae maris litoribus sunt propinqua post Montem Falconem, celso item in colle est Duinum nobile munitissimumque oppidum, et minore in colle Mocolanum. Deinde[49] est urbs Tergestum Romana colonia, cum vetusta tum etiam apud vetustos scriptores C. Caesarem in *Commentariis*, Plinium, et alios (cum historicos tum cosmographos) celebrata, tertioque[50] et tricesimo milliario, ut inquit Plinius, distans ab Aquileia. Ultra Tergestum autem[51] sex milia passuum[52] esse dicit idem[53] Plinius Formionem amnem, cui nunc Cisano est appellatio, a Ravenna undeducentesimo miliario distantem,[54] qui quidem amnis fuerit antiquus Italiae terminus. Labitur autem is amnis Formio (sive Cisanus) inter Muglam,[55] proximum Tergesto oppidum, et Iustinopolim urbem Caput Histriae[56] haud[57] improprie appellatam, quando ad praedictum Phormionem Histria[58] inchoetur.

12   Sed priusquam novae huic nobis[59] regioni manum apponamus, paucula explicemus quae retro in montibus de Foroiuliensibus sunt omissa. In ea montium parte quae in Adriaticum e regione Duini[60] oppidi est[61] versa, Goritia est sub Alpibus, quod oppidum, familiae nobili patrium comitatus titulum referenti subditum, populo et opibus est refertum. Supraque Tergestum aeque[62] sub Alpibus est Castrum Novum.

this party had not set out with the authority of their people, nor did they know what they were doing in Italy."[21] The city itself marks off Germany from Italy more clearly and decisively than any of the other Alpine border cities or towns that share boundaries with the French, Germans, or Slavs, since the customs of Cividale and its entire style of life are utterly different from that of the Germans. Above Cividale Sofimbergo lies on the Natisone. Up in the Alps Vapocco sits beside the source of the Torre, a river that flows into the Natisone below Cividale — according to Pliny the two rivers flow together past Aquileia.[22] Further down, about half way along the course of the Torre, is Dogrio, set on a high hill. Above Monfalcone, again high up under the Alps, is Cormons, a town often mentioned in my *History of the Lombards*.

But to turn now to those places beside the shore following 11 Monfalcone, there is the fine and strongly fortified town of Duino, also set on a high hill, and on a lower hill, Moncolano. Then there is the city of Trieste, a Roman colony ancient in itself and also celebrated in the ancient writers (Caesar in his *Commentaries*, Pliny, and other historians and geographers); it is situated thirty-three miles from Aquileia according to Pliny.[23] Pliny also says that the river Formio, now called the Risano, is six miles beyond Trieste and 199 miles from Ravenna, and that the river was anciently the terminus of Italy.[24] This river Formio or Risano flows between Muggia, the next town to Trieste, and the city of Justinopolis, called naturally enough Capodistria, because the province of Istria begins at the river Risano just mentioned.

But before I turn my hand to this new region, I should clear up 12 a few remaining details about Friuli that I passed over back in the mountains. In the mountainous district facing the Adriatic, opposite the town of Duino, lies Gorizia under the Alps: this town, which is subject to a noble family with the hereditary title of count, is populous and wealthy.[25] Above Trieste, and likewise at the foot of the Alps, is Castelnuovo.

Regio undecima. Histria

1   Histriam nunc, non quidem novam (quae ante Caesaris Augusti tempora Italiae censebatur) sed tamen[1] inter ceteras oras ultimo additam, inchoemus. Eam Plinius ut in[2] peninsulam excurrere dicit latitudine quadraginta circuituque centum et viginti quinque[3] miliarium, et quidem a Formionis (sive Cisani) ostio, ubi ultima est Tergestini sinus pars, ad Fanatici sinus,[4] quem nunc Carnarium appellant, intimam concavitatem, ubi est Castrum Novum (sive Arsiae fluminis ostium). Via difficilior quidem per arduos montes sed brevior vix quadraginta milia passuum[5] implet, cum circuitus[6] mari secundum litora factus supra dicta centum et viginti quinque[7] amplissime complectatur. Hinc pulchrum est cognoscere oram Adriatici maritimam supra a Venetiis Iustinopolim usque a nobis descriptam ubique sinuosissimam et adeo tortuosam esse ut iter id centum milium passuum mari directum e regione dimidio quam terra brevius sit.[8] A Formione autem fluvio ad Fanatici (sive Carnarii) promontorium, ea (sicut dicit Plinius) peninsula Histriae se in mare Italiam versus dextrorsum flectit.

2   Sed ad rem. Histriam regionem, Iapydiam[9] prius simul cum Foroiulio dictam,[10] vult ex Trogo Pompeio Iustinus sic fuisse appellatam ab Histri amnis (qui et Danubius) accolis, qui cum Argonautas Argon navim[11] a Danubio in Adriaticum mare humeris deferre adiuvissent, in ea Iapydum regione considentes Histriam de patriae regionis nomine appellarunt. Plinius vero cum aliquorum confutasset errorem dicentium (et quidem absurdissime) Histriam dici a parte Histri fluminis in Adriaticum delabente, subinfert Argon navim flumine in mare Adriaticum descendisse non procul Tergesto, nec iam constare quo flumine: Alpinosque diligentiores affirmare humeris fuisse transvectam, subisse autem His-

Region 11. Istria

Let us make a start now on the region of Istria, not indeed a   1
new addition to Italy, since it was reckoned to be part of the country before the age of Augustus, but the last of the provinces to
be added to it. Pliny says that Istria juts out like a peninsula 40
miles wide and 125 miles in circumference,[1] that is, from the
mouth of the river Formio or Risano at the furthest point of the
Gulf of Trieste to the innermost recess of the Gulf of Fanaticus,
or Quarnaro as it is now called, at Castelnuovo, in other words at
the mouth of the river Arsa. There is a difficult, though shorter,
road scarcely 40 miles long through daunting mountains, while a
circuit by sea along the coast takes a good 125 miles, as stated
above. It is worth knowing that the Adriatic coast from Venice to
Capodistria that I described above is so twisting and tortuous that
the hundred-mile voyage direct between the two places is shorter
by half than the land route. As Pliny says, the Istrian peninsula
from the river Risano to the promontory of Fanaticus (or Quarnaro) turns right into the sea to face Italy.[2]

But to return to the matter in hand. In his *Epitome* of Trogus,   2
Justin maintains that the region of Istria—which together with
Friuli had earlier been called Iapydia—was so named by the people who lived on the river Ister, i.e., the Danube. These men
helped the Argonauts to carry the ship Argo on their shoulders
from the Danube to the Adriatic, and then settled in that region
of the Iapydes, naming it Istria after their ancestral region.[3] Pliny
refuted the error of those who said (quite absurdly) that Istria was
named after a part of the river Ister that flowed into the Adriatic,
and he added that the ship Argo sailed down by river into the
Adriatic not far from Trieste, but there was no agreement about
which river it was. The more careful authors affirm that the Argo
was carried on shoulders across the Alps, but then first came up

tro, dein Sabo, dein Nauporto (cui nomen ex ea sit causa) inter Haemoniam Alpesque exorienti.

3   Prima Histriae urbs est (ut diximus) Iustinopolis, quam Iustinus, Iustiniani primi imperatoris filius atque imperii successor, in insula tunc Capraria sed prius Pullaria appellata aedificavit. Causam autem eius condendae urbis in *Historiis* fuisse ostendimus, ut in eo natura loci munitissimo loco tuti essent Histriae populi, variis diutinisque barbarorum incursionibus agitati. Iungitur tamen continenti ea insula brachio mille passuum[12] longitudine et ad decem latitudine ducto, in cuius medio arx valida Leoninum appellata Castellum oppidanis a terrestri oppugnatione praesidio est imposita. Magno fuit per aetatem nostram Iustinopoli ornamento Petrus Paulus Vergerius iure consultissimus et philosophus — quodque supra saepenumero[13] diximus inter primos huius saeculi eloquentissimus. A Iustinopoli[14] quinque passuum milibus[15] semotum est Insula oppidum, a quo tantumdem distat[16] Piranum civitas. Ab ea[17] Salodi promontorium totidem abest passus, a quo aeque distat[18] Humagum nobile oppidum, quod cursu prope recto et ad Italiam transverso per medium pelagus incurvari ferrique videtur. Exinde ad Fanaticum (sive Carnarium) promontorium aequaliore[19] et tamen sinuosissimo inter se prospectu cetera Histriae maritima oppida habentur. Ab Humago[20] quinque itidem passuum milibus[21] abest Haemonia civitas, cui nunc Civitati Novae est nomen. Prope quam sunt ostia Nauporti[22] fluminis (Quieti nunc appellati), in quem ex Alpibus oriundum[23] Argon navim Plinius asserit fuisse demissam. Post Nauportum prima est Parentium[24] civitas vetusta, cui Orsarium adiacet,[25] et mons et oppidum prominens illi impositum. Post haec Ruvignum[26] oppidulum.

4   Arduo deinde colli ac diffuso naturaque loci munitissimo imposita supereminet[27] urbs Pola, Romana colonia et Histriae ac Italiae urbium postrema. Ab ea vero urbe incipiens Fanaticum promontorium — postquam longo tractu contra Ariminum vel (sicut Plinio placet) contra Anconem[28] in mare se proripuit — sinum eiusdem

the Ister, then the Sava, then the Nauportus, a river that rises between Emona and the Alps and takes its name from this event.[4]

The first city of Istria, as I said, is Justinopolis.[5] The son of   3
Justinian I and his successor as emperor, Justinus built it on the
island then called Capraria, which was earlier known as Pullaria.
As I pointed out in my *Histories*, the city was built on a site that
was naturally well fortified to protect the people of Istria, who had
long suffered from barbarian incursions.[6] Though an island, it is
connected to the mainland by a causeway a mile long and about
fifty feet wide. In the middle a strong fortress called Castel Le-
onino has been built by the townsfolk to protect it from land attack. Pier Paolo Vergerio, lawyer, philosopher and (as I have often
said above) among the most eloquent men of our time, has graced
Justinopolis in my lifetime.[7] Five miles separate the city of Izola
from Justinopolis, and the city of Pirano is five miles further on
from Izola. The headland of Salvore is five miles from Izola, and
the fine town of Umago the same distance from Salvore. Projecting almost straight out diagonally, Salvore seems to curve through
the midst of the sea toward Italy. Then, as far as the promontory
of Fanaticus (Quarnaro), come the other maritime cities of Istria,
more similar in appearance though the coast here is highly in-
dented. The city of Emona, now known as Cittanova, is a further
five miles from Umago. At Cittanova is the mouth of the river
Nauportus, now called the Quieto, which rises in the Alps and
down which, Pliny tells us, the ship Argo was launched. The
first city beyond the Quieto is the ancient Parenzo, and next to
Parenzo is Orsera, the name of a mountain and the town set
prominently on it. After these comes the little town of Rovigno.[8]

Then on a high and broad hill well fortified by nature rises up   4
the Roman colony of Pola, last of the cities of Istria and Italy.
From Pola begins the promontory of Fanaticus. It projects out a
long way into the sea opposite Rimini (or, as Pliny has it, opposite
Ancona),[9] and then forms a gulf of the same name, which as I said

nominis efficit, quem nunc Carnarium diximus appellari. Estque eiusdem sinus novum prisco correspondens vocabulum, quod, Fanaticus a priscis a tempestatum frequentia atque (ut ita dixerim) insania, nunc vero Carnarius a multitudine cadaverum quae frequentibus ibi tempestatibus fiunt est appellatus.[29]

5   Prius vero quam ea[30] describamus quae Fanatico sinui apposita ad Arsiam amnem, certissimum atque notissimum Italiae ad Liburnos terminum, adiacent, mediterranea, quae altissimis in montibus a Iustinopoli ad Nauportum (sive Quietum) amnem interiacent,[31] explicabimus. Suntque in montibus Iustinopoli supereminentibus iurisdictionis eius[32] castella Rasponum et Rogium. Sunt item in montibus a mari longius quam praedicta loca[33] recedentibus in ea quam diximus flectentis se ad Italiam peninsulae curvitate: Bulea, Mimianum, Sanctus Laurentius, Portule, Grisiana et, superiori loco, Pimontum, Pigmentium, et Petra Piolosa,[34] Iustinopolitanorum oppida et castella.[35] Medioque ferme eorum omnium spatio Petram Pilosam inter et Portulam ac Pimontem est oppidulum nunc nomine Sdrigna, quod fuisse constat olim Stridonis oppidum, unde gloriosissimus Ecclesiae Dei doctor illustratorque Hieronymus originem duxit. Et trans Nauportum (sive Quietum) amnem ad Arsiam usque amnem, castella nunc in montibus oppidaque[36] exstant Vallis et[37] duo castra Iustinopolitanis supposita. Superiusque, Montona et Pisinum.[38]

6   Ne etiam superius promissum ulterius differamus: a Fanatico promontorio ad Arsiae amnis, nostri limitis Italiae, ostium, quo se[39] in Carnarium (sive Fanaticum) sinum derivat,[40] oppida ipsi supereminent sinui: Albona et Terranova, quae duo (et superius dictum Pisinum),[41] quod Arsiae et sinui Fanatico propinquent, Histriae atque Italiae ultima sunt censenda.

7   Adhibita est a nobis superiori loco describendis Histriae montium oppidis et castellis solito maior diligentia, quod quidem

is nowadays called Quarnaro. Quarnaro is a new word answering in sense to the old, because this bay, which the ancients called "Fanaticus" for the frequency and, so to say, craziness of its storms, is in fact now called "Carnarius" after the great numbers of cadavers that the numerous storms there bring about.[10]

However, before I survey the places that lie on the Gulf of 5 Quarnaro up to the river Arsa, which is the most definite and best known border of Italy with Liburnia, I shall give an account of the inland regions situated in the high hills between Capodistria and the river Nauportus (Quieto). In the hills that overlook Capodistria, and under its sway, are the castles of Raspo and Rozzo. In the hills further inland than the places already mentioned on the arc of the peninsula that (as we said) turns toward Italy, there are Buie, Momiano, San Lorenzo, Portole, Grisignana, and, on higher ground, Piedimonte di Taiano, Pinguente, and Pietrapelosa, all towns and castles of the Capodistrians. Almost at the center of all these, between Pietrapelosa, Portole and Piedimonte, is the little town now called Sdregna: this is generally thought to have formerly been the town of Stridon, where the glorious Doctor and Light of the Church, St. Jerome, was born.[11] On the other side of the river Nauportus (Quieto), as far as the Arsa, there are now in the mountains the castles and towns of Valle d'Istria and Dvori, subject to the people of Capodistria, and higher up in the hills, Montona and Pisino.

To put off no longer the promise I made above: from the Fa- 6 naticus promontory to the mouth of the Arsa—the boundary I have set to Italy—where the river flows into the gulf of Quarnaro (Fanaticus), are the towns of Albona and Terranuova set over the gulf. These, along with the Pisino mentioned above, have to be reckoned as the last towns of Istria and of Italy since they are so near the Arsa and the bay of Quarnaro.

I have described above the towns and castles of the mountains 7 of Istria with more than usual care only because I wanted to clarify

nulla[42] alia fecimus ratione quam ut rem minime nobis peritisque
regionum dubiam sed de qua multos ambigere vidimus praestantissimos Italiae atque orbis Christiani aliarum provinciarum viros
doceremus: Stridonem oppidum gloriosi Hieronymi patriam in
Italia, et quae nunc est[43] et quae Octavii Augusti imperatoris et
multo magis Plinii atque[44] etiam natalium ipsius Hieronymi temporibus erat, situm esse: ut tantum virum plane Italicum et non
alienigenam fuisse constet. Idque verba ipsius[45] de seipso scripta,
in libro *De viris illustribus*, certissimum efficiunt: 'Hieronymus pres-
byter patre natus Eusebio ex oppido Stridonis, quod a Gothis
eversum Dalmatiae quondam Pannoniaeque confinium fuit usque
in praesentem annum, id est Theodosii principis quartum decimum. Haec scripsit: *Vitam Pauli monachi, Epistularum ad diversos
librum*[46] unum, et cetera.'[47] Visitur vero apud Sdrignam (sive
Stridonem) praedicti Eusebii genitoris Sancti Hieronymi sepulchrum, et fama per aetatum[48] successiones tradita et litteris lami-
nae inscriptis plumbeae in eo, ut ferunt, repertae notissimum.

8   Videmus vero[49] multos in eam de qua diximus opinionem ductos fuisse ut crederent beatum Hieronymum Dalmatam fuisse,
quia litteras illis adinvenerit composueritque a Latinis Graecisque
diversas quae sint[50] postea appellatae 'Sclavonicae' a Sclavonibus
Germaniae olim populis, quos nunc appellant Bohemos. A quibus
(sicut in *Historiis* ostendimus) regio Dalmatiae Histris contermina
paulo post functum vita ipsum beatum Hieronymum fuit occupata et semper postea (ut nunc quoque)[51] Sclavonia est dicta. Et
quidem non solum eas praedictis composuit deditque Sclavonicas
litteras sed Officium quoque Divinum, quo Catholici utuntur
Christiani ex Graeco in id novum idioma traduxit quod gloriosus
Pontifex Eugenius quartus per nostras manus illis confirmavit.
Quo tempore apud Florentiam et[52] Graecorum unio cum Ecclesia
Occidentali est facta et Armenii, Iacobitae, Nestorini ac[53]
Aethiopes acceperunt ab eodem Eugenio[54] Catholicae Ecclesiae

a matter that is not in doubt to me and to experts in geography, but one about which I have noticed many excellent men of Italy and the rest of the Christian world were unsure. The town of Stridon, where the glorious St. Jerome was born, was located in Italy — Italy as it is today, and as it was at the time of the birth of the emperor Augustus, and more importantly, of Pliny and of Jerome himself too — to make it perfectly plain that this great man was an Italian and not a foreigner.[12] Writing about himself, Jerome's own words in *On Illustrious Men* make it as certain as it can be: "The priest Jerome, son of Eusebius, was born in the town of Stridon (which was destroyed by the Goths, and marks the frontier of Dalmatia and Pannonia up to the present time, the fourteenth year of Theodosius); he wrote a *Life of Paul the Monk* and a *Book of Letters to Various Persons*, etc."[13] The tomb of Eusebius, St. Jerome's father, mentioned above, can in fact be seen at Sdregna (Stridon): this is very well known, both from oral tradition handed down through successive generations and from an inscription on a lead tablet said to have been found in it.

It is clear that many men have come round to the view I mentioned, that St. Jerome was a Dalmatian, because he invented for them characters that differed from Latin and Greek, and composed works in them. These later came to be called "Slavonic" characters after the Slavs, once a German people but now known as Bohemians. Soon after Jerome's death, as I showed in my *Histories*, the Slavs seized the region of Dalmatia, which shares a border with Istria and which was ever after called Slavonia, as it still is.[14] Not only did Jerome devise and give to the Dalmatians those Slavonic characters, but he translated the Holy Office used by Catholic Christians out of Greek into this new tongue as well. The glorious Pope Eugenius IV confirmed this Office for them through my doing.[15] This was at the time when the Union of Greeks with the Western Church took place in Florence and the Armenians, Jacobites, Nestorians, and Ethiopians accepted from Pope Euge-

8

documenta. Illis vero qui pertinaces contenderent beatum Hieronymum, si in patria sua idiomate ab Italico penitus alieno usus fuit
et suos contribules Histros uti docuit atque voluit, videri fuisse
alienigenam,[55] respondemus maiorem melioremque quam sit Histria partem esse Italiae Calabriam atque Bruttios, quibus in regionibus sine controversia Italicis, et semper antea viguit, et nunc
quoque viget, Graecanicae linguae usus. Quin etiam circa Hastam,
Taurinos, Eporedienses,[56] et omnem eam Alpibus subiectam Italiae regionem cui gentes diu praefuerunt[57] Gallicae, alieno magis
populi illi quam proprio idiomate Italico abutuntur. Pariter apud
Vicentiam Veronamque praeclaras elegantissimasque moribus Italiae urbes, licet a Germania sint remotissimae, multi sunt vici,
multa oppida ipsis subdita civitatibus, quorum populi Teutonica
frequentius quam Italica locutione utuntur.

9   Sed iam ad nostrum ordinem revertamur. Gesta in Histris sigillatim suis locis referre[58] non expedit, sed satis fuerit ea quae supra
diversis in locis sunt dicta hunc in locum[59] colligere: primam scilicet eius regionis invasionem[60] ab Histris, qui Iapydas vel inde expulerunt vel dominio oppresserunt factam fuisse; et secundam,
qua Teutana muliere praestantissima in Histris regnante, barbari
supervenientes omnia[61] ferro ignique vastarunt; tertiamque his
populis maximam et horribilem cladem illam a Visigothis fuisse
illatam,[62] de qua nos in *Romanorum imperii inclinatione* initio scripsimus, quae quidem clades illa fuit de qua gloriosissimus ipse
Hieronymus apud Bethlehem degens voluit intellegi, et supra
dicto[63] in libro *De viris illustribus* et in *Expositionibus minorum*[64] *duodecim prophetarum*, ubi textum declarans prophetae Abacuch multarum urbium provinciarumque[65] desolationes spiritu prophetico
praedicentis in hanc[66] sententiam commentatus est. 'Nonne hoc
impletum esse audivimus in nostrae originis regione finium Pan

nius likewise the texts of the Catholic Church.[16] Now to those who stubbornly insist that St. Jerome appears to have been a foreigner, since he used in his own country an idiom wholly alien to any Italic language, and wanted his fellow Istrians to use it, and taught them to do so, I counter that Calabria and the land of the Bruttii is a bigger and better part of Italy than Istria: yet in these indisputably Italian regions the use of the Greek tongue has always flourished, and still does today. Not only this, but around Asti, Turin, Ivrea, and that whole region of Italy at the foot of the Alps, over which Gallic peoples have long held sway, the people use (or abuse) a foreign tongue rather than their native Italian. The case is similar with the famous and civilized Italian cities of Vicenza and Verona: though far from Germany, there are many villages and towns subject to those cities whose people regularly speak German rather than Italian.

But let us now return to our regular arrangement of things. 9 There is no need to relate the events that occurred in Istria severally, each in its place; it will suffice to gather together here the events described in various places above. That is, the region was first invaded by the Histri, who either drove the Iapydes out of the place or subjected them to their rule. The second invasion happened during the reign over Istria of an extraordinary woman, Teutana, her marauding barbarians laying waste to all before them with fire and sword.[17] The third invasion was the great and awful calamity that the Visigoths visited upon these people, which I wrote about at the beginning of my *Decline of the Roman Empire*.[18] It was this calamity that the glorious Jerome, while he was living in Bethlehem, wanted to make sense of, both in his *On Illustrious Men*, cited above, and in the *Expositions of the Twelve Minor Prophets*. There, in explicating the text of the prophet Habakkuk, where he foretold by prophetic inspiration the laying waste of many cities and provinces, Jerome makes this comment: "Have we not heard that this prophecy has been fulfilled in the region of my birth on

noniae atque Illyrici, ubi post varias barbarorum incursiones ad tantam desolationem perventum est[67] ut nec humana ibi manserit creatura nec animal superesse conversarique dicatur ex his quae hominibus amicari et convivere consueverunt?'

10   Quae quidem desolatio, cum ad annos centum continuasset, Iustinum impulit ut (sicut supra diximus) Iustinopolim munitissimo et tuto a barbarorum incursionibus loco aedificari curaverit. Proximae vero aetati nostrae[68] in bello quod Venetos inter et Genuenses acerrimum fuit, et Iustinopolis de Venetis in potestatem Genuensium est facta et ipsa[69] adiacentesque urbes maxima calamitate aliquamdiu pressae[70] ac conculcatae fuerunt.

11   Sed iam terminata sit Italiae nostrae latitudo ad hanc Alpium partem quam natura ei munimento adversus externas nationes a Varo ad Arsiam amnem per milia passuum quadringinta et quinquaginta opposuit[71] in recentem gloriosissimi Hieronymi doctoris commemorationem, qui sic eam et me sibi devotum ab omnibus tueatur adversantibus, sicut ad hos limites originem illum in ea habuisse ostendimus.

the borders of Pannonia and Illyricum, where, after various barbarian invasions, the land has been brought to such a pitch of
desolation that 'no human creature has been left nor is any beast
said to survive and exist there of those which are wont to befriend
and to live with men?'"[19]

This state of desolation lasted for a hundred years before Justi-   10
nus felt forced (as we said above) to have Justinopolis built in a
place that was well fortified and protected from barbarian invasion.[20] In the bitter war between the Venetians and the Genoese in
the generation before ours, not only did Justinopolis pass from the
Venetians into the hands of the Genoese but it and the neighboring cities were for some time crushed and oppressed by utter devastation.[21]

But now the breadth of our country of Italy, 450 miles from the   11
river Var to the Arsa, reaches its boundary and concludes at this
stretch of the Alps which was thrown up by nature to protect her
against foreigners, in fresh commemoration of the glorious Doctor
of the Church, St. Jerome. May he protect her, and me his devo-
tee, from all adversaries, as I in turn have shown that he was born
on these frontiers of Italy.

LIBER VII

Regio duodecima. Aprutium[1]

1   Absoluta[2] Istria regionum Italiae ad Alpes Liburnicas ultima, brevis a Fanatico eius sinu promontorioque (nunc Carnario) per Li-
burnicum mare in Troenti amnis ostia est traiectus ut alias a nobis
describendas septem[3] regiones aggrediamur: Samnium, Campaniam, Apuliam, Lucaniam, Salentinos,[4] Calabros, et[5] Brutios. Licet vero mihi hac in parte quod Livius Patavinus VII Libro habet
usurpare: maius solito negotium meis impendere humeris, cui
maiora deinceps sint pervestiganda, quod his in regionibus cele-
briora bella quam alibi in Italia fuere gesta et viribus hostium et
diuturnitate[6] temporum quibus bellatum est. Quas res tamen
Alexander Epirotas Pyrrhusve aut Hannibal Alaricusque et Totila,
vetustiores earum regionum hostes, quibusque in locis gesserint
facile erit nobis a maiorum aut nostris *Historiis* sumere et per singulas civitatum locorumque descriptiones (sicut supra fecimus)
edocere.[7] Quae vero a quadringentis annis postquam septem hae
regiones in unicam regni appellationem sunt confusae, in eo acci-
derint et qua ratione facta sit ipsa regni constitutio videtur unico
contextu diligentius enarrandum ne singulis postea in locis cogamur saepius dicta repetere.[8]

2   Per Ludovici Francorum regis tempora, Tancredus miles Normannus generosi vir animi, quod liberorum duodecim ex duabus
procreatorum uxoribus pondere premeretur, novas quaerere sedes
constituit, fortunam meliorem et opes sub alio caelo viribus sibi et
ingenio facere confisus. Qui cum in Italiam pervenisset, primum in

BOOK VII

Region 12. Abruzzo

Having now dealt with Istria, the last of the regions of Italy where it meets the Liburnian Alps, there is just a short crossing from Istria's Fanaticus gulf and promontory (nowadays the Quarnaro) across the Liburnian sea to the mouth of the river Tronto, in order to take on the seven regions that remain to be described: Abruzzo, Campania, Puglia, Lucania, and the territories of the Salentini, the Calabri, and the Brutii.[1] Well may I say what Livy of Padua says in Book VII: my shoulders are burdened with a responsibility heavier than usual and I have to investigate a succession of weightier matters, since these regions saw more celebrated wars than the rest of Italy, in terms both of the enemy forces in play and of the length of time the fighting took.[2] Yet what the ancient enemies of those parts — Alexander of Epirus, Pyrrhus, Hannibal, Alaric, Totila — did and where they did it may be easily gathered from the histories of our ancestors, or from my own, and will be easily expounded through the individual surveys of cities and sites, as I have done earlier. Now over the four-hundred-year period that these seven regions have been fused into a single entity called the Kingdom, what took place there and how precisely the Kingdom was established may be told in a single detailed narrative, so that I am not obliged to repeat in each individual place things already dealt with many times elsewhere.[3]

In the time of the French King Louis, the greathearted Norman soldier Tancred, crushed by the burden of twelve children by two wives, decided to seek a new home, trusting in his strength of mind and body to find a better fate and fortune in another land.[4] When he arrived in Italy, Tancred settled first in Romagna. Pan-

Romandiola substitit. Pandulfus per id temporis Capuanus princeps bello adversus Guaimarum Salernitanum principem multum[9] implicitus erat, cumque[10] auxilia undique conquireret, hanc gentem armis traditam[11] promisso stipendio accersivit, tantaque illico et talia Normanni gessere facinora ut eos viros fortes praestantissimosque esse[12] suo malo senserint hostes. Pandulfus vero hebetioris ingratique ingenii[13] ipsos spernebat. Unde factum est ut, tempore stipendii de quo in Romandiola convenerant[14] finito, transiverint ad Guaimarum, cuius principatum multis praeclare gestis brevi auxerunt. Premebat vero Normannos duces (ut assolet) aulicorum Guaimari invidia, cum peropportune accidit magistratus imperatoris Constantinopolitani in Calabris, Brutiis, Lucanis, et Neapolitana urbe petere a Salernitano (illi imperio subdito) auxilia[15] adversus Saracenos Siciliam opprimentes, cuius insulae pars maxima Graecis per id temporis erat subdita. Graecique, forti ac fideli Normanorum opera usi, Saracenos omni paene Sicilia deturbarunt.

3   Sed et ipsi Graeci, Normannorum virtute per singulos dies cum admiratione considerata, in eorum invidiam suspicionemque quam in accepti beneficii munerationem procliviores esse coeperunt. Id cum Normanni qua erant prudentia pervidissent, cupientibus Graecis facile[16] persuaserunt dimittendum esse in pinguis uberrimaeque rerum omnium Apuliae hiberna victorem exercitum, qui exhaustam belli diuturnitate et barbarorum crudelitate Siciliam instanti hieme consumpturus videbatur. Traductis in Italiam copiis, Normanni in Apuliam delati magnam illius partem sibi subegerunt. Atque[17] ut sedem haberent in qua mulieres pueros impedimentaque tuta conservarent, Melphim urbem arduo et natura communito loco aedificaverunt. Erat tunc temporis Constantinopoli[18] imperator Michael Ethiriachis,[19] qui, magnis per legatos ex

dolfo, the Prince of Capua at the time, was heavily involved in war against Guaimar, Prince of Salerno, and, in need of troops to support him wherever he could find them, he engaged the warlike Normans with the promise of wages. The Normans at once wrought such havoc on them that their enemies realized to their cost what superb and brave fighters they were. Pandolfo, on the other hand, stupid and ungrateful as he was, held the Normans in contempt. So it came about that once the period of their hire that they had agreed in Romagna was up, they went over to Guaimar, whose principality they soon enlarged by their many valiant actions. Now the envy of Guaimar's courtiers was beginning to turn against the Norman leaders, as tends to happen, when the officers of the Byzantine emperor in Calabria, Bruttii, Lucania, and the city of Naples providentially sought assistance from the prince of Salerno (a city subject to the empire) against the Saracens attacking Sicily (most of the island was subject to the Greeks at the time). With the aid of the brave and loyal Normans the Greeks succeeded in ejecting the Saracens from almost all of Sicily.

But observing with astonishment the Normans' prowess on a 3 daily basis, the Greeks themselves likewise began to feel more envy and suspicion toward the Normans than gratitude for the services they had received. With characteristic shrewdness the Normans noticed this, and had no difficulty in persuading the Greeks, eager for this outcome in any case, that their victorious army should be sent into winter quarters in Apulia; Apulia was a rich land and well provided for in all respects, whereas as winter approached the army seemed likely to devour a Sicily already exhausted by the long war and the savagery of the barbarians. Their troops transported to Italy, the Normans sailed to Apulia, and took control of a large part of it. In order to have a base where they could keep their wives, children, and baggage secure, they built the city of Melfi high on a hill in a spot that was naturally well fortified. Michael Ethiriacis[5] was the emperor of Constantinople at the time,

Graecia Siciliaque et Italiae sibi subditae regionibus comparatis exercitibus, in Normannos duci eos[20] curavit. Commissumque est secus Aufidum Cannarum Apuliae amnem et Oliventem[21] oppidum ingens proelium, in quo Normanni superiores victoresque evaserunt.

4   Multa hic de Normannorum successibus et gestis rebus dicenda omittimus, quae XIII *Historiarum* nostrarum Libro continentur. Tancredo patre et paulo post[22] Drogone filio, comite (ut tunc dicebant) Apuliae, mortuis, Hunfredus fratrum unus in eo comitatu successit. Hicque cum annis septem comitatum tenuisset, moriens Gothfredum fratrem habuit successorem, per quod tempus, Leone V[23] pontifice Romano, Guaimarus Salerni princeps a suis interfectus est. Gisulphusque Normannus[24] Salernitanum obtinuit principatum, ac[25] paulo post Beneventum Romanae ecclesiae urbem ut caperet est adnixus: quod cum rescisset[26] Henricus II[27] e Germania Romanorum imperator, Leoni pontifici per litteras et nuntios suasit ut, Teutonicorum copiis quas ipse Vercellis Italiae praesidio reliquerat acceptis, duceret in Normannos. Id cum fecisset, Leo pontifex superatus proelio et cum aliquot cardinalibus captus fuit. Normanni tamen (sicut decuit principes Christianos) maxima usi erga pontificem reverentia, eumque comites honore prosecuti ad urbem Romam qua venerat deduci curaverunt. Feliciusque fuit a Normannis et melius in Romanum pontificem quam in ceteros[28] quibus ad eam servierant diem collocata liberalitas, quod Romanae ecclesiae et pontificis auctoritate ea permissi sunt gubernanda tenere quaecumque de Italia tunc temporis obtinebant.

5   Exinde Gothfredus fato functus Bagelardum filium reliquit heredem, quod cum aegre tulisset Robertus cognomine Guiscardus, ex Tancredi filiis natu sextus virque[29] ingentis animi, nepote deiecto gentis Normanae principatum absumpsit. Erat tunc secundus Nicolaus pontifex Romanus. Is a capitaneis Romae (quos

and when his generals had gathered large armies from Greece and
Sicily and the other regions subject to him, he had them led
against the Normans. A great battle was joined beside the river
Ofanto of Cannae in Apulia and the town of Olivento, in which
the Normans proved stronger and came off the victors.[6]

I omit here a great deal that could be said about the successes   4
and achievements of the Normans, which may be found in Book
XIII of my *Histories*.[7] Following the death of Tancred and shortly
afterward of his son Drogo, the count of Apulia as he was called,
one of Drogo's brothers Humphrey succeeded him in that position. On Humphrey's death after seven years as count, his brother
Godfrey succeeded him. At that time, during the papacy of Leo V,
Guaimar prince of Salerno was killed by his own men. The Norman Gisulf then gained control of the principality, and soon attempted to capture Benevento, a city of the Roman Church. This
came to the attention of the German Holy Roman Emperor
Henry II, and by dint of envoys and letters he persuaded Pope
Leo to take over the German troops that he had left behind at
Vercelli to defend Italy and send them against the Normans. The
pope did so, but was defeated in battle and captured along with
several of his cardinals.[8] The Normans all the same treated the
pontiff with the greatest reverence, as befitted Christian princes,
and saw to it that he and his court were honorably escorted to
Rome, whence he had come. The Norman magnanimity had a
happier outcome, and was better spent on the pontiff than on the
others they had served up to that point, because by authorization
of the Church and pope, they were permitted to rule over all the
lands of Italy they controlled at the time.

Godfrey then died, leaving as his heir his son Bagelardus. Rob-   5
ert Guiscard, the sixth of the sons of Tancred and a man of great
spirit, took this very hard and toppled his nephew, seizing the
Norman principality for himself.[9] Nicholas II was the Roman
pontiff at the time, and being beset at Rome by captains (what we

nunc barones appellant) agitatus Guiscardum ad Aquilam urbem parum ante conditam in colloquium accersivit. Et cum Guiscardus Beneventum et cetera quae de iuribus[30] ecclesiae tenebat restituisset, papa illum terrae Apuliae et omnium quae in Italia obtinebat sub ducatus Apuliae titulo legitimum instituit possessorem. Robertusque *ligium* se (quod arctissimum servitutis vocabulum est) pontifici et ecclesiae iure iurando addixit.[31] Pauloque post in capitaneos Romanos proceres ducens,[32] eos omnes edomitos pontifici parere fecit. Nec multo post auctus animis Guiscardus Guilielmum fratrem Apuliae praefecit, et in Calabriam ducens Sancti Marci urbem communire aggressus est. Indeque[33] progressus et castra secus amnem Mocatum ad aquas calidas metatus, Consentinos Martiranensesque subegit. Secundum quam victoriam Sillaceum (sive, ut appellant, Squilaceum) accedens per Ionii maris litora pervenit Rhegium, quam dum obsidet civitatem Leucastrum, Maiam[34] et Cannalem[35] pactione recepit.

6   Rogerius interim fratrum Guiscardi natu minimus, castris aliquamdiu in Vibonensi monte[36] habitis, vallem Salinarum et multa ex eis quae in circuitu eius erant Normannorum[37] dicioni adiecit. Nicepholam vero oppidum communiens proprio curavit praesidio conservari. Quo item tempore Guiscardus Gaufredo[38] etiam fratri Guilliniacum et totam Teatinam in ea quae nunc est Aprutii regione[39] occupatam tribuit[40] gubernandam. Inde reversus ad Regii obsidionem Guiscardus, Calabris Brutiisque omnibus et ipso regno in suam et fratrum potestatem[41] redactis, tunc primum dux Calabriae et Apuliae fratrum consensu appellari coepit. Forte per id temporis Bettieminus, Bescavetti[42] Maurorum principis Siciliam pro Saracenorum soldano administrantis admiratus, Rogerium Guiscardi fratrem in Brutiis agentem occultus adiit et, praemio proditionis impetrato, eum impulit ut in Siciliam rebellare

would now call barons), he summoned Guiscard to the recently founded city of Aquila for a parley. Guiscard gave him back Benevento and the other towns subject to the Church over which he held sway, and the pope in return gave him lawful possession of the land of Apulia and all the lands that he controlled in Italy, under the title of the Duchy of Apulia. Guiscard declared himself by oath the "liege" (a very specific term of submission) of the pontiff and the Church.[10] Soon afterward he led his troops against the leading Roman barons, subduing them all and bringing them back to papal obedience. Not long after that, with his confidence enhanced, Guiscard left his brother William in charge of Apulia and taking his forces into Calabria, he began to fortify the city of San Marco Argentano. Leaving San Marco, he established a camp on the river Moccato by Acquacalda, and conquered Cosenza and Martirano. Following this victory, he advanced on Sillaceum (or Squillace, as they call it) and passed on down the coast of the Ionian Sea to Reggio Calabria; while he laid siege to Reggio, he won Nicastro, Mantea and Scalea by negotiation.

Meanwhile Roger, the youngest of Guiscard's brothers, who 6
had been for some time encamped on Monte Vibo, added the plain of Gioia Tauro and many towns around it to Norman territory. He ensured that the town of Nicefora was protected by its own garrison once he had fortified it. At that time too, Guiscard gave the governance of Guglionesi and all of the occupied district of Chieti in what is now the Abruzzo region to another of his brothers, Geoffrey. Guiscard then returned to the siege of Reggio[11] and, with all Calabria and the land of the Brutii and the Regno itself now in his and his brothers' power, he began to be called the Duke of Calabria and Apulia for the first time, with his brothers' consent. At that time it so happened that Bettieminus, the admiral of the Moorish prince Bescavettus who was governing Sicily on behalf of the Sultan of the Saracens, secretly approached Guiscard's brother Roger, who was campaigning in Calabria. Having

paratissimam duceret, quem Guiscardus navigio est subsecutus. Et
primam de Siculis in potestatem accepit urbem Messanam,[43] et[44]
ne plura hic quam tempus locusque postulet dicamus: brevi omnis
Sicilia in Guiscardi Rogeriique fratris potestatem venit.[45] Tuncque
Rogerius Alexandro II pontifici Romano, qui defuncto Nicolao
suffectus erat, camelos quatuor, partem praedae de Saracenis Sicilia pulsis factae, dono misit.[46]

7   Fuit vero mirabilis dicti Roberti et fratrum cursus victoriarum,
quandoquidem intra decem et octo annos (quorum ultimus fuit
septuagesimus post millesimum salutis annum) praedictis Italiae
regionibus et Sicilia sunt potiti. Paulo post cum Henricus tertius
imperator Germanus Gregorium septimum pontificem Romanum
acerrimo persequeretur bello, contulit se Aquinum dictus[47] pontifex et eandem concessionem quam secundus Nicolaus fecerat Roberto confirmavit — ea tamen adiecta condicione: ut Marchiam
Anconitanam, paulo ante Picenum appellari solitam, a suis Normannis occupatam dimitteret. Unde factum est ut, cum Gregorius
pontifex in Mole Hadriani, Castello nunc Sancti Angeli nuncu-
pato,[48] ab Henrico obsideretur, accedens cum copiis Guiscardus et
Romam porta Flumentana (sive Flaminia) ingressus[49] ceperit et,
Henrico vi expulso, pontificem obsidione liberatum deduxerit Salernum, ubi diem paulo post[50] obiit. Tantis tam multisque in Italia
et Sicilia gestis rebus, pellendo Constantinopoli Alexio imperatore
Graeco et quidem scelestissimo qui Christianis inimicaretur Guiscardus animum adiecit. Sed dum, Dyrrachio plurimisque Epiri[51]
et Acarnaniae ac Graeciae oppidis, castellis, et insulis vi captis,
maiora in dies molitur, Iulio mense apud Cassiobam insulam febre
correptus interiit.[52]

8   Cuius filio natu minori[53] nomine[54] Rogerio Urbanus secundus
pontifex Romanus in Melphiensi concilio paternum in Italia Apuliae et Calabriae ducatum concessit. Alter vero Roberti filius Boe-

been rewarded for his treachery, Bettieminus encouraged Roger to invade Sicily, which was ripe for insurrection, Guiscard following Roger with a fleet. Messina was the first city of Sicily to pass into the hands of the Normans, and (to put it briefly) all of Sicily was soon brought under the control of Guiscard and his brother Roger. Roger then sent four camels as a gift to Pope Alexander II (successor of the deceased Nicholas), part of the booty taken from the Saracens as they were being driven out of Sicily.[12]

The succession of victories won by Robert and his brothers was truly marvelous: within eighteen years, ending in 1070 CE, they had gained possession of the regions of Italy mentioned above and of Sicily. A little later, when the German emperor Henry III was pursuing a ferocious campaign against Pope Gregory VII, Gregory betook himself to Aquino and confirmed the grant that Nicholas II had made to Robert, but with the further condition that Robert was to give up the March of Ancona (usually known as Picenum in earlier times) which the Normans had seized. And so it happened that when Henry was besieging Gregory in the Moles Adriana (now called the Castel Sant'Angelo), Guiscard came up with his forces and entering Rome by the Porta Flumentana (or Flaminia), took the city. Forcibly expelling Henry, Guiscard lifted the siege and took the pope to Salerno, where he died soon afterward.[13] After so many momentous successes in Italy and Sicily, Guiscard threw himself into driving the Greek emperor Alexius Comnenus out of Constantinople—Alexius was, to be sure, a wicked man and an enemy of Christians. Guiscard captured Durazzo and many towns, castles and islands in Epirus, Acarnania, and Greece, but while he was making ever more ambitious plans with each passing day, he was seized by fever and died on the island of Cassiope in July.[14]

In council at Melfi, Pope Urban II granted Robert Guiscard's younger son Roger his father's Italian duchy of Apulia and Calabria. Another son of Robert, his eldest, Bohemund, was left heir

7

8

mundus natu maior[55] patris, quem semper secutus fuerat, dominii in transmarinis heres et exercitus ductor relictus est. Qui cum in Rogerium fratrem dominio Italico eum excludere cupientem traduxisset exercitum, meliorem fortunam sibi casu oblatam secutus est.[56] Gallicos enim, Germanos, Hispanos, et Anglicos proceres in Christianam expeditionem ab Urbano secundo[57] pontifice Romano apud Clarum Montem Alverniae institutam secutus, Antiochiam durissima trienni obsidione cepit, eiusque[58] ducatu et amplissimo principatu ab expeditionis magistratibus donatus fuit. Rogerio Normanno post quintum et vigesimum annum dufuncto, Guilielmus filius successit, qui Alexii imperatoris Constantinopolitani[59] filiam in matrimonium sibi[60] promissam habere sperans,[61] in Graeciam profecturus suos Apuliae et Calabriae ducatus secundo Calixto pontifici Romano commendavit. Sed Rogerius, altero genitus Rogerio Normanno Guiscardi germano fratre, comes Siciliae, nihil pontificem veritus Calabriam invasit. Et prius dimidiam cepit quam pontifex de ferenda ope potuerit cogitare. Misit tamen Ugonem cardinalem Calixtus, per quem sedis Apostolicae legatum Niceforam[62] arcem, quam obsideret in Calabris Rogerius, conservare et ipsum verbis comminationibusque ab incepto deterrere speravit. Ipseque pontifex cardinalium collegio et Romanorum copiis tumultuarie contractis sociatus, Beneventum usque se contulit, qua infausta in expeditione multos sibi carissimos febribus correptos amisit. Et ipse, adversa[63] pariter usus valitudine, lectica in urbem aeger moestusque relatus est. Qua fretus bene gerendae rei occasione Rogerius Calabriam omnem Apuliamque subegit.

9   Guilielmus vero uxoris spe fraudatus cum ad affines Salernitanos in Italiam reversus confugisset, diem ibi nullis relictis filiis obiit. Ex eoque tempore Rogerius tantarum rerum successu elatus non se ultra Apuliae et Calabriae ducem, Siciliaeque comitem, sed Italiae regem appellare coepit. Secundus vero Honorius pontifex

to the overseas dominions of his father (whom he had always supported) and made commander of his army.[15] Bohemund led this
army against his brother Roger, who wanted to keep him out of
his Italian domain, but chance offered him a greater piece of luck:
while he was accompanying the French, German, Spanish, and
English generals on the crusade that Pope Urban II had called at
Clermont in the Auvergne, Bohemund captured Antioch after a
hard three-year siege, and was rewarded by the Crusader chiefs
with the gift of the ample duchy and principality of Antioch.[16]
Roger the Norman died after twenty-five years and was succeeded
by his son William. As he was about to set out for Greece in the
hope of securing the hand of the emperor Alexius's daughter in
marriage, William entrusted the duchies of Apulia and Calabria to
the care of Pope Callixtus II. But Roger Count of Sicily (son of
the other Norman Roger, who was Guiscard's brother),[17] showed
the pontiff no respect: he invaded Calabria, and captured half of it
before the pope was able even to think of sending reinforcements.
All the same Callixtus sent Cardinal Hugo to Calabria as legate of
the Holy See, hoping that he would be able to protect the Rocca
Nicefora, which Roger had under siege, and deter him by words
and threats from carrying out his intentions. The pope himself,
accompanied by the College of Cardinals and hurriedly assembled
Roman troops, got as far as Benevento, but lost many who were
close to him on that unlucky expedition, carried off by fever. Callixtus's own health was just as poor, and he was taken back to
Rome in a litter, sick and depressed. Roger capitalized on this opportunity to advance his cause, and conquered all of Calabria and
Apulia.

   Disappointed in his hopes of a wife, William returned to Italy   9
and sought refuge with his relatives in Salerno, dying there without issue. Buoyed up by his great success, from that point onward
Roger began to call himself no longer Duke of Apulia and Calabria and Count of Sicily, but King of Italy. Pope Honorius II,

Calixto defuncto suffectus eam dissimulavit indignitatem, quam secundus Innocentius, Honorii successor, ferre non potuit adeo ut, iracundia magis ductus quam viribus ad tantam rem aggrediendam necessariis fretus, tumultuario contractum impetu exercitum in illum duxerit. Tanta vero profectus est celeritate ut Rogerium, qui nullos audiisset a pontifice factos apparatus, apud Sancti Germani oppidum ex improviso adortus repulerit. Et eo oppido vi capto, tyrannum in Castro Gallucio, in quod se de fuga receperat, obsederit. Sed Calabriae dux, Rogerii filius, cum exercitu veniens et patrem obsidione liberavit et pontificem cum cardinalibus, fusis eorum copiis, cepit. Usus tamen modestia Rogerius, pontifice cum suis omnibus liberato, quicquid voluit ab eo praeterquam regni titulum impetravit.

10   Reversus Romam Innocentius adulterinum pontificem novum sibi suffectum reperit, Petrum Petrileonis filium, qui se Anacletum pontificem appellaret. Quare Pisanorum triremibus conscensis in Franciam navigavit. Rogeriusque, novo et adulterino Anacleto in pontificem adorato, regni titulum et coronam ab eo[64] obtinuit. Primusque omnium Normannorum absurdum utriusque Siciliae regni titulum habuit. Ad tertium inde annum Innocentius pontifex Pisanorum auxilio Romam reversus, Lotharium Teutonicum imperatorem Romanum declaravit et in Lateranensi ecclesia coronavit. Amboque primarii Christianorum principes adversus Rogerium cum exercitu[65] profecti omnibus eum spoliarunt quae citra[66] fretum Siculum occuparat. Nec multi intercesserunt anni, cum Rogerius Innocentii pontificis occasione mortis fretus, secundo Celestino primum, dehinc[67] secundo[68] Lucio, pontificibus Romanis rem suam frigide administrantibus, et[69] demum Eugenio tertio Romano pontifice praestante quidem viro sed multis[70] agitato difficultatibus, omnia de integro cepit quae Innocentius ei[71] Lothariusque abstulerant.

11   Is[72] ad annum deinde[73] regni Siciliae assumpti quartum et vicesimum Panormi moriens, Guilielmum filium habuit successorem.

who succeeded Callixtus on his death, concealed his indignation, but his successor Innocent II took it so hard that he assembled an army and led it against Roger in a hastily conceived attack, driven more by anger than by possession of the forces required to undertake such an enterprise.[18] Indeed his attack was so speedy that he caught Roger unawares — for Roger had heard nothing of the pope's preparations — and drove him back at the town of San Germano. Innocent took the town by storm and laid siege to Roger in the castle of Galluccio, whither he had retreated. But Roger's son the Duke of Calabria came up with an army, delivered his father from the siege, and captured the pope and cardinals after routing their forces. Yet Roger behaved with restraint, released the pontiff and all his entourage, and got from him everything he wanted except the title of King of Italy.[19]

Returning to Rome, Innocent discovered that he had been newly succeeded by a false pope, one Pietro Pierleone who was calling himself Pope Anacletus.[20] On that account he took ship on galleys of Pisa and sailed off to France. Roger made obeisance to the new and bogus Anacletus as pope, and won from him the title and crown of king: he was the first of the Normans to hold the absurd title to the "Kingdom of the Two Sicilies."[21] Three years later Pope Innocent returned to Rome with Pisan help, declared the German Lothair Holy Roman Emperor, and crowned him in the church of St. John Lateran. This pair of supreme Christian princes took an army against Roger and deprived him of all the lands he had seized on this side of the Straits of Messina. Just a few years after that, taking advantage of the death of Pope Innocent and the mismanagement of their affairs by the successive popes Celestine II, Lucius II, and finally Eugenius III (an excellent pontiff certainly, but beset by many difficulties), Roger recovered all the lands that Innocent and Lothair had taken from him.

Roger died at Palermo twenty-four years after taking the title of the King of Sicily, and was succeeded by his son William.[22] Wil-

10

11

Cui, ab Hadriano quarto primum, post illumque[74] a tertio Alexandro, Romanis pontificibus, regni Siciliae et ducatus Calabriae ac Apuliae titulis ornato, ad annumque[75] sui principatus quintum decimum Panormi defuncto alter Guilielmus filius heres successorque fuit. Hic vero pacis quietisque amator cum in multitudinem pontificum Romanorum intra annos XXV inciderit, tertium Lucium, tertium Urbanum, octavum Gregorium,[76] tertium Clementem, nulla ab eorum quoquam molestia agitatus, Bono[77] cognomine est ornatus. Tandemque[78] et ipse Panormi sine liberis est defunctus. Erat tunc Panormi Tancredus, quem Rogerio supradicto ex concubina genitum omnes ad eam diem spreverant. Sed regni Siciliae proceres ne in Romani pontificis suum id regnum recipere adnitentis potestatem venirent[79] — vel[80] potius ut[81] Tancredo[82] in regium[83] sublato et praetenso signum propriam ipsi[84] conservarent tyrannidem, huic regni titulum demandarunt. Iamque Tancredus pro rege habitus Siciliam retinebat et Calabriae Apuliaeque manum iniicere conabatur, cum Celestinus III pontifex Romanus illi obsistere constituit. Sextum is Henricum Suevum, tunc in[85] imperatorem electum, ea confirmavit condicione ut regno Siciliae propriis recuperato sumptibus, et censum solveret annuum et terras iuris ecclesiastici sibi redderet. Idque quo facilius assequeretur, Constantiam Rogerii regis supradicti filiam virginem in monasterio Panormi agentem natuque[86] grandiorem quam quae filios procreatura videretur, dispensatione apostolica ab eo uxorem traduci permisit. Ingressi cum exercitu rex et regina primo imperii sui anno Neapolim obsederunt. Sed cum pestilentia exercitum invasisset,[87] re infecta abeuntes in Alemaniam se contulerunt. Annoque inde[88] quarto cum paratiore exercitu reversi, universo regno

liam was honored with the titles of the Kingdom of Sicily and of the Duchy of Calabria and Apulia by the successive pontiffs Adrian IV and Alexander III. He died at Palermo in the fifteenth year of his reign, leaving his son William II as heir and successor. William II was a lover of peace and quiet; he encountered a good many Roman pontiffs over the course of twenty-five years—Lucius III, Urban III, Gregory VIII, Clement III—but never had any trouble with any of them. In the end he too died at Palermo, without issue and hailed as "William the Good." At the time there was living at Palermo one Tancred, hitherto universally despised as having been born of a concubine to Roger. But the barons of the Kingdom of Sicily demanded the title of king for him, because they were disinclined to surrender themselves to the power of a pontiff who was striving to regain control of their kingdom—or rather because they wanted to preserve their own despotic rule by raising Tancred to royalty and having him claim the royal banner. Tancred, now regarded as good as king, kept control of Sicily and was trying to get his hands on Calabria and Apulia when Pope Celestine III decided to resist him. Celestine confirmed the Swabian Henry VI, the Holy Roman Emperor elect, in his position on condition that once Henry had recovered the Kingdom of Sicily at his own expense, he should pay the pope an annual tribute and restore to him the lands that had before been under papal jurisdiction. To make matters easier for him, Celestine gave Henry papal dispensation to take Costanza, King Roger's virgin daughter, to be his wife: she was living in a convent in Palermo and seemed too old to bear children. Having entered the Kingdom with an army, the king and queen spent the first year of their reign laying siege to Naples. But their army was stricken by plague, and Henry and Costanza took themselves off to Germany before the matter was concluded. Four years later they returned with a better equipped army and took control of the whole kingdom, capturing

potiti sunt, Tancredo et Margarito Epirotarum rege, qui praesidio illi advenerat, interceptis.

12   Henrico ad octavum imperii annum mortuo, electores imperii dissidentes, pars Philippum Henrici defuncti germanum fratrem, pars Ottonem Saxoniae ducem elegerunt,[89] quem Honorius III pontifex Romanus coronavit, et quia paulo post contra eius voluntatem regnum Siciliae hostiliter aggressus est, excommunicavit. Id enim regnum Federicus, Henrico sexto et Constantia monacha genitus, obtinebat, qui adulescens bonae (ut videbatur) indolis Saracenos omni Sicilia deturbaverat. Sed hic secundus Federicus, ab Honorio praedicto pontifice post Ottonis excommunicationem in imperatorem declaratus, Federico primo Barbarossa immanior, tam multa in pontificem Honorium machinatus est ut, qui eum coronaverat bonus pontifex, imperio ac regno privare atque excommunicare fuerit compulsus. Quemadmodum Gregorius quoque[90] IX pontifex, Honorio suffectus, pariter privatum excommunicavit. Isque scelestissimus Federicus pontifici Gregorio per annos XIIII quibus vixit adeo infestus molestusque fuit ut diem ille moestitia confectus obiise sit creditus.

13   Ferunt Senebaldum de Flisco[91] cardinalem Genuensem temporibus[92] Honorii et Gregorii pontificum supradictorum non vulgari cum Federico amicitia usum esse, et cum is in Romanum pontificem Innocentium quartum Gregorio successisset, dixisse Federicum malo eventu bonum se amicum cardinalem in vehementem hostem Romanum pontificem permutatum habere: quod quidem ipse rerum eventus[93] verum fuisse ostendit. Namque Innocentius, concilio apud Lugdunum congregato his quae praedecessores sui in Federicum gesserant approbatis, Langravium[94] Hassiae illi in imperatorem primo et paulo post, eo defuncto, Guilielmum Hollandiae comitem subrogavit. Solemnique sancivit decreto, quod distinctione quarta et sexagesima exstat: nullum de cetero, qui imperator sit Romanus, regno Siciliae, quod peculiare

Tancred along with Margaritus, the King of Epirus, who had come to help him.[23]

When Henry died in the eighth year of his reign, the Electors of the Empire could not come to an agreement, some voting for Henry's brother Philip, others for Otto, Duke of Saxony. Otto was crowned by Pope Honorius III, but excommunicated by him soon afterward for attacking the kingdom of Sicily against his wishes. The kingdom was held by Frederick, the child of Henry VI and the nun Costanza and apparently a youth of good character, who had expelled the Saracens from every part of Sicily. Honorius had declared this Frederick II emperor after excommunicating Otto, but Frederick — so much more inhuman than Frederick I Barbarossa — laid so many plots against him that the same good pontiff who had crowned him was forced to deprive him of his kingdom and empire and excommunicate him, as his successor Gregory IX also did after Frederick suffered those losses. The villainous Frederick was so hostile and troublesome to Pope Gregory for the remaining fourteen years of his life that it was believed that Gregory died of the grief that he had brought on.[24]

The Genoese cardinal Sinibaldo de' Fieschi is said to have enjoyed uncommonly good relations with Frederick during the papacies of Honorius III and Gregory IX.[25] When Cardinal Fieschi succeeded Gregory as Pope Innocent IV, Frederick is reputed to have said that it was his misfortune to have had a good friend in the cardinal turn into a bitter enemy as pope — and events proved it true. In fact once the Council called at Lyon had confirmed the actions taken by his predecessors against Frederick,[26] Innocent replaced Frederick as emperor, first with the Landgrave of Hesse and, when the Landgrave died shortly afterward, with Count William of Holland.[27] This he ratified with a solemn decretal that survives as "Distinctio LXIV," that no Roman emperor thenceforth was to rule over the Kingdom of Sicily, since it was the inalienable property of the Church of Rome. Frederick lived on for

est ecclesiae Romanae membrum, praefici posse. Supervixit postea
Federicus annis quinque, quo tempore multis agitatus est calami-
tatibus. Primo namque Henricum filium, quem sibi Constantia
regis Aragonum filia uxor pepererat, ob ancillae zelotypiam in
carcere necavit. Inde apud Parmam urbem proelio superatus, pre-
tiosissima[95] impedimenta et decem milia militum caesa[96] amisit.
Alterque filius legitimo matrimonio ex eadem uxore genitus, nomine Enisius, a Bononiensibus, quorum infestaret agrum, occisus
est.[97] Tandemque[98] a Manfredo filio ex ancilla suscepto, quem Ta-
renti praefecerat, cum leviter aegrotaret, suffocatus interiit.

14   Post cuius mortem electores illico Conradum eius[99] filium,
quem ex filia Iohannis Hierosolymitani regis uxore susceperat,
imperatorem declaraverunt. Qui nullo deterritus paternae privatio-
nis exemplo regnum Siciliae violenter ingressus est, et Neapolim
accedens, cum cives excommunicato deditionem facere obstinatius
recusassent, urbe per obsidionem famemque potitus moenia multis in locis aperuit civesque[100] (praesertim primarios) male habuit.
Subtractus tamen est paulo post morte quam Manfredus[101] frater,
dato veneno, accelerasse dictus est. At pontifex Innocentius quartus, qui sub ipsum necis Federici tempus exercitum parare coepisset, peropportune Conradi morte intellecta, Neapolim se contulit,
ubi apparuit illum,[102] etiam adversante magnis conatibus Manfredo, potiturum fuisse[103] regno, nisi eum mors brevi[104] subtraxis-
set. Per cuius mortis occasionem Manfredus—praetenso titulo
tutelae Conradini nepotis sui ex Henrico, quem patrem Frederi-
cum mori coegisse diximus, et Constantia Aragonensi[105]—regnum
omne mirabili celeritate subegit, adeo ut prius rem confecerit
quam Conradini pueri in Alemannia agentis tutores veri tanta de
victoria[106] certiores facti, aut venire potuerint[107] aut oratores mit-

five more years, wracked by a string of calamities: first from jealousy over a servant girl he had his son Henry killed in prison (the son born to him by his wife Constance, the daughter of the King of Aragon); then he was defeated in battle at Parma, losing his train of imperial treasure and ten thousand slaughtered soldiers;[28] and his second legitimate son, Enzo, also born of Constance, was killed by the Bolognese whose territory he was attacking; in the end Frederick died by suffocation at the hands of his son Manfred, the child of a maidservant, whom he had put in charge of Taranto when he was indisposed.[29]

After Frederick's death, the Electors straightaway declared Conrad emperor, Frederick's son born of his wife, the daughter of King John of Jerusalem.[30] Undeterred by the dispossession that his father had suffered, Conrad at once invaded the Kingdom of Sicily. When he reached Naples, the inhabitants stoutly refused to surrender to him, as being an excommunicate, but he took the city by siege and starvation, breached the walls in many places, and maltreated her citizens, the leading men in particular. Yet death took him not long afterward, an end which they say his brother Manfred hastened with a dose of poison. Innocent IV for his part had begun to ready an army around the time of Frederick's murder, and he now rushed to Naples on hearing the good news that Conrad had died. It seemed that for all Manfred's sterling efforts, Innocent was about to seize control of the Kingdom, but death quickly took him too.[31] Manfred took the opportunity of Innocent's death to subjugate the entire Kingdom with remarkable speed,[32] ostensibly acting as regent for his nephew Conradin, the son of Henry (whose death, as I said, their father Frederick had brought about) and Constance of Aragon.[33] So quickly, indeed, that Manfred had accomplished his task before the true guardians of the child Conradin (who was living in Germany) could come to Naples themselves, once they learned of Manfred's momentous victory, or send ambassadors to thank the barons and peoples of

tere principibus regni ac populis de facta celeriter deditione[108] gratiam a rege puero (sicut decuit) relaturos. Quod quidem ne posset accidere, Manfredus, dolo ex sua ingenii malignitate usus, nuntios derepente[109] simulantes advenisse subornavit, a quibus in regno palam est factum pueri regis Conradini interitum luctu omnia lachrymisque in Alemannia ipsis praesentibus replevisse. Moxque sub ipsum rumorem accurate disseminatum, Manfredus regio procedens apparatu sese regem appellari salutarique curavit.

15   Id cum rescisset quartus Alexander pontifex Romanus, qui Innocentio successerat, et Manfredum de more excommunicavit et paratissimum adversus eum duxit exercitum. Manfredus vero pecunia abundans quam in suorum caedibus et regni direptione cumulaverat, et multos ex Africa Saracenos et Florentiae aliarumque Lombardiae urbium extorres (qui tunc multi erant) mercede conduxit. Eoque[110] fretus exercitu Alexandrum papam cum ignominia reppulit. Creatus post Alexandri mortem, quae tunc forte accidit, pontifex IIII Urbanus, ex Trecis Gallicus, primum[111] Saracenos a Manfredo in Italiam Siciliamque perductos[112] per cruce signatos undique ex Christiano orbe coactos reppulit,[113] deinde[114] Carolum, Ludovici regis Francorum sancti fratrem germanum, Provinciae et Andegavorum comitem, regni Siciliae citra ultraque fretum regem declaravit. Carolus vero Romam veniens senatoriam dignitatem tam diu administravit quousque suus ex Galliis venisset exercitus. Coronamque Carolus et Beatrix uxor regnorum Siciliae et Hierusalem accepturi solemni stipulatione[115] annua[116] duodequinquaginta aureorum milia[117] pontifici et eius successoribus spoponderunt. Delatus ad Casinensem saltum cum copiis rex Carolus, Manfredum vi superatum ac resistentem[118] reppulit. Retrocedentemque[119] paribus castris usque Beneventum insecutus est, ubi pares[120] animis et viribus praestantissimi duces ad diem

the Kingdom on behalf of the boy king in return for their speedy profession of loyalty, as should have been done. To prevent that very thing, with his instinctive malicious guile Manfred played a trick on them by having messengers feign that they had just arrived from Germany: they made it known throughout the Kingdom that the death of the young king Conradin had brought universal grief to Germany, as they had themselves observed. Before long, as the rumor was assiduously disseminated, Manfred began to take on regal airs and made sure to have himself addressed and greeted as king.[34]

When Pope Alexander IV, who had succeeded Innocent, got to learn of this, he duly excommunicated Manfred and led a well-equipped army against him. But having acquired a great deal of wealth in slaughtering his people and plundering his kingdom, Manfred hired Saracen mercenaries from Africa, as well as exiles from Florence and other Lombard cities, who were at that time very numerous. With this army he drove back and humiliated Pope Alexander. Alexander by chance died at that point, and a Frenchman from Troyes was elected his successor as Urban IV. He first used crusaders gathered from all over the Christian world to beat back the Saracens that Manfred had brought to Italy and Sicily, and then declared the Count of Provence and Anjou, Charles (brother of the French king St. Louis), king of the Kingdom of Sicily on either side of the Straits of Messina.[35] In fact when Charles arrived in Rome, for a long time he merely held the rank of Senator, until his army came over from France. As Charles and his wife Beatrice were about to receive the crown of the Kingdoms of the Two Sicilies and of Jerusalem, they solemnly pledged to pay the pope and his successors forty-eight thousand ducats every year. King Charles with his forces passed down into the plain of Cassino, where he overcame Manfred in battle, and despite resistance drove him back. As Manfred retreated, Charles doggedly pursued him as far as Benevento; there, on April 28, 1266, the

15

quartum Kalendas Maii, anni sexti et sexagesimi supra millesimum ducentesimum salutis[121] conflixerunt. Manfredus vero, quem
aliquando variante proelio vicisse apparuit, superatus occisusque
est, in cuius exercitu duo milia[122] hominum ceciderunt.

16   Quarto Clemente paulo post in defuncti Urbani locum subro-
gato, cum Carolus adeptus,[123] nullo post Manfredi mortem resistente, regnum quietissime possideret, Conradinus adulescens
suis Alemannorum viribus (et quidem maximis) fisus, ut avitum
reciperet regnum adnixus est. Feruntque pontificem, qui habitus
sit sanctus, cum Alemanno adulescenti (ipse in Galliis oriundus)
manifesti periculi audaciam dissuadere sit veritus, multis dixisse ex
Romana curia et urbe contraria[124] sentientibus puerum pro vic-
tima ductum ingredi regnum. Sed erat tunc Romae senator Henricus, Castellae regis frater, ex cuius sorore Constantia Conradini
genitorem natum fuisse ostendimus. Quo suadente atque ex urbe
Roma (tunc sub Banderesiis) semilibera auxilium subministrante,
Alemanni furentes ingressi sunt regnum. Commissoque in campis
Palentinis proelio cui Henricus ipse senator interfuit, Carolus superior evasit. Cum[125] caedes in Alemannos[126] maxima committere-
tur, senator Romanis deducentibus in tuta evasit. Conradinus et
dux Austriae, servorum habitu fugientes, ad Asturam pervenerunt,
ubi ad diem a commisso proelio[127] octavam agniti[128] ad Caro-
lumque perducti sunt, in eosque[129] Carolus publice animadverti
iussit.

17   Ad annum postea[130] regnorum Caroli circiter octavum, Gallis[131]
in Sicilia pudicitiam mulierum lascive nimis et petulanter per-
temptantibus, Siculi omnium paene urbium ac oppidorum populi
coniurarunt quam primum die constituta advesperascere campanis
significari coepisset, confodiendos esse a singulis Gallos intra moe-

two outstanding generals, who were well matched in temper and resources, joined battle. Though as the fighting raged Manfred seemed at times to have carried the day, he was at length vanquished and killed, two thousand of his men falling in battle.[36]

Soon after that, with Clement IV elected pope on Urban's 16 death and Charles enjoying peaceful possession of the Kingdom (which he had gained without opposition after Manfred's death), young Conradin decided to put his faith in his very substantial army of Germans in an effort to recover his ancestral kingdom. Pope Clement is regarded as a saint: though as a Frenchman he shrank from trying to dissuade the young German from embarking on this obviously perilous action, he is said to have told many who believed otherwise in the court and city of Rome that the boy was being drawn into attacking the Kingdom like a sacrificial victim. But the Senator of Rome at the time happened to be Enrique, the brother of the king of Castile,[37] whose sister Constance, as I mentioned, was the mother of Conradin's father. With Enrique egging on Conradin and sending him reinforcements from Rome, which at that point was semi-autonomous under the Banderesi,[38] the Germans launched a furious attack upon the Kingdom. Battle was joined on the Piani Palentini, and the Senator Enrique himself took part, but Charles came off the victor. Though the Germans suffered much the greatest loss of life, the Senator with his Roman escort managed to escape to safety. Conradin and the Duke of Austria fled disguised as servants and made their way to Torre Astura, but they were recognized eight days after the battle and brought before Charles, who had them publicly executed.[39]

Some eight years into Charles's reign, with the French making 17 wanton and disgusting assaults on the virtue of the women of Sicily, Sicilians of practically all the towns and cities swore an oath that as soon as the bells began to toll vespers on a particular day, each and every one of them would slaughter any Frenchmen found

nia repertos. Quod cum esset non minus crudeliter quam constanter factum, dominio Gallis publice abrogato, Petrus Aragonum rex accersitus est, qui demandatum sibi Trinacriae regnum anno salutis millesimo ducentesimo octogesimo secundo[132] ea praetensa ratione audentius accepit: quod illud Constantiae uxori hereditario patris Manfredi iure diceret deberi. Carolo ad duodevicenum quam regnare coeperat[133] annum defuncto et Neapoli sepulto successit alter Carolus, qui regni Italiae partem Siciliae regnum nihilominus appellatum quatuor et viginti annis obtinuit. Is,[134] nulla re alia notior quam quia proletarius in regno quievisse videtur, annoque[135] aetatis quadragesimo moriens, quatuordecim filios ex Maria uxore, regis Hungariae filia, novem mares, foemellas quinque reliquit. E quibus[136] notiores fuere Carolus cognomento 'Martellus,' Hungariae regni titulo insignitus, Ludovicusque qui ex ordine[137] Minorum in sanctorum numerum translatus fuit, et tertius Robertus qui, parentis in regno[138] successor, Francisci Petrarchae amicitia[139] nobis est notus. Huicque ad annum Christi tertium et quadragesimum supra tredecies centenum diem obeunti Iohanna (quae prima est dicta) in regno successit. Ladislaus exinde diebus nostris, post eumque[140] secunda Iohanna, dehinc Ludovicus, demumque[141] Renatus, extremi Galliarum ex Andegavis regum nostri huius regni gubernacula diversis rationibus successibusque usi, quod in nostris *Historiis* diffuse apparet, obtinuerunt.

18   Et duodecim iam annis[142] quieta eius regni et Neapolitanae urbis possessione gaudet Alphonsus Aragonum rex inclytus, cui inter praedictos omnes soli contigit ut de capto maximis XX annorum laboribus et periculis tanto regno curru aureo Neapolim invectus triumphaverit. Si vero quod factitant mercatores calculum ex summis cogere[143] volumus, Normanni centum triginta quinque,[144] Germani sex et septuaginta, Galli centum septuaginta octo,[145] Alphonsus Arrago XII annis, quadringentos et unum conficientes, has, de quibus dicturi sumus, septem Italiae regiones sub unico

within their walls.[40] This was carried out with equal measures of determination and callousness, and so openly threw off the yoke of French domination. King Peter of Aragon was sent for and he boldly accepted the crown of Sicily that was offered him in the year 1282, the ostensible justification being that the realm was properly his wife Costanza's, who had inherited it from her father Manfred.[41] Another Charles succeeded Charles I of Anjou, who died and was buried in Naples in the eighteenth year of his reign. This Charles II held a portion of the kingdom of Italy (still called the "Kingdom of Sicily") for twenty-four years.[42] His reign was chiefly notable for the apparent quiescence of the populace; he died at the age of forty, leaving fourteen children (nine males and five females) born of his wife Maria, daughter of the King of Hungary. Of these the most well known were Charles Martel, distinguished by the title of King of Hungary,[43] the Franciscan Louis who became a saint, and Robert III, his father's successor as king, who is best remembered for his friendship with Francesco Petrarca.[44] When Robert III died in 1343, Joan of Naples (called Joan I) succeeded him as ruler. In our own time Ladislaus, and after him Joan II, then Louis II of Anjou, and finally René I of Naples were the last of the French Angevin kings to hold sway over this Kingdom of ours, each with their differing policies and varying success, as is made abundantly clear in my *Histories*.[45]

The famous King Alfonso of Aragon has enjoyed peaceful pos- 18
session of the Kingdom and city of Naples for twelve years now, and of all those mentioned above, he alone secured a triumph by capturing this great kingdom after twenty years of the utmost toil and danger, being carried into Naples on a chariot of gold.[46] If we want to draw up a balance sheet in the manner of merchants, the Normans held on to these seven regions of Italy of which I am about to speak under the title of "the Kingdom" (sometimes the "Kingdom of Naples," sometimes the "Kingdom of Sicily this side of the Straits of Messina") for 135 years, the Germans for 76, the

regni, quandoque Neapolitani quandoque Siciliae citra fretum dicti, titulo tenuerunt. Sed iam nostrum continuaturi ordinem ad Troentum amnem redeamus.

19   Adiacet[146] eius fluminis sinistrae Samnitum regio, cum amplissima tum etiam variis populis orisque distincta, siquidem Praetutini, Pinnenses, Frentani,[147] Paeligni, Marrucini, Furconenses, Amiternini, Vestini plurima possidentes loca populi, in Samnitibus adnumerati sunt. Pertinuitqe omnis ea regio (ut tandem nostrae aetatis nominibus utamur) ab hoc Troento amne ab Aquilaque Amiternensium, a Fregellis (ubi nunc dicitur Pons Corvus), ab Reate ab Suessaque Pometia (Vestinorum nunc Sessa), hinc ad Beneventum, quam inclusit civitatem, inde ad Larinates, Apulorum fines. Mutatumque ex Samnio praesentis Aprutii nomen magnam illius partem complectitur. Absurda vero est haec facta mutatio, et propter quam multi ex doctioribus viris, sed regionum imperitis,[148] credant Aprutium esse quod olim Brutii fuere, cum trecentis et alicubi pluribus passuum milibus Aprutium distet a Brutiis. Toleranda vero vel ea ratione videtur ipsa mutatio, quod ex particula licet tenui tam amplae Samnitium regionis id Aprutii corpus sumpsit nominationem, siquidem qui[149] Praetutinus dici fuit solitus ager, facta ab imperitissimis mutatione dici coepit[150] Aprutinus. Et quod prima inchoavit Samnii ad Picentum fines particula, ceterae Samnitium particulae atque orae sunt complexae ut omnis regio non Praecutium sed corrupte Aprutium vocaretur.

20   Nam Plinius ubi hanc describit regionem a superioribus inchoans, ut ad Picenum veniat sic habet ab Aterno amne, ubi nunc ager[151] Praetutinus Pennensisque idem Castrum Novum, flumen Iuvatinum, Truentum (cum amne quod solum Liburnorum in Italia reliquum est), flumen Albula, Tessuinum, quo finitur Prae-

French for 178, Alfonso of Aragon for 12, amounting to a total of 401 years. But now let us proceed in the order we laid down, and return to the river Tronto.

The region of the Samnites lies to the left of the river. It is very 19 extensive and divided up between various districts and peoples, since the Praetutini, Pinnenses, Frentani, Paeligni, Marrucini, Furconenses, Amiternini, and Vestini are peoples with widespread possessions who are all numbered among the Samnites.[47] To return at length to the current names, the whole region extended from the river Tronto and L'Aquila of the Amiternini, from Fregellae (now called Pontecorvo),[48] from Rieti and from Suessa Pometia (now Sessa of the Vestini) to Benevento (a city now encircled by the Tronto) on the one side, and on the other to Larino on the edge of Apulia. The present name "Abruzzo" has been changed from "Samnium" and comprises most of its territory. The change of name from "Samnium" to the modern "Abruzzo" is in fact absurd, and has induced many men of learning, though inexpert in Italian geography, to suppose that "Abruzzo" is what was formerly "the Brutii," though Abruzzo is three hundred miles from the land of the Brutii and in some places more. It seems that we must put up with the change because this entity of Abruzzo has taken its name from a small and unimportant fragment of the extensive Samnite region: what used to be called the *Ager Praetutinus* was transformed by the ignorant into *Ager Aprutinus*.[49] And because the first small section of Samnium began on the borders of Picenum, the other parts and districts of Samnium were embraced in it, so that the entire region was called not *Praetutium* but *Aprutium* by corruption.

In fact in describing the region, Pliny begins in its upper 20 reaches, from the river Aterno, so as to end up in Picenum with these words: "Here are the territories of Praetutia and Penne, the New Camp also, the river Juvatinum and Tronto with its river (the only Liburnian settlement left in Italy), the river Albula, and Tes-

tutina[152] regio et Picentum[153] incipit. Est vero haec via per quam duo omnium qui arma tractarunt exercitusque duxerunt praestantissimi duces, Hannibal primum et post eum[154] C.[155] Caesar, gerendis rebus maximis in huius regni loca regionesque venerunt. Livius namque[156] Libro XXII scribit Hannibalem post cladem ad Trasumenum Romanis inflictam, Spoleto nequiquam oppugnato, duxisse in agrum Picenum et, praeda omnifariam rerum per aliquot dies facta, profectum per Praetutinum et Adrianum agrum, Marsos inde Marrucinosque et Paelignos devastasse. Gaius autem Caesar, sicut in elegantissimis *Commentariis* suis habetur, maximo progressu omnem agrum Picenum percurrit. Cunctae earum regionum praefecturae libentissimis animis eum receperunt exercitumque eius omnibus rebus iuverunt. Inde Caesar, 'septem omnino dies ad Corfinium commoratus, per fines Marrucinorum, Frentanorum, et Larinatum in Apuliam pervenit.'

21   Sed iam urbes, oppida, et flumina, quae Plinius hic in Praetutianis nunc Aprutii initio fuisse dicit, nostris nominibus declarare[157] pergamus. Illudque in primis non omittamus Truentum oppidum, quod Plinius, a Liburnis Dalmatiae populis secus Truenti amnis ostia aedificatum fuisse indicat, non exstare nec aliquod in eius vestigio parum apparente subrogatum esse, vel oppidum vel castellum. Est vero primum ad dictam Troenti amnis sinistram oppidum Columnella, deinde sequuntur[158] Contraguerra, Ancaranum, Morrum, et nunc Trassinium,[159] quod vetus oppidum Plinius Tessuinum appellat. Cui proximum est Castellani (amnis Asculum ambientis) ostium, quo in Troentum derivat.[160] Et ad ipsius Castellani sinistram castella sunt: Mons Sanctus, Macula, Buffarium, Sanctus Vitus — cui oppido haeret vallis Castellana, ab eius fluvii fonte quem ibi habet appellata et aliquot viculis habitata. Ab eaque valle ad Amatricem, nobile Praetutino-

suinum, where the region of the Praetutini ends and that of Picenum begins."[50] This is actually the route taken by two of the
greatest military leaders ever to bear arms and command troops
when they came to this part of the world to perform their momentous deeds, first Hannibal and then Julius Caesar. Indeed Livy
writes in Book XXII that after he had inflicted the disaster of
Lake Trasimene on the Romans and laid siege in vain to Spoleto,
Hannibal led his army into Picenum. After several days of widespread looting, he set off through the lands of Praetutium and
Adria, laying waste successively to the territory of the Marsi, the
Marrucini and the Paeligni.[51] Caesar for his part, as he says in his
elegant *Commentaries*, traversed the whole territory of the Picen-
tines by forced marches. The commanders of all these regions
were very glad to welcome him, and assisted his army with provisions of all sorts.[52] Caesar then "stayed in Corfinium for a whole
week before making his way into Apulia through the lands of the
Marrucini, Frentani, and Larinates."[53]

But let us now proceed to list the contemporary names of the   21
cities, towns, and rivers that Pliny gives here as being in Praetutium, at the beginning of present-day Abruzzo. In the first place
we should note that the town of *Truentum* (said by Pliny to have
been founded at the mouth of the river Tronto by the Liburnian
people from Dalmatia) no longer exists, nor has any town or castle
occupied its scanty remains.[54] On the left bank of the Tronto that
I mentioned above the first town is Colonnella, then Controgu-
erra, Ancarano, Moro, and the modern Tesino, the ancient town
which Pliny calls Tessuinum.[55] Near Tesino is the mouth of the
river Castellano that encircles Ascoli, through which it passes as it
runs into the river Tronto. On the left bank of the Castellano itself are the castles Montesanto, Macchia da Sole, Monte Bufario,
San Vito, which sits beside the Valle di Castellano, named after
the source of the river which is found there and populated by a
number of small villages. From this valley to Amatrice, the famous

rum[161] oppidum, Troento amni montes imminent altissimi nullis castellis aut oppidis habitati.

22   Secundus sequitur in Praetutinis fluvius Librata, quem ab aquarum colore Albulam maiores appellavere. Estque passuum quinque milibus secundum litus a Troento semotus,[162] cui dextrorsum ignobilia haerent oppida[163] et castella: Caropolis, Neretium, et ad sinistram Torturetum, Sanctomerus, et Sanctus Egidius, ad quod castellum Libratae (sive Albulae) amnis fontes origoque habentur. Salinus deinceps est amnis ab Apennino defluens, a quo amne (vix duo milibus passuum a Librata recedente) remotiora sunt ad dexteram in mediterraneis montibus Rochetta[164] castellum et[165] Civitella oppidum arcem habens, omnium eius orae natura loci moenibusque munitissimam.[166] Sinistrorsum vero castella illi adiacent: Montorium, et superiore loco Poggium Morelli, superius Troia. Quinque dehinc milibus[167] passuum abest Tordinus amnis, quem Plinius Iuvantium[168] appellat quique habet[169] in Apennino ad radices Corni montis originem. Haeret vero ei dextrorsum in maris litore oppidum Flavianeum olim nobile, nunc paucis habitatum colonis, quod Ptolemaeus Pliniusque Castrum Novum appellant. Supraque Flavianeum in mediterraneis Tordino dextrorsum proxima sunt oppida: Mosanum, Ripatoni, et Villantum. Sinistrorsum vero eidem amni et pariter litori proximum est Castellum, Mons Paganus, supraque XII a mari milliario Viciola fluvius ex[170] Apennino ad Cornum oriundus Tordinum auget.

23   Ibique Teramum est nobilissimum regionis oppidum, quam Ptolemaeus Pliniusque Interamniam appellant. Paulo enim supra Teramum torrens nomine Flumicellus influit Tordinum ut tot circumdatum amnibus oppidum Interamnia debuerit appellari. Genuit is locus magnum regioni ornamentum Simonem patrem et Theodorum filium, iure consultissimos gente progenitos Lellia, ex

town of the Praetutini, high mountains bare of castles and towns overhang the river Tronto.

There follows the Vibrata, the second river of the territory of 22 the Praetutini, which our ancestors called the Albula because of the color of its waters. It is five miles from the Tronto along the coast. To its right are situated the undistinguished towns and castles of Corropoli and Nereto, and to the left Tortoreto, Sant'Omero, and the castle of S. Egidio, where the Vibrata (Albula) has its source and origin. Next is the river Salinello, which flows down from the Apennines scarcely two miles from the Vibrata. Somewhat more distant from it amid the inland mountains lie on the right the castle of Rocchetta and the town of Civitella del Tronto with its fortress, the best fortified place in the area thanks to the topography and its walls. To the left of the Salinello are the castles of Montone, and higher up Poggio Morello, and above that Troia. Five miles from the Salinello is the river Tordino, which Pliny calls the Iuvantium[56] and which originates in the Apennines at the base of Monte Corno. Along the right of the river Tordino on the seashore, lies the town of Castel San Flaviano (once well known, now the home of a few farmers), which Ptolemy and Pliny call Castrum Novum.[57] Further inland, beyond Castel San Flaviano, by the right bank of the Tordino are the towns of Mosciano Sant'Angelo, Ripattoni, and Bellante; on the left of the Tordino, close to the river and the coast alike, are Castellalto and Montepagano. Further up, twelve miles from the sea, the river Vezzola, which rises in the Apennines near Monte Corno, flows into the Tordino.

At that point is located the major town of the region, Teramo, 23 which Ptolemy and Pliny call "Interamnia."[58] Just above the town, in fact, a stream called Fiumicello flows into the Tordino, so that as it is surrounded by so many rivers, it was inevitably called "Interamnia." This place gave birth to great ornaments of the region in the jurisconsults Simone and Teodoro of the Lelli family. Sim-

quibus[171] ille in Pisana,[172] Constantiensi, et Basiliensi synodis pon-
tificumque Romanorum curia causas egregie peroravit, hic sacri
palatii causarum auditor est. Genitorque nunc[173] Venetias[174] natus
Romam incolunt.[175] Ad proximumque[176] Flumicelli ortum, tria
sunt[177] adeo[178] proxima et prope contigua ut unicum oppidum solo
Compli vocabulo nominentur. Supraque Viciolae ortum castella
sunt Burgum Novum,[179] Bisignum, et Rugnanum. Tordinum autem (sive Iuvantinum) inter et proximum vetusti praesentisque
nominis Vomanum amnem sex in litore milia passuum intercedunt, oppidaque et castella inter utrumque sunt plurima, partim
pariter ab utroque distantia, partim alterutris pro montium in
quibus sunt inaequalitate et alveorum utriusque amnis inflexu
proximiora. Quae ab infimo ad supremum, quo sita sint ordine,
satis fuerit explicare: Morrum, Lochariscum,[180] Custodia Vomani,
Castrum Vetus, Transmundum, Cancianum, Forcella, Mianum,
Rapinum, Collis Vetus, Fornariolum, Montorium, Ripa[181] Monto-
rii, Poggium Umbrechi, et Rossenum. Ad Vomanique fontem vici
sunt in Apennino populis frequentes: Campus Tostus, Poggium
Cancellum,[182] et Massionum. Habetque Vomanus sinistrorsum in
mediterraneis castella: Motulam, Montem Viridem, et Montem
Gualchum. Hucusque fuerunt Praetutini, quandoquidem Plinius
ad agrum Adriae coloniae et ad Aterni amnis fines agrum Praetutinum finiri dicit.

24   Deinceps versabimur in Marrucinis, quos Livius Libro
XXVIII[183] dicit dedisse voluntaria nomina in classem quam Scipio in Africam duxit. Et Libro LXXII bellum describens Italicum,
dicit Marrucinos Marsis rebellibus consensisse. Et Libro LXXVI
scribit Sulpicium legatum Marrucinos cecidisse. Post Vomanum
amnem fluvius Plumba sequitur, cui castellum haeret Hadriae
portus appellatum. Superius est Silva oppidum. Et tribus sicut
vult Plinius, ut nostri autem quinque, milibus passuum[184] a mari

one pled cases with great success at the Councils of Pisa, Constance, and Basel, and in the papal curia, while Teodoro is Auditor of Cases of the Holy Palace.[59] At present the father is living in Venice and the son in Rome. At the source of the Fiumicello nearby, there are three towns so close together, almost contiguous, that they are grouped together under the single name Campli. Above the source of the river Vezzola are the castles of Borgonovo, Bisenti, and Rocciano. There are six miles of coastline between the Tordino (*Iuvantinum*) and the next river, the Vomano, its ancient and still current name. There are numerous towns and castles between the two, some equidistant from both rivers, others closer to one or the other, depending on the undulations of the hills on which they are set and on the meandering of the respective river courses. It will be enough here to set out the order in which they are found, from the lowest to the highest: Morro d'Oro, Notarescho, Guardia Vomano, Castelvecchio, Castiglione Messer Raimondo,[60] Canzano, Forcella, Miano, Rapino, Collevecchio, Frondarola, Montorio al Vomano, Ripa, Poggio Umbricchio, and Roseto. At the river Vomano's source in the Apennines are the populous villages of Campotosto, Poggio Cancelli, and Mascioni. Inland the river Vomano has to its left Mottola, Monteverde, and Montegualtieri. This is as far as the Praetutini went, since Pliny says that their territory ended at the land of the colony of Atri and the borders of the river Aterno.[61]

Now we must turn to the Marrucini. In Book XXVIII Livy 24 says that they volunteered their names to serve in the fleet that Scipio took to Africa.[62] And in his account of the Social War in Book LXXII, he says that the Marrucini colluded with the rebellious Marsi.[63] In Book LXXVI he writes that the legate Sulpicius slaughtered the Marrucini.[64] After the Vomano comes the river Piomba, which has on its banks a castle called Porto d'Atri.[65] Further up than Porto d'Atri is the town of Silvi. Atri was three miles from the sea according to Pliny, but five miles as reckoned now,

et ab utroque fluvio pariter distat Hadria, vetus Romanorum colonia arduo in colle sita, quae cive ornatissima fuit Hadriano imperatore Romano. De quo Helius Spartianus: Hadrianus Hadria ortus, maiores suos, in Hispania ortos, per tempora Scipionis in Italia resedisse in libro vitae suae scribit. Et infra: 'Hadrianus apud Neapolim demarchus, in patria sua Hadria quinquennalis fuit.' Livius, Libro XXIV: 'Anno quinto belli Punici secundi Hadriae aram[185] in caelo speciesque hominum circa eam candida veste visas esse.' Supra Hadriam Plumbae fluvio ad dexteram castellum haeret Celinum. Superiusque ad ipsius fluvii fontem oppidum est Schiranum. Eidem autem Plumbae fluvio secundo supra mare millario sinistrorsum imminet oppidum nobile civitas Sancti Angeli appellata. Idque Plinius et Ptolemaeus Angolum dixere. Quod enim in multis contigisse videmus, tam facilis quam pia fuit 'Angoli' ad 'Angelum' Christianis temporibus facta mutatio. Et supra illud Plumbae amni Ilex oppidum pariter est propinquum.

25   Distat a Plumba fluvio secundum mare tribus milibus passuum amnis Salinus. Eique ad dexteram in litore haeret castellum Portus Sancti Angeli dictum. Supraque in mediterraneis Salinus fluvio augetur nomine Fino ex[186] Apennino ad Corni radices oriundo. Cui dextrorsum octo imminent oppida et castella quae satis fuerit ordine recensere: Cassilentum, Mons Siccus, Pignanum, Bisentum, Corvignanum, Serra, et Valvianum. Paulo etiam supra Fini amnis ostium altero Salinus augetur flumine[187] Tavo, quod pariter in Apennino ad Cornum exoritur. Interque haec flumina pari paene distantia et quarto a mari millario oppidum est in regione primarium civitas Penne appellata, Pennensium[188] nomine apud vetustissimos notissima. Sunt enim hi quos superius Plinium post Praetutinos Pennenses[189] diximus posuisse. Eaque in fluviorum peninsula Tavo dextrorsum imminent[190] Collis Corvinus et Lauretum nobile oppidum. Sequitur in litore Aterni amnis in regione

lying midway between the rivers Vomano and Piomba.[66] An ancient Roman colony set on a steep hill, Atri was given luster by its citizen, the Roman emperor Hadrian. Aelius Spartianus says that Hadrian, who was born at Atri, writes in his autobiography that his ancestors originated in Spain but had lived in Italy since the time of Scipio.[67] And below, "Hadrian was demarch at Naples, and duumvir of his native Atri."[68] Livy writes in Book XXIV: "Four years into the Second Punic War, an altar was seen in the sky at Atri, and human forms dressed in white surrounding it."[69] Above Atri, the castle Cellino Attanasio lies to the right of the river Piomba. Above Cellino, at the source of the Piomba is the town of Cermignano. To the left of the Piomba two miles inland sits Città Sant'Angelo, a fine town that Pliny and Ptolemy called Angolum.[70] This is the sort of change we see has often happened, the alteration in Christian times from "Angolum" to "Angelus" being as simple as it was pious. Above Città S. Angelo, and just as close to the river Piomba, is the town of Elice.

Three miles along the coast from the Piomba is the river Saline. 25 On its right bank is nestled the castle called Porto Sant'Angelo. Further inland a river known as the Fino is a tributary of the Saline, which rises at the base of Monte Corno in the Apennines. To the right of the river Fino sit eight towns and castles, which we need do no more than list in order: Castilenti, Monte Secco, Pignano, Bisenti, Corvignano, Serra, and Valviano. Just above the mouth of the river Fino, a second river joins the Saline, the Tavo, which again rises in the Apennines at Monte Corno. Pretty much midway between these rivers and four miles from the sea is the chief town of the region, the city known as Penne, or as the ancient authors call it, the city of the Pennenses. As I said earlier, these Pennenses were placed by Pliny after the Praetutini.[71] In the quasi-island formed by the Saline and the Tavo rivers, Collecorvino and the fine town of Loreto Aprutino sit on the right above the Tavo. The major river of the region is the Aterno, now known

primarii[191] ostium, quem amnem nunc Piscariam vocant. Is fluvio[192] Nuria apud monasterium Casae Novae secus Apenninum oriundo dextrorsum augetur. Suntque ad Nuriae dexteram Mons Sylvanus castellum, Spoltorium oppidum, et Moscufum, Planellumque et Cepagattum[193] castella. Et sub ipso fonte Abbatia Casae Novae, aedificiis et cetero ornatu (ut in ea montium asperitate) conspicua. Supra Nuriam fluvium Aterno (sive Piscariae) amni dextrorsum adiacent: Rosanum, Alandum, Petranicum, Turris Antonelli. Et superius est Castilionum.

26   Inde[194] ascendenti obvius est fluvius Caput Aquae dictus[195] uberrimo manans fonte, cui fluvio ad sinistram castella Buxum primum[196] et superius ad fontem Offenum adiacent.[197] Interque ea Capistranum duo milibus passuum ab eodem fluvio est semotum, quod oppidum viro nunc ornatur celeberrimo Iohanne Capistraneo seraphici Francisci ordinis (quem decorat) alumno, miraculis et quidem frequentibus, quod post apostolorum tempora rarum ac prope inauditum fuit, in vita coruscante. Supraque Capistranum in mediterraneis est oppidum Carapellum. Dehinc arduo ascensu Aterno amni adiacent Vetoritum et Raianum, et superius est Aquila urbs praeclara. Cuius[198] originem relaturi, quaedam nostri huius operis intentioni accommodata altiuscule repetamus[199] ut minori sit miraculo nostris hominibus tantam civitatem potuisse in ea montium asperitate tam brevi tempore coalescere. Roma sub consulibus atque etiam postea sub principibus florente, hi montes in quibus Aquilam nunc esse videmus duas habuere urbes, quarum unam nomine Amiternum populo quam nunc sit Aquila frequentiorem fuisse constat. Livius enim, Libro X, scribit Spurium Carvilium[200] alterum consulem Amiternum oppugnatum de Samnitibus cepisse, caesaque oppidanorum duo milia octingentos,[201] captos quater milia[202] ducentos septuaginta.[203] Et tamen postea

as the Pescara, which flows into the sea following the Tavo along the coast. It is joined on the right near the monastery of Casanova by another river, the Nora, which rises in the Apennines. On the right of the Nora there are the castle of Montesilvano, the town of Spoltore, and the castles of Moscufo, Pianella, and Cepagatti. Just below the source of the river Nora is the monastery of Casanova, very impressive for its buildings and other attractions, considering the rugged mountain terrain.[72] Above the Nora, and sitting on the right of the river Aterno (Pescara), are Rosciano, Alanno, Pietranico, Torre de Passeri. Further up is Castiglione a Casauria.

Going up from Castiglione, you come across a river called Capo d'Acqua, which pours forth from an abundant spring. To the left of the river are various castles, first Bussi and then, higher up at the source, Ofena. Between them, two miles from the river, is Capestrano, a town notable in our day for its famous son, Giovanni da Capestrano, raised in the Franciscan order which he now adorns, a man who glowed with miracles even while he was alive, something that since the apostolic age has been rare and practically unheard of.[73] Inland, above Capestrano, is the town of Carapelle. From there, after a steep climb, the villages of Vittorito and Raiano border the river Pescara, and further up is the illustrious city of L'Aquila. In accounting for its origin, we have to go back rather a long way to find material suited to the purposes of this work which will make the rapid formation of this great city in that rough mountain terrain seem less miraculous to our contemporaries. When Rome was at her height under the Republican consuls, and later under the principate too, the mountains where now we see L'Aquila had two cities, of which the one called Amiternum is known to have been more populous than L'Aquila is at present. Livy writes in Book X that Spurius Carvilius, the second consul, laid siege to Amiternum and took it from the Samnites, killing 2,800 of the inhabitants and taking prisoner another 4,270.[74] And yet Livy later lists the Amiternini, along with

26

idem Livius, populos Italiae enumerans qui Lucio Scipioni in Africam traducturo sponte auxilio fuere, dicit Amiterninos simul cum Umbris, Nursinis, et Reatinis milites illi dedisse. *Virgilius vero Amiternas appellat 'Turrigeras,'*[204] fuitque situm Amiternum in continuato ac plano montis dorso quinque milia passuum ab Aquila distans, cuius theatri templorumque et turrium, ingentis (ut apparet) urbis reliquiae, fundamenta cernuntur. Habuit vero ea urbs magni ornamenti civem, Salustium Crispum nobilem historicum.

27   Altera urbs in montibus Aquilae adiacentibus fuit Furconium appellata, quae, etsi Amiterno nominis vetustate, populi frequentia, et opum magnitudine fuit impar, suam tamen temporibus Christianis habuit dignitatem, quod omnibus conciliis, quae ante annos sexcentos Romae aut alibi per Italiam celebrata fuere, episcopum Furconensem ascriptum legimus. Eratque Furconium, diversa ab Amiterno regione octo milia passuum ab Aquila distans, in Aterni amnis fluenta proclivior, ubi etiam nunc exstantia quadrati lapidis fundamenta Furconium appellantur, videturque eius urbis agrum fuisse illum maiori ex parte quem nunc possident Aquilani. Itaque Amiternis ab ignoto nobis hoste et Furconio quod scimus a Longobardis solo aequatis, ipsarum urbium et suorum agrorum populi, quos soli montuosissimi aerisque salubritas multos gigneret conservaretque, in grumosis arduisque ascensu montibus, communitis oppidis, et castellis sese continuerunt. Et cum dispersi ea in locorum asperitate ipsi populi nullam regiminis formam communem possent retinere,[205] in tyrannorum subiectionem potestatemque venerunt, a quibus diu multumque lacerati oppressique sunt. Crediderimque quod tradita per quatuor aut ad summum quinque aetatum successionem publica nunc fama Aquilani affirmant factum esse ut, cum diu invisum tyrannidis iugum excutere statuissent, singuli castellorum populi quod prius coniuratione inita[206] se facturos spoponderant, suos quique tyrannos eadem trucidaverint hora.

the Umbri, Nursini, and Reatini, among the Italian peoples who spontaneously helped Scipio as he prepared to lead his army over to Africa.[75] *Vergil calls Amiternae "turreted."*[76] Amiternum was sited on a long flat mountain spine five miles from L'Aquila. The foundations of its theater, temples and towers, seemingly the remains of a vast city, can still be seen. The city in fact could claim as her own a citizen of great brilliance, the famous historian Sallust.

The second city in the mountains around L'Aquila was called 27 Furconium. In the Christian era it enjoyed some distinction (though it was no match for Amiternum in terms of antiquity, population, and wealth), since we read that all the church councils held in Rome or elsewhere in Italy over the last six hundred years were attended by the bishop of Furconium. The city, located opposite Amiterno eight miles from L'Aquila, was further downhill toward the streams of the Pescara, and even now there remain some foundations of dressed masonry that are called "Forcona."[77] It seems that the territory of this city for the most part corresponded to what is now held by the people of L'Aquila.[78] And so, though Amiternum was leveled by an unknown enemy and Furconium, as we know, by the Lombards, the people of these cities and their surrounding districts were bred and maintained in great numbers by the wholesomeness of the mountain air and soil. In this way they managed to keep themselves together in their mountain fastnesses, remote and difficult of access as they were, and in their fortified towns and castles. Isolated by the harshness of the terrain, these people were unable to share any particular form of government, and were consequently subjected to the power of tyrants who for a long time greatly maltreated and oppressed them. I am inclined to believe the story commonly told by the Aquilani, which has been passed down for four or at most five generations, that the individual people of these fortified towns formed a conspiracy to throw off the long detested yoke of tyranny and each agreed to slaughter their own tyrant all at the same time.[79]

28   Quod autem magis constat, liberati tot populi nihil duxere antiquius quam, hoc murorum orbe quem nunc habet Aquila inchoato, singulis castellorum populis, quos futura in urbe tenerent inhabitarentque vicos, qui hodie quoque internoscuntur, distribuere ut eo quisque ardentius operi intenderet quo sese domui et rei suae familiari studium impendere operamque navare intellegeret.[207] Nomen vero Aquilam non ab augurio (sicut gentiles olim) sed a similitudine indiderunt, quia speraverint eam urbem omnibus circa populis, haud secus quam aquila ceteris avibus, potentiorem dignioremque futuram. Quo autem anno Aquila urbs condi coeperit incertum omnibus esse videmus, sed eam scimus minus novam esse quam incolae opinentur et praedicent. Namque in secundi Nicolai pontificis Romani gestis rebus habetur (quod supra ostendimus) Robertum Guiscardum ad annum salutis decies centenum et sexagesimum accepisse ab eo pontifice in Aquila civitate ducatus Apuliae concessionem. Coeperat vero eius urbis fortuna rei publicae proximis temporibus a civium discordia labare adeo ut ad pristinam calamitatem reditura videretur, nisi maximo dei munere sanctum Bernardinum Senensem apud eos diem obire contigisset. Tantus namque ex omni orbe Christiano populorum concursus ad sancti eius sepulcrum miraculaque visenda est factus ut cum urbs Aquila opibus sit aucta tum maxime cives concordes unanimesque sint facti.

29   Supra Aquilam amnis Aterni (sive Pescariae) fonti subiacet in Apennino oppidum Mons Regalis, cui oppido incolae affirmant nobisque ostenderunt pirum esse proximam, colli innatam taliter fastigiato ut aqua in eam pluens arborem, triplici facta divisione, in tres magnos amnes diversas petentes regiones, Velinum, Troentum, Aternumque (sive Piscariam), dilabatur.[208]

What is rather more certain, however, is that all these different   28
peoples, once they had been liberated and had made a start on the
present city wall of L'Aquila, thought it best to assign to the individual peoples of the various castles particular neighborhoods of
the future city for them to own and live in, neighborhoods which
are still distinct today, in the belief that each man would turn to
the work with greater enthusiasm on the understanding that he
was spending time and effort on his own hearth and home. They
gave it the name Aquila not from augury (as the pagans used to
do) but from analogy, because they hoped that this city was going
to be more powerful and imposing than all the peoples around
them, just as the eagle is more powerful and imposing than all
other birds.[80] I observe that the year of L'Aquila's first foundation
seems to be quite unknown, but I do know that it is not as recent
as its inhabitants suppose and maintain. As I mentioned above, in
the account of the activities of Pope Nicholas II one finds that in
1060 Robert Guiscard was granted the Duchy of Apulia by that
pontiff in the city of L'Aquila.[81] In recent times, however, the city's
political fortunes began to totter through civil discord, to such an
extent that it appeared to be on the point of returning to the old
turmoil, when by God's great grace, San Bernardino of Siena happened to die in their midst. Such was the crush of people stream-
ing into the city from all over the Christian world to visit the tomb
of the saint and to witness his miracles that not only was there an
increase in L'Aquila's wealth but, more particularly, its citizens
were reconciled and harmony between them was restored.[82]

Above L'Aquila, the town of Montereale lies below the source   29
of the river Aterno (or Pescara) in the Apennines. Near the town
the citizens speak of a pear tree, which they showed me, that
grows on a hill whose summit is such that when it rains, the water
that falls on the tree divides into three and spills down into three
great streams that flow in different directions, the rivers Velino,
Tronto, and Aterno (Pescara).[83]

30   Habet sinistrorsum Aternus ostio in maris litore proximum Piscariam oppidum, cuius nomen (sicut fluvii) est mutatum, siquidem Aternum eam vetustissimam urbem Plinius Ptolemaeusque appellant. Superiusque urbs Theatina Marrucinorum a Plinio dicta septimo milliario a mari recedit,[209] episcopo nunc et cive suo ex nobili Volognanorum[210] familia oriundo ornata, quam Pipinus Caroli Magni filius, quod Longobardis obstinatiore favisset animo, demolitus est. Et tamen anno abinde paulo plus minus ducentesimo, Normanni eam duxerunt[211] dignam apud quam Aprutinorum gubernationis sedem tenerent. Nam (quod supra ostendimus) Gaufredus Roberti Guiscardi frater per[212] II Nicolai pontificis Romani tempora[213] occupatae regionis caput hanc urbem Guilliniacumque oppidum faciebat.

31   Auget superiore loco Aternum Alba fluvius, binis auctus torrentulis ex Maiella oriundis,[214] inter quos oppidum est Manupellum Urso ornatum comite, ex patricia Ursinorum Romana familia[215] oriundo litterisque[216] decorato. Et paulo superius Maiellae monti adiacet Rocha Morisii, inferiusque[217] Cusanum, et ad Aterni ripam est oppidulum Turris dictum. Lucus deinde oppidum Aterno est proximum ad ostium fluvii, quem unicum duo—Rufens inde, hinc Orta—torrentes[218] ex Maiella cadentes efficiunt, interque eos torrentes Caramanicum est oppidum non exile. Cantalupum deinde oppidulum ab Aterno recedens monti haeret, sub quo fons olei petronici perennis scatet. Quod quidem oleum Teutonici Hungarique diligentius quam Italici et colligunt et asportant. Proxime ad Aterni ripam Tochum est oppidum, et quatuor inde abest milia passuum Populium natura loci munitionibusque et populi frequentia nobilissimum. Nam cum eo confluant Aternum conficientes fluvii, hinc ab Aquila (sive a Monte Regali) inde a

Near its mouth on the coast the Aterno has on its left the town   30
of Pescara. Like the river, its name has been changed, since Pliny
and Ptolemy call this most ancient city Aternum.[84] Above Pescara,
seven miles from the sea, is the city that Pliny calls Teate of the
Marrucini,[85] to which its present bishop and native of the place,
scion of the noble family of the Valignani, adds luster.[86] Charlemagne's son Pepin demolished the city because of its obstinate
attachment to the Lombards. And yet about two hundred years
later, more or less, the Normans thought Chieti a fit place for
their seat of government of Abruzzo: as I mentioned above, in the
reign of Pope Nicholas II Geoffrey Guiscard, Robert's brother,
made this city the capital of occupied Abruzzo, along with the
town of Guglionesi.[87]

The river Alba joins the Aterno above Chieti, having itself been   31
joined by two smaller streams that rise in the mountains of the
Maiella. Between them is the town of Manoppello, distinguished
for its count Orso, the learned scion of the Roman patrician family of the Orsini.[88] Further up, Roccamorice lies alongside the
Maiella, while lower down is Cosano, and on the banks of the
Aterno a little town called Torre de' Passeri. Next on the Aterno is
the town of Luco at the mouth of a single river formed of two
smaller streams that flow down from the Maiella, on one side the
Rufento, on the other the Orta; between these two streams is
the not insubstantial town of Caramanico. Then set back from the
Aterno the little town of Cantalupo in Sannio nestles alongside
the Maiella, at whose base there is a petroleum spring that gushes
all year long. This oil is collected and exported more industriously
by the Germans and Hungarians than by the Italians.[89] Next, on
the bank of the Aterno, is the town of Tocco da Casauria, and four
miles from Tocco is Popoli, a very fine town in respect of its situation, fortifications, and teeming populace. The rivers that com-
bine to form the Aterno come together here, flowing down from
L'Aquila (i.e. Montereale) on the one side and from Sulmona on

Sulmone labentes, pons Aterno primum integro et nusquam inferius vadoso apud Populium est impositus. Et arces ductaque utrimque ad amnem murorum brachia claustrum efficiunt (ut in regione montuosissima) munitissimum. Hicque Marrucenis continere incipiunt Paeligni ad eum Aterni torrentem[219] hinc inde expositi,[220] quem[221] labi diximus a Sulmone.

32   Primum vero ad hunc amnem oppidum fuit Corfinium, cuius diruti ruinis tertio milliario a Populio distantibus Sancti Pelini[222] in Campis et Pentima est appellatio. Fuitque id Corfinium in quo Domitius Ahenobarbus sese C. Caesari ne Pompeium persequeretur opposuit. Ostendit vero Lucanus pontem, qui eum iungeret fluvium, fuisse prope Corfinium, ut non liceat suspicari eum fuisse qui nunc est sublicius ad Populium: 'Ite simul pedites, ruiturum ascendite pontem.' Paelignosque (quod diximus) continuisse Marrucinis, et his Frentanos, postea Larinates, Hirtius in *Civilis belli commentariis* sic ostendit: 'Caesar septem omnino dies ad Corfinium commoratus per fines Marrucinorum et Frentanorum et Larinatum in Apuliam pervenit.' Sed Aterni amnis quod est reliquum et illi adiacentes Paelignos priusquam Frentanos describamus. Is Aterni torrens, quem a Sulmone diximus[223] labi, geminum habet fontem, unum apud Pacentrum alterum apud Vallem Obscuram. E quibus delabentes rivi[224] apud Sulmonem coeunt in torrentem, qui[225] a Populio Sulmonem usque integer, planitiem XII miliarium[226] longitudine et vix sex[227] latitudine patentem intersecat, nec ipsi integro torrenti[228] praeter Corfinii (ut diximus) diruti ruinas aliud quam Pratula castellum adiacet.

the other, and so a bridge has been built at Popoli over the river where it is first a unified stream, and cannot be forded anywhere downstream. Forts and stretches of walls brought down to the river from either side create a very strong barrier, considering its mountainous position. It is here that the territory of the Paeligni, spread out on both sides of that tributary of the Aterno which I mentioned as flowing down from Sulmona, first abuts on the land of the Marruceni.

The first town on the river Aterno was Corfinium: the ruins of   32 this razed town are three miles from Popoli and are now called San Pelino and Pentima.[90] It was here in Corfinium that Aheno-barbus blocked Caesar's path to prevent him from pursuing Pom-pey. Lucan shows that the bridge that spanned the river was near Corfinium, so it must not be supposed that that bridge is the one set on piles at Popoli: "Advance, infantrymen, at the same time and mount the bridge before it collapses."[91] In the following passage from his *Commentaries on the Civil War*, Hirtius shows that Paelig-nian territory bordered on that of the Marrucini, as I said, and the Frentani bordered on the Marrucini, followed by the Larinates bordering on the Frentani: "Caesar spent seven days in all at Cor-finium, and then made his way into Apulia through the lands of the Marrucini, Frentani, and Larinates."[92] But let us survey what remains of the river Aterno and the territory of the Paeligni along it before coming to the territory of the Frentani. The tributary of the Aterno that we mentioned as flowing down from Sulmona has twin sources, at Pacentro and Vallescura.[93] The two streams de-scend from there and come together at Sulmona in a single water-course, which then flows undivided from Popoli to Sulmona, cut-ting through an open plain twelve miles long and a bare six wide. If we except the ruins of the razed Corfinium that I mentioned, the only castle that lies on the banks of the unified river is Pratola Peligna.

33   Sulmoque proximum rivo[229] ad Vallem Obscuram oriundo oppidum est celebre, quod civibus opificibusque praestantibus et populi multitudine frequentatur. Eoque nos viso Nasoni Ovidio
poetae excellentissimo congratulati sumus, qui patriam se dignam
tantopere exornaverit. Isque eam scribit aedificatam fuisse a quo-
dam Solymo,[230] Aeneae comite, his versibus 'Huius erat Solymus
Phrygia[231] comes unus ab Ida, a quo Sulmonis moenia nomen habent.' Erat vero Ovidius exsul in Scythia quando dictos et alios qui
sequuntur versus in *Fastis* scripsit. Sulmonis gelidi, patriae, Ger-
manice, nostrae. 'Me miserum, Scythico quam procul illa solo est!
Ergo ego tam longe—sed supprime, Musa, querelas.'

34   Supra Sulmonem Pectoranum oppidum, superiusque[232] est Vallis Obscura, vicus planitiei quinque miliarium,[233] ut[234] in ea montium celsitudine tam mirabili quam amplae adiacens. Fuit vero ea
planities aliquot habitata vicis, quod exstantes ruinae ostendunt.
Et Plinius eos populos Superaequanos Paelignorum appellat. Rivus[235] autem apud Pacentrum oriundus, cum Maiellam montem, a
quo cadit, linquere et in campos Sulmonenses labi incipit, monasterium attingit aedificiis ornatissimum, quod frater Petrus de
Morrono, quando in papam Celestinum electus fuit, inhabitabat.
Hanc oram et eam, quae a Populio Sulmonem usque campestris
est, et ipsam, unde geminos diximus torrentes[236] Aternum efficere,
montes undique altissimi (sinistrorsum Maiella, Apenninusque[237]
dextrorsum) claudunt adeo ut paucis (et quidem arduis praesidioque communitis) aditibus in eam sit accessus. Unde factum est
ut ab octingentis annis citra antiquato Paelignorum nomine dicta
sit Valvensis, qua ratione praepositum Sulmonensi ecclesiae et
omni olim Paelignorum orae episcopum Romana ecclesia Valven-
sem dicit. Sed haec[238] iam de Aeterno fluvio satis.

Next to the stream that rises at Vallescura lies the famous town   33
of Sulmona, bustling with throngs of citizens, excellent craftsmen,
and multitudes of people. When I saw the town, I congratulated
that fine poet Ovid for having lent luster to a native land that was
so deserving of him. Here in these verses he writes that Sulmona
was built by a companion of Aeneas, Solymus: "One of his companions was Solymus from Phrygian Ida, from whom Sulmona's
walls take their name."[94] Ovid was in fact an exile in Scythia when
he wrote the verses I quote and those that follow in the *Fasti*: "[the
walls] of chilly Sulmona, my fatherland, Germanicus: Alas for me,
how far from Scythian soil she is! And so am I just as far from
Sulmona—but stay your laments, Muse."[95]

Above Sulmona, is the town of Pettorano sul Gizio, and above   34
Pettorano Vallescura, a village lying on the Piano delle Cinquemiglia, an amazingly spacious plateau considering how high up in the
mountains it is. This plain was in the past settled by a number of
villages, as their ruins make clear. Pliny calls the people of the
plain the Paelignian Superaequani.[96] As it leaves its source in
Monte Maiella and flows down through the fields of Sulmona, the
river that rises at Pacentro passes by a magnificent monastery,
where Fra Pietro da Morrone was living when he was elected Pope
Celestine V.[97] On all sides very high mountains (Monte Maiella
on the left and the Apennines on the right) surround this river
valley, the stretch of plains from Popoli to Sulmona, and that district which I mentioned above where twin streams form the Aterno; there are consequently few means of access to it, and the few
passes are steep and closely guarded. And so for the last eight
hundred years, the entire region has ceased to be called Paelignum
and has been known instead as Valva.[98] For that reason the Roman Church calls the prelate with jurisdiction over the church of
Sulmona and the entire old district of Paelignum the bishop of
Valva. And let that suffice for the river Aterno.

35   Alia quae de Paelignis Superaequanis reliqua nobis sunt, ultra Maiellam ad dexteram Sari[239] nunc Sangri amnis melius describentur. Aterno (sive Piscariae) amni proximus est ad mare Lentus fluvius, ex Maiella oriundus, Frentanorum orae primus, cui dextrorsum et sub ipso monte Maiella adiacet monasterium Sancti Liberatoris, templo, aedificiis, et — quod nos illuc traxit — multis et elegantibus libris vetustissimis Longobarda scriptis littera ornatissimum. Eiusque fluvii[240] sinistrae in maris litore haeret nunc Francha Villa, quam prisci Frentanam appellavere urbem Frentanorum primariam. De qua Livius in IX: Aulus consul 'Frentanos uno secundo proelio debellavit, urbemque ipsam, quo se fusa contulerat acies, obsidibus imperatis in deditionem accepit.' Et infra: 'de Aequis triumphatum, exemploque eorum fuit ut Marsi, Marrucini, Frentani mitterent Romam oratores. His petentibus foedus datum est.' Frentanos vero omnium illius regionis[241] populorum solos fuisse fortissimos nonnulli opinantur, in eam ducti[242] sententiam male consideratis verbis Plinii hanc regionem, quae sibi fuit quarta, describentis. Ipse enim, ordine procedens[243] nostro huic contrario et a superioribus inchoans, dicit a Tiferno amne sequi regionem quartam gentium vel fortissimarum Italiae in ora Frentanorum, ut intellegi velit et ipsos Frentanos et, qui sequerentur adiacerentque, Marrucinos, Paelignos, et Praetutinos esse fortissimos. Notissimum vero est historias callentibus Romanas cohortes Paelignas ceteris Latini nominis fuisse praelatas. Lento amni in mediterraneis haeret Buchianicum nobile ditissimumque olea oppidum. Superius item sub Maiella est Rocha Montis Plani, et supra fontem Lenti est Castrum Menale.

The rest of what I have to say on the Paelignians and Superae- 35
quani will be more conveniently delivered once we are on the other
side of the Maiella on the right bank of the river Sagrus, nowadays
the Sangro. Next to the Aterno (Pescara) along the coast is the
river Alento, which rises in the Maiella. It is the first river of the
region of the Frentani. To its right at the foot of Monte Maiella is
the abbey of San Liberatore, with its fine church, buildings and
(what took me there more particularly) many elegant old books
written in Lombardic script.[99] To the left of the Alento on the
coast now stands Francavilla, which the ancients called Frentana,
the chief city of the Frentani. In Book IX Livy says of it: the consul Aulus "concluded in one successful battle the campaign against
the Ferentani, and having exacted hostages, received the surrender
of the city itself, in which their defeated army had taken refuge."[100]
And later: "A triumph was celebrated over the Aequi; and warned
by their example, the Marsi, Marrucini, and Frentani sent ambassadors to Rome. At their request, they were granted a treaty of
alliance."[101] Now some suppose that of all the peoples of this region only the Frentani were truly brave, and they have been led to
this belief by a statement of Pliny in describing this region (his
fourth) that they have misunderstood. Pliny follows an order contrary to mine, beginning further inland. He says that his fourth
region, home of the very bravest peoples of Italy, follows at the
river Biferno in the territory of the Frentani: so he wants it to be
understood that these Frentani *and* the neighboring tribes who
came next, the Marrucini, Paeligni, and Praetutini, are the bravest.[102] In fact it is well known to experts in Roman history that the
Paelignian auxiliaries were more highly regarded than the other
Latin peoples. Bucchianico lies on the river Alento in the interior,
a fine town that is rich in olive trees. Further up, under the Maiella massif, is Roccamontepiano, and above the source of the
Alento lies Castel Menardo.

36　　Ad Lentum in litore sequitur Forus amnis ex[244] Maiella pariter oriundus. Cui quinto a mari milliario proximum est dextrorsum Villa Maina oppidum, et superius sub Maiella Praetorium item oppidum. Foroque sinistrorsum est proximum Milianicum, et supra ad ipsum torrentem aliud oppidum Fara, superius Rapinum castellum, et ad Maiellam Penna. Recedit in litore a Foro Morus alter fluvius octo milia passuum. Et cum eo in spatio litori immineat et Foro proximum sit castellum Tullum, Moro proxima est ad bis[245] mille passus marique contigua vetustissima urbs Ortona, quam Ptolemaeus simul cum Aterni amnis ostio in Paelignis enumerat. Sed Plinius, cui in rebus Italiae magis credimus, quicquid est ab Aterni amnis ostio in Larinates Frentanorum orae attribuit. Quin ipse etiam Ptolemaeus (sicut et Plinius) Frentanam urbem Aterno sinistram, ubi nunc est Villa Francha, ponit, ut aut Ptolemaei picturam esse depravatam, quae contraria habeat,[246] aut eos qui retulerunt ei[247] errasse non dubitemus.

37　　Inter urbem Ortonam et Forum amnem adusque Maiellam montem, multa sunt oppida et castella, quae ab infimis ad suprema quo sint ordine sita docebimus. Tullo Vianum[248] supereminet, et Ortonae ad dexteram Arum, Aro Vacrum, supraque ea oppida est Casa Candidella castellum. Superius Sanctus Martinus, et illi sinistrorsum est Flettum. Ortonam vero inter et Morum fluvium in mediterraneis est Crechium. Superius sunt Ariellum atque Orsogna, Moroque fluvio ad sinistram haeret Sanctus Apollinaris. Supra est Frisium, et superius castrum novum Lanciani. At supra eius fluvii fontem ad bis[249] mille passus oppidum est Guardia Galli dictum. Parvus deinceps fluvius ad Morrum sequitur Feltrinus, cui unicum haeret in litore castellum, Sanctus Vitus Lanciani dictum, et in eo, quod quatuor milia passuum ad Sarum amnem intercedit, spatio Lancianum oppidum praestantissimum quatuor item mili-

On the coast the river Foro follows next upon the Alento, like-   36
wise rising in the Maiella. Next to the Foro on the right, five miles
from the sea, is the town of Villamagna, and, higher up under the
Maiella, the town of Pretoro. Next to the Foro on the left is Mi-
glianico, and above it on the river itself another town, Fara Filiorum Petri; above that are the castle of Rapino, and Pennapiedi-
monte by the Maiella. Eight miles along the coast from the Foro is
another river, the Moro. While the castle of Tollo overlooks the
shore in the area next to the river Foro, the ancient city of Ortona
lies about two miles away, on the coast next to the Moro. Ptolemy
lists Ortona, along with the mouth of the Aterno, as being in Paelignian territory.[103] But Pliny (who when it comes to Italian matters is in my view more trustworthy) assigned the whole stretch
from the mouth of the Aterno to the territory of Larino to the
land of the Frentani.[104] Not only that, but Ptolemy himself puts
the city of Frentana to the left of the Aterno, where Francavilla
now is, as Pliny does too, so that I am quite sure that either Ptolemy's map was distorted, since it is self-contradictory, or his infor-
mants were in error.[105]

Between the city of Ortona and the river Foro all the way to   37
Monte Maiella, there are many towns and castles, which I shall list
in order from the lowest to the highest. Viano sits overlooking
Tollo; above Ortona on the right is Ari, and above Ari, Vacri, and
above those towns the castle of Casacanditella. Higher still is San
Martino, and to its left Filetto. Inland, between Ortona and the
river Moro, is Crecchio. Further up are Arielli and Orsogna, and
on the left bank of the river Moro lies Sant'Apollinare. Above
there is Frisa, and above Frisa Castelnuovo di Lanciano. Two miles
above the source of the Moro is a town called Guardiagrele. Following the Moro, the next river is the Feltrino, on which at the
coast there is a single castle, San Vito di Lanciano.[106] In the four
miles from the Feltrino to the river Sangro is the famous town of
Lanciano, set back from the sea another four miles. Called Anxa-

bus a mari recedit, quod Anxanum[250] a maioribus appellatum magna populorum ad nundinas quotannis convenientium frequentia celebratur. Lancianoque dextrorsum ad Maiellae radices Palumbarium procul abest, cui oppido Penna[251] Castellum in montibus supereminet.

38   Saro amni, quem nunc corrupte Sangrum dicunt, dextrorsum in maritimis proximum est monasterium Sancti Iohannis ubi celeberrimum fuit Veneris templum. Supra sunt castella Fossa Caeca, et Rocha Sancti Iohannis in Venere. Superiusque Saro sunt proximae ingentes reliquiae urbis dirutae, quam Ptolemaeus et Plinius Bicam, nunc Secam incolae, appellant. Auget dextrorsum amnem Sarum (sive Sangrum) Aventinus fluvius in Superaequanis Paelignorum apud Furcam[252] Palenae oriundus. In ipsumque Aventinum item dextrorsum se exonerat Viridis torrens inter monasterium Sancti Martini et Faram oppidum ex Maiella monte oriundus. Et supra Sanctum Martinum Viridisque torrentis ortum Maiellae radicibus proxima sunt oppida Civitella et Lama.

39   Aventino autem amni postquam Viridi auctus est dextrorsum proxima sunt oppida Tarantum, Lectumque Paleni, et Palenum pro 'Paelignum' corrupte appellatum. Nam ea est Paelignorum altera pars, quos diximus Superaequanos a maioribus vocari. Sicque paulo superius Furca oppidum, ubi Aventinus oritur, Palenae pro Paeligna nunc dicitur, cui cernuntur proxima oppidi (ut apparet) vetustissimi fundamenta. Ornatum vero fuit Furca oppidum sancto et celebris famae Anchorita[253] Nicolao Furcensi, qui proximo anno apud urbem Romam centenarius est defunctus miraculisque plurimis coruscavit. Apudque haec loca (ut in amplissimis montibus) ampla et plana finit mons Maiella, quem (ut[254] diximus) separatum[255] ab Apennino Samnitium olim, nunc Aprutii,

num by our ancestors, great throngs of people nowadays descend on the town there for the annual fairs. A long way from Lanciano to the right lies the town of Palombaro at the foot of Monte Maiella, over which the castle of Penna looms up in the mountains.

On the coast to the right of the river Saro (or Sangro, as it is now corruptly called) is the monastery of San Giovanni, where there was a celebrated temple of Venus.[107] Above the monastery are the castles of Fossacesia and Rocca San Giovanni in Venere. Above them in turn, close to the Sangro, there are the extensive remains of a ruined city that Ptolemy and Pliny call Bica and the present inhabitants Seca.[108] The river Aventino, which rises in the territory of the Paelignian Superaequani at Forca di Palena, joins the river Saro or Sangro from the right. The Verde stream, which rises in the Maiella, also discharges into the Aventino from the right, between the monastery of San Martino in Valle and Fara San Martino. Above Fara San Martino and the source of the Rio Verde are the towns of Civitella Messer Raimondo and Lama dei Peligni at the foot of Monte Maiella.

After being joined by the river Verde, the next towns to the Aventino on the right are Taranta Peligna, Lettopalena, and Palena, a corruption of Paelignum. This is the other part of the territory of the Paeligni—the people called Superaequani by our ancestors, as I mentioned. A little higher up, the town of Forca, where the river Aventino rises, is now called Forca Palena (for "Paeligna"), near which can apparently be seen the remains of a very ancient town. The town was graced by the holy and famous hermit Nicola di Forca Palena: he died last year in Rome at the age of one hundred amid the glory of many miracles.[109] Around these parts, spacious and flat as far as they can be among such extensive mountains, Monte Maiella comes to an end, the highest mountain that the region (formerly the Samnite region, now the Abruzzo) has apart from the Apennines, as I said. A plain called

38

39

regio habet altissimum. Ad Furcam vero Palenae sive Paelignam planities sinistrorsum continet Furcae appellata, in qua sunt Peschum[256] Constantium et Rivus Sonulus oppida populis frequentata. Quae quidem loca brevibus sed arctissimis inter scabros montes semitis aditum habent ad planitiem Quinum Milium, quam, supra in Superaequanis, Paelignorum primariam esse diximus. Aventino amni sinistrorsum, qua eum influit torrens Viridis, proximum est Casale oppidum, superius Collis Macinarum et Falascusium. Inde altissimi montes Pitiorum Aventinum amnem usque ad[257] fontem magnis et inaccessibilibus rupibus superincubant.

40   Sed amni Saro (sive Sangro) supra Aventini amnis influxum item dextrorsum plurima adiacent oppida et castella, quae ascendendi ordo faciet notissima: Altinum, Rocha Scalogna, Gipsum, Turricella, Penna Hominis, Mons Niger, Bonanox villa, ubi ponte amnis est iunctus, Mons Lapianus, Fallum. Et paulo superius arduo inter montes altissimos aditu petitur Civitas Luparella oppidum, natura loci additis operibus et populi frequentia munitissimum. Supra sunt Quatrum, Misferatum, Gambatarum, Petra Ansuria, et secus Sari (sive Sangri) fluenta est oppidum Sancta Maria de Quinque Milibus, superius Rocha Quinque Milium. Deinde influit Sarum Rasinus torrens ad planitiem Furcae Paelignorum oriundus, cui castellum haeret Rocha Rasini dictum. Superius ad Sarum sunt item dextrorsum Scontronum, post villa Vallis Regiae Sari ipsius (sive Sangri) amnis fonti proxima. At iuxta mare Saro amni sinistrorsum eiusdem nominis civitas vetusta erat apposita, cuius pridem destructae vestigia dinoscuntur. Superiusque Castrum Palietti proximis temporibus novum est[258] suffectum a palearum copia dictum, quod in eum campestrem locum montanae adiacentis orae segetes demessae[259] ad trituram a vilicis congerantur.[260]

the Piano di Forca, ending on the left at Forca Palena (Paeligna), has on it the populous towns of Pescocostanzo and Rivisondoli. One may in fact get to these places along short but very tortuous paths through the rugged mountains at the Piano delle Cinquemiglia, which, as I said above in discussing the Superaequani, is the greatest plain of the Paelignian territory. Next to the river Aventino on the left, where it is joined by the Torrente Verde, is the town of Casale, and higher up Colledemacine and Fallascoso. Then the towering Monti Pizzi, with their great and inaccessible cliffs, overlook the river Aventino all the way to its source.

Likewise on the right, there are many towns and castles that lie   40 along the river Saro (or Sangro), above the junction with the Aventino, which the ascending order will render memorable: Altino, Roccascalegna, Gessopalena, Torricella Peligna, Pennadomo, Montenerodomo, the country estate of Buonanotte (where a bridge crosses the river),[110] Montelapiano, Fallo. A little further up a steep approach high in the mountains leads to Civitaluparella, a town well defended by nature as well as the fortifications it has had added to it and its teeming populace. Above Civitaluparella are Quadri, Pizzoferrato, Gamberale, Pietransieri. Beside the waters of the Saro (or Sangro) is the town of Santa Maria della Cinquemiglia, and higher up Roccacinquemiglia. Then the river Rasino, which rises in the plateau of Forca Palena and on which stands the castle called Roccaraso, joins the Sangro. Higher up, also to the right of the Sangro, are Scontrone, and then the estate of Villetta Barrea next to the source of the Saro (Sangro). On the coast to the left of the Saro there stood an ancient city of the same name, long destroyed, but traces of it can still be made out. Further up a town of very recent foundation, Palieta, has taken its place, so named for its abundant straw, since the laborers bring the corn harvested in the adjacent mountain region to these fields for threshing.[111]

41   Prius vero quam adeatur proximus mons arduus Palani dictus,
oppidum cui Archae appellatio est Saro proximum invenitur. In
monte autem Palani oppida sunt et castella: Bomia, Collis Medius,
et trans rivum Mons Ferrandus, inde Petra Ferraciana. Pertinent
vero superius ad Sarum plurima item oppida et castella, quae ascendendo in fontem ordine describemus. Petrae Ferracianae supereminet Castrum Pili, et post est Civitas Bucelli. Deinde sunt Pesculum[261] Pineatarii, Sanctus Angelus Pesculi, Castrum Iudicis
clarum in regione memoria Iacobi Caudolae, magni per aetatem
nostram exercituum ductoris, qui ex eo oppido duxit originem.
Supraque est sinistrorsum arduo in colle oppidum Capracotta, et
interius in depressa valle adiacet Maiellae Anglona, quod oppidum
nunc in regione primarium prisci Aquiloniam appellavere. Inde
Sanctus Petrus de Avelana, et postea ad Sari amnis fluenta oppidum est praestantissimum Castrum Sangri appellatum, opificibus
variis, sed in primis fabris ferrariis, frequentatum: hi enim minima
quaeque et maiuscula cuiusque[262] usus instrumenta ex ferro tam
fabre ducunt ut paris ponderis ac mensurae argentea pulchritudine
ac pretio vel superent vel aequent. Supra Castrum Sangri eidem
fluvio haeret oppidum Aufidena, de qua Livius in X: Cn.[263] Fulvii
consulis clara pugna ad Bovianum fuit. Bovianum[264] inde aggressus, nec multo post Aufidenam vi cepit. Deinceps sunt castella
Vallis Regia, Civitella, Rocha; inter montes Opum et Pesculum
Asserulum[265] in Apennini iugo amnis Sarni fontibus subiectum.

42   At in litore maris sequitur Sentus fluvius in monte Palario
oriundus, cui in mediterraneis dextrorsum Atissa et Tornaricum
oppida adiacent, et Sentum inter ac proximum Asinellam fluvium
Sancti Stephani monasterium est in litore. Intus vero castella sunt
et oppida: Turrinum, Casale Burdinum, Polutrum, Sernium, Ca-
salangra, Pilicornum. Ad Asinallaeque sinistram in litore est Penna

Before reaching the next steep mountain, called Monte Pallano, 41
one comes upon a town named Archi beside the Sangro. On
Monte Pallano itself there are towns and castles, Bomba, Colledi-
mezzo, and across a stream, Monteferrante, followed by Pietraferrazzana. Further up the Sangro there are likewise many towns and
castles, which I shall list in order as we move toward the source:
Castel di Pilo looming over Pietraferrazzana, and then Città Bu-
cello. Then there are Pescopennataro, S. Angelo del Pesco, and
Castel del Giudice, famous in the region for the memory of Jacopo
Caldora, one of the great military captains of our time, who was
born in this town.[112] Further up to the left is the town of Capracotta on a steep hill, and further inland in a low valley the town of
Agnone lies up against the Maiella; called Aquilonia by the ancients, it is now the chief town in the area. Then comes S. Pietro
Avellana, and later the fine town known as Castel di Sangro, on
the stream of the river Sangro itself. It is notable for various
handicrafts, especially blacksmithery: the smiths make iron tools
of every sort, both big and small, of such a high standard that in
terms of beauty and cost they are as good as, if not better than,
silverware of like dimensions. Above Castel di Sangro, the town of
Alfedena also lies on the Sangro.[113] Livy in Book X writes that
"The consul Cn. Fulvius fought a famous battle near Bovianum.
He then attacked and captured Bovianum, and not long afterward
Aufidena."[114] Next there are castles Villetta Barrea, Civitella Alfedena, Rocca; up in the mountains there is Opi, and Pescasseroli
on the Apennine ridge below the source of the river Sangro.

Next on the coast, meanwhile, comes the river Osento, which 42
rises on Monte Pallano. On the right of the Osento in the interior
are the towns of Atessa and Tornareccio. On the shore between
the Osento and the next river, the Sinello, there is the abbey of S.
Stefano in Rivomare.[115] Inland are the following towns and castles,
Torino di Sangro, Casalbordino, Pollutri, Scerni, Casalanguida,
Pilicorvo. On the left of the Sinello on the coast is the castle of

castellum, superiusque Vastum Aimonis nobile et vetus oppidum, quod prisci dixere Histonium. Idque theatri vetustissimi vestigiis et palatio est ornatum, quod Iacobus Caudola (ut in ea ora) superbissimum aedificavit. Asinellaeque fluvio in mediterraneis dextrorsum adiacet Mons Dorisius[266] oppidulum, comitatus ampli titulo insignitum. Superiusque ad Asinellae fontem tendenti castella sunt obvia: Gipsum, Carpinonum, Basilica, Gelinum, et Tripalum. Deinceps Asinellae proximus est in litore Trinius amnis, 'portuosus' a Plinio appellatus. Sinistrorsum vero Trinius habet Montem Nigrum oppidum quatuor milia passuum a mari et totidem ab ipso fluvio semotum. Superiusque sunt Castellutium, Rochavivara, Triventumque[267] nobile oppidum comitatus ampli titulum ditionemque habens, quod nunc Antonius, Iacobo genitus, Caudola et ipse fortissimus ductor possidet. Inde sunt Salcitum, Fossa Caeca, Bagnodum,[268] et Civitas Nova. Deinceps in ipsius Trinii amnis ortum montes altissimi Apennino continuantur, quibus in montibus castella sunt rara[269] et ipsa populis infrequentata.[270]

43   Post Trinium amnem Tifernus Samnitium in mare Adriaticum ultimus illabitur, qui fluvius apud Bovianum urbem vetustissimam in monte item Tiferno habet originem. De quo monte Livius, in decimo: 'Volumnius in Samnio interim res gerit. Samnitiumque exercitum in Tifernum montem compulsum non deterritus iniquitate loci fundit fugatque.' Est Tiferno[271] amni ad dexteram oppidum Termole mari proximum, quam Guido Ravennas Interamniam vult fuisse dictam, ut locus videatur fuisse in quo magnus philosophus Plato libros *De ideis* scripsit, quos in locis Italiae eius orae et in urbe Interamnia illum scripsisse constat. Intus octavo a mari milliario amni Tiferno ad mille passus haeret Guilliniacum oppidum nobile. Et superius octavo item milliario est Guardia

Penna, and higher up Vasto d'Ammone, a fine old town which the
ancients called Histonium. The town is notable for the remains of
an ancient theater and for a palace built by Jacopo Caldora, which
is magnificent by the standards of the region. Inland on the right
of the Sinello lies the little town of Monteodorisio, which enjoys
the grand title of "county." Higher up, as one proceeds to the
source of the Sinello, one encounters the castles of Gissi, Carpi-
neto Sinello, Basilica, Guilmi, and Tripalo. Next to the Sinello on
the coast there follows the river Trigno, which Pliny says is "well
provided with harbors."[116] On the left of the Trigno is Montenero
di Bisaccia, a town four miles from the sea and four miles from the
river. Further up are Castelluccio, Roccavivara, and the fine town
of Trivento, which enjoys the title and rights of an ample "county."
It is held by Jacopo's son Antonio Caldora, himself a valiant captain. Then there are Salcito, Fossacesia, Bagnoli del Trigno, and
Civitanova del Sannio. Then come mountains, the highest in the
Apennines, which stretch without interruption to the source of
the river Trigno; in these mountains the castles are sparse and
sparsely populated.

After the Trigno, the last river of Samnium to flow into the   43
Adriatic is the Biferno. The river originates near the ancient city
of Boiano on the mountain likewise called Biferno.[117] Of this
mountain Livy writes in Book X: "Volumnius is waging war at the
same time in Samnium, where, having driven the Samnite army
up Mount Tifernus, he routs and scatters them, undeterred by the
difficulties of the ground."[118] To the right of the Biferno is the
town of Termoli on the sea, which Guido of Ravenna claims was
called Interamnia.[119] So it seems that this was the place where the
great philosopher Plato wrote his books *On Forms*, a work which
he is generally supposed to have written in this part of Italy and in
the city of Interamnia.[120] Eight miles inland from the sea lies the
notable town of Guglionesi, a mile from the Biferno. And higher
up, another eight miles from Guglionesi, is Guardialfiera. Then

Alferi dicta. Inde Luparia, Carchabotatium, Lucitum, Lumesa-
num, Castrum Pignani, Rochetta,[272] Casale Riparanda, Lispine-
tum, Tornaquisium, et supremo (ut diximus) loco Bovianum, quae
urbs ditissima et paene omnium totius Samnii primaria aliquando
fuit habita. Livius enim, Libro nono: 'Consules, egregia victoria
parta, protinus inde ad Bovianum oppugnandum legiones ducunt
ibique hiberna egerunt.' Et infra: 'Inde victor exercitus Bovianum
ductus. Caput[273] hoc erat Pentriorum[274] Samnitum, longe ditissimum atque opulentissimum armis virisque. Spe praedae milites
accensi oppido potiuntur. Praedae plus paene[275] quam ex omni
Samnio umquam egestum,[276] benigneque omnis militi concessa.'
Et infra: cum Bovianum rebellasset, 'Cn.[277] Fulvii consulis clara
pugna ad Bovianum fuit. Bovianum inde aggressus nec ita multo
post Aufidenam[278] vi cepit.'

44   Sed iam finis adest Samnitium regionis, quae a Troento ad Tifernum amnem Apulis continentem Apennino et mari Supero
(sive Adriatico) concluditur, quamque nunc Aprutium (ut diximus) corrupto a Praetutinis verbo appellant. Ad aliam transeundum est partem Samnitium qui Transapenninum incoluere. Diffi-
ciliorem vero habet haec regio ceteris omnibus descriptionem, non
solum quod multis abundat rebus in ea gestis, verum quia haec
sola Apenninum hincinde complexa est, ut flumina quibus dividi-
turque[279] designaturque proxima regio Campania, prius dimidiata
in montibus, hinc[280] ipsi Samnio post in campos deducta, Campaniae sint attribuenda. Habebit tamen id commodi ipsa descriptio,
quod faciliorem reddet Campaniae descriptionem, quia quae Samnium ad hanc partem in montibus terminant flumina, eadem
quoque Campaniam in mediterraneis et ad mare complectuntur.

come Lupara, Castelbottaccio, Lucito, Limosano, Castropignano, Roccaspromonte, Casalciprano, Spinete, Tornaquisio,[121] and furthest up, as I mentioned, Boiano, once a very wealthy city and reckoned to be the most important of pretty much all the Samnite towns. For Livy in Book IX: "The consuls, who had won a brilliant victory, at once marched away to lay siege to Bovianum, where they remained in winter quarters."[122] And below: "From there he led his victorious army to Bovianum. This was the capital of the Pentrian Samnites, a very wealthy city and very rich in arms and men. The hope of plunder spurred the soldiers on to take the town. There was almost more booty carried out than was ever collected from all the rest of Samnium, and all of it was generously made over to the soldiers."[123] And below: after Boviano had rebelled, "The consul Cn. Fulvius fought a famous battle near Bovianum. He then attacked and captured Bovianum, and not long afterward Aufidena."[124]

But now we have reached the end of the region of Samnium,   44 extending from the Tronzo to the Biferno (which forms the border with Apulia), and bounded by the Apennines and the Upper Sea or Adriatic. This region they now call Abruzzo, the name being corrupted, as I said, from the Praetutini. Now we must turn to another part of the territory of the Samnites, those that dwelt on the other side of the Apennines. This region is in fact more challenging to describe than all the rest, not just because so many historical events took place here, but because this region alone embraces the Apennines on both sides, so that the rivers by which Campania (the next region) is articulated and defined, though they are first split up in the mountains and then descend into the plains from Samnium itself, are nevertheless to be given to Campania. But such a survey will have the advantage of making the description of Campania easier, because the rivers that form the boundaries in the mountains of this part of Samnium also define Campania, both inland and on the coast. For example, the river

Liris itaque (nunc Gaurianus) duos in Samnio habet fontes: unum ad Capistrellum, in Apennino castellum[281] et octavo supra Soram milliario; alterum ad Postam castellum quatuor a Sora milibus distans. Fonsque hic aquis copiosissimus esse videtur ille, quem Plinius asserit videri a lacu Fucino originem trahere. Duo hi rami cum infra Soram coeant, insulam efficiunt in qua sunt castella Peschum, Posta, et Lobrottulum.

45   Soram autem vetusti praesentisque nominis urbem Samnium primam hac in parte habet, de qua Livius in septimo: 'L. Genucio,[282] Ser.[283] Cornelio consulibus, Soram atque Albam coloniae ductae. Sora agri Vestini fuerat, sed possederant Samnites. Eo quatuor milia hominum missa.' Quod autem Soram dicit Livius fuisse agri Vestini hac ratione certum est, quia — cum Vestina urbs fuerit ad Lirim[284] in campis, qui nunc Sessae dicuntur, sicut in Campaniae descriptione dicemus — quicquid ab ostio Liris, quo in mare defluit, ad Soram usque ipsi adiacebat fluvio Vestinorum vocabulo est comprensum. Unde Lucanus Lirim describens dicit: 'Vestinis impulsus aquis.' Et Suessa Pometia, quae nunc est Sessa, Vestinorum est appellata. Cum vero Sorani ad suos Samnites defecissent, sic de eis dicit Livius: 'Mutata tamen belli sedes est ad Soram, et ex Samnio Apuliaque traductae legiones. Sora ad Samnites defecerat, interfectis colonis Romanorum. Quo cum prior Romanus exercitus ad ulciscendam[285] civium necem recuperandamque coloniam magnis itineribus pervenisset, sparsi per vias speculatores sequi legiones Samnitium nec iam procul abesse alii super alios nuntiant. Obviam itum hosti atque ad Lautulas ancipiti proelio dimicatum est.' Soram inde reditum. Novique consules M. Poetilius, C. Sulpicius. Quia[286] per difficilem urbis situm Sora-

Liris (nowadays the Garigliano) has two sources in Samnium, one at Capistrello, a castle in the Apennines eight miles beyond Sora, the other at Posta Fibreno, a castle four miles from Sora. It seems that the latter source with its great abundance of waters is the one that Pliny says originates in Lake Fucino.[125] When these two branches meet below Sora, they form an island on which are the castles of Pescosolido, Posta Fibreno, and Lobrottolo.

The first city in this part of Samnium is Sora, so named by ancients and moderns alike. Livy says of it in Book VII: "In the consulship of Lucius Genucius and Servius Cornelius, colonies were established at Sora and Alba. Sora had belonged to the territory of the Vestini, but the Samnites had taken possession of it; to this place were sent four thousand men."[126] Livy's statement that Sora was a city of the Ager Vestinus can be relied on: since there was a city Vestina beside the Garigliano on the present plain of Sessa (as will be mentioned in the description of Campania), all the land from the mouth of the Garigliano, where it flows into the sea, all the way to Sora is included in the term "Vestinian." Accordingly when Lucan describes the Liris, he says: "driven by the waters of the Vestini,"[127] and the present-day town of Sessa was called Suessa Pometia of the Vestini. In fact, when the Sorani had gone over to their kindred Samnites, Livy has this to say of them: "The seat of war now shifted, and legions were transferred from Samnium and Apulia into Sora, which had gone over to the Samnites after putting to death the Roman colonists. The Roman army, by a series of forced marches, undertaken to avenge their slaughtered fellow citizens and regain the colony, came first upon the ground. But the scouts who had scattered out along the roads reported one after the other that the Samnite legions were in pursuit and were already close at hand. Whereupon the Romans marched to meet the enemy and an indecisive battle was fought near Lautulae."[128] Then the Romans returned to Sora. The new consuls were M. Poetilius and C. Sulpicius. A deserter from Sora

45

nus transfuga decem Romanos in arcem duxit et, civibus per noc-
tem refractis vi portis fugientibus, ingressus est Romanus exercitus, trecenti viginti quinque, qui omnium consensu designabantur
nefandae colonorum caedis et defectionis auctores, vincti, Romam
ducti, et virgis in foro caesi et securi percussi summo gaudio plebis — cuius maxime intererat tutam ubicumque in coloniis multitudinem esse. Soram vero cum post praedictam cladem deducta a
Romanis fuisset nova colonia et diu satis floruisset, Federicus secundus imperator Germanicus per tempora Gregorii noni pontificis Romani eam destruxit. Nihilominus ipsa, nunc ducatus titulo
et duce optimo litterisque decorato ornata, mediocris oppidi populum divitiasque habet.

46   Insulae, quam bifurcatus in Samnio Liris (sicut ostendimus)
efficit, montes supereminent altissimi ad Apennini iuga perti-
nentes, in quibus nulla est hominum habitatio. Eisque dextrorsum
adiacet plaga (ut in ea montium asperitate) amoenissima, cui nunc
Cominum est appellatio. Montibus enim circumsaepta altissimis,
castella habet ad octo populis frequentia: Vicalvum, Alvetum,
Sanctum Donatum, Septem Fratres, Picinestum, Galinarium et
Casaliverum. Eam vero plagam vetustissimi Cominium appellavere
ab urbe eius nominis cuius locum incolae nunc ignorant. De qua
Livius, in decimo: Inde Carvilius[287] ad Cominium captum. Caesa
quatuor milia octuaginta. Accepta[288] in fidem quindecim milia
quatuor centum. Sed hac eadem in ora montibus dextrorsum subiecta est Atina urbs vetustissima, secus quam Melfa fluvius labitur
ex Apennino oriundus et apud Fregellas in Lirim defluens. Estque
Atina, quam Vergilius facit arma Aeneae fabricasse: 'quinque adeo
magnae positis incudibus urbes tela novant, Atina potens.' Et Li-

led ten Romans through the city's difficult terrain and into the citadel: the citizens fled at night through the gates that they had battered down, and the Roman army entered the city. And so 325 men, who were universally agreed to have been the ringleaders of the rebellion and to have instigated the dreadful murder of the colonists, were taken to Rome in chains, and flogged and beheaded in the Forum, to the delight of the plebs, who were most nearly concerned for the general safety of the masses that were sent out to form colonies.[129] Though the Romans sent out a new colony to Sora after the slaughter described above and it prospered for quite a long time, the German Emperor Frederick II destroyed it in the time of Pope Gregory IX. Notwithstanding, the city of Sora, now raised to the title of duchy under a duke of fine literary accomplishments, enjoys the population and wealth of a middling town.[130]

High mountains overlook the island formed by the splitting of   46
the Liris in Samnium, as I mentioned above.[131] These mountains, which are part of the Apennine range, are without human habitation. To the right of them there is a most pleasant stretch of land—considering the ruggedness of the mountain landscape—which is now called Comino. Shut in on all sides by high mountains, it has some eight castles, all well populated: Vicalvi, Alvito, San Donato, Settefrati, Picinisco, Gallinaro, Casalvieri. The ancients named the stretch of land Cominium after a city of that name, whose location is unknown to the present inhabitants. Livy writes about the city in Book X: Then Carvilius moved on to capture Cominium. Four thousand eight hundred men were slain. Fifteen thousand four hundred were received in surrender.[132] To the right at the foot of the mountains in the same area is the very ancient city of Atina, beside which runs the river Melfa, rising in the Apennines and flowing down into the Liris at Fregellae. Vergil has Atina taking part in the crafting of the arms of Aeneas: "Five great cities, no less, ready anvils and forge new weapons: mighty

vius in nono: C. Poetilius dictator 'cum audiisset arcem Fregella-
nam ab Samnitibus captam, omisso Boviano, ad Fregellas pergit.
Unde nocturna Samnitium fuga sine certamine, receptis Fregellis
praesidioque valido imposito, in Campaniam reditum maxime ad
Nolam[289] armis repetendam,' quae capta est a C. Cassio consule, a
quo etiam Atina et Calatia[290] captae.

47   Descendendo ad infima praedictae regionis montanae, fluvio
Melfae sub Casaliveri castello sinistrorsum haeret Schiavi oppidu-
lum. Inferius celso item in loco est Arpinum fama celeberrimum
M. Tullii Ciceronis et C. Marii, quos habuit gloriosissimos cives.
De qua Livius, in nono: 'eo anno Sora et Arpinum recepta a Samnitibus.' Et Libro decimo: 'Arpinatibus et Trebulanis civitas data.'
Et sub Arpino Melfae fluvio sinistrorsum proxima sunt castella
Fontana et Arce. At sub Sora, ubi bina Liris capita coeunt, est
Insula oppidum ab ipsis duobus fluviis circumdatum, quod maiores Interamniam appellavere. Et secundum eius fluvii decursum
castella Turris, Campus Latus, et Insuletta inveniuntur. Est etiam
nunc paulo superior parva nunc (sicut semper fuit) insula magno
eloquentibus gaudio invisenda, apud quam natus est — et non Ar-
pini — M. Cicero: sic enim ipse in suis *Legibus* scriptum reliquit:
'Sed ventum in insulam est: hac vero nihil est amoenius. Ut
enim[291] hoc quasi rostro finditur Fibrenus et divisus aequaliter in
duas partes latera haec adluit, rapideque dilapsus cito in unum
confluit. Et tantum complectitur quod satis sit modicae palaestrae
loci. Quo[292] effecto, tamquam id habuerit operis ac muneris ut
hanc nobis efficeret[293] sedem ad disputandum, statim praecipitat
in Lirim.[294] Et quasi in patriciam familiam[295] venerit, amittit no-

Atina . . ."[133] Livy writes in Book IX: The dictator Gaius Poetilius, "hearing that the citadel of Fregellae was captured by the
Samnites, raised the siege of Bovianum and proceeded to Fregellae. Having got possession of the place without a struggle after the
Samnites fled in the night, he installed a strong garrison there, and
leaving Fregellae, marched back into Campania, chiefly for the
purpose of winning back Nola by force of arms."[134] Nola was captured by the consul Gaius Cassius, who had captured Atina and
Calatia.[135]

As one reaches down into the lowest part of that mountainous   47
region, the little town of Schiavi lies on the left of the river Melfa,
below the castle of Casalvieri. Further down, though likewise sited
on a high hill, is Arpino, celebrated for the fame of her glorious
citizens Cicero and Marius. Of Arpino Livy writes in Book IX:
"That year, Sora and Arpino were won back from the Samnites."[136] And in Book X: "Citizenship was granted to the men of
Arpino and Trebula."[137] To the left below Arpino on the river
Melfa are the castles of Fontana Liri and Arce. Below Sora, where
the two branches of the Liris join up again, is the town of Isola di
Liri with the two streams on either side, called Interamnia by our
ancestors. On the lower reaches of this river are found the castles
of Torre Saracena, Campolato, and Isoletta d'Arce. A little further
up, there is an island, small now as it always has been, which can
only be looked upon by lovers of eloquence with great joy, for Cicero was born on this island, and not in Arpinum, as he himself
records in his work *On the Laws*: "But here we are on the island;
surely nothing could be more lovely. It cuts the Fibrenus like the
beak of a ship, and the stream, divided into two equal parts,
bathes these banks, flows swiftly past, and then comes quickly together again, leaving only enough space for a wrestling ground of
moderate size. Then after accomplishing this, as if its only duty
and function were to provide us with a seat for our discussion, it
immediately plunges into the Liris, and, as if it had entered a pa-

men obscurius. Lirimque multo gelidiorem facit. Nec enim ullum hoc frigidius flumen[296] attigi, cum ad multa accesserim, ut vix pede temptare id possim quod in *Phaedro*[297] Platonis facit Socrates.' Et infra secundo Libro: 'Quia si verum dicimus, haec est mea et huius fratris mei germana[298] patria: hic[299] enim orti stirpe antiquissima[300] sumus; hic sacra; hic genus; hic maiorum multa vestigia. Quid plura? Hanc vides villam, ut nunc quidem est, lautius aedificatam patris nostri studio. Qui cum esset infirma valetudine, hic fere aetatem egit in litteris. Sed hoc ipso in loco, cum avus viveret et antiquo more parva esset villa (ut illa Curiana in Sabinis), me scito esse natum. Quare id est[301] nescioquid quod[302] latet in animo ac sensu meo, quo me plus hic locus fortasse delectet.'

48   Succedit ordine describendus a nobis fluvius apud Pontem Corvum, ubi olim Fregellas fuisse diximus, cadens in Lirim et apud montis Casini radices labens. Cui fluvio haud longe remotum et Casino ad quinque milia proximum est campestre oppidum gloria Arpino nullatenus cedens Aquinum, Thoma primum sanctissimo atque doctissimo ecclesiae doctore, et Pescennio[303] Nigro imperatore Romano certe praestantissimo, ac Iuvenale poeta satirico civibus decoratum. Gregorius quoque septimus pontifex Romanus anno salutis tertio septuagesimo supra millesimum Roberto Guiscardo Apuliae et Calabriae ducatum in Aquino oppido solemniter concessit.

49   Ultra[304] Aquinum hinc est sinistrorsum Rocha Sicca[305] oppidum, inde celso in monte ubi urbs olim fuit Casinensis, est monasterium Casinense a sancto celebrique monachorum patre Benedicto aedificatum, quamquam ea quae nunc exstant ipsius

trician family, loses its less famous name, and makes the water of the Liris much colder. For, though I have visited many, I have never come upon a river which was colder than this one; so that I could hardly bear to try its temperature with my foot, as Socrates did in Plato's *Phaedrus*."[138] And below, in Book II: "To tell you the truth, this is really my own fatherland, and that of my brother, for we are descended from a very ancient family of this district; here are our ancestral sacred rites and the origin of our race; here are many memorials of our forefathers. What more need I say? Here you see our homestead as it is now—rebuilt and extended by my father's care; for, as he was an invalid, he spent most of his life in study here. It was in fact on this very spot, I would have you know, that I was born, while my grandfather was alive and when the house, according to the old custom, was small, like that of Curius in the Sabine country.[139] For this reason a lingering attachment for the place abides in my mind and heart, and causes me perhaps to feel a greater pleasure in it."[140]

We have next to describe the river at Pontecorvo (formerly the 48 site of Fregellae, as I mentioned), which runs down into the Liris and flows along the base of Montecassino.[141] Not far from the river and about five miles from Cassino is a town on the plain that by no means yields to Arpino in renown: Aquino, which glories in her citizens, principally Thomas, the saintly and learned Doctor of the Church, and then the outstanding Roman emperor Pescennius Niger, and the satiric poet Juvenal. It was also at Aquino that Pope Gregory VII solemnly ceded the Duchy of Apulia and Calabria to Robert Guiscard in 1073.

Beyond Aquino on the one side is the town of Roccasecca (on 49 the left), and on the other, on a high hill where the city of Casinum used to be, is the monastery of Montecassino. This was founded by the famous saint and father of monasticism Benedict, though the buildings that stand there now are not those which the good father Benedict himself erected, because shortly after his

monasterii aedificia non sunt illa quae bonus ipse pater Benedictus exstruxit, quod paulo post illius obitum Longobardi omnia funditus demoliti sunt. Contulit se ad id monasterium Tothila rex Ostrogothorum, fama ductus sanctimoniae[306] tanti viri et temptare volens si — quod sibi dictum erat — Benedictus spiritu prophetico occulta cognosceret. Sese famulum indumento mentitus alium praemisit qui regio ornatu et apparatu regem Tothilam simularet. Quem recognitum sanctus abbas cum placido vultu ad ceterum famulatum reiecisset, regem digito significatum (ut erat sordide indutus) ad se in monasterii vestibulum vocavit. Nec tamen haec et alia sanctitatis signa, quae Longobardi a Benedicto viderunt, adeo eos continere potuerunt quin, praescito et per sanctum ipsum[307] monachis praedicto Dei iudicio, crudelis et effera gens praedicta celebre id coenobium diruerit.

50 Ad Casini quoque montis radices novum est oppidum Sanctus Germanus, a[308] sancti abbatis conditoris sui nomine appellatum, intra cuius moenia et per circuitum scatentes uberrimi fontes amnem augent quarto supra milliario apud oppidum Sanctum Eliam oriundum, qui tertius Lirim amnem in Samnitibus efficit. Isque amnis duodecim expletis passuum milibus, in maiorem Liris cursum apud castellum Pontem Corvum (sicut ostendimus) cadit. Urbs vero, quam fuisse diximus in Casino monte republica florente, fuit Romana colonia, de qua Livius in nono: Volsci Pontiam insulam sitam in conspectu litoris sui incoluerant. Et vicerunt ut Casinum deduceretur colonia, sicut factum est. Traditque Plinius, 'L. Crasso, C. Cassio Longino consulibus, Casini puerum factum ex virgine sub parentibus, iussuque haruspicum[309] deportatum[310] in insulam desertam.' Et Livius Libro XXII: imperat duci ut se in agrum Casinatem ducat edoctus a peritis[311] regionis si eum saltum occupasset exitum Romano ad opem ferendam sociis interclusu-

death they were all utterly razed by the Lombards.[142] The king of the Ostrogoths Totila betook himself to the monastery, led on by reports of the holiness of that great man and wanting to see if—as he had been told—Benedict with his prophetic inspiration knew things hidden from other men. He disguised himself in servant's clothes and sent on another ahead to pretend with his royal apparel and insignia that he was king Totila. But the saintly abbot recognized the imposter and with a calm expression turned him back to join Totila's other servants, pointing to the king, meanly dressed as he was, and beckoning him to come to him in the monastery atrium. And yet these tokens of sanctity, and others that the Lombards saw performed by Benedict, were of no avail in restraining that cruel and wild race from destroying the famous monastery, God's judgment on them having been foreseen and prophesied to the monks by the saint himself.[143]

At the foot of Montecassino there is also the modern town of 50 San Germano, named after the saintly abbot who founded it. Within its walls and all around it copious springs bubble up to swell the river that rises four miles further up at the town of Sant'Elia.[144] This is the third Samnite river that goes to make up the Liris. After a run of twelve miles, it joins the main channel of the Liris at the castle of Pontecorvo, as I mentioned.[145] The city of Casinum, which as I said was on Montecassino in the heyday of the Republic, was a Roman colony, of which Livy writes in Book IX: "The Volsci had settled on Ponza, an island situated within sight of their own coast. And they won the day in getting a colony sent out to Casinum, as in fact happened."[146] Pliny tells us that "in the consulship of Licinius Crassus and Gaius Cassius Longinus, a girl at Casinum was changed into a boy under the eyes of her parents, and on the order of the augurs was sent off to a desert island."[147] And Livy writes in Book XXII: Hannibal "ordered his guide to conduct him to the territory of Casinum, for he had been told by those who knew the country that if he occupied that pass

rum. Viam quoque[312] describens qua Hannibal ex Campania Romam petiit, sic habet in XXVI: per Suessulam Alifanumque et Casinatem agrum in viam Latinam ducit. Sub Casinum biduo stativa habita et passim populationes actae. Inde praeter Interamniam Aquinumque in Fregellanum agrum ad Lirim fluvium. Interamniam vero fuisse credimus ubi sub Sancto Germano ad duo milia passuum[313] eidem fluvio magnae ingentesque vetustorum operum ruinae continent. Et Fregellas fuisse quem nunc Pontem Corvum dicimus satis constat.

51   Ultimo supradicti Liris fonte[314] apud Sanctum Eliam oriundo, haud longe Vulturni amnis origo distat. Nam cum, intra XII milia passuum,[315] Vallem Rotundam et Aquam Fundatam oppidula ad Apenninum pergens post tergum reliquerit, Sancti Vincentii oppidum reperit, quod monasterio eiusdem nominis (a quo id accepit nomen) ad mille passus est proximum. Idque monasterium olim frequentia monachorum opumque affluentia et magnificentia aedificii celeberrimum omnibus paene nunc temporum malitia spoliatum est. Circumdatum vero est nascentis loco Vulturni fluviolo, quod[316] brevi cursu maximum a scatentibus circumquaque fontibus accipit incrementum. Isque amnis, superiore parte (sicut diximus) per Samnites delapsus, Campaniam postea in mediterraneis et maritimis paene dimidiatam[317] dividit. Qua ratione cum ab ostiis quibus in mare defluit nunc ex more nostro non liceat, descriptionem econtra a fonte[318] incipimus. Primum descendentes ad dexteram oppidum Vulturno adiacens Montaquillum inveniunt, post Rocham Ravimolam, deinde Sanctam Mariam de Oliveto. Deinceps obvium est Venafrum in Campaniae partibus describendum. In montibus autem Apennino contiguis, qui Vulturni amnis fonti

he could keep the Romans from marching to the aid of their allies."[148] In describing the route taken by Hannibal on his way from Campania to Rome, Livy also has this to say in Book XXVI: "He led his army along the Latin Way through the territory of Suessa, Allifae and Casinum. Before Casinum he remained encamped for two days, and ravaged the country in all directions. Then he passed by Interamnia and Aquinum into the territory of Fregellae at the river Liris."[149] I believe in fact that Interamnia was where huge and massive remains of ancient buildings border on the river Liris two miles below San Germano. It is well known that Fregellae was what we now call Pontecorvo.

The river Volturno originates not far from the ultimate source   51
of the river Liris at Sant'Elia, as discussed above. As the traveler into the Apennines leaves behind the villages of Vallerotonda and Aquafondata, after twelve miles he comes upon the town of Castel San Vincenzo, a mile from the monastery of the same name, which it lends to the town.[150] By the injuriousness of time this monastery, which was once celebrated for its great numbers of monks, its splendid wealth, and magnificent buildings, has now been almost completely despoiled. In the place where the Volturno rises, the monastery is surrounded by a stream which in a short space is greatly augmented by the springs that bubble up on all sides. The river Volturno flows through Samnium in its upper reaches, as I said, and then divides Campania almost in two, both inland and by the coast. For that reason, being unable to begin with the mouths of the river where it flows into the sea in my usual manner, I shall start the description at the opposite end, at the source. To begin with, travelers coming down along the right bank of the Volturno find the town of Montaquila sitting on the river, and then Roccaravindola, and after that Santa Maria Oliveto. Then one comes to Venafro, which is to be described under Campania. In the mountains adjoining the Apennines that overlook the source of the river Volturno to the right, there are the

dextrorsum supereminent, sunt castella Mons Niger et Rivus Frigidus. Et inferius[319] est Forulum vetusti nominis castellum. Postea
secundum Vulturni decursum descendentes Fornellum ipsi amni
ad tria milia passuum[320] proximum inveniunt: quod oppidum novi
nominis, populo opibusque plenum, vini praestantiam in regione
habet. Vulturnoque e regione Fornelli continet vallis, quam Porcinam appellant, in qua vetusti et (ut apparet) magni olim oppidi
ruinae conspiciuntur. Pauloque inferius Vulturnum influit amnis
ab Aesernia delapsus vetusta olim Romana colonia, de qua Livius
in belli Italici (sive Socialis) LXXII: 'Aesernia et Alba coloniae ab
Italis obsessae.' Ad eum vero Aeserniae fluvium paulo priusquam
in Vulturnum labatur, vestigia cernuntur ingentia urbis usque ad
fundamenta dirutae, quam fuisse constat Telesiam urbem Samnitium potentissimam, de qua Livius in XXII: 'Hannibal ex Hirpinis in Samnium transit. Beneventanum depopulatur agrum. Telesiam urbem capit.' Et in XXIIII: Fabius in Samnio oppida vi
recepit Compulteriam Telesiamque. Et Compulteria quidem Tele-
siae dextrorsum vicina fuit, in ea tamen proclivior loca quae nunc
Capriatam[321] et Pratum appellant ac Mastratum.

52   Deinceps Beneventana sequitur ora totius Samnii primaria et
ceteris in[322] Italia rerum gestarum multitudine ac magnitudine
copiosior, quae montes habet[323] Apenninum sua celsitudine su-
perantes, rivis alicubi[324] rupibusque omnino insuperabilibus[325] se-
paratos. Est tamen fluviis, torrentibus, lacu, fontibusque[326] irrigua.
Protenditur vero haec ipsa Samnii pars, si Apennini iugum sequi-
mur, milibus passuum octoginta ab ipsis Vulturni fontibus ad Si-
laris Lucaniae fluvii ac limitis ortum. Et qui[327] ipsi insunt orae
fluvii praeter admodum paucos unico amne Sabbato excepti defluunt in Vulturnum ut Sabbatum parte infima stipes ceteri amnes
arboris rami esse videantur. Unde cogimur ab ipso incipientes sti-

castles of Montenero Val Cocchiara and Riofreddo. Lower down is Forlì di Sannio, an old-established castle. After that, continuing down the course of the Volturno one finds Fornelli about three miles from the river: this is a modern town, full of people and money and with the best wine in the region. Opposite Fornelli a valley known as Valle Porcina abuts the Volturno, where the ruins of an ancient and seemingly once great town are visible. A little further down a river joins the Volturno which flows down from Isernia, once an ancient Roman colony, of which Livy writes in Book LXXII of the Italic (or Social) War: "The colonies of Aesernia and Alba were put under siege by the Italians."[151] Shortly before this river joins the Volturno at Isernia, the vast remains of a city razed to its foundations can be seen, which are generally supposed to be those of the powerful Samnite city of Telesia, on which Livy writes in Book XXII: "Hannibal left the territory of the Hirpini and crossed into Samnium. He devastated the territory of Beneventum and captured the city of Telesia."[152] And he writes in Book XXIV that Fabius recovered by force the towns of Compulteria and Telesia in Samnium.[153] Compulteria did neighbor Telesia to the right, but lower down the slope, toward the places now called Capriati a Volturno, Pratella and Mastrati.

There follows the territory of Benevento, the chief district of Samnium and richer than the rest of Italy in the number and importance of the events that have taken place there. Its mountains surpass the Apennines in height, and they are in parts riven by streams and unscalable crags. Yet it is very well watered by rivers, torrents, a lake, and springs. If we follow the Apennine chain, this particular part of Samnium stretches for eighty miles from the wellsprings of the Volturno to the source of the Sele, a river that forms the border with Lucania. With very few exceptions, all the rivers of this district are tributaries of the Sabato alone, then flowing into the Volturno, so that the lower reaches of the Sabato look like a tree trunk and the other rivers its branches. We are

52

pite ramos, qui ad dexteram ascendendo inveniuntur primum, postea eos qui sinistrorsum Apennino dilabuntur ex superiore instituto nostro describere, intraque eam arboris amnium descriptionem quicquid regionis Samnitium nobis est reliquum comprehendemus. Attingamque prius eos amnes qui dextra[328] Sabbati confluentes[329] quam longe ab Apennino in mediterraneis oriuntur.

53   Primusque[330] post Aeserniensem Pratellus fluvius, a proximo eius nominis oppido appellatus, ex infimis Mathesii montis radicibus ortum habet. Nam Mathesium Apennini promontorium, et in sublime surgens et longe in[331] mediterranea lateque diffusum, sterile ut plurimum atque petrosum, unico ad hanc partem castello habitatum est Gallo, Pratelli amnis fonti proximo. Fuitque mons in quo primarii Samnitium habitavere viri fortes, utpote montani: unde 'Montesii' prius appellabantur a quibus, facta verbi corruptela, Mathesium dicitur promontorium. Hi autem montes sunt[332] de[333] quibus habet Livius IX:[334] 'Samnites ea tempestate in montibus vicatim[335] habitantes campestria et maritima loca contempto cultu molliore atque[336] (ut evenit) loci dissimilitudine ipsi montani atque agrestes depopulabantur.[337] Quae regio si fida Samnitibus fuisset, haud pervenire Arpos Romanus quivisset exercitus.' Sub Mathesio lacus est decem milia passuum[338] circuitu complexus, ad cuius inferiora parum a Vulturno distantia Aylanum est oppidum, inde Sancti Angeli castellum de Rupe Canina appellatum. A quo haud longe recedit Pes Montis oppidum colli superpositum[339] arduo, ex quo fluvius oritur, brevi quatuor milium cursu secus Allifas urbem decidens in Vulturnum, ut eum[340] collem esse oporteat illum in quo Fabius Maximus, Hannibalem insecutus, arduo consedit loco, sicut Livius in XXIII per haec verba habet: 'Hanni-

accordingly obliged to begin with the trunk and describe first the branches that one finds on the right going upstream, then the branches that descend from the Apennines on the left, in line with our earlier practice. I shall include in this description of the river network the parts of the Samnite region that I have not yet touched on. I shall first treat the rivers that join the Sabato from the right before going on to those that rise in the interior far from the Apennines.

The first river after the river of Isernia is the Pratello, so called 53 from the town that lies next to it, springing from the very base of Mount Matese.[154] Matese is a spur of the Apennines, rising up high and spreading far and wide into the interior, barren for the most part and rocky. Its habitations comprise a solitary castle, Gallo, which is situated beside the source of the river Pratello. It was the mountain where the chief Samnites used to live, tough men as mountain folk tend to be. From this circumstance they were first known as "Montesii," from a corruption of which the spur is named "Matesium." These are the mountains about which Livy writes in Book IX: "The Samnites lived at that time in villages in the mountains, and they would ravage the lowlands and the coast, since as rough mountain people they despised the way of life there as soft, and held the very different landscape in contempt, as often happens. If those parts had remained faithful to the Samnites, the Roman army could scarcely have managed to get as far as Arpa."[155] Under Matese there is a lake ten miles in circumference. Toward its lower reaches lies the town of Ailano close to the Volturno river, and then the castle of Sant'Angelo d'Alife, known as the Castello di Rupecanina. Not far from Sant'Angelo on top of a steep hill is the town of Piedemonte Matese, where a river rises that flows down a short four-mile course past the city of Alife into the Volturno. This, then, ought to be the hill where Fabius Maximus took up position on the heights as he pursued Hannibal, as Livy says in Book XXIII in the following words:

bal transducto per saltum et quibusdam in ipso saltu hostibus[341] oppressis in agro Allifano posuit castra.' 'Fabius quoque movit castra, transgressusque saltum super Allifas loco alto ac communito consedit.' Et de Allifis in IX: 'Dum haec in Etruria geruntur, consul alter C. Martius Rutilius Allifas de Samnitibus vi cepit.' Et infra: 'Fabius consul ad urbem Allifas cum Samnitium exercitu, signis collatis, conflixit.[342] Minime ambigua res fuit. Fusi hostes atque in castra compulsi. Postera[343] die, deditio fieri coepta et pacti qui Samnitium forent[344] cum singulis vestimentis emitterentur. Hi omnes sub iugum missi. Sociis Samnitium nihil cautum. Ad septem milia sub corona venerunt. Qui se civem Hernicum diceret, in custodia habitus.' Fluvius inde sequitur supra[345] Petram Roiam oppidum ex Mathesio oriundus, Cusanum Correctium[346] habens oppositum, qui prope Puianellum[347] oppidum labitur in Vulturnum. Habetque sinistrorsum is fluvius oppidum Faviculum et Loium in mediterraneis propinquum.

54   Sed iam ad Sabbati stipitem est perventum. Is amnis primo dextrorsum Seritella augetur ex Caudinis montibus oriundo, et in valle quam Seritella toto efficit cursu haec sunt oppida: Castrum Potonis, Pesolia, Mons Saticulus, de quo Vergilius, in VII: 'Saticulus asper,' et Livius XXIII: Marcellus 'a Casilino Calatiam[348] petit. Inde, Vulturno amne traiecto, per agrum Saticulanum Trebulanumque super Suessulam pervenit Nolam.' Et superius vallis est Caudina, in qua apparent vetustae urbis Caudii fundamenta. Nec longe abest Harpadium nunc, quod prius Hirpinum dicebatur. Id oppidum furculis proximum est Caudinis clade Romanorum insig-

"Hannibal had conveyed his army through the pass — surprising some of his enemies in the pass itself — and had pitched his camp in the district of Allifae."[156] "Fabius, too, broke camp, and marching through the pass established himself in a lofty and naturally strong position above Allifae."[157] On Allifae itself he writes in Book IX: "While this was going on in Etruria, the other consul Gaius Marcius Rutilius took Allifae from the Samnites by storm."[158] And below: "The consul Fabius fought near the city of Allifae a pitched battle with the army of the Samnites. The result was anything but doubtful, as the enemy were routed and driven into their camp. Next day they began to surrender. The Samnites among them bargained to be dismissed in their tunics. All these were sent under the yoke. The allies of the Samnites were protected by no guarantee, and were sold into slavery, to the number of seven thousand. Those who said they were Hernician citizens were kept under guard."[159] Next comes a river that rises in the Matese above the town of Pietraroia opposite Cusano Mutri, and flows into the Volturno near the town of Puglianello. The river has on the left the town of Faicchio, and nearby Gioia Sannitica further inland.

Now we have come to the "trunk" of the Sabato. The Seritella, which rises in the Caudine mountains, is the first river to flow into the Sabato from the right, and in the valley that the Seritella forms along its entire course there are these towns, Castelpoto, Pesoglia, Mount Saticula, which Vergil calls in Book VII "the rugged Saticulan."[160] And Livy, in Book XXIII: Marcellus "went to Caiatia from Casilinum,[161] and thence, after crossing the river Volturnus, made his way to Nola through the territories of Saticula and Trebia, above Suessula and through the mountains."[162] Further up is the Caudine valley, where the foundations of the ancient city of Caudium can be seen, and not far away is the present-day Arpaia, which used to be called Hirpinum. This town is close to the Caudine Forks, famous for the disastrous defeat of

54

nibus. De hisque duobus locis sic habet Livius, in IX: 'Samnites eo anno consulem C.[349] Pontium, Herennii filium, habuerunt.' 'Exercitu educto, circa Caudium quam potest occultissime ducit. Inde ad Caiaciam,[350] ubi iam consules Romanos castraque esse audiebat, milites decem pastorum habitu misit, pecoraque diversos alium alibi haud procul Romanis pascere iubet, praecipiens ut ubi inciderint in praedatores, idem omnibus sermo constet: legiones Samnitium in Apulia esse; Luceriam omnibus copiis circumsedere, nec procul esse[351] quin vi capiant.' 'Saltus duo alti, angusti silvosique montibus circa perpetuis inter se iuncti. Latet inter eos satis patens clausus in medio campus herbidus aquosusque, per quem medium iter est. Sed antequam venias ad eum, intrandae primo angustiae sunt. Et aut eadem qua te insinuaveris retro via repetenda aut, si ire porro pergas, per alium saltum altiorem impeditioremque evadendum.' T. Veturius Calvinus, Spurius Postumius consules erant. Item Livius de Hirpino, Libro XXIII: 'Hannibal post Cannensem pugnam ex Apulia in Samnium moverat, accitus in Hirpinos a Statio pollicente se Compsam traditurum.' Item infra: Eadem aestate Marcellus a Nola, quam praesidio obtinebat, crebras excursiones in agrum Hirpinum et Samnites Caudinos fecit.' Et infra: 'Hannibal profectus Arpis ad Tifata.' Et Livius item in bello Sociali Libro LXXV: 'Lucius Sulla Hirpinos domuit. Samnites fudit.' *Et ne tam in orbe celebrem notitiam ratio habenda cursus fluviorum faciat his qui non viderint obscuriorem,*[352] absunt haec loca a Benevento (fluviis ubi expedit transmissis) decimo, vallis Caudina milliario, et furculae quarto decimo. Ad alteramque vallis

the Romans there. Of these two places, Livy has the following to say in Book IX: "In that year the Samnites had as consul C. Pontius, son of Herennius."[163] Pontius "led his army out and encamped with all possible secrecy in the vicinity of Caudium. Thence he dispatched in the direction of Calatia,[164] where he heard that the Roman consuls were already in camp, ten soldiers in the guise of shepherds, with orders to graze their flocks — scattered here and there — at no great distance from the Romans. On encountering pillagers, they were all to tell one story, namely, that the Samnite levies were in Apulia, where they were laying siege with all their forces to Luceria, and were on the point of taking it by assault."[165] "Two deep defiles, narrow and wooded, are connected by an unbroken range of mountains on either hand; shut in between them lies a fairly extensive plain, grassy and well-watered, with the road running through the middle of it. But before you come to it, you must enter the first defile, and afterward either retrace the steps by which you made your way into the place, or else — should you go forward — pass out by another ravine, which is even narrower and more difficult."[166] The consuls were Titus Veturius Calvinus and Spurius Postumius.[167] Livy again on the territory of the Hirpini in Book XXIII: "After the battle of Cannae, Hannibal had moved out of Apulia into Samnium, being invited into the land of the Hirpini by Statius, who promised that he would turn over Compsa to him."[168] And below: "That same summer Marcellus made frequent raids into the territory of the Hirpini and the Caudine Samnites from Nola, which he held with a garrison."[169] And below: "Hannibal set out from Arpi to Tifata."[170] Livy again in Book LXXV on the Social War: "Lucius Sulla subdued the Hirpini. The Samnites he put to rout."[171] *And in case a detailed account of the course of these rivers makes apprehension of them more difficult for those who have not seen them, famous as they are,* these places are ten miles from Benevento (taking into account convenient river crossings, the Caudine valley one mile from it,

Caudii partem oppida sunt Sanctus Martinus, Penna Scurmina, et
Sanctangelus ad Scalas.

55   Fluvius deinde sequitur dextrum illabens Sabbatum, ex Monte
Virginis arduo quidem et late diffuso nascens. Ad cuius vallem
Alta Villa primum est oppidum, post Mons Freddunus castellum,
et in proxima valle Avellinum civitas vetusta, quam Ptolemaeus[353]
Abellam, Plinius Abelinum vocat. Et tamen ab avelana nuce appel-
latum dicit, quae ibi plurima habebatur.[354] Superius est Mercuriale
castellum, et longe supra Virginis monasterium, quod ex Magnae
Matris deum[355] fano in gloriosae Virginis Mariae Dei Genitricis
ecclesiam Christianis temporibus est mutatum. Nam Antoninus
Pius in *Itinerario* viam describens a Benevento ad Columnas, ad
Mercurialem primum, post ad Matrem Magnam posuit. Altera
item vallis superior torrenti apposita in Sabbatum defluenti hinc
Atram Paludem inde Serenum oppida habet. Deinceps sunt Apennini iuga Montes Tremuli appellata, a quibus Sabbatum habet ortum.

56   Inferius ad Sabbati sinistram urbs est Beneventum. Quam urbem[356] Servius in Vergilii octavum,[357] super verbo, 'Diomedis ad
urbem,' dicit a Diomede conditam fuisse. De qua Livius in IX:[358]
Ad Beneventum, quod tunc Maleventum, XXX milia Samnitium
caesa aut capta, Sulpicio et Petilio consulibus. Et Libro decimo
quarto scribit coloniam a Romanis cum Arimino fuisse deductam.
Et Libro XXII: 'Hannibal ex Hirpinis in Samnium transit, Beneventanum depopulatur agrum.' Et Libro XXIV (ubi et amnis
proximi mentio est): Et ad Beneventum, inquit, parte altera
Hanno[359] ex Brutiis cum magna peditum manu, altera Gracchus a
Luceria accessit, qui[360] prius oppidum intravit. Inde ut Hannonem

and the Caudine Forks fourteen. At the other end of the Caudine valley are the towns of San Martino, Penna, Pietrastornina, and Sant'Angelo a Scala.

There follows a river that rises on the steep and sprawling 55 Montevergine and flows into the Sabato from the right. The first town in the valley is Altavilla, then the castle Montefredane, and in the next valley the ancient city of Avellino, which Ptolemy calls Abella and Pliny Abelinum. Yet Pliny says that Avellino was named after the hazel nut, which was found there in great quantities.[172] The castle Mercogliano is further up, and high above that the Santuario di Montevergine. In Christian times this was turned from a temple of Cybele, Great Mother of the gods, into a church of the glorious Virgin Mary, Mother of God, for when Antoninus Pius in his *Itinerary* described the road from Beneventum to Columnae, he puts Mercogliano first and then Mater Magna.[173] There is also a second valley higher up, around a torrent that flows down into the Sabato. On this side it has the town of Atripalda, and on the other the town of Serino. Then there are the Apennine ridges called Monte Terminio, where the Sabato originates.

Farther down, on the left bank of the river Sabato, is the city of 56 Benevento. In commenting on the phrase "to the city of Diomedes" in *Aeneid* Book VIII, Servius says the city was founded by Diomedes.[174] Livy says of it in Book IX that in the consulship of Sulpicius and Petilius, thirty thousand Samnites were killed or captured at Beneventum, then known as Maleventum.[175] In Book XIV he writes that the Romans planted a colony at Beneventum and another at Ariminum.[176] And in Book XXII: "Hannibal left the territory of the Hirpini and crossed into Samnium, devastating the territory of Beneventum."[177] And in Book XXIV, where the nearby river is mentioned, he writes that on one side Hanno came to Beneventum from the land of the Brutii with a large infantry force, while from the opposite direction Gracchus arrived from Luceria and got into the city first. Then, on *discovering that*

ad amnem Calorem *venisse comperit*[361] tria milia passuum[362] ipse egressus mille ferme passus ab hoste castra locat. Nec hostes moram dimicandi fecerunt. XVII[363] milia peditum erant maxima ex parte Brutii et Lucani, equitum tria milia ducenti. Pugnatum est quatuor horis. Volones[364] facti sunt liberi. Minus duo milia hominum ex tanto exercitu evasere. Ex victoribus Romanis ferme duo milia ceciderunt. Quam pugnam Gracchus Romae pingi fecit in atrio Libertatis in Aventino. Et Libro XXV:[365] Hanno ex Brutiis cum Benevento appropinquasset, ad tria miliaria[366] castra communivit, quo Campani duo milia plaustrorum duxerunt ut frumentum Capuam deferrent. Fulvius consul ex Boviano Beneventum cum venisset, castra vi cepit. Caesa sex milia. Capti septem milia. Et Libro XXVII: Beneventanos Livius ponit inter colonias ex rebellibus decem et octo, quae in potestatem senatus sunt factae.

57   Beneventanam urbem nos *Historiarum* sexto ostendimus a Tothila Ostrogothorum rege destructam fuisse. Et Libro XII[367] scripsimus Saracenos montem Garganum tenentes Beneventum, quae pridem fuerat instaurata et a Longobardis ducibus per annos supra ducentos possessa, iterum spoliatam dirutamque solo aequasse. Et infra diximus Guilielmum Normannum, Siciliae regem ab Adriano tertio pontifice Romano in ecclesia Sancti Martini apud Beneventum declaratum, sese ligium hominem fecisse Romanae ecclesiae, et, dimissa urbe ipsa pro peculiari et propria Romanae ecclesiae, in regno fuisse quod occupaverat confirmatum.

58   Est autem Beneventum in campestri solo, cui colles sunt proximi fertiles villis longe et[368] late frequentati. Hisque in collibus sexto a Benevento distat milliario Mons Fusculus oppidum, supra quod est Turris et oppidum Mons Militum appellatum. Sabbati amnis vallis, quam sinistrorsum efficit, castella hoc ordine continet.[369] Mons Falconis est primitus, Candida deinde et Serpitum.

Hanno had moved up to the river Calore three miles from the city, Gracchus left the city and made camp about a mile from the enemy.[178] Nor was the enemy slow to give battle. He had 17,000 infantry, Bruttians and Lucanians for the most part, and 3,200 horse. They fought for four hours.[179] The slave volunteers were freed. Out of these great armies fewer than two thousand men survived. Nearly two thousand of the victorious Romans fell.[180] Gracchus arranged for the battle to be depicted in the atrium of the temple of the goddess Liberty on the Aventine.[181] And from Livy Book XXV we learn that when Hanno arrived near Beneventum from the land of the Bruttii, he built and fortified a camp about three miles from the town, whither the Campanians brought two thousand wagons to take grain to Capua.[182] When the consul Fulvius got to Beneventum from Bovianum, he took the camp by force, six thousand men being slain and seven thousand captured.[183] In Book XXVII Livy has Beneventum among the eighteen rebellious colonies that the Senate brought back under their control.[184]

In Book VI of my *Histories*, I mentioned that the city of   57 Benevento was destroyed by Totila, king of the Ostrogoths.[185] And in Book XII I wrote that the Saracens in possession of Monte Gargano again sacked and destroyed Beneventum and razed it to the ground, long after it had been revived and held for over two hundred years by Lombard dukes.[186] In a later passage I said that the Norman William was declared king of Sicily by Pope Adrian III in the church of San Martino in Benevento, made himself vassal of the Roman Church, and, letting go of the city of Benevento itself as the feud and property of the Roman Church, was confirmed in the Kingdom which he had seized.[187]

Benevento lies on the plains, but the nearby fertile hills have   58 extensive and widespread country farms. In these hills six miles from Benevento is the town of Montefusco, and above it Torre le Nocelle and a town named Montemiletto. The valley of the river Sabato on the left has castles in this order, first Montefalcione,

Superioribusque in montibus arduis Tremulis appellatis,[370] Vulturaria habetur oppidum. Calor fluvius tertio ferme supra Beneventum stadio Sabbatum influit, ad cuius dexteram in colles mon-
tesque vergentem, quos Benevento diximus supereminere, castella
et oppida inveniuntur: Iapygium, Cusanum, Castrum Vetus, et
superius Montella oppidum nobile. Calorique amni secundo supra
Sabbatum miliario Valentinus pons fuit in via Appia positus, a
Valente imperatore appellatus, nunc dirutus. Et ipsi fluvio sin-
strorsum adiacent oppida, primo Apicium, ubi alter dictae viae
pons fuit eximius, post Mirabella, Taurasum, Cusanum, Balneo-
lum, Cassianum, Nuscus, et superiori loco insurgit Apenninus ubi
dictus oritur Calor amnis.

59   Quo item in loco alter fluvius habet originem, Aufidus, quem
per Apuliam labi in mare Adriaticum ostendemus. Tropoaltus
inde fluvius Calorem dextrum influit. Cui Tropoalto dextrorsum
silva eiusdem nominis latissima continet, supra quam castella eidem fluvio haerent: Bonetum, Grypta Mainardi, Flomarium,[371] et
Vicus civitas. Sinistrorsum vero castella habet is fluvius apposita[372]
Miletum, Amandum, Iunculum,[373] et superius in Apennino Grumus[374] est Mons, Crepacorius appellatus, ex quo is fluvius ortum
ducit. Myscanus inde fluvius, a Crepacorio nascens, Calorem eodem loco quo et superior Tropoaltus influit, cui dextrorsum adiacent Cursanum et Mons Calvus. Eoque quod praedictos Mysca-
num et Tropoaltum interiacet spatio in colle[375] est Arianum civitas,
Ara Iani priscis temporibus appellata. Et Myscani dexterae valli
insunt oppida et castella Mons Malus, Bonus Albergus, Casale
Albulum, Castrum Franchum. Sed et Calorem paulo priusquam
ipse Sabbatum ingrediatur ad Valentini pontem Tamarus influit
amnis, nulli praedictorum quos auget aquarum copia inferior. Ab

then Candida and Sorbo Serpico. The town of Volturara Irpino is located in the steep hills called Monte Terminio above this valley. The river Calore flows into the Sabato nearly three stades above Benevento. On its right bank as it turns toward the hills and mountains which overlook Benevento, as I mentioned above, these castles and towns are found: Giapigio, Chiusano di San Domenico, Castelvetere sul Calore, and further up the fine town of Montella. Two miles above the Sabato, the Appian Way passed over the river Calore on the Pons Valentinus, named after the emperor Valens and now destroyed. The towns that lie to the left of the Calore are, firstly, Apice, where the Appian Way had a second excellent bridge, then Mirabella Eclano, Taurasi, Cusano, Bagnoli Irpino, Cassano, Nusco. Higher still the Apennine ridge rears up, where the river Calore originates.[188]

Another river has its origin there too, the Ofanto, which as I shall show flows through Apulia into the Adriatic Sea.[189] Then the stream Tropoalto flows into the Calore from the right. The Tropoalto is bordered by a considerable forest of the same name on its own right, above which these castles lie on the same river, Bonito, Grottaminarda, Flumeri, and the town of Trevico. On the left of the river are situated the castles of Melito Irpino, Torreamando, Zungoli. Higher up in the Apennines is Mount Grumus, known as Crepacore, where the river originates. Then the river Miscano, which rises at Crepacore, flows into the river Calore at the same spot that the upper Tropoalto joins it; on its right bank are Corsano and Montecalvo Irpino. On a hill in the stretch between these rivers Miscano and Tropoalto is the city of Ariano Irpino, called Ara Jani in ancient times.[190] In the valley to the right of the river Miscano, there are towns and castles, Montemalo,[191] Buonalbergo, Casalbore, Castelfranco in Miscano. Shortly before the Sabato joins the Calore, the Calore is itself joined by the Tammaro at Pons Valentinus, a tributary the equal of any of the rivers men-

59

ipsisque duobus fluviis pari paene spatio abest Padulae oppidum in regione primarium.

60   Superiusque dextero haerent Tamaro oppida et castella: Sanctus Georgius, Molinaria, Casale Iohannis, Reganum, Sancta Maria, Collis, apud quem Iacobus Caudola apoplexi interiit, Cercellum, Coffianum, Sancta Crux. Quo in loco silva incipit amplissima Apenninum hincinde complexa, ut pars in Fortorium Apuliae amnem, pars in hunc Tamarum se extendat, quae latitudine[376] quatuor milliaria, longitudine[377] viginti implet. Suntque illius quernae arbores sublimitate insignes, ramis omnino in vertice carentes. Tamaro sinistro haec adiacent loca: Petra Pulcina, Pavum, Pestulum, Farnetum, Campus Lotharius, monasterium Guiletti, Marconum, Saxum Honorii, et in Apennino Sepinum vetusti nominis oppidum. De quo Livius XXI: 'Papirio ad Sepinum maior vis hostium obstitit, obsidendoque vi ac operibus urbem expugnat. Uno de quadringentis captis minus tria milia caesi.' Et post sequitur Alta Villa, et supra est Castrum Vetus in Grumo, ad quem Tamarus fontem habet.

61   Sed iam ad sinistram stipitis Sabbati amnis est redeundum. Telesia urbs vetusta colli[378] in planitie subiacet milliario uno a Sabbati stipite remota. Eaque in urbe fluvius oritur cadens in Sabbatum tantae frigiditatis ut nullos gignat pisces. De qua[379] Livius XXI: 'Hannibal ex Hirpinis[380] in Samnium transit. Beneventanum depopulatur agrum. Telesiam[381] urbem capit.' Limataque oppidum proxime Sabbato haeret. Quatuor dehinc torrentes ad Castrum Pontis oppidum unicis ostiis in Sabbatum cadunt, quorum torrentum fontibus ab Apennino remotissimis quatuor haerent castella: Sanctus Laurentius, Sanctus Lupus, Pons Landulphi, et Casaltonum.

tioned in abundance of water. Nearly equidistant from the two rivers Calore and Tammaro is Paduli, the chief town of the region.

Above Paduli, towns and castles lie on the right bank of   60
the Tammaro, San Giorgio La Molara, Molinara, Casale, Reino, Santa Maria, Colle Sannita (where Jacopo Caldora died of a stroke),[192] Circello, Cuffiano, Santa Croce del Sannio. Here begins an extensive forest which lies on both sides of the Apennines: part of it spreads out to the Fortore, a river of Apulia, and another part to the river Tammaro, covering an area four miles wide and twenty miles in length. The oak trees there are extraordinarily high, entirely lacking branches at their tops. On the left bank of the Tammaro are situated the following places, Pietrelcina, Pago,[193] Pesco Sannita, Fragneto Monforte, Campolattaro, the monastery of Guglietto, Morcone, Sassinoro, and in the Apennines the ancient town of Sepino. Of Sepino Livy writes in Book XXI: "Papirius, before Saepinum,[194] had a larger body of the enemy to reckon with, and by assault and siege works he captured the city. Three hundred and ninety-nine were captured and less than three thousand slain."[195] After Sepino comes Altavilla Irpina, and above Altavilla is Castelvetere in Grumo, where the river Tammaro has its source.

But we have now to return to the left side of the trunk of the   61
river Sabato. The ancient city of Telese lies on the plain at the foot of a hill, a mile from the trunk of the Sabato. A stream rises in this city that flows down into the Sabato, and it is so cold that it bears no fish. Of Telese, Livy writes in Book XXI: "Hannibal left the territory of the Hirpini and crossed into Samnium. He devastated the territory of Beneventum and captured the city of Telesia."[196] The town of Limotola lies close to the Sabato. Then four torrents flow down into it through separate mouths at the town of Ponte. Four castles are situated at their sources, which are very far from the Apennines, San Lorenzo Maggiore, San Lupo, Pontelandolfo, and Casalduni.

62   Sabbato amne cum suis fluviorum torrentumque ramis descripto, ad finem Samnitium regionis est perventum, ut Campaniam ab ipso Sabbato in Capuanam urbem verso hac in parte inchoantem describendam aggredi possimus.[382]

With this description of the river Sabato and its network of   62
streams and torrents, we have come to the end of the region of
Samnium. So now we can turn to the survey of Campania, beginning from the river Sabato as it turns in this part toward the city
of Capua.

LIBER VIII

Regio tertia decima. Campania[1]

1   Samnii regione ad utramque Apennini partem absoluta, ad proximam continentemque atque connexam illi in Cisapenninis[2] Campaniam est transeundum vel ea maxime ratione, ut inchoatos in Samnitium montibus fluviorum cursus, qui Campaniam quoque intersecant, expediamus. Cur autem eam 'Felicem Campaniam,' postea alii 'Terram Laboris' appellaverint[3] suo tempore et loco dicemus. Licet vero tota haec regio vetustissimis celebrata sit omnium dignitatum monumentis, nullum tamen locum nec ipsa nec alia pars Italiae habet in quo[4] maior quam in hoc Campaniae initio dignarum[5] relatu rerum mutatio sit facta.

2   Inchoat Campania ad dexteram Liris fluvii, quem nunc Gaurianum diximus appellari. Quem quidem Lirim Strabo dicit ferri desuper ex Apennino et a Vestinis labique in mare ad Fretealas[6] vicum, quae fuerit urbs praeclara. Cui concordat Lucanus: 'et umbrosae Liris per regna Maricae Vestinis impulsus aquis.' Cur autem[7] 'Maricae regna' Lucanus dicat, Servius in Vergilii septimo sic ostendit: 'Marica fuit uxor Fauni, quae est dea litoris Minturnensium iuxta Lirim fluvium.' De Vestinis et Minturnensibus qui fuerint dicturi prius Ausones docebimus, a quibus Italia olim Ausonia fuit appellata, et proximum mare Ausonium pelagus est dictum. De his tribus populis Livius sic habet in nono: 'Consules Sora profecti Ausonibus bellum intulerunt.' Et infra: 'Ausonum gens proditione civium, sicut Sora, in potestatem venit. Ausonia et

BOOK VIII

Region 13. Campania

Having dealt with the region of Samnium on both sides of the Apennines, we must pass on to the neighboring part of Campania which abuts and connects to it on the western side of the Apennines, chiefly with a view to explaining the courses of the rivers that start in the mountains of Samnium and cut across Campania as well.[1] At the proper time and place I shall address the question why this region was called "Campania Felix," and later by others "Terra di Lavoro."[2] The whole region is celebrated for its excellent ancient monuments of every sort; but neither Campania nor any other part of Italy has anywhere that has undergone greater vicissitudes in historic events than this first portion of the region.

Campania begins on the right-hand bank of the river Liris, which, as I said, is now called the Garigliano. Strabo says that the Liris is carried down from the Apennines and flows out of the land of the Vestini into the sea at the village of Fregellae, once a famous city.[3] Lucan agrees: "the river Liris, driven by the waters of the Vestini through the realm of shady Marica."[4] Servius on Vergil's Book VII explains why Lucan says "the realm of Marica" in these words: "Marica was the wife of Faunus, and she is a goddess of the shore of Minturnae on the river Liris."[5] Though I shall speak about the Vestini and the Minturnenses and who they were, I shall treat first of the Ausonians, after whom Italy was once called Ausonia and the neighboring sea was called the "Ausonian Main."[6] Livy writes about these three peoples in Book IX as follows: "The consuls set out from Sora and made war on the Ausonians."[7] And below: "The Ausones were brought into subjection by the betrayal of their cities, as had happened in the case of Sora.

Vestina et Minturnae urbes erant ex quibus principes iuventutis duodecim numero in proditionem urbium coniurati ad consules venerunt.' 'Quibus auctoribus mota propius castra missique milites, partim armati partim inermes. Ita portae occupatae triaque oppida eadem hora eodemque consilio capta, sed quia absentibus ducibus impetus factus est, nullus modus caedibus fuit. Deleta Ausonum gens, vix certo defectionis crimine.' Ausonibus et eodem impetu Vestina urbe deletis, Vestinum nihilo minus nomen ab ipso Liris ostio usque Soram mansit regioni et Ausonum omnino interiit.

3   Minturnaque, quam Liris divideret, fuit Romana colonia, de qua Livius in decimo: 'Ita placuit ut duae coloniae circa Vestinum Falernumque agrum deducerentur, una ad ostium Liris fluvii, quae tunc Minturnae appellata.' Fuit Marcellini papae temporibus generali concilio Ecclesiae decorata, cuius ingentia nunc vestigia[8] cernuntur ubi ad turrim scaphamque[9] Gauriani prope Traiectum oppidum exstat[10] theatrum paene integrum et aquaeductus forma. Inchoavit vero pridem Minturnarum urbis desolatio. Nam in Beati Gregorii *Registro* epistula est, quam scribit Bacaudae[11] episcopo Formiensi in haec verba: 'Et ideo quoniam Minturnensium ecclesiam funditus tam cleri[12] quam plebis[13] destitutam desolatione[14] cognovimus, tuam pro eo petitionem quatenus Formianae ecclesiae, in qua corpus Beati Erasmi martyris quiescit cuique Paternitas[15] tua praesidet, adiungi debeat exaudiri necessarium duximus.' Fuit Minturna una ex urbibus quae, propter aëris gravitatem, sacrosanctam vacationem a Romanis habuit. Estque locus apud quem C. Marius (sicut Valerius Maximus scribit) Urbe profugus cum in palustri canna delitesceret, viso asino aquas hilarius pe-

From Ausonia, Minturnae, and Vescia, twelve young nobles who had conspired to betray their cities came to the consuls."[8] "At their urging, the consuls moved their camp nearer and dispatched soldiers, some armed and some not. Thus the gates were captured, and three towns were taken in one hour and by a single stratagem. But because the leaders were not present when the attack was made, there was no limit to the slaughter, and the Ausonian nation was wiped out — though it was not quite clear that it was guilty of defection."[9] Though the Ausonians were wiped out in the same assault as the city of Vestina, the name of the region from the mouth of the Liris to Sora nonetheless remained Vestinum while the name of the Ausonians entirely disappeared.

Minturnae, which the Liris ran through, was a Roman colony, of which Livy writes in Book X: "They resolved to plant two colonies in the Vescinian and Falernian country, one at the mouth of the river Liris, which was then named Minturnae . . ."[10] Minturnae was graced by a general church council in the time of Pope Marcellinus.[11] Extensive remains of the colony can still be seen today near the town of Traetto, at the tower and ferry of the Garigliano, where an amphitheater survives nearly entire and the channels of an aqueduct. The decline of the city of Minturnae actually began a long time ago, for in the *Registrum* of St. Gregory the Great, he writes these words in a letter to Becauda, Bishop of Formia: "We understand that the church of the Minturnesi has been left completely destitute by the abandonment of clergy and laymen alike, and so we have decided that we must heed your petition on its behalf: namely, that the church of Minturnae must be attached to the church of Formia, where the body of St. Erasmus the martyr reposes and over which Your Worship presides."[12] Minturnae was one of the cities that, because of her bad air, enjoyed from the Romans a sacrosanct exemption.[13] It is the place where Gaius Marius, as Valerius Maximus tells us, hid as a fugitive from Rome among the reeds of a swamp and saw an ass cheer-

3

tente, bonum concepit omen, et inde transvectus mare copiis repa-
ratis victor in patriam est reductus. De quo Livius LXXVII sic
dicit: C. Marius pater cum in palude Minturnensium lateret, ex-
tractus est ab oppidanis, et cum missus ad eum occidendum ser-
vus natione Gallus maiestate tanti viri perterritus recessisset, impositus publice navi delatus est in Africam. Hunc eundem locum
duodecimo *Historiarum* docuimus illustratum fuisse insigni proelio
quod X Johannis Romani pontificis temporibus gestum fuit in
Saracenos maxima occidione ibi superatos et tunc Italia penitus
exactos. Sicque[16] videmus duas urbes olim praeclaras, primo Fretealas,[17] post Minturnas, ad Liris ostia interiisse et pariter omnino
deletam esse omnem memoriam Ausonum et Maricae.

4   Mons vero praedicto Liris ostio in Campaniae initio proximior
varias et fama celebres habet nominationes, qui alicubi Gaurus,
alicubi Massicus, alicubi Gallicanus est dictus. Primaque pars et
eidem ostio proximior Gaurus dicta Gaurelianum, ut diximus, illum appellari facit. Quem quidem Gaurum montem Plinius dicit,
sicut et Vesaevum Campaniae item montem, sulphura sudare,
quod aquae ostendunt callidae paulo superius etiam nunc scatentes,
ubi Turrim Balneorum et balnea[18] videmus. Ceterae montis nominationes cum adiacentibus locis et urbibus ostendentur. Secundum adiacens Minturnis oppidum in Gauro et Campaniae initio
fuit Trifanum, quem locum Livius in octavo dicit medium fuisse
inter Minturnas et Sinuessam. Tertio loco fuit Sinuessa stadiis
quadraginta (sicut Strabo ait) sed (sicut nunc) octuaginta a Minturnis semota. De qua habet Livius in octavo, quod supra de Minturnis diximus: 'Ita placuit ut duae coloniae circa Vestinum Faler-

fully making for the water, which he interpreted as a good omen. From there he sailed back over the sea with his troops restored to him and returned victorious to his fatherland.[14] Livy in Book LXXVII, has the following to say on this matter: "When the older Gaius Marius was hiding in a swamp at Minturnae, he was dragged out by the townsmen. A Gallic slave was sent to kill him, but he balked at the deed, deterred by the majesty of the great man, and so Marius was put on a ship at the city's expense and taken to Africa."[15] In Book XII of my own *Histories* I showed that this place also became famous in the time of Pope John X for the notable battle fought against the Saracens, who were overcome with great loss of life on their part and then driven out of Italy completely.[16] And so we see that two once famous cities, first Fregellae and then Minturnae, disappeared at the mouth of the Liris, and that all memory of the Ausonians and Marica was likewise lost.

Closer to the mouth of this river Liris in the first part of Campania is a mountain with various well known names, called in places Monte Gauro, elsewhere Monte Massico, and in yet other parts Monte Gallicano. The first part, known as Monte Gauro, is closest to the mouth of the Liris, and is the reason the Liris is called the Garigliano, as I mentioned.[17] Pliny says that Monte Gauro, like that other Campanian mountain Vesuvius, exudes sulfur, as is indicated by the hot springs which still today bubble up a little higher up, where we see Torre di Bagni and the baths themselves.[18] The other names for the mountain will appear when we come to the places and cities adjacent to it. A second town by Minturnae in the first part of Campania on Monte Gauro was Trifanum: Livy says in Book VIII that its location was midway between Minturnae and Sinuessa.[19] The third town was Sinuessa, forty stades from Minturnae according to Strabo, but eighty stades as is reckoned now.[20] On Sinuessa, Livy in Book VIII writes (as I observed above on Minturnae): "They resolved to plant two colo-

4

numque agrum deducerentur, una ad ostium Liris (quae nunc
Minturnae), altera in saltu Vestino Falernum agrum contingente,
ubi Sinope Graeca urbs dicitur fuisse, Sinuessa deinde a colonis
Romanis appellata.' Huius vero civitatis ad caput nunc Montis
Draconis deletae, ingentes et late diffusae in continenti sed maiores
in mari, quae portus moles fuerunt, apparent nunc ruinae. Livius
etiam XXII scribit Fabium Maximum per iuga Massici montis
ducentem prohibuisse Hannibalem ad Romanae coloniae moenia
tendentem, cum supra dixerit Hannibalis milites praedatum ivisse
usque ad aquas Sinuessanas: unde patet aliam montis partem,
quae a Suessa Pometia (vel Aurunca nunc Sessa) ad Calenum oppidum (nunc Carinulam)[19] protenditur, fuisse Massicum, per
cuius iuga Fabius tunc ducebat. Supplet autem vices Sinuessae
oppidum Arx Mons[20] Draconis dictum, vel potius eius suburbium
mille passus a mari semotum. Et paulo inde absunt supradicta
Gauri Balnea, quae Strabo dicit morbis quibusdam prodesse plurimum.

5   Post Montis Draconis arcem in Massico monte vicis villisque
plurimis frequentato ad partem in mare versam nullum est oppidum vel castellum. Ad eam vero partem, qua adverso Liri et dextro
Massico itur, solum est octo milia passuum[21] quaqua versum inter
mare, viam Appiam, Lirim, et Massicum patens nuncque cultissi-
mum et vicis villisque frequentissimum, quae Suessae Casalia appellantur, quod quidem solum, stante Romana Republica, silis sive
trifoliis herbis prata conficientibus optima abundavit. Unde Valerius Martialis poeta: 'Caeruleus nos Liris amat, quem silva Maricae protegit. Hinc[22] silae maxima turba sumus.' Et quidem etiam
nunc ea regio maximum habet in faeno quaestum. M. Cicero in

nies in the Vescinian and Falernian country, one at the mouth of the river Liris, which was then named Minturnae, the other in the forest of the Vestini bordering on Falernian territory, where the Greek city of Sinope is said to have been, later called Sinuessa by the Roman colonists."[21] At the tip of present-day Mondragone there can be seen today the remains of the ruined city of Sinuessa, extensive on the land side but still more so in the sea, where they formed the moles of a harbor. In Book XXII Livy again writes that Fabius Maximus led his army along the ridges of Mons Massicus to stop Hannibal as he made for the walls of the Roman colony,[22] though he had earlier said that Hannibal's army had gone plundering as far as the baths of Sinuessa:[23] thus it is clear that it was another part of the Mons Massicus along whose ridges Fabius was leading his army, extending from Suessa Pometia (or Aurunca, nowadays Sessa)[24] to the town of Calenum, nowadays Carinola. But the town known as Rocca di Mondragone (or rather a suburb of Mondragone a mile from the sea) has taken the place of Sinuessa. Not far from Rocca di Mondragone are the baths of Monte Gauro that were mentioned above, which Strabo says are very effective in the treatment of a number of ailments.[25]

After Rocca di Mondragone, there are no towns or castles on 5 the seaward side of Monte Massico, which itself has a great many villages and estates. But if one travels toward the facing Liris with Monte Massico on the right, in that part there is open ground that stretches for eight miles in every direction between the sea, the Appian Way, the Liris, and Monte Massico, land much cultivated and well populated with towns and estates called the Casali di Sessa, and indeed in the days of the Roman Republic, it had abundant snub-nosed or trefoil clovers that made fine meadows. And so the poet Valerius Martial: "The sea-blue Liris, which Marica's grove protects, loves us: we snub-nosed grasses come from here in great masses,"[26] and in fact the land produces hay very profitably even now. When Cicero in the second speech

oratione *Contra legem agrariam Rulli* secunda cum vellet dissuadere venditionem agri Campani, montis Gauri, praedictique campestris soli in pratis tunc culti et Viae Herculaneae[23] a Gaieta ad ipsa prata productae, sic habet: 'Hac lege tribunicia decemviri vendent agrum Campanum. Accedit et mons Gaurus. Accedent sileta[24] ad Minturnas. Adiungitur et illa Via vendibilis Herculanea[25] multarum divitiarum et magnae pecuniae.'

6   In via autem Appia ubi ea primum attingit Massicum montem urbs est vetus, Suessa olim Pometia et quandoque Auruncorum dicta, quae varias fecit regionum mutationes—quod Auruncorum olim (qui et Ausones) Sidicinorumque, et post Volscorum, demum fuit Vestinorum, prout ex sequentibus faciliter apparebit. Livius in primo: 'Anci liberi Suessam Pometiam exsulatum ierant.' Et infra de Tarquinio Superbo: 'Is primum Volscis bellum in ducentos amplius post suam aetatem annos movit, Suessamque Pometiam ex his vi cepit.' Et infra idem Livius eandem Suessam rebellem praedae militi Romano datam ostendit. Et in octavo: 'Aurunci metu oppidum deseruerunt, profugique cum coniugibus ac liberis Suessam commigrarunt, quae nunc Aurunca appellata. Moenia eorumque urbs ab Sidicinis deleta.' Item in nono: Suessam eodem anno colonia deducta. Fuerat Auruncorum.

7   Progressi Suessa Pometia (sive Aurunca) per Appiam silicibus stratam et per cavas vias dextro Massico Calenum octavo milliario inveniunt vetustam urbem, quae nunc Carinula dicitur. Estque hinc Falerno agro inde Massico monti contigua, quamquam vetusta Caleni oppidi vestigia aliquantulum a nunc Carinula sunt remota; de qua urbe Iuvenalis:[26] 'molle Calenum' continet sinis-

Against the Agrarian Law of Rullus wanted to argue against selling off the Campanian district, Monte Gauro, the fields mentioned above which were at the time cultivated as meadowlands, and the Via Herculanea that extended from Gaeta to these meadows, he has this to say: "The decemvirs will sell the Ager Campanus in accordance with this tribunician law. Add to that Monte Gauro. Add to these the meadows of Minturnae. And join all that to that very sellable road to Herculaneum, a road of great riches and considerable value."[27]

Where the Appian Way first reaches Monte Massico is the an-   6
cient city of Sessa (once called Suessa Pometia, sometimes Suessa Aurunca). Sessa has undergone various changes in the region it was attached to, being at one time a city of the Aurunci (that is, the Ausonians)[28] and the Sidicini, then of the Volscians, finally of the Vestini, as will be perfectly clear from the following passages. Livy writes in Book I: "Ancus's sons had gone into exile in Suessa Pometia."[29] And later, on Tarquinius Superbus: "It was he who first set off the war with the Volsci that lasted two hundred years beyond his own time and who captured Suessa Pometia from them by storm."[30] Further on Livy also shows that a rebellious Suessa was given to the Roman soldiers to plunder.[31] And in Book VIII: "The Aurunci abandoned the town out of fear, and with their wives and children they migrated as refugees to Suessa, now renamed Suessa Aurunca. Their walls and city were destroyed by the Sidicini."[32] Again in Book IX: the same year, a colony was planted at Suessa. It had been a town of the Aurunci.[33]

Making your way from Suessa Pometia (or Aurunca) along the   7
paved Appian Way and the sunken roads, and keeping Monte Massico on your right, after eight miles you come upon the ancient city of Calenum, now called Carinola. Carinola sits up against Falernian territory on one side and Monte Massico on the other, though the ancient remains of the town of Calenum are some little way from the Carinola of today. Juvenal's "luxurious

trorsum Appiae viae, qua Calenum urbem a Suessa peti diximus, et ipsi pariter civitati mons item Massicus supra Teanum civitatem, ut diximus, Calesque usque ad Calatiam continuatus. Et licet mons ipse dorso uno a Calibus sinistrorsum ad Venafrum et inde ad Vulturnum recto cursu protendatur, altera pars, fracta alicubi viis cavis et silvosa, ad Caliculam (sive nunc Caianellum) se dextrorsum flectit et Vulturnum, sed inferiori loco, petit, adeo ut inter praedictos montes et Vulturnum, sed superiorem Samnitibus continentem, campi relinquantur Venafrani semper antea (sicut et nunc) a civitate illis contigua appellati. Namque Plinius de olivis tractans Venafranos campos dicit glareosos sed pingues feracissimosque oleae esse. Hisque campis adiacent hinc Gallucium, Conca, Ronca Mosini,[27] Mignanum, Pesantianum Varianumque, inde Sextum, et superius (sicut diximus) ultra Vulturnum sunt Allifae.

8   Sed alia parte, Vulturnum inter interiorem[28] contra Caianellum labentem, quousque per Capuam et olim Casilinum fertur in mare, et omnem superius dictum montis tractum et alteram eiusdem Massici partem, quae a[29] Carinula ad maris litora et Sinuessanum olim agrum, nunc Montis Draconis suburbium, pertinet, campestre est solum totius Italiae amoenissimum, quem olim campum Stellatem appellavere. Eidemque campo partim imminent partim insunt Calenum primo (sive Carinula), Turris Francolisii, Teanum Sidicinum, Cales (sive Calvi), et Calicula (sive Caianellum). Sed quod Massico monti contigisse diximus ut ad Liris ostia pars eius appellaretur Gaurus, pariter ad aliam contigit partem ut inter Carinulam Turrimque Francolosii Gallicanus olim sit dictus, ubi Cascanum incolae nunc appellant. De campo autem Stellatae sic habet Livius in nono: 'In campum Stellatem agri Campani

Calenum,"³⁴ is bordered on the left by the Appian Way (the road you take to get to Calenum from Sessa, as I said), and is similarly bordered by Monte Massico, which extends, as I said, beyond Teano and Cales all the way to Galazze. Though one ridge of Monte Massico turns leftward from Cales toward Venafro, and then from Venafro in a straight line to the river Volturno, a second stretch, which is broken by sunken roads here and there and covered with forest, turns to the right toward Callicula (present-day Caianello) and heads for the river Volturno, but lower down, so that between the mountains mentioned earlier and the higher reaches of the Volturno, where it meets Samnite territory, one leaves the plain of Venafro, now and always so called after the neighboring city. In dealing with olives, Pliny says that the plain of Venafro is full of gravel but rich and highly productive of olives.³⁵ Beside the plain are on one side Galluzzo, Conca Casale, Roccamonfina, Mignano, Presenzano and Vairano; on the other there is Sesto, and further up, on the other side of the Volturno, is Alife, as I mentioned.

But in the other direction, between the river Volturno inland   8
as it flows by Caianello before emptying into the sea by way of Capua and the former Casilinum³⁶ and the whole stretch of Monte Massico that was dealt with above, and the other portion of Monte Massico that runs from Carinola to the coast and the former territory of Sinuessa (now in the outskirts of Mondragone), there is the pleasantest plain in all of Italy, which was formerly called the Campus Stellatis. Partly on this plain and partly above it are first Caleno (or Carinola), Torre Francolise, Teano Sidicino, Cales (Calvi), and Callicula (Caianello). But just as I noted in the case of Monte Massico, that the part by the mouth of the Liris was called Monte Gauro, so it happens that in the opposite direction, between Carinola and Torre Francolise, it was formerly called Monte Gallicano, and is now known to the inhabitants as Monte Cascano. Livy in Book IX has this to say about the Campus Stellatis: "The Samnites made forays into the Campus

Samnitium incursiones factae.' Idem in decimo: 'Samnitium legiones, cum partem Appius Claudius praetor partem L. Volumnius proconsul persequeretur, in agrum Stellatem convenerunt. Pugnatum infestis animis. Caesa Samnitium sexdecim milia trecenti.'[30] Item XXII: Hannibalem Telesia potitum auditis Capuanis duobus alternis fidentem ac diffidentem ut Campaniam ex Samnio peteret moverunt. Ipse imperat duci ut se in agrum Casinatem ducat, edoctus a peritis regionum, si eum saltum occupasset, exitum Populo Romano ad opem ferendam sociis interclusurum. Sed Poenum abhorrens ab Latinorum prolatione nomen 'Casilinum' pro 'Casino' ducem accipere fecit. Aversusque ab itinere per Allifanum Calatinumque et Calenum agrum in campum Stellatem usque ad Casilinum descendit, ubi cum montibus fluminibusque clausam regionem circumspexisset, vocatum ducem virgis caesum in crucem sustulit. Castris ad Vulturnum amnem communitis, Maharbalem cum equitibus in agrum Falernum praedatum dimisit. Usque ad aquas Sinuessanas ea populatio pervenit. Ut vero ad Vulturnum amnem castra sunt posita, exurebatur amoenissimus Italiae ager villaeque passim incendiis fumabant, per iuga Massici montis Fabio ducente. 'Ut vero in extrema iuga Massici montis ventum[31] est, hostes sub oculis erant Falerni agri colonorumque Sinuessae tecta urentes.' Qui ergo a Telesia, nunc etiam id retinente nomen et a nobis in Samnio supra Vulturnum dextro Aeserniensi amne descripta, movebat, Hannibal, ut ad Casinum iret, per Allifanum quidem primo, sed inde dextrorsum ad Venafrum, ab eoque oppido Casinum fuit ducendus. Sed dux errore nominis, averso (sicut proprie dicit Livius) itinere, sinistrorsum flexit in Calatinum, cuius urbem nunc Caiaciam pro Calatia di-

Stellatis in Campania."[37] In Book X he further says: "The Samnite legions, as the praetor Appius Claudius was pursuing some of them and the proconsul Lucius Volumnius others, assembled on the Campus Stellatis. There was a murderous battle. Of the Samnites, 16,300 were slain."[38] And in Book XXII: "After taking Telesia, Hannibal listened to the two Capuans, whom he trusted and distrusted by turns, but they persuaded him to march from Samnium into Campania. He ordered his guide to lead him into the territory of Casinum, for he had been told by those who knew the country that if he occupied that pass, he could keep the Romans from marching to the aid of their allies. But the difficulty the Carthaginians had with Latin caused the guide to understand the name 'Casilinum' instead of 'Casinum.' Leaving the proper route, Hannibal came down through the territories of Allifae, Calatia, and Cales onto the Campus Stellatis and all the way to Casilinum. There, looking round on the mountains and rivers that enclosed the plain, he summoned the guide, and had him flogged and crucified. He fortified his camp on the river Volturno and dispatched Maharbal with the cavalry to ravage the Falernian countryside. The devastation extended even to the Baths of Sinuessa. But when Hannibal had encamped by the river Volturno, the fairest district in all Italy was in flames, and the smoke went curling up from burning farmhouses as Fabius continued to march along the ridges of Monte Massico. But when they reached the farthest extremity of the range, they saw the enemy down below them setting fire to the farms of the Falernian district and the colony of Sinuessa."[39] Hannibal, then, was marching from Telesia (a place with the same name today, which I described under Samnium, above the river Volturno and with the river of Isernia on the right),[40] and to get to Casinum he needed to be guided first through Allifae, and then turning to the right to Venafro, and from there to Casinum. But the guide mistook the name and, just as Livy says, took the wrong route, veering leftward into the Calatinum — its city is now called

cunt. Et transmissis — quod evitari non potuit — angustiis cavarum silvosarumque viarum, quae ad Caliculam nunc Caianellum[32] ducunt, pervenit ad Calenum agrum, eius scilicet civitatis quae pro Cal⟨ibus⟩ Sidicin⟨is⟩[33] dicta est Calvi. Et per ipsum Stellatem procedens campum, non prius viae intellexit errorem quam, ad propinquum Casilini (quod nunc Castellutium appellant) Vulturnum perductus, clausam montibus et fluminibus Vulturno ac Saono regionem moestus circumspexit.

9 Castris itaque ad Castellutium vel ibi prope positis, facile fuit Maharbali[34] usque ad aquas Sinuessanas, ubi scilicet Saonus in stagnum effusus labi incipit in Vulturnum, praedatum ire. Ut vero ad praedictum Vulturnum castra sunt posita, exurebatur amoenissimus Italiae ager: is scilicet, qui Falernus tunc appellatus, pertinebat a Carinula ad Castellutium (sive tunc Casilinum). Quod Livius agrum Falernum a Campano[35] divisisse asserit per iuga Massici montis: ea videlicet, quae a Carinula ad Maritimam oram protenduntur, Fabio ducente. Ut vero ad extrema ipsius Massici montis pervenit Fabius, hostes sub oculis erant, quod ab ipso monte Massico vix quatuor milia passuum[36] Castellutium et Vulturni fluenta distant.

10 Prius vero quam Hannibalis reditum in Samnites describam, aliqua referre[37] libet ex quibus campus Stellatis[38] qualis quantusque fuerit patebit. Marcus Cicero legem dissuasurus Agrariam, qua Rullus Cornelius decemvir et collegae agrum Campanum Stellatemque campum et supradicta ad Gaurum Lirimque[39] sileta cum[40] via Herculanea,[41] vendere intendebat, sic habet: 'At enim ager Campanus hac lege amittitur[42] orbis terrae pulcherrimus.' Et infra: 'Adiungit Stellatem campum agro Campano et in eo duo-

Caiazzo rather than Calatia. After crossing, as was unavoidable, the passes of hollow, wooded roads that lead to Callicula (present-day Caianello), Hannibal arrived at the territory of Cales, that is, of the city now called Calvi instead of Cales Sidicinae. As he made his way over the Campus Stellatis, Hannibal did not realize that he had gone astray until he was brought up against the river Volturno near Casilinum, which is now called Castelluccio; looking around despondently he saw the region shut in by mountains and by the rivers Volturno and Savone.

And so once camp had been set up at Castelluccio or nearby, it 9 was easy for Maharbal to go pillaging as far as the baths of Sinuessa, which is where the Savone drains into a swamp and begins to flow into the Volturno. When Hannibal made camp on the Volturno, as I mentioned, the fairest district of Italy was set on fire: this land, at that time known as the Falernian territory, stretched from Carinola to Castelluccio, ancient Casilinum. Livy says that the Volturno marked the boundary between the Falernian territory and Campania,[41] as Fabius continued to march along the ridges of Monte Massico, that is, those ridges which stretch from Carinola to the coast. When Fabius reached the farthest extremity of the range, the enemy were in full view, for scarcely four miles separate Monte Massico from Castelluccio and the waters of the Volturno.[42]

But before I describe Hannibal's passage back to Samnite terri- 10 tory, I should report on some other matters, from which the nature and extent of the Campus Stellatis will become clear. When Cicero was about to speak against the agrarian law which the decemvir Cornelius Rullus, along with his colleagues, was going to use to sell off the Campanian territory, the Campus Stellatis and the above-mentioned meadows at Monte Gauro and the river Liris, along with the road to Herculaneum,[43] he has this to say: "But with this law we shall lose Campania, the most beautiful region in all the world."[44] And below: "Rullus adds the Campus

dena distribuit[43] in singulos homines iugera, quasi vero paulum
non differat ager Campanus a Stellati.[44] Nam dixi antea lege per-
mitti ut quae velint municipia, quas velint veteres colonias, colonis
suis occupent. Calenum municipium complebunt. Teanum oppri-
ment et Atellam.' Ostendit vero praedictis in orationibus Cicero
non solum viam Herculaneam[45] Gaurumque et sileta ad Minturnas sed campum quoque Stellatem peculiares fuisse populi Romani fundos, ex quibus alerentur exercitus. Quod quidem Suetonius Tranquillus innuere videtur, cum dicit C. Caesarem in
consulatu suo ad gratiam Romani populi comparandam divisisse
campum Stellatem viginti milibus civibus Romanis quibus tres
sive plures filii essent.

II   Ut autem ad Hannibalem redeamus. Dicit Livius Fabium tam
diu extraxisse reliquum aestatis ut Hannibal, destitutus ab spe
summa appetiti certaminis, iam hibernis locum circumspectaret,
quia ea regio praesentis erat copiae non perpetuae: arbusta vineae-
que et consita omnia magis amoenis quam necessariis fructibus.
Itaque cum sciret Hannibali per easdem angustias quibus intrave-
rat redeundum esse, Gallicanum montem et Casilinum occupat
modicis praesidiis. Et infra: 'Inclusus deinde videri Hannibal, et
ad[46] Casilinum obsessus. Cum Capua et Samnium et tantum a
tergo divitum sociorum Romanis commeatum subveherent, Poenus tunc intra fortunae minas, saxa ac Linterni arenas, stagna
perhorrida situ hibernaturus esset. Itaque cum per Casilinum eva-
dere non posset et iugum Caliculae superandum esset, ludibrium
oculorum in[47] speciem terribilem ad frustrandum hostem com-

Stellatis to the Campanian district, and in the two together he allots twelve acres to each settler — as if there were no difference at all between the Campanian district and the Campus Stellatis! For I have said before that leave is given by the law for them to occupy with their settlers whatever municipalities and old colonies they choose. They will fill up the township of Cales. They will overrun Teanum and Atella."[45] In the orations mentioned above, Cicero shows that not only the road to Herculaneum and Monte Gauro and the meadows at Minturnae, but the Campus Stellatis as well were the personal property of the collective Roman People, from which their armies were nourished and sustained. Indeed, Suetonius seems to intimate as much when he says that as consul Julius Caesar parceled out the Campus Stellatis among twenty thousand Roman citizens with three or more sons apiece so as to gain popularity with the people.[46]

But to come back to Hannibal: Livy says that Fabius dragged   II
out the remainder of the summer for so long that Hannibal was disappointed in his hopes of the battle which he had made every effort to bring on, and was now looking round for a place to winter in; for the country where he was, though a land of plenty for the time being, could not support him permanently, being taken up with orchards and vineyards, and planted everywhere with agreeable fruits rather than staple ones. And so when Fabius learned that Hannibal would have to return through the same passes he had entered by, he seized and occupied Monte Gallicano and Casilinum with fair-sized garrisons.[47] And below: "Hannibal seemed then to be hemmed in and blocked at Casilinum. The Romans had Capua and Samnium at their backs and all their wealthy allies to furnish them with provisions, so it seemed the Carthaginians were set to go into winter quarters under threat from Fortune[48] — the rocks and sands of Liternum, the marshes dreadful in their filth. And so, since he could not make his way out through Casilinum and the ridge of Callicula had to be

287

mentus, duo milia boum cornua fascibus sarmentorum igni accen-
sorum in montem Gallicanum (nunc Cascanum Turri, sicut diximus) Francolisii imminentem a Fabio praeoccupatum egit. Et
interea Romani qui ad transitum saltus insidendum locati erant,
ubi in summis montibus ac super se quosdam ignes conspexerunt,
praesidio excessere. Interea toto agmine Hannibal transducto in
agro Allifano posuit castra. Fabius quoque movit castra, transgressusque saltum super Allifas loco alto consedit. Tum Hannibal, si-
mulans se per Samnium petere Romam, usque in Paelignos pervenit.' Fuitque via nunc etiam trita et qua nuper Neapolim ivimus
ipsi ab Allifis, traiecto amne Vulturno sub Formelo, monasterii
Sancti Vincentii (sicut in Samnio ostendimus) castello, ad Castrum Sarni (sive, ut dicunt, Sangri). Eo exinde superato qui adiacet colle, profectus Hannibal. Amnem Rasinum[48] sinistrorsum relinquens, ad Furculas Paelignorum,[49] nunc Palenae dictas, pervenit,
unde flexo itinere per Frentanos, Ortonenses, Aprutinos retro
Apuliam repetiit.

12   Sed iam ad nostrum ordinem redeamus. Vulturni amnis ostio
dextrorsum urbs olim adiacebat ipsius nomine Vulturnum appellata. Livius XXVI: 'Capua interim summa vi a consulibus obsideri
coepta est, quaeque in eam rem opus erant comportabantur
parabanturque: Casilinum frumentum convectum; ad Vulturni
ostium ubi nunc urbs est castellum communitum. Ante Fabius
Maximus communierat praesidium impositum ut mare proximum
et flumen in potestate esset.' Item Livius[50] libro XXXII ostendit
coloniam Romanam fuisse deductam Vulturnum, urbem ad ostia
Vulturni amnis sitam ubi nunc oppidum Castellum ad Mare dic-

climbed, he contrived a visual trick of awesome power to delude the enemy: he drove two thousand head of cattle, their horns tied to bundles of brushwood which were set alight, on to Mount Callicula (nowadays Monte Cascano, as I said), which overlooks Torre Francolise and which had been occupied previously by Fabius. Meanwhile the Romans took up station to occupy the pass, but when they saw fires on the mountain peaks right above them, they abandoned their position. While this was happening Hannibal led his whole army through the defile and made his camp in the territory of Allifae. Fabius too broke camp, passed through the defile, and stationed himself in the heights above Allifae. Feinting as if to pass through Samnium and head for Rome, Hannibal then went all the way to the country of the Paeligni."[49] This was and is the regular route, and the one I myself recently took when going to Naples from Alife, passing over the river Volturno below Formelo, a castle of the Abbey of San Vincenzo, as I mentioned in my discussion of Samnium,[50] at the Castrum Sarni, or, as they now call it, Castel di Sangro. After scaling the hill beside Formelo, Hannibal set out from there. Leaving the river Rasino behind him on the left, he arrived at Furculae of the Paeligni, now called Forca di Palene, where he changed direction to make his way back to Puglia through the lands of the Frentani, Ortonenses, and Aprutini.

But let us now return to our regular progression. There used to   12
be a city lying to the right of the mouth of the Volturno, called Vulturnum after the river. Livy writes in Book XXVI: "The siege of Capua was undertaken with great intensity by the consuls, and all that was needed for the purpose was brought together and made ready. Casilinum was the depot for grain. At the mouth of the Volturnus, where there is now a city, there was a fortified stronghold. Fabius Maximus had previously strengthened the garrison there so that they could control the river and the sea in those parts."[51] In Book XXXII, Livy also mentions that a Roman colony was established at Vulturnum, a city located at the mouth of

tum videmus. Supraque Castellum ad Mare Vulturno dextrorsum
adiacet viculus Castellutium appellatus, ubi Casilinum fuisse non
coniecturis modo sed multis quoque ducimur argumentis. Primumque nominis similitudo in ceterarum concursu rationum non
parum valet, sed et cetera habet Castellutium, quae de Casilino
apud Livium scripta videmus: propinquitatem castello, quod Fabius ad Vulturni ostium communiverat ut in his duobus maritimis
oppidis vix tertio in vicem distantibus milliario frumentum deponi
potuerit Sardinia avectum, quod postea Capuam importaretur.
Castellutium quoque dividit supra descriptum Falernum agrum a
Campano, et propinquum est Sinuessano olim (nunc Montis Draconis) agro.

13 Nec moveat quemquam ruinarum veteris aedificii paucitas quae
nunc in Castellutio apparet.[51] Casilinum enim parva urbs nequaquam moenium structurarumque munimento sed Praenestinorum
Perusinorumque, qui forte praesidio inerant, virtute eam pertulit
durissimam obsidionem. Si vero fuerint qui apud vicos superiore
loco appositos Vulturno, Cancellum et Arnonum, fuisse Casilinum ideo opinentur, quod in praedictorum aliquo maiusculae
cernantur vetustates, considerare debebunt solam eorum a mari et
a Vulturno castello distantiam ne maritima appellari potuerint
adversari et praeterea[52] esse apud Castellutium non apud Cancellum aut Arnonum eam amnis Vulturni tortuositatem, quam Livius
apud Casilinum fuisse dicit. Arnonum etiam paululum a prisco
mutatum est vetus Romanum nomen quo et non Casilino Livius
si voluisset uti potuisset.

14 Nam Petrus noster Candidus in *Parallelarum Plutarchi* transla-
tione vitam Fabii Maximi et gesta Hannibalis ad Casilinum describens, sic habet: 'In ultimas Campaniae oras Casilinum usque

the Volturno, where now we see the town called Castellammare.[52] And above Castellammare, on the right of the Volturno lies the little village called Castelluccio: there are many good reasons, and not just guesswork, to make us suppose that this was the site of Casilinum. In the first place, in combination with all the other reasons, the similarity of the names has no little weight, but Castellucio has other features too which we read in Livy applied to Casilinum: its proximity to the fort that Fabius built at the mouth of the Volturno, so that grain shipped from Sardinia could be stored in the two coastal towns barely three miles from one another, which was later taken to Capua. Castelluccio also separates the Falernian district described above from Campania,[53] and it abuts the neighboring territory of the former Sinuessa, now Mondragone.

No one should worry about the scant ruins of ancient buildings   13 to be seen nowadays at Castelluccio. It was not the protection of walls and structures that saved the little city of Casilinum from that cruel siege, but the courage of the Praenestines and Perusines who happened to be manning the garrison. Granted there have been those who reckon that Casilinum was one of the villages on the Volturno farther inland, Cancello and Arnone, because in one or other of them rather more in the way of antiquities is to be seen:[54] but they should consider that the distance of these towns from the sea and from the fort of Vulturnum alone forbids their being called "maritime" towns, as does the further fact that the bend in the river Volturno, which Livy says was at Casilinum, is at Castelluccio and not at Cancello or Arnone. Also, the old Roman name Arnonum has changed little from its ancient form, and Livy could have used it, and not Casilinum, had he wanted to.

In fact my friend Pier Candido Decembrio, in the account of   14 the life of Quintus Fabius Maximus and Hannibal's exploits at Casilinum in his translation of Plutarch's *Parallel Lives*, has the following passage: "He was carried to the very edge of Campania, as

delatus est, qua Vulturnus fluvius (quem Nataronum Romani appellant) defluit. Ea regio montibus undique obsessa versus mare,
dumtaxat importuosum, ac fluminis ostia aperitur.' Cetera de Casilini obsidione notiora sunt quam ut ea hic poni oportere iudice-
mus, sed id unum in Casilini praeconium libet dicere: Casilini
obsidione factum esse ut salva fuerit ab Hannibale res Romana,
quandoquidem eius loci obsidionis causa Hannibalis animi ex re-
centi victoria Cannensi ardentes refrixerunt, et inclusus Capuae
exercitus ille ferocissimus Campanis deliciis enervatus est. Et ne[53]
Arnonum post amissam Casilini nominis vetusti gloriam, qua a
non nullis ornari consuevit, suo etiam careat praeconio, rem novam ipsius vici occasione dicemus: falconis avis aëreae et rapacissi-
mae aucupium, quo inclytus rex Alphonsus Arago apud Arnonum
plurimo utitur, ante ducentos annos omnino incognitum fuisse.
Nam etsi Servius grammaticus Capuam dicit ab augurio Falconis
eo nomine appellatam, quod Etrusci eius urbis conditores 'Capim'
inaugurantes viderint (quo nomine falconem appellabant), tamen
quis fuerit hominibus dictae avis usus non scribit. Pariter Plinius
cum multa ponat rapacium avium nomina, accipitres (scilicet
maiores et minores) ac 'chiluones' — quos aliqui falcones fuisse volunt —, tamen nullam aucupii usus earundem avium facit mentionem, ut etiam non sit dubitandum quin, si temporibus Vergilii
eius aucupii usus fuerit, Aeneam facturus fuisset[54] et Didonem eas
quoque aves in venationem ferre,[55] ubi dixit: 'Massilique ruunt
equites et odora canum vis.' Audemusque confidenti assertione
dicere ante ducentesimum (ut diximus) annum nullam gentem aut
nationem consuevisse rapaci aliqua ave mansueta alias aves (ter-
restres aut aquatiles aut aëreas) capere.

15   Supra Castellutium (sive Casilinum) et duodecimo a mari milliario amni Vulturno adiacet urbs Capua novo quidem loco, qui

far as Casilinum, by which flows the river Vulturnus, called the Nataronus by the Romans. This district is hemmed in by mountains on all sides, but is open toward the sea, though it has no anchorages, as well as to the mouths of the river."[55] The rest of the siege of Casilinum is too well known for me to think it worth recording here, but I may just mention one thing in commendation of it. The siege of Casilinum saved the Roman Republic from Hannibal: the siege of this place cooled Hannibal's spirits, which had been set afire by his recent victory at Cannae, and penned in at Capua, that ferocious army of his was emasculated by the charms of Campania. And lest Arnone be deprived of its own praise, after losing the luster that goes with the ancient name of Casilinum, which some have been in the habit of bestowing on it, the town may serve as an opportunity to address a novelty: two hundred years ago a sport which the famous King Alfonso of Aragon often practices at Arnone, hunting with falcons, those predatory birds of the skies, was quite unknown. It is true that the commentator Servius says that Capua got its name from augury of a falcon, since the Etruscans who founded the city saw a *capys*, their word for a falcon, as they were taking the auspices, but he does not say what use men made of the bird.[56] Pliny likewise records the names of many predatory birds — hawks large and small, and *chilyones*, which some maintain were falcons — but he makes no mention of the use of the birds for fowling:[57] and if this kind of fowling had been practiced in Vergil's time, he would doubtless have had Aeneas and Dido take the birds out hunting in the passage where: "the Massilian horsemen rush forth and a pack of keen-scented hounds."[58] We may confidently venture to say that, as I mentioned, two hundred years ago no tribe or people were accustomed to catch other birds (be they birds of ground, water, or air) with trained predators.[59]

Above Castelluccio (that is, Casilinum) and twelve miles from the sea, the city of Capua lies on the river Volturno at a new loca- 15

duo milia passuum[56] a priori[57] Capua est semotus. Nec id multis disseri oportet, quando vetustae urbis fundamenta, portae, theatra, templa, et cetera aedificia, moles magnae apud Sanctae Mariae basilicam cui 'de Gratia' est cognomen internoscuntur. De Capuae autem origine et nomine sic habet Livius in quarto: 'Peregrina res sed memoria digna traditur eo anno facta: Vulturnum Etruscorum urbem, quae nunc Capua est, ab Samnitibus captam, Capuamque ab duce eorum "Capye"[58] vel — quod propius est vero — a campestri agro appellatam. Cepere autem, prius bello fatigatis Etruscis, in societatem urbis accepti.[59] Deinde festo die graves[60] somno epulisque incolas veteres novi coloni nocturna caede adorti.' Notissima vero sunt et relatu longiuscula quae Livius de Capua tradit, sed digniora summatim accipiemus.

16   Libro XXIII dicit Hannibalem, cum descendisset ad Mare Inferum oppugnaturus Neapolim, flexisse iter in Capuam luxuriantem longa felicitate et indulgentia fortunae eamque recepisse. Et infra: eundem Hannibalem, castris apud Casilinum communitis praesidioque modico imposito, in hiberna Capuam concessisse, ubi exercitus ille Campanis emarcuit deliciis. Quem vero finem habuerit Capuanorum cum Hannibale amicitia (etsi vulgo notissimum est) paucis dicemus. Capua a Romanis capta, dicit Livius quosdam ex Romanis censuisse delendam esse urbem praevalidam, propinquam, inimicam. Ceterum praesens vicit utilitas: nam propter agrum, quem omnium fertilitate terrae satis constabat in Italia primum esse, urbs servata est ut esset aliqua aratorum sedes. Urbi frequentandae multitudo incolarum libertinorumque et institorum opificumque retenta. Ager omnis et tecta publica populi Romani

tion two miles from the original Capua.[60] Not much needs to be said about the ancient city because its foundations, gates, amphi-theaters, temples, and the great mass of other buildings can be seen from the Basilica of Santa Maria delle Grazie. And on the origin and name of Capua, Livy has the following to say in Book IV: "A foreign episode, but worth relating, is ascribed to this year, namely, that Volturnum, the Etruscan city which is now Capua, was taken by the Samnites, and named Capua from their leader Capys, or, as is more probable, from its plains. Now they captured it after being admitted by the Etruscans—who were worn out with fighting—to a share in the city and its fields; then, on a holi-day, when the old settlers were heavy with sleep and feasting, the newcomers fell upon them in the night and slaughtered them."[61] What Livy hands down to us about Capua is well known and lengthy to relate, but I shall rehearse the more important points in summary fashion.

In Book XXIII Livy says that when Hannibal had come down 16 to the Tyrrhenian Sea on his way to attack Naples, he directed his march toward Capua, a town that was indulging in its long-continued prosperity and the favor of fortune, and received its surrender.[62] Further on he says that once Hannibal had set up camp at Casilinum and had placed a small garrison in it, he with-drew into winter quarters at Capua, where that famous army of his wasted away amid the pleasures of Campania.[63] We should say something about the outcome of the friendship between the Capuans and Hannibal, well known though it is. According to Livy, some of the Romans wanted Capua to be destroyed, as being a city that was powerful, close by, and hostile. But the immediate advantages that the city offered won the day. The city was saved for its land, which was widely agreed to be the most fertile in all Italy, so that it might form a settlement for farmers. The great mass of the inhabitants—freedmen, merchants, and craftsmen—was kept to populate the city. All the land and buildings became

facta. Ceterum habitari tantum[61] urbem Capuam frequentarique placuit, corpus nullum civitatis, nec plebis concilium, nec senatus esse sine consilio publico, sine imperio. Nec saevitum incendiis ruinisque in tecta innoxia murosque.

17   Marcus autem Cicero, cum legem agrariam supradictam dissuaderet qua Capuam deduci coloniam volebant, oratione prima habet aliqua quae non dubitamus Titum Livium, quando supradicta scribebat, perlegisse. 'Capuam deduci coloniam volunt, illam urbem huic urbi rursus opponere. Qui locus propter ubertatem agrorum, abundantiamque rerum omnium, superbiam et crudelitatem genuisse videtur. Maiores nostri Capua[62] magistratus, senatum, consilium commune, omnia denique insignia rei publicae sustulerunt, neque aliud quicquam nisi inane nomen Capuae reliquerunt, quod videbant si quod rei publicae vestigium illis moenibus contineretur, urbem ipsam imperio domicilium praebere posse.' Et in oratione item *In Rullum* secunda: 'At enim ager Campanus dividitur orbis terrae pulcherrimus, et Capuam colonia deducitur urbem amplissimam atque ornatissimam.' Et infra: 'Unumne fundum pulcherrimum populi Romani, caput vestrae pecuniae, pacis ornamentum, subsidium belli, fundamentum vectigalium, horreum legionum, solatium annonae disperire patiemini. At vero hoc agri Campani vectigal, cum eius modi sit ut domi sit et omnibus praesidiis oppidorum tegatur, neque bellis sit infestum nec fructibus varium nec caelo et loco calamitosum.' Et infra: 'Campani semper superbi bonitate agrorum et fructuum magnitudine, urbis salubritate ac pulchritudine. Ex hac copia et omnium rerum affluentia primum illa nata est arrogantia quae a maioribus

the property of the Roman people. But they decided that the city of Capua should only be inhabited and populated; there was to be no civic government or popular council or senate—no public deliberation, no military authority. Nor was rage vented on innocent buildings and city walls by burning and demolition.[64]

In arguing against the previously mentioned agrarian legislation 17 that proposed planting a colony at Capua, Cicero has some things in his first speech that I am sure Livy read closely when he was writing the passages quoted above: "They want to plant a colony at Capua, to set that city once more against this one. The very fertility of its fields and the general abundance of produce seems to have engendered arrogance and cruelty in the place. Our forefathers deprived Capua of magistracies, a senate, public assemblies—in short all the marks of governance, and left it with nothing but an empty name, because they realized that if any vestige of self-government was left within those walls, the city could again become a base of power."[65] And likewise in the *Second Speech against Rullus*: "But the Campanian territory, the most beautiful in the world, is being divided up, and a colony sent to Capua, that magnificent and splendid city."[66] And then below: "Will you let the single most beautiful estate of the Roman people perish—the mainstay of your finances, the adornment of your peace, your support in war, the foundation of your revenues, the granary of your legions, your consolation in time of scarcity? But as our revenues derived from the territory of Campania are of such a nature that they are always at home, and protected by the garrisons of all our Italian towns, so they are neither hostile to us in time of war, nor variable in their productiveness, nor exposed to accidents of climate or location."[67] And below: "The Campanians were always proud from the excellence of their soil, and the luxuriance of their crops, from the healthiness and beauty of their city. From that abundance, and from this affluence in all things, in the first place, originated those qualities; arrogance, which demanded of our an-

nostris alterum consulem postulavit, deinde ea luxuries quae ipsum Hannibalem (armis etiam tunc invictum) voluptate vicit.'

18   Hanc ipsam urbem (contra ac Cicero suaserat) Julius Caesar coloniam deduci voluit. De quo Suetonius: 'Cum in colonia Capua deducti lege Julia coloni, ad exstruendas villas vetustissima sepulchra disicerent idque eo studiosius facerent quod aliquantum[63] operis antiqui scrutantes reperiebant, tabula aenea in monumento, in quo dicebatur Capys, conditor Capuae, sepultus, inventa est.' Eandem vero Capuam urbem, quam Romanus Populus in tam iusto odio servavit et quam Cicero tantis extulit laudibus, rex Vandalorum Gensericus, ad annum sexcentesimum postquam Romanis fuerat subdita, ferro ignique destructam, reliquit habitatoribus destitutam. Et cum, Ostrogothis a Narsete omni potentatu deiectis, eodem loco eosdemque inter parietes et muros Capua rehabitata esset, ad annum inde circiter centesimum a Longobardis sub triginta ducibus tunc agentibus iterum destructa fuit. Quis[64] autem et quo tempore postea eam ad hunc in quo nunc est duos mille passus remotum transtulerit locum, nec alicubi legimus nec ab his qui inhabitant civibus scire potuimus.

19   Plinius in Italiae descriptione cum ad Capuam pervenit, campum illi adiacere dicit Leborinum[65] totius Italiae amoenissimum. Et libro XVII de terrarum diversitate tractans, Leborinum Capuae campum nobilem appellat, eiusque solum dicit, arduum opera et difficile[66] cultu, bonis quam vitiis uberius pascere. Est vero hoc totum campestre solum, quod a Tifatis monte urbi imminente ad Neapolitanos Puteolanosque colles pertinens, Vulturno ab ipsa urbe Capua ad eius ostia, quibus se in mare exonerat, est

cestors that one of the consuls should be chosen ⟨from Capua⟩: and in the second place, that luxury which conquered Hannibal himself by pleasure, who up to that time had proved invincible in arms."[68]

Contrary to what Cicero had been urging, Julius Caesar sup-   18 ported the foundation of a colony in the city of Capua. On this Suetonius writes: "When the colonists assigned to the colony of Capua by the Julian Law were demolishing some tombs of great antiquity to build country houses, and were applying themselves to the task all the more energetically because as they rummaged about they kept finding quantities of ancient handiwork, a tablet of bronze was discovered in a tomb in which the founder of Capua, Capys, was said to have been buried."[69] Six hundred years after it came under Roman control, this city of Capua, which the Roman people so justly hated and Cicero so highly praised, was destroyed with fire and the sword by Genseric, king of the Vandals, and left deserted. About one hundred years after that, when Capua had been repopulated in the same location and within the same houses and walls after Narses had utterly destroyed the power of the Ostrogoths, it was destroyed a second time by the Lombards, operating at that time under the thirty dukes.[70] But who later effected the relocation of the city to a spot two miles away, where it now is, and when, I have been unable to find out, either from reading or from the local inhabitants.

When Pliny gets to Capua in his survey of Italy, he says that it   19 lies next to the Leborine plain, the loveliest in all Italy.[71] And in Book XVII, in dealing with the difference between soils, Pliny calls the Leborine plain at Capua "famous," and says that in terms of productivity the good points of its soil, hard to work with and difficult to cultivate though it is, outweigh the bad.[72] In fact the land of the entire plain — extending from Mount Tifata,[73] which overlooks Capua, to the hills of Naples and Pozzuoli — is bounded by the stretch of the Volturno from the city of Capua to the

clausum. Et periti regionis Capuani cives affirmant campos, qui
Adversam urbem novam ad Atellae urbis vetustae ruinas aedificatam circumstant, in trecentorum annorum publicis privatisque
monumentis dici Leborios: eam vero vim habuit Leborinae terrae
appellatio ut Campaniae nomen in suum mutari obtinuerit. Idque
nos meliuscule quam a pravis chronicorum scriptoribus est tradi-
tum referre confidimus.

20   Capua urbe vetusti in eam Romanorum odii et binae desolatio-
nis exsecrabili infamia laborante, vicini urbium oppidorumque populi Campanos se appellari ignominiosum periculosumque ducen-
tes id declinarunt patrium nomen et sese Leborinos pro Campanis
dixere, effecitque obstinata eorum perseverantia ut quicquid urbium et locorum in Campania censeri solebat de terra Leboris di-
ceretur. Sed corruptum nunc 'laboris' verbum in eam partem ab
ignorantibus accipitur, ut Laboris Terram cui labor utiliter impen-
datur dictam existiment: quamquam non desunt qui magis absurde dicant terram hanc a labore, quem illi capiendae et dominio
subigendae impendi oporteat, sic a maioribus appellatam.

21   Atella vero urbs, cuius saepe meminit Livius et quam Cicero
supra, *De Lege Agraria*, cum Teano opprimi aegre ferendum ostendit, fuisse ubi nunc est nova urbs Adversa praeter alias rationes
hoc uno constat argumento: quod Sanctae Mariae ecclesia haud
longe ab Adversa cognomen 'in Atella' vetustum retinet. Libetque
utriusque urbis (et veteris et novae) dignitates referre: primum
Atella haudquaquam minora in re parva quam Capua in magnis
praebuit Campanae luxuriae documenta, siquidem pro superbiae
et crudelitatis origine, quam Cicero tribuit Capuae, haec Atellana-

mouth of the river where it discharges into the sea. Citizens of Capua who are experts in the local geography affirm that the plains surrounding the modern city of Aversa (built on the ruins of the ancient city of Atella) are called Leborine in public and private documents of the last three hundred years: the name "Terra di Leborie" has proved so powerful that it has been able to get the name "Campania" replaced by its own. I am sure that this explanation is better than that handed down in the writings of ill-informed chroniclers.

The city of Capua suffered from the dreadful notoriety of the   20 ancient hatred of the Romans and the double destruction it had undergone. The peoples of the nearby cities and towns accordingly thought it shameful and dangerous to be called Campanians, and they rejected their ancestral name and called themselves "Leborini" instead of "Campani." Thanks to their dogged persistence all the cities and sites traditionally reckoned Campanian were said to belong to the "Land of Lebor." But the name, now corrupted into "Labor," is taken by the ignorant to mean that the land was called "Laboris" because labor is well spent on it — though there are those who say even more improbably that this land was so named by our ancestors from the "work" that one needs to spend on it to take it and tame it.[74]

The city of Atella is often mentioned by Livy, and Cicero in his   21 speech *On the Agrarian Law* (cited above) mentions that it had the misfortune of being overwhelmed along with Teanum.[75] It is fairly agreed that Atella was where the modern city of Aversa now is, among other reasons, from this single piece of evidence, that the church of Santa Maria not far from Aversa retains its ancient name of Santa Maria in Atella. I will here record the distinctions of both cities, old and new. In the first place, Atella has given us ample proofs — on a small scale, as Capua does on a large one — of Campanian lasciviousness: if Capua was the source of the cruelty and arrogance that Cicero ascribes to it, Atella devised the lubri-

rum carminum lasciviam modulationemque (quod nomen indicat et Macrobius affirmat) invenit. Quid vero hae fuerint Atellanae M. Varro, Aulus Gellius Macrobiusque, et Iuvenalis satiricus saepe indicant, earumque artis cum non expediat nec sit huius temporis et loci inquirere documentum, satis superque fuerit obscoenam notare lasciviam. Pueri et puellae luxuriemque spumantes natu maiores compositum metro ac musica, modulatione, lascivis et omnia dictu factuque[67] pudenda exprimentibus verbis carmen, motu quoque corporis et gestu quaqua versum etiam resupinato,[68] ita in choreis et ad impudicorum mensas pronuntiabant gesticulabanturque ut nihil praeter ipsum coeundi exquisitissimum deesset effectum.[69] Meliora autem originis et disciplinae rudimenta habuit urbs Adversa.

22   Robertus Guiscardus, vir gloria et laude dignissimus, magnam et praestantem eam Italiae partem, quae regnum Siciliae aut Neapolitanum est appellata, a Saracenis Graecisque laceratam, ad regni ipsius formam primus redegit. Qui Neapolim Capuamque una eademque premens obsidione castra apud Atellam habuit communita, in quibus cum aliquot perseverasset annis[70] civitatem condidit ab ipsoque adversandi praeclaris et potentibus urbibus effectu[71] 'Adversae' illi nomen in rei gestae memoriam dedit.

23   Sed iam ad maris litora[72] est redeundum. Post Vulturnum sequitur Clanius amnis, apud Suessulam oppidum medio paene inter Capuam et Nolam urbes tractu in montibus oriundus. Estque is fluvius de quo Vergilius: 'Clanius non aequus Acerris,' quia Acerrarum urbis agrum (sicut et Capuanum et olim Atellanum, nunc Adversanum) multis inundat in locis: adeo ut longiusculis pontibus eum Capuam inter et Adversam urbem oporteat iungi, ad quos pontes molas esse multas videmus.

ciousness and rhythmic measures of the Atellan farces, as the name suggests and Macrobius confirms.[76] Just what these Atellan farces were is often suggested by Varro, Aulus Gellius and Macrobius, and by the satirist Juvenal.[77] There is no point in examining a specimen of this art form here, this being neither the time nor place; it is more than enough merely to note their lewd smuttiness. Boys and girls and old men in a lather of debauchery would declaim in troupes and at the tables of the shameless a play composed in meter and set to music and melody, in filthy language and words expressing every sort of disgraceful behavior in word and deed, with bodily movements and gestures of every sort, even laid out on their backs, and would gesticulate in such a way that nothing was left to the imagination save an explicit act of sexual intercourse.[78] The city of Aversa, however, had better beginnings in her origin and culture.

The glorious and much-lauded Robert Guiscard was the first to reduce into the form of a kingdom that large and magnificent portion of Italy known as the Kingdom of Sicily, or the Kingdom of Naples, which the Saracens and Greeks had shattered. While he was putting pressure on Naples and Capua with one and the same siege, he had his military camp at Atella. After he had spent a number of years in this camp, he founded a city there, and from the very fact of having these famous and powerful cities as *adversaries* he gave it the name Aversa to commemorate the event.[79] 22

But now we must return to the coast. The river Clanio comes next after the Volturno. It rises in the mountains at the town of Castel di Sessola, at a spot almost halfway between the cities of Capua and Nola. This is the river of which Vergil writes: "Clanius unfriendly to Acerrae,"[80] because in many places it floods the territory of the city of Acerrae, as it does the territory of Capua and of the city that was once Atella and is now Aversa, so that it had to be crossed by quite long bridges between Capua and the city of Aversa; there are many mills to be seen by these bridges. 23

24   Eidem Clanio haud longe a Mari Infero turris apposita est parum vetusta, nunc Patriae[73] appellata et in ruinis Linterni Scipionis Africani villae aedificata. Namque Ptolemaeus Pomponiusque
Mela, Plinius et Guido Ravennas, Iginii imitator, Linternum inter
Vulturnum et Cumas ponunt. Livius autem uno in loco cum supradictis sentire, in alio discrepare videtur. Nam, libro XXII, cum
difficultates afferret quibus Hannibal coactus videretur ex Falerno
agro, qua venerat angusta via, in Samnium rediturus (quod supra
diximus), sic habet: 'Poenus tunc intra fortunae minas ac Linterni
arenas perhorridas[74] situ hibernaturus esset.' Cum ergo ad sinistram Vulturni tunc ageret Hannibal nec ipsum amnem ibi praeal-
tum vado neque ponte ad Casilinum communito ac praesidiis fir-
mato transmissurus videretur, oportuit ad Falerni agri partem esse
Linternum, ubi eum Livius nisi angustias superasset hiematurum
fuisse dicit. Et, libro vigesimo tertio, idem Livius[75] cum fraudem
scribit qua Capuani Cumas suis partibus adiicere sint[76] conati, sic
habet: 'Interim Titus Sempronius cos., Sinuessae (quo ad conve-
niendum diem edixerat) exercitu lustrato, transgressus Vulturnum
flumen circa Linternum posuit castra.'

25   Ex quibus nulli dubium fuerit constare Linternum fuisse (sicut
dicti asserunt cosmographi) ad eam Vulturni partem quae spectat
in Cumas. Necessariumque erit et dicere et tenere Livium, qui
loca perambulaverit et Linterni (sicut infra ostendimus) Scipionis
statuam tempestate disiectam viderit, scivisse villam quidem ultra
Vulturnum sed eius agrum arenosum[77] stagnosumque citra exsti-
tisse. Est vero Linternum locus in quo P. Cornelius[78] Scipio Africanus voluntarium egit exsilium, quem fama est morientem sepulchro inscribi iussisse: 'Ingrata patria, ne ossa quidem mea habes.'

On the Clanio not far from the Tyrrhenian Sea a tower has in 24 recent times been erected, now called Torre di Patria and built on the ruins of the villa of Scipio Africanus at Liternum. In fact Ptolemy and Pomponius Mela, Pliny and Guido of Ravenna (the imitator of Hyginus) all place Liternum between the Volturno and Cumae.[81] Livy, however, seems to agree with these authors in one place and to differ from them in another: in Book XXII, recounting the difficulties that seem to have constrained Hannibal as he prepared to return to Samnium by the same narrow road along which he had come from Falernian territory (as I said above), Livy has this to say: "the Carthaginians were set to go into winter quarters under threat from Fortune and amid the sands of Liternum bristling with filth."[82] Hannibal was therefore operating on the left bank of the Volturno and it seems he did not intend to cross the river, which was very deep there, by fording it nor by the bridge at Casilinum, which had been fortified and reinforced by a garrison: so Liternum—where Livy says Hannibal was going to spend the winter, had he not managed to get through the passes—must have been toward Falernian territory. And writing in Book XXIII of the trick that the Capuans used to try to win Cumae to their side, Livy also says the following: "The consul Titus Sempronius meanwhile reviewed the army at Sinuessa (where he had announced a date for mobilization), crossed the river Volturno, and made camp near Liternum."[83]

All this should dispel any doubt that Liternum was located on 25 the part of the river Volturno facing Cumae, as the geographers mentioned above assert. We are obliged to state and affirm that Livy, who walked over the ground and saw a statue of Scipio that weather had shattered at Liternum (as I shall mention), indeed knew that his estate had been on the far side of the Volturno but on this side of the river's sandy and swampy land. Liternum is the place where Scipio Africanus spent his voluntary exile. As he lay dying he is said to have ordered his tomb inscribed with these

Quae facta in monumento ingratitudinis patriae inscriptio effecit[79] ut locum nuper certius exploratiusque invenerimus.[80] Namque ad dictum amnem Clanium paulo supra ostium quod habet in mari,[81] turris est ruinis aedificiorum veterum superaedificata, quam (ut diximus) Turrim Patriae vocant, ubi id monumentum fuisse tenemus. Et praeter id patriae vocabulum praeterque supradicta Ptolemaei, Plinii, Livii, et aliorum testimonia, certitudinem quoque attulit nobis evidentiorem[82] fons aquae acidulae quem Plinius Linterni fuisse dicit, cuius aqua vini modo faciat temulentos. Scatet enim nunc etiam inter praedictas aedificiorum ruinas aqua, quam pastores affirmant epotam omnes capitis languores curare. Nosque, ea accurate gustata, saporem quidem (ut ceterarum quae bibuntur) bonum esse cognovimus. Sed quamvis fumos[83] ab ea in nares (sicut a vino consuevit) non ingratos olfecerimus,[84] quos potatio habeat effectus — forte ob haustus moderationem — intellegere nequivimus. Seneca, *Epistula*[85] LI: 'Linterni honestius Scipio quam Baiis exsulabat.' Sepulchri autem eiusque inscriptionis et monumenti ac statuae si nullum nunc exstat certum indicium, minus miror, quod Livius Patavinus, qui minus centum annis ab illius aetate abfuit, quid ipse viderit, libro XXVIIII, scribit: 'Scipionem alii Romae alii Linterni et mortuum et sepultum ferunt, utrobique monumenta ostenduntur et statuae. Nam et Linterni monumentum, monumentoque statua superimposita fuit quam tempestate disiectam nuper vidimus ipsi. Et Romae extra portam Capenam in Scipionum monumento tres statuae sunt: duae Publii et Lucii Scipionum dicuntur esse, tertia poetae Q. Ennii.' Et Seneca, *Epistulae*[86] LXXVII initio, videtur id ignorasse sepulchrum. Nam dicit 'in

words: "Ungrateful fatherland, you do not even get my bones."[84]
The inscription about his fatherland's ingratitude on the monument recently led me to make a more certain and definitive identification of the site of Liternum, for a little way above the mouth of the Clanio where it empties into the sea, there is a tower built on top of the ruins of some ancient buildings. They call it Torre di Patria, as I mentioned, and this I believe to be the site of Scipio's tomb. Apart from the word "Patria" and the statements of Ptolemy, Pliny, Livy, and others cited above, a spring of mineral water also gave us plainer testimony: Pliny says it was at Liternum and that its water made men tipsy like wine.[85] The water wells up even now among the ruins of the buildings that I mentioned, and shepherds say that drinking it is a cure for all kinds of headaches. I carefully tasted it and realized that its flavor, as of other such waters that people drink, was indeed good. But though I inhaled its not unpleasant vapors into the nostrils, as one does with wine, I could not detect any effect that drinking it had, perhaps because I took only a moderate draft. Seneca writes in *Epistle* LI: "It was more honorable for Scipio to spend his exile at Liternum than at Baiae."[86] It is not so surprising if no certain evidence of Scipio's tomb and its inscription, the monument and the statue still survives, since Livy of Padua, who lived less than a hundred years after Scipio's time, writes about what he himself saw in Book XXVIII: "Some say that Scipio died and was buried at Rome, others at Liternum, and tombs and statues can be seen in both places. Recently I myself saw at Liternum a tomb with a statue set on it that had been toppled in a storm. And there are three statues in the tomb of the Scipios outside the Porta Capena at Rome: two are said to be those of Publius and Lucius Scipio, and a third of the poet Q. Ennius."[87] At the beginning of *Letter* LXXVII, Seneca seems to have been unaware of this tomb at Rome, for he says: "I am resting at the villa which once belonged to Scipio himself, and

ipsa Scipionis villa iacens haec tibi scribo, adoratis Manibus eius et ara, quam sepulchrum esse tanti viri suspicor.'

26 Linterno[87] Cumae ad quintum adiacent milliarium,[88] interque utrumque locum, qua in parte litus inter stagnum et mare incurvatur, villa fuit Servilii Vatiae, quam Seneca, *Epistula* LV, describit, dicitque: praetorium hominem illum divitem nulla alia re notum fuisse quam eius villae otio, in quo consenuerit, ut occupati aliquando clamaverint: 'O Vatia, solus scis vivere,' cum tamen ille iudicio Senecae sciret latere non vivere. Unde dicit de se ipso Seneca solitum quotiens illac transiret iocando dicere, non de vivo sed tamquam de mortuo: 'Hic situs est[89] Vatia.' Cumanae urbis originem hanc tradit Livius in VIII: 'Cumani a Chalcide Euboica originem trahunt. Classe, qua advecti domo fuerant, multum in ora maris eius quod incolunt potuere. Primo in insulam Aenariam et Pithecusas[90] egressi, deinde in continentem ausi sedes transferre.' Vergilius: 'Et tandem Euboicis Cumarum allabitur oris.' Et 'hic, ubi delatus Cumaeam accesseris urbem,' super quo Servius: 'Euboea insula est, de cuius civitate Chalcide profecti sunt ad novas sedes quaerendas. Et haud longe a Baiis, qui locus a Baio, Ulyxis filio,[91] illic sepulto nomen accepit, invenerunt vacuum litus ubi, visa muliere gravida, civitatem condiderunt.'

27 Livius in secundo: 'Accersita deinde auxilia et a Latinis populis et a Cumis. Cumanae cohortes arte adversus vim usae declinavere paululum. Effuseque palatos hostes conversis signis a tergo adortae sunt.' Et infra: 'Insignis hic annus nuntio Tarquinii mortis. Mortuus est Cumis, quo se post fractas opes Latinorum ad Aristodemum tyrannum contulerat.' Et libro quarto: 'Eodem anno a Cam-

I write to you after doing reverence to his spirit and to an altar which I am inclined to think is the tomb of that great warrior."[88]

Five miles from Liternum lies neighboring Cumae. Servilius   26 Vatia's villa was between the two places, where the beach curves round between the lagoon and the sea.[89] Seneca describes it in *Letter LV*, saying that that wealthy praetorian was known for nothing so much as the leisure he took in that villa where he passed his old age — so much so that people with busy lives sometimes used to cry aloud: "O Vatia, only you know how to live!" Though in Seneca's judgment, what he knew was how to lie low, not how to live. So Seneca says about himself that whenever he passed that way, he used to say in jest, as of a corpse and not a living man: "Here lies Vatia!"[90] Livy gives us this account of the city of Cumae's foundation in Book VIII: "The men of Cumae came from Chalcis in Euboea. Thanks to the fleet in which they had sailed from their home, they enjoyed much power on the coast of that sea by which they dwell. Having landed first on the island of Aenaria and the Pithecusae, they afterward ventured to transfer their seat to the mainland."[91] Vergil: "And at long last he slid to the shores of Euboean Cumae," and "here when on your voyage you reach the city of Cumae."[92] On this line, Servius writes: "Euboea is an island, and from the Euboean city of Chalcis they set out in search of a new place to live. Not far from Baiae — a place which got its name from Baius, the son of Ulysses who was buried there — they found an empty beach, where, after seeing a pregnant woman, they founded their city."[93]

Livy writes in Book II: "Auxiliaries were then summoned both   27 from the Latin peoples and from Cumae. The Cumaean levies, employing skill to meet force, swerved a little to one side, and facing about attacked the enemy stragglers in the rear."[94] And below: "This year was marked by the announcement of Tarquinius's death. He died at Cumae, whither he had gone to the court of the tyrant Aristodemus after the downfall of the Latin cause."[95] And

panis Cumae, quam Graeci tunc urbem tenebant, capiuntur.' Et
octavo: 'Cumanos Suessulanosque eiusdem iuris condicionisque
cuius Capua esse placuit.'

28   Est vero celsus in urbe Cumana collis in cuius cacumine fuit
templum Apollinis, de quo Vergilius: 'Arces quibus altus Apollo
praesidet.'[92] Et quidem nunc ea in urbe, quam vidimus omni destitutam habitatore, praeter rupes saxo stupendas vivo, pennae cernuntur murorum excelsae. Et ubi Apollinis arx fuit, sacellum est
Christianum et ipsum vetustate consumptum. Nihilque exstat integrum nisi caverna frontispicio decorata manufacto, quam Sibyl-
lae antrum fuisse socius itineris noster[93] Prosper Camuleius, vir
doctus, eam ingressus quibusdam coniecturis affirmavit. Fuit quoque Cumis propinquus ad tria milia passuum[94] Hamarum locus
sacer, de quo Livius XXIII: 'Campani adorti sunt rem Cumanam
suae iurisdictionis facere, primo sollicitantes ut ab Romanis defice-
rent. Ubi id parum processit, dolum ad capiendum eos comparant.
Sacrificium ad Hamas nocturnum erat.' Huius vero olim celebris
loci mons arduus, qui a balneis nunc Tripergulanis vix mille
quingentos abest passus, ruinis ad verticem tegitur conspiciendis
et quibus nulla est propior Tripergulis hominum habitatio aut
cultura. Ad partem vero qua Cumae spectant in Avernum et Baias,
distat pariter ab utrisque urbibus fornix latericio opere sublimibus
columnis sustentatus cuicumque Romano operi comparandus.

29   Abest deinde quinto a Cumis Misenus mons Vergilii carmine
celebratus: et 'nunc Misenus ab illo dicitur.' Eidemque, qua spectat
in Cumas, lacunae adiacent nunc 'Mare Mortuum' appellatae, circa
quas in continentis supercilio ruinae et fundamenta cernuntur
eximia. Fuit namque locus in quo Suetonius Tranquillus scribit
Octavianum Augustum classem apud Misenum instituisse ingentem quae versas in Tyrrhenum mare imperii Romani provincias,

in Book IV: "In the same year Cumae, a city which the Greeks then held, was captured by the Campanians."[96] And in Book VIII: "They voted to give the people of Cumae and Suessula the same rights and the same terms as the Capuans."[97]

In the city of Cumae there is a high hill, at the summit of 28 which there was a temple of Apollo, of which Vergil says: "citadels over which high Apollo presides."[98] The city is now bare of human inhabitants, as I observed, but lofty pinnacles of walls may still be seen beside dizzying crags of living rock. Where Apollo's citadel once stood there is a Christian chapel, likewise destroyed by time. Nothing remains intact, except a cavern with an ornamental entrance which my traveling companion, the learned Prospero da Camogli, entered, concluding from certain pieces of evidence that it was the cave of the Sybil.[99] Three miles from Cumae was the holy place of Hamae,[100] on which Livy writes in Book XXIII: "Campanians attempted to reduce the state of Cumae to subjection, at first tempting them to revolt from the Romans. When that failed, they contrived a ruse to entrap them. A nighttime sacrifice took place at Hamae."[101] The top of the steep mountain of this once celebrated place, barely a mile and a half from the baths of the present-day Tripergole, is covered in conspicuous ruins — there is no human dwelling or cultivation closer than Tripergole.[102] In the area where Cumae looks toward Lake Avernus and Baiae, equidistant from both cities, there is a brickwork arch supported on high columns which is comparable to any Roman work.

Then five miles from Cumae comes Mount Misenus, celebrated 29 in Vergil's poem: and "now Mount Misenus is named after him."[103] Lagoons now called the "Dead Sea" lie along the side of Mount Misenus facing Cumae,[104] and around them on the shore of the mainland remarkable ruins and foundations can be seen. This in fact was the spot where Suetonius tells us that Octavian stationed a huge fleet at Misenum to protect the provinces of the Roman empire that face onto the Tyrrhenian Sea, on one side Gaul and

hinc Galliam et utramque Hispaniam inde Mauritaniam[95] Africamque, et interiectas insulas tutaretur. Eratque eius classis praefectus Plinius Veronensis quando apud Vesaevum montem incendio est absumptus. Distant a Miseni promontorio hinc Cumae (sicut diximus) quinque[96] — inde Lucrinus Avernusque totidem — milibus passuum.[97] Et cum a Cumis vix quatuor milibus et[98] terrestri via absit Avernus, illa quinum undique milium maritima longitudo terram ambit omnium olim Italiae pulcherrimam, in qua Baiae fuerunt, civitas opulenta. Idque omne solum etsi quinis (ut diximus) productum est milibus, latitudine tamen parum variata, duo alicubi et minus alibi milia explet ut digiti unius speciem[99] prae se ferat. Quo in terrarum, ut ita dixerim, digito tam multa cernuntur, partim integra in subterraneis, partim superius semiruta, partim in ruinas collapsa veterum operum monumenta ut, extra urbis Romae moenia, nihil illi toto in orbe terrarum aedificiorum magnitudine ac pulchritudine par credam existimemque fuisse, ut non iniuria dicat Horatius: 'Nullus in orbe[100] locus[101] Baiis praelucet amoenis.' Cumque Misenus e regione Puteolos spectet, mare quo invicem dirimuntur, ex Suetonii Tranquilli in *Vita Gaii Caligulae*[102] sententia, vix tria milia passuum[103] et sescentos implet: unde sinus utrobique (dictus olim Baianus) a Miseno in intimum Averni sinum quinis et totidem ab Averno in Puteolos milibus est productus. Fuerit vero operosum singula describere quae aut digitus ille terrestris aut sinus Baianus habet, sed digniora (quantum fieri poterit) breviter attingemus.

30   Primum Misenus ipse mons, qua in promontorium coarctatur, etsi natura cavernosus fuit,[104] tamen tantis excavatus est operum laboribus, tantis vel marmoreis vel latericio et lapide quadrato compactis in sublime ductis sustentatur columnis, ut ubique pensilis videatur. Erantque (ut apparet)[105] intus balnea, erant natato-

the two Spains, on the other Mauritania and Africa, and the islands between them.[105] The elder Pliny was admiral of this fleet
when he was killed in the eruption of Mount Vesuvius. On the
one side Cumae is five miles from Capo di Miseno, as I said, and
on the other the Lucrine Lake and Lake Avernus are the same
distance from the cape. Though Lake Avernus is scarcely four
miles from Cumae by the land route, the journey along the coast
of five miles each way encompasses terrain that was once the most
beautiful in all Italy, including the wealthy city of Baiae. This
whole tract of land, though five miles in length, as I said, is fairly
uniform in width, being two miles across in some places and in
others less, so that it bears the appearance of a finger. On this
"finger" of land there are so many monuments of ancient workmanship to be seen — some intact beneath the ground, some half-
ruined above ground, some collapsed in ruins — that apart from
the walls of Rome, I cannot think that there is anything in the
whole world to equal it in the extent and beauty of its buildings.
So Horace was quite right to say, "No place on earth outshines
lovely Baiae."[106] Since Punta di Miseno sits directly opposite Pozzuoli, the sea which separates them, according to Suetonius's esti-
mate in the *Life of Caligula*, measures not quite three and a half
miles,[107] and so it follows that the bay formerly known as the Gulf
of Baiae extends five miles on both sides, from Misenum to the
innermost inlet of Lake Avernus and from Lake Avernus to Pozzuoli. It would be laborious to describe every individual feature of
this finger of land or of the Gulf of Baiae, but as far as possible I
shall touch briefly on the more important ones.

In the first place Mount Misenus, where it narrows and turns   30
into a promontory, though it is naturally cavernous, has nevertheless been hollowed out by such vast construction projects, and is
held aloft by so many columns of marble or brick and dressed
stone that the whole mountain seems suspended in air. It appears
that there were baths inside it, there were swimming pools, and

ria, erant ad cenas luxumque triclinia. Superius vero, in continenti et qua vergit in praedictum Misenatium classis locum, fundamenta visuntur his, qui non viderint, incredibilia, ubi 'Piscinam' vulgo 'mirabilem' dicunt. Nam cum ea pulcherrimae (ut constat) aedis desuper destructae fundamenta fuerint, pars haec exstans subterranea, sublimibus sustentata latericiis columnis, ducentos quinquaginta longitudine centumque et sexaginta latitudine passus patet. Et ita est integra ut nova videatur, quam Lucii Luculli domum, quae illi erat in Baiano, fuisse tenemus. Et quia in loco omnium Italiae calido est sita, videtur esse illa de qua Plutarchus scribit Lucullum perbelle cum Cn. Pompeio ac Marco Cicerone et plerisque illius saeculi principibus viris iocatum fuisse, cum, ipsis omnibus Romanis in Lucullano (nunc Frascato) apud Lucullum aestate cenantibus, Pompeio imperitiam aedificandi in Lucullo damnanti quod domum, pulcherrimam sumptuosissimamque ⟨et⟩ nimis multis porticibus fenestrisque apertam, aestati quidem idoneam sed hiemi omnino inhabilem[106] fecisset, ille respondit virtuti suae Pompeium detrahere, qui grues se prudentiores existimet, aestiva loca hiemaliaque alternis inhabitantes. Sese enim dixit,[107] qui hanc in Lucullano aestati idoneam fabrefecerit, alteram in semper vernanti Baiano hiemalem pulcherrimamque exaedificasse.

31   Sepulchra vero et villarum aliorumque monumentorum vestigia, partim omnino prostrata partim semiintegra, tam multa eo in quinum milium peninsulae et digiti territorio cernuntur ut continuatam ibi urbem potius quam dispersas per agrum villas fuisse appareat.

32   Sed iam sinum describamus Baianum, de quo nihil est quod admirabilius dicere possumus[108] quam quod omnia eius litora decem milia passuum[109] a Miseno ad Puteolos in circuitu protensa aedificiis (et quidem omnium quae[110] raro alibi viderimus maxi-

couches for banquets and debauchery. Up on the mainland, toward the location of the fleet of Misenum mentioned earlier, the foundations can be seen—incredible till you have seen them—of what was generally known as "the amazing pool." Though it is believed that these were the foundations of a beautiful building that was destroyed above ground, the part of it that survives underground is held up on lofty brick columns and measures 250 feet in length and 160 feet in width. It has suffered so little damage that it appears as new, and I am convinced that it was Lucius Lucullus's Baian home.[108] Being built in one of the hottest parts of Italy, it seems it is the residence that Plutarch writes about, where Lucullus exchanged graceful banter with Pompey and Cicero and some of the leading men of the age. All these Romans were dining with Lucullus in the summer at the Lucullanum, nowadays Frascati,[109] when Pompey criticized Lucullus's inexperience in building, since he had constructed a beautiful and expensive home which, because it lay open to the weather with too many porticos and windows, was fine for summer but impractical in winter. Lucullus replied that Pompey was slighting him in thinking that cranes were brighter than he was, as they lived in one place in the summer and another in winter. He said that though he had indeed had this Lucullanum home constructed for summer, he had built another very beautiful home for the winter on his estate at Baiae, where it was always springtime.[110]

Tombs and the remains of villas and other monuments—some 31 completely ruined, others fairly intact—are to be seen in such great numbers in the five-mile stretch of this peninsula and "finger" of land that it gives the appearance of having been a continuous city rather than country estates scattered over the land.

But now let us turn to the description of the Gulf of Baiae. I 32 can best convey its wonders by saying that in its ten miles circumference from Miseno to Pozzuoli, its entire shoreline was blanketed with uninterrupted buildings, as big as the biggest I have

mis) contecta ac continuata fuerunt, cum eorum pars collibus imposita celsissimis et in apertum prominentibus pelagus bracchiis sustentata fuerit, insanarum molium opere in profundissimum mare iactis. Exstant tamen aliqua paene integra, thermae scilicet, ad ipsum Baiani[111] sinum intimum, qui unicus nunc locus priscam Baiani appellationem memoriamque conservat. Sunt et aliae paene similes thermae illis propinquae, quarum conditoris et nominis notitiam habere nequivimus. Sed balneum longe infra Avernum petentibus et Lucrinum est obvium, nedum aedificii structuram sed et picturam quoque aliqua ex parte integram conservans. In quo versuum pars pictorum exstat, ex quorum verbis carptim lectis conicere licet id fuisse Ciceronis balneum, cui id carmen libertum eius adscripsisse Plinius asserit. Supraque illud idem Ciceronianum aliud est balneum in longam tortuosamque fossam saxo excavatum, quod sine aliquo aquae calentis[112] usu solo vapore sudores provocat copiosissimos et (sicut ferunt medici) saluberrimos. Fuit vero maioribus thermarum huius modi usus, quas ab actu fricandi[113] tergendique necessario 'frictolas' appellarunt. Easque aeque ac balneas viduis et virginibus Christianis vitandas[114] esse gloriosus[115] Ecclesiae doctor Hieronymus admonuit. 'Tritolam' nunc corrupte appellant.

33   Incipitque[116] ad eam sinus Baiani partem Lucrinus esse, de quo in Vergiliani versus expositione, 'An memorem portus Lucrinoque addidita claustra,' Servius sic habet: 'In Baiano sinu Campaniae contra Puteolanam civitatem lacus sunt duo, Avernus et Lucrinus, qui olim propter copiam piscium vectigalia magna praestabant. Sed cum maris impetus plerumque perrumpens exinde pisces excluderet et redemptores gravia damna paterentur, supplicaverunt Senatui. Et profectus Caesar ductis bracchiis exclusit partem maris quae ante infesta esse consueverat, reliquitque breve spatium per

occasionally seen elsewhere: some of them were set on the tops of high hills and held up on piers projecting out into the open water and set in the depths of the sea on immense piles. Some buildings survive almost whole, on the other hand, in particular a thermal bath complex on the inmost reach of the Gulf of Baiae, a place that is the only one to preserve the name and memory of ancient Baiae. There are other baths nearby much like these, but I was unable get any information on their builder or their name. But there is a bath far below these which those making for Avernus and Lucrinus come across. It preserves not just the structure of the building, but a panel too, in parts still undamaged: some of the panel's painted verses survive, and from the words that can be read here and there, one gathers that this was the bath of Cicero, on which Pliny says Cicero's freedman wrote this poem.[111] Further up, above the bath of Cicero, there is another bath, carved out of the rock into a long and winding trough, which by steam alone and without using any hot water, brings on abundant and very healthy sweating, according to the physicians. To be sure, our ancestors did use thermal spas of this kind, which they called *frictolae* from the action that is needed of rubbing or wiping. Jerome, the glorious Doctor of the Church, admonished widows and maidens to steer clear of these rubbing baths, as also of conventional baths.[112] Now they call this *frictola* "Tritola" by corruption.[113]

On this stretch of the Gulf of Baiae begins the Lucrine Lake, on which Servius in his explication of the Vergilian verse, "Should I tell of the harbors and the barriers placed on the Lucrine Lake?," has this to say: "On the Gulf of Baiae in Campania, opposite the city of Puteoli, there are two lakes, Avernus and Lucrinus, which were once very profitable thanks to their plentiful fish. But the sea often broke through into them, and one invasion left them without any fish, bringing heavy losses to the contractors. When they appealed to the Senate, Caesar set out to keep back the part of the sea which had been persistently dangerous by constructing break-

33

Avernum quo et copia piscium posset intrare et fluctus non essent molesti. Quod opus Iulium dictum est.' De eodem Suetonius: 'Portum Iulium apud Baias immisso in Lucrinum et Avernum mari lacum effecit.' Et Servius in Vergiliani versus expositione, 'Divinosque lacus,' sic dicit: 'Avernus et Lucrinus lacus antea silvarum densitate sic ambiebantur, ut exhalans inde per angustias aquae sulpureae odor gravissimus[117] supervolantes aves necaret: unde et Avernus dictus. Quam rem Caesar audiens deiectis silvis amoena reddidit loca.' Et infra in Vergilianum versum, 'Acheronte refuso':[118] 'Acheron fluvius dicitur infernorum. Sed constat locum esse haud procul a Baiis undique montibus saeptum adeo ut nec orientem solem possit aspicere nec occidentem, sed tantum meridionalem.'

34   Baiani sinus latitudinem, de qua diximus, Suetonius in Caligulae[119] vita sic ostendit: 'Baianum medium intervallum et Puteolanas moles trium milium et sexcentorum fere passuum ponte iunxit, contractis undique onerariis navibus et ordine duplici ad ancoras collocatis, superiecto aggere terreno ac directo in Appiae viae formam. Per hunc pontem ultro citroque commeavit biduo continenti, primo die phalerato equo, insignis quoque civica corona, et scutum tenens, et gladio aureaque chlamyde, postridie quadrigario habitu curriculoque biiugi famosorum equorum.' Sed et Nero, illius successor, maiores circa Baianum excogitavit insanias. De quo Suetonius: 'Inchoabat[120] piscinam a Miseno ad Avernum lacum contectam porticibus, quasi conclusam, quo quicquid totis Baiis calidarum aquarum esset converteretur. Fossam ab Averno Ostiam qua navibus necnon via iretur, longitudine centum

waters, leaving a short channel through to Avernus by which fish could enter in quantity without the waves causing damage. This was known as the 'Julian works.'"[114] Suetonius writes of it: "He created the Julian Harbor at Baiae by allowing the sea passage into the lakes of Lucrinus and Avernus."[115] Servius in commenting on the verse of Vergil, "and the lakes haunted by gods," says: "Lakes Avernus and Lucrinus used formerly to be so ringed about by dense forests that an oppressive odor of sulfurous water arose from them through tiny openings, and would kill birds flying over-head. It was therefore called 'Avernus.' When Caesar heard this, he had the trees cut down and made the place much pleasanter."[116] And below on the Vergilian verse, "where Acheron comes flooding up," he says: "They say that Acheron is a river of the Underworld. But it is generally agreed that its location — which is so hemmed in by hills all around that the sun can be seen neither rising nor set-ting, but only at midday — is not far from Baiae."[117]

As to the breadth of the Gulf of Baiae, which I mentioned above, Suetonius deals with it thus in his *Life of Caligula*: "He bridged the gap between Baiae and the piers of Puteoli, a distance of about three and half miles, by bringing together merchant ships from all sides and anchoring them in a double line, after which a mound of earth was heaped upon them and fashioned in the man-ner of the Appian Way. Over this bridge he rode back and forth for two successive days, the first day on a caparisoned horse, him-self resplendent in a civic crown and holding a shield, with a sword and cloak of cloth of gold; on the second, in the dress of a chari-oteer in a chariot drawn by a pair of famous horses."[118] But Calig-ula's successor, Nero, dreamed up even greater extravagances at Baiae. On this Suetonius writes: "He also began a pool, extending from Misenum to the lake of Avernus, roofed over and practically enclosed in colonnades, into which he planned to turn all the hot springs in every part of Baiae, and laid foundations for a canal from Avernus to Ostia, to enable the journey to be made by ship; 34

sexaginta milium, latitudine qua contiguae quinqueremes comme-
arent.' De eodemque scelestissimo imperatore Suetonius: Agrippi-
nam matrem 'litteris Baias evocavit ad solemnia Quinquatrium simul celebranda. Datoque negotio trierarchis[121] qui liburnicam qua
advecta erat velut fortuito concursu confringerent, protraxit con-
vivium.' Sed cum nando evasisset, ⟨eam⟩ iugulari fecit. Servius
Vergilianum exponens versum, 'Infernique lacus,' dicit 'Lucrinum
et Avernum significari, inter quos est spelunca per quam ad inferos
descendebatur.' Sed iam satis de vetustioribus: ad recentiora veniamus. Helius Spartianus de Alexandro imperatore optimo, Mamaeae Christianae[122] filio, sic habet: 'In Baiano palatium fecit cum
stagno Mamaeae matri, quod[123] Mamaea tunc dictum hodieque[124]
vocatur. Fecit et alia opera in Baiano magnifica in honorem affi-
nium suorum et stagna stupenda admisso mari.' Fuit Baiano sinui
propinquus, Bauli, locus Herculis, quem Servius dictum putat
quasi 'bouali,' quod illic habuerit animalia. Haec sunt quae de
Baiano sinu (sive vetusta sive recentiora) duximus dicenda. Restat
ut ea praesentibus applicemus.

35   Ad Frictolas (nunc Tritolam) Lucrinus incipiebat. Cernuntur
enim e regione illius in litore bracchia murorum quae[125] Caesar, ut
violentum excluderet mare, iecit. Avernus vero a Lucrino nunc se-
paratus est. Quod breve spatium a Caesare relictum, quo piscium
copia posset intrare mare, superinducta arena conclusit. Quae quidem clausura diligentissime de industria conservatur ne crescentes,
accedente[126] mari, aquae balneis officiant, quae vicus, nunc Triper-
gula appellatus, plurima et (ut medici perhibent) omnium Italiae
saluberrima habet. Adiacent vero ea omnia Averno lacui salsum in

its length was to be a hundred and sixty miles and its breadth sufficient to allow ships with five banks of oars to pass each other."
On this same criminal emperor, Suetonius also writes: "He invited
his mother Agrippina in a letter to come to Baiae and celebrate the
feast of Minerva with him. On her arrival, instructing his captains
to wreck the galley in which she had come, by running into it as if
by accident, he detained her at a banquet. But when she had
swum to safety, he had her murdered."[119] Explaining Vergil's verse,
"the lakes of hell," Servius writes: "He means Lucrinus and Avernus, and the cave between them through which one descended to
the underworld."[120] But that is quite enough about the ancient
times: let us pass on to more recent history. Aelius Spartianus
writes as follows on that good emperor Alexander Severus, the son
of the Christian Mamaea: "He built a palace on the bay of Baiae,
together with a pool, for his mother Mamaea, which was then
called 'Mamaea,' as it still is today. He built other magnificent
works on the bay of Baiae in honor of his relatives, and let in the
sea to create enormous lagoons."[121] Near the Gulf of Baiae there
was a place of Hercules, Bauli, that Servius supposes was named
as if it were "bouali"[122] because Hercules kept his cattle there.[123]
Such are the ancient and more modern points of interest that I
thought I should mention in connection with the Gulf of Baiae. It
remains to connect them with the current situation.

The Lucrine Lake used to begin at Frittole (present-day Tri-   35
tola), for the ramparts of the walls that Caesar built as a barrier
against the ravages of the sea can be seen on the beach opposite
the Lucrine Lake. Nowadays Lake Avernus is separate from the
Lucrine Lake. The short stretch of water that Caesar suffered to
remain to allow fish to reach the sea has been blocked by deposits
of sand. This blockage is carefully maintained so that waters swollen by the incoming sea do not damage the baths of the village
now called Tripergola, which are very numerous and, according to
the doctors, the most salubrious in all Italy. All these baths sit on

aquis retinenti saporem, quas quidem aquas ita habet altas ut nullis etiam longissimis funibus, saxo aut plumbo magni ponderis ad perpendiculum colligato, eius profunditas tangi possit. Mirumque est cernere stupendi et insani operis aedificia quae, aut in circuitu Averni aut in eius aquis ripae proximioribus, fuerunt iacta, cum tamen viae silicibus in circuitum stratae et aquarum formae dulcium superioribus in collibus paene sint integrae.

36   Egressi depressa haec Lucrini et Averni loca et Puteolos petituri, via incedunt silicata,[127] ad quam undique maiorum supradictis aedificiorum in Baianum superne despectantium ruinae cernuntur quousque ad viam est ventum Atellanam, quae[128] ab urbe Roma Atellas per Appiam et post ab Atellis ducebat ad Baias. Qua quidem in via haud longe a Puteolis et Baiano medioque ad nunc Adversam spatio, tam integra adhuc sunt veterum operum monumenta ut, si ostia addantur et fenestrae, videantur habitationem non incommodam praestatura. Eademque via ad Baiani supercilium, ubi Sanctae Mariae sacellum est, post tergum relicta, maiorum etiam omnium quae[129] hactenus circa Baianum descripsimus aedificiorum ruinae in sublimi[130] erectae cernuntur, quas incolae Belgermanum appellant. Fueruntque opera, sicut litterae pila incisae marmorea ostendunt, quae Tiberius Caesar, bello Germanico feliciter perfecto (unde 'Germanicus' est appellatus), ad facti eius famam memoriamque exstruxit. Eique pulcherrimo etiam nunc operi proximum est paene integrum exstans theatrum, cuius occasione factum esse dicit Suetonius ut, cum celeberrimis ludis, quibus Caesar intererat Augustus, senatorium virum frequenti consessu nemo recepisset, idem princeps spectandi[131] modum correxerit.

37   Dehinc sunt Puteoli, de qua civitate vetusta sic habet Livius in quarto: 'Exitu eius anni, Q. Fabius ex auctoritate Senatus Puteolos per bellum captum[132] frequentari fecit, emporiumque communivit,

Lake Avernus, whose waters still have a salty taste. These waters are so deep that the bottom cannot be reached by even the longest ropes, sent straight down by heavy stone or lead weights attached to them. It is a wonder to behold the ruins of the extraordinary and extravagant buildings built on the shores of Lake Avernus or in waters close to its banks, though the roads paved with stone around the lake and aqueducts to carry fresh water in the hills above it are nearly intact.

Leaving the low-lying neighborhood of Lucrinus and Avernus 36 on the way to Pozzuoli, you take a paved road, on which ruins of buildings overlooking the Gulf of Baiae — greater than those mentioned above — are to be seen on all sides, until you come to the Via Atellana. This road used to run from Rome to Atella as the Appian Way, and then from Atella to Baiae. Not far from Pozzuoli and the Gulf of Baiae, and in the area between them and the present Aversa, the remains of ancient structures on this road are so little damaged that if you added doors and windows, it seems they could provide a not uncomfortable place to live. Leaving this road behind you at the edge of the Gulf of Baiae, where there is the chapel of Santa Maria, you can see ruins of tall buildings even more extensive than any so far described on the Gulf, which are called by the locals Belgermano. These works were erected by Tiberius, as an inscription on a marble pillar declares, when his war with the Germans had been successfully concluded (hence his title Germanicus), to glorify and commemorate that achievement.[124] Beside these buildings, which are very handsome even now, an amphitheater survives nearly intact. Suetonius says it occasioned the emperor Augustus's amendment of the way games were viewed, when at a crowded games attended by the emperor himself, no one would make a place in the packed seating area for a senator.[125]

There follows the ancient city of Pozzuoli, on which Livy 37 writes in Book IV: "At the end of that year Quintus Fabius, by the authority of the senate, increased the population of Puteoli, which

atque praesidium imposuit.' Et infra de Hannibale: 'Ad lacum Averni per speciem sacrificandi, re ipsa ut temptaret Puteolos, descendit. Sacro deinde perpetrato ad quod venerat et dum ibi moratur pervastato[133] agro Cumano usque ad Misenum promontorium, Puteolos repente agmen convertit ad opprimendum praesidium Romanum.' Et infra: 'P. Cornelius Scipio Africanus et C. Aelius[134] Paetus magna inter se concordia senatum sine ullius nota regebant et portoria navalium Capuae Puteolisque instituerunt.' Et infra: Consul Atinius tulit ut quinque coloniae in oram maritimam deducerentur, quarum una fuit deducta Puteolos. Helius Spartianus dicit Hadrianum imperatorem cum mortuus esset apud Baias, sepultum fuisse Puteolis in villa Ciceroniana, ubi Antoninus[135] successor templum pro sepulchro illi[136] consecravit.

38   Puteolis nostro ordine transmissis, locus occurrit medio inter ipsam et urbem Neapolitanam spatio fama apud veteres celebratus. Namque villa, quam Plutarchus tradit Lucium Lucullum habuisse prope Neapolim — et apud eam montem excidisse atque ita excavasse ut mare introduceret, unde Cn. Pompeius et M. Cicero illum appellare soliti fuerint[137] Xerxem togatum — ea est cuius ruinae ingentes balneo supereminent Agnani dicto, quamquam non balnea loco sed alterae sunt frictolae superioribus meliores. Et, qui rerum huius modi magnarum ingenio viribusque factarum peritiam habent, facillime scissuram pervident[138] intelleguntque manu factam ⟨esse⟩, unde defossus reiectusque mons viam praebuit (nunc etiam levi opera reparabilem), qua mare nunc Agnani lacum ita impleret ut ad villae muros porticusque navigari possset.

had been captured in war, and fortified and garrisoned the commercial center."[126] And later, on Hannibal: "He came down to Lake Avernus on the pretext of making a sacrifice, in reality to attack Puteoli and the garrison which was there. Then, after accomplishing the rite for which he had come, and devastating the territory of Cumae as far as the promontory of Misenum, while he lingered there, he suddenly headed his column toward Puteoli, to surprise the Roman garrison."[127] And below: "P. Cornelius Scipio Africanus and C. Aelius Paetus were managing the Senate in perfect harmony without passing censure on any one member; they also let out the port duties at Capua and at Puteoli."[128] And below: The consul Atinius had a motion carried to establish five colonies on the coast, one of which was established at Puteoli.[129] Aelius Spartianus says that when the emperor Hadrian died at Baiae, he was buried at Cicero's villa at Puteoli, where his successor Antoninus Pius dedicated a temple to him instead of a sepulcher.[130]

Now that we have duly finished with Puteoli, we come upon a 38 place that was famous among the ancients, midway between Puteoli and the city of Naples. This is the villa that Plutarch tells us Lucius Lucullus owned near Naples, the one where he cut into a mountain and hollowed it out so that the sea came in: hence, Plutarch says, Pompey and Cicero used to call him "Xerxes in a toga."[131] Its vast ruins loom over the so-called Bagni di Agnano, though the place does not have baths as such but more of the vaporous *frictolae*, better than the ones mentioned above.[132] Those who have an understanding of this sort of grand undertaking of brain and brawn can clearly see that the fissure is man-made: when the mountain was dug out and pared back it offered the possibility of the sea filling the lake of Agnano so as to allow boats to go right up to the walls and colonnades of Lucullus's villa — and it could even be brought back into use today with no great effort.

39   Procedentesque eo itinere ad cavernam perveniunt Griptam
nunc appellatam, ubi Pausilypus mons pulcherrimis[139] olim, sicut
Plinius tradit, villis habitatus, ad sexcentos passus excavatus pla-
num via Puteolana curribus iter praebet. Quis autem id memora-
bile opus fecit ignotum est nobis, qui tamen legimus factam[140]
apud Senecam Cordubensem[141] ipsius loci mentionem *Epistula*
LVII, ubi dicit: 'Excepit me Gripta Neapolitana: nihil illo carcere
longius, nihil illius faucibus[142] obscurius, quae nobis praestant non
ut per tenebras videamus sed ut ipsas cernamus. Si locus haberet
lucem, pulvis auferret, in aperto quoque res gravis et molesta.
Quid illic, ubi in se volutatur[143] et cum sine ullo inspiramento sit
inclusus, in ipsos a quibus excitatus est recidit?' Et Donatus[144] in
Vergilii expositione tradit ipsum poetam sepultum fuisse Neapoli
via Puteolana ad secundum lapidem. Quod sepulchrum circa praedictam Griptam saepe quaesitum nequivimus invenire.

40   Sequitur Neapolis urbs vetusta atque praeclara, cuius originem
Livius in octavo refert in Cumanos his verbis: 'Palaepolis fuit haud
procul ubi nunc Neapolis est. Duabus urbibus idem populus habi-
tabat. Cumis erant oriundi.' Palaepolimque, quam tenerent Graeci,
dicit infra Livius[145] a Publio Plautio[146] consule captam fuisse. Et
infra: 'Iam Publius, inter Palaepolim Neapolimque loco opportune
capto, diremerat hostibus societatem auxilii mutui.' Et infra item
dicit Neapolim auxilio Nolanorum Romanis deditam fuisse. Usi
vero sunt semper postea Neapolitani erga Romanos et alios domi-
nos constantissima fide. Primum Romana re publica Cannensi

As you proceed along this road, you come to a cavern now 39
called the Grotta di Posillipo, where Mount Pausilypus (once
populated with handsome villas, Pliny tells us) was tunneled
through for six hundred feet to provide a level carriageway for traf-
fic on the Via Puteolana.[133] I do not know who built this remarkable work, though I have read the mention that Seneca of Cor-
duba made of the place in his *Letter LVII*, where he says: "The
Crypta Neapolitana[134] swallowed me: No place could be longer than
that prison; nothing could be gloomier than its jaws,[135] which en-
abled us, not to see amid the darkness, but to see the darkness.
But even supposing that there was light in the place, the dust,
which is an oppressive and disagreeable thing even in the open air,
would destroy the light. How much worse the dust is there, where
it rolls back upon itself, and, being shut in without ventilation,
blows back in the faces of those who stir it up!"[136] Donatus in his
commentary on Vergil passes on to us the tradition that the poet
himself was buried at Naples, on the Via Puteolana two miles out
of the city.[137] Though I have often searched for the tomb in the
vicinity of the Grotta mentioned above, I have never been able to
find it.[138]

Next after Pozzuoli comes the famous old city of Naples. In 40
Book VIII, Livy traces the origin of Naples back to the men of
Cumae in these words: "Palaepolis was not far from where Naples
is today, and the two cities were inhabited by one people. Cumae
was their mother city."[139] Livy says below that the consul Publilius Paetus captured Palaepolis, which was in the power of the
Greeks.[140] And below: "By taking up a favorable position between
Palaepolis and Neapolis, Publilius had already deprived the enemy
of the mutual exchange of assistance."[141] And further on again, he
says that Naples was betrayed to the Romans with the help of the
men of Nola.[142] In fact thereafter the Neapolitans' loyalty to the
Romans and to their other masters has always been steadfast, in
the first place when the Roman Republic was laid low by the di-

clade consternata, 'cum ad Gereoneum[147] iam hieme impendente consisteret bellum, Neapolitani legati Romam venerunt. Ab his quadraginta paterae aureae magni ponderis in Curiam delatae,' quas quidem senatus contra morem suum accepit et Neapolitanis gratias egit. Cumque Hannibal Neapoli summo opere potiri quaesiverit, Neapolitani in Romanorum partibus perstiterunt. Livius in XXIII, de Hannibale: 'Ipse per agrum Campanum mare Inferum petit oppugnaturus Neapolim ut urbem maritimam haberet.' Et infra: 'Hannibal, Capua recepta, cum iterum Neapolitanorum animos partim spe partim metu nequiquam temptasset, in agrum Nolanum exercitum duxit.' Et infra quarto: 'Inde ad populandum agrum Neapolitanum magis ira quam spe potiundae urbis duxit.'

41 Floruit autem semper postmodum Neapolitana urbs Romana re,[148] sub consulibus et pariter sub principibus, integra adeo ut apud eam graves viri animorum a curis laxamentum, discoli vero lasciviae deversorium, quaererent.[149] Suetonius de Nerone: 'Reversus e Graecia Neapolim, quod in ea primum artem musicam protulerat, albis equis introiit, disiecta parte muri.' Et infra: 'Nero de motu Galliarum Neapoli cognovit die ipso quo matrem occiderat.'

42 Sed et viros videmus litteris celebratos Vergilium diu, Titum Livium aliquando, et Horatium Neapoli[150] moratos fuisse. Et Servius asserit Vergilium scripsisse *Georgica* Neapoli, quam Parthenopen[151] appellavit ac otii ignobilis notavit. Franciscus quoque Petrarcha praestanti vir ingenio, a Roberto rege Neapolitano Gallicana oriundo progenie rogatus, Neapolim bis se contulit nulla quidem maioris lucri spe suasus quam ut optimo atque humanissimo regi doctos et virtuosos viros unice amanti gratificaretur.

saster of Cannae: "With winter already approaching, the war at Gereonium had come to a standstill when the Neapolitan legates arrived at Rome. They brought with them into the senate house forty massive golden bowls,"[143] which contrary to their usual practice the Senate accepted with a vote of thanks to the Neapolitans.[144] Though Hannibal tried with might and main to take Naples, the Neapolitans stood fast on the side of the Romans. In Book XXIII Livy writes of Hannibal: "He himself made his way to the Tyrrhenian Sea by way of Campania, intending to attack Naples so that he might have a seaport."[145] And below: "Hannibal, after gaining possession of Capua and vainly trying, partly by hope, partly by fear, to work for the second time upon the feelings of the Neapolitans, led his army over into the territory of Nola."[146] Below, in Book IV: "Then he led out his army to ravage the territory of the Neapolitans, more out of anger than in hope of taking their city."[147]

Indeed, the city of Naples always prospered thereafter while the Roman state stood undiminished, under consuls and under emperors equally, so much so that important men would seek there relaxation from their cares, and scoundrels a place of diversion for their pleasures.[148] Suetonius on Nero: "Returning from Greece, since it was at Naples that he had made his first appearance, he entered that city with white horses through a part of the wall which had been thrown down."[149] And below: "He was at Naples when he learned of the uprising of the Gallic provinces, on the anniversary of his mother's murder."[150]   41

But we observe that famous literary men sojourned at Naples, too — Vergil a great deal, Livy from time to time, and Horace. Servius tells us that Vergil wrote the *Georgics* at Naples, which he called Parthenope and criticized for its "ignoble leisure."[151] At the invitation of the French King Robert of Naples, that extraordinary genius Francesco Petrarca twice betook himself to Naples, with no more thought of profit than to oblige a good and humane king   42

Eamque vim habuit inita inter divitem regem et doctum integru-
mque sed rerum inopem virum et tamen animo et virtute divitem
poetam: ut per unicam eius modi amicitiam conservatus nunc vi-
vat rex Robertus. Nam quod omnibus in quorum manus haec ve-
nient faciliter ostendere ac (quoad vixerimus) probare poterimus:
extra urbem Neapolitanam paucissimi ac paene nulli sunt viri
(quantumvis docti) qui Robertus rex, quis et unde aut quo tempore fuerit, alia noverint ratione vel causa quam quod eum in
amicissimi Francisci Petrarchae operibus sive Latinis sive vulgari-
bus legendo recognoverunt.[152]

43   Servius in Vergiliani versus expositione, 'Nec tu carminibus
nostris indictus abibus, Oebale,' dicit: 'Oebalus filius est Telonis et
nymphae Sebetridis. Hic autem est iuxta Neapolim, sed Telo diu
regnavit Capreis filiusque eius transiit ad Campaniam et, multis
subiugatis populis, suum dilatavit imperium.'

44   At postquam Romani imperii inclinatio coepit, crebrescenti-
bus arbarorum insultibus, Neapolitani partes Romanorum pro
posse[153] supraque secuti sunt. Et, quod in *Historiis* copiose ostendimus, rex Vandalorum Gensericus, classe ingenti ab Africa ducta,
Romanam[154] urbem captam spoliatamque et omni humano habitatore destitutam reliquit, qui et Capuam quoque evertit. Ad Neapolim vero cum venisset, eam diu obsidione pressam capere nequivit.
Paucis abinde annis Belisario Justiniani imperatoris duci adeo
constanti animo restiterunt Neapolitani ut, cum postea per lapi-
deum aquaeductus foramen scalpris dilatatum urbs in eius potestatem facta esset, Neapolitani sola principis humanitate ab excidio
sint servati.

45   Multis postea interiectis annis, cum Saraceni omnem oram
maritimam quae a Caieta Rhegium usque protenditur per bellum
obtinuissent, Neapoli quoque sunt potiti, quam ad annos triginta
possederunt quousque Johannes X pontifex Romanus, vir excel-

who above all others loved learned and virtuous men. The relationship that formed between the wealthy king and the learned and upright man, poor in wealth but rich in virtues of the spirit, has had the effect that King Robert lives on today, preserved by a friendship unique of its kind. I can demonstrate and (while life remains) provide easy proof to all those into whose hands these writings may come, that outside Naples itself, very few men — almost none, in fact, no matter how learned — know who King Robert was, whence he came or when he lived, except by reason of having read about him in the Latin or vernacular works of his close friend Francesco Petrarca.[152]

Servius in commenting on Vergil's verse, "Nor will you pass   43
unmentioned in my song, Oebalus," says: "Oebalus is the son of Telon and the nymph Sebetris. Now the stream Sebetris is hard by Naples, but Telon long ruled over Capri, and his son crossed over into Campania and enlarged his realm by subjugating many nations."[153]

As the decline of the Roman Empire set in and assaults of the   44
barbarians grew ever more frequent, the Neapolitans stuck with the cause of Rome to the utmost of their powers and beyond. As I showed at length in my *Histories*, the king of the Vandals, Genseric, brought a great fleet from Africa and captured and sacked Rome, leaving it bare of every human inhabitant, and destroying Capua as well. But when he got to Naples, he was unable to take it despite a long siege.[154] A few years later the Neapolitans stood so firmly against Belisarius, the general of the Emperor Justinian, that when he subsequently gained control of the city after having chisels widen a gap in the stone of an aqueduct, only the humanity of the emperor saved the Neapolitans from destruction.[155]

Many years later, when the Saracens had taken in war the entire   45
coast from Gaeta to Reggio Calabria, they took possession of Naples too. They held the city for thirty years, until the excellent Pope John X applied himself to driving the Saracens out of It-

lentissimus, pellendis Italia Saracenis animum adiecit. Quo hortante et auxilia subministrante, Neapolitani omnium primi id diu invisum abiecerunt iugum, secutique eius urbis exemplum ceteri Campaniae, Lucaniae, et Brutiorum populi (eam scilicet incolentes oram quae a Neapoli continetur[155] freto Siculo), dominio[156] Saracenorum abiecto, sese in Christianam vindicarunt libertatem. Qua afflicti clade Saraceni, auxiliaribus copiis ex Africa Mauritaniaque accersitis, oppida et urbes, quae sibi erant in Italia reliquae, praesidiis confirmatas maioribus retinere conati sunt: Formias, Minturnas, Sinuessam, Vulturnum, Linternum, Cumas, atque Baianum. Nam Puteolani Neapolitanis ab initio in rebellione consenserat.

46   Perstitit vero perseveravitque sanctissimus pontifex in sua expellendae barbariei aeternis digna laudibus voluntate, et Italos omnes, quantumvis inter se aliis rationibus laceros atque discordes, in fidei Christianae tutelam orando suadendoque — magis quam quod[157] nequisset iubendo — armari obtinuit. Quibus in magnum coactis exercitum, pontifice Johanne duce, ventum est ad Minturnas, et (quod in eius urbis descriptione diximus) proelium apud eam gestum est in quo Saraceni maxima clade superati sunt. Unde factum est ut ea gens, impia et non magis Christiano quam Italico nomini inimica, regionem praedictam a Formiis ad Baianum (et quicquid urbium, oppidorum, munitorumque locorum in ea praesidiis obtinebant) incendiis et toto conatu reliquerint dirutum adeo ut ea, quam hucusque vix conando potuimus singulis in locis ad nominis antiqui notitiam perducere, manserit solitudo.

47   Aucta vero est semper postea opibus urbs Neapolitana, et feliciter sub Johanne X inchoatas in barbaros inimicitias felicissime retinuit. Namque cum Leonis quarti papae temporibus Saraceni Sanctorum[158] Petri et Pauli Apostolorum utrasque urbis Romae

aly.[156] At his instance and with his support the Neapolitans were the first to throw off the yoke they had long detested, and the remaining peoples of Campania, Lucania, and the land of the Brutii (that is to say, the inhabitants of the coastlands from Naples to the Straits of Messina) followed Naples' example, cast off Saracen domination, and reclaimed their Christian freedom. Downcast by this defeat, the Saracens summoned reinforcements from Libya and Morocco and sought to hold on to the Italian towns and cities that were left to them by strengthening their garrisons: Formia, Minturnae, Sinuessa, Castel Volturno, Liternum, Cuma, and Baia—not Pozzuoli, whose people had been allies in rebellion with the Neapolitans from the beginning.

But the holy pontiff stood his ground and persevered in his 46 never sufficiently praised resolve to expel the barbarians. More by entreaty and persuasion than by ordering them, which he had been unable to do, he managed to get all the Italians to arm themselves in defense of the Christian faith, however divided and at odds with one another they were otherwise. When they were all assembled in a great army under Pope John's leadership, they came to Minturnae, where a battle took place in which the Saracens suffered a calamitous defeat, as I said in my description of the city.[157] And so it came about that that impious and hostile people—hostile to the Italians as much as to Christians—abandoned the region mentioned above, from Formia to Baiae, destroying by fire all the cities, towns, and garrisoned castles that they had held, so far as they could, and with such success that it has remained a wasteland where, for all my efforts, I have hardly been able to identify the individual places with their ancient names.

After that the city of Naples grew ever more prosperous, still 47 stoutly maintaining its hatred of the barbarians that had begun with such success under John X. And in fact during the papacy of Leo IV, when the Saracens had taken and burned down the two Roman basilicas of the Apostles, St Peter's and St. Paul's, and

basilicas vi captas incendio absumpsissent urbemque Romam diu obsessam capturi viderentur, nullis maioribus ex omni Italia quam Neapolitanorum viribus et servata est Roma et barbari sunt expulsi. Nimis multa huic operi et loco essent illa quae de Neapolitanorum variis casibus scribi possent, dum Guiscardis Germanisque et Gallicis regibus qui Neapolim a trecentis annis regia ornarunt dignitate oboedientissime parent. Sed omnes eorum laudes accumulat gloriosa calamitas in magnam conversa[159] felicitatem: dum pro servata[160] Gallico Andegavensi principi Renato fide durissimam ab Alphonso Aragonum rege obsidionem pertulerunt quousque (pari cum Belisarii temporum eventu) per aquaeductus cuniculum ab ipso rege capti, atque ad hanc, in qua nunc beati florent, felicitatem eiusdem regis praesentia clementiaque servati sunt, ut non immerito is rex triumphi consuetudinem diutissime intermissam longo tandem postliminio in Italiam revocaverit.

48   Habet urbs Neapolitana basilicas, moenia, et arces, ac publicas privatasque aedes superbas et ceteris Italiae maioribus comparandas, in quis praeclarum est Virginis Clarae monasterium, quod a Sanctia Aragone regina, Roberti regis inclyti uxore, aedificatum facile omnia Italiae monasteria antecellit, eique[161] proximum esse videtur Sancti Martini extra urbis moenia Carthusiense coenobium aedificii magnificentia pulcherrimum. Constat tamen arcem unam, Castellum Novum appellatum, mari imminentem, Alphonsi regis laude et memoria dignum opus, ceteris quae in Italia nunc exstent veteribus sive novis operibus, monumentis, et structuris praeferendum esse, sive[162] turrium eius murorumque altitudinem ac crassitudinem et pulchritudinem, sive aularum cubiliumque et singularum eius partium amplitudinem et ornamenta peritus eius modi rerum existimet.

49   Ornata fuit Neapolis patrum nostrorum aetate Bonifacio IX pontifice Romano ex Tomacella gente oriundo, qui primus non

seemed on the point of capturing Rome itself after a long siege, it was the Neapolitan forces more than any other Italians that saved Rome and drove out the barbarians.[158] This is not the time and place to rehearse the many vicissitudes of Naples while it was subject to the Guiscards and to the German and French kings who have given the city the luster of regal grandeur for the last three hundred years. But a glorious calamity that was transformed into a piece of great good fortune caps all their distinctions: thanks to the loyalty they showed toward the French king René of Anjou, the Neapolitans were enduring a terrible siege at the hands of King Alfonso of Aragon when there occurred an event reminiscent of what happened in Belisarius's day: having been captured by the king entering through the channel of an aqueduct, they were brought by the king's protection and clemency to the good fortune that they presently enjoy. At last, then, King Alfonso has quite properly restored to Italy the long-abandoned custom of celebrating triumphs after a lengthy exile.[159]

The city of Naples has basilicas, city walls, and fortresses, and 48 splendid private and public buildings which are a match for any in Italy. Among them is the famous convent of Santa Chiara built by Queen Sancha of Aragon, wife of the famous King Robert, and far outstripping all the monasteries of Italy.[160] Near it outside the walls of the city one may see the Carthusian monastery of San Martino, a magnificent and beautiful building.[161] Yet all agree that one particular fortress which overlooks the sea, called the Castel Nuovo, a work worthy of the glorious memory of King Alfonso, is superior to all other works, monuments, and edifices ancient or modern now extant in Italy, no matter whether the experts in such matters consider the height and massiveness and beauty of its towers and walls or the spaciousness and ornament of its halls, rooms and individual parts.[162]

In our fathers' time, the Roman Pontiff Boniface IX of the 49 Tomacelli family lent luster to Naples. He was the first to bring

modo urbem Romam sed et ipsum quoque pontificatum in dominii potestate continuit. Pauloque[163] post alterum Neapolis pontificem Romanum habuit, Johannem XXIII[164] ex gente Cossea, quem
alioquin prudentem Sigismundus imperator in Germaniam seduc-
tum a concilio Constantiensi pro ecclesiae facienda[165] unione pri-
vari curavit. Magno item per id temporis ornamento Neapolitanae
urbi fuit Ladislaus rex Galliae regum prosapia, Neapoli genitus et
nutritus, qui militiae omnino deditus, praeter id Neapolitanum
omne regnum armis quaesitum, urbem quoque Romam Perusi-
amque[166] et Assisiam de iuribus ecclesiae, et Cortonam de Etruria, cepit, quam vendidit Florentinis. Constansque fuit omnium
eius aetatis prudentium opinio, ipsum Italico regno et (quod postea facillimum erat)[167] imperio Romano, nisi florentem eum mors
intercepisset, brevi potiturum fuisse.

50   Neapolitanae urbi secundum litus Pompeii a vetustis scriptoribus proximi describuntur, qui vicus olim fuit amoenissimus Ro-
manisque gratissimus, adeo ut M. Cicero legem (de qua saepe
diximus) dissuadens Rulli agrariam aegre[168] ferendum ostendat
Pompeios a decemviris venum dari. Et quia doctos qui hoc tempore Neapoli apud regem in pretio habentur errare videmus, Pompeios et Herculaneum ubi nunc Turris est Octavii fuisse affir-
mantes, vetus testimonium ostendendo certius Pompeiorum loco
afferemus. Primumque dicimus ubi nunc Annuntiata et Castellum
est ad Mare Pompeios,[169] vicum oblongum villisque speciosissimis
frequentissimum fuisse. Livius in IX: Per idem tempus classis
Romana a P. Cornelio, quem senatus maritimae orae praefecerat,
in Campaniam acta cum appulsa Pompeios esset, socii navales, ad
populandum Nucerinum agrum profecti, facta praeda exuti[170]

not only the city of Rome but also the pontificate itself under his personal control.[163] Soon after Naples had a second pontiff in John XXIII of the Cossa family. Cautious in other respects, John was inveigled into Germany by the emperor Sigismund, who saw to it that he was deprived of his office by the Council of Constance that had been convened to unify the Church.[164] At this time, too, King Ladislaus, of French royal stock, though born and bred in Naples, was a great ornament to the city: wholly given over to military life, in addition to taking by force of arms the entire Kingdom of Naples, he wrested from Church control the city of Rome as well, and Perugia and Assisi, and from Tuscany Cortona, which he sold to the Florentines.[165] It was the firm conviction of experts of the day that Ladislaus would soon have gained possession of the Kingdom of Italy and — an easy thing once that had been done — of the whole Roman Empire, had death not caught him in his prime.[166]

Following the city of Naples, ancient authors describe Pompeii   50
as being next along the coast, a town that was once very agreeable and attractive to the Romans. Cicero, for example, in arguing against the agrarian legislation of Rullus (which I have often mentioned) conveys his shock at the decemvirs putting Pompeii up for sale.[167] Since I see that learned men who are today held in high regard at the king's court in Naples are wrong in maintaining that Pompeii and Herculaneum were where Torre del Greco is now, I shall adduce surer ancient evidence bearing on the site of Pompeii. In the first place I assert that Pompeii, an elongated town studded with pretty villas, was where Torre Annunziata now stands, and Castellammare di Stabia.[168] Livy writes in Book IX: At about this time a Roman fleet, commanded by Publius Cornelius, whom the senate had placed in charge of the coast, sailed for Campania. And when they put into Pompeii, the sailors who had set out to pillage the territory of Nuceria were stripped of the booty they had taken.[169] It would have been sensible, then, for marines who in-

sunt. Qui ergo Nucerinum praedaturi fuerunt agrum navales milites Sarni ostia potius ingredi oportuit quam ad distantem sexto
milliario Turrim Octavii facere excensionem. Herculaneum vero
ulterius et multis distans milibus fuisse infra ostendemus. Et quidem Turris Octavii nominis novi vicus, cui distantia ab urbe
Neapolitana dederit appellationem, nullas habet vetustatis reliquias — praeter superioris Plinii mortis locum, quem ibi fuisse necessarium tenemus. Nulla enim in parte alia Vesaevi montis incendia, quibus imprudenter inspiciendis Plinius est necatus, navi
potuerunt adiri. Et quidem ea omnis ora ubicumque saxa etiam in
litoris supercilio terrae supereminent, incendii vestigia ostendit
adeo certa[171] ut nihil praeter flammam fumumque desit, quo illa
passim nunc etiam ardere advena suspicetur.

51   Fuitque id incendium de quo Suetonius Tranquillus in *Vita Titi
Vespasiani* sic dicit: 'Quaedam suo tempore tristia acciderunt, ut
conflagratio Vesaevi in Campania. Curatores restituendae Campaniae consularium numero sorte duxit. Bona oppressorum in Vesaevo quorum heredes non exstabant restitutioni afflictarum civitatum attribuit.' Vesaevum vero montem vitium agrorumque
cultura ditissimum nunc appellant summum, quod in conspectu
Neapolitanae urbi positus et hinc campis inde mari maiore parte
circumdatus videtur esse summus. In mediterraneis campestribus,
quae Adversam urbem Vesaevumque montem interiacent, duo exstant loca veterum memoria celebrata: Merelanium olim nunc
Marlianum[172] oppidum et urbs Acerrae.[173] De qua Livius XXIII:
'Hannibal Acerras cepit vacuas et incendit.' Et libro XXVII: 'Acer-
ranis permissum est ut aedificarent quae incensa erant.' Ad quam
historiam allusit Vergilius in *Georgicis*, ubi terras laudans culturae
excellentioris dicit: 'Talem dives arat Capua, et vicina Vesaevo ora
iugo, et vacuis Clanius non aequus Acerris.' Quo in loco Vergilius

tended to plunder Nuceria to enter the mouth of the river Sarnus rather than disembark at Turris Octavii six miles away. (I shall show below that Herculaneum was further on and many miles away.) Certainly Turris Octavii is a town of recent foundation (its name deriving from its distance from Naples) and has no traces of antiquity, beyond being the place of the elder Pliny's death, which I am sure must have occurred there. There was no other direction from which a boat could have approached the flames of Mount Vesuvius — the foolhardy inspection of which killed Pliny. In fact this entire stretch of coast, wherever rocks lie on top of earth, even on the edge of the beach, displays such clear signs of fire that only the absence of flames and smoke stops a stranger supposing that they are burning even now.

This was the conflagration about which Suetonius writes as fol- 51 lows in his *Life of Titus:* "Some sad events took place in his time, such as the eruption of Mount Vesuvius in Campania. He picked overseers for the revival of Campania by lot from the class of consulars. The goods of those who were buried in Vesuvius and had no heirs, he assigned to the restoration of the destroyed cities."[170] Mount Vesuvius, which is very rich in vines and agricultural land, is now called Monte Somma, because being set in full view of the city of Naples and surrounded on one side by plains and on the other mostly by the sea, it seems very large. In the plains of the interior lying between the city of Aversa and Mount Vesuvius, there are two places celebrated in ancient history: the town now known as Marigliano, in former days Merelanium, and the city of Acerra. On Acerra Livy writes in Book XXIII: "Hannibal seized Acerrae, which was empty, and put it to the torch."[171] And in Book XXVII: "The citizens of Acerrae were allowed to rebuild what had been burned down."[172] Vergil alluded to this historical episode in the *Georgics,* where in praising land that was good for farming he says: "Rich Capua plows such land, and the region bordering the ridge of Vesuvius, and Clanius unfriendly to de-

id quod supra diximus de Terra Leboris innuit: omnem eam regionem quae undique Clanio amni adiacet, Leborinam olim appellatam, feracissimi esse soli. Sicut de ea Plinium scripsisse ostendimus—qui tamen, de terris tractans ad sationem vitium optimis, dicit Campaniam ubique optimam vitibus esse, quae tenues exhalat nebulas, et cretam in Pompeianorum agro ac argillam[174] cunctis ad vineas generibus anteponi, quoniam excipitur cum illis in vicem sabulum album.

52   Sed iam ventum est ad superiorem Clanii amnis partem, cum ab Acerris distet quatuor milia passuum[175] Suessula oppidum nunc vacuum, iuxta quod (sicut a principio diximus) fontem is fluvius habet. Sarnusque posthac nobis describendus ordine videtur occurrere, cum cetera explicuerimus de[176] Suessula. De qua Livius in VII: 'Tertia pugna ad Suessulam commissa est, qua fugatus a M. Valerio Samnitium exercitus.' Et in VIII: 'Cumanos Suessulanosque eiusdem iuris condicionisque cuius Capuam esse placuit.' Et infra: 'Inter Capuam et Suessulam castra castris conferamus.' Et libro XXIII: 'Hannibal super Suessulam per montes Nolam pervenit.' Et infra: 'M. Claudius proconsul ad eum exercitum, qui supra Suessulam Nolae praesideret, missus.' Et inferius: Claudiana castra erant supra Suessulam.

53   Sed iam aliqua de Campanis propter dimidiatum in Samnio (sicut ostendimus) Vulturnum superius omissa[177] repetenda sunt. Ea in parte ad quam, Sabati amnis stipite utrimque descripto, Samnium omne[178] finitum esse ostendimus, Isclerus sequitur, omnium Campaniae hac in parte fluviorum primus[179] in Vulturnum supra Capuam quinto ferme milliario cadens. Qui Isclerus ex montibus Caudinam vallem claudentibus ortum habet. Et inter Soritellam fluvium superius in Samnio descriptum et ipsum Is-

serted Acerrae."[173] In this passage Vergil is suggesting what I said above regarding the *Terra Leboris*:[174] the entire region that lies on both sides of the river Clanio, once called Leborine, has extremely fertile soil. Though Pliny in discussing the best land for planting vines says that all Campania, which "emits thin clouds of vapor," is very good for the best vines, I mentioned above that he wrote that in the land about Pompeii the chalk and clay are preferable to all other kinds of soil for growing vines because white sand is in turn extracted with them.[175]

But now we have come to the upper reaches of the river Clanio, 52 since the now deserted town of Sessola is four miles from Acerre, and as I said at the outset, the source of the river Clanio is next to Sessola.[176] Following the Clanio in order, it seems that the river Sarno is the next I have to describe, once I have explained some remaining details about Sessola. Livy writes of it in Book VII: "There was a third battle at Suessula, where M. Valerius routed the Samnite army."[177] And in Book VIII: "The Senate voted to give the people of Cumae and Suessula the same rights and the same terms as the Capuans."[178] And below: "Let us set up our camp opposite theirs between Capua and Suessula."[179] And in Book XXIII: "Hannibal made his way through the mountains above Suessula to Nola."[180] Below again: "M. Claudius the proconsul was dispatched to the army above Suessula to protect Nola."[181] And farther down: Claudius's camp was above Suessula.[182]

But we must now return to some matters about Campania that 53 were omitted above, because as I mentioned the river Volturno is split into two parts in Samnium.[183] Here, at the point where Samnium finishes altogether at the "trunk" of the river Sabato (of which I described both sides), the river Isclero follows.[184] It is the first river in this part of Campania, flowing into the Volturno nearly five miles above Capua. The Isclero has its source in the hills that surround the Caudine valley. Between the river Soritella, described above under Samnium,[185] and the Isclero there are very

clerum sunt montes altissimi, in quibus primum est Gripta oppidum. Cui supereminet mons nunc Tabor, olim Taburnus, quem Servius, Vergilium in *Georgicis* exponens, Campaniae montem esse dicit, qui vites ab[180] industria contra naturam alat. Et idem super versu item Vergilii *Aeneidos* XII, 'Ac velut ingenti Sila summove Taburno,' dicit 'Taburnus mons est Campaniae.' Valli autem ex monte Taburno in Isclerum vergenti imminet Collis Pacis. Et vallis quam Isclerus efficit dextrorsum habet Limatulam[181] et Ducentium. Superiusque in monte est Airola nobile oppidum comitatus titulo insigne, duobus milliaribus a Furculis Caudinis distans. Pertinent in haec usque loca montes ardui Capuae ad adversam regionem imminentes, qui et longiusculo tractu ad Nolam urbem feruntur, Tifata olim appellati, in quibus oppida sunt: Moronia,[182] Caserta comitatu insigne, Magdalonum, et superius Duraganum. In proximaque valle Furculis Caudinis superiore Argentum est, et infra, Marilianum, vetusti (ut diximus) nominis oppidum. Proxime ad medium montem est Cancellum oppidum, superius Forinum.

54   Sunt vero hi montes Tifata, de quibus sic habet Livius in VII: 'Nam Samnites, omissis Sidicinis, ipsam arcem finitimorum Campanos adorti, unde aeque facilis victoria praedae atque gloriae plus esset, Tifata, imminentes Capuae colles, cum praesidio firmo occupassent. Descendunt inde quadrato agmine in planitiem quae inter Capuam Tifataque interiacet.' Et idem infra: Proelium ad Tifata atrox, 'in quo oculos Romanis ardere dixerunt.' Fusi caesique Samnites. Et libro XXIII: Hannibal ad Tifata[183] castra habebat, qui raptim[184] currens Gracchum non invenit. Et infra: 'Inter Capuam castraque Hannibalis, quae in Tifatis erant.' Et inferius:[185] Hanni-

high mountains in which the first town you come to is Grotta. Looming above it is Monte Taburo, formerly Mons Taburnus,[186] which Servius in his commentary on Vergil's *Georgics* says is a Campanian mountain that tricks nature into growing vines artificially.[187] Servius again writes on a line of Vergil's *Aeneid* XII, "And as in vast Sila or on lofty Taburnus," that "Taburnus is a mountain in Campania."[188] Collepasso overlooks the valley that stretches down from Monte Taburo to the river Isclero. This valley created by the Isclero has on its right side Limatola and Dugenta. Higher up on Monte Taburo is the well-known town of Airola, notable for its designation as a "county," two miles from the Caudine Forks. The steep mountains that overlook Capua in the opposite direction extend all the way to these places, and a lengthy extension takes them on to Nola, in a range formerly known as Tifata.[189] Here are the towns of Meronida, Caserta (a distinguished "county"), Maddaloni, and higher up Durazzano. In the valley next to them, above the Caudine Forks, is Arienzo, and below Arienzo the ancient town of Marigliano, as I mentioned above. Nearby, in the middle of Monte Tifata is the town of Cancello, and above that Forino.

These mountains are the Monte Tifata, on which Livy has the 54 following in Book VII: "The Samnites ignored the Sidicini and attacked the Campanians as the strongest of their neighbors: victory over them would be just as easy, and the booty and glory greater. Having secured Tifata, a ridge of hills overhanging Capua, with a strong garrison, they march down from there with their army formed in a square onto the plain which lies between Capua and Tifata"[190] Livy writes further on: There was a fierce battle at Tifata, in which "they said the eyes of the Romans flashed with fire."[191] The Samnites were put to rout and slaughtered. And in Book XXIII: Hannibal had his camp at Tifata, but despite his rapid progress he did not find Gracchus.[192] Below again: "Between Capua and Hannibal's camp, which was on Tifata."[193] And farther

bal, 'praesidio modico relicto in Tifatis, profectus cum exercitu toto.' Et libro XXIV: Hannibal profectus Arpis, ad[186] Tifata in veteribus castris super Capuam consedit. *Et libro XXVI: Hannibal in valle post Tifata montem consedit.*[187] Livius[188] item libro XXXII: 'Cornelius[189] Scipio Africanus, C. Aelius[190] Paetus sub Tifatis Capuae agrum vendiderunt.' Ad eiusdem montis declivia, quae aversa a Capua regione in Caudinae vallis suprema desinere incipiunt, Sarnum est oppidum, a Sarno fluvio ibi fontes copiosissimos habente dictum. In quibus fontibus scribit Plinius ligna et folia, cum ceciderunt,[191] in lapides durescere.

55 Sed inter eos fontes et Vesaevum montem longe supra a nobis descriptum Nola est urbs vetustissima et in historiis celebrata, quam Justinus a Iapygis conditam fuisse asserit. Cuius agrum esse fertilissimum Vergilius in *Bucolicis* sic scribit: 'Talem dives arat[192] Capua, et vicina Vesaevo ora[193] iugo'—licet 'ora' posuerit pro 'Nola,' Nolanis, sicut Servius scribit, iratus, quia[194] eum aut hospitio non acceperant aut aquulam[195] noluerant ei concedere in suum[196] agellum Vesaevi radicibus subiectum derivandam. Livius in IX: 'In Campaniam reditum[197] maxime ad Nolam armis repetendam, quae capta est a C. Junio[198] consule.' Et libro XXIII: Hannibal, 'Capua recepta, cum iterum Neapolitanorum animos partim spe partim metu nequicquam temptasset, in agrum[199] Nolanum exercitum duxit.' Item infra: 'M. Claudius proconsul ad eum exercitum, qui supra Suessulam Nolae praesideret, missus.' Item inferius: 'Et Nolae, sicut priore anno, senatus Romanorum, plebs Hannibalis erat.' Item inferius: 'Eadem aestate Marcellus ab Nola, quam praesidio obtinebat.' Et inferius: Hannibal, 'praesidio

down: Hannibal "left a modest garrison on Tifata and set out with the rest of his army."[194] In Book XXIV: "Having set out from Arpi, Hannibal settled into his old quarters at Tifata above Capua."[195] *And in Book XXVI: Hannibal encamped in a valley behind Mount Tifata.*[196] Livy once more in Book XXXII: "Cornelius Scipio Africanus and Gaius Aelius Paetus also sold the lands of Capua, which lie at the foot of Mount Tifata."[197] On the slopes of this mountain range, which from the region opposite Capua begin to merge with the uppermost reaches of the Caudine Valley, is the town of Sarno, named after the river Sarno, which has very copious springs there. Pliny writes that when pieces of wood and leaves fall into these springs, they harden into stones.[198]

Between those springs and Mount Vesuvius, which I described 55
a while back,[199] lies Nola, a very ancient city much celebrated in history, which Justin asserts was founded by the Iapyges.[200] Vergil writes in his *Eclogues* that the territory of Nola is most fertile, thus: "Rich Capua plows such land, and the region bordering the ridge of Vesuvius," — though the poet substituted "ora" for "Nola," because he was angry with the Nolans, according to Servius: either because they had not shown him a hospitable welcome or because they refused to allow him to divert a rivulet onto his estate below the foothills of Vesuvius.[201] Livy writes in Book IX: Poetelius "returned to Campania, chiefly with a view to recovering Nola by force of arms," which was then captured by the consul Gaius Iunius.[202] And in Book XXIII: "Hannibal, after gaining possession of Capua and vainly trying, partly by hope, partly by fear, to work for the second time upon the feelings of the Neapolitans, led his army over into the territory of Nola."[203] Again below: "Marcus Claudius was sent as proconsul to the army which was above Suessula, in order to guard Nola."[204] Likewise, farther down: "At Nola, just as in the previous year, the senate sided with the Romans, the common people with Hannibal."[205] And below: "The same summer Marcellus from Nola, which he held with a garrison

modico relicto in Tifatis, profectus cum cetero[200] exercitu ire Nolam[201] pergit.' Et libro XXIV: 'Adventu Hannibalis Nolana mota
est plebs.' Livius item libro undenonagesimo:[202] Sulla Nolam in
Samnio recepit et agros eius legionibus divisit. Si autem Livius
hoc in loco Nolam in Samnitibus adnumeravit, minime mirandum, quia[203] eo in Sociali Bello quod tunc is[204] scribebat, Nola
vicinis Samnitibus ita obstinate consenserat ut ex ea regione haberi[205] potuerit. Suetonius Tranquillus, mortem Octavii Caesaris
Augusti describens, eum dicit a Capreis Nolam delatum in eodem
cubiculo in quo pater Octavius obiisset,[206] et centuriones eum a
Nola Bovillas humeris detulisse.

56   Fluvius[207] vero Sarnus—cuius descriptio bis supra a nobis est
inchoata—in mare Inferum cadit ad loca Annuntiatae nunc
proxima, ubi olim Pompeios fuisse ostendimus. Isque fluvius,[208] de
quo Vergilius in VII, 'et qua rigat[209] oppida Sarnus,' et 'nocturnae
aurae editor' a Lucano appellatus, nunc dicitur Scafati a 'scaphis'
quae[210] ibi tenentur viatoribus in agrum Nucerinum traiiciendis.
Nam proxima ad quatuor mille passus est urbs Nuceria, quam M.
Cicero, legem dissuadens agrariam a Rullo[211] Cornelio proposi-
tam, queritur in decem virorum libidinem perventuram, his verbis:
'Neapolim, Pompeios, Nuceriam suis praesidiis devincient.' Livius
autem, libro XXVII, sic habet: 'Nucerini Atellam, quia id malue-
rant, Atellani Calatiam[212] migrare iussi.' Nuceriae dextrorsum
montes imminent, in quorum medio oppidum est a situ nomen
nactum: Intermontes enim appellatur. Vallisque his montibus sinistrorsum proxima Sanctum Severinum habet nobile oppidum, a
quo clara eius cognominis familia originem habet. Eaque vallis,
omnigenum fertilis frugum, vinis praesertim vermiculis abundat.

. . ."[206] And further on: Hannibal "left a modest garrison on Tifata and set out for Nola with the rest of his army."[207] In Book XXIV he writes: "The coming of Hannibal aroused the common people of Nola."[208] Livy again in Book LXXXIX: Sulla won back Nola in Samnium and divided its lands among his legions.[209] It is no surprise if Livy reckons Nola as being in Samnium in this passage, since in the Social War of which he was writing at that point, Nola had been so firmly in the camp of its Samnite neighbors that it might well be considered as part of that region. In describing the death of the emperor Augustus, Suetonius says that he was brought from Capri to Nola after dying in the same room as his father Octavius, and that centurions bore him on their shoulders from Nola to Bovillae.[210]

I have twice above begun to give an account of the river Sarno.[211] It flows into the Tyrrhenian Sea at a place close to the present Torre Annunziata, which I showed was once the site of Pompeii.[212] Vergil speaks of the river in Book VII, "where the Sarnus waters the towns,"[213] and it is said by Lucan to "send forth exhalations by night."[214] It is now called Scafati, from *scaphae*, or "skiffs," which are kept there for travelers crossing over into the territory of Nocera—the neighboring city of Nocera being four miles away. When Cicero is speaking against the Agrarian Law proposed by Rullus, he complains that Nuceria will be held at the whim of the decemvirs in these words: "They will tie down Naples, Pompeii, Nuceria with their garrisons."[215] Livy, too, in Book XXII, has the following: "the Nucerians, having so elected, were conducted to Atella, while the Atellans were ordered to migrate to Calatia."[216] Mountains rise above Nocera on the right, in the middle of which is a town that takes its name from its situation, as it is called *Intermontes*, or Tramonti. The valley hard by these mountains on the left has the notable town of Mercato San Severino, whence the distinguished family of that name originated.[217] This valley is fertile in every kind of crop, but abounds particularly

56

347

Ad infimam vero eius vallis partem apud oppidum quod Aqua Malorum appellatur, fluvius est qui, paucis delapsus passuum milibus, hiatu terrae absorbetur, et post centum ferme passuum[213] spatium—integer et quantus fuerat[214]—in amplam scaturiginem evomitur. Cavaque urbs a situ appellata valli et fluvio[215] dextrorsum in monte imminet.

57 Sed a Nuceria urbe ad praedictas cavas progressi, montes dextrorsum linquimus celsos amplissimosque in mare Inferum excurrentes et promontorium facientes, quod Minervae cognomen priscis temporibus habuit, nunc ab[216] Amalfi oppido appellatum. Cuius oppidi nomen nullo in veteri loco invenimus. Primaque eius loci mentio nobis occurrit ubi in *Historiis* ostendimus, ad annum salutis quintum vigesimum undeciesque centenum, Ottonem imperatorem Teutonicum ab Innocentio II pontifice Romano contra Rogerium Siciliae comitem fuisse vocatum, Rogerioque Italiae continenti pulso Amalfim civitatem et Rivellum cum castellis circumvicinis spoliatum fuisse. Sed fama est qua Amalfitanos audimus[217] gloriari, magnetis usum, cuius adminiculo navigantes ad Arcton diriguntur, Amalfi fuisse inventum. Quicquid vero habeat in ea re veritas: certum est id noctu navigandi auxilium priscis omnino fuisse incognitum. Nam licet legamus Hispanos ad Hesperi sideris directionem navigasse in Italiam, unde (sicut operis principio diximus) Italia Hesperiae appellationem habuit, nullum tamen ad eam rem, caelo nubibus obscurato, a magnete aut ab alio instrumento petebatur auxilium.

58 Ipsis vero in montibus Amalfitanis vini oleique feracissimis, qua in mare Inferum desinunt et meridianum[218] excipiunt solem, regio est omnium Italiae amoenissima: cedri malique quod arantium[219] vocitamus et punicorum ceterorumque malorum ferax, quibus Neapolitana urbs in primis gaudet. Suntque hoc in promontorio praeter Amalfim oppida in mare pariter versa, Maius et Minus

in red wines. Deep in the floor of the valley is a town called Acquamela, where there is a river that runs for a few miles and is then swallowed up by a hole in the ground; after an interval of almost a hundred feet it gushes forth in full spate, just as it was and just as voluminous. Set on a mountain to the right the city of Cava de' Tirreni, so called from its situation, overlooks the valley and river.

As we make our way from the city of Nocera to the caves I   57
mentioned above, we leave behind us on our right lofty and extensive mountain chains that run off into the Tyrrhenian Sea, forming a promontory which in ancient times was called the Promontory of Minerva and is now named after the town of Amalfi, though I do not find the town's name in any ancient source.[218] The first mention of this place I have come across is in the passage from 1125 mentioned in my *Histories*, where Pope Innocent II summoned the German emperor Otto against Count Roger of Sicily;[219] once Roger was beaten back from mainland Italy, the city of Amalfi was plundered, and Ravello, together with the castles lying round about in the vicinity. The story is, and I have heard them say it, that the men of Amalfi boast that the use of the magnet to guide those sailing northwards was discovered at Amalfi.[220] Whatever the truth of the matter, it is certain that this aid to navigation at night was quite unknown to the ancients. For though I read that Spaniards have sailed to Italy in the direction of the Evening Star (which is why Italy had the name Hesperia, as I said at the beginning of this work),[221] they found no help in the magnet or any other device when the sky was obscured.

Where these mountains of Amalfi with their bountiful vines   58
and olives fall away into the Tyrrhenian facing the midday sun is the loveliest of all the regions of Italy: fertile in cedar and the fruit of the orange (as we call it) and in the pomegranate and other fruits in which Naples rejoices more than any other city. On this promontory, besides Amalfi, there are towns that face on to the sea

nomine appellata, inde Caput Ursi, et ulterius Veterum,[220] vicus villis amoenissimis habitatus.

59   Post promontorium est Salernum urbs ad Silerim fluvium, oriturque is fluvius in Apennino, qua in parte Drumentum in mare Superum currens suos habet fontes. Vallem nunc describi oportuit, quam Siler amnis sinistrorsum a mari ad Apenninum oppidis alicubi castellis et vicis habitatam[221] habet. Sed eam dexteramque simul, Lucaniae regionis contiguae descriptionem aggressuri, describemus[222] ut montes Lucaniae, excelsos et pleraque insuperabiles, melius ostendamus. Sunt enim illi de quibus dicit Livius in IX, cum difficultates enumerans quas inventurus fuisset[223] Alexander Magnus si in Italiam traiecisset, interrogat quis illi habitus fuisset Lucanos montes et saltus Apuliae cernenti. Sed iam Apuliae manum[224] apponamus.[225]

Regio quartadecima. Apulia[1]

1   Oportuit supra[2] Samnitium regione ad Tiferni amnis dexteram a nobis expedita ad eiusdem fluvii sinistram transire et ibi inchoantem Apuliam exordiri, sed connexam (sicut ostensum est) Samnio Campaniam prius describere coacti fuimus. Itaque ad Apuliam, finita Campania, redeundum est. Eam regionem a duce eiusdem nominis sic appellatam Ptolemaeus bifariam dividit ut Apulos, Daunos, et Tifernos ad Barium urbem, Peucetios[3] inde usque ad Salentinos esse velit. Servius vero, in Octavo,[4] Vergilii verba exponens, 'Diomedis ad urbem,' sic habet: 'Diomedes tenuit

in the same way, Maiori and Minori by name, then Capo d'Orso, and beyond them, the village of Vietri sul Mare populated by charming country villas.

After the promontory comes the city of Salerno on the river 59 Sele. The river rises at the place in the Apennines where the river Drumento, which flows into the Adriatic, also originates. I should properly now describe the valley to the left of the Sele, populated with scattered towns, castles and villages from the sea to the Apennines. But I shall describe together the valley to the left and to the right when I undertake the survey of the neighboring region of Lucania, so as to give a better account of the lofty and in many places impassable Lucanian mountains. Those in fact are the mountains of which Livy speaks in Book IX when he enumerates the difficulties that Alexander the Great would have encountered had he crossed over into Italy, and asks what Alexander's frame of mind would have been as he beheld the mountains of Lucania and the passes of Puglia.²²² But let us now set our hand to Puglia.

Region 14. Puglia

Having dealt above with the region of the Samnites on the right 1 bank of the river Biferno, I should have passed over to the left bank and started on Puglia, which begins there.¹ But I was obliged to describe Campania first, because Campania is adjacent to Samnium, as I showed.² And so with Campania completed, we must go back to Puglia. Ptolemy says this region was named after an eponymous chief, and he divides it into two parts, the Apulians, Dauni and Tiferni as far as the city of Bari, then the Peucetians reaching into the Salentine peninsula.³ Servius in his commentary on Vergil's words in Book VIII, "to the city of Diomedes," has this to say: "Diomedes ruled over parts of Apulia and, once

partes Apuliae et, edomita omni Gargani montis multitudine, in eodem tractu multas condidit civitates Beneventum Aequitucium,[5] et Arpos, quae et Argyrippa[6] est dicta. Pars vero, ad quam Vergilius facit missum fuisse Mesapum, Mesapia, et Peucetia[7] a fratre, item Daunia a Dauno rege.'

2   Gesta in Apulis referre operosum esset, sed aliqua ex more nostro summatim attingemus. Apuli prius bello quam amicitia[8] Romanis noti fuerunt. Nam Livius libro VIII dicit C. Sulpicio, Q. Aemilio consulibus, ad defectionem Samnitium accessisse novum Apuliae bellum, cuius tunc ager sit vastatus. Et libro IX Publium consulem in Apuliam profectum aliquot expeditionibus[9] populos aut vi subegisse aut condicionibus in societatem accepisse. Et infra: 'Inclinatis semel in Apulia rebus, Teatini[10] quoque Apuli ad novos consules, Q. Iunium Bubulcum, Q. Aemilium Barbulam, foedus petitum venerunt, pacis per omnem Apuliam praestandae populo Romano auctores. Id audacter spondendo impetravere ut foedus daretur, neque ut aequo tamen foedere, sed ut in dicione[11] populi Romani essent. Sicque Apulia est perdomita.' Libro autem X: 'Magnus motus servilis eo anno in Apulia fuit. Tarentum provinciam L. Postumius praetor habebat. Is de pastorum coniuratione, qui vias latrociniis pascuaque publica[12] infesta habuerant, quaestionem severe exercuit. Ad septem milia hominum condemnavit. Multi inde fugerunt. De multis sumptum est supplicium.'

3   Sunt prima Apulorum ad Tiferni sinistram oppida: Campus Marinus in litore, et intus decimo milliario Larinum, novum oppidum alteri suffectum vetustissimo eiusdem nominis proxime ad duos mille passus demolito. De quo Livius, libro XXII, post de-

the mass of peoples on Monte Gargano had all been subdued, founded many cities in the region, Beneventum, Aequum Tuticum, and Arpi, which was called Argyrippa. The part of Apulia to which Vergil has Messapus being sent, on the other hand, was called Messapia, and Peucetia was named after a brother of Diomedes, and Daunia, too, from the king Daunus."[4]

It would be a wearisome undertaking to recount the whole history of Puglia, but as is my custom I shall touch on some of the major points.[5] The Apulians were known to the Romans for their warfare before they were known for their friendship. Livy says in Book VIII that in the consulship of Gaius Sulpicius and Quintus Aemilius, a new war opened up in Apulia with the rebellion of the Samnites, and its territory was then laid waste.[6] In Book IX he says that the consul Publius made several incursions into Apulia, and either subjected its peoples by force or made them allies by granting terms.[7] And below: "When affairs had taken a turn for the worse in Apulia, the Apulian Teatines also came to the new consuls, Quintus Junius Bubulcus and Quintus Aemilius Barbula, to sue for a treaty, engaging to ensure the Roman people peace throughout Apulia. By this bold pledge they prevailed so far as to obtain a treaty — not, however, on equal terms, but on terms that made them subject to the Romans. Thus was Apulia subdued."[8] And in Book X: "That year there was a great uprising of slaves in Apulia. The praetor Lucius Postumius had Tarentum as his province. He carried out a strict investigation into a conspiracy of shepherds who had endangered the highways and public grazing spaces by their banditry. He found about seven thousand men guilty: many of them escaped, but many were put to death."[9] 2

The first towns of Puglia on the left bank of the river Biferno are Campomarino on the coast, and ten miles inland Larino, a modern town that has replaced a very old one of the same name, no more than two miles away and now demolished. Of Larino, Livy in Book XXII, after describing Hannibal's retreat from Faler- 3

scriptam Hannibalis fugam ab agro Falerno sic habet: 'Hannibal ex Paelignis flexit iter, retroque Apuliam repetens, Galeranum[13] pervenit ad urbem. Dictator in Larinate agro castra communivit.' C. Caesar in *Commentariis*: Inde Caesar 'septem omnino dies ad Corfinium[14] commoratus per fines Marrucinorum, Frentanorum, et[15] Larinatum in Apuliam pervenit.' Quarto supra Larini Veteris ruinas milliario est Casacalenda oppidum, cui ad duos mille passus proximae sunt ruinae Gerionis oppidi vetustissimi, de quo Livius, libro XXII: 'Cum ad Gerionem, iam hieme impendente, consisteret bellum, Neapolitani oratores venerunt Romam.' Et infra: 'quam diu pro Gerionis Apuliae castelli inops,[16] tamquam pro Carthaginis moenibus, pugnavit.' Superius sunt: Loveniscum,[17] Morronum, Castellum Lineum, Petrella,[18] Mons Saganus,[19] Iacobi copiarum ductoris egregii patria, a qua[20] cognomen habet. Inde: Coacta, Rochetta, Ratinum, Bussum, Baranellum, Vinculatorium, quod a Boviano et[21] Tiferni amnis origine quinque milia passuum[22] abest. Medioque in montium a mari ad Bovianum tractu Monti Sagano[23] ad sinistram quarto proximum est milliario Campus Bassus, a quo oppido patriam quoque et cognomen[24] habent comites Campi Bassi, quorum Carolus copias cum prudentiae et fortitudinis laude ducit.

4   A Tiferno autem fluvius nunc Fortorius viginti milia passuum[25] in litore distat. Qui quidem fluvius in mare se exonerat prope lacum Lesinae appellatum, passuum[26] quadraginta milia in circuitu complexum. Lesinaque oppidum quatuor a mari[27] milibus[28] distans, lacui, cui dat nomen, mille passibus est propinquum. Intus autem quarto supra Lesinam milliario proximum est ad mille passus amni Fortorio et arduo in colle oppidum in regione egregium, Serra Capriola appellatum. Superius sunt oppida et castella: Sanctus Iulianus, Collis Tortus, Machia, Petra Cratelli, Campus Petrae, Geldonum, et in summo Circus Maior, cui proximum Fortorius

nian territory, has this to say: "Hannibal altered his line of march as he left the Paelignian land, and turning back to Apulia again, he reached the city of Galeranum. The dictator established his camp in the territory of Larinum."[10] Caesar writes in his *Commentaries* that he "stayed in Corfinium for a whole week before making his way into Apulia through the lands of the Marrucini, Frentani, and Larinates."[11] Four miles beyond the ruins of old Larinum is the town of Casacalenda, and about two miles further on are the remains of the very ancient town of Gereonium, on which Livy writes in Book XXII: "The approach of winter had already put a stop to the fighting around Gereonium when envoys from Neapolis arrived in Rome."[12] And below: "How long has Hannibal fought for the walls of the castle of Apulian Gereonium, bare of resources though he is, as if for the walls of Carthage?"[13] Further up there are Loveniso, Morrone del Sannio, Castellino del Biferno, Petrella, and Montagano, home of the famous captain Giacomo da Montagano, who takes his name from there.[14] Then come Coatta, Rocchetta, Oratino, Busso, Baranello, Vinchiaturo, which is five miles from Boiano and from the source of the river Biferno. In the middle of the stretch of mountains that runs from the sea to Boiano, just four miles from Montagano on the left, is the town of Campobasso, homeland of the Counts of Campobasso and origin of their name: one of them, Carlo di Campobasso, is a military captain renowned for his sagacity and bravery.[15]

Twenty miles along the coast from the Biferno is the present-day river Fortore; it debouches into the sea near the Lago di Lesina, which is forty miles in circumference. The town of Lesina is four miles from the sea, and just a mile from the lake to which it gives its name. Four miles inland from Lesina on a steep hill, and about a mile from the river Fortore, is a famous town of the region called Serracapriola. And beyond Serracapriola are these towns and castles: San Giuliano di Puglia, Colle Torto, Macchia Valfortore, Pietracatella, Campodipietra, Gildone, and at the very high- 4

amnis habet ortum. Ad sinistram vero Fortorii[29] Sanctus Nicander, oppidum quinque milia passuum[30] a mari distans, lacui Lesinae imminet ad eam partem quae monti Gargano est proxima. Interiusque Porcina oppidum quindecim a Fortorio et[31] duo a Gargani Montis radicibus milia passuum[32] abest. Sextoque supra Porcinam milliario oppidum Sanctus Severus sexdecim a Fortorio et sex a Gargano milibus recedit.

5   Prius vero quam ultra procedamus, Garganum prisci praesentisque nominis montem fama notissimum describamus. Is ad infimas radices in planitiem desinentes ducentorum milium in[33] circuitu patet. Qua vero in parte ad occidentem solem versa Fortorium amnem et maris Adriatici sinum spectat, lacum habet Varrani appellatum triginta milia passuum[34] in circuitu complexum. Cui quidem lacui castella circum imminent Caprinum, Cagnatum,[35] et Scitella,[36] et qua mons ipse in mare prominet Rodium (ut nunc appellant) oppidum inferiora obtinet. Quod quidem promontorium et oppidum Ptolemaeus Pliniusque et ceteri omnes prisci Tirium appellarunt. Supra est oppidum Vicus dictum. Et superius montis summitatem obtinet praeclarum Sancti Angeli oppidum, a quo mons ipse praesentis temporis ut plurimum nominationem habet. Ornaturque templo cum aedificiis ceteroque apparatu tum[37] maxime[38] ipsa religiositate[39] conspicuo, quod archangeli Michaelis patrocinium apud Deum nostrum imploraturi totius Christiani orbis populi, maximo per universa anni tempora concursu, frequentant.[40] Qua vero Garganus spectat in orientem solem, oppidum est portuosum nunc Bescia (olim Vestice) appellatum. Unde ostendimus in *Historiis* Alexandrum tertium pontificem Romanum, a Guilielmo secundo Normannorum[41] gentis rege adiutum, solvisse cum tredecim triremibus ut pacem cum Federico primo, imperatore pessimo, compositurus, Venetias navigaret.

6   Eoque in loco cum sit secundum Gargani promontorium, Ptolemaeus Adriatici maris sinum finire ac Ionium mare asserit[42] in-

est point Cercemaggiore, near which the Fortore has its source. On the left bank of the Fortore five miles from the sea, the town of San Nicandro Garganico overlooks the part of the Lago di Lesina nearest Monte Gargano. Further inland the town of Apricena is fifteen miles from the Fortore and two from the foot of Monte Gargano. Six miles above Apricena is the town of S. Severo, which is sixteen miles from the river Fortore and six from Monte Gargano.

Before we go farther, we must deal with the famous Monte 5 Gargano — the name it had in antiquity as it does today. Monte Gargano is two hundred miles around at its base where it merges into the plains. Where it faces west toward the river Fortore and the Adriatic gulf, it has a lake called Lago di Varano, thirty miles in circumference.[16] Overlooking this lake is a circle of castles, Carpino, Cagnano, and Ischitella, and where the mountain juts out into the sea, the town of Rodi (as it is now called) sits on the lowland parts. Ptolemy and Pliny and all the other ancient authors called the promontory and town Tirium.[17] Above Rodi is a town called Vico, and above Vico the famous town of Sant'Angelo occupies the top of Monte Gargano — in fact the mountain itself is nowadays mostly called Monte Sant'Angelo from the town. This summit is graced by a church with buildings and other trappings of conspicuous splendor — most splendid of all is its atmosphere of sanctity — where people come in throngs from all over the Christian world and at all seasons of the year to implore the intercession of the Archangel Michael with Our Lord.[18] On the east-facing side of Monte Gargano there is a town with a harbor, Vieste, formerly called Vestice: from here, with the help of the Norman king William II, Pope Alexander III set sail for Venice with thirteen galleys to make peace with that terrible emperor Frederick I, as I mentioned in my *Histories*.[19]

Since there is a second promontory of Gargano at this spot, 6 Ptolemy states that the Adriatic gulf comes to an end and the

choare. Qui etiam dicit Diomedis[43] insulam Gargano[44] ad triginta milia passuum[45] e regione proximam esse. Estque haec insula, de qua Beatus Aurelius Augustinus *De civitate Dei* scribens, aliqua dicit: quibus ab ipso transcriptis unusquisque pro auctoris gravitate fidem quam volet[46] poterit adhibere. 'Diomedem ferunt deificatum et socios suos in aves[47] esse conversos, non fabuloso poeticoque mendacio sed historica attestatione. Quin etiam templum eius esse aiunt in insula Diomedica non longe a monte Gargano, et hoc templum circumvolare atque incolere has alites tam mirabili obsequio ut aquam impleant et aspergant. Et eo si Graeci venerint (aut Graecorum stirpe progeniti), non solum quietas esse verum et insuper advolare;[48] si autem alienigenas viderint, subvolare ad capita cum[49] gravibus ictibus ut etiam perhibeant[50] vulnerare. Nam duris et grandibus rostris satis ad haec proelia perhibentur armatae.' Eam vero insulam, Tremiti appellatam,[51] et Diomedis, ut videtur, templum illud nunc inhabitant religiosi canonici regulares[52] appellati, quos non minus hoc in loco quam Venetiis (sicut ostendimus) et fovit et auxit gloriosus pontifex IV Eugenius. Quorum vitae austeritas et sanctimonia adeo cunctis est admirabilis ut, cum advenis omnibus sint hospitales ac munifici, a nullis vel perditissimis quarumcumque gentium et nationum piratis, ullam hactenus acceperint laesionem. Eorum nos quosdam narrare audivimus has aves Diomedis nomen retinentes magnitudine anseris insulam habere multas, sed omnino omnibus innocuas, nec aliquod eis aut templo praestantes obsequium.

7   De Gargano monte habent aliqua Vergilius et Servius quae ad universae Apuliae notionem plurimum faciunt. Nam cum Vergilius in nono dicat, 'Gargani[53] condebat Iapygis arces,' exponit Servius: 'Iapygia est pars Apuliae in qua est mons Garganus, qui

Ionian Sea begins there.[20] Ptolemy also says that the Island of
Diomedes is opposite Gargano some thirty miles out.[21] This is
the island about which St. Augustine in his *City of God* makes
some statements, to which (quoted verbatim from Augustine)
each reader can give as much credence as he cares to in view of the
author's importance. "Diomedes is said to have become a god and
his companions transformed into birds, and not in a lying fable
devised by poets but in historical fact. Indeed, they say that he has
a temple there on the island of Diomedes, not far from Monte
Gargano, and that the birds that fly round and roost in his temple
display such marvelous devotion that they fill their beaks with
water and sprinkle the temple with it. Also, when Greeks or men
descended from Greek stock come to that place, the birds not only
behave quietly but even hover over them; but if they see non-
Greeks, they fly at their heads with such forceful blows that they
say the birds actually cause them physical harm. For, it is said,
they are well armed for these encounters with hard and large
beaks."[22] Nowadays religious known as Canons Regular live on
this island, which is called Tremiti, and in the supposed temple of
Diomedes:[23] the illustrious pontiff Eugenius IV supported and
advanced them here no less than he did in Venice, as I mentioned.[24] The strictness of their life and their piety are so wonderful for everyone to behold that though they are hospitable and
generous to all comers, no one, not even the most desperate pirates
of any tribe or race whatever, has to this day ever done them
harm. I have heard some of them say that the Island of Diomedes
has many such birds, still called the birds of Diomedes, the size of
a goose, but harmless to all and showing no particular devotion to
the canons themselves or to the temple.[25]

Vergil and Servius have some information on Monte Gargano 7
which is very helpful in forming an idea of Puglia as a whole.
When Vergil in Book IX says "he was founding the citadel of Ia-
pygian Garganus," Servius explains: "Iapygia is the part of Apulia

usque in Adriaticum protenditur pelagus.'[54] Lucanus etiam dicit:
'Apulus Adriacas[55] Garganus exit in undas.' Garganum montem
adiacentiaque oppida Saraceni per Grimoaldi Longobardorum regis tempora ad annum salutis paulo plus septingentesimum ceperunt, quos idem rex expulit, populis Christianis ubique conser-
vatis, ut nullam[56] gens Longobarda in ducentis regnorum suorum
annis talem praestiterit[57] Italiae operam. Ad annum exinde paulo
plus minus centesimum Carolus Magnus, imperator et Francorum
rex, Saracenos Garganum opprimentes cum expulisset, omnia pa-
cifice possedit quae ab ipso Gargano ad Cordubam Hispaniae urbem intercedunt.

8   Prius autem quam exposita mari post Garganum montem
prosequar, alia describam quae ad amnem Fortorium inchoavi.
Supra Sancti Severi oppidum quarto milliario est Turris Maior
castellum duodecim milibus a Fortorio recedens. Et supra, totidem[58] milibus a Turri Maiore abest Castellutium oppidum, unde
parvo distat spatio Mons Rotanus. Et supra est Cellentia, post
oppidum Sanctus Marcus, inde Vulturaria, et proxime Sancti oppidum quod dicitur Gaudii. Supraque id est Rossetum, superius
Fortorii[59] amnis fonti Mons Falco castellum est proximum.[60]

where Mount Garganus is located, a mountain that stretches out into the Adriatic Sea."[26] And Lucan says: "Apulian Garganus juts out into the waters of the Adriatic."[27] The Saracens captured Monte Gargano and the towns that flank it in the time of the Lombard king Grimoald, about 700 CE: Grimoald expelled them, but preserved all the Christian communities, a service such as the Lombard nation had not performed for Italy in the two hundred years of their rule here. A century later, more or less, when the emperor and king of the Franks Charlemagne had driven out the Saracens who were attacking Monte Gargano, all the land between Monte Gargano and the city of Cordoba in Spain was peacefully in his control.

Before I continue with the coastal towns after Monte Gargano, I shall describe the others that I began with back at the river Fortore.[28] Four miles beyond the town of San Severo and twelve miles from the Fortore lies the castle of Torremaggiore. The town of Castelluccio Valmaggiore is likewise four miles beyond Torremaggiore, and Monte Rotano is but a short way from Castelluccio. Beyond Monte Rotano is Celenza Valfortore, and after that the town of San Marco la Catola, then Volturara Appula, and quite close by the town called San Bartolomeo in Galdo. Beyond that is Roseto Valfortore, and higher up, very near the source of the river, is the castle of Montefalcone di Val Fortore.

8

APPENDIX

BLONDI FLAVII FORLIVIENSIS ADDITIONES CORRECTIONESQVE
ITALIAE ILLVSTRATAE

1.1 Interrogasti me in minoribus agens, Pater Beatissime, cur *Italiam* meam nondum absolutam ediderim. Subticui tunc indignabundus, certo proposito non prius animi dolorem publicandi quam illatum eo in opere vulnus (post adhibitam medelam) indicasset edocuissetque cicatrix.

1.2   Creverat ingens ea multiplex et multi laboris Italiae descriptio ab Alpibus (id est, a suae latitudinis principio) hinc ad Garganum Apuliae promontorium sinistra, inde dextera ad Salernum, cum, multis eam videre petentibus, evicit unus dignitate episcopus ut, singulos schedarum quinterniones legendos accipiens, iure iurando promiserit nec exemplum inde transcribere nec[1] illos cuiquam ostendere. Et tamen tanta fuit praesumptione atque perfidia ut viros aetatis nostrae in catalogum principio promissum multis in operis urbibus et oppidis a me positos[2] (praeter paucissimos sibi amicos) abraserit et quaedam alia in locorum descriptione mutaverit. Promiseratque quibusdam codicem litteris ornatuque elegantissimum ex ea mutilatione confectum concedere transcribendum.

1.3   Quo ego perculsus[3] nuntio, tantae iniuriae per editionem vel praecipitatam censui occurendum, grataque et iucunda effecit operis a me editi materia ut brevi plures quam dicere ausim diversis in

APPENDIX

BIONDO FLAVIO OF FORLÌ
ADDITIONS AND CORRECTIONS
TO THE *ITALIA ILLVSTRATA*

While you were not yet in orders,[1] Most Holy Father, you asked   1.1
me why I published my *Italia illustrata* when it was still unfinished.
I kept an indignant silence at the time, because I had firmly resolved not to make my grievance public until a remedy had been
applied and the scar alone revealed the wound I had received with
that work.

My description of Italy, from the Alps (that is, from the begin-   1.2
ning of their transverse extent) to the Gargano promontory of
Puglia on the left in the first place, and secondly to Salerno on the
right, had grown to an enormous size, and was both complex and
laborious. Many people were asking to see it, but only one, of
episcopal rank, prevailed upon me.[2] He promised on oath that as
he received the gatherings of sheets for perusal one after the other,
he would neither have a copy made of them nor let anyone else see
them. And yet he showed such effrontery and untrustworthiness
that he deleted the contemporaries that I had included in a catalog
promised at the beginning in connection with many of the towns
and cities of the work, except for a handful of his friends, and he
altered some other things in the description of places. He had
further promised to lend certain people a finely written and illuminated manuscript made on the basis of this mutilated text, so that
they could copy it.

I heard the news with consternation, and determined to coun-   1.3
ter that great wrong with an edition of my own, even if it was a
hurried one. The material in the edition put out by me proved so

provinciis visi sint *Italiae* codices *illustratae:* unde meam apud multos haberi videns editionem ab adulterini operis publicatione deterritus est episcopus.

1.4   Sed dum ego hanc arceo repelloque inferendam a levi homine iniuriam, ipse ego maiorem operi mihique inflixi. Nosti tu, qui multa et quidem dignissima historico oratorioque charactere hactenus scripsisti (prout superatis cum omnium admiratione pontificatus Romani laboribus singulos per dies scribere continuas), oportere, scripta cum ad finem perducta sint extremaque videatur apposita manus, parumper editionem differre ut ea nos postmodum relegentes tamquam in alienum veniamus opus et errata melius acutiusque recognoscamus nostra. Quam ob rem prudenter dixit Horatius 'nonumque prematur in annum' editio.

1.5   Et falso episcopi titulo insignitus, vulpecula meus in eam me impulit editionis praecipitationem ut nec errata corrigere nec manca supplere nec[4] nova (quae relegenti venissent in mentem mihi) addere potuerim. Supplebit vero hic liber *Italiae* nostrae additus et uno eodemque die episcopi vitium intelleges et tibi solitam placere meliorem, pinguiorem, correctiorem videbis *Italiam.*

1.6   Nec inconvenire existimabo, si non nulla quae post factam editionem nova fieri gerive contigit digna referam, sequarque operis ordinem ut singulas percurrenti provincias facile sit ubi vel correctio vel additio facta sit inspicere. Novusque hic labor meus id—multis quod scio gratissimum—efficiet ut, postquam accepto ab invido vel potius insano homine vulneri necessariam mihi videor

popular and welcome that in a short while more copies of *Italia illustrata* than I would have dared to claim were seen in the various provinces of Italy. Seeing that my edition was now in the hands of a good many people, the bishop was deterred from publishing his pirated work.

But in warding off the injury the scoundrel had done me, I inflicted a greater one on my work and on myself. As a writer yourself of many high-quality historical and oratorical works (works that you continue to write every day, after dealing with papal business to universal admiration), you know that we must delay publication for a while when a piece of writing seems to have reached the end and has had the finishing touches put to it, in order that in reading it over later, we may come to it as if it were the work of someone else, and so recognize its defects better and more readily. On this score Horace was quite right to say of publication, "Hold it back for eight years."[3]

This little fox of mine, then, wrongly given the distinguished title of bishop, forced me into this precipitate publication, so I wasn't able to correct mistakes, fill in gaps, or add the new material that would have occurred to me if I had reread it. This appendix tacked on to the *Italia illustrata* will supply these wants, and on one and the same day you'll understand the wrong the bishop did me and find an *Italy* that you have been wont to enjoy better, richer, and more correct.

I think it will be best to report some new matters of importance that happened or were accomplished after I published my edition, keeping to the order of the book, so that it will be easy for anyone running through the individual regions to see at a glance where a correction or addition has been made. Now that I have applied, as I believe, the required remedy to the injury I received from that jealous or rather unhinged man, this new labor of mine, which I know will be welcome to many, will enable me to carry on

adhibuisse curam, describere ac absolvere pergam quod a Gargano et Salerno in mare Ionium fretumque Siculum Italiae est reliquum, nulla ratione alia hactenus quam concepta indignitate dilatum.

De Ligvria incipit

2.1 Prima et sola additio in Liguribus ad Saonam et Genuam utrique urbi communis facienda occurrit. Diximus in prima descriptione Saonae urbis gubernationi et dominio tunc praepositum fuisse Thomam Fregosum, ducatu Genuensi bis functum: qui vir inter paucos primosque aetatis nostrae gravissimus prudentissimusque sit habitus, Ludovicusque Fregosus illi nepos ducatui praeerat Genuensi. Quo in loco inter ennarandam Genuae urbis amplitudinem magnificentiamque, ipsam diximus in Scythico, in Pontico, in Thracico litoribus habuisse tunc colonias, per quarum occasionem barbaros Christiani praesertim Italici nominis hostes terreret, et cum saepenumero repulisset tum maxime in dies magisque⁵ afflictura videretur. Sed praestantissimae ac celeberrimae urbis fortuna derepente mutata est. Uno enim ferme ac eodem tempore multa inciderunt quae — in historia a nobis alibi⁶ aut ab alio quopiam diligentius enarranda — nunc parva et adstricta hic commemoratione ex opusculi huius natura complectemur.

2.2 Petrus Fregosus Baptista genitus, ambitione ductus, Ludovicum Fregosum consobrinum suum Bartholomaeo genitum, mitioris quam ipse esset ingenii, alioquin probum et Genuensi populo gratissimum, insidiis appetitum ducatu deiecit et in patrimonii oppida quae ad Sarzanam possideret illaesum abire permisit. Thomas paulo post senio confectus obiens Saonam aliis nepotibus suis di-

and conclude my description of the rest of Italy, from Gargano and Salerno to the Ionian Sea and the Straits of Messina:[4] the only reason it has been put off until now is precisely the slight I suffered.

Region 1. Liguria

The first and only addition that needs to be made to Liguria applies equally to Savona and Genoa. In my original description of Savona, I said that Tommaso Fregoso, twice doge of Genoa, was then in charge of the city as governor and ruler.[5] He was one of those rare men of the utmost gravity and wisdom, among the foremost of our era; his nephew Ludovico Fregoso was doge of Genoa.[6] In my account of the greatness and grandeur of the city of Genoa,[7] I said that it had colonies at that time on the coastlines of Scythia, Pontus, and Thrace, which served to strike fear into the barbarian enemies of Christendom, of Italy in particular, and it had not only often beaten them back but seemed poised to inflict more harm on them with each passing day. But the fortunes of this exceptional and famous city changed all at once. A great many things happened at almost the same time, of which, due to the nature of this little work, I can give here no more than a summary account, though their history will be told elsewhere in greater detail by me or by someone else.

Pietro Fregoso, son of Battista, was ambitious.[8] His cousin Ludovico, son of Bartolomeo, was of a gentler disposition than Pietro, but in other respects honorable and very popular with the Genoese. Pietro laid a trap for Ludovico, ejected him from his ducal office, and allowed him to go off unharmed to some towns that he had inherited at Sarzana. Shortly afterward Tommaso, worn out by old age and dying, gave up Savona to other nephews for

2.1

2.2

misit gubernandam. Interea Alphonsus Arago—praeter Hispaniae Citerioris, Sardiniae, et Corsicae, Neapolitanumque[7] et Trinacrium (quae utraque Siculum appellant) regna obtinens—habitas aliquando leviores cum Ludovico Fregoso[8] duce tributi contentiones in apertum adversus[9] Petrum et Genuam urbem bellum exasperavit, Franciscusque Sfortia Mediolani dux regi ad id favit: adeo ut Petrus ipse Alphonso regi et, eo per id temporis mortuo, regi Ferdinando eius filio ac successori et semper simul Mediolanensium duci resistendi desperatione adductus, quod multotiens omnibus eis comminatus fuerat,[10] urbem Genuam cum arce Castellecto appellata regi Francorum tunc Carolo in liberum permiserit[11] dominium, per quam permutationem Novium et Gavium[12] oppida et aureorum viginti quinque milia dono accepit.

2.3   Sed dum ea sic aguntur, Maumettus[13] Turchorum rex potentissimus, Christianorum praesertim Graecorum ignavia et avaritia potius quam viribus suis et potentu fretus, urbem ceperat Constantinopolitanam. Ac proximam illi Peram[14] de Genuensibus ditissimam rebusque Genuensium opportunam urbem primo, post alias ad Ponticum Bosphoranumque[15] et Scythicum litora occupaverat. Visumque est per eam tempestatem iram Dei in populum Genuensem desaevire: duodecim namque et eo amplius ceteas ingentes eximii valoris naves per Mediterraneum mare vi tempestatis afflictas demersasque et diversis perditas modis fuisse constitit.

2.4   Quibus tot tantisque Dei comminationibus illatisque vulneribus dum Genuenses ad bonam vitae frugem adduci oportuit, novis de industria scandalis data est opera. Petrus enim Fregosus, Gallico regi quam sibi non servari diceret fide falsa, Genuam impetiit. Et a Gallico principe, qui regis vices gereret, Iohanne Lotharingo duce, Renati regis nato probe resistente, occisus est.

them to govern. Having gained control of the kingdoms of Naples and Trinacria (as they call the two Sicilies), in addition to eastern Spain,[9] Sardinia, and Corsica, Alfonso of Aragon in the meantime blew up some initially trivial disputes about tariffs with doge Ludovico Fregoso into open war against Pietro and the city of Genoa, with the encouragement in this of the Duke of Milan, Francesco Sforza. Things came to a head. Pietro himself saw the hopelessness of standing up to King Alfonso—and on Alfonso's death in that period to his son and successor King Ferdinand—while at the same time constantly opposing the Duke of Milan, because all of them had often been threatened by him. Pietro accordingly gave the king of France, at that time Charles, free dominion over Genoa and its fortress, known as the Castelletto.[10] In exchange for this Pietro got the towns of Novi and Gavi and a gift of twenty-five thousand florins.

But while all this was going on, Mehmed, the mighty Turkish king, captured the city of Constantinople, relying not so much on his own resources and power as on the cowardice and greed of the Christians, the Greeks in particular.[11] Very close to Constantinople, he had first taken over Pera from the Genoese, a rich city invaluable for Genoese trade,[12] and then other cities along the coasts of Pontus, the Bosporus, and the Black Sea. It seemed that in that period the wrath of God was raging against the Genoese: we know that twelve or more huge merchant ships of enormous value were buffeted by the force of a storm in the Mediterranean, and were sunk or lost in various ways.

With all these dreadful warnings and afflictions laid on them by God, the Genoese ought to have turned to a more virtuous way of life, but instead they devoted themselves with a will to new scandals. Pietro Fregoso attacked Genoa, accusing the king of France of the bad faith which he himself showed. He was killed during the stout resistance of the king of France's regent at Genoa, the French prince Jean, duke of Lorraine, the son of King René.[13]

2.3

2.4

2.5   Eo exinde Lotharingo duce regnum Neapolitanum adversus Ferdinandum regem ingresso, Genua novos habuit motos, inter quos Ludovicus Fregosus a populo dux creatus est. Sed cum recuperandae per arcem civitati Renatus rex magnas a Saona[16] immitteret Gallorum copias, caedes duorum milium in illas[17] a Genuensi populo commissa. Et cum recuperatam post arcem populus Genuensis, duce Ludovico Fregoso, urbemque retineat, Saonam copiis communitam novus retinet genitori Carolo suffectus rex Francorum Ludovicus.

2.6   Sic brevi tempore urbis Genuae potentia, Italiae cumulo gloriae accedere solita, ad id deducta est, ut de servandis portu et moenibus Genuae saepius quam de invadendis Scythis, Bosphoranis,[18] et Thracibus cogitetur.

De Etrvria incipit

3.1   Ad Etruriam cum veniendum sit, primas additiones in maritima Saenensium regione incipiemus. Dehinc ab[19] Umbronis fluvii ostiis in eius mediterranea, operis primi ordinem sequemur. Primaque est additio ad Castilionum Piscariae castellum, quod paene litoreum ad paludis caenosae emissarium[20] esse diximus. Id autem castellum, aliquamdiu ab Alphono Aragonum rege possessum, eo vita functo, in manibus et potestate remansit Ferdinandi Aragonis, Neapolitani regis illius filii et successoris. Qui, gratitudine usus in tuam Sanctitatem (cuius iustitiae et beneficentiae beneficio id suum regnum a Gallicis et suis rebellibus subditis agitatum retinet), Antonium Piccolomeum, nepotem tuum, Amalphitanum ducem, eius generum ipso donavit castello, quod aliis eiusdem Antonii ducis et fratrum villis ac possessionibus agri Saenensis proximum esse intellegeret.

Then as the duke of Lorraine entered the Kingdom to attack 2.5
Ferdinand,[14] Genoa experienced fresh upheavals, in the course of
which the Genoese made Ludovico Fregoso doge. But when King
René sent a great force of Frenchmen from Savona to take back
the city by means of the Castelletto, two thousand of them were
slaughtered by the Genoese. And though the Genoese under Doge
Ludovico Fregoso kept control of the city after they recovered
Castelletto, the new King Louis of France, who succeeded his father Charles, kept control of a Savona garrisoned by his troops.[15]

Thus in short order the might of Genoa, which had been ac- 2.6
customed to adding to Italy's store of glory, was reduced to this:
they had to give more thought to keeping the harbor and the walls
of Genoa safe than to invading the lands of the Black Sea, the
Bosporus, and Thrace.

Region 2. Tuscany

When we come to Tuscany, my first additions begin with the 3.1
maritime territory of Siena. Then I shall follow the order of the
original work, from the mouth of the river Ombrone to its hinterland. The first addition is the castle at Castiglione della Pescaia,
which I said was almost on the shore at the outlet of a silted-up
lagoon.[16] This castle was long owned by King Alfonso of Aragon,
and when he died, his son and successor Ferdinand of Aragon,
king of Naples, kept it in his own hands. Out of gratitude to Your
Holiness, since he retains his kingdom thanks to your evenhand-
edness and support, troubled as it was by the French and by rebellion among his own subjects, Ferdinand gave the castle itself to
your nephew, and his own son-in-law, Antonio Piccolomini, the
duke of Amalfi, knowing that it was close to other Sienese estates
and properties of Duke Antonio and his brothers.[17]

3.2   Non[21] longe a praedicto maritimae regionis loco montem Amia-
tam excelsum diximus multis in circuitu castellis frequentari, inter
quae unum esse hic addendum inspeximus, eximiae inter cetera
amoenitatis castellum, Abbatiam Sancti Salvatoris appellatum.
Quod quidem, a divitibus habitatum colonis, multos nostrae Curiae praestantes viros anno praesenti[22] commode in saluberrimam
habitationem excepit. Et cum tua Sanctitas in eo monasterio bene
fuerit, non nulli ex magnatibus etiam laute et iucunde in circuitu
habuerunt.

3.3   Continent vero inde monasterio inde castello silvae in montes
sursum altissimos in decliviaque et rivos longe lateque multis se
milibus extendentes. Sed cum longius progressi quercus prope solas inveniant, pars nemoris castello monasterioque propinquior
solas habet abores castaneas sublimitate quidem eximia visendas
sed densitatis vastitate mirabiles. Quarum multae sex aut octo,
plurium aliae, hominum, in id expansis bracchiis, se vicissim extre-
mis digitulis contingentium, impleant complexum. Facit vero ramorum diffusa et amplissima in singulis latitudo ut, cum omnem
per aestatem subiectum longissimo spatio campum numquam sol
irradiet, natae licet in feracissimo natura solo humiliores herbae
gratissimam praebeant viriditatem sed tenuem animalibus pastionem. A quo item loco tam multis tam diversisque ramorum (ut
apparet) fornicibus contecto, id hominibus aeque ac animantibus
ceteris provenit quandoque commodum ut, cum perpetua ibi per
aestatem fruantur umbra, si quando derepente (ut fit) rapidior
violentiorque fusus sit caelo imber, minima aut nulla (et quam
alicubi declinare possint) infusione tangantur.

3.4   In ea amoenissima omnium tecta — quae prius saepenumero
'stabula,' sicut poeta inquit, fuerant 'alta ferarum' — tua Sanctitas
saepe convenit, ubi, assistentibus sibi selectis pridem in id munus
doctissimis celebribusque viris referendariis tuis, gravem accura-
tumque habuisti conventum, examinatisque singulorum petitioni-

Not far from the coastal region of Siena mentioned above, I   3.2
said that lofty Monte Amiata was dotted with a ring of castles,[18]
and one of them I consider should be added here: a castle of extraordinary charm compared to the rest, the Abbadia San Salva-
tore. Populated by prosperous farmers, the town this year gave a
fitting welcome to many distinguished men of our Curia with
wholesome accommodation.[19] With Your Holiness happily settled
in that monastery, a number of eminent curialists lived well and
agreeably in the vicinity.

The forests stretch unbroken from the monastery and castle up   3.3
into the high mountains and down the slopes and gullies, extending far and wide for many miles. Those who carry on farther find
oaks almost exclusively, but the part of the woods nearer the castle
and monastery has only chestnuts, well worth seeing not only for
their remarkable height but also for their sheer girth. Many of
these trees could take the embrace of six or eight men with arms
spread wide and fingertips touching—some of them even more.
The spreading mass of branches of each individual tree ensures
that all summer long the sun will never shine on to the ground
lying underneath to any great extent, and consequently that the
stunted grass that grows there, though planted in very fertile
soil, will offer welcome greenery but scant pasturage for animals.
From this spot too, protected as it were by these many and various
overarching branches, there sometimes comes to men and beasts
alike this blessing, that since they enjoy continuous shade there
throughout the summer, if the heavens ever open up with a sudden and violent shower, as happens, they get very little or no
drenching, or one at any rate that can be diverted elsewhere.

Your Holiness has frequently resorted to these pleasant abodes,   3.4
which often in the past served as "the high coverts of wild animals," as the poet says.[20] Here you have held grave and careful
meetings assisted by your referendaries, learned and celebrated
men specially selected for the task.[21] Here responses were made to

bus pridem exhibitis, non magis in iure et iustitia quam in gratiis et concessionibus, est responsum. Ab his vero aliisque pontificii oneris muneribus cum ibi cessatum erat, ceteri praestantes Romanae Curiae viri per eam amoenitatem incessu, deambulatione, et honestissimis agitationibus se exercebant.

3.5   Sed iam ad Umbronem veniendum est. Is fluvius apud olim Populoniam secusque nunc Grossetum urbem in mare labitur Inferum. In opere enim edito, postquam sita ad eius fluvii dexteram describentes Ischiam et Insulam castella posuimus, Bonconventum ad eius fluvii superiora esse diximus, ubi nunc bene additur Arbiam torrentem secundo infra Bonconventum miliario cadere confundique in Umbronem. Qui Arbia torrens, ubi viam interrumpit ab urbe Roma Saenas recta ducentem, ponte iungitur lateritio, quem, ab aquarum alluvionibus bis eversum, praesenti anno populus instaurat Saenensis—molibus illi firmius substentando iactis, qui priscorum Romanae olim rei publicae operum speciem prae se ferunt.

3.6   Et ad textus praedicti continuationem, supra Bonconventum de Umbrone fluvio diximus. Paulo sub eius amnis fonte Assianum est oppidum, ad quem locum addimus: id oppidum praesenti anno salutis secundo sexagesimo supra quaterdecies centenum id nactum[23] esse ornamentum ut, te pontifice Pio II urbis Romae pestilentiam declinante et Pientiam urbem tuam inhabitante, Cancellaria Apostolica, viris frequentata praestantibus, Assiani quatuor fuerit mensibus, apud quod[24] has nos destinavimus additiones.

3.7   Lucam item describentes Etruscam urbem, Lucio III eam et Alexandro II pontificibus Romanis civibus suis ornatam fuisse diximus[25] et tres tantummodo saeculi nostri viros ad eiusdem civitatis decus tunc attulimus. Sed quo tempore ea descriptio in nostris haerebat latebatque manibus, magnum etiam Lucae urbis ornamentum domi apud nos crescebat, nobis aeque ac ceteris tunc incognitum: Iacobus Lucensis, quem diu post e nostro Secretaria-

petitions of individuals after earlier consideration and examination, as matters of grace and favor as much as of justice and right. When time could be spared from these and other functions of the papal office, the rest of the distinguished men of the Roman Curia would take advantage of this delightful spot to exercise — taking walks and promenades, engaging in dignified physical exertions.

But now we must turn to the river Ombrone, which flows into 3.5
the Tyrrhenian Sea at the former city of Populonia and alongside the present city of Grosseto. In the published work, I located the castles of Istia d'Ombrone and Isola on the right bank of the Ombrone. I then said that Buonconvento was on the upper reaches of this river,[22] where now it is as well to add that the stream Arbia descends and flows into the Ombrone two miles below Buonconvento; and that the Arbia, where it meets the road that leads directly from Rome to Siena, is crossed by a bridge of brick which has twice been destroyed by flooding.[23] The people of Siena are this year restoring it by setting up buttresses to stabilize it, work reminiscent of the feats of engineering of the Roman Republic long ago.

To continue the above text, I spoke about the river Ombrone 3.6
above Buonconvento. A short distance below the source of the river is the town of Asciano. To its description I now add that in this year of grace 1462 the town obtained the following honor: while you, Pope Pius, were escaping the plague at Rome by residing in your city of Pienza, the Apostolic Chancery with all its eminent men in attendance spent four months at Asciano, where I conceived these additions to my work.

Similarly, when I described the Tuscan city of Lucca, I said that 3.7
she had been graced by her own citizens as Popes Lucius III and Alexander II,[24] and I mentioned only three men of our time as adding to the city's luster. But while that description was as yet still in my hands and unpublished, another great adornment of his hometown Lucca was arising in our midst, unknown to me as to

tus Apostolici Collegio ad episcopatum Papiensem inde ad cardinalatus fastigium tua Sanctitas digne extulit, acris quidem ingenii
et multae studiorum humanitatis peritiae virum, meliora de se
cum rerum experientia praestaturum.

3.8 Sed et Pistoria civitas sicut loco et situ Lucae urbi[26] proxima est
sic illi similem hoc tempore nacta est fortunam, quando Nicolaum
de Forteguerris Pistoriensem, tibi pridem domesticum, tu etiam,
Pater Sancte, cardinalem creasti: virum vel ideo multifaciendum
quod, quaecumque iussu tuo magna aggreditur, non minus bene
quam celeriter et magnifice conficit et sese probum Ecclesiae pugi-
lem in cunctis exhibet.

3.9 Continuandae vero sunt nobis ad operis ordinem inchoatae superius in Saenensium ditionis agro additiones. Diximus eos, qui
secundum Umbronis fluvii sinistram regionem maritimam Sae-
nensibus subditam emensi sint, hinc Petrioli balneum invenire
inde dextrorsum in Montis Amiatae finibus Montalcinum. Nunc
ad Petriolum addimus magno eius oppidi cessisse decori tuam,
Pater Sancte, et aliquot Romanae Ecclesiae cardinalium moram
(bis terve proximis temporibus) lavandi causa ibi factam. Per quam
vero magis bonae valetudini quam vitae prorogationi tuae et
multorum consultum esse existimant physici periti. Et quando
moderatas delectationes virtutem balneorum ad comparandam
confirmandamve sanitatem corporum iuvare constat, rem in vena-
tionum genere dicemus non solum eis qui inspexerunt sed audien-
tibus quoque laetam.

3.10 Monasterium est Sancti Antonii appellatum, Petriolo[27] maritimam versus regionem mille quingentis passibus supereminens.
Quam fragosam celsi silvosique montis viam cum paene confece-
ris, paululum[28] de ascensu ⟨est⟩ remittendum ut ad parum sump-
tuose et minus laute aedificatum te conferas monasterium quod, e

everyone else, Jacopo da Lucca.[25] Much later Your Holiness raised him from our ranks of the College of the Apostolic Secretaries to the see of Pavia, and then to the eminence of the cardinalate — a man of keen intellect and great expertise in humanist studies, to be sure, and one who will only give better of himself with growing experience.

There is the city of Pistoia, too, the nearest city to Lucca in loca-   3.8
tion and situation.[26] It has had in our day a similar destiny to that city's, Holy Father, for you also made Niccolò Forteguerri of Pistoia a cardinal after long service as your domestic familiar: a man of such talents that whatever great enterprises he takes on at your bidding he accomplishes with efficiency, speed and splendor, showing himself a worthy champion of the Church in every respect.[27]

But we must continue in the proper order with the additions   3.9
that I earlier started on in the territory under Sienese rule. I said that those who traverse the coastal land under Sienese control, on the left of the river Ombrone, find on one side the baths of Petriolo, and on the other, to the right at the edge of Monte Amiata, Montalcino. On Petriolo we can add the great glory that was given that town by your stay there to take the waters, Holy Father, and that of a number of cardinals of the Roman Church, two or three times recently.[28] Skilled physicians reckon that the stay will have been made for its health-giving properties rather than to prolong life, yours and many others'. Since pleasures in moderation assist the beneficial effects of the baths in obtaining and retaining physical health, as everyone agrees, I'll tell you a hunting story that was found amusing not just by those who saw it but by those that heard it too.

There is a monastery dedicated to Sant'Antonio that overlooks   3.10
Petriolo a mile and a half toward the coast.[29] When you have climbed the uneven road of the high wooded mountain, the ascent slackens off a bit as you reach the monastery, cheaply and by no means luxuriously built. Of our leading cardinals, it had been able

nostris summis viris cardinalibus, solum excipere potuisset eum, qui per hanc aestatem inhabitat, Alexandrum Saxoferratensem, Sanctae Susannae presbyterum cardinalem, vitae semper hactenus monasticae innutritum.

3.11   Continet monasterii illius hortulo terrae particula silvis aliunde conterminata, quae, cultura raro alias habita nunc penitus destituta, solis[29] filicibus (malignis agro herbis) rubisque fecunda est. Hanc vero herbam, durioris sublimisque calami, radices quas alte iacit densas et dulces habere hinc scimus quod, carestia populos per Italiam premente, pauperes vidimus ex contritis filicum radicibus atri coloris pane confecto avide vesci.

3.12   Ad eam itaque dulcium filicis radicum pastionem aper quinum pondo centenariorum cum noctu et quandoque interdiu venire assuevisset, cepit libido monachos, quorum oculis saepe subiectus erat, illius aliqua potiundi. Accersitusque cervos et apros sagitta petere medicata assuetus venator accessit, qui sedens ad auroram in cellula cum monachis per rimulam apri consuetudinem contemplatus est. Exspectatum inde cum in claram lucem fatisceret diluculum, delinitam medicamine sagittam scorpioni (sive balistae) in ictum aptari coeptum erat. Cum subtilius ⟨sint⟩ contemplati iuniores qui aderant, monachi et confratres, venatorem[30] submissa admonent voce cerni, inter herbas apro proximas et ab illo pedibus minime conculcatas, lupum toto prostratum corpore, qui, radices tenacissimo exstirpanti dente et in pasturam totis sensibus aeque ac toto capite et pectore demersae bestiae intentissimas strueret insidias. Quotiens vero in excavatam scrobem corrosurus radices aper anteriorem demisisset corporis partem, elevatiores subinde factos, qui in solido manserant solo,[31] clunes et maxime coleos extra femur in ea semper bestia prominentes lupus ut aggrederetur sensim movit. Sed cum mota se intorsisset pascens bestia, substitit

to receive only the one who is living there this summer, Alessandro of Sassoferrato, cardinal priest of Santa Susanna, a man nurtured all his days in the monastic life.[30]

Part of the grounds of the monastery, elsewhere bounded by woods, forms a little garden: seldom looked after in earlier times and now utterly abandoned, it produces only bracken (plants damaging to horticulture) and brambles. We know that this plant with its tough and tall stalks has deep-rooted tubers that are thick and sweet, since when famine oppresses the people of Italy, we see the poor greedily feeding themselves on black bread made of ground-up bracken roots. 3.11

And so when a five-hundred-pound boar had got into the habit of coming to feed on the sweet bracken roots at night, and sometimes during the day, the monks would often have him in their sights, and were overcome by a desire to somehow get their hands on him. They sent for a hunter experienced at taking stags and boars with poisoned arrows. When he came, he sat with the monks at dawn in one of their cells, observing the behavior of the boar carefully through a chink in the wall. When the dawn that they had been waiting for started to brighten into the light of day, he began to fit a poisoned arrow into his crossbow, or *balista*, to get a shot. When the younger monks and lay brothers looked more closely, they told the hunter under their breath that they could see a wolf, its whole body stretched out in the grass closest to the boar and where it was least trampled by its hooves. It was preparing an all-out surprise attack on the beast, which was crouched down doggedly digging up roots with its tusks with all its senses, heart and soul, intent on feeding. Whenever the boar's foreparts sank down into the hole he had dug to gnaw on the roots — its haunches and scrotum staying on level ground and so raised up — the wolf would slowly move forward intending to attack them, the scrotum especially, always prominent in this beast, extending as it does beyond the thighs. But whenever the 3.12

demisso capite insidiator. Tandem, oblata iterum occasione derepente usum[32] animal rapacissimum arreptos vasto morsu bestiae
coleos tenacissime tenuit. Quo percitus dolore, ingenti aper saltu
se quam longe proripiens connexum traxit et lupum.

3.13   Vertit vero ocius hiantes fauces in clunes proprios laesum animal, prementem[33] tenacissime lupum anhelans morsu reciproco
remordere. Et quo magis spe[34] sua et intentione frustrari se cerne-
ret, eo saepius, urgente simul cum coleorum dolore mortis metu,
in gyrum et vanam remordendi rabiem se rotavit. Econtraque lupus (tamquam vehiculo) coleis apri innixus et toto contractus
corpore, id in primis curare ab inspicientibus cernebatur: ne dis-
tracta per motus violentiam posteriora eius (praesertim crura) re-
curvus in id aper occiperet.

3.14   Facta vero est, dura filice et multis obtecto sentibus in loco (qui
multo erat cruore conspersus), area adeo conculcata obtritaque ut
conserendo eius modi duello constratam praeparatamque fuisse
quis dixerit. Vix horae dimidium[35] ea duraverat beluarum pugna,
cum ponderosi corporis aper, pendentem a visceribus suis iustae
magnitudinis lupum non magis trahens quam versans et in gyrum
volutans, dissoluta intestinorum compagine, exanimis corruit.

3.15   Quam primumque lupus plane victor se erexit, inchoatam
continuans ad inguina voraginem, rictum et fauces ad usque oculos in iacentis praedae ventrem abscondit, tuncque, plaudentis ad
cellulae rimulas hortantibus monachis, paratam prius[36] adversus
aprum sagittam venator libratissime in lupum scorpione contorsit.
Lupusque ictu ventrem confossus saltu primum edito extra proelii

beast shifted its ground as it fed and turned around, the attacker stopped short and lowered its head. At last, as opportunity presented itself again, the rapacious predator suddenly seized the scrotum of the beast with a great bite and held on tight. Stung by the pain, with a huge leap the boar spun away as far as it could, dragging the wolf still attached with it.

Soon the wounded animal turned its gaping jaws toward its own haunches in an effort to return the bite as the wolf held on remorselessly. The more it saw its hopes and designs frustrated, the more the boar twisted back on itself in a frenzied but vain attempt to bite back, driven on by fear of death and the pain in its scrotum. The wolf for its part bore down on the boar's scrotum, treating it as if it were a cart, with its whole body squeezed tight together — the onlookers thought it chiefly wanted to avoid the boar getting hold of its hind quarters when it bent back to do so, its legs in particular, forced apart as they were by the violent agitation. 3.13

Covered with tough bracken and many brambles, and spattered with a lot of gore, the space was so trampled and crushed that one might have thought it specially prepared with coverings strewn about for just this sort of fight. The battle of these beasts had lasted scarcely half an hour when the heavy boar, now not so much dragging the wolf hanging from his guts (itself of a fair size) as twisting and turning in circles, collapsed lifeless when the membrane holding his innards together gave way. 3.14

As soon as the wolf, the clear winner, picked himself up, he continued to feast on the loins where he had begun, burying his muzzle up to his eyes in the belly of his fallen prey. With the encouragement of the monks at the chinks of the cell, which rang with applause, the hunter shot the arrow prepared earlier for the boar from his crossbow powerfully into the wolf. Struck in the belly, the wolf first burst out of the clearing where the battle had taken place with a great leap. It collapsed after receiving a second 3.15

aream se proripuit, ad secundumque debiliter intentatum cum ce-
cidisset, ter quaterque potius se volutans quam progrediens, vi
medicaminis faciente, interiit: ut implendae delectationis spe frus-
trati sint iuniores monachi, quibus erat constitutum semivivam (ut
opinati erant) bestiam cruciatibus conficere. Sed hoc ad Petriolum
satis.

3.16   In Monte Ilcinio nihil decentius additur quam hunc amoenissimi elegantissimique situs locum Cancellariam Apostolicam nuper commodissime tenuisse priusquam pestis inde illam Assianum
venire compulerit. Optimeque factum vidimus ut, quo tempore
Pientiam et hanc Ilciniam civitates in unum coniunctas episcopatum declarasti, Ilciniam sua praesentia divina re agendis Deo et
tibi gratiis laetius celebranda multi et honoratiores quique honora-
verint curiales. Nobis vero non parva iucunditatis accessio in Ilci-
nia[37] fuit. Ibi nosce: propinquo ad Sancti Antonii monasterium in
loco fodinas esse alabastri, ex quibus ingens eius marmoris cum
alias educta vis est tum maxime in dies educi posset.

3.17   Nunc maiori incumbendum est additioni in primis futurae novi
huius operis ornamento. Postquam Saenensis urbis peracta descriptione Clusii veterrimae urbis et Montis Policiani nobilis oppidi memoriam expedivimus, alia raptim collegimus circumstantia,
quae tunc minutiora sunt visa, inter quae posuimus Corsignanum
hinc Policiano inde Quirico proximum. Effecerat vero tardiuscula
per Etruriam et in Saena urbe conversatio nostra — primum enim
Saenam Eugenio IV pontifice Romano vidimus — ut multa eius
urbis[38] dignissima ignorarem.[39] Hinc celebratam ibi vetere fama
Piccolomeae gentis conditionem referre[40] omisimus. Ea namque
multiplicum (ut ita dixerimus) stipitum nobilis gens tua viris pridem fecunda fuit armis et doctrina celebribus: quibus, sicut et aliis
nobilibus suis Saenae urbis saeculorum quae diu fuerunt, facul-

shot weakly launched at it, spinning round three or four times rather than advancing, and as the power of the poison took hold, it perished. As a result the younger monks, who had agreed to kill the beast by tormenting it while it was still half alive (as they imagined), were frustrated of their hopes of amusement. But that is enough on Petriolo.

As for Montalcino, the only worthwhile addition is to mention   3.16
the recent happy stay of the Apostolic Chancery in this pleasant and elegant spot, before plague compelled it to leave for Asciano.[31] When you proclaimed the merger of the cities of Pienza and Montalcino into one bishopric, it was a fine sight to see many notable members of the Curia honoring Montalcino with their presence when divine service was celebrated and joyful thanks offered to God and to you. Indeed, I myself felt no small access of joy coming over me in Montalcino. Concerning this site, you should know that in a place near the monastery of S. Antonio, there are alabaster quarries where vast quantities of the stone have been mined in the past, and which could still be mined today.[32]

We must now turn to a very important addition which will   3.17
prove to be the major ornament of this new supplement.[33] After I concluded my description of the city of Siena, and related the history of the ancient city of Chiusi and the noble town of Montepulciano, I quickly touched on some other towns in the vicinity, which seemed at the time of smaller consequence. Among those I included Corsignano, which is near Montepulciano on one side and San Quirico on the other.[34] My rather late acquaintance with Tuscany and the city of Siena (which I saw for the first time in the pontificate of Eugenius IV) made me ignorant of many notable features of the city. That was why I neglected to mention the situation of the Piccolomini family, which has been celebrated from time immemorial. This noble family of yours with its multiple branches, so to say, has long been prolific in men famous for arms and learning; but as with other Sienese nobles of generations long

tates parum suffecerant continua praebere exercitia virtuti singulorum praemia honores et amplitudinem praebitura. Hinc nonnulli
ex vestratibus, haud secus quam ex alia Saenensi nobilitate plurimi, diversas per castella et oppida urbi subdita cepere sedes in
quibus, cum urbani civilis otii cepisset satietas, venatione, aucupio,
piscatione et multiplici alia temporis traducendi libertate uterentur
et aliquid agerent in quo mentis et animi laetitia simul cum sani-
tate corporea fruerentur. Sic factum est ut, dum Silvius Piccolo-
meus genitor[41] tuus dicta de causa apud Corsignanum conversatur,
tu, sive in urbe sive ibi genitus, quod certum est, in Corsignano sis
natus, ad cuius consuetudinem oppidi te adeo traxisse videtur natalis soli amor ut, puer primo post adulescens, quicquid temporis
a liberalium artium et legum studiis atque a gravi virorum in Saenensi gymnasio agentium consuetudine subterfurari ac succidere
potuisti, in Corsignaneum effuderis diversorium.

3.18   Abfuisti postea diutissime non solum a Saena et Etruria sed
etiam ab Italia, apud summos orbis Christiani principes, imperatores et reges, apud summosque conciliorum et potentissimorum
populorum conventus pro maximis summisque causis conversatus:
quousque, tua te ducente ingenti virtute, Tergestinus primo post
Saenensis episcopus, deinde Romanae Ecclesiae cardinalis, et demum Romanus pontifex es creatus.

3.19   Sed quod in rebus contingit humanis, diversa ab ea quae Sil-
vium olim Piccolemeum traxit fatorum series effecit[42] ut tua Beati-
tudo, causis intentissima Christianae fidei et Ecclesiae, urbem
Mantuam ad conventus habendos, ab urbe Roma et propria pontificum maximorum sede petitura, recto per mediam Italiam itinere
Corsignanum originis suae patriam repetere sit coacta. Gratissima-
que fuit non magis tibi quam ceteris qui in celeberrimo comitatu
tuo erant, cardinalibus, praelatis, nobilibus, et aliis Curiae Romanae praestantissimis viris, tuorum decoratum natalium fortuna

past, their wealth was insufficient to provide regular occasions that could offer their talents rewards, honors, and distinctions. And so like many other nobles of Siena, some of your family took up residence in various castles and towns of the Sienese district where, when they had had enough of civilian ease in the city, they would take to hunting, fowling, fishing, with freedom to enjoy many other ways of passing the time and do something in which they could get mental and spiritual refreshment alongside bodily health. So it came about that your father Silvio Piccolomini was staying at Corsignano for just such reasons when you were born there — this much is certain, whether you were conceived in Siena or Corsignano. Love of your native land seems to have drawn you to such prolonged intimacy with the town that, first as a boy and later as a young man, whatever time you could steal or pare away from your studies in the liberal arts and the law and from grave association with the men of the University of Siena, you devoted to your lodgings at Corsignano.

After that you spent much time away not just from Siena and 3.18 Tuscany but from Italy itself, dealing with the highest princes, emperors, and kings of Christendom at the high assemblies of councils and mighty nations in matters of the greatest and highest moment, until under the guidance of your own outstanding virtue, you were made first bishop of Trieste and later bishop of Siena, then cardinal of the Roman Church, and finally pope of Rome.[35]

But as happens in human affairs, a different set of chance cir- 3.19 cumstances from that which took your father Silvio there caused Your Holiness, in your eagerness for the cause of the Christian Faith and Church, to be obliged to return to the land of your birth at Corsignano, as you made your way from Rome (the proper seat of popes) straight through the heart of Italy to the city of Mantua to hold a congress there.[36] It was a stroke of chance just as welcome to the cardinals, prelates, noblemen, and other distinguished curialists in your numerous retinue as it was to you, and not just

oppidum non inspicere magis quam aliquot diebus inhabitare. Per quos dies nullus ingenii, nullus generosi inter nos animi, nullus vel mediocris ingenii fuit qui non Corsignano amplas ornatissimasque et fortuna sua dignissimas[43] optaverit aedes.

3.20   Itum est inde Mantuam, et maior celebriorque ibi Christianorum principum, oratorum, et populorum habitus est conventus ceteris omnibus quos nostra alibi per Italiam viderit aetas. Ad decimum inde mensem, redeunti ad propria tecum Romanae Curiae iter rectissimum per Corsignanum fuit, ubi alia et prima maior aedium tenuitatis oppidi illius quaerela passim inter nostros audita est: illudque ostensum a curialibus desiderium tuam movit Sanctitatem ut quam omnibus exhibet genio quoque suo benignitatem impartiretur.

3.21   Postquam vero ibi a te destinatum est aedificium, fecisti quod non magis Iesu Christi vicarium et Petri Apostolorum principis successorem quam omnes decet Christianos. A divinis namque inchoans, destinatae basilicae (qualem Romani pontificis opus esse deceat), per diem martyris Laurentii solemniis celebrem, lapidem primum tu ipse manu tua fundamentis[44] iecisti. Reditum est inde Romam, unde tertio post anno pestilentia nos dispersos abire coegit. Qua diversis in Etruriae locis debacchante, collegia Curiae et quandoque singulos curiales diversas habere et mutare sedes oportuit, sicque tuam Beatitudinem aliam saepius quam Corsignanum sedem habere oportuit. Ad diem vero Apostoli Matthaei festo celebrem, absolutam omnium opinione celerius basilicam dedicasti eiusque Apostoli vocabulo insignisti. Civitatem quoque de[45] pontificatus nomine Pientiam et dici debere et haberi deinceps decrevisti, quod oppidum hactenus fuerat Corsignanum. Cui civitati cum episcopum dioecesimque dedisses, Ilcinium (quod oppidum

to get a look at the town graced by the good fortune of your birth but to stay there for several days. Throughout those days, there was no one among us of talent, no one generous in spirit, no one of even middling abilities, who did not desire that Corsignano should have spacious and ornate buildings to match its good fortune.

From there we went on to Mantua, where a congress of Christian princes, envoys, and nations was held which was larger and better attended than any other that our age has witnessed in Italy. Ten months later, as the Roman Curia returned home with you, the route went straight through Corsignano, where there was heard among us a general lament, greater than before, about the poverty of the town's buildings. The longing expressed by the members of the Curia moved Your Holiness to treat his own person with the favor he showed everyone else.

3.20

When you planned a building there, you did something that all Christians should do, no less than the vicar of Christ and successor of Peter, prince of the Apostles. Starting with divine service on the feast of St. Lawrence Martyr,[37] you laid with your own hand the first stone of the foundations of the planned cathedral, work that befits a Roman Pontiff. From Corsignano we returned to Rome, from which we were forced to disperse and flee three years later by an outbreak of plague. With pestilence raging all over Tuscany, colleges of the Curia and sometimes their individual members were obliged to keep moving among different residences, and thus Your Holiness was forced to reside elsewhere more often than at Corsignano. The cathedral was finished faster than anyone had thought possible, and on the feast day of the St. Matthew you dedicated it and named it after the Apostle.[38] Then you decreed that the city, hitherto the town of Corsignano, was now and in future to be called Pienza from your pontifical name. Giving Pienza a bishop and a diocese, you declared the town of Montalcino

3.21

tunc inhabitabamus) in civitatem Ilciniam, Pientiae episcopatu
sociam, declarasti.

3.22   Eo[46] die, primo cum absolutam inspicerem contemplarerque[47]
basilicam, assistentem lateri meo et singulis respondentem eius
architectum infinitis prope quaestiunculis agitavi. Quarum uni,
celeritatis perficiendi operis, numquam potuisset facere satis, nisi
subiecta oculis ipsa absolutio comprobasset. Quod vero Sanctitai
tuae dixisse tunc memini: ea basilica multas in aliquibus Italiae
urbibus habet magnitudine ipsi[48] pares atque etiam ampliores; non
nullas habet marmorum crustamentis musivique pictura insigni-
ores; sed nullam quis facile memorabit, quae Pientiae Sancti Matthaei basilicae, subterranei superiorisve totius aedificii proportione
et partium inter se singularum convenientia, aequetur.

3.23   Palatium tuo natali cubiculo superaedificatum basilicam cui
continet magnitudine superat, et cum eiusdem architecti opificium
sit, parem in singulis sui partibus proportionis et dimensionum
gratiam prae se fert. Quam quidem gratiam cum architecto dice-
rem totam in operis summa minorem esse illa quam basilicae tri-
buebam, retulit ipse in tuos culpam, qui, quas passi principio non
fuerant ab eo fieri particulas, perfecto[49] iam operi addendas evice-
rint. Habet autem palatium et vestibulum et porticus et aulas tri-
plices cubiculaque in utraque contignatione cum ampla tum ornatissima suis commodissima officinis, ut etiam qui auctorem ignoret
vel habitatorem, si non omnino socors sit, utrumque munus in
Romanum pontificem referat.

3.24   Ea nos, Pater Sancte, ingentia pulcherrimaque opera inspexisse
delectavit, non solum quia tali sumus animo geniti ut saeculi nostri ornamenta amare non nequeamus sed quia bono ea exemplo
facta recognoscimus: optimos namque e principibus viris quosque[50]

(where I was then staying) raised to the status of a city which was to share the diocese jointly with Pienza.

On the day that I first inspected and examined the finished ca- 3.22 thedral, I troubled the architect with any number of little questions as he stood at my side, answering them one by one.[39] He could never have given a satisfactory answer to one of them, about how quickly the building would be finished, had not the actual finished work spread out before our eyes backed him up. I recall what I said to Your Holiness on that occasion: "There are many cathedrals in Italian cities that are the size of this one, or even bigger; some have more remarkable marble paneling or scenes in mosaic; yet no one would find it easy to name any that match the cathedral of St. Matthew of Pienza for the proportions of the whole structure, above and below ground, and for the harmony of its individual elements."[40]

The palazzo built over the bedroom where you were born is 3.23 bigger than the cathedral next to it, and, being the work of the same architect, it shows a similar gracefulness in the scale and dimensions of the individual parts.[41] Yet when I told the architect that I felt the overall grace of the design was inferior to the cathedral's, he retorted that the blame lay with your people, who had won the day in having features added to the work at completion which they had not allowed him to execute at the beginning. The palazzo has a courtyard and loggias, and on each floor sets of three spacious and ornate rooms and cubicles, very well adapted for offices: so that even if someone did not know who was the builder or tenant, he would suppose (short of being a complete fool) that both roles were filled by the Pope of Rome.

I was delighted, Holy Father, to have examined these imposing 3.24 and beautiful works, not only because my nature is such that I cannot but love the works of art of our own time, but also because I realize that they were made so as to set a good example: I know that all the best princes have lavished examples of their love

scimus amorem suum (quo naturaliter abundarunt) in omnes passim sed in suos et sua propensius ostendisse.

3.25   Sic Severus Afer imperator Romanus doctrinae, praesertim eloquentiae, ingentis, morum gravitate, continentia, et bonitate meliores, qui umquam fuerunt, Romanos principes aut aequans aut superans, non dissimili tuae causa quae te Mantuam duxit, in Africam se contulit. Qui ad Leptim natalis sui soli locum perveniens, destinatas in accessu aedes ibi rediens extruere coepit et Romae agens amplissimas perfici curavit.

3.26   Marcus vero Antoninus Aurelius philosophus, laudatissimae imperator probitatis, aedes in quibus natus educatusque est avitas apud Lateranensem, nunc basilicam orbis Christiani primariam, adeo dilexit ut eas postea imperator (quantum per occupationes licuit) libentius maioribus melioribusque palatiis aedibusque Romanis inhabitaverit.[51]

3.27   Et e nostris pontificibus Christianis Innocentius III, doctrina, humanitate, et ceteris virtutibus nulli paene pontificum Romanorum secundus, aedes paternas avitasque in quibus aut natus aut (quod indubitatum est) ab infantia nutritus erat in excelsam amplamque exstantem Romae turrim a gente sua Comitum dictam exstruxit.

3.28   Et si huius operis condicio volumenque pateretur, facile mihi fuerit principum[52] et praestantissimorum hominum—atque etiam pontificum Romanorum et ecclesiasticorum virorum—mille in exemplo affere, quibus pro posse et supra studium cura[53] fuit opera exstruere ingentia, quibus suam et suorum saeculi ac regionum virtutem et gloriam posterorum memoriae commendarent. Sed de his nunc satis.

3.29   Non sunt parvo Pientiae nostrae decori aedes iam multae in ea aedificatae, quales deceat magnos viros inhabitare. Quarum unam Iohannis Ioffridi Burgundionis, cardinalis Atrebatensis,[54] alteram Iacobi Lucensis, cardinalis Papiensis, vidimus absolutas, cum duas

(which they have naturally in abundance) on men in general, but more readily on persons and things of their own.

Thus a man of great learning, in eloquence in particular, and in dignity, continence, and virtue the equal or superior of the best Roman princes who ever lived, the Roman emperor Severus Afer went off to Africa for much the same reason as took you to Mantua.[42] When he got to his native land of Leptis, he began the construction of temples on his return which he had planned on his accession, and while in Rome he saw to their completion on the grandest scale.[43]   3.25

As for Marcus Aurelius, the philosophical emperor much praised for his integrity, he was so attached to the ancestral house in the Lateran in which he had been born and brought up, now the foremost basilica in Christendom, that as emperor he later preferred to live in it than in grander and superior palaces and buildings, whenever demands on his time allowed.[44]   3.26

Of our Christian popes, Innocent III, who among the Roman pontiffs was second to none in learning, humanity, and the other virtues, built up the house of his father and forefathers (in which he was either born or — and this is beyond dispute — brought up from infancy) into a soaring and spacious tower, which still stands in Rome, called the Tor de' Conti after his family.[45]   3.27

If the design of this volume allowed, it would be easy for me adduce the precedent of a thousand princes and potentates, even popes and prelates, who were not just enthusiastic but strained all their powers to see that vast monuments were raised up to commit their prowess and glory, and those of the men of their time and place, to the memory of posterity. But that is enough now on these matters.   3.28

It is no small glory for our town of Pienza to have such palaces built there that are fitting for great men to live in. Two of them I have seen completed, one of Jean Jouffroy of Burgundy, the Cardinal of Arras, the other of Jacopo of Lucca, the Cardinal of Pavia,   3.29

ab illustribus nepotibus tuis a nonnullisque alias audiverim[55] destinatas.

3.30 Pientiam praetergressi, operis nostri ordine Politianum, Clancianum, Lucinianum et alia vallis quam Clanarum vocant castella repetentes, id in illis additionum faciemus ut cardinales dicamus qui huius anni pestilentiae Romanae causa[56] illa inhabitaverunt: Guilielmum enim de Estoutevilla[57] Gallicum, cardinalem Rothomagensem, episcopum Portuensem Monspolitianus, Alanum de Coaetivis Britonem, cardinalem Avinionensem Lucianum, Nicolaum de Cusa Germanicum, cardinalem Sancti Petri ad Vincula Clancianum hospites habuere. Ad quam regionem cum montis Cabioni castellum arduo in colle situm nos cum familia sedem trimestri habuerimus, tam salubrem quam amoenam, id contemplati didicimus quod, pridem hoc nostrum *Illustratae Italiae* opus describentes, a Plinio dictum credere non potuimus. Ille enim, de nebula tractans, eam scribit uvas nutrire et in locis Pado proximis, quod ad Ravennam tunc diximus contrarium esse videmus. Nullus enim Italiae regionum quae ad Padum pertinent locus, ubi nebula saepe oritur, vinum gignit non malum. Sed in hac Clanarum Etruriae regione, ubi frequentiores densioresque oriuntur nebulae, optima gignuntur vina. Quin incolae dixerunt ostenderuntque nobis vineas in collibus sitas, ad quos Clanas[58] hinc inde supereminentes nebula ascendit,[59] meliora multo gignere vina illis quae in amoenioribus collibus aut planitie a nebula remotioribus sitae sunt.

3.31 Longo post supradicta tractu per Etruriam discurrentes ad descriptionem fontis et originis Tiberini amnis pervenimus, ubi Anglarium,[60] oppidum tribus ab eo fluvio millibus distantem, hinc Cotulo aëreae arci praedicto fonti proximo, inde Burgo ad Sepulchrum praeclaro Umbriae loco propinquum esse diximus. Sed anno proximo additionem faciendam vidimus quae referatur di-

though I was told of two others planned by your illustrious nephews and some other persons.[46]

As we pass beyond Pienza and revisit in the same order as before Montepulciano, Chianciano, Lucignano, and the other castles in the valley known as Valdichiana,[47] here I shall mention as an addition the cardinals who lived in these towns owing to plague in Rome this year: Montepulciano had as its guest the Frenchman Guillaume d'Estouteville, cardinal of Rouen, bishop of Ostia;[48] Lucignano, the Breton Alain de Coëtivy, cardinal of Avignon;[49] Chianciano, the German Nicholas of Cusa, cardinal of San Pietro in Vincoli.[50] When I was resident here with my family for three months in Montegabbione, a castle set on a high hill and a place as healthy as it was attractive, I learned by observation something that, although it was said by Pliny, I could not quite believe as I was writing my *Italia illustrata* some time ago.[51] Speaking of mist, Pliny says that it nourishes grapes, and in places close to the Po,[52] whereas I see that what I said under Ravenna contradicts this, for no place in the regions of Italy that lie along the Po, where mist often rises, produces wine of any quality. But in this district of the Valdichiana in Tuscany, where there are frequent dense mists, very good wines are produced. What is more, the inhabitants have told me and shown me that vineyards planted on hills overlooking the Valdichiana on both sides, to which the mist rises up, produce finer wines by far than vineyards planted on gentler hills or on the plain well away from mist.

A long way from the places mentioned above, I cross Tuscany and come to describe the origin and source of the river Tiber: here, as I said, is Anghiari three miles from the river, close on one side to the lofty stronghold of Cotolo (which lies beside the source of the Tiber mentioned above), and on the other to the famous Umbrian town of Borgo Sansepolcro.[53] But I realized last year that I needed to make an important addition: gaining considerably in size from the various streams and springs that flow into it as it

3.30

3.31

gnissimam. Tiberis namque fluvius, cum ad duodecim passuum milia per varios montium anfractus diversis torrentibus fontibusque aucta non parum excreverit, oppido appropinquat Sancti Sepulchri, ubi per mediam aestatem ita se in terram sabulumque abscondit, ut tribus et quandoque quatuor millibus delitescat nusquamque (etiam ab effodientibus)[61] reperiatur, et tandem postea, totus simul consueto in alveo scaturiens, in mediocrem magis fluvium quam torrentem discurrit.

winds through a twelve-mile stretch of mountains, the Tiber approaches Borgo Sansepolcro. There in the middle of summer it hides itself in the earth and sand, so that for three and at times four miles it becomes invisible and is nowhere to be found, even if you dig down for it. Later, when it at length wells up entire in its usual bed, it runs off as a moderately sized river rather than a stream.

Note on the Text[1]

Dr. Paolo Pontari, in the first volume (2011) of his magisterial critical edition of the Istituto Storico Italiano per il Medioevo's *Italia illustrata*, has made great strides forward in the areas of codicology and stemmatics. But what we know now, thanks largely to his refinements, about the chronology of the transmission of Biondo's text and about the complexity of the interrelationships of the manuscripts and print witnesses, seems almost to make us even less sure of ourselves, if anything, as we try to decide just what *Italia illustrata* Biondo Flavio meant to leave behind him.[2]

Nevertheless, as the basis for my text of the *Italia illustrata* of Volume 2, I have again used the Roman 1474 *editio princeps* of the *Italia illustrata* (the work of Biondo's son Gaspare, founded on manuscripts left him by his father, he claims), despite misgivings.[3] Identification of the manuscripts on which Gaspare based his edition (as has happened with his edition of the *Roma instaurata*) is still possible, certainly, but seems less likely now. In any case, I think that in establishing the text of the *Italia illustrata*, a somewhat more generous quotient of *divinatio* than is usual in traditional textual criticism will have to be tolerated. The present is still a provisional edition rather than a fully critical edition.

r   The *editio princeps*, published in Rome by Johannes Philippus de
     Lignamine in 1474. (Pontari's RM)

Also, I have collated four significant manuscripts of three important phases of the author's composition and revision of the work against the 1531 Froben edition (Pontari's FR₁) and used their readings as a check against Gaspare.

B   Vatican City, Biblioteca Apostolica Vaticana, MS Ottob. lat. 2369.
     Mid-fifteenth century. Contains a dedication to Nicholas V
     and numerous marginal and interlinear additions in the au-
     thor's hand. After Nicholas' death in 1455, the author scored
     the dedication and all passages relating to him. (Pontari's V)

F   Florence, Biblioteca Nazionale Centrale, MS Magl. XIII 38 (Gaddianus 739). Early sixteenth century. Contains a dedication to Piero de' Medici and, in Region 2, Tuscany, numerous passages that have passed out of the textual tradition. Lacks the entire Region 14, Puglia. (Pontari's N)

H   Vienna, Österreichische Nationalbibliothek, MS Series Nova 2960 (*olim* Staatsarchiv 711). Dated 1466. Contains a dedication to Pius II, and has the author's new stand-alone *additiones correctionesque* to Region 1, Liguria, and Region 2, Tuscany, and other new revisions (incorporated into the text). Marginal annotations in the hand of the owner, the learned bishop of Trent Johannes Hinderbach. (Pontari's W)

Q   Vatican City, Biblioteca Apostolica Vaticana, MS Pal. lat. 948. Late fifteenth century. Lacks the distinctive matter of B, F, and H. (Pontari's V3)

For Region 7, Lombardy, and Region 8, Venice, only, I have included readings from two other manuscripts.

C   Ravenna, Casa Cavalli, s.n. Mid-fifteenth century. Has the Nicholas V dedication, as also many of the passages scored by Biondo in the text and margins of B. Contains some of the revisions of H. (Pontari's Cav)

E   Florence, Biblioteca Riccardiana, MS Ricc. 1198. Mid-fifteenth century. Contains the stand-alone dedication to Pius II and additions to Liguria and Tuscany, and the revisions (added in the margins) of H. (Pontari's R)

The text printed here in roman type is, in principal, the text that Gaspare Biondo transmits in r as his father's final recension, although many readings have been imported from other redactions where these seemed to offer a better text. Departures in the *princeps* from the other witnesses are very numerous, but mostly stylistic, and could not all be accounted for in my Notes on the Text: but, almost always, the same matter and meaning are being communicated. A sufficient number of variant readings of all kinds are offered in the notes so that, it is hoped, the reader

has a generalized sense of a very complicated textual situation. Since Gaspare's text omitted a number of readings and passages found in other earlier redactions, these have been included in italics for the reader's convenience, with notes to indicate their source.

Verse passages in the Latin and the English texts are printed as prose, following Biondo's own practice, and I have not attempted to reduce to good grammatical order the numerous sentence fragments that Biondo quotes. In accordance with the preference of this series, spelling has been modernized, and modern conventions of punctuation and capitalization have been followed. In the Latin text, editorial additions are indicated by angle brackets, deletions by square brackets; in the translation, editorial additions are indicated by square brackets.

APPENDIX

After his estrangement (ca. 1450–53) from the Curia of Nicholas V, Biondo continued to come back into his own professionally under Callixtus III and Pius II and to maintain a program of scholarly writing. He finished the *Roma triumphans* (1459) and the *Borsus sive de militia et iurisprudentia* (1460) during the period, and he continued to rework the *Italia illustrata*. In Vienna, Österreichische Nationalbibliothek, MS Series Nova 2960 (my *H*, Pontari's *W*),[4] transcribed in 1466, we have evidence of what is certainly Biondo Flavio's final stratum of revision, undertaken in the papacy of Pius II, in the cultural and professional environment most congenial to him since Eugenius IV: the manuscript contains (1) a letter to Pius II, giving this stratum a *terminus post quem* of 1458, the date of Pius's election; and (2) longish addenda to *Liguria* and *Etruria*, updating those *regiones* to 1462. The text of this manuscript was transcribed by Hugo Haemste and was owned and extensively annotated by a friend of Pius II, Johannes Hinderbach, bishop of Trent. The latter was in Rome from 1465 to 1466, where he arranged for the manuscript's transcription. Only one other manuscript, Florence, Riccardianus 1198 (my *E*, Pontari's *R*), whose transcription we can date to 1477–78, contains the Pius letter and the two addenda, along with some two dozen marginal revisions (some already in the text of the Viennese manuscript) — which give out

in *Lombardia* (Biondo's *Regio Septima*).[5] Three other manuscripts have the marginal *additiones* and *correctiones* only, without the letter and addenda.[6]

The letter to Pius, which has the aroma at least of the author's other three dedications,[7] tells the story of the piratical bishop who had forced Biondo into premature publication of the *Italia illustrata* at the beginning of the 1450s. The addendum to *Liguria* deals principally with the sad decline of the fortunes of the city of Genoa over the interim, a favorite theme. The addendum to *Etruria* serves, among other things (including a boar-wolf animal fable and a sketch of Pius's building program at Pienza), to link Tuscan places to Pius — as the author had done before with *Etruria*, *Umbria*, and *Picenum* to Nicholas. The additions and corrections of the five manuscripts are mostly new or updated information. The overall impression of this redaction, in my judgment, is of an author still open, even a year before his death, to the fluid nature of the *Italia illustrata*. Biondo died on June 4, 1463.

Nogara printed in 1927 (from MS E only) the new material meant to go into the text and the freestanding letter to Pius and the addenda to *Liguria* and *Etruria*.[8] Given in the Appendix is my Latin text and English translation of the letter and the two addenda based on the manuscripts *HE*. The other material of this last recension is printed within the text in italics in both I Tatti volumes of *Italy Illuminated*.

NOTES

1. See also my "Note on the Text" of Volume 1 (ITRL 20), pp. 357–61, which this Note is not meant significantly to supersede.

2. I did not have Pontari's Volume 1 (or his Volume 2 [2014]) in time to use when I constituted the text for this Volume 2 of the I Tatti edition.

3. For my discussion of this incunable, see Volume 1, p. 357f. And cf. Pontari (2011), pp. 321–26 and 498–510 (509, particularly). I am still unable to share Pontari's absolute conviction that this edition cannot represent the author's ultimate intentions.

4. Blondus Flavius, *Italia illustrata*, ed. Pontari, 1:304–6, and White, "Towards a Critical Edition," pp. 286–89.

5. Nogara, *Scritti*, pp. 225–39; Pontari, 1:287–89; White, "Towards a Critical Edition," pp. 280–81, 286.

6. Bologna, Biblioteca Universitaria, 1139, and Vatican City, Biblioteca Apostolica Vaticana, Reg. lat. 729, my *ZR* (Pontari's BV2). See White, "Towards a Critical Edition," pp. 287–88. Pontari (1:269–75, and Tavola 9), includes the Dresden, Sächsische Landesbibliothek F66 (my *X*, Pontari's *D*) among the representatives of this redaction: it was once owned by Girolamo Biondo and contains his compilation of his father's letters.

7. To Piero de' Medici, Malatesta Novello, and Nicholas V.

8. Nogara, *Scritti*, pp. 225–39.

Notes to the Text

❧❧❧

7. LOMBARDY

1. Blondi Flavii Forliviensis Italiae Illvstratae Liber Qvintvs, et Regio Septima, Lombardia: Incipit Foelicissime *r*

2. fuerint CF

3. ei *r*

4. Decium *Fr*

5. Caesar *mss.*, *r*

6. Decium *Fr*

7. Carpam *r*

8. imminent BC

9. Salcinium *r*

10. Salcinium *Fr*

11. Volongum *r*

12. Frontinus enim . . . lugere fas esset *omitted (added by B²) in* B¹C

13. in aetate *mss.*

14. Viros habuit ea urbs praeclara praestantes *mss.*

15. amplissimi *mss.*, *r*

16. et magnum BC

17. disturbii *mss.*, *Froben*

18. ubi *mss.*, *Froben*

19. Ramugola *mss.*, *r*

20. Bussetum *r*

21. lardae BEFHQ, largae C

22. Rovengonum BCHr: ravengonum E, *Froben*: rovegnonum Q

23. mixti *Livy*, QF: mixtis *in the other witnesses and* r

403

24. supraque *mss.*: superque *Fr*

25. illi *r: omitted in the mss.*

26. Cum tamen . . . peditumque habuisse] Cum tamen populus inesset magnus, milia virorum octo, Mediolanensium vero exercitui (praeter Sfortianos milites) decem milia inerant: Franciscus Piccininus, Guidatius Manfredus, Ludovicus Vermes, Carolus Gonzaga, et alii minores copiarum ductores, quos omnes constat supra XV milia equitum peditumque habuisse *mss., Froben*

27. qui unis castris . . . omnes tenderent *omitted in BC*

28. Runchivierum *Q*

29. Adaloaldi *BC*: addolaldi *r*: Addoaldi (adualdi *Q*) *in the other witnesses*

30. Oganascum *r*

31. Rovenum *BC*: Jovenum *in the other witnesses and r*

32. *omitted in r*

33. *omitted in r*

34. nimis *BCr*

35. Brundusino *r*: blundisino *BC*

36. *mss., r*

37. Celeiates Cerdiciatesque *Livy*

38. Castellarium *mss., r*

39. Terdona *EHQr*: Tertona *in the other witnesses*

40. Pedemontium incipit Ferrariensisque ora. paene omnes marchionibus (marchionibus *omitted in C*) sunt subiecti in Italia nobilissimis, qui, ex Palaeologis oriundi Constantinopolitanis imperatoribus, quinquaginta iam et centum annis eam possident oram *BC*

41. Moncalerium] Castillionum et Moncalerium *BC*

42. Pavonum *r*

43. eam urbem *BC*

44. novum *BC*

45. Gn. Plancus *EHr*, C. Plancus *BCQ*

46. continentur *Froben*

47. Damianium *r*

48. Arduus ab eo fons scatens *r*

49. illi] Transpadanae *r*

50. Adiacet Mincio ad sinistram prope Padum Governum oppidum *mss.*

51. Intra mille passuum *Froben*: infra mille passuum milia *mss.*, *r*: Infra eum locum duo milia *Livy*

52. Superestque Paula uxor, mulierum aetatis nostrae a religionis, sapientiae, et humanitatis partibus celeberrima *mss.*

53. Malsoninum *r*: Malsosinum *BC*

54. Rivolta *r*

55. Garganum *r*

56. Lucioninum *BC*

57. Tiennium *BHQr*: sunt Tiennum *C*: trennium *E*

58. Estque *mss.*

59. ipse *mss.*

60. Brocium *CEQr*, Brocum *BH*: Brenum *Froben*

61. diffinire *r*

62. Abduam amnem *BC*: amnem *EHQ*: *omitted in r*

63. olium amnem *r*

64. Planorium *C*

65. Intra mille passuum *Froben*: infra mille passuum milia *mss.*, *r*: Infra eum locum duo milia *Livy*

66. reddita per aetatem nostram obsidione quam *mss.*

67. bello et Francisco Barbaro insigni Veneto praefecto defendente pertulit *mss.*

68. a torrentibus quatuor *mss.*

69. lodrium *BQr*

70. *omitted in r*

71. abest *mss.*

72. incurrit *mss.*

73. Vitelliani *mss.*

74. ab Agilulfo *BC*: a gissulpho *H*: a Gillupho *F(-pbo)r*

75. Francisco Sfortiae per Blanchae Mariae uxoris dotem subiecta est *mss.*

76. quoque Cremonensem *mss.*

77. quoque *mss.*

78. habet *EHr*: habuit *in the other witnesses*

79. fundulis *r*

80. *omitted in r*

81. Picilionum *r, mss.*

82. Bardoinum *r*

83. bucca *r, mss.*

84. *omitted in r*

85. magnae *r*

86. autem *BC*

87. Liviis *r*

88. fuerint *BC*: fuerunt *EFHQr*

89. apud veteres *r*: in veteribus scriptis *mss.*

90. Primusque praeter *mss.*

91. Post *r*

92. in convalle *r*: convalli *mss.*

93. insunt castella *mss.*

94. *mss., r*

95. emissiorium *r*

96. et *BC*: *omitted in the other witnesses*

97. Colongum *r*

98. Bergomus *mss.*, *r*: Bergomum *Q*

99. dicimus *BC*

100. cui oppida insunt et castella *BC*

101. equites duodecim pedites quatuor milia *mss.*

102. Sequitur *Froben*: Sequuntur *mss.*, *r*

103. eius nominis] in eo *mss.*

104. cognomen] Comensem appellationem *mss.*

105. Civemque] Civem ea civitas *mss.*

106. Oromoniorum *mss.*, *r*

107. tradere ac fateri] tradidisse, qui fassus fuerit *mss.*

108. fuisse eam gentem a Graecis, interpretatione nominis indicante quod vitam in montibus *mss.*

109. Plinius autem] Isque Plinius *mss.*

110. conversatus *mss.*

111. qui *EHr*: quae *BCQ*

112. basilicam *mss.*

113. Baptistae sumptuosissimi operis superbissimaque in eodem exstructa] Baptistae ac palatium superbissimum sumptuosissimo opere in eodem exstruxit *mss.*

114. At secundum lacus *CQr*: Ad secundum latus *in the other witnesses*

115. Senolengum *r*

116. et dehinc castellum Clavenna (et *omitted in F*) *mss.*: et Clavenna *r*

117. Raetiorum *r*

118. Curiae latus *r*: mire latus *mss.*

119. huic amni *mss.*

120. propulsatum *Q*

121. abesse *mss.*

122. aliquo loco] aliqualiter *mss.*

123. ea *CEFH*

124. fuitque in ea tum caedes maxima] ubi tunc caedes maxima fuit (fuit caedes maxima *F*) *mss.*

125. nusquam *BC*

126. Cuius rei similem] Pariterque *mss.*

127. circa *mss.*

128. a comite suo, viro bono] a bono viro comite suo *mss.*

129. propositum *mss.*

130. Rodulfo *r*, Redulfo *F*

131. possessam *C*

132. tuncque *BCE*

133. oppressa *FQ*

134. Luithprandus *Fr*

135. Sancti *FQ*

136. Luithprandi *r*

137. haec] praedicta *mss.*

138. eam vero] eandem *mss.*

139. iurium *F*

140. Ticinio *mss.*

141. sinistram *Q*

142. illum] uerbanum lacum *F*

143. ex quibus *mss.*: quorum *F, Froben*

144. cui *mss.*

145. Ticinium *mss.*

146. multis] in multis *F*

147. *omitted in r*

148. *BC: omitted in the other witnesses*

149. a Vertamacoris . . . Plinius aedificata *omitted in (added in E^2) E^{1}Q, Froben*

150. Octaviani imperatoris temporibus] per Octaviani imperatoris aetatem *F*

151. supra millesimum trecentesimum] quater decies centenum *F*

152. abduci *C*

153. habeant *r*

154. Dulcidini *r*

155. nuncupatum *E*

156. Ad Ticini item undas est Castellettum, et paulo supra ad lacus Verbani (seu Maioris) emissorium, a quo Gravalonus ortum habet, sinum efficit ipse lacus quem Mergotii lacum dicunt *F*

157. eorumque alter] quorum unus *F*

158. quibus] unde *mss.*

159. itur] traiicitur *mss.*

160. accepit *BCF*

161. sebuino *mss., r:* Verbano *Froben*

162. Sed alia est eiusdem nominis civitas in Gallia (asia *F*), cuius fines nullis amnibus similiter sunt coerciti *mss.*

163. quam *mss.*

164. iuraverant *Florus mss., r:* iuraverunt *FQ*

165. post *mss.*

166. per omne saeculum *mss.*

167. Roma enim (enim: etiam *F*) non modo non genuit quem habuit multo maiorem Mediolanensi populum, sed, faciente aëris semper ab ipsa condita insalubris dispositione, confluentem ex tota Italia comportatamque, et inductam ex toto orbe, mortalium exuberantiam male conservavit *mss.*

168. *omitted in r*

169. *omitted in r*

170. Ab urbe condita *omitted in r*

171. Romanorum *mss.*

172. vulneratam *r*

173. revocaretur *C*

174. xxxii *EFHQr*

175. per annos ferme quingentos *mss.*

176. Maxentii *E*

177. iuxta intolerabiles *H*

178. durante *FQ*

179. annis trecentis et sexaginta] per annos LX et CCC *mss.*

180. quintum et sexagesimum supra millesimum et centesimum] LXV et undecies centenum *mss.*

181. miliario *mss.*

182. centum et quinquaginta annis] per annos CL *mss.*

183. millesimum et ducentesimum] duodecies centenum *mss.*

184. Candianus *Froben*: Candidus *mss., r*

185. *omitted in F*

186. post *F*

187. nomine *mss.*: *omitted in r*

188. Johannes ipse Galeacius *mss.*: Galeacius *r*

189. Venceslao *Froben*: Ladizlao *mss., r*

190. ex *Hr*: *omitted in the other witnesses*

191. robur atque *Froben*

192. Datium quoque *BC*

193. *BC*: *omitted in the other witnesses*

194. e quibus] quorum *F*

195. valuerunt *BC*

196. oppida *Q*

197. M *Pliny, H²*, *Froben*: *omitted in BCEFH^iQr*

198. celeberrimo militum ductore et monasterio Lucedi amplissimo ornatum *mss.*

199. Et Duria Baltea *mss.*

200. adiacet] continet *mss.*

201. Hipporhedia *r*

202. dicta *Q*

203. angustae *r*

204. alteras . . . alteras *BCFr:* alteram . . . alteram *in the other witnesses*

205. Isara *BC:* Isera *in the other witnesses*

206. Balteae amnis *BC: omitted in the other witnesses*

207. Clavasium *BCF:* Davasium *in the other witnesses*

208. Ad dexteramque superius Sancti Martini, ad sinistram vero Sancti Benedicti de Fructeria, habentur oppida *r:* Et superius Sancti Martini ad dexteram ad sinistramque Sancti Benedicti de Fructeria habentur oppida *in the other witnesses*

209. Taurinensium *F*

210. Taurinus *F*

211. quia *r, Livy:* quae *BC:* qui *EFHQ*

212. *omitted in BC*

213. Ciriacum *E,* (cu-) *F,* (Cy-) *HQr,* tir- *BC:* Cariacum *Froben*

214. superius *BC*

215. Clausiola *r*

216. cui *F*

217. passus *mss.*

218. Cui amni . . . dextrorsum haeret *mss.:* Dextrorsum vero Bricariasium *(sic),* deinde Mons Bobius haeret *r*

219. Augustae a taurinorum *r:* augustae taurinorum *F*

220. antiquae Ligurum (ligurium *F*) stirpis *mss.*

221. hostia *F*

222. Cricium *mss., r*

223. rupit *r:* irrupit *mss.*

8 . VENICE

1. Blondi Flavii Forliviensis Italiae Illustratae Regio Octava Venetiae Liber Sextus *r*

2. appellatis ad stagnantes . . . (sive Foroliviensem)] appellatis Venetiarum urbis ducatus fines ad quas Gradatas stagnantes mari Adriatico aquae salsae obtineant, in quas Athesis fluvius, post Meduacus, inde Timavus defluunt amnes, ipsarum Venetiarum civitatem eisdem salsis circumdatam aquis priusquam Marchiam Tarvisanam sive Foroiuliensis *F*

3. Postmodo namque ostia cursusque fluviorum in sicco melius persequemur *F*

4. easdem *F*

5. ipsarumque loca] et earum particulas *F*

6. terminos longitudine *mss.*, *Froben*

7. Gradatis *EFHQr*: Gradatis ubi est Gradus civitas *BC*

8. *omitted in Fr*

9. adeustinique *Fr*

10. *omitted in r*

11. Castellarum *r*

12. per annos *mss.*, *Froben*

13. certius *BCEH*

14. Rotarit *r*, patirith *F*

15. eodemque *mss.*, *Froben*

16. civitatum *r*

17. habere coepere *mss.*, *Froben*

18. pariter *mss.*

19. duci *BCr*

20. ad Clavum] ad annum *Froben*: annales *Q*

21. *omitted in BCEHQ*

22. Eo denique anno *BC*

23. creatus fuit, qui *mss., Froben*

24. Quibus in foederibus actum est *mss., Froben*

25. deinde *F*

26. ubi eius] inibique eiusdem *mss., Froben*

27. Bargadinus *r*

28. Fr: *omitted in mss., Froben*

29. BC: *omitted in EFHQr, Froben*

30. indecenter attonsus] tonsoratus (censoratus *F*) *mss., Froben*

31. Anno postmodum qui secutus est, tricesimo sexto et octingentesimo *mss., Froben*

32. *omitted in F*

33. quadragesimo] sexagesimo *BFQ: omitted in CEH, Froben*

34. Pupiliam *mss., Froben*

35. qui et *BC*

36. septuagesimo septimo *F*

37. hae *mss., Froben*

38. gratia *it seems in r*

39. gradu *mss*

40. *omitted in r*

41. fatiscente *r*

42. inde tertio] qui inde tertius est secutus *mss., Froben*

43. hic dux Petrus Tribunus *mss., Froben.*

44. *omitted in r*

45. hinc in praedicta ecclesia inde in Sancto Gregorio obserabantur *mss., Froben*

46. per cuius tempora *mss., Froben*

47. Alemannus rex *F*

48. per Italiam *F*

49. qui nactus per debilitatem imperii et Italiae occasionem *mss., Froben*

50. Veneti in Italis mari potentiores *mss., Froben*

51. nova aedificia] fabricas locorum *mss., Froben.*

52. igne *r*

53. *omitted in r*

54. funditus *mss., Froben*

55. compluribus *F*

56. restaurarunt *EFHQ, Froben*

57. *omitted in r*

58. *omitted in r*

59. situm *r*

60. civitatis *omitted in mss.*

61. Duodecimo deinceps anno Veneti *F*

62. *omitted in r*

63. continuare *mss., Froben*

64. primum et septuagesimum supra millesimum et centesimum] septuagesimum primum supra undecies centenum *mss., Froben*

65. Ad annum namque *BCEH*: Nam ad annum *Fr, Froben*

66. sextum et nonagesimum supra millesimum et centesimum] quartum de duodecies centeno *mss., Froben*

67. iis *r*

68. quinquagesimo *r*

69. Venetorum] vir inter Venetos *mss., Froben*

70. appellaretur *H*: appelletur *mss., edd.*

71. felicissime gesto *omitted in r*

72. Trivisanus *r*

73. duodecimo *omitted in Fr*

74. multos ipsi ac praestantissimos novimus] multos praestantissimosque vidimus *mss., Froben*

75. Petrum Aemilianum, episcopum Vicentinum litteris multum, plurimum prudentia, decoratum *mss.*, *Froben*

76. Leonardum Iustinianum, magni nobilisque ingenii virum, qui inter alia humanitatis Latina et Graeca studia, musicae adulescens iuvenisque deditus, dulcissimis carminibus et peritissime vulgariter compositis *mss.*, *Froben*

77. vulgari et materna] vulgari *mss.*, *Froben*

78. *omitted in the mss.*

79. paucisque] qui et paucis *F*

80. *omitted in r*

81. Victorius *B*

82. *omitted in r*

83. Latinas litteras grammaticales *mss.*

84. *BC*: portuositates *EFHQ, edd.*

85. suus *mss.*, *Froben*

86. quoque *mss.*: quosque *r*

87. pontificem paulo post habuere Veneti ex Condulmaria gente *mss.*, *Froben*

88. per *Historias* nostras *mss.*, *Froben*

89. notissima pontificibus Romanis qui ante se fuerunt praestantissimis parem et aliorum turbae multo digniorem eum reddiderunt *mss.*, *Froben*

90. potest *r*

91. doctrinae praecipue] scientiae particulariter *mss.*

92. adiecit *mss.*

93. oratorum historicorumque *mss.*

94. subtilissime *mss.*

95. isque unicum . . . obtinet locum *in the first hand of B before deletion*: *omitted in the mss. and r*

96. Et pariter . . . administrari voluit *in the first hand of B before deletion* (isque humo . . .) C: *omitted in the mss. and r*

97. patriae *r*

98. ingenii *r*

99. Superque sunt Venetiis dux Franciscus Foscaris, omni virtutum praeterquam litterarum gloria ornatissimus, et cives: Franciscus Barbarus, excellentissimi vir ingenii, cuius litterarum Graecarum et Latinarum doctrinae (an eloquentiae) editis operibus celebratae, aut in administranda re publica sapientiae et pietatis aut gestarum (praesertim apud Brixiam) rerum gloriam anteponas haud facile possis discernere *mss., Froben*

100. sapientiae et gubernanda re publica peritiae gloriam habet *mss., Froben*

101. gerenda *mss., Froben*

102. *omitted in the mss., Froben*

103. pariter *mss., Froben*

104. Trivisanus *Fr*

105. Barbanus *r*

106. *omitted in the mss., Froben*

107. sunt *mss., Froben*

108. *omitted in the mss., Froben*

109. *omitted in r*

110. Et Paulus Barbus, equestris ordinis, germani fratris sui Petri Barbi Romanae ecclesiae cardinalis integerrimi humanissimique ac ductae ab Eugenio pontifice originis maternae gloriam bonarum artium, in quibus excellit, studiis accumulat *mss., Froben*

111. summo viro Francisco patre dignus] Francisci praedicti filius *mss.*

112. quod alterum in narrationis ordine *mss., Froben*

113. incurrimus (in curribus *F*) *r*

114. *omitted in Fr*

115. solum iuris] modo iurium *F*

116. professionem abunde pleni sed eloquentia quoque ornatissimi sunt ut ei nuncipatorum studio peritiorum multos aetatis nostrae scribendo discendoque (dicendoque *F, Froben*) aequent *mss., Froben*

117. Petrus Thomasius medicorum non magis Venetorum quam ceterorum aetatis nostrae eloquentissimus habetur *mss., Froben*

118. habita ratio quae] respectus qui *mss., Froben*

9. MARCH OF TREVISO

1. Blondi Flavii Forliviensis Italiae Illvstratae Nona Regio Marchia Tarvisina Incipit Foelicissime *inscr. r*

2. -sanam *FQ*

3. Melariae] meridiem *FQ*

4. litoris dexteram] dexteram lit(t)oralem *mss., Froben*

5. -sana, *etc. FQ*

6. sui *r: omitted in mss., Froben*

7. umquam *r: omitted in mss., Froben*

8. pertinuerit *mss., Froben*

9. maximas atque amplissimas urbes Veronam et Patavium barbaro Marchiae vocabulo Tarvisiique titulo subiici] barbaro marchiae vocabulo maximas atque amplissimas urbes Veronam Pataviumque titulo subiici Tervisino *mss., Froben*

10. *mss., Froben*: invaserunt *r*

11. locutionis Latinae Romanorum] locutionis Romanae Latinis verbis *mss., Froben*

12. non solum *r*: nedum *mss., Froben*

13. in Italia *Q*

14. eam *r: not in mss., Froben*

15. cuius Italicis communis est usus, Longobardorum temporibus] Italicam nunc appellatam per Longobardorum tempora *mss., Froben*

16. vocabuli *Froben*: vocabulis *mss., r*

17. ipsius *mss., Froben*

18. *Br:* Romanorum *FHQ, Froben*

19. charactere litterarum *mss., Froben*

20. postposito *mss., Froben*

21. sua ineptia gentis barbariem *mss., Froben*

22. adinvenerint *mss., Froben:* -erunt *r*

23. fuit *not in mss., Froben*

24. -siuntha *FHQr*

25. et Theodatus *B*

26. doctissimus fuere *mss., Froben*

27. ducum filiis *B*

28. qui regum aut gentis Longobardorum concilii permissione et decreto impetrasset eas *mss., Froben*

29. impetrassent . . . haberent *FQ*

30. appellatus *r*

31. ad Padum] Pado tenus *mss., Froben*

32. familiae nobilis Caprianensium villa *mss., Froben*

33. A qua] unde *mss., Froben*

34. et *not in mss., Froben*

35. *Br:* circuitu *FHQ, Froben*

36. iurium *omitted in r*

37. quinquagesimum undeciesque centenum *B:* millesimum quinquagesimum *r,* quinquagesimum deciesque centenum, (L.M.) *FHQ, Froben*

38. ad vigesimum inde miliarium] vigesimo inde miliario *mss., Froben*

39. pertinentque *mss., Froben*

40. ex quibus] quorum *mss., Froben*

41. sinistrum *r*

42. quod *mss., Froben*

43. Insulaque *mss., Froben*

44. Cretam *FQ*

45. pro *mss., Froben*

46. in Bucolicis *mss., Froben: omitted in r*

47. illi *not in Froben, mss.*

48. Aricinam Zavedensi Brassicae Zavedensibusque cauliculis *B*

49. vicenos *mss., Froben*

50. eam *mss.*

51. undeseptuagesimo *r*

52. B*r*: occupaverant *HQ*, -erunt *F, Froben*

53. ei *not in mss., Froben*

54. *Froben*: Ariulfus *mss., r*

55. *Froben*: Bavariorum *FHQr*, baioariorum *B*

56. *Froben*: Ariulfus *mss., r*

57. Veronam *r*: Veronae *mss., Froben*

58. subtilitate *mss., Froben*

59. Oleum quoque] oleumque *mss., Froben*

60. frumentaque *mss., Froben*

61. vero *not in mss., Froben*

62. namque *not in mss., Froben*

63. *not in mss., Froben*

64. grata odore] odorantia *FHQ, Froben*, odoratia *B*

65. Sunt enim ex eis non nullae *omitted in mss., Froben*

66. immixta *mss., Froben*

67. Vellerum vero] lanae *mss., Froben*

68. ab herbarum et pascuae praecipua nobilitate] et armenta [et armenta *omitted in Froben*] a pastionis [pastionibus *F*] proprietate *mss., Foben*

69. qua *r*

70. *omitted in mss., Froben*

71. prospectu *mss., Froben*

72. naturae munere] naturaliter *mss., Froben*

73. *not in mss., Froben*

74. et multo maiorem vim habeat. Cuius rei gratia herbilegi] ingenitam et multo maiorem virtutem praestaret quae [quod *F, Froben*] herbilegi *mss., Froben*

75. Multae etiam ac variae] diversae etiam *mss., Froben*

76. Br: ipse *FQ, Froben*

77. *omitted in r*

78. sunt ad aequam muliebribus formam de saxo productae] ad iustam muliebrium formam de saxo fabre sunt ductae *mss., Froben*

79. aquulae *mss.*: aquae *Froben*

80. et *mss., Froben*

81. infuderit] asperserit atque laverit *mss., Froben*

82. Sed iam solidiora Veronae (sicut et ceteris urbibus) ornamenta, viros omnis aetatis praestantes [praestantes *omitted in FQ*] attingamus [-gemus *F*]. Zenoque, sicut religionem Christianam et suam ipsius decet sanctitatem, primus erit. Qui, Veronae praesul celebris sanctimoniae, multa scripsit exstantia sacras utriusque testamenti litteras declarantia et Ambrosianam (quam imitatus est) eloquentiam redolentia. Aemilium Macrum Veronensem poetam Eusebius in Asia obiisse asserit. Paulo post Catullus poeta, subinde uterque Plinius saepe a nobis hac in *Italia* celebrati Veronenses fuere *mss., Froben*

83. *omitted in r*

84. coniunxerat *mss., Froben*

85. *omitted in Fr*

86. sui saeculi *mss., Froben*

87. parvum *BFQ*

88. physicus *F*

89. afficiet *FQ*

90. Monticulenses [*sic*] . . . comites *mss., Froben*

91. duodecies centenum *mss., Froben*

92. vi eiectus Mantuanorum armis] per arma eiectus, armis Mantuanorum *mss., Froben*

93. campo *r*: vico *mss., Froben*

94. duodecies centenum *mss., Froben*

95. saevissimus *FQ*

96. *Froben: omitted in mss., r*

97. sibi *mss., Froben: omitted in r*

98. Patavinos *mss., Froben*

99. *Froben:* Suncinum *mss., r*

100. paucis . . . annis *mss., Froben*

101. novi per *mss., Froben*

102. anno uno et quinquagesimo *mss., Froben*

103. tenuerit *mss., Froben*

104. civitates *mss., Froben*

105. per quas contentionum occasiones *mss., Froben*

106. ab annis]annos *mss., Froben*

107. recepit *mss., Froben*

108. profectus *r: omitted in mss., Froben*

109. Qui Armeniaci *mss., Froben*

110. reparavit *mss., Froben*

111. nunc superest *B*

112. faciliter *mss., Froben*

113. cremonenses *F*

114. eorumque exemplo omnem regionem] quorum exemplo omnis regio *mss., Froben*

115. dedit *mss., Froben*

116. *text in italics in B (only) and deleted by a second hand*

117. addidit, *first hand of B, r: omitted in FHQ, Froben*

118. Pontonam *B,* pontem *FQ*

119. superius *mss.*, *Froben*

120. superius *mss.*, *Froben*

121. Adrianorum *mss.*, *Froben*

122. pertinet *mss.*, *Froben*

123. eius *r*

124. quas 'Fossiones' appellant] ubi appellant Fossiones *mss.*, *Froben*

125. praesidium *mss.*, *Froben*

126. institutae eius rei publicae initio ea in parte fuit constructum] ea in parte institutae rei publicae initio fuit impositum *mss.*, *Froben*

127. Interiusque *B*

128. *omitted in mss.*, *Froben*

129. Deinceps *mss.*, *Froben*

130. *omitted in B*

131. conficiendas chartas comminuendis] in scriptum coagulandis *Froben*

132. aedificata *F*

133. *omitted in mss.*, *Froben*

134. deinceps *mss.*, *Froben*

135. arctum *mss.*, *Froben*

136. *Hr*: Secconzanum *Froben*: Segunzanum *BFQ*

137. supra *mss.*, *Froben*

138. *mss.*: Parclasium *edd.*

139. Menumque et ad sinistram Cavalesium et Visum ac Chanacium *omitted in FQ*

140. sunt dextrorsum] dextrorsum haerent *B*: dextrorsum *FHQ*, *Froben*

141. *omitted in mss.*, *Froben*

142. Serrentino *FQ*

143. fonte *FQ*

144. eius *B*

145. fluvio *FQ*

146. proximum amnem Meduacum *B*

147. fuit *H*

148. *omitted in Fr*

149. instar fluvii currens fossa est] fossa est incurrentem [incurrentes *F*] fluvium *mss., Froben*

150. Montognana *r*

151. illum sinistrorsum] primo Bachilionem sinistrorsum *mss., Froben*

152. ad similliam *r*

153. consueverint *mss.,* -verunt *Foben*

154. Guilielmum Ravennatem archiepiscopum, apostolicae sedis legatum, deseruerunt Bononienses milites, quorum opera usus Ecelinum de Romano Patavio eiecerat: qua ex re factum est] Bononienses milites, quorum opera Guilielmus Ravennas archiepiscopus, sedis apostolicae legatus, Ecelinum de Romano eiecerat Patavio, eundum deservuerunt legatum: unde factum est *mss., Froben*

155. Encellinus *r*

156. Supra Custodiam] Superiusque *mss., Froben*

157. Alius item fluvius Vincentiam illabitur, Tesina appellatus, qui apud Landrigum oppidum oriundus et apud Luxanum oppidum scissus alterum ramum, cui Barcanum haeret oppidum, facit. Eoque] Et altero item fluvio urbem Vicentiam illabente, Tessina appellato apudque Landrigum oppidum oriundo Meduacus augetur amnis, qui Tesina apud Luxanum oppidum scissus, alterum ramum, cui Barcanum haeret, oppidum [oppidum haeret *FQ*], facit. Isque *mss., Froben*

158. stillam et guttam *mss., Froben*

159. rhetorica practice *r*

160. paene *mss., Froben*

161. ornatissimos *mss., Froben*

162. *omitted in mss., Froben*

163. in munimentum Patavio *r:* munimento Patavii *mss., Froben*

164. ad *mss., Froben*

165. vel tractus *Br*: retractus *FHQ, Froben*

166. Teriorum *r*

167. *Mss., edd.*

168. *omitted in mss., Froben*

169. decessisse *BH, Froben,* disc- *FQ*

170. Circumvenit *F*

171. medio *mss., Froben*

172. terrerent *mss.*: terrent *edd.*

173. praetereundum] ita praetentum *r*

174. ostiis *mss., Froben*

175. vidisset *mss.*

176. *Froben*: graves summas *mss., r*

177. alteram *mss.*

178. videbatur *mss., Froben*

179. *omitted in mss., Froben*

180. *omitted in mss., Froben*

181. in terra] interea *mss.*

182. *B*: refugientibus *FHQr, Froben*

183. itaque *mss., Froben*

184. praeteritum a Cleonymo *mss., Froben: not in r*

185. litus ita protentum (quod praetergressis stagna a tergo essent aestibus maritima irrigua) ostiumque amnis praealti, quo invecta sit flumine
adverso classis prope Patavium ad quatuordecim miliaria, satis ostendere]
litus transgressa stagna ostium amnis praealti, in quem circumacta sit
adverso flumine classis et ad quartuodecim milia oppido Patavio propin-
quata satis ostendere *mss., Froben*

186. adductos *F, Froben*

187. *italicized passage in B only*

188. apperturae *r*

189. Patavi *mss.*, -avii *Froben*

190. a *omitted in* r

191. poeta *mss.: omitted in edd.*

192. *Froben:* lineus *mss.*, r

193. haec] infrascripta *mss.*, *Froben*

194. supradictas *mss.*, *Froben*

195. non solum] nedum *mss.*, *Froben*

196. *not in mss.*, *Froben*

197. regola *Qr*

198. peragrum *r*

199. Patavi *r*

200. humanissime *FQ*

201. similem ei] sibi similem *mss.*, *Froben*

202. trigesimum et quadringentesimum *mss.*, *Froben*

203. per Caroli Magni et filiorum nepotumque imperii tempora *mss.*, *Froben*

204. trigesimum septimum et duodecies centenum *mss.*, *Froben*

205. propter *H*

206. ingressus *B*

207. interemptus est *second hand of B*

208. munitissima atque etiam ornatissima *B*

209. tanemus *sic r*

210. lic(h)ostrota *mss.*

211. *Froben:* Lacedemonis *mss.*, r

212. et paleariam] palearem *mss.*, *Froben*

213. eius quoque] eiusque *B*

214. f. *omitted in r*

215. Et *omitted in B*

216. ascriptum *F*

217. regionis *Q*

218. halys *r*, halis *mss.*: alis *Froben*

219. priore *B*

220. filiae *B*

221. magius *F*

222. Spaniarum *F*

223. Iule *r*

224. secutus] ad *mss.*, *Froben*

225. Velusi *r*

226. cupidine *F*

227. dedissemque *Qr*

228. iocosis *Catullus*

229. movere *H*

230. urios *H*: variosque *FQ*

231. ametunta *FQr*

232. Golgos *Catullus*: alcos *Fr*, altos *H*, Aleos *Froben*, alios *Q*: *omitted in B*

233. quaeque *omitted in B*

234. Apono *r*: ap(p)ano *mss.*: Abano *Froben*

235. magicae *r*

236. Iohannesque *BQ*

237. nec *mss.*, *r*: et *Froben*

238. arboribus *not in mss.*, *Froben*

239. *Froben*: tectos *mss.*, *r*

240. ultimo *B*

241. hisque *mss.*

242. prior *Martial*

243. Helicaonis *Martial*

244. in auras *mss.* (in aras *Froben*), *edd.*: oras *Martial*

245. his etiam r: quibus *mss., Froben*

246. dulces *FHQ*

247. physicus celebris *not in mss., Froben*

248. quartum de duodecies centeno *mss., Froben*

249. Deinceps *mss., Froben*

250. quem *B*

251. *Froben:* Arcinagus *BHr,* -nogus *FQ*

252. *mss., r:* Navoriusque *Froben*

253. Pemechum *Froben*

254. iuvanum *F*

255. ravennatem *F*

256. veterum] apud veteres *mss., Froben*

257. *not in mss., Froben*

258. dehinc] et post *mss., Froben*

259. quod *B, Froben:* qui *HQr*

260. Per tempora vero Ostrogothorum *mss., Froben*

261. videtur initium fuisse dignitatis eius] dignitatem inchoasse videtur *mss., Froben*

262. illius] ipsius *FQ*

263. Ravenna *mss., Froben*

264. filio *FQ*

265. a naso *F*

266. mardirium *F*

267. Superius *mss., Froben*

268. *omitted in FQ*

269. Resega *B*

270. Feltro *Froben:* Filtro *mss., r*

271. convallium *B*

272. *omitted in mss., Froben*

273. Cordovalus amnis *mss., Froben*

274. ostii bifariam divisi partem] ostia bifariam divisa quorum parte *B*

275. Alteraque parte ad proxima Caprularum] altera ad proxima crapularum *B*

276. delectam *F*

277. Mut(t)egique *BFQ, Froben:* Mutegidique *Hr*

278. *omitted in mss., Froben*

279. *mss., r:* Civiolonum *Froben*

280. superius *mss., Froben*

281. Caprulas] ad Caprulas *in the second hand of B*

282. Habetque . . . Sextum *omitted in B*

10. FRIULI

1. Regio Decima. Forvmivlivm *inscr. Froben*

2. inque] neque *FQ*

3. Iapidium *Froben:* Iapigum *mss., r*

4. Liminis *FHQr:* Limini *B, Froben*

5. primum *omitted in mss., Froben*

6. post *mss., Froben*

7. Proclanum *r*

8. Deinceps *mss., Froben*

9. post *mss., Froben*

10. superius *mss., Froben*

11. stagnum illabenti] id illabenti stagnum *mss., Froben*

12. in ipsa] ipsa in *FH, Froben,* ipsa *BQ*

13. semota *mss., Froben: omitted in r*

14. haudquaquam *mss., Froben*

15. eam *r: omitted in mss., Froben*

16. Baebii *Livy*

17. venisset] venisset spem ademit eum qui in Gallia esset *B*

18. negavit *Froben*: negabat *r*: *omitted in mss*

19. nuntium] Cumitium *as it seems in r*

20. Marsilia *Froben*

21. comportatio *mss., Froben*

22. in ea] ibidem *mss., Froben*

23. mercandisque] mercandis coemendisque *mss., Froben*

24. Eademque *mss., Froben*

25. Petro et *Froben*

26. eius exaratus] exaratus sua *mss., Froben*

27. beatoque *BHr*

28. de *r*

29. mira *mss., edd.*

30. *BH Froben*: scripsit *FQr*

31. secundas *r*

32. *Froben*: suae *mss., r*

33. delectus *B, Froben*

34. *Froben*: qui *mss., r*

35. *r*: neque in *mss., Froben*

36. neque *r*: aut *mss., Froben*

37. proximioribus *mss., Froben*

38. gestis] gestis non *mss.*: gestis id *Froben*

39. *Froben*: eum *mss., r*

40. Iacobum *FQ, Froben*

41. Fasagna *Froben*

42. superiori *H, Froben*

43. propinquus *r*

44. celsos inter montes] celso inter montes loco *second hand of B*

45. Hanstriae *r*

46. civili et *F*

47. Sofin-/Sophin- *BFr*

48. Cromona *Froben*

49. Deinceps *mss., Froben*

50. tertio *r*

51. *Froben*: Ultraque Tergestum *mss., r*

52. passus *mss.*

53. idem *not in mss., Froben*

54. a Ravenna undeducentesimo miliario distantem] et undeducentesimo passuum milliario a Ravenna distantem *mss., Froben*

55. Mulgam *Q, Froben*: mugla *H*

56. Istria *Froben*

57. haudquaquam *mss., Froben*

58. Istria *Froben*

59. nobis *edd.*: omitted in *mss.*

60. divini *r*

61. est *omitted in FH*

62. pariter *mss., Froben*

II. ISTRIA

1. tamen *not in mss., Froben*

2. *omitted in r*

3. centum et viginti quinque] viginti quinque [xxv] et centum *mss., Froben*

4. sisinus *FQ*

5. passus *mss., Froben*

6. circuitas *r*

7. centum et viginti quinque] XXV et centum *mss., Froben*

8. iter id centum milium passuum mari directum e regione dimidio quam terra brevius sit] dimidia brevior [dimidio brevis *Froben*] sit mari quam terra directum [diretius *H*] e regione centum milia passus [-uum *Froben*] iter *mss., Froben*

9. *Froben*: Iapigiam *mss., r, etc.*

10. appellatam *mss., Froben*

11. Argonautas Argon navim] Argon navim ab Argonautis *mss., Froben*

12. passus *mss., Froben*

13. saepe *FQ*

14. A Iustinopoli] Primum a Iustinopoli *mss., Froben*

15. passuum milibus] milia passuum *Froben*: milia passus *mss.*

16. a quo tantumdem distat] et post tantumdem inde distans *mss., Froben*

17. Ab ea] et tertio loco *mss., Froben*

18. a quo aeque distat] Quartumque paris a superiori distante [distantiae *Q*] *mss., Froben*

19. Deinceps aequaliore ad Fanaticum sive Carnarium promontorium *mss., Froben*

20. Ab Humago] Ab Humagoque *BFH Froben*, et ab Humago *Q*

21. itidem passuum milibus] pariter milia passus *mss., Froben*

22. Nauporti sunt ostia *mss., Froben*

23. ex Alpibus oriundum] Alpibus exorientem *mss., Froben*

24. Parentum *r*

25. continet *mss., Froben*

26. Post est ruingnum *B*

27. Arduo deinde colli ac diffuso naturaque loci munitissimo imposita supereminet] deinde sinu supereminet amplo colli imposita arduo naturaque loci munitissimo *mss., Froben*

28. Anconem] -nam *H*, -ne *Q*

29. appellatum *Q*

30. ita *F*

31. pertinent *mss.*, *Froben*

32. eius] suae *mss.*, *Froben*

33. loca *not in mss.*, *Froben*

34. Pilosa *mss.*, *Froben*

35. Iustinopolitanorum oppida et castella] quae omnia Iustinopolitanorum sunt oppida et castella *mss.*, *Froben*

36. oppidaque] et oppida *B*

37. et *not in mss.*, *Froben*

38. pissinum *B*: pissium *mss. edd.*

39. se *not in r*

40. exonerat *mss.*, *Froben*.

41. Pissinum *FQ*: pissium *BH, edd.*

42. uulla *r*

43. est *added by the second hand of B: not in mss.*, *Froben*

44. itaque *B*

45. ipsius] sua *mss.*, *Froben*

46. libros *H*

47. cetera] quae *FQ*

48. aetatis *Froben*, -tem *H*

49. ergo *H*

50. sunt *FQ*

51. ut nunc quoque] sicut nunc quoque fit *mss.*, *Froben*

52. et *not in FQ*

53. atque *FQ*

54. ingenio *r*

55. docuit atque voluit, videri fuisse alienigenam *mss.*, *Froben*: docuit videri eum fuisse alienigenam *r*

56. *Froben*: I(p)por(h)edienses *mss.*, *r*

57. praefuerunt diu *FQ*

58. Histris sigillatim suis locis referre] Istris particulatim referre *mss.*, *Froben*

59. in suum hunc locum *mss.*, *Froben*

60. eius regionis invasionem] invasionem factam in regionem *mss.*, *Froben*

61. factam fuisse; et secundam, qua Teutana muliere praestantissima in Histris regnante, barbari supervenientes omnia] Teutanaque muliere praestantissima [potentissima *B*] in Histris regnante barbaros supervenisse qui omnia in Histris *mss.*, *Froben*

62. maximam et horribilem cladem illam [illam *omitted in r*] a Visigothis fuisse illatam] fuisse maximam et horribilem cladem illam a Visigothis illatam *mss.*, *Froben*

63. supra dicto *not in r*

64. minorum *omitted in r*

65. multarum urbium provinciarumque] multas in urbes provinciasque *mss.*, *Froben*

66. hanc] hanc maxime *mss.*, *Froben*

67. est perventum *mss.*: perventum *Froben*

68. aetatem nostram *r*

69. ipsa] ea *mss.*, *Froben*

70. praeesse *r*

71. Sed iam terminata sit Italiae nostrae latitudo ad hanc Alpium partem quam natura ei munimento adversus externas nationes a Varo ad Arsiam amnem per milia passuum quadringinta et quinquaginta opposuit] Finita iam ad hanc Alpium per milia passuum [passus *mss.*] quadringenta et quinquaginta ab Varo ad Arsiam amnem externis nationibus munimento Italiae oppositarum partem [partem *omitted in F*] sit Italiae nostrae latitudo *mss.*, *Froben*

12. ABRUZZO

1. Blondi Flavii Forliviensis Italiae / Illvstratae Aprvtivm Regio Dvo / Decima et Liber Septimvs Incipit Fe / Licissime *r*: Regio duode-

cimo. Aprutium (sive Samnium), Campania, Apulia, Lucania, Salentini, Calabria, et Brutii *mss., Froben*

2. Absoluta hucusque *B*

3. sex *B*

4. Salatinos *r*: Palentinos *B*

5. et Calabros atque *B*

6. longinquitate *mss., Froben*

7. Facile tamen erit Alexander Epirota [-thas *BQ*, -tas *H*], Pyrrhus, Hannibal, Alaricus, Totila [Totila et Longobardi *B*] vetustiores earum regionum hostes quas res et quibus in locis gesserint a maiorum aut nostris *Historiis* sumere et per singulas civitatum locorumque descriptiones (sicut supra fecimus) edocere *mss., Froben*

8. saepe dicta identidem replicare *mss., Froben*

9. *omitted in FQ*

10. cumque] qui cum *mss., Froben*

11. deditam *mss., Froben*

12. ut viros fortes praestantissimosque eos *mss., Froben*

13. hebetiori (*sic*) ingratique ingenii *r*: hebetioris ingenii ingratusque *mss., Froben*

14. convenerat *mss., Froben*

15. accidit imperatoris Constantinopolitani in Calabris, Brutiis, Lucanis, et Neapolitana urbe magistratus petere Salernitanum illi subditum imperio auxilia *mss., Froben*

16. faciliter *mss., Froben*

17. Atque] Qui *mss., Froben*

18. Constantinopoli *mss., Froben*: Constantinopolis *r*

19. Ethiriachis *mss., edd.*

20. *omitted in mss., Froben*

21. Oluientem *r*

22. paulo post] post parum *mss., Froben*

23. V *mss., edd.*

24. Gisulphusque (-sol-) Normannus *mss., edd.*

25. qui *mss., Froben*

26. restitisset *F*

27. II *mss., edd.*

28. Feliciorque fuit Normannis et melius in Romano pontifice quam in ceteris *mss., Froben*

29. filiorum Tancredi ordine sextus, vir *mss., Froben*

30. de iuribus] iurium *mss., Froben*

31. adduxit *H*

32. ducens Romanos proceres *mss., Froben*

33. Inde *mss., Froben*

34. Maianum *B*

35. Cannalem *Froben*: Canaleam *FHQr*, Caneleam *B*

36. agro *FQ*

37. multa in circuitu Normannorum *mss., Froben*

38. Gaufredo *mss., r*, Ganfredo *Froben*

39. in nunc Aprutii regione *mss., Froben*

40. ea quae nunc est Aprutii regione occupatam tribuit] nunc Aprutii regione occupata attribuit *mss., Froben*

41. sua . . . potestate *F*

42. bittiminus belcanetti *FQ*

43. Et prima de Sicilis in Normannorum potestatem venit urbs Messana *mss., Froben*

44. et ac *r*

45. omnis Sicilia in Guiscardi fratrisque Rogerii potestatem brevi est facta *mss., Froben*

46. praedae de Saracenis Sicilia pulsis factae partem dono misit *mss., Froben*

47. *omitted in* r

48. Castello Sancti Angeli *mss., Froben*

49. porta . . . ingressus] per portam Flumentanam (sive Flaminiam) *mss., Froben*

50. post parum *mss., Froben*

51. Cypri H

52. Iulio . . . interiit] ad Cassiopam insulam febri per Iulium mensem ex caumate correptus interiit *mss., Froben*

53. maiori B

54. *omitted in* H

55. filius natu maior Boemundus *mss., Froben*

56. exercitum meliorem (meliorem exercitum H) sibi a casu oblatam secutus est fortunam *mss., Froben*

57. *omitted in* F

58. cuius *mss., Froben*

59. -tam BH

60. *omitted in* FQ

61. ut haberet *corrected (from* habere [sperans *omitted*] *of the first hand of B) by the second hand of B*

62. Nicephorim (et Nicephorim B) *mss., Froben*

63. mala *mss., Froben*

64. ab eo *omitted in* FHQ

65. cum exercitu *omitted in* H

66. circa F

67. post *mss., Froben*

68. *omitted in* BQr

69. *omitted in* H

70. tertio praestanti Romano pontifice multis *mss., Froben*

71. omnia de integro cepit quae Innocentius ei] omnia de Italia recepit [receperit *Froben*] quae Innocentius sibi *mss., Froben*

72. *omitted in r*

73. *omitted in mss., Froben*

74. *omitted in mss., Froben*

75. annum *mss., Froben*

76. octavum Gregorium B: *omitted in FHQ, edd.*

77. Boni *Froben*

78. Tandem *mss., Froben*

79. fierent *mss., Froben*

80. vel eum *Q*

81. *omitted in F*

82. Tancredo] hoc *BH, Froben*: eo *FQ*

83. regnum *Froben*

84. propriam ipsi] suam *mss., Froben*

85. *omitted in FQ*

86. natu *mss., Froben*

87. invadisset *H*

88. Qui anno inde *mss., Froben*

89. delegerunt *mss., Froben*

90. Quemadmodum Gregorius quoque] Quem Gregorius *Froben*

91. Flisco *r*: Fisco *mss., Froben*

92. per tempora *mss., Froben*

93. successus *mss., Froben*

94. Langravium *Froben*: lanthcravium *BHr*, lantheravium *Q*, lantheranium *F*

95. ditissima *mss., Froben*

96. militum caesa] milites ferro occisos *mss., Froben*

97. Occisus est] diu carcere tentus fuit *B*

98. Tandem *mss., Froben*

99. eius] dicti *H, Froben*: praedicti *B*: dicti Henrici *F*, dicti hennam *(sic) Q*

100. et cives *Froben*

101. Manfredus, *corrected (out of* Conradinus *in the first hand of B) by the second hand of B, Froben: mss., r*

102. ubi apparuit illum] quem apparuit esse *mss., Froben*

103. fuisse *omitted in mss., Froben*

104. brevi apud Neapolim *mss., Froben*

105. praetenso Conradini ex Henrico, quem patrem Federicum mori coegisse diximus, et Constantia Aragonensi nepotis tutelae titulo *mss., Froben*

106. tanta de victoria] tantae victoriae *mss., Froben*

107. potuerunt *Froben*

108. de facta celeriter deditione] factae celeriter deditionis *mss., Froben*

109. repente *r*

110. Eoque] quo *mss., Froben*

111. *omitted in mss., Froben*

112. ductos *BF*: conductos *H*

113. primum reppulit *mss., Froben*

114. post *BH, Froben*, postea *FQ*

115. per solemnem stipulationem *mss., Froben*

116. annuos *BQ, Froben*, annos *F: omitted in H*

117. aureorum milia] mille aureos *BH*, mille ducatos *FQ, Froben*

118. Manfredum vi superatum ac resistentem] eo vi superato, Manfredum quoque resistentem *mss., Froben*

119. Retrocedentemque] quem retrocedentem *mss., Froben*

120. ubi pares] paresque *mss., Froben*

121. supra millesimum ducentesimum salutis] supra duodecies centenum salutis *mss.*, *Froben*

122. mille *mss.*

123. adeptus *Froben*: adeptum *Br*: adeptam *FHQ*

124. ex Romana curia et urbe contraria] contraria in Romana curia et urbe *B*

125. Cumque *B*

126. Alemannis *FH*

127. commissi proelii *mss.*, *Froben*

128. recogniti sunt *mss.*, *Froben*

129. eosque] quos *mss.*, *Froben*

130. vero *H*

131. Gallis suis *mss.*, *Froben*

132. anno salutis millesimo ducentesimo octogesimo secundo]secundo octogesimo et duodecies centeno salutis anno (salutis anno *omitted in H*) *mss.*, *Froben*

133. inceperat *BH*, *Froben*: receperat *F*

134. *om. r*

135. anno *mss.*, *Froben*

136. E quibus] quorum *mss.*, *Froben*

137. Ludovicusque qui ex ordine] Ludovicus qui ordinis *mss.*, *Froben*

138. parentis in regno] illi et patri in regno *H*, (regna) *Froben*: patri in regno *BFQ*

139. amicitia nunc *H*

140. *omitted in mss.*, *Froben*

141. demum *mss.*, *Froben*

142. duodecimo iam anno *mss.*, *Froben*

143. calculum ex summis cogere] calculum in summas [calculas . . . summam *H*] redigere *mss.*, *Froben*

144. quinque et centum triginta *HQ, mss.*, quinque et cxxx *F*, quinto et centum triginta *B*

145. octo et centum septuaginta *mss., Froben*

146. Continet *mss., Froben*

147. Ferentani *Froben*, Frentatii *H*

148. imperiti *r*

149. ubi *mss., Froben*

150. incepit *Foben*, occepit *mss.*

151. *After* ager, *B has*: Adrianus et Adria colonia a mari tria millia passus flumen Vomanum ager

152. Praetutiana *BFH, Froben*, praecunciana *Q*

153. Picentinum *Froben*

154. *omitted in mss., Froben*

155. Caius *r*

156. Namque Livius *mss., Froben*

157. *After* declarare, *B has*: aut ubi interierunt eorum loca et vestigia indicare

158. sequitur *H*

159. et Minotrassinium *Froben*

160. se in Troentum exonerat *mss., Froben*

161. Praetutiorm *FQ*

162. remotus *F*

163. oppidula *B*

164. Rocheta *r*

165. ac *mss.*

166. munitam *mss., Froben*

167. milia *mss., Froben*

168. iuvantinum *BH*, iuvatium *FQ*: Vivantium *Froben*

169. quique habet] habetque *mss., Froben*

170. ex] in *mss.*, *Froben*

171. ex quibus] quorum *mss.*, *Froben*

172. persana (?) *r*

173. *omitted in mss.*, *Froben*

174. nunc Venetias] Venetiis *Froben*

175. nunc incolunt *BFQ*, *Froben*

176. proximum *r*

177. *After* sunt, *B has*: castella Camplum, Castellum Novum, et Nucella adeo in vicem proxima

178. *omitted in mss.*, *Froben*

179. Burgum Novum *omitted in mss.*, *Froben*

180. Locharistium *Froben*: rochariscum *B*

181. rocha *B*

182. castellum *r*

183. xxvii *r*

184. oppidum. Et tribus sicut vult Plinius, ut nostri autem quinque, milibus passuum] oppidum [oppidula *B*]et tria [Troia *Froben*], sicut Plinius. Ut nunc autem quinque milia passus *mss.*, *Froben*

185. aram] in aram *r*

186. in *mss.*, *Froben*

187. fluvio *FQ*

188. Pinnensium *r*

189. Pinnenses *FHQr*

190. imminent *BHQ*: imminet *F*, *Froben*, minet *r*

191. primarium *r*

192. fluvius *Q*, *Froben*

193. *B*: Capagattum *FHQ*, *edd.*

194. Deinceps *mss.*, *Froben*

195. Aquaeductus *Froben*

196. primo *mss., Froben*

197. adiacet *mss., Froben*

198. eius *BFH, Froben,* huius *Q*

199. repetemus *mss., Froben*

200. *Froben:* Cornelium *mss., r*

201. octingenta *Froben*

202. mille *mss., Froben*

203. octuaginta *FHQ, Froben*

204. *omitted in r*

205. continere *Froben*

206. unita *Froben*

207. intellegeret operamque navare *Froben*

208. dilabatur *Froben,* delabatur *mss., r*

209. recedit] semota *FQ*

210. Valognanorum *r,* -ganorum *Q*

211. duxerint *r*

212. per tempora *FHQ*

213. *omitted here in FHQ*

214. oriundis *mss., r,* oriundus *Froben*

215. gente Romana *QF,* gente *H*

216. et litteris *mss., Froben*

217. inferius *mss., Froben*

218. ad ostium fluvii quem unicum duo Rufens inde hinc Orta torrentes] ad fluvii unius ostium, quem hinc [nunc *FHQ*] Rufens [Rufeus *Froben*] inde Orta torrentes *mss., Froben*

219. Hicque Marrucenis continere incipiunt Paeligni ad eum Aterni torrentem] Hicque Paeligni Marrucenis continere incipiunt ad eam Aterni partem *mss., Froben*

220. appositi *Froben*

221. quam *mss., Froben*

222. Sancti Pelini] Scimpelini *Froben*

223. Ea Aterni pars quam diximus ad Sulmonem *mss., Froben*

224. Delabentesque inde fluvii *mss., Froben*

225. in torrentem, qui] et Aternus *mss.*

226. miliarium] milia passuum *mss., Froben*

227. sex] dimidio *Froben*

228. amni *mss., Froben*

229. fluvio *Froben*

230. Solimo *r*: sulmone *mss.*

231. Phrygia (frigia)] frigida *F*, frigidus *Q*

232. superius *mss., Froben*

233. quinum milium *mss., Froben*

234. et *Froben*

235. Fluvius *mss., Froben*

236. fluvios *mss., Froben*

237. Apenninus *mss., Froben*

238. hoc *Q*

239. Sari *mss., edd.,* recte Sagrus

240. fluminis *FQ*

241. illius regionis *omitted in mss., Froben*

242. adducti *Froben*

243. praecedens *r*

244. *omitted in FHQ, Froben*

245. duos *mss., Froben*

246. habet *B*

247. sibi *mss., Froben*

248. Iuanum *r*: Iuianum *mss., Froben*

249. duos *mss.*, *Froben*

250. Anaxanum *H*, *Froben*, -sanum *F*

251. pella *B*: pennam *H*

252. Furcham *Hr*

253. Anachorita *mss.*, *Froben*

254. et *FHQ*

255. sepe- *mss.*: superatum *Froben*

256. pecum *BFQ*

257. ad *Froben*: in *mss.*, *r*

258. *om. r*

259. de messe *Hr*

260. congregantur *F*, *Froben*

261. pesculum *B*, pesulum *FHr*, persulum *Q*: Praesulum *Froben*

262. Cuiuscunque *F*

263. Cn. *Livy*: Cornelii *mss.*, *r*: C. *Froben*

264. Bonaianum *Hr*

265. Asserrulum *r*

266. odorisius *H*

267. Triventum *mss.*, *Froben*

268. Bagnolum *B*

269. rata *Hr*

270. infrequentata *H*: infrequentia *BFQ*, *edd.*

271. Tiferno] in Tiferno *Froben*

272. Orchetta *Froben*

273. Captum *Froben*

274. Pentriorum *Livy*: Pent(h)eorum *mss.*, *edd.*

275. paene *Livy*: ibi *mss.*, *edd.*

276. egestum *r*, *Livy*: est gestum *mss.*: est egestum *Froben*

277. Cn. *Livy*: C. *Froben*: Cornelii *mss.*, r

278. Aufidiam *FQ*

279. dividitur *mss.*, *Froben*

280. hinc *HQFr*: huic *B*, *Froben*

281. castello *r*

282. Genucio *Livy, mss., Froben*: Gemitio *r*

283. Servio *Livy*: Sergio *Froben*: Servilio *mss.*, *r*

284. Lirum *r*

285. ulciscendam *Livy, Q*: -dum *BFHr, Froben*

286. qui *FQ*: qua *H*

287. Cariulius *Hr*: canulius *B*

288. accepti *FQ*

289. Molam *BHr*

290. *Froben*: Collatia *mss.*, *r*

291. Ut enim] Etenim *Lambin*

292. loci. Quo] Lonquo *as it seems*, r

293. efficeret *r*: effecerit *mss.*, *Froben*

294. in Lirim praecipitat *r*

295. familiam patriciam *Cicero*

296. flumine *FQ*

297. Phedio *r*

298. germani *FQr*

299. hinc *Cicero*

300. antiquissima *omitted in* r

301. id est] inest *Cicero*

302. quod] et *Cicero*

303. Pescenino *mss.*, *Froben*: Pesinino *r*

304. At ultra *mss.*, *edd.*

445

305. sicha *Br*

306. sancti nomine *FQ*

307. ipsis *H*

308. *omitted in FHQr*

309. auruspicum *r*, -cem *H*: auspicium *(before correction by a second hand)* B

310. deportatam *H*

311. petitis *Hr*

312. Livius quoque, viam *mss., Froben*

313. *Froben*: passus *mss., r*

314. *Froben*: fonti *mss., r*

315. passus *mss., r*

316. qui *B, Froben*

317. dimidiam *mss., Froben*

318. fronte *B, Froben*

319. interius *Q*

320. passus *mss., r*

321. crapriatam *mss.*, Crapiatam *(as it seems) r*: Trapiata *Froben*

322. de *mss., Froben*

323. habent *r*

324. rivis altis *F,* (altibus) *Q*

325. inseparabilibus *r*

326. fontibus quam *mss.*

327. quot *BFQ,* quo *H*

328. dextra] ad dext(e)ram *FQ*

329. confluentia *BH, Froben*

330. Primusque est *Q*

331. a *Q*

332. Hi tamen montes nicati proprio nomine dicebantur *B*

333. e *FQ*

334. in viiii *FQ*

335. nicati *B*

336. ac *r*

337. *Froben:* depopulantur *mss., r*

338. *Froben:* passus *mss., r*

339. superimpositum *BQ, Froben*

340. eum *BFQ, Froben:* enim *Hr*

341. hostium *B*

342. confligit *Livy*

343. postero *Livy*

344. forent ut *Livy*

345. sequitur supra *BHQ:* sequitur super *F, Froben:* supra *r*

346. correctum *Froben*

347. Pugi- *H*

348. Calatiam *Froben*

349. *Froben:* Cornelium *mss., r*

350. callatiam *r*

351. abesse *FQ*

352. *italicicized passage from B: omitted in other mss., edd.*

353. Ptolomaeus *r*

354. habeatur *FQ*

355. deum *mss., edd.*

356. *omitted in r*

357. octavo *BFQ*

358. in IX (nono) *omitted in Froben*

359. *omitted in* r

360. et B

361. *added above by the second hand of B*

362. passus *mss.,* r

363. Decem et septem *Froben*

364. Voloni *mss.,* r

365. Et Livius vigesimo quinto *mss., Froben*

366. tria miliaria] xxx milia *Br,* triginta mil(l)iaria *FHQ*

367. xxii *FQ*

368. ac *mss.*

369. hoc ordine continet] insunt hoc ordine ascendendo *B*

370. Tremulis appellatis] quibus est tremulis appellatio *B*

371. Flomarium *mss.,* Flornarium *r,* Flormarlum *Froben*

372. opposita *mss.,* r

373. vinculum *FQ*

374. Grunius *r*

375. colle arduo *BH*

376. cum latitudine *mss., Froben*

377. tum longitudine *mss., Froben*

378. colle *r*

379. quo *r*

380. B^2Q: Arpinis, *first hand of B, HF, edd.*

381. Telesiem *r*

382. Finit liber Septimus et Regio duodecimo *r*

13. CAMPANIA

1. Blondi Flavii Forliviensis Italiae Illvstratae Liber Octavvs, et XIII. Regio, Campania Vetvs, Incipit Felicissime *r*

2. cisalpeninis *r*

3. Cur autem eam Felicem Campaniam postea alii Terram Laboris appellaverint *mss.*, *Froben*: Cur autem eam plus foelicem campaniam postea terram laboris appellaverint *r*

4. *Froben*: qua *mss.*, *r*

5. digna *r*

6. *mss.*, *edd.*: Φρεγέλλας *Strabo*

7. Cur autem] Et cur *mss.*, *Froben*

8. vestigia nunc *FHQ*

9. Scaphanique *Froben*

10. exstet *r*

11. Becardae *Froben*: Bacardae *BHr*: Bacardo *FQ,*

12. clericis *Froben*

13. plebeiis *Froben*

14. *Froben*: consolatione *mss.*, *r*

15. Paternitas *H*: fraternitas *mss.*, *edd.*

16. Sicutque *r*

17. *mss.*, *edd.*

18. balnea nunc *HQ*, *Froben*

19. carmulam *B¹r*

20. montis *FQ*

21. passus *mss.*, *edd.*

22. hic *r*

23. herculanteae *mss.*, *r*

24. sil(l)eta *mss.*, *edd.*: salicta *Cicero*

25. herculantea *mss.*, *r*

26. Iuvenalis *B*, *r*, *Froben*: Oratius *FHQ*

27. Gallucium, Conca, Ronca Mosini *omitted in B¹FHQ*, *Froben*

28. *Froben*: inferiorem *mss.*, *r*

29. aut *r*: in *FQ*

30. trecenti *mss., r*: trecenta *Froben*

31. montis ventum] perventum *FQ*

32. cavanellum *Froben*

33. cales sidicino *mss., edd.*

34. maherbali *BHQr*: adherbali *F*

35. Campano Vulturnum *FQ*

36. *Froben*: passus *mss., r*

37. afferre *B*

38. stellates *r*: Stellas *mss., Froben*

39. Lirimque et *Froben*

40. quoque cum *Froben*

41. Herculantea *mss., Froben*, -lentea (*sic*) *r*

42. dimittitur *B*

43. distribuit *mss., r*: discribit *Froben, Cicero*

44. a Stellati *Froben*: ac stellatis *mss., r*

45. herculanteam *mss., r*

46. *omitted in r*

47. *omitted in mss., r*

48. resinum *Q*: rasivum *r*

49. pelingnorum *r*

50. *omitted in r*

51. appareat *B*

52. praeter id *mss., Froben*

53. Et ne *r*: Ne etiam *mss., Froben*

54. fuerit . . . fuisset *r*: fuisset . . . fuerit *mss., Froben*

55. *r*: tulisse *mss., Froben*

56. passus *mss., Froben*

57. *Froben*: priore *mss., r*

58. capi *r*: Capuo *mss., Froben*

59. *Froben*: acceptis *mss., r*

60. B²: graveis *Froben*: gravi B¹FHQ

61. tamquam B: tamen F

62. Capuae *Froben*

63. *mss. edd.*: aliquantum vasculorum *Suetonius*

64. quid *r*

65. lebornium *r*

66. difficilem *r*

67. factoque BHQ

68. resupinando F

69. deesset effectum] actum deesset F

70. annos H

71. affectu FQ, *Froben*

72. litus *Froben*

73. patria *r*

74. perhorridas *Livy*: perhorrida *mss., edd.*

75. idem Livius *omitted in r*

76. sunt Q

77. agrum eius est harenosum *r*

78. p. cor. FQ: gn. BHr: P. *Froben*

79. fecit *r*

80. inveniremus QF

81. QF: mare BH, *edd.*

82. firmiorem QF

83. fumus *r*

84. *Froben*: olefecerimus *r*: olphaverimus B, (olfa-) FHQ

85. epistularum libro F

86. epistularum *F*

87. linterni *r*

88. mil(l)iare *mss., Froben*

89. es *BHr*

90. petacusas *mss., r*

91. a socio Ulixis Baio *Servius*

92. praesidet *B²F, Froben, Vergil*: praeminet *B¹HQr*

93. nostri *FQ*

94. passuum *Froben*: passus *mss., r*

95. mauritimam *r*

96. quinto *mss., Froben*

97. mille passus *mss., Froben*

98. *omitted in Froben*

99. formam *FQ*

100. urbe *r*

101. sinus *Horace*

102. Caligulae *Froben*, gal(l)iculae *mss.*: galliculaeque *r*

103. *Froben*: passus *mss., r*

104. fuerit *Froben*

105. apparent *FQ*

106. inhabitabilem *BF*

107. dicit *Froben*

108. possimus *BFQ Froben*

109. *Froben*: passus *mss., r*

110. qua *r*

111. baianum *Froben*

112. cadentis *FQ*

113. fabricandi *r*

114. evitandas *BFHQ, Froben*

115. gloriosissimus *FQ*

116. incipit *r*

117. suavissimus *Froben*

118. refulso *F*

119. Caligulae *Froben*, gal(l)iculae *mss.*

120. inchoavit *r*

121. *Froben*: tetrarchis *mss.*, tetrachis *(sic) r*

122. christiani *r*

123. quae *Froben*

124. hodie *r*

125. qua *r*

126. *Froben*: cedente *mss., r*

127. salicata *r*

128. qua *r*

129. qua *r*

130. sublime *(rightly?) FQ*

131. spectaculi *B*

132. captum *mss., edd.*: coeptum *Livy*

133. pervo stato *(sic) r*

134. Aelius *Livy, Froben*: Laelius *mss., r*

135. Antonius *BFHr*

136. *Froben*: ibi *BHr: omitted in FQ*

137. fuerunt *Froben*

138. praevident *Froben*

139. pulcherrimus *FHr*

140. factum *r: omitted in Q*

141. corduensem *r*

142. facibus *(before correction)* B¹: facilius H

143. re p(ublica) F

144. ipse Donatus H

145. Livius *omitted in* r

146. plancio BF

147. gerionem B, *Froben*: ierionem HQr: hieronem F

148. re p. F

149. laxamentum quaererent et discoli lasciviae diversorium B, (laxamenti) FHQ, *Froben*

150. Neapolim r

151. Parthenope *mss.*

152. recognoverint F

153. propasse r

154. Romam FQ

155. continet *mss., Froben*

156. domino r

157. quod quidem Q

158. Saraceni Sanctorum] sarraceni magna barbarorum alluvio sanctorum B

159. conversam r

160. pro servata] perseverata *(rightly?)* F

161. eaque r

162. sive *Froben*: si *mss., r*

163. Paulo r

164. xxii r

165. faciendae r

166. Perusiam r

167. erit H

168. egere *(as it seems)* r

169. pompeius r

170. exciti F

171. torta F

172. marilianum r

173. Acerra BFHr

174. agrillam r

175. mil(l)ia passus *mss., r:* mille passus *Froben*

176. de *omitted in* r

177. obmissa r

178. omnium r

179. primum *Froben*

180. absque *added superscript* B²: *omitted in* FQ

181. Lunatulam *Froben*

182. Moronia r: Moronida *mss.,* Meronida *Froben*

183. *Froben:* tiphatis *mss., r*

184. raptim *Froben:* rapidum *mss., r*

185. Et inferius] inferis r

186. ac B

187. B: *omitted in mss. and edd.*

188. Livius *om.* r

189. Cornelius] Cornelius paetus *mss., r*

190. Aelius] Laelius BHQr

191. ceciderint F: deciderint B

192. erat *first hand in* B, r

193. Nola BF, *Froben*

194. qui FQ

195. aquilam *BHr*

196. suum] sinum *r*

197. reditu *r*

198. Livio *Froben*

199. agri *r*

200. cicero *r*: toto *B*

201. Nolam] Nolam iam *mss., r*

202. undenonagesimo *B*: quarto de nonagesimo *mss., Froben*

203. quod *BFQ, Froben: omitted in H*

204. *omitted in r*

205. habere *r*

206. obiisset *F*: obiisse *mss., r, Froben*

207. Plinio *Froben*

208. Isque fluvius *mss., Froben*: Estque *r*

209. riget *r*

210. quae] quae et *r*

211. a Rullo] arula *r*: Rullo *Froben*

212. callanam *r*

213. centum . . . passuum *corrected superscript* B^2: centesimi . . . passus *mss., edd.*

214. fuerit *r*

215. fluvio praedicto *B*

216. ab *omitted in r*

217. audivimus *Froben*

218. meridionalem *FQ*

219. ciracium *(as it seems) F*

220. returium *(as it seems) H*: veterium *Q*: veturvium *r*

221. habitata *BFQr*

222. describimus *BHQr*

223. fuit *r*

224. manus *FQ*

225. apponemus *F*

14. PUGLIA

1. Blondi Flavii Forliviensis Italiae Illvstratae Regio XIIII Apvlia Incipit Feliciter *r*

2. supra *omitted in r*

3. *Froben:* pencetios *B:* penceticos *HQr*

4. Octavum *BH*

5. *Froben:* equmtutium *BHr,* equntutium *Q*

6. *Froben:* agrippa *mss., r*

7. *Froben:* pecentia *mss., r*

8. amicitiae *r*

9. expeditionibus *Froben:* expeditione una *BHr,* expeditio una *Q*

10. *Froben:* reatini *mss., r*

11. dictione *Hr*

12. pascuaque publica] pascua *H*

13. Galeranum *Froben:* -enum *mss., r*

14. confinium *r*

15. et et *H:* omitted in *Q*

16. B *Froben:* inopis *HQr*

17. Loveniscum *HQr:* Ioveniscum *B Froben*

18. *Froben:* petella *r,* perella *H,* perrella *Q*

19. Mons Saganus *B Froben:* mons aganus *HQ:* monsganus *r*

20. et a qua *Q*

21. et] in *Q*

22. passuum *Froben:* passus *mss., r*

23. Monti Sagano *Froben:* montiagano *mss., r*

24. cognomentum *Q*

25. *Froben:* passus *mss., r*

26. *Froben:* passus *mss., r*

27. mare *r*

28. quarto . . . miliario *Q*

29. Fortorii amnis *B*

30. *Froben:* passus *mss., r*

31. et *B: omitted in HQ, edd.*

32. *Froben:* passus *mss., r*

33. in *omitted in Froben*

34. *Froben:* passus *mss., r*

35. Cognatum *Froben*

36. Sitella *Froben*

37. cum *r*

38. maximae *r*

39. religione *r*

40. frequentatur *Q*

41. Normandorum *B*

42. asserit] incipit *H*

43. dimedis *r*

44. Garganeo *Froben*

45. *Froben:* passus *mss., r*

46. volit *(sic) r*

47. naves *Q*

48. adulare *Augustine*

49. tamque *Augustine*

50. perimant *Augustine:* perhibeant *BH,* -bent *Q*

51. appellant *Q*

52. canonici regulares *HQ, edd.*: ordinis Sancti Georgii in Alga *B*

53. *Froben*: garganii *mss., r*

54. *B, Froben*: pelagum *HQr*

55. *Froben, Lucan*: adriaticas *mss., r*

56. *Froben*: nullum *mss.*, nulla *r*

57. *r*: praestiterint *mss., Froben*

58. tostidem *r*

59. Fortori *r*

60. Rome in domo Nobilis viri Iohannis Philippi de Lignamine Messanensis. S. D. N. familiaris. hic liber impressus est Anno domini MCCCCLXXIIII Die vero lune quinta Mensis Decembris. Pont. Sixti IIII Anno Quarto. *subscribed in r*

APPENDIX

1. neque . . . neque *H*

2. propositos *H*

3. perclusus *before correction H*

4. ne *H*

5. magis magisque *H*

6. alibi a nobis *H*

7. Neapolitanum quoque *H*

8. fergoso *H*

9. *H*: adversum *E*

10. fuerat comminatus *H*

11. permisit *H*

12. Gravium *H*

13. Maumethus *H*

14. Peyram *H*

15. Bosphoraneumque *H*

16. Savona *H*

17. illis *H*

18. Bosphoraneis *H*

19. ad *H*

20. emissorium *H*

21. Nam *H*

22. praesenti anno *H*

23. iactam *H*

24. quam *H*

25. diximus fuisse *before correction H*

26. urbi *H: omitted in E*

27. Putriolo *H*

28. *E*: paulum *H*

29. et solis *H*

30. et venatorem *H*

31. solo *omitted in E*

32. versum *E*

33. promentem *H*

34. se *H*

35. dimidiam *H*

36. prius *H: omitted in E*

37. Alciniam . . . Alciniam . . . Alcinia *H*

38. urbe *H*

39. ignoraremus *H*

40. referri *H*

41. genitor *H*: genitor pater *E*

42. effecit *H*: efficit *E*

43. dignas *H*

44. fundamenta *H*

45. de] de tuo *H*

46. Ea *E*

47. contemplarerque *H*: contemplaremque *E*

48. ipsa *H*

49. profecto *H*

50. quoque *H*

51. inhabitaverit *H*: inhabitavit *E*

52. principium *H*

53. et cura *H*

54. attrebatensis *H*

55. audiverimus *H*

56. causam *EH*

57. stoutevilla *H*

58. Clanes *H*

59. ostendit *before correction H*

60. Anglariam *H*

61. offendentibus *H*

Notes to the Translation

꙲ᠻᠻ꙲

ABBREVIATIONS

Biondo, *History*	Biondo Flavio, *Historiarum ab inclinato Romanorum libri XXXII*, in *Blondi Flavii De Roma triumphante libri X* . . . (Basel: Froben, 1559)
Castner	Catherine J. Castner, *Biondo Flavio's Italia illustrata: Text, Translation, and Commentary*. 2 vols. (Binghamton, NY, 2005–10)
CIL	*Corpus inscriptionum latinarum* (Berlin: G. Reimer, 1894–)
DBI	*Dizionario biografico degli italiani* (Rome: Treccani, 1960–)
RE	*Paulys Real-Encyclopädie der classischen Altertumswissenschaft: neue Bearbeitung . . . von Georg Wissowa* (Stuttgart, 1894–1980). With *Supplement* (1903–80)
R.I.	Biondo Flavio, *Roma instaurata*, in *Blondi Flavii De Roma triumphante libri X* . . . (Basel: Froben, 1559)
RIS	Rerum italicarum scriptores
S.H.A.	Scriptores Historiae Augustae

7. LOMBARDY

1. The *torrente* Scoltenna, ancient *Scultenna*, becomes the Panaro on the plain, where it feeds into the Po (as Biondo says in §2). See *Romagna* §66, and note.

2. See *Romagna* §3. Adrian was pope from 772 to 795. Charlemagne met him at Rome immediately after his defeat of the Lombards, while his army was still besieging Pavia, at Easter 774, resulting in the "Donation of Charlemagne."

3. Pliny the Elder, *Natural History* 3.122: the town of "Bodincomagus" was on the river "Bodincus," the Ligurian name for the Po; it was not at Bondeno, however, but far away in the present province of Turin.

4. Biondo, *History* 126h.

5. Livy 39.55.6–7.

6. Livy, *Periochae* 118.7–9.

7. A condensation of Livy, *Periochae* 119.11–18.

8. Pliny the Elder, *Natural History* 2.240, who speaks of spontaneous eruptions of fire from the earth on days sacred to Vulcan, *statis Volcano diebus*. Biondo understands the *Vulcanum* of his text of Pliny to mean *ignis* or *flamma*.

9. O. Cuntz, ed., *Itineraria Antonini Augusti et Burdigalense* (Leipzig, 1929), p. 281.9.

10. *Romagna* §77, where Biondo expresses his belief that this branch had formed in the last hundred years. The branches of the Po have greatly altered again since his time.

11. Lodovico III (d. 1478), student of Vittorino da Feltre, humanist-prince, and patron of the arts.

12. Originally from Modena, the Pio held Carpi from the times of the dynast Manfredo Pio (d. 1348) until 1527.

13. The Torrente Dragone.

14. The Abbey of S. Benedetto di Polirone on the Po, a Benedictine foundation of 1007, was actually built by Matilda of Canossa's grandfather, Tedaldo, a century before she made her benefactions.

15. §3 above.

16. Frontinus, *Strategemata* 4.138, who means the Calabrian Regium (Reggio di Calabria): Frontinus omits *Lepidum* and reads *sepelire* for Biondo's *sepeliri*.

17. Biondo, *History* 200f, referring to the days January 25–27, 1077.

18. Of 1095 (Urban) and 1106 (Paschal, his successor).

19. Rothari was king from 636 to 652.

20. See §21 below, with note 91.

21. Compare Livy 21.25.3–13.

22. *Romagna* §17. Biondo means he is reusing the quotation of Livy.

23. Livy 32.30.4. Modern texts read at the end *tutandum*, "to protect their country," not *Tannetum*.

24. In 552; Biondo, *History* 90g-h.

25. Buccellinus was preparing to winter in Campania in 554. This *Tannetum*, in the vicinity of Capua, cannot be the Emilian Taneto. See Paulus Diaconus, *Historiarum Langobardorum libri VI* (in L. Bethmann and G. Waitz, *Pauli Historia Langobardorum* [Hannover, 1878]), 2.2. Paul the Deacon (d. ca. 799), member of an old Lombard family, was a monk of Benevento and Montecassino, and at the Aachen of Charlemagne: scholar, poet, chronicler, homilist, his widely read *History of the Lombards* covers the period 568 to 744.

26. Biondo writes Livy in error for Pliny (*Natural History* 7.163, quoted again in §8).

27. The strategically important town of Colorno was under the lordship of the Correggio of Parma till 1612.

28. Livy 39.55.7.

29. Cassius Parmensis (*RE* 47), the tyrannicide, whom Horace has as a poet (*Epist.* 1.4.3), and Cassius Chaerea (*RE* 37), the centurion, one of the murderers of Caligula.

30. Astrologer and mathematician, teacher of Vittorino da Feltre, died 1416. For the confusion of his tomb in Parma cathedral with that of Macrobius, see Roberto Weiss, *The Renaissance Discovery of Classical Antiquity* (Oxford: Blackwell, 1969), pp. 121–22.

31. Pliny the Elder, *Natural History* 7.163.

32. Martial 5.13.8.

33. The first three towns cannot be identified, as Bonaventura Angeli complained more than four centuries ago (*Historia della città di Parma et descrittione del fiume Parma* [Parma, 1591], p. 753). Belforte in the province of Parma is not on the Parma River but on the Taro (downstream from Borgo Val di Taro). It looks as if Biondo's geographical information is more than usually confused at this point.

34. An eighth-century Benedictine foundation. Liutprand (r. 712–744) was the ablest of the kings of Lombardy.

35. Borgo San Donnino was renamed Fidenza (the Roman *Fidentia*) in 1927.

36. "S. Colombano" appears to refer to Vernasca in the Apennines, with its ancient church dedicated to St. Columban. Since Biondo refers to present-day Fidenza as "Borgo S. Donnino," he presumably regards *Fidentiola* as modern Fiorenzuola (d'Arda), the next town along on the via Aemilia.

37. Livy, *Periochae* 88.1–2: For *Fidentiolamque*, Livy's text has *Fidentiamque*.

38. Asconius 3.5–10. The triumvirs of the (vexed) text are: P. Cornelius Asina, P. Papirius Maso, Cn. Cornelius Scipio; the year was 218 BCE.

39. Livy, *Periochae* 20.18.

40. Livy 27.39.11. Livy says that the colony's celebrity had "led him (*induxerat eum*) to think that by destroying it he would strike terror into the rest," the last clause omitted in Biondo's quotation.

41. Paraphrasing Livy 28.11.10–11.

42. Historia Augusta, *Aurelian* 21.1–2.

43. Livy 21.57.6–14.

44. Cicero, *Brutus* 172.

45. The words attributed to Cicero are not in *Pro Murena* but in *In Pisonem*, 87 (and cf. frags. ix–x). Caesar's father-in-law was Lucius Calpurnius Piso Caesoninus (*RE* 90), the object of Cicero's invective; his father, the Placentine armorer, was Gnaeus Calpurnius Piso.

46. Tedaldo Visconti (r. 1271–76). The (second) Council of Lyon opened in May 1274.

47. Pliny the Elder, *Natural History* 7.163.

48. §8 above.

49. In 1402.

50. See §41, with note 185 below.

51. In 1447.

52. Hannibal's first Italian victory, over Tiberius Sempronius Longus, in 218 BCE.

53. Biondo seems to be confusing the Irish missionary companions Sts. Gall and Columban: St. Columban founded the monastery of Bobbio in 614. Under the influence of his wife, Theodolinda (d. 628), the Lombard king Agilulf gave Columban the land for his abbey. When Agilulf died, Theodolinda ruled for the last ten years of her life with her son Adoald.

54. It seems likely that Biondo here means to refer not to S. Giovanni (Castel S. Giovanni, mentioned in the next sentence, is on the Po west of Piacenza), but to S. Stefano (d'Aveto), near which is the present-day village of Allegrezze.

55. Livy 21.48.8–9.

56. Livy 32.29.6–8, a close paraphrase, with textual discrepancies. *Litubium* has traditionally been identified with Retorbido, five miles southwest of Casteggio.

57. Borso, who succeeded his brother Leonello in 1450 as duke of Ferrara, Modena, and Reggio, ruled over Castelnuovo until his death in 1471. The gift of Filippo Maria Visconti, third duke of Milan (d. 1447), must have preceded Borsos's ascent to the dukedom.

58. Moncalieri is now a southern suburb of Turin.

59. The dynasty lasted in Monferrato from 1306 to 1533.

60. Later cardinal of S. Teodoro (1467–84).

61. Pliny the Elder, *Natural History* 3.49 (where *Valentinum* is read, not *Valentium*).

62. Called the Casale of St. Evasius by our author, the saint of Asti having supposedly been executed there under Julian the Apostate in 362.

63. Cane effectively controlled the duchy of Milan from the death of Gian Galeazzo Visconti in 1402 until his own death at Pavia in 1412.

64. Ludovico I, 1406–75.

65. Alexander III (Orlando Bandinelli, a Sienese) was pontiff from 1159 to 1181.

66. The *casane astigiane* were the major banking families of Asti in the Middle Ages, taking advantage of their location on the trade routes to the fairs of Champagne. In 1389 the town was given to the duke of Orlé-

ans (Louis de Valois) as the dowry of his wife, Valentina, daughter of Gian Galeazzo Visconti, duke of Milan.

67. Pliny the Elder, *Natural History* 3.49. Gnaeus Plancius (*RE* 4), friend and client of Cicero (see Cicero, *Pro Plancio*).

68. Pliny the Elder, *Natural History* 3.49, that is, *Alba Pompeia.*

69. The Scarampo were a prominent Ghibelline family of Asti and feudatories of towns in the Langhe district south of Alba; their ancestral home, the "Caminata," survives in Cairo Montenotte. For the Del Caretto, see *Liguria* §23 and note. On the Ligurian *riviere*, see *Liguria* §29.

70. Distrusted by the Visconti (under whom he had established himself as captain), Carmagnola went over to the Venetians: they suspected him of collusion with his old employers and beheaded him in St. Mark's Square in 1432

71. Pliny the Elder, *Natural History* 2.229 and 3.117. Biondo seems to have teased a proper noun *Visundum* out of the epithet *visendum* ("worth a look") in the second passage of Pliny.

72. Servius ad *Aen.* 6.659, relating *apud inferos* (among the dead) to *Mare Inferum*, the usual Roman name for the Tyrrhenian Sea, as *Mare Superum* for the Adriatic.

73. Ibid. See also Ovid, *Metamorphoses* 2.324; Hyginus, *Fabulae* 154; compare Vergil, *Aeneid* 10.190. Phaëthon, son of the Sun (Helios), fell from heaven into the river Eridanus, identified by the Romans with the Po.

74. Pliny the Elder, *Natural History* 18.101, discussing the use around the Po of Italian millet, to which beans are added but no water: *circumpadana* [*Italia panico utitur*] *addita faba sine aqua* (Biondo read with the manuscripts *sine qua*).

75. Pliny the Elder, *Natural History* 18.128, after grapes and wheat.

76. After defeat at Chalons (451) by Aëtius, Attila turned to Italy. In 452 he was met at the Mincio by Pope Leo I and a deputation, which in the legend included Sts. Peter and Paul, and was mysteriously discouraged from continuing on to Rome.

77. *Tuscany* §2. Livy 5.33.9–10.

78. Vergil, *Aeneid* 10.201.

79. Martial 1.61.2.

80. Livy 32.30.4–5. Also cited at §7 above, where see note.

81. Livy 24.10.7.

82. *Eclogues* 9.28. Vergil alludes to land confiscations carried out by the Second Triumvirate at the end of the Roman Republic, which were extended from Cremona to neighboring Mantua.

83. Biondo, *History* 117d, 176f.

84. St. Longinus, the soldier who pierced Jesus's side on Calvary, brought Christianity and Christ's blood to Mantua, where it was kept in a reliquary in the church of Sant'Andrea. Leo II was pope in 682–83. Biondo means Pope Leo III (d. 816), who established a diocese of Mantua and who had cordial relations with Charlemagne. Leo IX recognized the blood's genuineness in 1053.

85. See *Tuscany* §42, with note. Biondo here confuses Nicholas II (r. 1058–61), who passed the decree concerning papal elections at the Lateran synod of April 1059, with his successor Alexander II (r. 1061–73), who convened a synod at Mantua in May 1064.

86. The Gonzaga ruled over Mantua from 1328 into the eighteenth century. Gianfrancesco, the first marquis (d. 1444), married Paolo Malatesta da Rimini (d. 1449) and brought Vittorino to Mantua to educate their children, setting him up in the famous Ca' Giocosa; he founded the university (*Studio pubblico*) at Mantua and was a patron of humanists. His son Ludovico Gonzaga (d. 1478) succeeded him and proved to be an even more generous patron of learning, to Vittorino, Guarino, Platina, Filelfo among others.

87. Cavriani (sometimes recorded as Capriani) was bishop of Mantua from 1444 till his death in 1466, a favorite of Eugenius IV and Pius II.

88. Particularly by Mastino II della Scala in the fourteenth century. The della Scala (or Scaligeri) were lords of Verona from 1277 to 1387.

89. Vergil, *Aeneid*, 10.205–6.

90. Biondo, *History* 541d–42g. The episode was known as *galeas per montes* and became famous throughout Europe.

91. The place-names are more than usually shaky here. The small lake may be either the Lago di S. Massenza or the neighboring Lago di Toblino; above them is Vezzano, presumably Biondo's *Vocianum*. *Pontionum* seems to represent modern Pinzolo, a long way up the Sarca valley, and *Sancta Maria* is doubtless Madonna di Campiglio, still further into the Dolomites.

92. Paulus Diaconus, *Historia Langobardorum* 5.5: "qui locus, ubi hoc gestum est proelium, Francorum usque hodie Rivus appellatur, nec longe distat ab Astensis civitatis liminibus." The location of the battle in 663 was actually Refrancore in the province (as Paulus indicates) of Asti.

93. Just as the neighboring Marquis d'Este did at Stellata, §4 above.

94. Nothing in the vicinity closely responds to the Latin name *Brocium* (the same problem attaches to *Brotium* in §9). It most likely stands for Berzo (Inferiore) just to the south of Cividate, or conceivably Borno to the west; *Brenum* in Froben's text looks like a banalization to accord with the larger settlement of Breno to the northeast.

95. Justin, *Epitome* 20.5.7–9.

96. Livy 32.30.6 and 5.35.1.

97. Livy 21.25.9–14, in paraphrase. Livy's text says that Lucius Manlius was the Roman commander and that seven hundred Roman soldiers were lost (eight hundred in some manuscripts, and so in the first use of this passage in §7 above).

98. Livy 32.30.5–6, and see §17 above. Livy has *agrum suum tutandum* for *agrum suum*, *Tannetum*.

99. Biondo's old friend, humanist, and statesman (d. 1454); see his praises sung in *Venice* §26, below. He was the Venetian *capitano* (governing magistrate) of Brescia in the years 1437 to 1440, when Piccinino's Milanese forces had it under siege. See his life by G. Gualdo in *DBI* 6 (1964): 101–3, and on his friendship with Biondo, P. Gothein, *Francesco Barbaro* (Berlin, 1932), pp. 126–39.

100. Aulus Vitellius (*RE* Suppl. 9, 7b), emperor in 69 CE, destroyed Cremona in the same year. Viadana derives as a name from *Vitelliana*.

101. Among the *condottieri* of the late Duke Filippo Maria Visconti, there was a Broccardo Persico, an enemy of the Sforza.

102. Livy 21.25, 2.

103. Vergil, *Eclogues* 9.28, "Alas for Mantua, too close to poor Cremona!" as in §18 above (with note).

104. §41 below.

105. Bibaculus (b. 103 BCE, according to Jerome), pupil of Valerius Cato, connected with the *novi poetae*. Quintilius was a friend of Horace and a kinsman of Vergil. Eusebius of Cremona (d. after 420) was a friend of Jerome and his unscrupulous ally against Rufinus: Biondo seems to have mixed him up with Eusebius of Caesarea, the "Father of Church History."

106. Also Rhazes, or Razi (Mohammed-abu-Bekr-ibn-Zacaria; d. 923). Physician, philosopher, alchemist, his medical text was called the *Almansor*.

107. Biondo runs together the minor astrologer Gerardo da Sabbioneta with his better known contemporary Gerardo da Cremona (the correct ascription of some of their scientific works is still controversial). Gerardo da Cremona lived in Toledo for forty years, where he died in 1187 after prodigious labors in the translation of Arab scientific works into Latin, as well as Greek works, Aristotle especially, from Arabic into Latin; see the unsigned life in *DBI* 53 (2000): 620–33. By "Chaldean," Biondo presumably means Syriac.

108. Niccolò later became archbishop of Milan (1453) but died soon afterward. His brother was the secretary of Francesco Sforza, duke of Milan.

109. On July 25, 1406, Ugolino and Carlo Cavalcabò, successive *signori* of Cremona, were murdered along with other members of the family by their captain Gabrino Fondulo, who took over the city himself.

110. Or Ambrogio da Vignate, of the noble Guelf family of Lodi, professor at the University of Turin in the middle of the fifteenth century.

111. Born at Lodi in 1407, studied in Milan, taught at the University of Pavia. A lover of Vergil, he composed a Book 13 for the *Aeneid*. He con-

nected professionally (as notary, datary, canon of St. Peter's) with Martin V, Eugenius IV, Nicholas V, and after 1455 was an Augustinian.

112. Servius on Vergil, *Georgics* 4.127; Lucan, *Pharsalia* 1.344–45.

113. Pliny the Elder, *Natural History* 3.124. Pliny says that Lodi Vecchio was founded by Transalpine *Boii*, that the *Laevi* and *Marici* founded *Ticinum* (now Pavia), not Lodi, and that the city was called *Laus Pompeia*.

114. Biondo, *History* 30e. Odoacer, a Scirian German, leading mutinous German troops of the Roman army against Orestes, checked him at Lodi, besieged him within Pavia, and had him beheaded at Piacenza. He allowed Orestes's son, the teenaged Romulus Augustulus (nominally the last Roman Emperor of the West), to live. Odoacer ruled Italy from 476 to his death in 493.

115. §20 above.

116. Poschiavino is, at least nowadays, the name of the river (largely in the Swiss canton of Graubünden) that flows through the town of Poschiavo and the lake of the same name.

117. Justin, *Epitome* 20.5.7–9.

118. Pliny the Elder, *Natural History* 3.124, also drawn on in §28 below. Modern texts read *Oromobiorum* or *Orumbiviorum*.

119. The famous humanist educator. On his role in the transmission of the text of Cicero's long-lost *Brutus*, see *Romagna* §29. Also, J. White, *Latomus* 38 (1979): 223–24.

120. In §24.

121. In the battle of Caravaggio (September 15, 1448), Francesco Sforza's Milanese troops routed the Venetian forces under Colleoni.

122. Biondo, *Romagna* §§ 40, 46, and 51. Alberico da Barbiano (d. 1433), the nephew and namesake of the great *condottiere*, received Belgioioso as a fief from Filippo Maria Visconti (= Filippo Maria Angelo) in 1431; his son Luigi (d. after 1471) was lord of Belgioioso at the time of writing: Alberico III and Malatesta will be his sons.

123. §27 above, with note.

124. §27 above, with note.

125. Pliny the Elder, *Natural History* 3.124. By "Cornelius Alexander," Biondo means the "Polyhistor," Alexander of Miletus, whom Pliny quotes.

126. Catullus 35.1–7.

127. Pliny the Elder, *Natural History* 2.232.

128. Pliny the Elder, *Natural History* 3.131.

129. Pliny the Elder, *Natural History* 36.159.

130. Paulus Diaconus, *Historiae Langobardorum* 3.27, 4.3.

131. Strangely, Biondo was unaware that the Isola Comacina lay just off Ossuccio on the western shore of the western arm of lower Lake Como. What he goes on to say is equally strange, if the text is right.

132. Pliny the Elder, *Natural History* 10.77.

133. Supposedly Charlemagne's, the iron portion of it beaten out of a nail from the True Cross.

134. King of the Ostrogoths, Theodoric killed Odoacer and ruled Italy from 493 to 526.

135. St. Gregory the Great, Pope Gregory I (590–604). The *Dialogues* are not universally accepted as genuine. On Theodolinda, see §34 below, with note.

136. It seems that the text is defective, since the geography does not make sense: the *torrente* Breggia flows into Lake Como from the west below Cernobbio and above the town of Como, while the Lago di Pusiano (*Eupilus*) and the Lambro flowing out of it lie to the east of the lake.

137. This information, which really relates to the present Chur in Graubünden, Switzerland (capital of the Raeti, or the Roman province of Raetia), is not found in Pliny's *Natural History*.

138. Justin, *Epitome* 20.5.7–10 (their leader was named Raetus).

139. Pliny the Elder, *Natural History* 3.124: and see §25 above, with note.

140. Livy 21.39.10.

141. Livy 21.45.1–2.

142. Livy 21.46.7–8.

143. As above, §25. Attila had sacked the city in 452.

144. Alboin (r. 565–572) laid the city under siege for three years. In 569, Pavia succumbed, and Alboin made it his capital.

145. Pope from 924 to 926.

146. Alonda, that is, Adelheid, or St. Adelaide (d. 999).

147. Biondo's Latin rendering of S. Pietro in Ciel d'Oro, which preserves St. Augustine's remains, and those of Boethius.

148. That is, Corteolona.

149. Perctarit (d. 688) championed Catholicism over Arianism and kept peace with the Byzantine Greeks, as also with the Roman element of his population. Gondiberta (Gundiperga) was the daughter of Agilulf and Theodolinda.

150. For example, *History* 60g and index s.v. *papia*.

151. From the Burgundian Gondebald (Gundobad), shortly before Epiphanius's death in 496. Epiphanius had rebuilt Pavia after its destruction by Odoacer.

152. In April 984, the antipope Boniface VII, restored from Constantinople by followers of Crescentius and reinstalled in Rome, imprisoned the legitimate pope, John XIV (not XVIII), in the Castel Sant'Angelo (as he had Benedict VI), where he died, probably murdered by Boniface's adherents.

153. A friend and contemporary of Valla, Sacco taught law at the Studio of Pavia, where he founded a college for the needy. He was a central figure in Pavian humanism. For the jurist Sillano Negri (d. 1457), see the entry by C. Storti in *Dizionario biografico dei giuristi italiani*, ed. I. Birocchi et al. (Bologna, 2013), pp. 1417–18.

154. The Naviglio Grande.

155. P. C. Decembrio (1392–1477) was a student of Chrysoloras, broadly learned and prolific. He was variously attached to Filippo Maria Visconti, Alfonso I d'Aragona, Nicholas V, and Pius II, and he acted as a literary agent of Humfrey, Duke of Gloucester. Decembrio had, through Iñigo d'Avalos and Bessarion, sought help for Biondo from Alfonso at the beginning of his financial troubles in 1448 (see Fubini in *DBI* 10 [1968]: 548 f.).

156. Paulus Diaconus, *Historia Langobardorum* 3.35.

157. Theodolinda or Theodelinda (d. 628), an effective champion of Athanasian Christianity against Arianism.

158. That is, the region called Lomellina.

159. Pliny the Elder, *Natural History* 19.9.

160. Perhaps owing to a defective text, Biondo distorts what Pliny says in the *Natural History* 3.124: "Novaria ⟨orta⟩ ex Vertamacoris, Vocontiorum hodieque pago" ("Novara was founded from Vertamacori, a place belonging to the Vocontii and nowadays a village").

161. Eusebius 250.12–13: and see Seneca the Elder, *Controversies* 9, *Preface* 1–9, and Suetonius, *On the Rhetoricians* 6.

162. Fra Dolcino Tornielli assumed leadership of the sect of the "Apostolici" after its founder, Gherardo Segarelli, was burned at the stake at Parma in 1300. It stressed apostolic poverty and penance. Clement's crusade against the sect concluded with Dolcino's death on March 23, 1307. On "Dolcin," see Dante, *Inferno* 28.55–60.

163. Now known as Monte Rosa, the tallest mountain in Switzerland, where its highest peak lies (4637 meters) and the second highest massif in the Alps after Mont Blanc.

164. Biondo regards the name, Gazzada, *Mons Gazarorum*, as an etymological expression of Apostolic heretical beliefs, from Italian *gazzari*, "Cathars."

165. Castelletto sopra Ticino, set on the river like Abbiategrasso in §34.

166. The geography is confusing here, Mergozzo being at the northwest tip of the lake and Castelletto at the very bottom, where the Ticino exits. What Biondo calls the Gravellone must be the torrent now called Strona, which flows through the town of Gravellona Toce from the river Toce before the latter enters Maggiore. The Gravellone, which flows into the Ticino near Pavia (§34), is a different watercourse.

167. Such language (*coruscare, vibrare*, etc., with *miraculis*, as often) communicating the curative or restorative powers, the magical energies, that the relics possess. The lake is today the Lago d'Orta (Biondo's mention

of Lago di Mergozzo in the next sentence seems rather to refer to Lago d'Orta).

168. Biondo names the lake here as Lago d'Iseo (*Lacus Sebuinus:* see §20), but the lake that the Ticino enters at Magadino is Maggiore, more than one hundred miles from Iseo.

169. Mediolanum, in Biondo's view wrongly taken to denote something "in the middle" (*medio*), is in fact one of the commonest and oldest Celtic place-names: thirty-six are recorded, mostly within modern France.

170. Livy 5.34.9 and 3, and Justin, *Epitome* 20.5.7–9.

171. Florus, *Epitome* 1.20.1 and 3, paraphrased, where the Gaulish leader is named as Brittomarus. Literally, the Gauls would "not loosen their sword belts" till they were on the Capitol, the heart of Rome.

172. Eusebius 220.20–24.

173. Livy, *Periochae* 20.9, referring to 222 BCE (which would be 532 AUC., the year from the foundation of Rome).

174. Livy 30.18.1–19.5.

175. Livy 31.21.1–18.

176. Livy 31.47.6–49.7.

177. That is, Constantius Gallus 325–54.

178. Eusebius 322.4.

179. Eusebius 329.16–18. Auxentius, the Arian bishop of Milan who was declared a heretic after his death, was able to hold his see until he died in 374, being succeeded by the Catholic Ambrose. The passage in Ambrose's *Homilies* regarding his exile has not been traced.

180. The canonist Orlando Bandinelli, Alexander III (r. 1159–81), whose support of the Lombard league against Barbarossa led to an eighteen-year schism and a succession of imperial antipopes.

181. The rivalry was bitter and gruesome. The Torriani (della Torre), lords of the Valsassina, had been eclipsed by the Visconti by the end of the thirteenth century. Biondo's date of 1276 probably refers to the battle of Desio of January 21, 1277, and the victory of Ottone Visconti, archbishop of Milan, over Napo della Torre and his kin and allies.

182. Clement VI was pope from 1342 to 1352: his appointees, Luchino (d. 1349) and Giovanni (d. 1354) were the uncles of the moderate Azzo Visconti (1302–39), whose rule over Milan reverted to them when he died childless. Gian Galeazzo (Duke of Milan from 1395, d. 1402), was a generous patron of learning, as well as an astute, vicious, and complex ruler.

183. Candia was the Venetian name for Crete. Candiano (Pietro Filargo) acted as Gian Galeazzo's ambassador on many diplomatic missions. As antipope, he reigned 1409–10. An unlikely hypothesis has him coming from Candia in Piemonte (Clavuot, *Arbeitsmethoden*, p. 122 and n. 326).

184. Muratori *RIS* 16.821c–d.

185. The "Ambrosian Republic" of 1447–50.

186. Alexander I (r. 1061–73), Urban III (1185–87), Celestine IV (October–November 1241). Bishop Datius (d. 552) opposed the Arian Ostrogoths, who imprisoned him in his city. He was a friend of Cassiodorus and exiled to Constantinople. Gregory writes of him in *Dialogues* 3.4; see also Clavuot, *Arbeitsmethoden*, p. 298 and n. 384.

187. *S.H.A.*, *Didius Julianus* 1.2.

188. *S.H.A.*, *The Two Valerians* 8.3.

189. *S.H.A.*, *Aurelian* 18.3. Biondo mistakenly writes of the younger Valerian instead of the later emperor Aurelian.

190. Twelfth-century jurist, an imperial judge under the emperor Lothair (1133–37), to whom was attributed the first redaction of the precedents of feudal law, the *Libri feudorum*.

191. A Milanese (d. 1425), he taught law at Parma, Pavia, and Siena. An advisor to the Duke of Milan.

192. Andrea Biglia of Milan (d. 1435), grammarian, historian, philosopher, theologian, he knew Greek and possibly some Hebrew, and taught at Bologna, Milan, Perugia, and Siena. He was a friend of Aurispa and Traversari. See *DBI* 10 (1968): 413–15. He wrote *Libri novem historiae Mediolanensis et Lombardicae*. Da Rho (*Raudensis*), a Conventual Franciscan (1395–ca. 1447), succeeded Barzizza as professor of eloquence at Milan in 1431 (see *DBI* 3 (1961): 574–77). Biondo would have known and admired his *De imitatione Latinae eloquentiae*.

193. Brippio or Brivio, poet, died 1457; his sculpted tomb survives in the church of St. Alessio, Rome. See the life by M. Miglio in *DBI* 14 (1972): 355–58.

194. Martial 10.12.1.

195. Pliny the Elder, *Natural History* 3.124: "Vercellae Libiciorum ex Salluis ortae" ("Vercelli of the Libicii, founded by the Sallui") — the Sallui, or Salluvi, were the first inhabitants, followed by the related Celtic or Ligurian Libici.

196. Pliny the Elder, *Natural History* 33.78: the text of Pliny has *cavebatur*.

197. Eusebius 321.25–326.3 and 324.20.

198. The emperor Constantius III (d. 421).

199. Biondo, *History* 18e–f. Joannes was executed and Valentinian III established as Western emperor in 425: Ardaburus (sent by Theodosius) and Castinus (Joannes's *Magister militum* and Galla Placidia's enemy) would have clashed then.

200. Ceccolo Broglia (Broglia da Tridino), *condottiere* and captain, alumnus of Alberico's Compagnia di San Giorgio, dead in July 1400.

201. The Cistercian foundation of 1123.

202. Pliny the Elder, *Natural History* 3.123.

203. Ibid.; that is, the Little (Hercules) and Great (Carthaginians) St. Bernard passes.

204. Pliny the Elder, *Natural History* 3.136–38.

205. That is, San Benigno Canavese, with the Benedictine abbey of Fruttuaria, founded in 1003, on its outskirts.

206. Livy 21.38.5–6, 21.39.1, 4.

207. Towns on either side of the river Stura di Lanzo, in its lower reaches, now forming the northern boundary of Turin.

208. A twelfth-century foundation of the monks of the Hospitaller Order of St. Anthony of Vienne.

209. The abbey of Santa Maria di Pinerolo, founded by Countess Adelaide in 1064.

210. Modern Turin. Pliny the Elder, *Natural History* 3.123.

211. Livy 21.37.2.

8. VENICE

1. See *Romagna* §70.

2. As, for example, *Lazio* §19.

3. Biondo, *History* 31a.

4. *Andreae Danduli Chronica per extensum descripta*, in RIS² 12.1 (Bologna, 1938), 220, 2–5 (henceforth cited as Dandolo, *Chronicle*, with page and line number).

5. Dandolo, *Chronicle* 96, 24–29.

6. O. Cuntz, ed., *Itineraria Antonini Augusti et Burdigalense* (Leipzig, 1929), p. 126.6.

7. Vergil, *Aeneid* 1.244–46. See *March of Treviso* §27 below, where Biondo develops a mistaken identification of the ancient Timavus with the Brenta.

8. Biondo, *History* 31a–b.

9. Dandolo, *Chronicle* 58, 24–25 and 29.

10. Dandolo, *Chronicle* 59, 11–13.

11. Dandolo, *Chronicle* 60, 1–2.

12. Pliny the Elder, *Natural History* 3.121.

13. Dandolo, *Chronicle* 54, 6–7.

14. Biondo, *History* 89c–d. The Broglio (a medieval word for park or grove) later became the Piazza S. Marco; both churches have disappeared.

15. Dandolo, *Chronicle* 87, 20–26.

16. Vergil, *Aeneid* 6.743, "quisque suos patimur manes."

17. Dandolo, *Chronicle* 89, 20–22, 29, and 88, 19; and Biondo, *History* 116f.

18. Dandolo, *Chronicle* 95, 7–11.

19. Dandolo, *Chronicle* 95, 15–96, 1.

20. Dandolo, *Chronicle* 96, 9–11.

21. Dandolo, *Chronicle* 96, 24–29.

22. Dandolo, *Chronicle* 98, 30.

23. Dandolo, *Chronicle* 99, 27–28.

24. Dandolo, *Chronicle* 104, 40–106, 4.

25. On the river Piave, see *March of Treviso* §§41–44. Dandolo, *Chronicle* 108, 24–27.

26. Dandolo, *Chronicle* 112, 3–7, and 114, 18–19.

27. Dandolo, *Chronicle* 114, 21–24, and 115, 6–7.

28. Dandolo, *Chronicle* 116, 6, 10–11.

29. He was actually termed "Consul," according to Dandolo, *Chronicle* 116, 13–17.

30. Usually known as Teodato Ipato, the latter element, as with his father, Orso Ipato, in reality a Byzantine title, *hypatos*, the Greek equivalent of *consul*. Dandolo, *Chronicle* 117, 37–39.

31. Dandolo, *Chronicle* 118, 12–14.

32. Dandolo, *Chronicle* 118, 16–20.

33. Dandolo, *Chronicle* 119, 18–19.

34. Dandolo, *Chronicle* 122, 33–123, 3.

35. Dandolo, *Chronicle* 121, 22–25.

36. Dandolo, *Chronicle* 126, 19–22.

37. Dandolo, *Chronicle* 127, 33–40.

38. Dandolo, *Chronicle* 128, 1–5.

39. Biondo, *History* 165a–b and 166h.

40. Dandolo, *Chronicle* 129, 20–27.

41. Dandolo, *Chronicle* 139, 34–140, 7.

42. Biondo means that the town was deserted but retained a titular bishop. Dandolo, *Chronicle* 141, 23–25.

43. Dandolo, *Chronicle* 142, 10.

44. Dandolo, *Chronicle* 142, 32–143, 3.

45. Dandolo, *Chronicle* 144, 41–145, 6.

46. Dandolo, *Chronicle* 146, 1–3, 8–10.

47. Dandolo, *Chronicle* 146, 11, 14–15.

48. Dandolo, *Chronicle* 146, 24–25; and Biondo, *History* 172h–73c.

49. Dandolo, *Chronicle* 148, 14–17.

50. Dandolo, *Chronicle* 149, 1–4.

51. Dandolo, *Chronicle* 149, 15–16, 24–26.

52. Dandolo, *Chronicle* 149, 30–150, 3.

53. Dandolo, *Chronicle* 150, 5–6, 9–12.

54. See *Piceno* §15, with note 56. Dandolo, *Chronicle* 152, 18–19, 25–26.

55. Dandolo, *Chronicle* 153, 19–20.

56. Dandolo, *Chronicle* 155, 3–7.

57. Dandolo, *Chronicle* 155, 13–21.

58. Dandolo, *Chronicle* 160, 10–13; and Biondo, *History* 177d.

59. Biondo, *History* 177a and c–d.

60. Dandolo, *Chronicle* 161, 6–7, 9–10, 15–17.

61. Dandolo, *Chronicle* 163, 1–2, 4–6, 17–20.

62. Dandolo, *Chronicle* 163, 22, 30–33.

63. Dandolo, *Chronicle* 164, 5–8, 13–14.

64. Dandolo, *Chronicle* 164, 16, 25–27.

65. Dandolo, *Chronicle* 165, 29–34.

66. Dandolo, *Chronicle* 167, 29–37, 41–42.

67. Dandolo, *Chronicle* 168, 9–10, 13, 21–23, 30, 31.

68. Dandolo, *Chronicle* 170, 30.

69. Dandolo, *Chronicle* 179, 12–34.

70. Dandolo, *Chronicle* 179, 1, and 180, 14–16.

71. Dandolo, *Chronicle* 195, 12–13.

72. Dandolo, *Chronicle* 185, 23–26.

73. Dandolo, *Chronicle* 204, 1–2.

74. Dandolo, *Chronicle* 206, 1–5.

75. Dandolo, *Chronicle* 206, 9–15.

76. Dandolo, *Chronicle* 208, 12–15.

77. Dandolo, *Chronicle* 208, 17–19.

78. Dandolo, *Chronicle* 209, 27–210, 10.

79. Dandolo, *Chronicle* 213, 33–35 ("olibolensi litore").

80. Dandolo, *Chronicle* 225, 13–27; and Biondo, *History* 231b–c.

81. Dandolo, *Chronicle* 230, 16–22.

82. Dandolo, *Chronicle* 232, 1–3 (marginalia).

83. Dandolo, *Chronicle* 235, 5–6.

84. Dandolo, *Chronicle* 239, 10–11.

85. Dandolo, *Chronicle* 243, 20 (marginalia)

86. Dandolo, *Chronicle* 252, 28–253, 3.

87. Dandolo, *Chronicle* 278, 17–279, 25; and Biondo, *History* 271c.

88. Dandolo, *Chronicle* 295, 25–27.

89. Dandolo, *Chronicle* 296, 32–34.

90. Dandolo, *Chronicle* 313, 1–4.

91. Dandolo, *Chronicle* 314, 13–25.

92. Petrarch, *Letters* 8.5.14: ". . . miraculosissima civitas Venetia eiusque dux illustris, honoris quoque causa nominandus, Andreas, non minus bonarum artium studiis quam tanti magistratus insignibus vir clarus," and 19.9.13: "Atque utinam dux Andreas, qui tunc summe rerum preerat, hodie viveret. . . . bonum enim virum atque integrum sueque rei publice amantissimum michique amicissimum sciebam, doctum preterea et facundum et circumspectum et affabilem et mitem" (Francesco Petrarca, *Le Familiari*, ed. V. Rossi, 4 vols. (Florence, 1933–42), 2:172, 3:328). Dandolo came from an old ducal family and was doge himself (1343–54). Trained in letters and law, he had taught at the University of Padua. His *Chronica*

per extensum descripta (above, note 4) covers Venetian history down to 1280, and his *Chronica brevis* to 1342. See also *Liguria* §28, with note 69. On the procession of Venetian learned men that follows, see Margaret L. King, *Venetian Humanism in an Age of Patrician Dominance* (Princeton, 1986). The defining characteristic of their humanism is its civic and non-contemplative character; some common and distinctive features are high birth and connections by blood or marriage, education in the law at the University of Padua, participation in the governance of the city and colonial administration, ambassadorial service, military service, a focus on Church hierarchy.

93. Jean II Boucicault.

94. See *Funebris praestantissimi viri Leonardi Justiniani pro Carolo Zeno oratio*, in RIS² 19.6, pt. 2 (Bologna, 1941), pp. 141–46. In addition to his military service (he was author of the great victory over the Genoese at Chioggia in 1380), Zeno (1334–1418) had been student, businessman, traveler, envoy: a late-in-life humanist, he began Greek at eighty, and he was a friend of Chrysoloras, Vergerio, Guarino.

95. See Pier Paolo Vergerio, *Epistolario*, ed. L. Smith (Rome, 1934), epp. 87 and 104. On Pier Paolo Vergerio the Elder, see *Romagna* §25, with note 62. He wrote a history of Venice, *De republica Venetorum*, possibly at the suggestion of Zaccaria Trevisan (as next note).

96. Zaccaria Trevisan il Vecchio (d. 1414, of plague), studied at Padua and Bologna, was politician, diplomat (including in the service of the Venetian pope Gregory XII, Angelo Correr), scholar, collector of Greek and Roman manuscripts, teacher of Barbaro, friend of Barzizza, Bruni, Guarino, Salutati.

97. Pietro Miani or Emiliani (d. 1433), an influential humanist bishop of Vicenza from 1409. He had been a student of Chrysoloras and collected Greek as well as Latin texts. He knew Francesco Barbaro, Bruni, Guarino, Pietro del Monte (in whose *De nobilitate* he is an interlocutor), Ambrogio Traversari, and Pier Paolo Vergerio.

98. Leonardo Giustinian (ca.1389–1446), patrician brother of Lorenzo, the patriarch of Venice, and student of Guarino and Barzizza: consummate Venetian statesman-humanist, diplomat, merchant, soldier. He was

friend, patron, and correspondent of humanists, and a collector of Latin and Greek manuscripts. The ascription of various songs to him is problematic, yet the vernacular songs described by Biondo here are called *giustiniani*, after him. See also note 94 above.

99. Lippomano (d. after 1446), a legal expert, acquainted with oriental languages, including possibly Syriac (*Chaldaeas . . . litteras*). A politician and a soldier, he had wealth enough to collect books. He was a friend of Filelfo, Barbaro, and Ognibene Scola.

100. Paolo Nicoletti (d. 1429), always called "Paulus Venetus," or in English "Paul of Venice," an Augustinian, teacher, and voluminous and tireless writer in philosophy and theology. Some 279 titles are ascribed to him: see Alan R. Perreiah, *Paul of Venice: A Bibliographical Guide* (Bowling Green, OH, 1986).

101. Barbarigo (ca. 1380–1448/49), of a distinguished ducal family, held numerous posts within the Republic (Procurator of St. Mark's 1442). He enjoyed a scholarly and personal relationship with Guarino Veronese, was a student of Lactantius, a fine Latin prose stylist, and a composer of Latin verses. Daniele Vettori, a contemporary and political associate of Barbarigo, was probably a student of Barzizza and later of Lorenzo Bonzio in Venice.

102. Admiral, with great victories over the Turks (Gallipoli, 1416) and Genoese (Rapallo 1431), generalissimo, geopolitical strategist: Loredan unsuccessfully aspired to become doge as a rival of Francesco Foscari and was assassinated in 1439. Biondo served him as secretary (1427) at Brescia.

103. Gregory XII (Angelo Correr; pope 1406–15), advanced four nephews to the College of Cardinals (including Gabriele Condulmer, the future Eugenius IV). Antonio Correr (1369–1445) had an early connection with S. Giorgio in Alga (see *Tuscany* §42) and later became Latin Patriarch of Constantinople, and Cardinal Treasurer of the Holy Roman Church.

104. Cardinal Francesco Lando (d. 1427), patrician and jurisconsult, was Camerlengo of the Sacred College of cardinals. Pietro Morosini (d. 1424), canon of Treviso, jurisconsult (studied law at Bologna, professor

of law at the University of Padua), was appointed cardinal by Gregory XII in 1408.

105. Francesco Condulmer was cardinal from 1431 until his death in 1453. (Biondo uses *unicus* to contrast him with Gregory XII, who made four cardinalatial appointments from a single family.) He was cardinal bishop of Porto and, like Antonio Correr, Camerlengo of the Holy Roman Church. Biondo's *primum . . . locum* means that Condulmer was Dean of the College of Cardinals. (Condulmer is generally supposed to have forced Biondo to premature publication of the *Italia Illustrata*: see Introduction, vol. 1 [ITRL 20], p. xxi.)

106. Ludovico Trevisan (1401–65), Patriarch of Aquileia 1439–40, and his father, Biagio. Like his father, Ludovico was a physician: at Rome he became Cardinal Gabriele Condulmer's physician, and when Condulmer became Eugenius IV, Trevisan embarked on a distinguished and varied ecclesiastical career (including as soldier) and was eventually named cardinal and Camerlengo by Eugenius. He was the subject of a remarkable portrait by Mantegna now in Berlin.

107. Eutropius 7.21, regarding Titus, the son of Vespasian: Barbo was immensely popular as a cardinal. A businessman originally, Barbo's advancement through a church career was very quick once his uncle became pope. Though generally unfriendly to humanist learning and thought, it was in his reign as Pope Paul II (1464–71) that printing came to Italy and Rome, with Sweynheym and Pannartz and Ulrich Han.

108. Foscari was doge from 1423 to 1457, years consumed in land wars of very unhappy outcome — for the family of the Foscari and for imperial Venice — against Milan.

109. Francesco Barbaro (1390–1454), Biondo's great friend and patron (Biondo served as Barbaro's secretary at Vicenza [1425], for example, and Barbaro had written Alfonso d'Aragona for help with notices on the Regno for Biondo's ongoing work [1451]), was the very perfect type of Venetian aristocrat humanist/civil servant. He was Senator of the Republic and held numerous governorships and ambassadorial posts. A student of John of Ravenna and Guarino, he knew and translated from Greek (Plutarch) and was patron and friend of George of Trebizond.

110. For Andrea Morosini as mayor of Padua and dedicatee of a Lauro Quirini dialogue, see King, *Venetian Humanism*, pp. 164 and 419.

111. Ermolao Donato (d. 1450, murdered), aristocrat, was a civil servant, ambassador and soldier, friend of Francesco Barbaro. He was said to have written a verse history of his times in Latin.

112. The younger Zaccaria Trevisano, jurisconsult, was active politically in the mid-fifteenth century, as Biondo was writing.

113. On the lawyer, orator, and admiral Barbone Morosini (ca. 1414–ca. 1457), see King, *Venetian Humanism*, pp. 407–8. Ludovico (Alvise) Foscarini (1409–80) was an aristocrat and lawyer, and he served the Republic in Feltre, Vicenza, and Verona. His learning in the law was admired by Cyriac of Ancona and Pius II. He collaborated with Isotta Nogarola on a dialogue on gender identity (*De pari aut impari Evae atque Adae peccato*) in Verona in 1453 and enjoyed a Platonic friendship with her that Ermolao Barbaro discouraged. Vitale Lando (1421–ca. 1482) was the great-nephew of Cardinal Francesco Lando (note 104 above). He had a doctorate in laws from Padua, was Senator of the Republic, ambassador to Siena (1452), and governor and captain of Ravenna (1461). He knew Foscarini and Pietro Perleone. Candiano Bollani (1413–78) served the Republic as legate (Ferrara in 1452, Pordenone 1455) and colonial administrator (Belluno in 1460). He wrote a lost commentary on the *Rhetorica ad Herennium* and an extant commentary in the first three books of Genesis. Niccolò Canal (1415–83) was a student of literature and laws at Padua. He was a friend of Barbaro, Filelfo (who dedicated to him his translation of Xenophon, *Cyropaedia*), and Foscarini. He pursued with distinction the traditional Venetian civic *cursus*, for example, head of the Council of Ten in 1446, legate (Florence and Perugia in 1444, Constantinople 1460), captain (Brescia in 1451, Bergamo in 1456). As admiral, he was prosecuted by Bollani for his failure to recapture the island of Negroponte from the Turkish fleet in 1470. See A. Ventura in *DBI* 17 (1974): 662–68.

114. Lauro Quirini (1420–ca. 1475–79), born in and eventually returned to Crete, was a student of law at Padua (1443–48), taught Aristotle's *Ethics* at Venice, and Rhetoric and Moral Philosophy at Padua in 1451. He

collected Greek and Latin manuscripts; corresponded with Francesco and Zaccaria (son) Barbaro, Isotta Nogarola; and carried on literary feuds with Bruni and Poggio. See King, *Venetian Humanism*, pp. 419–21, and *Lauro Quirini umanista*, ed. Vittore Branca (Florence, 1974).

115. Giovanni Corner (ca. 1370–1452), a student of Cicero's rhetorical works and correspondent of Barzizza, collected manuscripts, friend of Cyriac and Pietro Perleone, patron of Filelfo: see King, *Venetian Humanism*, pp. 354–55.

116. Paolo Barbo (1416–62) was the nephew (through his mother) of Eugenius IV (Gabriele Condulmer), whom he served in Rome, and the brother of Paul II (Pietro Barbo, above §25, with note 107). On Eugenius's death in 1447, Barbo returned to Venice and devoted himself to Venetian political life and foreign service.

117. Andrea Giuliani (ca. 1384–1452) was a student of Barzizza and Guarino, served the Republic in Venice and abroad, and was correspondent and friend of Francesco Barbaro, Filelfo, and Leonardo Giustinian (§21). In 1415 he delivered the funeral oration for Chrysoloras. See King, *Venetian Humanism*, pp. 379–81.

118. Bernardo Giustiniani (1408–89) studied with Filelfo and Guarino and pursued political, trade, and learned interests. He was a passionate proponent of crusade against the Turks, translated from Isocrates, and wrote *De origine urbis Venetiarum rebusque gestis a Venetis*, printed in 1493. See King, *Venetian Humanism*, pp. 381–83.

119. Girolamo Barbarigo (ca. 1410–67, poisoned), politician, diplomat, of a ducal family: two brothers (Marco and Agostino) were doges. He was a correspondent of Decembrio, Barbaro, and Filelfo and a literary patron. He was an advocate of crusade against the Turks. See King, *Venetian Humanism*, pp. 319–20.

120. Niccolò Barbo (ca. 1420–62), student of George of Trebizond, and legate and colonial administrator. Letters and, particularly, an *Oratio in laudem Francisci Contareni* of his survive. He was a correspondent of Trebizond, Isotta Nogarola, Panormita, and Guarino. See King, *Venetian Humanism*, pp. 328–29.

121. Fantino Dandolo (1379–1459), student of Vittorino, and early humanist and collector of manuscripts. He was legate and administrator of the Republic, and later, archbishop of Crete, bishop of Padua. See King, *Venetian Humanism*, pp. 357–59.

122. Gregorio Correr (1409–64) was the nephew and, later, secretary of Cardinal Antonio Correr and great-nephew of Gregory XII, Angelo Correr. He studied with Vittorino and was made protonotary by Eugenius IV, another uncle. He wrote satires, hexameter songs, Aesopic fables, and a Senecan verse tragedy *Procne* (in *Humanist Tragedies*, ed. Gary Grund, I Tatti Renaissance Library 45 [Cambridge, MA, 2011], pp. xxvii–xxx, 110–87). He knew Biondo from Florence in 1434. Named Patriarch of Venice by Paul II, he died before taking up the appointment.

123. Ermolao Barbaro (the Elder, ca. 1410–71) was the nephew of Francesco Barbaro. He studied Latin and Greek with Guarino da Verona, and law at the University of Padua. Eugenius IV made him protonotary in 1435 and bishop of Treviso in 1443. Nicholas V made him bishop of Verona in 1453. See E. Bigi in *DBI* 6 (1964): 95–96.

124. Pietro da Monte (1404–57), student at the University of Padua, canon lawyer. He was a correspondent of Francesco Barbaro, Poggio, Traversari, and Decembrio, was bishop of Brescia (1442), and was papal governor of Perugia (1451–53). See King, *Venetian Humanism*, pp. 405–6.

125. Jacopo Zeno (ca. 1418–81), bishop of Feltre and Belluno (1447–60), and following Fantino Dandolo's death in 1459 bishop of Padua. A humanist with a large personal library of manuscripts, Guarino dedicated his Latin translation of Plutarch's *Themistocles* to him. See King, *Venetian Humanism*, pp. 447–49.

126. Domenico Dominici (1416–78), bishop of Torcello (1448–64) and from 1464 bishop of Brescia. He served Calixtus III, Nicholas V, Pius II, and Paul II. A learned and wealthy collector of manuscripts, he was a friend of Biondo and encouraged the publication of *Italy Illuminated* (he welcomed printing); Biondo's son Gaspar dedicated his edition of the *princeps* to him in 1474. See King, *Venetian Humanism*, pp. 363–65, and H. Smolinsky's life in *DBI* 40 (1991): 691–95.

127. Pietro Tommasi (1375/80–1458), physician and humanist, educated at the University of Padua. He was with Carlo Zeno's fleet, possibly as physician, and lived briefly in Crete and Vicenza. He treated humanists and eminent Venetians in his practice, corresponded extensively with the important learned men of the time (e.g., Poggio, Filelfo, Guarino), and was a collector of manuscripts, including Greek ones. See King, *Venetian Humanism*, pp. 434–36.

9. MARCH OF TREVISO

1. That is, at the top of the Adriatic. The Roman province of Dalmatia, roughly modern Croatia, Bosnia-Herzegovina, and Albania, reached no further toward Italy than the Istrian peninsula, where Croatia now meets Slovenia.

2. *De verbis Romanae locutionis* (*On the Expressions of Roman Speech*) of 1435 (Nogara, *Scritti*, pp. 115–30).

3. Biondo's §§2, 3, 5, and 6 on the barbarousness of the Lombards are thrown into instructive relief by what our author has to say in §4 about the deference of the Romanizing Ostrogoths to the old culture.

4. Vergil, *Aeneid* 10.205–6, "Quos patre Benaco velatus harundine glauca / Mincius infesta ducebat in aequora pinu," as at *Lombardy* §19.

5. From 1391 onward.

6. *Romagna* §77.

7. *Romagna* §§75 and 76.

8. Biondo might have mentioned here the important woman humanist Isotta Nogarola (1418–66), a one-time student of the Veronese Martino Rizzoni, himself a pupil of Guarino da Verona.

9. Compare *Romagna* §76.

10. Ibid.

11. Actually, *Aeneid* 9.680.

12. See Pliny the Elder, *Natural History* 19.140–42, and compare 20.78.

13. Florus 1.38.11, 13–14, 16–18, 20. Modern texts give the number of Romans that fell in the battle as less than three hundred (*hinc trecentis minus*) and the name of the Cimbrian king as Boiorix.

14. Both battles took place in 489. Odoacer retreated to Ravenna where, after a three-year siege, Theodoric murdered him in 493.

15. This in 936.

16. Justin 20.5.8.

17. Cassiodorus, *Variae* 12.4.4. On Cassiodorus, see *Romagna* §24.

18. Fourth-century bishop of Verona and local devotional favorite (possibly Mauretanian, possibly martyred) mentioned in Ambrose (*Epistles* V) and Gregory (*Dialogues* 3.19): homilies ascribed to St. Zeno survive.

19. Didactic poet (d. 16 BCE), of whose work only fragments survive: R. Helm, ed. *Die Chronik des Hieronymus*, 2nd ed. (Berlin: Akadamie Verlag, 1956), *Eusebius Werke*, 7:166.

20. Compare *Lombardia* §28.

21. Rinaldo da Villafranca, mid-fourteenth-century prehumanist scholar and grammarian, poet, and occasional writer. He attached himself early on to the court of the della Scala at Verona, where he was long esteemed and had many mostly highborn students. He knew Petrarch (with whom he had a personal and professional friendship) and Dante.

22. Giovanni Maggio was a judge in the Verona of the della Scala. On his son (d. 1445), Biondo's friend, see F. Scarcella, "Maggio Maggio giurista veronese," in *Atti e memorie dell'Accademia di Agricoltura Scienze e Lettere di Verona*, ser. 6, 29 (1977–78): 247–58.

23. Jacopo Lavagnola: grandfather (a physician) and grandson (student of Guarino and lawyer, Senator of Rome). Avanzi (Avantius) is unidentified.

24. See J. M. M. Hans Thijssen, "The Book-Collection of Bernardus a Campanea de Verona (fl. end 14th/beginning 15th century)," *Scriptorium* 44 (1990): 299–312. For Themistocles's prodigious memory, see Cicero, *De oratore* 2.299.

25. Giannicola Salerno da Verona (d. 1426), another student of Guarino and very active in public affairs. See M. C. Davies, "The Senator and the

Schoolmaster: Friends of Leonardo Bruni in a New Letter," *Humanistica Lovaniensia* 33 (1984): 1–21 (3–5).

26. The Ghibelline family Montecchi (Shakespeare's Montagues) and Guelf Sambonifacio arose and quarreled together in Verona from the beginning of the twelfth century. The Sambonifacio were driven out of the city in 1225.

27. Staunch supporter and son-in-law of Frederick II, Ezzelino (d. 1259) ruled over much of the Marca Trevigiana (including Verona, Padua, Vicenza) by main force, attempting and failing to conquer Milan; he is also found at *Romagna* §72. Azzo VI d'Este died in 1212, and his son Azzo VII in 1264.

28. The Ghibelline Cangrande I della Scala (1291–1329), grandson of Mastino I (the first Capitano del Popolo, acclaimed in 1362), expanded his rule from Verona to include Padua, Feltre, Belluno, and Treviso. He established a Scaligeri despotism over Verona that lasted from 1277 to 1387. Cangrande's Veronese court was brilliant and generous culturally, and his patronage included Dante (see *Paradiso* 17), Petrarch, and Giotto.

29. Lucchino I dal Verme, condottiere (d. 1372), captured Crete in 1364.

30. Jacopo dal Verme (1350–1409) served the Venetians, like his father.

31. Alessandria, or the battle of Castellazzo, on June 25, 1391. The famous English condottiere Sir John Hawkwood (Giovanni Acuto, d. 1395) appears here for the first time in *Italy Illuminated*, an odd postponement from Biondo's discussion of mercenary captains and armies in Italy, with its emphasis on Alberigo da Barbiano, in *Romagna* §§44–51.

32. A very different picture of Giorgio Cavalli's integrity and relations with Venice is given in the life by L. Miglio in *DBI* 22 (1979): 736–39: see Castner 1:323. He died in exile in Crete around 1406.

33. *Romagna* §31.

34. Altichiero di Domenico da Zevio (ca. 1330–ca. 1390) worked in Verona and Padua; he was notable particularly for his narrative fresco cycles in the naturalistic style of Giotto.

35. Antonio Pisano or Pisanello (ca. 1395–ca. 1455), son of a Veronese mother and a Pisan father, painter and medalist influenced by Giotto and

Altichiero, who worked at Venice, Rome, Ferrara, Mantua, Milan, Rimini, and for Alfonso V at Naples, where he died. He may have assisted Gentile da Fabriano (*Romagna* §§11 and 14, with notes 44 and 49). During the Council of Florence in 1438–39 (on which see *Tuscany* §30), he executed a medal of John VIII Palaeologus. In 1427 Guarino wrote a ninety-line hexameter poem thanking Pisanello for a painting of St. Jerome, now lost: see *Epistolario di Guarino Veronese*, ed. Remigio Sabbadini, 3 vols. (Venice, 1915–19), ep. 386: 1:554–57 (text), and 3:209–10 (commentary).

36. Biondo, *History* 102h–103d. As often when Biondo cites his *Decades*, the citation will support only a portion (usually a subordinate clause) of his statement in *Italy Illuminated* and not the rest (usually the main clause).

37. Biondo, *History* 111d. This was her brief first marriage to Autari, king of the Lombards, in 589.

38. Biondo, *History*, 156h.

39. Eugenius IV's nephew, hence the deletion. See *Venice* §25 above. Condulmer's title was from 1445 cardinal bishop of Porto, but he was at the same time bishop of Verona.

40. *Romagna* §76.

41. *Venice* §3 (the lagoons of Venice).

42. *Romagna* §§75–76.

43. §15 above, with note 26.

44. As in §13 above. Guarino had a country property in the Valpolicella and often wrote letters from there. The reference appears to be to his praise of the land in ep. 157 Sabbadini (cf. note 35 above).

45. Justin 20.5.7–9.

46. Now known as the Adigetto: Castner 1:183.

47. §18 above.

48. Known in humanist circles as Omnibonus Leonicenus (1412–74), he succeeded his teacher Vittorino as master at Mantua until 1453, where Platina (Bartolomeo Sacchi) was his pupil and successor.

49. Quintus Remmius Palaemon (b. at Vicenza: Eusebius 262.19–23) was a first-century CE grammarian of great talent and eccentricity, the first to produce a genuinely systematic and comprehensive Latin grammar.

50. Antonio Loschi of Vicenza (b. ca. 1365), *contubernalis* of Barzizza at Pavia, ordained, served the Visconti and the Venetians, and served in the Curia. He was an influential scholar and prolific author and controversialist who knew Bruni, Poggio, Guarino, Barbaro, Filelfo, Panormita, Niccolò Niccoli, and Salutati. The analytical and widely studied Ciceronian work Biondo praises is generally entitled *Inquisitio super duodecim orationes Ciceronis*. His *Epistulae metricae* are a Vergilian exercise. Loschi is an interlocutor in Biondo's *De verbis Romanae locutionis* (note 2 above).

51. Bissaro died in 1466. Leandro Alberti, *Descrittione di tutta Italia* (Venice, 1561), fol. 473v, suggests that he was also a poet. He took a pro-Venetian line, which Biondo goes on to praise in the next sentence and which as an observation may have been suggested to him by Bissaro's career.

52. Pliny the Elder, *Natural History* 3.121.

53. Livy 10.2.1–10 (trans. B. O. Foster, Loeb edition, 1926). Biondo's identification of the *Meduacus* with the *Bacchiglione* is correct.

54. Vergil, *Aeneid* 1.244, and Servius *ad loc.*

55. Servius, *In Aeneidem* 1.245.

56. Servius, *In Aeneidem* 1.246. For *multitudine*, Servius has *abundantia*.

57. Marcus Antoninus Pius, *Itinerary* 126.6. This whole passage is a reworking of *Venice* §3.

58. Lucan 7.192–94. Lucan was himself misled by Vergil's *hic*, "in these parts," just after the reference to Timavus in *Aeneid* 1.247 (R. G. Austin, commentary *ad loc.*).

59. Vergil, *Aeneid* 1.242–46.

60. The Paduan Mussato (1261–1329), a follower of Lovato Lovati, wrote the Senecan verse tragedy *Ecerinis* on the tyrant Ezzelino III da Romano; text and translation by Gary Grund in *Humanist Tragedies*, I Tatti Renaissance Library 45 (Cambridge, MA, 2011), pp. xx–xxiv and 2–47. He was another prehumanist, historian (of nearly contemporary events), and politician. See §36 below.

61. Martial 13.89.

62. Biondo's identification of the *Timavus* with the Brenta, laborious and bookish in development, is mistaken. It is the Timavo in the region of Trieste, as it was in Biondo's day. For a discussion of Biondo's procedure here, with both the *Meduacus* and *Timavus*, see Castner 1:325–27.

63. Martial 1.61.3.

64. Florus 1.21.3–4, not an exact quotation, and modern texts read *Titiumque* for *et Timavum*. The Arsa is the Italian name for the river Raša in the Istrian region of Croatia.

65. Pliny the Elder, *Natural History* 2.229.

66. Vergil, *Aeneid* 1.247.

67. Livy 1.1.1–3.

68. Cicero, *Philippics* 12.10.

69. Macrobius, *Saturnalia* 1.11.22; Asconius 3.1–5.

70. §5 above.

71. An ancient Lombard Ghibelline family of builders and developers, as Biondo notes, prominent in the affairs of the city for almost three hundred years, and actually running it from 1337 to 1405. They were patrons of Petrarch. See B. G. Kohl, *Padua under the Carrara, 1318–1405* (Baltimore, 1998).

72. Livy 10.2.1–10.

73. The medieval Duomo of S. Maria Assunta, the second on the site and now in turn replaced by the Renaissance cathedral, was consecrated in 1180.

74. The medieval Palazzo della Ragione was rebuilt after the fire of 1420.

75. Misguided local pride led the Paduans to identify bones dug up at S. Giustina in 1413 as those of Livy: see B. L. Ullman, "The Post-Mortem Adventures of Livy," in his *Studies in the Italian Renaissance*, 2nd ed. (Rome, 1973), pp. 53–77.

76. Livy 10.2.14.

77. Acts 1:26, where Matthias takes the place of Judas among the Apostles.

78. CIL V.2975.

79. *CIL* V.2865. The stone in fact marks the burial place of a freedman of Livia Quarta, the daughter of Livy, *Quartae L(ibertus)* being misunderstood as *Quartae L(egionis)*.

80. Seneca the Elder, *Controversies* 10, *Preface* 2. Biondo omits the essential words preceding his quotation: "Pertinere ad rem non puto."

81. Pliny the Younger, *Ep.* 2.3.8; Jerome, *Ep.* 53.1.3.

82. The false belief that the eminent jurist Julius Paulus, early third century CE, was Paduan was owed to a statue inscribed with his name that was found there (see *Scriptores Historiae Augustae* 18.26).

83. Martial 1.7.2–5. Biondo must have in mind Martial 1.61.4, where the two poets are linked and associated with Padua.

84. Martial 1.76.

85. Catullus 95.7–8.

86. Catullus 36.1–20. The transmitted reading is *turis* (frankincense, "smoke") for the correct *ruris* (the countryside, "rustic boorishness"), which is first found in the Venice edition of 1496.

87. Pietro d'Abano (ca. 1257–ca. 1316) was a student of medicine and philosophy at Constantinople and Paris who enjoyed a distinguished teaching career at the University of Padua. His great work, *Conciliator differentiarum philosophorum et praecipue medicorum*, was an attempt to synthesize the beliefs of the Latins, Greeks, Jews, and Arabs on medicine and natural philosophy. He was twice tried by the Inquisition (the second trial concluding posthumously). On Mussato, see §24 above, with note. Lovato Lovati (1241–1309) was another of the Paduan prehumanists, an older contemporary of Mussato.

88. Francesco Zabarella (1360–1417), canon lawyer and teacher of canon law, prolific writer, diplomat, cardinal in 1411 under John XXIII; he was a friend of Coluccio Salutati and teacher of the elder Pier Paolo Vergerio. Pietro Pileo da Prata (ca. 1330–1400) taught at Padua and Pavia; was a diplomat, bishop, and archbishop (Treviso, Padua, Ravenna); and was cardinal under Urban VI. As bishop of Padua he knew Petrarch.

89. All three, Marsilio, Gian Galeazzo, and Guglielmo, were members of the Santa Sofia family of Padua (the *Sophilici*) and academic physicians

(Marsilio was professor of medicine there in the second half of the fourteenth century).

90. Giovanni Dondi dall'Orologio (1330–88) was a physician and a lecturer on medicine at Padua and Pavia, as well as a physical scientist, mathematician, historian, antiquarian, and poet. He built the famous astronomical clock (whence the family's name) at Padua or Pavia, perhaps for Gian Galeazzo Visconti, whose physician he was; he was also a friend of Petrarch and inheritor of some of his books. Antonio Cermisone (d. 1441), Jewish by legend, taught medicine at Pavia and Padua and wrote numerous medical tractates on plague, fever, baths, and the like.

91. Pliny the Elder, *Natural History* 14.67.

92. Blessed Beatrice d'Este (d. 1226, in her nunnery on Monte Gemmola), daughter of Azzo VI d'Este, Benedictine nun and abbess, focus of the courtly love poems of Rambertino Buvalelli.

93. Martial 10.93.1–2. Helicaon, Antenor's son, is confused by Biondo (or his manuscripts) with Helicon, haunt of the Muses.

94. Book 7 of the *Pharsalia*, in fact, vv. 192–93. And see §27 above, where vv. 194–95 (a misinterpretation of *Aeneid* 1.24) are included.

95. On land that was given him by the Carrara (§32 above), where he lived from 1370 to 1374, the last years of his life.

96. Cassiodorus, *Variae* 2.39.9–12.

97. Pliny the Elder, *Natural History* 2.227.

98. Martial 6.42, on the baths of Abano (Castner 1:334).

99. Michele Savonarola (1385–1464), physician and natural scientist, grandfather of the heretical Dominican reformer Girolamo. He taught medicine at the Universities of Padua and Ferrara and was court physician to Leonello and Borso d'Este (Castner 1:334). He wrote *De aegritudinibus a capite usque ad pedes* (*On Medical Complaints from Head to Toe*). Here Biondo is thinking of his *De balneis et thermis naturalibus*.

100. Pliny the Elder, *Natural History* 3.126.

101. See *Venice* §8 for the diocese, and §28, with note, for Dominici (1416–78).

102. Pliny the Elder, *Natural History* 3.126.

103. Martial 4.25.1.

104. O. Cuntz, ed., *Itineraria Antonini Augusti et Burdigalense* (Leipzig, 1929), 126.6 and 281.9 (see also *Venice* §3 above).

105. Pliny the Elder, *Natural History* 3.126 (*ex montibus Tarvisanis*, "from the mountains of Treviso").

106. Totila (r. 541–52) was the last king but one of the Ostrogoths.

107. In 569: a kind of doublet of the Attila and Leo I legend of *Lombardy* §17 (with note).

108. Ermolao Barbaro (the Elder, 1410–71) is mentioned at *Venice* §28 (q.v.) as bishop of Treviso and nephew of Francesco Barbaro. Biondo's entry seems here to take on a tinge of personal affection.

109. Compare *Friuli* §1, below.

110. Pliny the Elder, *Natural History* 3.127.

111. Pliny the Elder, *Natural History* 3.126.

112. Pliny the Elder, *Natural History* 3.127. The historical area of Friuli known as Carnia is centered on Udine. Like Carinthia in Austria, it derives its name from the Celtic tribe of the Carni.

113. The river *Anaxum* mentioned by Pliny (3.127) is nowadays identified with the Stella, which flows into the Laguna di Marano well to the north of the mouth of the Piave (ancient *Plavis*).

114. In *Venice*, Biondo several times connects the name of Eraclea with the emperor Heraclius, but he never says that the citizens of these destroyed cities built Eraclea; he insists rather that in concert with Eraclea they created Venice, and so too at *History* 165b.

115. On Zeno, see *Venice* §28, with note 125.

116. Pliny the Elder, *Natural History* 3.130 (Belunum).

117. Pliny the Elder, *Natural History* 3.126.

118. §42.

119. Biondo, *History*, 130f.

120. See *Romagna* §20, with note.

10. FRIULI

1. That is, living on the "far side" of the Po: Pliny the Elder, *Natural History* 3.130.

2. Pliny the Elder, *Natural History* 3.126. The branches seem no longer to exist.

3. At *Venice* §2, Biondo says that the other limit of Venetian territory is the town of Loreo near the Po.

4. See Biondo, *History* 101b, and *Venice* §§3 and 18.

5. Pliny the Elder, *Natural History* 3.126.

6. The Basilica of Santa Maria Assunta.

7. That is, Poppo (or Poppone), of Bavarian origin, Patriarch of Aquileia (1019–ca. 1042–45).

8. Compare Livy 40.26.1–3.

9. Livy 40.34.2.

10. Compare Suetonius, *Augustus* 20.

11. Suetonius, *Tiberius* 7.3.

12. S.H.A., *The Two Maximini* 33.1–2.

13. S.H.A., *The Two Maximini* 25.2–3 (earlier, of course, not "later").

14. Pliny the Elder, *Natural History* 3.120.

15. Biondo's admiration for emporiums is unreserved: compare, for example, Genoa at *Liguria* §26. But his linking here of the once great but now near-ghost-town Aquileia with the eclipsed Spina and Adria sounds a note of mutability that he particularly enjoys producing.

16. In saints' legends of Biondo's time and later, Hermagoras and his deacon Fortunatus were martyred in the reign of Nero, around 70 CE, at Aquileia, but they probably lived toward the end of the third century. A thread of saintly continuity, connecting them with Peter and Mark and on to Syrus, is made to pass rather creatively through the needle's eye of Aquileia. (Mark is supposed to have written his gospel in Rome and then to have produced a *copy* of it in Aquileia for her citizens.) St. Chromatius, late fourth-century bishop of Aquileia and theologian, in addition to

his relationship with Jerome, was a correspondent of Ambrose, Chrysostom, and Rufinus. This Tyrannius Rufinus of Aquileia (ca. 345–410) was a monk, theologian, pamphleteer, and controversialist. He was a friend and fellow student of St. Jerome (a friendship broken in the Origen controversy) and lived and studied in Egypt. His translations into Latin of Eusebius, Origen, Gregory of Nazianzus, and Clement helped promote Western acquaintance with the Greek Fathers' religious thought.

17. G. B. Brusin, *Inscriptiones Aquileiae*, 3 vols. (Udine, 1991–93), no. 2892a (the Augustus is Maximinus Thrax, who repaired the via Annia at Aquileia about 238 CE).

18. In Biondo's time the Venetians had held Udine by conquest since 1420; it had been acquired by the dukes of Austria by a treaty of 1362.

19. Jacopo da Udine (White, "Towards a Critical Edition," p. 272, n. 17), whom Francesco Barbaro solicited for regional information to help Biondo with the work, composed *De nobilitate et antiquitate civitatis Aquileiensis*. Biondo kept his eye on it as he went along (particularly for his account of the Christianizing of Aquileia), but he did not take it wholesale into his text, as he did Bracelli's *Descriptio orae ligusticae* in Liguria (see *Liguria*, notes 40 and 57). See also Gian Giuseppe Liruti, *Notizie delle vite ed opere scritte da' letterati del Friuli*, vol. 1 (Venice, 1760), pp. 365–69: Liruti expressly denies that Jacopo da Udine was surnamed Simeoni.

20. Like Udine, Monfalcone had been held by the Venetians since 1420. The city's foundation by Theodoric cannot be substantiated.

21. Livy 39.22.6–7.

22. Pliny the Elder, *Natural History* 3.126 (which reads *praefluente Aquileiam*).

23. Pliny the Elder, *Natural History* 3.127, notes its location in the region of the Carni and its thirty-three mile distance from Aquileia. Caesar (Hirtius), *Gallic War* 8.24, mentions its being attacked and looted by neighbors. Mela, Strabo, and Ptolemy also mention it as *Tergeste, Tergestum, Tergestini*.

24. Pliny the Elder, *Natural History* 3.127.

25. The Bavarian Meinhardiner, conti di Gorizia, prominent in Friuli from the early twelfth century onward.

II. ISTRIA

1. Pliny the Elder, *Natural History* 3.129.

2. Pliny the Elder, *Natural History* 3.127. The manuscripts of Pliny in Biondo's time read *Fanaticus* for the correct *Flanaticus* (see note 10 below).

3. Justin 32.3.13–15. *Iapydia* was the land of the *Iapydes* (Pliny the Elder, *Natural History* 3.127 and 140; Vergil, *Georgics* 3.475), a part of the Roman Illyricum, on the edge of modern Croatia.

4. That is, Nauportus, from *navem portare*, "carrying the ship" (the modern Istrian river Quieto): Pliny the Elder, *Natural History* 3.128. Castner (1:340) notes here Biondo's neglect of Martial 4.25 and 8.28 to qualify Pliny's mythological account.

5. Capodistria to the Italians, modern Koper in Slovenia.

6. Biondo, *History* 93d.

7. For example, *Romagna* §§25–28 with note 62, where Pier Paolo Vergerio the Elder (d. 1444) is defined and elevated by the company he keeps. See J. M. McManamon, *Pierpaolo Vergerio the Elder: the Humanist as Orator* (Tempe, AZ, 1996).

8. Pliny the Elder, *Natural History* 3.128. South of Justinopolis (Capodistria/Koper), Izola and Piran in Slovenia begins modern Croatia. The Croatian names of the places here given in the Italian form, which Biondo would have known, are Savudrija (Salvore), Umag, Novigrad (Cittanova), Porec (Parenzo), Vrsar (Orsera), Rovinj.

9. Pliny the Elder, *Natural History* 3.129.

10. The true readings *Flanates, Flanaticus* were only discovered by Ermolao Barbaro after Biondo's death (*Castigationes Plinianae*, ed. G. Pozzi, 4 vols. [Padua, 1973–79], 3:165). Biondo associates the name *Carnarius* with *carnes*, "flesh."

11. The identification of Stridon with Sdregna/Zrenj is by no means assured.

12. St. Jerome is the patron saint of Capodistria, and Vergerio's family was particularly devoted to him; Jerome was Biondo's name-day saint, to whose help, as he tells Francesco Barbaro, he attributed his own return to

Nicholas V's curia (White, "Towards a Critical Edition," p. 279). At *March of Treviso* §16, Biondo mentions Guarino's poem on Pisanello, which thanks the artist for a painting of St. Jerome. Biondo's loyalty to Jerome is primarily loyalty to their (that is, Jerome's, Biondo's, Vergerio's) *shared* citizenship of language, learning, and history: a citizenship that attaches properly only to *Italia*. Biondo's demonstration, using Jerome as an article of evidence, that Istria is thus part of Italy is the centerpiece of this diminutive *regio*.

13. St. Jerome, *On Famous Men* 135.1–5.

14. Biondo, *History* 115d.

15. For another example of professional pride in his Curial service (and persistent affection for Pope Eugenius IV), see Biondo's statement about his management of the documents for that pontiff's canonization of Nicholas of Tolentino in 1446, at *Piceno* §18, with note 68.

16. See on the Council of Ferrara-Florence, *Tuscany* §30 and *Romagna* §73.

17. Florus 1.21.3–4. Teutana, or Teuta, was ruler of an alliance of Illyrian tribes in the third century BCE, was regent for her stepson, and was ultimately deprived of power by the Romans. She earlier appears in *March of Treviso* §27.

18. Biondo, *History* 8g–h.

19. St. Jerome, *Commentary on Habakkuk*, Prologue 59–63.

20. In §3 (the building of Justinopolis).

21. In 1380, Maruffo Doria captured Capodistria (Justinopolis) for the Genoese, but in the next year the city (along with Trieste, Cittanova, Parenzo, Pirano, Pola) was restored to the Venetians by treaty, following the War of Chioggia.

12. ABRUZZO

1. Biondo promises to deal with *Samnium* (the Abruzzo), *Campania* (the Terra di Lavoro), *Apulia* (the northern part of modern Puglia), *Lucania* (modern Basilicata), the *Salentini* (the Salentine peninsula, also known as the Terra d'Otranto, of southern Puglia), the *Calabri* (northern and cen-

tral modern Calabria), and the *Brutii* (the parts of southern Calabria facing Sicily), though in the event he completed only the first three (see the Introduction, pp. xx–xxi; Castner 2:405; *Liguria* §9).

2. Livy 7.29.1.

3. Biondo here (§§2–18) lays down a common historical structure for the remainder of *Italy Illuminated*, that is, Alfonso of Aragon's Kingdom of Naples, or the Regno, without bringing it to completion as he had hoped (see note 1 above).

4. As he says in §4, Biondo makes great use of Book 13 of his *Histories* in this section. On the Normans in Italy, see G. A. Loud, *The Age of Robert Guiscard: Southern Italy and the Norman Conquest* (Harlow, Essex, 2000). The career of the eleventh-century dynast Tancred of Hauteville (d. 1041) is mainly legendary. His sons, however, established the Normans as a lasting presence in Italy, though there were Normans in Italy from 1017. In what follows, Biondo and his sources do capture well (with some inaccuracies and confusion) the continuous realignments of Norman, residual Lombard, Byzantine, German, and Saracen forces across Sicily and the Mezzogiorno, and the steady rise to power of the Normans.

5. Michael IV Paphlagon. *Ethiriachis* seems to be a version of the military title ἑταιριάρχης, "commandant of the palace guard."

6. The battle of Olivento (really a river, a tributary of the Ofanto north of Melfi) took place on March 17, 1041. The catastrophic Roman defeat at Cannae in 216 BCE was much further down the river Ofanto, toward its mouth at the coast near Barletta.

7. Biondo, *History* 192e–96h.

8. This was at Civitate, northwest of Foggia, in 1053. The pope involved was Leo IX, not Leo V, and the emperor was Henry III; Humphrey led the Normans.

9. See *Campania* §22, with note.

10. These were the terms of the famous Conference of Melfi (not Aquila) of 1059.

11. Which he took possession of in 1060.

12. By 1091, with the fall of Noto, the Normans controlled all of Sicily. Biondo must have in mind here the fall of Messina in 1060, or of Palermo in 1071: Alexander succeeded Nicholas in 1061 and was pope until 1073.

13. In 1084, after a three-year war with Henry.

14. July 17, 1085.

15. That is, Robert's possessions on the eastern Adriatic, which the Byzantines soon captured.

16. A pious aside in keeping with the aims of the eventual author of four crusading tractates (*Italy Illuminated*, vol. 1 [ITRL 20], p. x, with note 11). Bohemond secured Antioch in 1099.

17. Roger II.

18. In 1128.

19. The dramatic and rapid reversals at Galluccio (a village about ten miles southeast of San Germano, the medieval name for Cassino) took place in the summer of 1139; and by the Treaty of Mignano of the same year, Innocent declared Roger king of Sicily, duke of Apulia, and prince of Capua.

20. Antipope Anacletus II (d. 1138).

21. Roger was crowned in Palermo on Christmas Day 1130. The Two Sicilies were Sicily proper and the Mezzogiorno (Apulia, Calabria, and Campania, or "peninsular Sicily").

22. In 1154, having extended his Sicilian and Italian dominion into North Africa.

23. Henry was crowned king of Sicily in Palermo on Christmas Day 1194.

24. Gregory died in Rome in 1241. Castner remarks on Biondo's silence regarding "the cultural richness of Frederick II's kingdom" (2:411), just as he had shown no appreciation of the culture of his grandfather Roger II's court. See David Abulafia, *Frederick II: A Medieval Emperor* (London, 1988).

25. See *Liguria* §30, with note 70 there.

26. Convened June 24, 1245.

27. Henry Raspe, Landgrave of Thuringia (d. February 17, 1247); Count William II of Holland (1228–56) was elected King of the Romans in 1247.

28. A genuine calamity, on February 18, 1248.

29. Frederick died in 1250 in Castel Fiorentino (Puglia), probably of dysentery. Biondo's account of his troubled last days is mostly anti-imperial embroidery.

30. Isabella II of Jerusalem, Frederick II's second wife, whom he married in 1225.

31. Conrad IV (son of Frederick and Isabella II) died in May 1254, and Innocent in December of the same year.

32. By 1257.

33. Conradin (1252–68) was the son of Conrad IV and Elizabeth of Wittelsbach.

34. He was crowned king of Sicily in Palermo on August 10, 1258.

35. Charles of Anjou, King Charles I of Sicily (but from 1282 to his death in 1285, king of Naples only), was the son of Louis VIII of France and younger brother of Louis IX (St. Louis).

36. Ending Hohenstaufen ascendancy in Italy.

37. "El Senador," Enrique (Henry of Castile), brother of Alfonso IX (1230–1303), who fought with Conradin at Tagliacozzo and was captured and imprisoned for over twenty years.

38. "Banderesi," faction leaders effectively running the city, so called after their war banners.

39. Tagliacozzo (see *Lazio* §9, with note 46), on August 23, 1268. Conradin's companion was Frederick, Margrave of Baden (b. 1249).

40. The Sicilian Vespers of 1282, which dislodged the Angevins from the island.

41. The Spaniard Peter III (Pero lo Gran), king of Aragon and Sicily (d. 1285), was not only Manfred's heir by marriage but could trace his own line back to Robert Guiscard.

42. Charles II (d. 1309, having given up Sicily in 1302), Charles I's son, count of Anjou, and king of Naples.

43. Charles Martel d'Anjou (Carlo Martello; d. 1295), a friend of Dante whose claim to Hungary was unfulfilled; St. Louis of Toulouse, Franciscan archbishop of Lyons and bishop of Toulouse (d. 1297); for Robert III, see *Campania* §42, with note 174.

44. See *Campania* §42 particularly.

45. Joanna I of Naples (1328–82), Robert's granddaughter, intriguer and much married, she countenanced the murder of her first husband (her cousin Andrew of Hungary) and was murdered by another cousin, Charles III of Durazzo, whom Biondo skips; Ladislaus the Magnanimous (1377–1414), son of Charles III, an expansionist; Joanna II of Naples (1373–1435), sister of Ladislaus; for his military help she first promised rule of Naples to Alfonso V of Aragon (by adopting him) in 1421; Louis II of Anjou (1377–1417), son of Louis I of Anjou, crowned king of Naples by the antipope Clement VII and ruled for ten years; René of Anjou, king of Naples (1409–80), son of Charles II (Ladislaus's rival), another adoptive son of Joanna II, returned to France in 1441 when Alfonso put Naples under siege.

46. On February 26, 1443. Compare *Campania* §47, with note 159. See also J. H. Bentley, *Politics and Culture in Renaissance Naples* (Princeton, 1987), pp. 54–62, as cited by Castner 2:412.

47. Pliny the Elder, *Natural History* 3.38.

48. Actually Ceprano: compare also *Lazio* §55, with note 273.

49. *Praetutianus* rather: see Clavuot 1:43.

50. Pliny the Elder, *Natural History* 3.110–11 (with omissions and variants in Biondo's quotation).

51. Livy 22.9.1–5, and compare *Umbria* §8.

52. Caesar, *Civil War* 1.15.

53. Caesar, *Civil War* 1.23.5.

54. Pliny the Elder, *Natural History* 3.110.

55. Ibid.

56. §20 above (Iuvatinum), with note.

57. Ptolemy, *Geographia* 3.1; Pliny the Elder, *Natural History* 3.110, now Giulianova.

58. Pliny mentions several places as inhabited by *Interamnenses* (i.e., people between two rivers, *amnes*), but not Teramo. Biondo is probably thinking of Terni in Umbria or Termoli in Molise.

59. The son Teodoro (1427–66), bishop of Feltre and of Treviso, died before he could take up the cardinalate to which Paul II had appointed him. He edited Jerome's letters and tracts. As a doctor of civil and canon law, he worked as an advocate and judge in the papal courts.

60. See Castner 2:231.

61. Conflating passages in Pliny the Elder, *Natural History* 3.110–11.

62. Livy 28.45.19.

63. Livy, *Periochae* 72.2.

64. Livy, *Periochae* 76.3.

65. *Scerne*: see Castner 2:233.

66. Pliny the Elder, *Natural History* 3.110 (modern texts read six miles).

67. S.H.A., *Hadrian* 1.1, not an exact quotation (see next note).

68. S.H.A., *Hadrian* 19.1. Biondo has got the story back to front: Hadrian's ancestors came from Adria in Picenum but settled in Italica in Spain (not Italy) in the time of the Scipios. The second quotation collapses Hadrian's native Italica into the Adria of his ancestors.

69. Livy 24.10.10–11.

70. Ptolemy, *Geography* 3.1.52; Pliny the Elder, *Natural History* 3.107 (Angulani).

71. See §20 above.

72. The Cistercian Abbazia Santa Maria di Casanova, founded in 1197, now ruined.

73. See *Piceno* §13. S. Giovanni Capistrano died in 1456.

74. Livy 10.39.1–4.

75. Livy 29.45.19.

76. Vergil, *Aeneid* 7.631, where modern texts read *Antemnae*.

77. See Castner 2:237.

78. Along with Amiterno.

79. An echo of the Sicilian Vespers as told in §17. Compare Clavuot 1:94, n. 246.

80. The foundation legend probably comes from regional chronicles, such as that of the local poet Buccio di Ranallo (d. 1363). Modern toponomy sees the name as deriving from the many streams for which the preceding *castellum* S. Maria de Acquilis was named.

81. In §5.

82. Shifting and conflicting allegiances, mostly of Kingdom of Naples and papal interests, compounded by *condottieri* involvement and by earthquakes and pestilence, had weakened the city. After the death of the Franciscan Minister-General Bernardino there, on May 20, 1444, the order under the guidance of Giovanni Capistrano and Jacopo della Marca began an extensive construction program, and a time of prosperity and peace for the city followed.

83. Leandro Alberti (ed. 1550, fol. 235) repeats this curiosity; compare also Biondo on Serravalle in *Umbria* §9.

84. Pliny the Elder, *Natural History* 3.110, speaking of the river, not the city; Ptolemy, *Geography* 3.1.17.

85. That is, Chieti (Pliny the Elder, *Natural History* 3.106).

86. Colantonio Valignani, bishop from 1445 to 1488.

87. See §6 above.

88. In 1450, Orso Orsini became count of Manoppello and was also granted the Abruzzo districts of Valle Siciliana and San Valentino by King Alfonso.

89. Petroleum (literally, "rock oil") was supposed to have medicinal properties.

90. Modern Corfinio was in fact named Pentima (site of the abbey of San Pelino) till 1927, when it assumed again the ancient name.

91. Lucan 2.499.

92. Caesar, *Civil War* 1.23.5.

93. The Gizio and (apparently) the Vella. The village named Vallescura, or Roccavalleoscura, is the present Rocca Pia, south of Sulmona.

94. Ovid, *Fasti* 4.79–80, and compare Silius Italicus 9.72.

95. Ovid, *Fasti* 4.81–83.

96. Pliny the Elder, *Natural History* 3.106.

97. The Eremo di Santo Spirito di Maiella near Roccamorice. On Celestine V, see *Lazio* §28, with note 144.

98. *Valvae*, Biondo thinks, in the sense of "door;" as having *paucis aditibus . . . accessus*, "few means of access."

99. One of the oldest foundations (by tradition from the time of Charlemagne) of the Monte Cassino Benedictines. By "Lombard" handwriting, the humanists understood what we call Beneventan script.

100. Livy 9.16.1 (modern texts read *Ferentanos*).

101. Livy 9.45.18 (modern texts read *oratores pacis petendae amicitiaeque*).

102. Pliny the Elder, *Natural History* 3.106.

103. Ptolemy, *Geography* 3.1.16.

104. Pliny the Elder, *Natural History* 3.106.

105. Ptolemy, *Geography* Map of Italy; and compare Pliny the Elder, *Natural History* 3.106.

106. The Castellum Novum or Castrum Novum of the Middle Ages is now (since 1864) Castel Frentano. San Vito di Lanciano is nowadays S. Vito Chietino.

107. The abbey of San Giovanni in Venere, a sixth-century Benedictine foundation with its later medieval buildings now partially restored.

108. Pliny the Elder, *Natural History* 3.106: *Buca*, whose location is much disputed; perhaps Penna di Vasto.

109. Died as a Hieronymite hermit in the convent of S. Onofrio, Rome, in 1449. See his life by Giovanna Casagrande in *DBI* 78 (2013): 446–48.

110. Originally Malanotte, in the twentieth century this place was renamed Montebello sul Sangro.

111. That is, Palieta takes its name from *paglia*, Italian for "straw."

112. Condottiere, also known as Caudola (1368–1439). Not previously mentioned, even at *Romagna* §48, though his first service was under Braccio da Montone. He initially served Alfonso V in his campaign for the throne of Naples but shifted his support to Alfonso's rival René of Anjou.

113. Alfedena is not the site of the ancient Aufidena, which was closer to Castel di Sangro.

114. Livy 10.12.9, modern Boiano.

115. An ancient (842) Benedictine foundation on the site of a pagan temple, periodically rebuilt.

116. Pliny the Elder, *Natural History* 3.106.

117. Part of the massif now known as the Monti del Matese in present-day Molise.

118. Livy 10.30.7.

119. The statement is not found in the chorographical works of the anonymous Geographus Ravennas, or Guido Ravennas, edited together by Pinder and Parthey (Berlin 1860); nonetheless it does seem well founded, according to an inscription first presented in Domenico Romanelli, *Antica topografia istorica del regno di Napoli* (Naples, 1819), parte III, pp. 26–27.

120. Plato was said in ancient sources such as Diogenes Laertius and Cicero to have visited Pythagoreans in the far south of Italy (Apulia, or *Magna Graecia*), but Biondo's association of the *Republic* ("De ideis") with Interamnia seems to have no ancient or medieval authority: A. Riginos, *Platonica* (Leiden, 1976), p. 62.

121. Castner 2:253.

122. Livy 9.28.1–2.

123. Livy 9.31.4–5.

124. Livy 10.12.9 (repeated from the end of §41 above).

125. Pliny the Elder, *Natural History* 2.224.

126. Livy 10.1.1–2.

127. Lucan 2.425.

128. Livy 9.23.1–4.

129. Livy 9.24.1–15, paraphrased.

130. Niccolò Cantelmo (d. 1454?), who obtained the title from Alfonso V in 1443.

131. The *Isola di Liri* of §44.

132. Livy 10.43.8.

133. Vergil, *Aeneid* 7.629.

134. Livy 9.28.3–4.

135. Livy 9.28.6. The city's name is represented in the name of the church of S. Giacomo alle Galazze in the comune of Maddaloni, six miles southeast of Capua.

136. Livy 9.44.16.

137. Livy 10.1.3.

138. Cicero, *On the Laws* 2.6; Plato, *Phaedrus* 230B.

139. See Cicero, *On Old Age* 55; Plutarch, *Cato* 2.

140. Cicero, *On the Laws* 2.3.

141. The river Melfa. Biondo mentions Pontecorvo in *Lazio* §§18 and 55 (with note).

142. Benedict (*Lazio* §39, with note 207) founded the monastery circa 529, and it was destroyed by the Lombards circa 577. The saint died in 543.

143. See Gregory the Great, *Dialogorum libri IV*, II.14 and 15.

144. Now Sant'Elia Fiumerapido. The Rapido becomes the river Gari at Cassino (the old San Germano) and below the town flows into the Liri to form the Garigliano.

145. §48 above.

146. Livy 9.28.7–8 (the place was actually Interamna Sucasina, a modern conjecture).

147. Pliny the Elder, *Natural History* 7.36.

148. Livy 22.13.5–6.

149. Livy 26.9.2–3.

150. The monastery of San Vincenzo al Volturno was founded in 731. The prime source for its medieval history is the *Chronicon Vulturnense*, a Beneventan manuscript in the Vatican Library edited by V. Federici as *Chronicon Vulturnense del monaco Giovanni*, 3 vols. (Rome, 1925–38).

151. Livy, *Periochae* 72.7.

152. Livy 22.13.1.

153. Livy 24.20.5. The site of Compulteria was near Alvignano in the present province of Caserta.

154. The Pratello is now the river Lete: it took its old name from the village of Pratella. As above (§51), Biondo seems uncertain of the name of the stream on which Isernia sits.

155. Livy 9.13.7–8. Biondo has a different text from ours and perhaps works from memory here. I have tried to reproduce what I think was his understanding of his text.

156. Livy 22.17.7.

157. Livy 22.18.5–6. Today Allifae is Castello d'Alife. The modern Alife is somewhat lower down from the ancient site.

158. Livy 9.38.1.

159. Livy 9.42.6–9.

160. Vergil, *Aeneid* 7.729.

161. The site of present-day Capua, ancient Capua now being Santa Maria Capua Vetere.

162. Livy 23.14.13.

163. Livy 9.1.2.

164. Biondo has confused Caiatia (Caiazzo) and Calatia (compare the church of San Giacomo alle Galazze in Maddaloni; see above, §46 note).

165. Livy 9.2.1–4.

166. Livy 9.2.7–8.

167. Livy 9.1.1.

168. Livy 23.1.1.

169. Livy 23.41.13.

170. Livy 24.12.3. (Mons) Tifata is the modern Monti di Maddaloni.

171. Livy, *Periochae* 75.10.

172. Ptolemy, *Geography* 3.1.3; Pliny the Elder, *Natural History* 15.88. Pliny actually says that the nuts were named at first *Abellinae* after their place of origin (Abella), and only later *abellanae*.

173. Antoninus Pius, *Itinerarium* 103.3, mentions "Ad Matrem magnam," but not in connection with Benevento.

174. Servius, *In Aeneidem* 8.9

175. Livy 9.27.14.

176. Livy, *Periochae* 15.5–6.

177. Livy 22.13.1 (as above, §51).

178. Livy 24.14.1–3. Only *B* has the italicized matter, which paraphrases Livy.

179. Livy 24.15.1–3.

180. Livy 24.16.9, 4, 5.

181. Livy 24.16.19.

182. Livy 25.13.4–10, paraphrased.

183. Livy 25.14.10–11.

184. Livy 27.10.7–10. Livy's point is rather that the eighteen colonies stood by Rome against Hannibal.

185. In 545 CE. Biondo, *History* 71a.

186. Biondo, *History* 181a.

187. Biondo, *History* 245d–46e. Compare §11 above, where the pope is Adrian IV.

188. In the Croci di Acerno.

189. At Altopiano Irpino.

190. Biondo gives the same explanation for the name of Rignano Flaminio at *Tuscany* §58.

191. So known until 1861, when the place became Sant'Arcangelo Trimonte, now (since 1978) in the province of Benevento.

192. In November 1439. A famous condottiere and duke of Bari (note 112 above).

193. Pago Veiano (Castner 2:277).

194. The ancient town, about two miles from the Sepino of today.

195. Livy 10.45.12–14.

196. §51 above. Livy 22.13.1.

13. CAMPANIA

1. Compare *Abruzzo* §44. Bordered above by the Garigliano, below by the Sele, by the seacoast to the west, and (vaguely) by the Apennines behind, the *regio* Campania has not been very crisply defined.

2. Biondo does not in fact deal with the appellation "Happy Campania" (compare Pliny the Elder, *Natural History* 3.60), but for Terra di Lavoro, see §§19–20 below.

3. Strabo 5.3.6 (the correct reading being *Fregellas*, past which in Strabo the river flows, to enter the sea at Minturnae). See *Lazio* §2, with note.

4. Lucan 2.424f.

5. Servius, *In Aeneidem* 10.145. A nymph goddess local to the Minturnae district, mother of Latinus by Faunus. She had a temple and sacred grove near the mouth of the Garigliano (Valentina Livi in *Religion in Republican Italy*, Yale Classical Studies 35 [2006]: 105–13).

6. Strabo 5.3.6. See also *Lazio* §11.

7. Livy 9.25.1–2.

8. Livy 9.25.3–4.

9. Livy 9.25.7–9.

10. Livy 10.21.7–8.

11. He reigned 296 to 304 CE. It may be that Biondo has in mind the pseudo-Council of Sinuessa (some miles south of Minturnae), a fabrication of later centuries, at which Marcellinus was supposed to have been condemned for idolatry.

12. Gregory the Great, *Registrum*, in *Corpus Christianorum, Series latina* cxl, ed. Dag Norberg (Turnhout, 1972), October 590.

13. From the obligation to provide levies of troops; compare Livy 27.38.3–5 and 36.3.5–6.

14. Valerius Maximus, *Memorable Sayings and Doings* 1.5.5.

15. Livy, *Periochae* 77.14–17.

16. Biondo, *History* 179d, also recounted at §45–46 below. The battle was fought in June 915, Pope John himself taking the field. See also *Romagna* §55, with note.

17. The Garigliano is formed by the Gari joining the Liri, to use their modern names, the name of the united river being an amalgam of "Gari-Lirano." See §2 above.

18. Pliny's *Natural History* mentions the mountain more than once, but not in connection with sulfur.

19. Livy 8.11, 11.

20. Strabo 5.3.6. A stade is a little less than one-eighth of an English mile.

21. §3 above. Livy 10.21.7–8.

22. Livy 22.7.1–2 and 7.

23. Livy 22.13.10.

24. The town known in the Middle Ages and later as Sessa has since 1864 been Sessa Aurunca again. The site of Suessa Pometia is not known, not necessarily close to modern Pomezia in Lazio. Biondo does not distinguish the two towns (see §6 below).

25. Strabo 5.3.11.

26. Martial 13.83. But Martial's topic is *scillae*, "prawns," not the *silae herbae* above.

27. Cicero, *On the Agrarian Law* 2.36. Compare *Lazio* §16.

28. *Ausones* was no more than the Greek form of the Latin *Aurunci*.

29. Livy 1.41.7.

30. Livy 1.53.2.

31. Livy 2.25.5.

32. Livy 8.15.4–5.

33. Livy 9.28.7.

34. Juvenal (1.69) is correctly identified as the source of the phrase *molle Calenum* ("luxurious Calenum") in B, r, and in Froben's edition; this is presumably a correction of Biondo's original reading, *Horatius* (as given in FHQ). In the earlier draft he may have been thinking of the phrase *molle Tarentum* in Horace's *Satires* 2.4.34.

35. Pliny the Elder, *Natural History* 17.31.

36. The site of modern Capua.

37. Livy 9.44.5.

38. Livy 10.31.4–7, abbreviated.

39. Livy 22.13.1–14.3, abbreviated. Biondo's rough telescoping of Livy's text has left several syntactical incoherencies, further muddied by a differently drafted version below. See also Plutarch, *Fabius Maximus* 6.1–2, which Biondo had in Decembrio's translation (Clavuot 1:162, with note 94).

40. At *Abruzzo* §51.

41. Livy 22.14.3 and 22.15.4.

42. For the tone and treatment of Livy's Hannibal on the Campus Stellatis, compare Hannibal in the Casentino, *Tuscany* §§34–35.

43. Cicero, *The Second Speech on the Agrarian Law* 2.36 (above, §5).

44. Ibid. 2.76.

45. Ibid. 2.85–86.

46. Compare §5 above; Suetonius, *The Deified Julius* 20.3.

47. Livy 22.15.1–4

48. *fortunae minas, saxa*: the reading of the manuscript tradition, corrected to *Formiana saxa* ("the cliffs of Formiae") by Sabellico fifty years later; this complicates matters in §24 below, but does not deflect Biondo from Liternum and the proper site of Scipio's tomb.

49. Livy 22.16.4–18.7: loosely quoted from manuscripts, partly paraphrased and misunderstood or misremembered.

50. *Abruzzo* §41 (Castel di Sangro) and §51 (the town and abbey of S. Vincenzo al Volturno).

51. Livy 25.20.1–2.

52. Livy 32.29.3. Castellammare is now Castel Volturno.

53. In §9.

54. Now a single commune, Cancello ed Arnone.

55. Plutarch, *Q. Fabius Maximus* 6.1–2. On Decembrio and his native town Vigevano, see *Lombardy* §34, with note.

56. Servius, *In Aeneidem* 10.145.

57. See Biondo at *Lazio* §7, with note: Pliny treats predatory birds in *Natural History* 10.21–28. A manuscript variant of Pliny's *cybindis* (nighthawk), at 10.24, is probably the source of Biondo's *chilyones* (here, and in the *Lazio* passage).

58. Vergil, *Aeneid* 4.132.

59. Frederick II's *De scientia venandi per aves* falls right on the edge (ca. 1250) of Biondo's two-hundred-year limit, the Bayeux Tapestry (1070s) comfortably outside it, and Boccaccio's Federigo degli Alberighi of the *Decameron* (ca. 1353) well within, but falconry is far older than that in Western consciousness, and particularly its aristocratic connections. For Biondo, linking Alfonso with Aeneas and Dido, even negatively, is thus instinctive.

60. See Jacques Heurgon, *Recherches sur l'histoire, la religion et la civilisation de Capoue préromaine des origines à la deuxième guerre punique* (Paris, 1942),

p. 441 (cited in Castner 2, *ad loc*.) The ancient city was on the site of the modern Santa Maria Capua Vetere.

61. Livy 4.37.1–2. Livy thinks it more probable that *Capua* was named for its *campi* (*campestris ager*), "plains." Compare Servius, *In Aeneidem* 1.242.

62. Livy 23.1.5 and 2.1.

63. Livy 23.18.9. *Emarcuit*, perhaps echoing church Latin: Livy likes the uncompounded *marcere* and *marcescere* in this sense (as at 23.45.2).

64. Livy 26.16.7–10 and 12.

65. Cicero, *Second Speech on the Agrarian Law* 2.85–86. Biondo refers to his earlier mention of the speech in §10.

66. Ibid. 2.76.

67. Ibid. 2.80–81.

68. Ibid. 2.95.

69. Suetonius, *Deified Julius* 81.1. Suetonius says the workmen found quantities *of vases* of ancient workmanship, omitted in Biondo's text.

70. The Vandals destroyed the city in 456. The interregnum of the thirty Lombard dukes was from 574/75 to 584/85.

71. Pliny the Elder, *Natural History* 18.111.

72. Pliny the Elder, *Natural History* 17.28. Pliny means here that it is precisely the good features, and not the imperfections, of the rich alluvial Leborine soil that make it hard for farmers to work with. Biondo misses Pliny's point.

73. Comprehending a twelve-mile projection of the Apennines (the Monti Tifatini), straddling Campania and Abruzzo and looking down on the Campanian plain to the south, near Capua.

74. That is, the plain of Leboria is the origin of the term *Terra di Lavoro* widely applied to Campania, rather than a literal "Land of Work," *Terra Laboris*.

75. Cicero, *The Second Speech on the Agrarian Law* 2.86, cited in §10 above.

76. Macrobius, *Saturnalia* 1.10.3.

77. Juvenal 3.173–75 and 6.71–72.

78. Whatever his sources, Biondo's overheated language here recalls his treatment of the *barilotto* of the Fraticelli at *Piceno* §13. See, for example, Livy 7.2.12 for a more measured view of the Atellan farces.

79. Aversa, which became the nerve center of an expanding Norman territory in Italy, is not quite the ancient Atella. The Norman freebooter Rainulf Drengot held Aversa in fief from the Duke of Naples, Sergius IV, in 1030. Guiscard did not come into Italy until 1046/47. Both worked to strengthen the town's fortifications. Guiscard first appears in *Piceno* §1, then in *Abruzzo* §§1, 5–8, 28–29, 48, and in *Campania* §§22 and 47.

80. Vergil, *Georgics* 2.225.

81. Ptolemy, *Geography* 3.1.6 (326.9–11); Pomponius Mela 2.4.70; Pliny the Elder, *Natural History* 3.61; Guido Ravennas 33 (472.20–22).

82. Livy 22.16.4–5. See §11 above, with note. Biondo ignores the seeming discrepancy in Livy and uses a triangulation of other literary evidence and personal observation to locate Liternum in the area of the Lagno and Torre di Patria (the early fifteenth-century defensive work on the coast between Cumae and the mouth of the Volturno); see Castner 2:430f.

83. Livy 23.35.5.

84. Valerius Maximus, *Memorable Doings and Sayings* 5.3.2.

85. Pliny the Elder, *Natural History* 2.230, where the "slightly acid" spring Lyncestis (or *Lincestis*) is the right reading, though Biondo seems to have read or remembered *Linternum* (or *Lincernum*).

86. Seneca, *Moral Epistles* 51.11.

87. Livy 38.56.3–5.

88. Seneca, *Moral Epistles* 86.1.

89. Near the present-day Torregaveta and the Villa Vazia restaurant: see James Ker, *The Deaths of Seneca* (New York, 2009), pp. 326ff.

90. Seneca, *Moral Epistles* 55.3–4.

91. Livy 8.22.5–6.

92. Vergil, *Aeneid* 6.2 and 3.441.

93. Servius, *In Aeneidem* 3.441.

94. Livy 2.14.6–7.

95. Livy 2.21.5–6.

96. Livy 4.44.12.

97. Livy 8.14.11.

98. Vergil, *Aeneid* 6.9–10.

99. On Prospero Schiaffino da Camogli, later a Sforza diplomatic agent and secretary of Emperor Frederick III (and a surprising bishop of Caithness in Scotland), see Clavuot 1:50 and note 90.

100. A pan-Campanian ritual site, usually located in the area of the present-day Torre San Severino (*CIL* 10.3792; M. W. Frederiksen, *Campania* [London, 1984], p. 33f.).

101. Livy 23.35.2, 15, and 18.

102. A village obliterated in the eruption and creation of Monte Nuovo in 1538, which drastically transformed the landscape that Biondo visited.

103. That is, after Aeneas's trumpeter Misenus: Vergil, *Aeneid* 6.234. Mount Misenus is the present Punta di Miseno. On the area in general, see M. Borriello and A. D'Ambrosio, *Baiae-Misenum*, vol. 14 of *Forma Italiae* (Florence, 1979), as cited in Castner 2:433.

104. A portion of the Gulf of Baia gradually separated off from the bay by a bar, now Lago di Miseno.

105. Suetonius, *The Deified Julius* 49.1.

106. Horace, *Epistles* 1.1.83. It may be that Biondo's looseness of interpretation (still repeated in guidebooks) here is intentional and didactic (but compare Castner 2:433).

107. Suetonius, *Caligula* 19.1.

108. Mistakenly: see Clavuot 1:195f, and Castner 2:434.

109. Lucullus's estate in Tusculum, and compare *Lazio* §44.

110. Plutarch, *Lucullus* 39.4.

111. Pliny the Elder, *Natural History* 31.7–8. See Morgan Llewelyn, "*Natura narratur*: Tullius Laurea's Elegy for Cicero," in *Classical Constructions: Pa-*

pers in Memory of Don Fowler, Classicist and Epicurean, ed. S. J. Heyworth (Oxford, 2007), pp. 113–41.

112. St. Jerome, Letters 107.11, to Laeta, 403 CE.

113. The Stufe di Tritola (also known as Bagni di Tritoli or di Nerone, between Baia and Pozzuoli) come from Italian tritolare, to "pound" (Latin tritus from terere), whereas frictolae derives from fricare, to "rub" or "massage."

114. Vergil, Georgics 2.161, and Servius ad loc.

115. Suetonius, The Deified Augustus 16.1. The project was rather undertaken by Agrippa in 37–36 BCE and named Portus Iulius, after Octavian.

116. Vergil, Aeneid 3.442, and Servius ad loc. The etymology of Avernus was supposed to be ἄορνος, "birdless."

117. Vergil, Aeneid 6.107, and Servius ad loc.

118. Suetonius, Caligula 19.1–2.

119. Suetonius, Nero 34.3, and see Tacitus, Annales 14.4–8.

120. Vergil, Aeneid 3.386, and Servius, ad loc.

121. S.H.A., Alexander Severus 26, 9–11. For Mamaea, see Italy Illuminated, vol. 1 (ITRL 20), Preface §1 and Lazio §52.

122. Present-day Bacoli; Latinized from βοαύλια in Servius, which Biondo read as from bovalis.

123. Servius, In Aeneidem 6.107 (and see at 7.662).

124. See Fynes Moryson, Itinerary (Glasgow, 1907), 1:248, who repeats Biondo here — as does Leandro Alberti. "Belgermano" as if from Bellum Germanicum, "the German War."

125. Suetonius, The Deified Augustus 44.1.

126. Livy 24.7.10–11. Biondo has a different text here (notably captum for coeptum), and his understanding of it is unclear.

127. Livy 24.12.4–5 and 24.13.6–7.

128. Livy 32.7.2–5.

129. Livy 32.29.3.

130. *S.H.A.*, *Hadrian* 25.6–8 and 27.3. The Puteolanum of Cicero, as in *On Fate* 2 (the dialogue's setting) and *Letters to Atticus* 16.1.1.

131. Echoing Herodotus, *Histories* 7.22–24, where Xerxes cuts a channel through Mount Athos for his fleet. See Plutarch, *Lucullus* 39.3–4; Pliny the Elder, *Natural History* 9.170; and Strabo, 5.4.5. On the Lucullanum, see above, end of §30, with note.

132. In §32.

133. Pliny the Elder, *Natural History* 9.167 (compare 3.82). The tunnel's length is in fact more than seven hundred meters.

134. As the tunnel was called in antiquity. An element of the same program of construction of Agrippa (note 115 above), engineered by Cocceius, that produced the Portus Iulius.

135. Seneca's text has *facibus* (torches) for Biondo's and some manuscripts' *faucibus* (jaws).

136. Seneca, *Epistles* 57.1–2. Petronius (frag. xvi) also complained about the Grotta.

137. Aelius Donatus, *Life of Vergil* 36, based on the life by Suetonius.

138. Biondo takes this statement over verbatim from his *Roma triumphans* (ed. Basel 1559, p. 146). By legend Vergil was buried at the Piedigrotta entrance of the tunnel, undiscovered and unverified still. See J. B. Trapp, "The Grave of Vergil," in his *Essays on the Renaissance and the Classical Tradition* (Aldershot, 1990), art. V.

139. Livy 8.22.5. Palaepolis simply means the "old city," gradually replaced by Neapolis, the "new city" of Naples.

140. Livy 8.23.1.

141. Livy 8.23.10.

142. Livy 8.23.1.

143. Livy 22.32.4.

144. Compare Livy 22.32.9.

145. Livy 23.1.6.

146. Livy 23.14.5–6.

147. Livy 24.13.7.

148. *Discoli* is an Italianism, rare in Biondo.

149. Suetonius, *Nero* 25.1.

150. Suetonius, *Nero* 40.4.

151. Servius, *In Georgica* 4.563 (where Vergil self-deprecatingly contrasts Augustus's martial energy with his own quiet studiousness at Naples).

152. On Robert, see *Abruzzo* §17; also *Romagna* §68 and §77, with note, on Robert of Anjou and Petrarch's lost map of Italy. Robert ruled over Naples from 1309 to 1343; he was a legendary patron of learning and the arts. Biondo's sentiments here are heartfelt and at the same time programmatic: Alfonso is meant to see himself in Robert, and Biondo in Petrarch.

153. Servius, *In Aeneidem* 7.733–34. The nymph's name is properly Sebethis, her stream the Sebethus.

154. Biondo, *History* 26e–h. The sack of Rome took place in 455 and of Capua in the following year.

155. In 536. See §47 below.

156. See note 16 above.

157. See §3 above.

158. In 846.

159. Alfonso concluded his six-month siege of Naples in the summer of 1442 and entered the city in triumph on February 26, 1443. For the Belisarius episode, see §44 above, with A. Ryder, *Alfonso the Magnanimous* (Oxford, 1990), pp. 244–45.

160. A church-convent complex of the Poor Clares, founded by King Robert and constructed over thirty years by the queen in the early fourteenth century. On the king's death, Sancha entered the convent. Both are buried in the church.

161. The charterhouse (Certosa), now a museum, completed and consecrated by the ill-starred Queen Giovanna I in 1368, was dedicated to St. Martin, bishop of Tours.

162. Angevin castle, completed by Charles I in 1282 as seat of government and court and expanded by King Robert. Alfonso restored and reinforced it to withstand improving artillery, later adding the sculptural main gate in celebration of his triumphal entry (§47 above, with note).

163. Pietro Tomacelli of Casarano, pope from 1389 to 1404. A reasonable appraisal: the pope established temporal control over the Rome *comune* and created the Papal States in the form that Biondo knew in his time.

164. Baldassare Cossa of Procida, antipope from 1410 to 1415. John had been rightly reluctant to call a council for fear that it would depose him. Compare *Romagna* §28 on literary discoveries during the Council of Constance.

165. See *Tuscany* §48. Ladislaus took Cortona in 1409, selling it to Florence in 1411.

166. King of Naples (1386–1414) and dead at age thirty-seven, Ladislaus was energetic, adroit, and murderous. It *was* his ambition to conquer all Italy.

167. Cicero, *On the Agrarian Law* 2.86.

168. Torre del Greco (older name: *Turris Octava*), Torre Annunziata (*Oplontis*), Castellammare di Stabia (near the ancient *Stabiae*, where the elder Pliny, the admiral, died): in the circumstances of the time, none is an unreasonable guess for the site of ancient Pompeii, which was not to be rediscovered for another three hundred years.

169. Livy 9.38.2.

170. Suetonius, *Titus* 8.7.9.

171. Livy 23.17.7.

172. Livy 27.3.7.

173. Vergil, *Georgics* 2.224–25, quoted in part in §23 above and again at §55 below.

174. In §§19 and 20.

175. Pliny the Elder, *Natural History* 17.25 (Biondo's text is here defective).

176. See §23 above and *Abruzzo* §54.

177. Livy 7.37.4.

178. Livy 8.14.11–12.

179. Livy 8.23.9.

180. Livy 23.14.13, about Marcellus, not Hannibal.

181. Livy 23.32.2.

182. Livy 23.48.2.

183. *Abruzzo* §51.

184. Its ancient name is unknown. See *Abruzzo* §52 for the "lower reaches of the Sabato looking like a tree trunk."

185. That is, the Seritella of *Abruzzo* §54.

186. A mountain group to the west of Benevento between the Calore and Isclero valleys.

187. Servius, *In Georgica* 2.37–38.

188. Servius, *In Aeneidem* 12.715.

189. Now called Monti di Maddaloni after the town (compare *Abruzzo* §54).

190. Livy 7.29.6–7.

191. Livy 7.33.17.

192. Livy 23.36.1, 4.

193. Livy 23.39.8.

194. Livy 23.43.5–6.

195. Livy 24.12.3–4.

196. Livy 26.5.4.

197. Livy 32.7.3.

198. Pliny the Elder, *Natural History* 2.226, of leaves and twigs in the river Sele beyond Sorrento: "virgulta . . . et folia lapidescunt."

199. In §§50f.

200. Compare Justin, *Epitome of Trogus* 20.1.13: "Iam Falisci, Nolani, Abellani nonne Chalcidensium coloni sunt?"

201. Not the *Eclogues* but *Georgics* 2.224–25 (as in §51), and Servius *ad loc.*, with Aulus Gellius, *Attic Nights* 6.20.1–4.

202. Livy 9.28.3–6 (recomposed fragments).

203. Livy 23.14.5–6, also used in §40 above.

204. Livy 23.32.2.

205. Livy 23.39.7.

206. Livy 23.41.13.

207. Livy 23.43.5–6, also used in §54 above.

208. Livy 24.13.8.

209. Livy, *Periochae* 89.26–27: "Sylla Aeserniam in Samnio recepit. XL-VII legiones in agros captos deduxit et eos his divisit."

210. Suetonius, *The Deified Augustus* 100.1–2.

211. §§52 and 54 above.

212. In §50.

213. He is thinking of *Aeneid* 7.738: "et quae rigat aequora ['flatlands'] Sarnus."

214. Lucan 2.423.

215. Cicero, *On the Agrarian Law* 2.86.

216. Livy 27.3.7.

217. The Valle dell'Irno. The Sanseverino were one of the great magnate families of the Regno.

218. But see Clavuot 1:203.

219. Biondo, *History* 241a. In the 1559 Froben edition, the emperor is correctly called Lotharius, not Otto.

220. The magnetic compass was probably a third-century Chinese invention: Amir D. Aczel, *The Riddle of the Compass: The Invention that Changed the World* (Boston, 2002). See also John Vardalas, "A History of the Magnet Compass," *The Institute* (November 8, 2013), online at http://theinstitute.ieee.org/technology-focus/technology-history/a-history-of-the-magnetic-compass; and Barbara M. Kreutz, "Mediterranean

Contributions to the Medieval Mariners Compass," *Technology and Culture* 3 (July 1973): 367–83.

221. *Liguria* §2: Hesperia from Hesperus, the Evening Star.

222. Livy 9.17.17.

14. PUGLIA

1. *Abruzzo* §§43–44.

2. *Abruzzo* §62 (Samnium = Abruzzo).

3. Ptolemy, *Geography* 3.1.13–14.

4. Vergil, *Aeneid* 8.9, and Servius, *ad loc.*

5. Biondo's treatment of *Regio XIV*, Puglia, is the skimpiest (compare Alberti's *Descrizione d'Italia* [Venice, 1596], fols. 242v–51r on the region) of the fourteen *regiones* he managed to complete—apart from four others originally planned that he let go entirely. In addition to motivations for abbreviation cited above at *Abruzzo* note 1, Castner 2:441 hypothesizes the Turkish threat and the propaganda work that Biondo was doing to counter it, as well as his absorption in a new work, *Roma triumphans.* We may also take seriously Biondo's use of the adjective *operosum* here as a sign of simple scientific and artistic fatigue with the project at hand. See also Domenico Defilippis, "La Daunia degli umanisti," in *18° Convegno Nazionale sulla Preistoria, Protostoria, Storia della Daunia, San Severo 29–30 Novembre 1997. Atti*, ed. Armando Gravina (San Severo, 1999), pp. 147–92 (http://www.archeologiadigitale.it/attidaunia/pdf/18-defilippis.pdf).

6. Livy 8.37.3 and 6.

7. Livy 9.15.2–3: Biondo has before him, or remembers, a different text; the consul was actually Publilius.

8. Livy 9.20.7–9.

9. Livy 39.29.8–10.

10. Livy 22.18.7–8, with omissions.

11. Caesar, *Civil War* 1.23.5, as at *Abruzzo* §20.

12. Livy 22.32.4.

13. Livy 22.39.16–17. Livy has: *Quam diu pro Gereoni, castelli Apuliae inopis, tamquam pro Carthaginis moenibus . . .* ("How long ⟨has Hannibal been sitting⟩ before the walls of the miserable castle of Gereonium as if before the walls of Carthage?"). Our author sees the aposiopesis but has a different text.

14. Soldier of fortune who served the Angevin cause in the Kingdom against the Aragonese (d. 1477).

15. Or Carlo Gambatesa (d. 1459). He served Alfonso V, as well as the Visconti and Sforza.

16. Like the Lago de Lesina (§4), a saltwater lagoon with two outlets to the sea, though fed by freshwater springs.

17. Ptolemy, *Geography* 3.1.14: *Urion;* and Pliny the Elder, *Natural History* 3.103: *Teanum.* But it may be that the *Tirium* of Biondo's statement is a garbling of *-turium* in Pliny's *promunturium.*

18. This is the Santuario di San Michele Arcangelo in the town of Monte Sant'Angelo, on Monte Gargano (now generally called Monte S. Angelo). The saint's connection with the place (and with Siponto in particular) as its guardian angel is noted by Jacobus de Voragine, which was probably Biondo's source: compare *Liguria* §23, with note: see *Legenda Aurea,* ed. G. P. Maggione (Florence, 1998), pp. 986–1001. The Christian shrine probably goes back to the early sixth century, and building continued almost into Biondo's time. It became a very popular pilgrimage destination, as Biondo says.

19. Biondo, *History* 251a.

20. Ptolemy, *Geography* 3.1.14.

21. Ptolemy, *Geography* 3.1.69.

22. Augustine, *City of God* 18.16.9–12 and 15–23: Augustine has *insuper adulare* ("fawn on them besides") and *ut etiam perimant* ("enough even to kill them").

23. San Domino (the island of Diomedes itself in Augustine's account), San Nicola, Capraia, Cretaccio, and Pianosa are the islands that make up the Tremiti archipelago.

24. *Tuscany* §42, mentioning the Venetian foundation of the canons of S. Giorgio in Alga.

25. Jelena Marohnić, "The birds of Diomedes" (2010), examines the myths and the likely identification of the birds as shearwaters: http://hrcak.srce.hr/index.php?show=clanak&id_clanak_jezik=93243&lang=en.

26. *Aeneid* 11.247 (a different text from Biondo's), and Servius *ad loc.*

27. Lucan 5.380.

28. At §4 above.

APPENDIX

1. An artful allusion to Pius's apologetic Bull of Retractation of April 26, 1463, the famous *In minoribus agentes*, which explained his rejection of his previous conciliarist views and which Biondo would have seen beforehand and discussed with the pope. See T. A. Izbicki, G. Christiansen, and P. Krey, eds., *Reject Aeneas, Accept Pius: Selected Letters of Aeneas Sylvius Piccolomini (Pope Pius II)* (Washington, DC, 2006), pp. 389ff.

2. Most often supposed from internal evidence to be Cardinal Francesco Condulmer (d. 1453), Eugenius IV's nephew: see *Venice* §25, with note, and P. Pontari ed., *Blondus Flavius, Italia Illustrata*, 2 vols. to date (Rome, 2011–), 1:422–24. Frances Muecke notes in a private communication Biondo's contemptuous treatment of Condulmer (who is not named) at *Roma triumphans* 2.36; see her forthcoming I Tatti edition (Volume 74 in this series [2016], p. 372, n. 111).

3. Horace, *Ars Poetica* 388.

4. Biondo's present appendix ends with material on Borgo Sansepolcro, Anghiari, Cotolo, and the source of the Tiber, corresponding to §51 in *Tuscany* (his *regio secunda*) in the main text. His additions, which he means to go into the text proper, give out in *Lombardy* (his *regio septima*). His language here suggests that he intended not only to continue to expand, as in *Liguria* and *Tuscany*, the remaining regions of the work already published but to break new ground and cover *regiones* 15–18, Alfonso's

Regno (*Lucania,* Terra d'Otranto, Calabria, *Terra Brutiorum*), which he had earlier given up on.

5. *Liguria* §23, with note. He was governor of Savona from 1450 to 1458. See L. Amelotti in *DBI* 50 (1998): 448–51.

6. For Ludovico, see *Liguria* §30, with note.

7. *Liguria* §29.

8. Pietro di Campofregoso (doge, disastrously, from 1450 to 1459), grandson of Tommaso, vassal and soldier of the Visconti.

9. *Hispania Citerior,* the old Augustan *Hispania Tarraconensis*: eastern maritime Spain, effectively Aragon and Catalonia.

10. Charles VII (1403–61), Valois king of France. Genoa remained in French control from 1458 to 1461.

11. The Ottoman Sultan Mehmed II, May 29, 1453.

12. That is, Galata, a *fondaco* (emporium), and eventually a fortress of the Genoese by concession of the Byzantine emperor, on the Golden Horn opposite Constantinople.

13. Jean II of Anjou (1424–70), called the Duke of Calabria, was like his father, René of Anjou, the titular king of Naples; René (1409–80) had lost his kingdom to Alfonso V of Aragon in 1442.

14. Ferdinand I (1423–94), son of Alfonso V, commonly known as Ferrante.

15. The Duke of Orleans (1423–83), who succeeded his father Charles VII as Louis XI of France.

16. At *Tuscany* §17. The former Lake Prile. It was later drained and reclaimed for farming.

17. Pius II (Enea Silvio Piccolomini) legitimated Ferdinand's possession of the Kingdom of Naples, though Calixtus III had wanted to make it a Church protectorate. Ferdinand still had to protect it against foreign enemies, such as Jean d'Anjou, as well as internal ones. Pius's nephew Antonio Todeschini Piccolomini, the Duke of Amalfi (1437–93), married Ferdinand's daughter, Maria d'Aragona. Among Antonio's brothers,

landowners in Sienese territory, was the future Pius III, Francesco Todeschini Piccolomini.

18. *Tuscany* §52.

19. 1462.

20. Vergil, *Aeneid* 6.179.

21. Curial officials who received and advised on petitions directed to the pope.

22. *Tuscany* §§18–19.

23. The road is part of the Via Francigena, the old pilgrimage route to Rome. The bridge gives the town of Ponte d'Arbia its name.

24. *Tuscany* §24.

25. On Jacopo Piccolomini Ammannati (b. 1422 in Lucca–1479), one of Pius's most trusted advisors, cardinal from 1461, see the sketch by Charles R. Mack, *Pienza: The Creation of a Renaissance City* (Ithaca, NY, 1987), pp. 118–25.

26. Pistoia is some twenty-four miles from Lucca in a straight line, but it is the nearest substantial town and treated by Biondo following Lucca in *Tuscany* §25.

27. Forteguerri (1419–73), prelate-soldier, diplomat, humanist, in addition to being Pius's maternal kin. Pius made him bishop of Teano in 1458 and cardinal of Santa Cecilia in 1460.

28. Petriolo is mentioned only in passing at *Tuscany* §41. For Pius's own account of his stay at the baths, see Pius II, *Commentaries*, vol. 2, bks. 3–4, ed. M. Meserve and M. Simonetta, I Tatti Renaissance Library 29 (Cambridge, MA, 2007), 4:15–16.

29. The Eremo di Sant'Antonio in Val d'Aspra near Petriolo: the following episode (§§11–15), a disturbing animal fable, seems a kind of Curial allegory difficult to decipher: but, save for his treatments of the Fraticelli (*Umbria* §§12–13), of Dolcino and Margherita (*Lombardy* §35) and of Atellan farces (*Campania* §21), Biondo's prose in the *Italy Illuminated* is never so heated as here.

30. Alessandro Oliva of Sassoferrato (1407–63), a preacher attached to the Order of Augustinian Hermits as an oblate, that is, from childhood. Eugenius made him Procurator General of his order, and brought him to the Council of Florence in 1439. He was made cardinal in 1460.

31. §6 above.

32. Biondo presumably means Sant'Antimo, a Benedictine monastery of great wealth in the Middle Ages, suppressed by Pius in this very year, 1462, along with his creation of the joint diocese of Montalcino/Pienza. Montalcino was earlier a feudal property of S. Antimo, which still has columns with capitals carved from local alabaster.

33. The following, §§17–28, on Pienza-Corsignano are the centerpiece of the author's revisions. Mack, *Pienza: The Creation of a Renaissance City* (note 25 above) is invaluable here. There is a text and annotated translation of §§18–27 by Catherine Castner in an Appendix to Mack, pp. 166–70.

34. All in *Tuscany* §45, between Siena (§§42–44) and Arezzo (§§46–47).

35. Pius's *Commentarii*, though not always trustworthy, are the best source for Pius's biography. On his family and early life, see Pius II, *Commentaries*, vol. 1, bks. 1–2, ed. Meserve and M. Simonetta, I Tatti Renaissance Library 12 (Cambridge, MA, 2003), 1:1–6.

36. Pius's Congress of Mantua of 1459 was a failed call to Christian princes for a crusade against Mehmed II and the Turks, which eventually (1464) killed him.

37. August 10, 1459.

38. September 21, 1462. The cathedral was actually dedicated to Santa Maria Assunta (built over an earlier church of the same name). See Mack, *Pienza*, pp. 76–99.

39. Bernardo Rossellino of Settignano (1409–64), mason, sculptor, architect, associate of Leon Battista Alberti, on whom see Mack, *Pienza*, pp. 42–76 and *passim*.

40. The "underground" church is the baptistry of St. John (see Mack, *Pienza*, pp. 77–78).

41. The Palazzo Piccolomini, another work of Rossellino (note 39 above) and owned by the Piccolomini family for the next five hundred years.

42. Septimius Severus "The African" (145–211 CE).

43. Probably a hint, too, at the *Septizonium* (compare *S.H.A., Severus* 19.5), a finishing touch to the Palatine imperial residence. For other Roman projects of Severus, see ibid. 21.12, 23.1, 24.3. On Severus's African building projects, see Anthony R. Birley, *Septimius Severus: The African Emperor* (London, 1971), p. 218. For these, Biondo may have looked also at a Latin version of Cassius Dio, for example, *History, Epitome* 77.16. 3–4, on the emperor's fondness for seeing his name carved on his building and restoration projects.

44. By legend, the emperor's childhood home on the Caelian hill was in the neighborhood of the Basilica of St. John Lateran, the cathedral of the bishops of Rome, which itself went back to the fourth century CE.

45. Lotario dei Conti di Segni (1160/61–1216, pope 1198–1216). The tower, built in 1238 by the pope's brother, still exists near the Roman Forum.

46. On Jouffroy (1412–73, theologian and canon lawyer, diplomat, cardinal from 1461) and the Palazzo Jouffroy, see Mack, *Pienza*, pp. 125–30. For Jacopo Ammannati of Lucca and his palace, see note 25 above. For the papal nephews, see note 17 above.

47. *Tuscany* §45.

48. The Benedictine Guillaume d'Estouteville (1403–83), among other titles, was archbishop of Rouen (1453) and cardinal bishop of Ostia (1461). He was a candidate for pope at the conclave (1458) that elected Pius II. All three of the cardinals mentioned here attended Pius at the Congress of Mantua in 1459.

49. Alain de Coëtivy (1407–74) was from 1437 bishop of Avignon (though usually called the "Cardinal of Avignon") and cardinal priest of Santa Prassede (1449).

50. Nicholas Cusanus (1401–64), polymathic scientist, mathematician, theologian, textual critic, diplomat. He went to Constantinople and with Eugenius IV to the Council of Florence in 1439. He was at Mantua with Pius. In 1447, he was elevated to cardinal by Eugenius, then by Nicholas

publicly in the next year. He owned a manuscript (Bk) of the *Italia illustrata*, Bernkastel-Kues, Bibliothek des Sankt Nikolaus-Hospitals, 157: Pontari (note 2 above), pp. 263–66.

51. *Romagna* §32.

52. Pliny the Elder, *Natural History* 14.34.

53. *Tuscany* §51. Sansepolcro is very much Tuscan, but Umbria for Biondo included all of the Tiber valley, most of which is in Umbria, until it was joined by the Aniene (*Umbria* §2).

Bibliography

༄༅༄

EDITIONS OF THE LATIN TEXT

Rome: Johannes Philippus de Lignamine, 1474. (See Note on the Text in volume I.)

Verona: Boninus de Boninis, 1481–1482.

Venice: Bernardinus de Vitalibus, 1503.

Venice: [Gregorius de Gregoriis], 1510.

Turin: Bernardinus Sylva, 1527.

Basel: Hieronymus Frobenius, 1531.

Basel: Hieronymus Frobenius and Nicolaus Episcopius, 1559.

Biondo Flavio: Italy Illuminated I (Books I–IV). Edited and translated by Jeffrey A. White. Cambridge, MA: Harvard University Press, 2005. (I Tatti Renaissance Library 20.)

Castner, Catherine J. *Biondo Flavio's Italia illustrata: Text, Translation, and Commentary*. 2 vols. Binghamton, NY: Global Academic Publications, 2005–10. Latin text of the 1559 edition, with facing English translation; introduction and commentary in English.

Italia illustrata, edited by Paolo Pontari. 2 vols. to date (1. Introduzione, Nota al testo; 2. Liguria, Etruria, Latium). Rome: Istituto storico italiano per il Medio Evo, 2011–14.

ITALIAN TRANSLATIONS

There is an Italian translation/paraphrase by "Lucio Fauno" (i.e., Giovanni Tarcagnota) that was printed in the following editions:

Venice: Michele Tramezzino, 1542; reprinted in 1543, 1544, 1548, and 1549.

Venice: Domenico Giglio, 1558.

Alberti, Leandro. *Descrittione di tutti Italia*. Bologna: Giaccarelli, 1550. (In many senses a reworking and expansion of the *It. ill.* in the *volgare*.)

STUDIES

Albanese, Gabriella, and Paolo Pontari. "*De pictoribus atque sculptoribus qui hac aetate nostra claruerunt. Alle origini della biografia artistica rinascimentale.*" *Letteratura & Arte: rivista annuale* 1 (2003): 59–110.

Cameron, Alan. "Biondo's Ammianus: Constantius and Hormisdas at Rome." *Harvard Studies in Classical Philology* 92 (1989): 423–36.

Campana, Augusto. "Biondo Flavio da Forlì." *La Romagna*, n.s. 16 (1927): 487–97.

——. "Passi inediti dell' *Italia Illustrata* di Biondo Flavio." *Rinascita* 1 (1938): 91–97.

Cappelletto, Rita. "*Italia Illustrata* di Biondo Flavio." In *Letteratura Italiana: Le Opere*. Vol. 1: *Dalle origini al Cinquecento*, a cura di Alberto Asor Rosa, pp. 681–712. Torino: Einaudi, 1992.

——. "Per la storia del testo dell' *Italia illustrata*: interpolazioni e note di lettura nel cod. Marc. lat. X 21 (3523)." In *Commemoratio: Studi di filologia in ricordo di Riccardo Ribuoli*, edited by Sesto Prete, pp. 13–24. Sassoferrato: Istituto internazionale di studi piceni, 1986.

Castner, Catherine J. "Direct Observation and Biondo Flavio's Additions to *Italia Illustrata*: The Case of Ocriculum." *Medievalia et Humanistica*, n.s. 25 (1998): 93–108.

Clavuot, Ottavio. "Flavio Biondos *Italia illustrata*: Porträt und historisch-geographische Legitimation der humanistischen Elite italiens." In *Diffusion des Humanismus: Studien zur nationalen Geschichtsschreibung europäischer Humanisten*, edited by Johannes Helmrath, Ulrich Muhlack, Gerrit Walther, pp. 55–75. Gottingen, 2002.

——. *Flavio Biondos "Italia Illustrata": Summa oder Neuschöpfung? Über die Arbeitsmethoden eines Humanisten*. Tübingen: M. Niemeyer, 1990. (Bibliothek des Deutschen Historischen Instituts in Rom, Band 69).

——. "Italien endeckt sich selbst: Über die historischen und antiquarischen Studien des Biondo Flavio (1392–1463)." In *Feconde venner le carte: Studi in onore di Ottavio Besomi*, edited by Tatiana Crivelli, pp. 145–59. Bellinzona: Casagrande, 1997.

DeFilippis, Domenico. *La Rinascita della corografia tra scienza ed erudizione*. Bari: Adriatica, 2001.

Fubini, Riccardo. "Biondo Flavio." In *Dizionario biografico degli italiani*, 10:536–59. Rome: Treccani, 1968.

——. "La Geografia storica dell' *Italia illustrata* di Biondo Flavio." In *La cultura umanistica a Forlì fra Biondo e Melozzo*, edited by Luisa Avellini and Lara Michelucci, pp. 89–112. Bologna: Il Nove, 1997.

Granata, Giovanna. *La vicenda editoriale dell' Italia illustrata di Biondo Flavio*. Pisa: [s.n.t], 1997.

Hay, Denys. "Flavio Biondo and the Middle Ages." *Proceedings of the British Academy* 45 (1958): 97–125.

Jacks, Philip. *The Antiquarian and the Myth of Antiquity: The Origins of Rome in Renaissance Thought*. Cambridge: Cambridge University Press, 1993.

Lucarini, Carlo Martino. "La tradizione manoscritta dell'*Italia illustrata* di Biondo Flavio." *Giornale italiano di filologia* 55 (2003): 59–80.

Lucarini, Carlo Martino, and Paolo Pontari. "Nuovi passi inediti dell' *Italia Illustrata* di Biondo Flavio." *Rinascimento*, n.s. 42 (2001): 225–57.

Mack, Charles R. *Pienza: The Creation of a Renaissance City*. Ithaca, NY: Cornell University Press, 1987.

Mazzocco, Angelo. "Petrarca, Poggio, and Biondo: Humanism's Foremost Interpreters of Roman Ruins." In *Francis Petrarch, Six Centuries Later: A Symposium*, edited by Aldo Scaglione, pp. 353–63. North Carolina Studies in the Romance Languages and Literatures Symposia 3. Chapel Hill: Department of Romance Languages, University of North Carolina, 1975.

——. "Some Philological Aspects of Biondo Flavio's *Roma Triumphans*." *Humanistica Lovaniensia* 28 (1979): 1–26.

Miglio, Massimo. "Incunaboli come fonte: il manoscritto utilizzato in tipografia della *Roma instaurata* del Biondo." In Massimo Miglio, *Saggi di Stampa: Tipografi e cultura a Roma nel Quattrocento*, edited by Anna Modigliani, pp. 115–28. Rome: Roma nel Rinascimento, 2002.

Nogara, Bartolomeo. *Scritti inediti e rari di Biondo Flavio*. Vatican City: Tipografia Poliglotta Vaticana, 1927. (Studi e Testi 48.)

Pontari, Paolo. "Ancora su passi inediti dell'*Italia illustrata* di Biondo Flavio." *Rinascimento* n.s. 43 (2003): 357–415.

——. "*Picturae et elocutiones*: fonti storiche e geografiche del *Italia illustrata* di Biondo." In *Da Flavio Biondo a Leandro Alberti. Corografia e antiquaria*

tra Quattro e Cinquecento. Atti del Convegno di studi (Foggia, 2 February 2006), edited by Domenico Defilippis, pp. 99–130. Bari: Adriatica, 2009.

Viti, Paolo. "Umanesimo letterario e primato regionale nell' *Italia illustrata* di Flavio Biondo." In *Studi filologici e storici in memoria di Guido Favati*, II, edited by Giorgio Varanini and Palmiro Pinagli, pp. 711–32. Padua: Antenore, 1977.

White, Jeffrey A. "Biondo Flavio as Henry James' Dencombe (?): Revising the *Italia Illustrata*." In *A New Sense of the Past: The Scholarship of Biondo Flavio (1392–1463)*, edited by Angelo Mazzocco and Marc Laureys. (Supplementa Humanistica Lovaniensia). Leuven: Leuven University Press (forthcoming, 2016).

———. "Towards a Critical Edition of Biondo Flavio's *Italia Illustrata*: A Survey and an Evaluation of the MSS." In *Umanesimo a Roma nel Quattrocento*, pp. 267–93. New York: Barnard College (Columbia University), 1984.

Cumulative Index to Volumes I and II

꙳ɕ꙳

Locators are given by region and paragraph number. The preface is cited by "Pr" and paragraph number. Biondo Flavio's Additions and Corrections in the Appendix are cited by "AC," section number, and paragraph number. Notes to the Translation are cited by the region and paragraph number to which they refer.

Publication of this volume has been made possible by

The Myron and Sheila Gilmore Publication Fund at I Tatti
The Robert Lehman Endowment Fund
The Jean-François Malle Scholarly Programs and Publications Fund
The Andrew W. Mellon Scholarly Publications Fund
The Craig and Barbara Smyth Fund
for Scholarly Programs and Publications
The Lila Wallace–Reader's Digest Endowment Fund
The Malcolm Wiener Fund for Scholarly Programs and Publications

COMPREHENSIVE CHEMICAL KINETICS